COMPLETE DICTIONARY
OF ENGLISH AND HEBREW
FIRST NAMES

ALSO BY ALFRED J. KOLATCH

The Jewish Book of Why
The Jewish Child's First Book of Why
The Jewish Home Advisor
Jewish Information Quiz Book
The Jewish Mourner's Book of Why
The Jonathan David Dictionary of First Names
The New Name Dictionary
Our Religion: The Torah
The Second Jewish Book of Why
These Are the Names
This Is the Torah
Today's Best Baby Names
Who's Who in The Talmud

Complete Dictionary
of
English and Hebrew
First Names

ALFRED J. KOLATCH

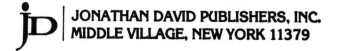
JONATHAN DAVID PUBLISHERS, INC.
MIDDLE VILLAGE, NEW YORK 11379

COMPLETE DICTIONARY OF
ENGLISH AND HEBREW FIRST NAMES

Copyright © 1984
by
Alfred J. Kolatch

JONATHAN DAVID PUBLISHERS, INC.
68-22 Eliot Avenue
Middle Village, New York 11379

10   9   8   7

Library of Congress Cataloging in Publication Data

Kolatch, Alfred J., 1916-
    Rev. ed. of: the name dictionary. 1967.
    Bibliography: p.
    1. Names, Personal—English. 2. Names, Personal—Jewish.
    3. Names, Personal—Hebrew. 4. English language—
    Etymology—Names. 5. Hebrew language—Etymology—
    Names. I. Title. II. Title: Complete dictionary of English and
    Hebrew first names.
    CS2367.K63   1984   929.4'4'03924   82-23454
    ISBN 0-8246-0295-1
    ISBN 0-8246-0302-8 pbk

Printed in the United States of America

DEDICATED
TO THE MEMORY OF
ANNA and SAMUEL RUBIN

Table of Contents

Preface

This dictionary contains modern English and Hebrew names together with an analysis of their meanings and origins. Included among the more than 11,000 main entries are a large number of biblical names that are suitable for use today, plus practically every Hebrew first name in use in Israel today. These biblical and modern Hebrew names have been transliterated into English, and for those who can read Hebrew and are eager to know the correct Hebrew spelling and exact pronunciation of these names, the Hebrew script is provided immediately following each main entry.

Since there are many who, after choosing an English name for a child, would like to select a Hebrew name with the same meaning, a Hebrew Name Vocabulary is included in a separate section following the masculine and feminine main entries. In this section one can find transliterated Hebrew (and Yiddish) names grouped according to meaning. Thus, for example, if one has selected Helen, meaning "light," as the English name for an offspring, by consulting the Vocabulary section, under the category "Light," he will find a variety of Hebrew first names that match the English name's basic meaning.

In studying this book to find an appropriate name, one should not be surprised by the large number of names that may appear to be unusable. These are primarily biblical appellations, some of which have been revived in modern Israel. They are presented with their variant spellings and variant forms, thus offering the namer a greater choice. These names might not appeal to a large segment of the population, but nonetheless they are basic Jewish names.

It should be pointed out that it is not improper (or less Jewish) to select a name that does not have a Hebrew entry after it (in parentheses). Those names accompanied by Hebrew entries are basically Hebrew (or Yiddish) names. Names like Arthur or Thelma or Mae will not have a Hebrew name after them, because they are derived from other languages. To find a corresponding Hebrew name for such entries one will have to consult the Hebrew Name Vocabulary.

Finally, a word of thanks is due to the many researchers, scholars, editors, and typists who have been so helpful in the preparation of this dictionary. Hagai Lev of the Institute of Contemporary Jewry at the Hebrew University in Jerusalem did some of the initial work back in 1966, when he combed through some 100,000 names listed in the Registry of Births in Israel and in public school, high school, and university records. This past year Elinor Slater helped by compiling lists of the newer names that have come into use over the past few years.

Special thanks to my two editors, Jonathan Kolatch and David Kolatch, who checked the manuscript before and after typesetting and have helped immensely in making this a more readable piece of work. And, finally, to Florence Weissman and Mary McGee I extend my profound thanks for typing the manuscript and making many useful suggestions.

ALFRED J. KOLATCH

January 1984
Wassaic, NY

Introduction

I

Where Our Names Come From

Old Testament Names

The earliest personal names on record are found in the Bible. Many are still in use in their original form. For the most part, biblical names (which were often based on life experiences of the individual) are easy to understand because their roots are easily traced, usually to the Hebrew; in fact, many are explained in the Bible itself.

The Hebrew root of the name Cain, for example, is *kanoh*, meaning "to acquire, to buy." Genesis 4:1 explains: "And she [Eve] conceived and bore Cain, and said, 'I have *acquired* a man [Cain] with the help of the Lord.' "

Abraham and Sarah named their son Isaac. Abraham was 100 years old at the time, and when Sarah was told she was to bear a child, she said, "Everyone who hears about it will *laugh*." The Hebrew root of the name Isaac, *tzachok*, means "laughter."

Scores of such examples can be found in the pages of the Bible. Names sometimes describe a physical attribute (Korach, meaning "bald," or Charim, meaning "flat-nosed"), an inspiring or unusual experience (Moshe was so named because he was "drawn out of the water"), resemblance to or reminders of animal features or characteristics (for example, Yona, meaning "dove," or Devora, meaning "bee"), or affection or affinity to plants or flowers (Tamar, meaning "palm tree," or Tzemach, meaning "plant"). The Bible also contains many God-centered names (such as Yonatan, meaning "gift of God," or Yoel, meaning "God is willing") and names that express hope for a bright future or better conditions (Yosef, meaning "may God increase").

Christian Names

Christians of the first centuries used Old Testament Hebrew names. In time, however, these were abandoned by many New Testament figures as a form of protest against Judaism. Thus, the man once known as Simon bar Jonah came to be called Peter, and Saul of Tarsus became known as Paul.

During those early centuries many Christian parents followed the pattern of choosing names associated with mythology and idolatry, even though they abhorred both. Phoebe, Olympius, and Jovianus were commonly used. The seventh-century Bishop of Seville was outraged by the use of these names. In his *Etymologiae* he wrote of the significance of biblical names, urging Christians to use them, but to no avail.

The Reformation

Not until the Reformation, in the 1500s, when as a rebellion against the Catholic Church and its authority Protestantism came into being, did biblical names—particularly Old Testament names— again become popular. In seventeenth-century Puritan England, where the Reformation turned into a crusade against all Church dogma and ceremonials, New Testament names in particular were renounced in favor of Old Testament names.

Many Puritan extremists, even those living as late as the eighteenth and nineteenth centuries, went so far as to use the most obscure and odd-sounding names they could find; they even took phrases from Scripture and used them—in their entirety—as names. Ernest Weekley, in his book *Jack and Jill,* reports that at the beginning of the twentieth century there was a family with the names Asenath Zaphnath Paaneah, Kezia Jemima Keren Happukh, and Maher Shalal Hashbaz. The average Puritan, however, was satisfied with Old Testament names as well as those derived from abstract virtues, such as Perseverance, Faith, Hope, Humility, Charity, and Repentance. A pair of twin girls born to the English Wycliffe family in 1710 were named Favour and Fortune.

Opposition to New Testament Names

The Quakers (Society of Friends), like the Puritans, preferred Old Testament names and despised the nomenclature of the New Testament, probably as part of their protest against the Church of England, with which they broke in 1648. The Quakers disapproved of the elaborate ceremonies of the established Church.

The life of John Bunyan (1628-1688), author of *Pilgrim's Progress,* epitomizes the conflict between the Quakers and Puritans and their opponents. In his early years, Bunyan was an antagonist of the Quakers. For this reason he named his children Mary, John, Thomas, and Elizabeth—all but the last being New Testament names. By the time of Bunyan's second marriage his philosophy had changed. No longer an opponent of the Quakers, he had become intensely opposed to the established Church and its bishops. His children by his second wife were named Joseph and Sara, after Old Testament figures.

Current Use of Biblical Names

Although biblical names have fallen in and out of favor in the course of history, over the last two generations they have proven to be among the most popular names in use, irrespective of religion or race. In a study of 10,000 personal names appearing in the birth columns of *The New York Times* between 1943 and 1946 (as reported in the author's earlier book, *The Name Dictionary*), of the ten most popular masculine names six were biblical or of biblical origin—two (Michael and David) from the Jewish Bible and four (Stephen, Peter, Steven, Mark) from the Christian Bible. Among the female names, five of the ten most popular were biblical or of biblical origin: Jane, Ann, Joan, Nancy, Judith (Jane, Joan, and Nancy are variant forms of Ann). The 1948 New York City birth records reveal a striking similarity: among the ten most popular masculine names in that year were John, James, Michael, Joseph, Thomas, Stephen, and David—three Old Testament names and four New Testament names. The ten most popular feminine names included two names of biblical origin: Mary and Nancy.

Studies of the 1980 and 1981 birth rolls of New York City, Detroit (with a large black population), and the State of Pennsylvania reveal an amazing consistency in the selection of biblical names by parents.

The 1981 list of New York City births shows seven biblical names (Michael, David, Jason, Joseph, John, Daniel, James) to be among the ten most popular male names, and five biblical names (Jessica, Michelle, Elizabeth, Lisa, Danielle) to be among the ten most popular female names.

The Detroit 1981 birth records show five biblical names (Michael, Jason, James, David, Joseph) among the ten most popular male names, and three biblical names (Jessica, Sarah, Andrea) among the ten most popular female names.

The 1980 report from Pennsylvania includes seven biblical names (Michael, Jason, Matthew, David, John, James, Joseph) among the ten most popular male names of that year, and two biblical names (Jessica and Sarah) among the ten most popular feminine names, with the next four names on the list (Rebecca, Stephanie, Elizabeth, Lisa) also biblical or of biblical derivation.

Names from Places

Many first names, like surnames, have been borrowed from the names of places. The Bible, of course, has many such examples.

Efrat is the place where Rachel died and was buried; Efrata is the name of Caleb's wife in the Book of Chronicles. Afra, the name of a city in the Book of Joshua, is also a masculine first name. Ur, a place-name in the Book of Genesis, is a masculine first name that appears in the Book of Chronicles.

In more recent times, Myrna Loy, the actress, was named after the whistle-stop Myrna, a name her father found intriguing. Portland Hoffa, the radio comedienne and wife of Fred Allen, was named after Portland, Oregon. Florida Edwards is the name of a radio actress. Actress Tallulah Bankhead was named after her grandmother, who in turn was named after Tallulah Falls, Georgia. Philadelphia Levy was the daughter of a Philadelphia family prominent at the end of the eighteenth century.

Calendar and Holiday Names

Among the Christian holidays, Easter and Christmas have long served as sources for forenames. Pentecostes was the name of a servant of Henry VIII. Easter is commonly used and can be found as a character in Lillian Smith's novel *Strange Fruit*, and Christ and Christmas are the backbone of names such as Chris, Christopher, Christina, Christine, Natalie, Noel, and Noelle.

Among Jews, too, many names now in use are derived from the calendar and holidays. In fact, the Hebrew term for holiday, *yom tov*, is sometimes used as a personal name. In the Middle Ages, it was common to call boys who were circumcised on Purim by the name Mordechai, in honor of the hero of the holiday. Those born on Tisha B'Av were often named Menachem, meaning "comforter," because the ninth *(tisha)* day of the month Av is a fast day commemorating the destruction of the Temple in Jerusalem, and in the Prophetic portion (Isaiah 40) read in the synagogue on the Sabbath following that fast day the Prophet *comforts* Israel. Children born on Yom Kippur were sometimes called Rachamim ("mercy"). Among the Jews of Eastern Europe a son born on Chanukah was usually called by the name of the holiday. Pesach (Passover) was a name given to boys born on that holiday, and Shabetai (Sabbatai) was often used for a boy born on a Sabbath. One rabbi, the father of twelve sons, is reported to have named each son after a different Hebrew month. The above names continue to be used today, but they are not as closely associated with the holidays or the calendar as they were in the past.

Among the general population in America and elsewhere, names associated with holidays as well as names of the days of the week and the months of the year are used: Noel, Tuesday, April, May, June, and so on.

Numeral Names

Numbers are another source for names that were used a great deal in the past and are used in some rare instances today. The Romans were the first to take numeral names. Among the more common are Quintus (5), Octavius (8), and Septimus (7). Among Tripolitan Jews in North Africa, Hmessa and Hammus, meaning "five," are used as feminine and masculine personal names respectively. Recently a Michigan family with the surname Stickaway named their three boys One, Two, and Three; and their three girls, First, Second, and Third.

One of the rare present-day examples of a number being used as a personal name made its appearance recently in the case of a young rabbi who, having difficulty finding a satisfactory Hebrew name for his first daughter, decided to name her Rishona (first).

It is interesting to note that the Puritans, and especially the Quakers, refrained from using the names of months and substituted numbers in their place. They believed that since most months had names of pagan origin, it would be best to avoid using them as personal names. For this reason we find, as we study some of the official records and tombstone engravings of the seventeenth century, that months are referred to by number rather than name—January referred to as 1, February as 2, and so on.

Occupational Names

Many occupational names have become first names, although the vast majority have come down to us as last names. Most fall into the category of the name Wright, which is an Old English name meaning "artisan, worker." It is used occasionally as a first name (e.g., Wright Morris, author), but for the most part it has remained a surname (e.g., the Wright brothers, Orville and Wilbur).

Middle English names were often occupational names. Bannister, meaning "one who draws a crossbow," and Brewster, meaning "one who brews beer," are used from time to time. Newly created names are rarely based on occupation.

Celebrity Names

Many names in use today have been adopted because they are the names of celebrities. In this category we include not only contemporary celebrities in the fields of entertainment, sports, music, and politics, but also the great figures of history, political as well as religious, whose charisma was so great that parents named children after them.

Alexander the Great entered Palestine in 333 B.C., and according to legend all Jewish boys born in that year were named Alexander in his honor. Although we do not have records indicating how popular that name became among the masses in the years immediately following Alexander's visit, we do know that one Jewish king (Alexander Janneus) and one queen (Salome Alexandra) did use the name. A bit later, in talmudic times, we find the name being used by the scholar Rabbi Alexandri (Yoma 53b).

Over the years many Jewish boys have been named Theodor Herzl, after the founder of modern Zionism, and more recently the names of Israel's popular prime ministers (Ben-Gurion and Golda) have been used. Inspired by the Israel-Egypt Peace Treaty, signed in Washington, D.C., in March 1979, Mr. and Mrs. Hotam El Kabassi named their triplets born on April 5, 1979, Carter, Begin, and Sadat—in honor of U.S. President Jimmy Carter, Israeli Prime Minister Menachem Begin, and Egyptian President Anwar Sadat, the three principals at the signing.

The custom of naming children after celebrities, however, has never been particularly popular among Jews. In fact, in scanning the Bible one finds that the names of heroes mentioned early in the Bible are not used again by anyone later in the biblical narrative. No one but the original Abraham, Sarah, Isaac, Rebecca, Jacob, Rachel, Leah, Joseph, Moses, Aaron, Miriam, Isaiah, and Jeremiah carry those names. The reason for this strange circumstance has not been explained. Nor has it been explained why at least a few of the Rabbis of the Talmud were not named after some of the most revered personalities in the Bible. Not one scholar in the Talmud is named Abraham, Israel, or David. Some of the names of Jacob's sons are used, but Dan, Gad, and Aşher are not among them. Of the Prophets, Isaiah, Hosea, Joel, Amos, Obadiah, Micah, Habakkuk, Zephaniah, and Malachi are not used in the Talmud at all.

It is indeed difficult to explain why many Rabbis of the Talmud are named Ishmael, but not one is named Abraham and only one is named Moses. Attempts have been made to explain the use of the name Ishmael, but they are not satisfying. Rabbi Jose (Genesis Rabba 71:3) finds some justification in the explanation that Ishmael is an example of a person whose "name was beautiful but whose actions were ugly." The commentary (Tosafot) on Berachot 7b justifies the use of the name by observing that Ishmael, Abraham's son by his concubine Hagar, was a sinner who repented, and it was, therefore, quite proper to use his name.

Name Changes

Since early Bible times it has been customary to somewhat modify an individual's name, or change it entirely, when a change in the status of the individual was anticipated or had been achieved. Among the more prominent examples: Abraham (from Abram), Sarah (from Sarai), Jacob (to Israel), Joshua (from Hosea), Gideon (to Jerubaal), Zedekiah (from Mattaniah), and Jehoiakim (from Eliakim).

Though name-changing is no longer common, there is an old Jewish custom of changing a person's name in time of serious illness, which persists in certain circles. It is hoped that the change of name will cause the angel of death to question whether the person he is about to visit (who has a different name than expected) is the correct target. Sometimes, if the patient is young, the name Alter ("old one" in Yiddish) or Alterke (for a female) is added to or substituted for the original name. The thought is that the angel of death would be confused if, when he is assigned to take action against, say, Alter or Chayim Alter, and he finally finds him, the person turns out to be young rather than old as his name implies.

Masculine/Feminine Interchanges

Many names in contemporary usage have been "borrowed" from the opposite sex, sometimes without modification but more often with a slight change. The practice of interchanging names between the sexes is an old one. The Bible contains many examples of names common to both sexes. In II Kings 8:26 Athaliah is the daughter of Ahab and Jezebel, while in I Chronicles 8:26 Athaliah is used as a masculine name. Efah, the concubine of Caleb, is also used as a masculine name. Shlomit appears in both a masculine and feminine form, as do Tzivya, Bilga, Chuba, Noga, Chupa, Gover, Buna, Bina, Abijah, Afra, Reenah, Chavila, and Simcha.

A number of outstanding contemporary male personalities have been given names that are characteristically feminine: polar explorer Richard Evelyn Byrd, noted author Evelyn Waugh, Congressman Clare Hoffman of Michigan, among others.

Among women's names we find a large number adopted from the masculine forms. In many instances, the feminine name is so long established and accepted that we no longer realize that it had its origin in a masculine name. In this group we find Alexandra and Alexandria from Alexander; Charlotte and Charlene from Charles; Davi, Davida, and Davita from David; Erica from Eric; Frederica from Frederic; Georgia, Georgine, and Georgette from George; Harriet and Harri from Harry; Henrietta, Henri, and Henria from Henry; Herma and Hermine from Herman; Josepha and Josephine from Joseph; Louise and Louisa from Louis; Roberta from Robert; Stephanie from Stephan; and Willa and Willene from Will or William.

Unconventional Spellings

For the past two or three decades many new first names have come into being as a result of a desire on the part of parents to be different or distinctive. They have increasingly been taking popular names and spelling them differently.

The most common characteristic of this new fad is substituting a "y" for an "i" or adding an "e." Fannye was once Fannie, and Mollye was formerly Mollie. Likewise, Sadie has become Sadye, and Edith has become Edyth or Edythe. Shirley has become Shirlee, Shirlie, or Sherle. Similarly, the letter "i" has been substituted for "y" and new spellings like Tobi, Toni, and Ricki have become common.

Sometimes letters are dropped or added to old names to form new ones. Consequently, names like Sarah and Hannah have become Sara and Hanna. Esther can now be found as Ester and sometimes as Esta or Estee.

Among the many feminine names that have, because of a new spelling, made their appearance of late are Rosalin, Rosaline, Rosalyn, Roselyn, Roslyn, Roslyne, and Rosylin from Rosalind; Debra and Dobra from Deborah; Karolyn and Carolyn from Caroline; Alyce and Alyse from Alice; Gale from Gail; Arlyne from Arline; Arleyne from Arlene; Lilyan from Lillian; Elane and Elayne from Elaine; Ilene and Iline from Eileen; Ethyl and Ethyle from Ethel; Janis from Janice; Jayne from Jane; Madeline, Madelon, Madelyn, Madelyne, and Madlyn from Madeleine; Marilin and Marylin from Marilyn; and Vyvyan and Vivien from Vivian.

Changes in spelling also account for a large number of new masculine names: Allan, Alyn, Allyn, and Allen from Alan; Frederic, Fredric, and Fredrick from Frederick; Irwin, Erwin, Irving, and Irvine from Irvin; Isidore, Isador, and Isadore from Isidor; Laurance, Laurence, Lawrance, and Lorence from Lawrence; Maury, Morey, and Morry from Morris; Murry from Murray; and Mervyn from Mervin.

The Complete Dictionary of English & Hebrew First Names includes many names that were created by spelling existing names unconventionally.

Pet Forms (Diminutives)

Pet forms, often called diminutives, make up a large portion of our contemporary first names. This group grows larger and larger as the desire for self expression grows stronger. Often, the given first name of an individual is completely abandoned and the pet name becomes the real name. James Earl Carter, the thirty-ninth president of the United States, is a prime example. Although his original and legal name is James, Jimmy is the name he prefers and the name he used when signing official documents.

II

The Naming Process

Hebrew and Secular Names

Throughout most of Jewish history, Jews have used both secular, non-Jewish names and Hebrew names. In the Talmud (Gittin 11b) it is noted that "the majority of Jews in the Diaspora have Gentile names." This observation can be applied to every period in Jewish history, from the Babylonian Exile (586 B.C.E.) onward. Daniel (of lions' den fame) and his friends had Hebrew and Aramaic (Babylonian) names. Daniel's Aramaic name was Beltshatzar. His friends, popularly known as Shadrach, Meshach, and Abed-nego, were known also by their Hebrew names—Chananya, Mishael, and Azarya. (Biblical names ending in "a" or "ah" are generally Aramaic: Ezra, Nehemiah, etc.)

In the fourth century, with Alexander the Great's conquest of Palestine, Jews came into closer contact with Greek (Hellenistic) culture. As a result they soon began using Greek names. This practice spread, and some of the greatest among the Sages of the early talmudic period, as well as some of the most revered leaders of the Jewish people in the early centuries B.C.E., carried Greek names such as Antigonus, Avtalyon, Jason, Onias, and Alexander. Some used both a Hebrew and a Greek name; thus someone with the name Netanel or Yonatan would choose Dositheus or Theodotian as his Greek name, based on a similarity of meaning. In the same manner, Tobiah (Tuviya) also became known as Agathou, Uri as Phoebus, and Tzadok as Justus.

The practice of Jews using both Hebrew and secular names grew in popularity with the passage of time. Among Italian Jews in early times we find Diofatto used for Asael, and Tranquillo and Tranquillus for Manoach and Menachem. Among French Jews we find a great leader of the thirteenth century, Rabbi Yechiel of Paris, also known as Vivant. Frenchmen with the Hebrew name Matityahu also were known as Dieudonne, Chaim as Vive, Ovadya as Serfdieu, and Gamliel as Dieulecresse.

Jews living in the Arab world used Arabic names along with their Hebrew names. Thus, Abraham also was called Ibrahim, David was also known as Daoud, Eliezer as Manzur, Matzliach as Maimun.

(The Jews of India, known as Bene Israel, modified their Hebrew names so they would have a Hindi sound. Thus, Benjamin became Benmanjee, Abraham became Abrajee, David became Dawoodjee, and Jacob became Akkoobjee.)

The practice of giving a child both a Hebrew (or Yiddish) and a secular name continues to this day. More often than not, the only association between the Hebrew and secular name is a similarity in sound, and the similarity is most often confined to the first letter or syllable.

Names to Be Avoided

Although there are no strict religious rules dictating which names may or may not be used, there are Jewish traditions suggesting the wisdom behind avoiding certain names. The Sages (Midrash Genesis Rabba 49:1) suggest, for example, that one avoid using the names of wicked people—including Pharaoh, Sisera, and Sennacherib. This practice seems to have been observed over the centuries.

Rabbi Chayim Azulai, an eighteenth-century scholar, author of an encyclopedia containing the biographies of 1,300 scholars and writers, suggested that Jews avoid using all names that appear in the Bible before the time of Abraham. He considered it improper to name a child after Adam or Noah or Shem or Ever—people who preceded Abraham. Azulai also condemned anyone who would select the name Yafet (Japheth), a name already belonging to the father of third-century Palestinian scholar Benjamin ben Yafet (Berachot 33a).

A noted contemporary of Azulai, Elazar Fleckeles, disagreed, asserting that it was quite proper to use pre-Abrahamitic names. Fleckeles calls attention to the talmudic scholars Benjamin ben Yafet and Akavya ben Mehalalel (both Yafet and Mehalalel are pre-Abrahamitic biblical names).

The cautions of Rabbi Azulai have been largely ignored, and for the past two centuries many illustrious persons have carried pre-Abrahamitic names.

Naming Children After Relatives

Ashkenazic Jews—the Jews of Germany, France, Russia, England, etc., and their descendants—adhere closely to an old Jewish belief that a man's name is the essence of his being; the name is his soul. When a child is given a relative's name, he is also being given the relative's soul. If the relative is still alive, the soul would have to be shared by two people—the older living relative and his namesake. For that reason, Ashkenazic Jews discourage naming a newborn after a living relative, for it might result in the shortening of the older person's life.

While Ashkenazim refrain from naming their offspring after living relatives, they generally do name them after deceased relatives.

In the twelfth century, the noted mystic Judah ben Samuel of Regensburg (popularly known as Rabbi Yehuda Hechasid, meaning "Judah the Pious One") introduced a practice which forbade a man from marrying a woman with exactly the same name as his mother. Rabbi Yehuda was fearful that this might lead to the embarrassing situation of a man's mother answering when he is actually addressing his wife. This concern aside, Ashkenazic Jews in particular consider such marriages ill-advised, because if a man were to marry a woman with the same first name as that of his mother, and his mother were to die, the man would not be able to honor his deceased mother by naming a future daughter after her (because his wife—still living—carries that same name.

Generally, Yehuda Hechasid disapproved of naming any child after a living relative; but he also disapproved of naming a child after a deceased relative, out of fear that the soul of the deceased might be disturbed. In his will, the rabbi instructed that none of his descendants be called by his name or the name of his father, Samuel.

Sephardic Jews—from Spain, Portugal, Italy, North Africa, and the Middle East—do not share the Ashkenazic belief that a person's life will be shortened if a newborn is named after him. Sephardim therefore do not hesitate to name their offspring after living grandparents, and occasionally, though infrequently, even after themselves.

There is a longstanding tradition justifying the Sephardic practice. As far back as the fourth century B.C.E., at the height of Greek influence in Palestine, Jews used the names of living relatives. In the family of the High Priests, the names Onias and Simon were used alternately, between 332 and 165 B.C.E. In the early talmudic period (beginning with the first century B.C.E.), Hillel the Great's family repeated the names Gamaliel and Judah for several generations, with occasional use of the names Simon and Hillel.

The practice continued through the Middle Ages, and many examples can be cited. Generally, the eldest son in a family was named after the paternal (and sometimes maternal) grandfather. The grandson of the eminent eleventh and twelfth-century philosopher and poet Yehuda Halevi was also named Yehuda (during the poet's lifetime). In the family of the twelfth-century philosopher Moses Maimonides, we find that the name of Maimonides' grandfather was Yosef son of Isaac, son of Yosef, son of Ovadya, son of Shlomo, son of Ovadya. And the same pattern of naming after living relatives can be seen in the family of the thirteenth-century Italian talmudist Rabbi Isaiah ben Elijah deTrani, whose maternal grandfather's name was Isaiah, and in the family of thirteenth-century Spanish-born Moses ben Nachman (Nachmanides), whose grandson had the same name as his maternal grandfather, Jonah (Girondi).

Naming Children After Non-Relatives

The Talmud cites instances where, for a variety of reasons, children were named after persons—living or dead—not within their own family. In one case (Shabbat 134a), the second-century scholar Nathan of Babylonia (Natan HaBavli), a contemporary of Judah the Prince, advised a mother who had lost two sons at the time of their circumcision to wait until her third son was older (and healthier) before circumcising him. She followed the scholar's advice and her son survived. In gratitude she named him Nathan, meaning "He [God] gave [life]." In another case (Bava Metzia 84b), Rabbi Eliezer ben Hyrcanus, a first-century C.E. scholar and a disciple of Yochanan ben Zakai, was considered so helpful by several women in answering their questions that the women later named their children after him.

As mentioned above, the idea of naming a child after a celebrated person did not take root in Jewish tradition. Aside from Chasidim who have occasionally named children after a deceased *rebbe* whom they adore, and Jews who have named their offspring after personal heroes (such as Herzl, Balfour, Ben-Gurion, Golda), the practice has never been widespread. Quite likely, the reason for this hesitancy is linked to the belief that a man's name is his person, that a man's name is his soul. Jews who may have wanted to name a child after a celebrity did not do so out of fear that the soul of that person would be acquired along with his name, that is, that it would occupy the body of the infant. This would place a very grave responsibility on the child, who would have to measure up to the life of the great soul now occupying his body.

When and Where Is a Boy Named?

Although there is a tradition that girls and boys are to be named in the synagogue on the first Sabbath after their birth, today it is established custom to name a boy at his *brit* (circumcision), which is held on the eighth day after birth. However, neither the Bible nor the Talmud mentions this fact. In the few instances in the Bible where the circumcision rite is mentioned (Genesis 17:24 for Abraham; Genesis 17:25 for Ishmael; Genesis 21:4 for Isaac; and Exodus 4:25, where Tzipora, wife of Moses, circumcises her son), no mention is made of naming the child. What appears to be the rule is that children in the Bible were named at the time of birth, not later: all of Jacob's sons were named at the time of birth (Genesis 29 and 30);

Tzipora named her son Gershom at the time of birth (Exodus 2:22); Samson was named immediately after birth (Judges 13:4).

Only in the New Testament do we find references to people being named at the time of their circumcision. In Luke 1:59 Zacharias and Elizabeth have a son who is named John at the time of his circumcision, and in 2:21 Jesus is named at the time of his circumcision.

There are at least two references in talmudic literature that describe what transpires at a circumcision ceremony. In the Midrash (Ruth Rabba 6:6), a detailed description is given of the proceedings at the *brit* of Elisha ben Avuya. All segments of the population of Jerusalem—rich and poor—are invited. A banquet is prepared and much merrymaking ensues after the ceremony. Some stay on for hours and sing and dance and play games, while the more learned gather in a separate room to discuss Tora. But no mention is made of the naming of the child at the ceremony.

Similarly, another celebration of this kind was held about 100 years later in Sepphoris, a city in northern Palestine. Here again the Midrash (Kohelet Rabba 3:4) describes all the merriment that ensues, but no mention is made of naming the baby.

Scholars are of the opinion that the actual practice of naming a child formally at the *brit* began some time in the middle of the twelfth century, but no information is available to explain why the practice began precisely at that time. By the sixteenth century, the practice was commonplace, as indicated in the *Shulchan Aruch*. The *brit* being the first major religious event in the life of a male child, it is quite understandable that his naming should take place at that time.

When and Where Is a Girl Named?

The first opportunity for naming a female child publicly is at the first Sabbath service following birth, when a *minyan*—a quorum of worshippers—is assembled. On that occasion the father is honored with an *aliya* (called to the Tora), after which the baby girl is named. The naming can also take place at the morning service on a Monday, Thursday, or on Rosh Chodesh (New Moon), since the Tora is read on those occasions as well and the new father can therefore be given an *aliya*.

In naming boys and girls, the name of the newborn is mentioned in the blessing, together with the name of the father. Today, in many instances, the name of the mother is mentioned at the ceremony as well.

Naming an Adopted Child

The Talmud (Sanhedrin 19b) says: "Whoever raises an orphan may be considered to be his parent." From this statement later authorities concluded that if one adopts a child, and the child has not yet been named, he or she may be called by the name of the adoptive father. Thus, for example, a girl is to be called _____ bat Moshe (adoptive father's name) and a boy _____ ben Moshe. If the child was named before being given up for adoption, the name of the natural father is to be retained.

The Talmud also arrives at this conclusion from the biblical account of King Saul and his daughters Michal and Merav. Merav had several children, who were raised by her younger sister Michal; and the Bible refers to these children as Michal's children even though she was not their real mother. Based on this, it was concluded that it is proper for a child who has been adopted to be called by the name of his adoptive parents. It must be said, however, that in Jewish law the natural parents never lose their rights or status, and a child must mourn for them when they die. The child is also obligated to say Kaddish for adoptive parents when they die, because of the strong emotional ties that normally develop between children and those who have cared for them all or most of their lives.

Names for Converts

Although there is no legal requirement mandating that a convert use the name of Abraham or Ruth or Sarah as a first name, there is a longstanding tradition to this effect. In most cases, a male convert is named Avraham ben Avraham Avinu (Abraham the son of Abraham our father), and a female convert is named Sara bat Avraham Avinu (Sarah the daughter of Abraham our father) or Rut bat Avraham Avinu (Ruth daughter of Abraham our father). The use of "ben Avraham" and "bat Avraham" is generally insisted upon for purposes of identifying an individual as a proselyte (Shulcan Aruch, Even Haezer 129:20).

Two reasons are offered for naming converts Avraham. First, the Bible (Genesis 17:5) speaks of Abraham as being "the father of a multitude of nations"; and since proselytes come from diverse peoples and backgrounds, it is appropriate that they be called sons of Abraham.

A second explanation is offered in the Midrash: Since the Children of Israel are called God's "friends"—as it is written, "the seed of Abraham My [God's] friend" (Isaiah 41:8)— and since proselytes are called God's "friends"—as it is written, "God is the friend of the proselyte" (Deuteronomy 10:18)—it was concluded that Abraham has a special relationship to proselytes. In Jewish tradition, Abraham became known as "the father of proselytes," because once they have converted to Judaism, they have forsaken all previous family connections, and the family of Abraham becomes their family. The Talmud (Yevamot 22a) calls them "newborn babes."

Offering the convert the name of Abraham is explained by the Midrash to be an expression of deep love. The Midrash says: "God loves proselytes dearly. And we too should show our love for them because they left their father's house, and their people, and the Gentile community and have joined us" (Deuteronomy Rabba 8:2).

It is, of course, a matter of history that not all proselytes have taken the name Abraham. The scholar Onkelos was a proselyte. Flavius Clemens, nephew of the Roman Vespasian, was a proselyte. The Talmud (Berachot 28a) also refers to a proselyte named Judah the Ammonite.

Female converts take the name of Sarah because she was the First Lady of Israel, the wife of Abraham; and they take the name of Ruth because Ruth of the Bible is the epitome of loyalty to Judaism. Ruth is famous for swearing her eternal allegiance to her mother-in-law Naomi, which was expressed in these immortal words (Ruth 1:16):

> Whither thou goest, I will go,
> Where thou lodgest, I will lodge,
> Thy people shall be my people,
> And thy God my God.

Using the Matronymic Form When Praying for Good Health

As a rule, in Jewish life a person is identified by his or her father's name; he or she is referred to as _____ ben/bat _____ (his/her father's name). This, for example, is the form used when writing a person's name in a Jewish marriage contract (ketuba) or a Jewish divorce document (get). There is, however, one notable exception: when a person is sick and a prayer for recovery is recited, the mother's name (matronymic) is used.

Apparently, the practice of using the matronymic form on this occasion developed quite early and was already in vogue in talmudic times. The fourth-century talmudic scholar Abaye said: "My mother told me that all incantations [prayers for recovery] which are repeated several times must contain the name of the mother . . ." (Shabbat 66b).

The Zohar (on the Bible portion "Lech Lecha") makes a similar point when it says that all appeals to supernatural beings, whether in prayers or on charms, must be made in the name of the mother.

To find biblical justification for the practice, the Sages pointed to the verse, "I am the servant, the son of Thy handmaid, Thou hast loosened my bonds [saved me]" (Psalms 116:16). From this verse the inference is drawn that in an emergency, when one prays to be saved, the matronymic rather than the patronymic form should be used.

Using the Matronymic Form to Avoid Confusion

There are times when the matronymic form is used to identify a person simply to avoid confusion and misunderstanding. Thus, we find, for example, that the talmudic scholar Mari, who was a proselyte, was named Mari ben Rachel (mother's name). His status as a proselyte was immediately known to all.

It is considered important that the individual's status as a Jew be readily known because that status in large part determines his or her legal rights. A proselyte, for example, may not marry a *Kohayn* (*Shulchan Aruch, Even Haezer 6:8*). Since the status of one named Mari ben Rachel, for example, would be immediately known to all, no one would introduce him to the daughter of a *Kohayn* with an eye towards marriage.

The noted eighteenth-century Polish scholar Ezekiel Landau made the point that when one writes a document of divorce *(get)* for a proselyte, the matronymic rather than the patronymic should be used because many proselytes are generally named _____ *ben Avraham,* and this could conceivably lead to some confusion at a future date (many born Jews are also named _____ *ben Avraham*). By using the matronymic form, a misunderstanding might be avoided. In fact, some scholars favor using the matronymic form in the divorce document in cases where, in general, the mother in the family is better known than the father.

In the same way, to avoid error and misunderstanding, the child of a Jewish mother and a non-Jewish father was called by the matronymic (_____ *ben* _____ [the mother's first name]). Using the matronymic form at a *Pidyon Haben* (Redemption of the Firstborn), for example, makes it evident that the father is probably not Jewish and that as a non-Jew he should not be called upon to recite the prayers that a Jewish father normally recites.

Using a Grandfather's Name

Rabbi Moses Isserles, in his Notes on the *Shulchan Aruch, Orach Chayim 139:3,* suggests that one should assume his grandfather's name if his father has converted to another religion. When given an *aliya,* it is suggested that the convert's son be called to the Tora by the name of his maternal grandfather. By so doing, the son would be making a clear statement that he disapproves of his father's action. Isserles also indicates that when in the past the son has received many *aliyot* in that community and is well known by his father's name, he should continue to be called as he was in the past (before his father's conversion).

Naming a Child Born Out of Wedlock

If a child is born out of wedlock to a Jewish mother and the father's identity is unknown, the child should be named at the appropriate time and place (at the *brit* for a boy or in the synagogue for a girl), and he or she should be named after the mother—for example, _____ *ben Rachel* or _____ *bat Rachel*. According to Moses Isserles, in his Notes on the *Shulchan Aruch, Orach Chayim 139:3*, such a child (called a *shetuki* in Hebrew), when given an *aliya*, should be called to the Tora by the name of his maternal grand-father in order to avoid embarrassment that might be caused by those wondering why the individual was using his mother's name.

The Naming Ceremony for a Boy

Before commencing the actual circumcision, the *mohel*, who is the surrogate of the father, recites the following blessing in Hebrew: "Blessed art Thou, O Lord our God, King of the universe, Who hast hallowed us by Thy commandments and commanded us to circum-cise [our sons]." The father then recites: "Blessed art Thou, O Lord our God, King of the universe, Who hast hallowed us by Thy commandments and commanded us to enter this child into the Covenant of Abraham our father."

Upon completing the operation, the *mohel* holds up a cup of wine and pronounces the blessing for wine. He then continues with a prayer for the welfare of the child and his parents, which includes the words, "And may he henceforth be known in Israel as _____ son of _____." This prayer, which includes verses from Proverbs 23:25, Ezekiel 16:6, Psalms 105:8-10 and 118:1, and Genesis 21:4, concludes with the words, "This little child named _____, may he grow to be great! Even as he now enters the Covenant [of Abraham], so may he enter the world of Tora study, a life of connubial bliss, and a life in which he will perform good deeds."

The *sandek* ("godfather"), who holds the baby during the circum-cision, then drinks some of the wine and a few drops are dabbed on the lips of the infant.

The Naming Ceremony for a Girl

The naming ceremony for a girl is simpler. On the Sabbath following the birth of the child, the father visits the synagogue and receives an *aliya* (a Tora honor). After his portion of the Tora is read, the father recites the final Tora blessing. The sexton or rabbi then recites a special prayer for the welfare of the mother, asking for her return to good health now that the delivery is over. This prayer is known as a *Mi Shebayrach*, which are the first two words of the prayer, meaning "May He who blessed." A second *Mi Shebayrach* is then recited, and as part of this prayer the baby is named. The general wording of the prayer is, "May He who blessed our forefathers Abraham, Isaac, and Jacob bless _____ and his daughter just born to him, and she shall henceforth be known in Israel by the name _____ daughter of _____. Guard and protect her father and mother. May they live to rear her to be a God-fearing person, and may they raise her to achieve connubial bliss and a life of meritorious deeds."

In some Reform congregations today, the child is named on the first Sabbath that the mother and child are well enough to visit the synagogue together. A similar custom seems to have been followed in some communities in medieval Germany.

MASCULINE NAMES

Aaron The Anglicized form of Aharon. *See* Aharon.

Abahu (אַבָּהוּ) From the Aramaic, meaning "God is my father." In the Talmud (Bava Kama 117a), a fourth-century Palestinian scholar.

Abaya A variant spelling of Abaye. *See* Abaye.

Abaye (אַבָּיֵי) From the Aramaic, meaning "little father." The name of several third- and fourth-century talmudic scholars. In the Talmud (Horayot 14a), Nachmani was Abaye's nickname. He was named after Rabba's father, in whose house Abaye was reared. Abaya is a variant spelling.

Abba (אַבָּא) From the Arabic, Syriac, and Aramaic, meaning "father." The name of scores of Babylonian and Palestinian talmudic scholars. The most famous Abba was the fourth-century Babylonian-born scholar (Berachot 24b), who settled in Palestine. Abbie and Abby are pet forms. Akin to Avi. *See* Avi.

Abba Yudan (אַבָּא יוּדָן) A variant form of Avdan. *See* Avdan.

Abbe, Abbey From the Old French and Latin, meaning "the head of a monastery, an abbot." *See* Abbot. Or, a short form of Abiel (Aviel). *See* Aviel. Used also as feminine names. Abbie and Abby are variant spellings.

Abbie A variant spelling of Abbey. *See* Abbey. Also, a pet form of Abba. Popular as a feminine name. Abby is a variant spelling.

Abbot, Abbott From the Hebrew and Aramaic, meaning "father." Akin to Abba. Popularized in the Middle Ages after being adopted as names by the heads of religious orders. Abbe is a French form. *See* Abbe.

Abby A variant spelling of Abbe, Abbey, and Abbie. Used more commonly as a feminine form. *See* Abby (feminine section). Also, a pet form of Abba.

Abda A variant spelling of Avda. *See* Avda.

Abdan A variant spelling of Avda. *See* Avda.

Abdel A variant spelling of Avdel. *See* Avdel.

Abdi A variant spelling of Avdi. *See* Avdi.

Abdiel A variant spelling of Avdiel. *See* Avdiel.

Abdima A variant spelling of Avdima. *See* Avdima.

Abdimi A variant spelling of Avdimi. *See* Avdimi.

1

Abdon   A variant spelling of Avdon. *See* Avdon.

Abe   A pet form of Abraham. *See* Abraham.

Abednego (עֲבֵד נְגוֹ)   An Aramaic name, meaning "servant of [the god] Nego (Nebo)." In the Bible (Daniel 1:7), the Aramaic name of Azariah, one of the three men who miraculously escaped unharmed from a blazing furnace.

Abel (הֶבֶל)   From the Assyrian, meaning "meadow," or from the Hebrew, meaning "breath." In the Bible (Genesis 4:2), the brother of Cain, son of Adam and Eve. Able is a variant spelling. Abeles is a variant form.

Abelard   From the Anglo-Saxon, meaning "noble, nobly resolute."

Abeles   A variant form of Abel. *See* Abel.

Aberlin (אַבֶּערְלִין)   A Yiddish form of Abraham. *See* Abraham.

Abi, Abie   Pet forms of Abraham. *See* Abraham. Also, variant spellings of Avi. *See* Avi.

Abia, Abiah   Variant spellings of Avia. *See* Avia.

Abiasaph   A variant spelling of Aviasaf. *See* Aviasaf.

Abida   A variant spelling of Avida. *See* Avida.

Abidan   A variant spelling of Avidan. *See* Avidan.

Abiel   A variant spelling of Aviel. *See* Aviel.

Abiezer   A variant spelling of Aviezer. *See* Aviezer.

Abihu   A variant spelling of Avihu. *See* Avihu.

Abihud   A variant spelling of Avihud. *See* Avihud.

Abimelech   A variant spelling of Avimelech. *See* Avimelech.

Abimi   A variant spelling of Avimi. *See* Avimi.

Abin   A variant spelling of Avin. *See* Avin.

Abina   A variant spelling of Avina. *See* Avina.

Abinadab   A variant spelling of Avinadav. *See* Avinadav.

Abinoam   A variant spelling of Avinoam. *See* Avinoam.

Abir (אַבִּיר)   From the Hebrew, meaning "strong."

Abiram   A variant spelling of Aviram. *See* Aviram.

Abiri (אַבִּירִי)   From the Hebrew, meaning "courageous, gallant."

Abishai   A variant spelling of Avishai. *See* Avishai.

Abishua   A variant spelling of Avishua. *See* Avishua.

Abishur   A variant spelling of Avishur. *See* Avishur.

Abital   A variant spelling of Avital. *See* Avital.

Abituv   A variant spelling of Avituv. *See* Avituv.

Able   A variant spelling of Abel. *See* Abel.

Abner   A variant spelling of Avner. *See* Avner.

Abraham   The Anglicized spelling of Avraham. *See* Avraham. Aberlin is a variant form. Abe, Abi, and Abie are pet forms. Abram is a contracted form.

Abram   A variant spelling of Avram. *See* Avram. A popular name among New Englanders of Puritan stock.

Absalom   A variant spelling of Avshalom. *See* Avshalom.

Abtalyon   A variant spelling of Avtalyon. *See* Avtalyon.

Abuha   A variant spelling of Avuha. *See* Avuha.

Ach (אָח)   From the Hebrew, meaning "brother."

Acha (אָחָא)   From the Aramaic, meaning "brother." The name of many Babylonian talmudic scholars over the centuries. Achai is a variant form.

Achai (אָחָאִי)   From the Aramaic, meaning "brother." A variant form of Acha. A nickname given to several talmudic scholars named Acha, prominent among them being a fifth-century Babylonian scholar (Ketubot 47a).

Achan (עָכָן)   Possibly from the Aramaic, meaning "snake." In the Bible (Joshua 7:1), a member of the tribe of Judah.

Acharon (אַחֲרוֹן)   From the Hebrew, meaning "last, latest." Often the name of the last son in a family.

Achav (אַחְאָב)   From the Hebrew, meaning "father's brother." In the Bible (I Kings 16:33), a king of Israel who reigned from 874 to 853 B.C.E., husband of the evil Jezebel. Ahab is a variant spelling.

Achaz (אָחָז)   From the Hebrew, meaning "to hold, detain, restrain." In the Bible (II Kings 15:38), the son of Jonathan and a king of Judah. Ahaz is a variant spelling. Achazai and Achzai are variant forms.

Achazai (אַחְזַי)   A variant form of Achaz. *See* Achaz. In the Bible (Nehemiah 11:13), a Priest whose sons lived in Jerusalem in the time of Nehemiah.

Achazia, Achaziah   Variant spellings of Achazya. *See* Achazya.

Achazya (אֲחַזְיָה)   From the Hebrew, meaning "God has grasped." In the Bible (I Kings 22:40), a king of Israel and a son of Ahab. Achazyahu is a variant form. Achazia, Achaziah, Ahazia, and Ahaziah are variant spellings. Akin to Achaz.

Achazyahu (אֲחַזְיָהוּ)   A variant form of Achazya. *See* Achazya. Ahaziahu is a variant spelling.

Achban (אַחְבָּן)   From the Hebrew, meaning "brother of an intelligent one." In the Bible (I Chronicles 2:29), a member of the tribe of Judah.

Achbor (עַכְבּוֹר)   From the Hebrew and Aramaic, meaning "mouse." In the Bible (II Kings 22:12), an officer of King Josiah of Judah.

Acher (אַחֵר) From the Hebrew, meaning "other, another person." In the Bible (I Chronicles 7:12), a descendant of Benjamin.

Achi (אֲחִי) From the Hebrew, meaning "my brother." In the Bible (I Kings 5:15), a leader of the tribe of Gad. The name of a fourth-century Palestinian talmudic scholar.

Achia, Achiah Variant spellings of Achiya. *See* Achiya.

Achiam (אֲחִיאָם) From the Hebrew, meaning "the brother of my mother, uncle." In the Bible (II Samuel 23:33), one of King David's warriors. Achiem is a variant form.

Achiasaf (אֲחִיאָסָף) From the Hebrew, meaning "my brother has gathered in."

Achiav (אֲחִיאָב) From the Hebrew, meaning "the brother of my father, uncle." Akin to Achav.

Achichud (אֲחִיחוּד) From the Hebrew, meaning "a riddle."

Achida (אֲחִידָע) From the Hebrew, meaning "my brother is knowledgeable."

Achidan (אֲחִידָן) From the Hebrew, meaning "my brother is just."

Achidod (אֲחִידוֹד) From the Hebrew, meaning "my brother is an uncle" or "my brother is a friend."

Achiem (אֲחִיאָם) From the Hebrew, meaning "the brother of my mother, uncle." Achia is a variant form.

Achiezer (אֲחִיעֶזֶר) From the Hebrew, meaning "my brother is my helper." In the Bible (Numbers 1:12), a leader of the tribe of Dan.

Achihud (אֲחִיהוּד) From the Hebrew, meaning "brother of majesty" or "God is praised." In the Bible (Numbers 34:27), a leader of the tribe of Asher. Its contemporary meaning is "friend of the Jews."

Achikam (אֲחִיקָם) From the Hebrew, meaning "established" or "resurrected." In the Bible (Jeremiah 40:5), the father of Gedaliah, who was appointed by the king of Babylonia to be governor of Judah.

Achikar (אֲחִיקָר) From the Hebrew, meaning "my brother is precious."

Achilud (אֲחִילוּד) From the Hebrew, meaning "my brother is born." In the Bible (II Samuel 8:16), the father of Jehoshaphat, King David's chronicler.

Achimaatz (אֲחִימַעַץ) From the Hebrew, meaning "my brother is wrath, anger." In the Bible (II Samuel 15:27), a son of Zadok.

Achiman (אֲחִימָן) From the Hebrew, meaning "my brother is a gift." In the Bible (Numbers 13:22), a son of Anak.

Achimelech (אֲחִימֶלֶךְ) From the Hebrew, meaning "the king (God) is my brother." In the Bible (I Samuel 21:2), a Priest who befriended David.

Achimot (אֲחִימוֹת) From the Hebrew, meaning "my brother is death." In the Bible (I Chronicles 6:10), a Levite.

Achina (אֲחִינָא) From the Aramaic, meaning "brother." A fourth-century talmudic scholar.

Achinadav (אֲחִינָדָב) From the Hebrew, meaning "noble brother." In the Bible (II Kings 4:14), an officer of King Solomon's royal court.

Achiner (אֲחִינֵר) From the Hebrew, meaning "my brother is a light (candle)."

Achinoam (אֲחִינֹעַם) From the Hebrew, meaning "my brother is a delight, sweet." Used in the Bible as a feminine name (I Samuel 4:13).

Achipelet (אֲחִיפֶּלֶט) From the Hebrew, meaning "my brother is a fugitive" or "my brother is a deliverer."

Achira (אֲחִירַע) From the Hebrew, meaning "my brother is evil." In the Bible (Numbers 1:15), a leader of the tribe of Naphtali.

Achiram (אֲחִירָם) From the Hebrew, meaning "my brother is noble, princely, lofty." In the Bible (Numbers 26:38), a son of Benjamin.

Achisamach (אֲחִיסָמָךְ) From the Hebrew, meaning "my brother is my support." In the Bible (Exodus 31:6), the father of Oholiav, who helped in the construction of the Tabernacle.

Achisar (אֲחִישָׂר) From the Hebrew, meaning "my brother is a prince."

Achishachar (אֲחִישַׁחַר) From the Hebrew, meaning "my brother is [the] dawn." In the Bible (I Chronicles 7:10), a member of the tribe of Benjamin.

Achishai (אֲחִישַׁי) From the Hebrew, meaning "my brother is a gift" or "my brother's gift."

Achishalom (אֲחִישָׁלוֹם) From the Hebrew, meaning "my brother is peace."

Achishar (אֲחִישָׁר) From the Hebrew, meaning "my brother is song." In the Bible (I Kings 4:6), the officer in charge of Solomon's royal palace.

Achishur (אֲחִישׁוּר) From the Hebrew, meaning "my brother is a wall."

Achisofel A variant pronunciation of Achitofel. See Achitofel.

Achitofel (אֲחִיתֹפֶל) From the Hebrew, meaning "my brother is folly." In the Bible (II Samuel 15:12), an advisor to King David. Achisofel is a variant form.

Achitov (אֲחִיטוֹב) From the Hebrew, meaning "my brother is goodness." Akin to Achituv.

Achituv (אֲחִיטוּב) From the Hebrew, meaning "my brother is goodness." In the Bible (I Samuel 14:3), the grandson of Eli the High Priest. Akin to Achitov.

Achitzedek (אֲחִיצֶדֶק) From the Hebrew, meaning "my brother is just."

Achitzur (אֲחִיצוּר) From the Hebrew, meaning "my brother is a rock (strong)."

Achiya (אֲחִיָּה) From the Hebrew, meaning "God is my brother." In the Bible (I Chronicles 11:36), one of King David's warriors, and (I Kings 11:29) a Prophet in the time of King Jeroboam. In the Talmud, a variant form of Chiya. See Chiya. Ahia and Ahiah are variant spellings. Achiyahu is a variant form.

Achiyahu (אֲחִיָּהוּ)   A variant form of Achiya. *See* Achiya.

Achlai (אַחְלַי)   From the Aramaic, meaning "sick, diseased." In the Bible (I Chronicles 2:31), a member of the tribe of Judah.

Achlav (אַחְלָב)   From the Hebrew, meaning "fat." In the Bible (Judges 1:31), a town assigned to the tribe of Asher.

Achli (אַחְלִי)   From the Hebrew, meaning "I have a brother" or "my brother."

Achran (עָכְרָן)   From the Hebrew, meaning "disturbed, troubled." In the Bible (Numbers 1:13), a member of the tribe of Asher.

Achumai (אֲחוּמַי)   From the Hebrew, meaning "black." In the Bible (I Chronicles 4:2), a member of the tribe of Judah.

Achuzam (אֲחֻזָּם)   From the Hebrew, meaning "possessor, owner." In the Bible (I Chronicles 4:6), a member of the tribe of Judah.

Achuzat (אֲחֻזַּת)   From the Hebrew, meaning "possession." In the Bible (Genesis 26:26), a friend of Avimelech.

Achva (אַחְוָה)   From the Hebrew, meaning "brotherhood, friendship."

Achyan (אַחְיָן)   From the Aramaic, meaning "fraternal," and from the Hebrew, meaning "nephew." In the Bible (I Chronicles 7:19), a member of the tribe of Manasseh.

Achyo (אַחְיוֹ)   From the Hebrew, meaning "fraternal, brotherly." In the Bible (II Samuel 6:3), a son of Aminadav.

Achzai (אַחְזַי)   A variant form of Achaz. *See* Achaz.

Adabel (אַדְבְּאֵל)   From the Hebrew, meaning "God has established." In the Bible (Genesis 25:13), Ishmael's third son and a grandson of Abraham.

Adad (אֲדַד)   A variant form of Hadad (I Kings 11:17). *See* Hadad.

Adael (עֲדָאֵל)   From the Hebrew, meaning "God is witness" or "adorned by God." Akin to Adaya.

Adaia, Adaiah   Variant spellings of Adaya. *See* Adaya.

Adair   From the Celtic, meaning "oak ford." Also, a Scottish place-name.

Adalia, Adaliah   Variant spellings of Adalya. *See* Adalya.

Adalya (אֲדַלְיָא)   From the Persian, meaning "respectable," or from the Arabic, meaning "refuge." In the Bible (Esther 9:8), the fifth son of Haman. Adalia and Adaliah are variant spellings.

Adam (אָדָם)   From the Hebrew, meaning "earth." Also ascribed to Phoenician and Babylonian origins, meaning "man, mankind." In the Bible (Genesis 2:7), the name of the first man. Not used among Christians until the seventh century, or by Jews until recent centuries. Adamina is a Scottish feminine form created in the 1800s.

Adar, Addar (אַדָּר)   From the Babylonian *daru*, meaning "darkened," or from the Hebrew, meaning "noble, exalted." The name of the Hebrew month that ushers in springtime. In the Bible (I Chronicles 8:3), the son of Bela and a grandson of Benjamin. Adara is a feminine form. Ard is a variant short form.

Adaya (עֲדָיָה)   From the Hebrew, meaning "adorned by God" or "God's witness." In the Bible (I Chronicles 8:21), a leader of the tribe of Benjamin. Adaia and Adaiah are variant spellings. Akin to Adael.

Adda (אַדָּא)   From the Hebrew, meaning "vapor" or "cloud." Used primarily as a modern feminine name. In the Talmud (Shabbat 48a), a fourth-century Babylonian scholar. Akin to Ido.

Adelbert   A variant form of the Old High German, meaning "noble" and "bright," hence "an illustrious person." Albert is a French form.

Aden   A variant spelling of Adin. See Adin.

Adi, Addi, Addie (עֲדִי)   From the Hebrew, meaning "my adornment" or "my witness."

Adiel (עֲדִיאֵל)   From the Hebrew, meaning "adorned by God" or "God is my witness." In the Bible (I Chronicles 27:25), King David's treasurer.

Adif (עָדִיף)   From the Hebrew, meaning "the choicest." Adiph is a variant spelling.

Adin (עָדִין)   From the Hebrew, meaning "beautiful, decorative, pleasant, gentle." In the Bible (Ezra 2:15), a man who returned from exile with Zerubbabel. Also (II Chronicles 29:12), a Levite. Aden is a variant spelling. Akin to Adna. Adina is a variant form.

Adina (עֲדִינָא)   A variant form of Adin. See Adin. In the Bible (I Chronicles 11:42), one of King David's warriors. Used also as a feminine name.

Adino (עֲדִינוֹ)   A variant form of Adin. See Adin. In the Bible (II Samuel 23:8), one of King David's warriors.

Adiph   A variant spelling of Adif. See Adif.

Adir (אַדִּיר)   From the Hebrew, meaning "noble, majestic."

Adiv (אָדִיב)   From the Hebrew and Arabic, meaning "pleasant, gently-mannered."

Adlai (עַדְלָי)   From the Aramaic, meaning "refuge of God" or "God is witness." Or, from the Arabic, meaning "to act justly." In the Bible (I Chronicles 27:29), the father of Shaphat, overseer of King David's flocks.

Adler   From the German, meaning "eagle."

Admata (אַדְמָתָא)   From the Persian, meaning "unrestrained, free." In the Bible (Esther 1:14), one of King Ahasueros's favorite counselors.

Admon (אַדְמוֹן)   From the Hebrew *adom*, meaning "red." The name of the red peony flower in Upper Galilee, Israel. In the Talmud (Ketubot 105a), a judge in Jerusalem in Second Temple times.

Adna, Adnah (עַדְנָה)   From the Aramaic, meaning "all good fortune" or "delight" or "adorned." In the Bible (II Chronicles 17:14), a member of the tribe of Judah and an officer in King Jehoshaphat's court. Akin to Adin. Also spelled עָדְנָא. Edna is a variant feminine form.

Adni (עַדְנִי)   From the Hebrew, meaning "my delight."

Adolf, Adolfo   Variant forms of Adolph. Adolf is an Old High German form. *See* Adolph.

Adolph   From the Old German, meaning "noble wolf" or "noble helper." Dolf and Dolphus are pet forms. *See also* Adolf. Adolphe is the French form.

Adolphe   The French form of Adolph. *See* Adolph.

Adon (אָדוֹן)   From the Hebrew and Phoenician, meaning "lord" or "master." In Hebrew literature, the name is often used as a synonym for God. In Greek mythology, Adonis was a young man of godlike beauty.

Adonia, Adoniah   Variant spellings of Adoniya. *See* Adoniya.

Adonikam (אֲדֹנִיקָם)   From the Hebrew, meaning "my God is exalted". In the Bible (Ezra 2:13) an ancestor of a family of Babylonian exile returnees.

Adoniram (אֲדֹנִירָם)   From the Hebrew, meaning "God is exalted" or "my master is mighty." In the Bible (I Kings 4:6), a tax collector during the reign of David, Solomon, and Rehoboam. Also known as Adoram (I Kings 12:18) and Hadoram (II Chronicles 10:18).

Adoniya (אֲדֹנִיָּה)   From the Hebrew, meaning "the Lord is my God." In the Bible (II Samuel 3:4), the fourth son of David and his wife Chagit (Haggith). Adonia and Adoniah are variant spellings. Adoniyahu is a variant form.

Adoniyahu (אֲדֹנִיָּהוּ)   A variant form of Adoniya. *See* Adoniya.

Adoram (אֲדֹרָם)   A short form of Adoniram. From the Hebrew, meaning "God is exalted" or "my master is mighty." In the Bible (II Samuel 20:24), an official during King David's reign. Adoniram is a variant form.

Adrian   A short form of the Latin name Hadrian. From the Greek, meaning "rich." Also, from the Latin, meaning "black." The seaport of Adria, which gave its name to the Adriatic Sea, was known in ancient times for its black sand.

Adriel (עַדְרִיאֵל)   From the Hebrew, meaning "God is my majesty." In the Bible (I Samuel 18:19), King Saul's son-in-law.

Aduk (אָדוּק)   From the Hebrew, meaning "committed, religious."

Afra   A variant spelling of Ofra. *See* Ofra.

Afri   A variant spelling of Ofri. *See* Ofri.

Agel (אָגֵל)   From the Hebrew, meaning "I will rejoice." Agil is a variant form.

Agil (אָגִיל)   A variant form of Agel. *See* Agel.

Agmon (אַגְמוֹן)   From the Hebrew, meaning "reed."

Agnon (אַגְנוֹן) A variant form of Ogen. *See* Ogen.

Agron (אַגְרוֹן) From the Hebrew, meaning "correspondence" or "vocabulary." Igron is a variant form.

Agur (אָגוּר) From the Hebrew, meaning "knowledgeable, learned" (Proverbs 30:1). According to the Talmud it is the pseudonym for Koheles, author of the Book of Ecclesiastes. Also, a name ascribed to King Solomon.

Ahab A variant spelling of Achav. *See* Achav.

Ahaba A variant spelling of Ahava. *See* Ahava.

Aharon (אַהֲרֹן) From the Hebrew, meaning "teaching" or "singing." Also, from the Hebrew, meaning "shining" or "mountain." Or, from the Arabic, meaning "messenger." In the Bible (Exodus 4:14), the older brother of Moses and Miriam. In the Talmud (Menachot 109b), a fifth-century Babylonian scholar. Aaron is the Anglicized form. Aron is a variant form.

Ahava, Ahavah (אֲהָבָה) From the Hebrew, meaning "love." In the Talmud (Rosh Hashana 29a), a third-century Palestinian scholar. Ahaba is a variant spelling.

Ahaz A variant spelling of Achaz. *See* Achaz.

Ahazia, Ahaziah Variant spellings of Achazya. *See* Achazya.

Ahaziahu A variant spelling of Achazyahu. *See* Achazyahu.

Ahud (אָהוּד) From the Hebrew, meaning "sympathetic."

Ahuv (אָהוּב) From the Hebrew, meaning "beloved."

Ahuvam (אֲהוּבָעָם) From the Hebrew, meaning "beloved by the nation."

Ahuvia, Ahuviah Variant spellings of Ahuvya. *See* Ahuvya.

Ahuviya (אֲהוּבִיָּה) A variant form of Ahuvya. *See* Ahuvya.

Ahuvya (אֲהוּבִיָּה) From the Hebrew, meaning "beloved of God." Ahuvia and Ahuviah are variant spellings. Ahuviya is a variant form.

Ain From the Scotch, meaning "belonging to one." Used also as a feminine name.

Ainsley From the Scotch, meaning "one's own meadow, one's own field." Used also as a feminine name.

Akashya (עֲקַשְׁיָא) From the Aramaic, meaning "stubborn" or "distorted." In the Talmud (Eruvin 87b), the father of a second-century Palestinian scholar, Chananya.

Akavel (עֲקַבְאֵל) A variant form of Akiva. *See* Akiva.

Akavia, Akaviah Variant spellings of Akavya. *See* Akiva.

Akavya (עֲקַבְיָא) The Aramaic form of Akiva. *See* Akiva. Akavya ben Mehalalel was a leading first-century talmudic Palestinian scholar. Akavia and Akaviah are variant spellings.

Akevy   The Hungarian form of Jacob. *See* Jacob.

Akiba   A variant spelling of Akiva. *See* Akiva.

Akim   A Russian short form of Yehoyakim. *See* Yehoyakim.

Akiva (עֲקִיבָא)   A variant form of the Hebrew name Yaakov (Jacob), meaning "to hold by the heel." *See* Jacob *and* Yaakov. Kiba and Kiva are pet forms. Akavel, Akavya, and Akuv are variant forms. Akiba is a variant spelling. The famous Rabbi Akiva (ben Joseph) was a talmudic scholar of the first century.

Aksel   From the Old German, meaning "small oak tree."

Akub, Akkub   Variant spellings of Akuv. *See* Akuv.

Akuv (עָקוּב)   From the Hebrew, meaning "to hold by the heel" or "to over-reach." Akin to Akiva and Yaakov (Jacob). In the Bible (I Chronicles 3:24), a descendant of Zerubbabel. Akub and Akkub are variant spellings.

Al   A pet name for many first names, including Alan, Albert, Alfred, and Alexander.

Alan   From the Middle Latin name Alanus. Of doubtful origin, but usually taken from the Celtic, meaning "harmony, peace," or from the Gaelic, meaning "fair, handsome." Allan, Allen, Allyn, and Alyn are variant spellings.

Alard   A variant form of the Old German name Adalhard, meaning "of noble ancestry." Allard is a variant spelling.

Alastair   From the Greek, meaning "the avenger." In Greek mythology, Alastor personified revenge. Alastair is also considered a Gaelic form of Alexander. *See* Alexander. Alistair and Allistair are variant spellings. Allister is a variant form. Altie is a pet form.

Alba   A variant form of Alban. *See* Alban.

Alban   From the Latin, meaning "white." Albanus is the original form. Alben and Albin are variant spellings. Alba, Albino, and Albion are variant forms. Akin to Alpin.

Alben   A variant spelling of Alban. *See* Alban.

Alberic, Alberich   From the High German, meaning "wise king, wise leader." Introduced into England as Alberi, which later became Aubrey.

Albert   A French form of the Old High German name Adelbrecht (Adelbert), meaning "high nobility" or "nobly bright." Albrecht is a variant form.

Albie   A pet form of Albert. *See* Albert. Elbie is a variant form.

Albin   A variant spelling of Alban. *See* Alban.

Albino   An Italian form of Alban. *See* Alban.

Albion   A variant form of Alban. *See* Alban. The ancient name for Britain (which included Scotland), so named because of its white cliffs.

Albrecht   An early German form of Albert. *See* Albert.

Aldan   A variant spelling of Alden. *See* Alden.

Alden   From the Middle English, meaning "old age, antiquity." Aldan and Aldon are variant spellings.

Alder   From the Old English, meaning "old." Aldo is a variant form. Akin to Alter. Aldren is probably a variant form.

Aldo   An Old German and Italian form of Alder. *See* Alder. Aldus is a variant form.

Aldon   A variant spelling of Alden. *See* Alden.

Aldous   A variant spelling of Aldus. *See* Aldus.

Aldred   From the Old English name Ealdred, meaning "old, wise counsel." Eldred is a variant form.

Aldren   Probably a variant form of Alder. *See* Alder.

Aldus   A Latinized form of the Old German Aldo. *See* Aldo. Aldous is a variant spelling.

Aldwin   From the Old English, meaning "old friend."

Alec, Aleck   Short forms of Alexander, popular in Scotland. *See* Alexander.

Alef, Aleph (אָלֶף)   From the Hebrew, meaning "number one" or "leader." The first letter of the Hebrew alphabet.

Alemet (עָלֶמֶת)   From the Hebrew, meaning "concealed, hidden." In the Bible (I Chronicles 8:36), a member of the tribe of Benjamin.

Alex   A popular short form of Alexander. *See* Alexander. Alix and Allix are variant spellings.

Alexander (אֲלֶכְּסַנְדָר)   From the Greek name Alexandros, meaning "protector of men." According to legend in the Talmud (Tamid 31b), when the Greek monarch Alexander the Great conquered Palestine in 333 B.C.E. all Jewish boys born in that year were named Alexander in his honor. Alexandri, Alexis, Sander, and Xander are variant forms. Alec, Aleck, and Alex are among the many short forms. Sacha and Sasha are Russian pet forms. Sandy is an American pet form.

Alexandri (אֲלֶכְּסַנְדְרִי)   A variant form of Alexander. *See* Alexander. In the Talmud (Berachot 99a), a fourth-century Palestinian talmudic scholar.

Alexis   A form of Alexander. Used also as a feminine name. *See* Alexander.

Alf, Alfeo, Alfie   Pet forms of Alfred. *See* Alfred.

Alfonse, Alfonso, Alfonzo   Variant spellings of Alphonso. *See* Alphonso.

Alfred   From the Old English, meaning "elf counsel" or "wise counsel." Became popular in the ninth-century when the English king, Alfred the Great, curbed Danish conquests in England. One of the most popular names in northern Europe prior to the sixteenth century. Alf and Alfie are common pet forms.

Alger   From the Anglo-Saxon, meaning "noble spearman" or "warrior."

Ali From the Arabic, meaning "exalted." Ali Halevi was the head of the academy (the *gaon*) of Baghdad in 1140.

Alian A variant spelling of Alyna. *See* Alyna.

Alis A pet form of Alistair. *See* Alistair.

Alistair A variant spelling of Alastair. *See* Alastair. May also be derived from the Arabic, meaning "the bird." Alis is a pet form.

Alitz (עָלִיץ) From the Hebrew, meaning "joy." Aliz is a variant spelling.

Alix A variant spelling of Alex. *See* Alex.

Aliz (עָלִיז) From the Hebrew, meaning "joy, joyful." Also, a variant spelling of Alitz. *See* Alitz.

Allan A variant spelling of Alan. *See* Alan.

Allard A variant spelling of Alard. *See* Alard.

Allen A popular variant spelling of Alan. *See* Alan.

Allison A masculine name derived from Alice, meaning "Alice's son." *See* Alice (feminine section).

Allistair A variant spelling of Alastair. *See* Alastair.

Allister A variant form of Alastair. *See* Alastair.

Allix A variant spelling of Alex. *See* Alex.

Allon A variant spelling of Alon. *See* Alon.

Allston From the Old English, meaning "Al's (elf's) town." *See* Alfred. Alston is a variant spelling.

Allyn A variant spelling of Alan. *See* Alan.

Almog (אַלְמוֹג) From the Hebrew, meaning "coral," a reddish stone. Also, the name of a tree that grows in India.

Almon (אַלְמוֹן) From the Hebrew, meaning "forsaken" or "widower."

Alon (אַלוֹן) From the Hebrew, meaning "oak tree." In the Bible (I Chronicles 4:37), one of the sons of Simeon. Also, a short form of Alphonso. *See* Alphonso. Allon is a variant spelling.

Alpha The first letter of the Greek alphabet, meaning "the beginning." Derived from the Hebrew *alef. See* Alef.

Alphonse The French form of Alphonso. *See* Alphonso.

Alphonso From the Old High German, meaning "of noble family." Alphonse is a French form. Alfonse, Alfonso, and Alfonzo are other variants. Alon is a short form. Lon, Lonnie, and Lonny are pet forms.

Alpin From the Latin name Alpes (Alps), meaning "high mountain." Akin to Alban, meaning "white." *See* Alban.

Alroy From the Latin and Old English, meaning "royal ruler."

Alsie   Probably a form of Alson. *See* Alson.

Alson   From the Anglo-Saxon, meaning "noble stone." Or, a patronymic form meaning "the son of Al." Alsie is probably a variant form.

Alston   A variant spelling of Allston. *See* Allston.

Alta   From the Latin and Spanish, meaning "tall, high." Alto and Altus are variant forms. Used also as a feminine name. Altie is a pet form.

Alter (אַלְטֶר)   From the Old English and the Old High German, meaning "old, old one." Among Jews, a supplementary name given to a critically ill young man so as to confuse the angel of death into thinking that the man called "old one" could not possibly be the young sick person he was after. Akin to Alder. Also spelled אַלְטָער.

Altie   A pet form of Alta or Alastair. *See* Alta *and* Alastair.

Alto   A variant form of Alta. *See* Alta.

Alton   From the Old English, meaning "old town."

Altus   A variant form of Alta. *See* Alta.

Aluf, Aluph (אַלּוּף)   From the Hebrew, meaning "master, prince, ruler." Also from the Hebrew, meaning "loyal friend" or "scholar."

Alva, Alvah (עַלְוָה)   From the Latin, meaning "white." Also, from the Hebrew, a transposed form of *avla*, meaning "sin." In the Bible (Genesis 36:40), a leader of the family of Esau. Also (I Chronicles 1:51), an Edomite.

Alvan (עַלְוָן)   From the Latin, meaning "white," or from the Old High German, meaning "old friend" or "noble friend." In the Bible (Genesis 36:23), an Edomite, not related to the modern name.

Alvin   A variant form of Alvan. *See* Alvan.

Alvis   From the Old Norse, meaning "wise."

Alvon (עַלְבוֹן)   From the Hebrew, meaning "an insult." In the Bible (II Samuel 23:32), one of King David's warriors.

Alwin, Alwyn   From the Old English, meaning "noble friend" or "elf friend." Akin to Alvan.

Alyan (עַלְיָן)   From the Hebrew, meaning "heights." In the Bible (I Chronicles 1:40), one of the sons of Seir.

Alyn   A variant spelling of Alan. *See* Alan.

Amadore   From the Greek and Italian, meaning "gift of love."

Amal (עָמָל)   From the Hebrew, meaning "work, toil." In the Bible (I Chronicles 7:35), a member of the tribe of Asher. Akin to Amel.

Amali (עֲמָלִי)   A variant form of Amal. From the Hebrew, meaning "my work, my toil."

Amand   A French form of the Latin name Amandus, meaning "worthy of love."

Amaria, Amariah Variant spellings of Amarya. *See* Amarya.

Amariahu A variant spelling of Amaryahu. *See* Amaryahu.

Amarya (אֲמַרְיָה) From the Hebrew, meaning "the speech (word) of God." In the Bible (I Chronicles 5:37), a Priest in the time of King Jehoshaphat. Amaria and Amariah are variant spellings. Amaryahu is a variant form.

Amaryahu (אֲמַרְיָהוּ) A variant form of Amarya. *See* Amarya. Amariahu is a variant spelling.

Amasa (עֲמָשָׂא) From the Hebrew, meaning "work, deed." In the Bible (II Samuel 17:25), a nephew of King David. Akin to Amasai.

Amasai (עֲמָשַׂי) From the Aramaic, meaning "work, deed." In the Bible (I Chronicles 12:19), one of King David's military leaders. Akin to Amasa.

Amasia, Amasiah Variant spellings of Amasya. *See* Amasya.

Amasya (עֲמַסְיָה) From the Hebrew, meaning "burden of God." In the Bible (II Chronicles 17:16), one of King Jehoshaphat's military leaders. Amasia and Amasiah are variant spellings.

Amati From the Italian, meaning "love."

Amatzia, Amatziah Variant spellings of Amatzya. *See* Amatzya.

Amatzya (אֲמַצְיָה) From the Hebrew, meaning "strength of God." Amatzia and Amatziah are variant spellings. In the Bible (II Kings 12:22), a king of Judah. Amatzyahu is a variant form.

Amatzyahu (אֲמַצְיָהוּ) A variant form of Amatzya. *See* Amatzya.

Ambert From the German, meaning "bright, shining."

Ambrose From the Greek, meaning "immortal, divine."

Amdiel (עַמְדִּיאֵל) From the Hebrew, meaning "God is my pillar, my support."

Amel (עָמֵל) From the Hebrew, meaning "to work." Akin to Amal.

Amemar (אַמֵימָר) A hybrid of the Hebrew *ami*, meaning "my people," and the Aramaic *mar*, meaning "lord, master." In the Talmud (Bava Batra 31a), a leading fifth-century Babylonian scholar.

Amery From the Latin, meaning "the loving one." May also be a form of the Hebrew name Amal. Amory is a variant spelling.

Ames Probably from the Latin and French, meaning "love."

Ami (עַמִּי) From the Hebrew, meaning "my people." In the Bible (Ezra 2:57), a servant of King Solomon whose descendants were among the Babylonian Exile returnees. Also, from the Aramaic, meaning "mother," and spelled אִמִּי or אַמִּי. In the Talmud (Yevamot 80a), a fourth-century talmudic scholar who was also called Imi. Ammi is a variant spelling. Used also as a pet form of Amiel and Amikam.

Amiad (עַמִּיעַד) From the Hebrew, meaning "my nation is eternal."

Amiasaf, Amiasaph (עֲמִיאָסָף) From the Hebrew, meaning "my people has been gathered in, reunited."

Amiaz (עֲמִיעָז) From the Hebrew, meaning "my nation is mighty."

Amichai (עֲמִיחַי) From the Hebrew, meaning "my nation lives."

Amichen (עֲמִיחֵן) From the Hebrew, meaning "my nation is gracious."

Amichur (עֲמִיחוּר) A variant form of Amihud (II Samuel 13:37). *See* Amihud.

Amidan (עֲמִידָן) From the Hebrew, meaning "my people (nation) is just, righteous."

Amidar (עֲמִידָר) From the Hebrew, meaning "my nation is alive."

Amidor (עֲמִידוֹר) From the Hebrew, meaning "my generation of people."

Amidror (עֲמִידְרוֹר) From the Hebrew, meaning "my nation is free."

Amiel (עֲמִיאֵל) From the Hebrew, meaning "God of my people." In the Bible (II Samuel 9:4), the father of Machir, who befriended King David. Ammiel is a variant spelling.

Amiezer (עֲמִיעֶזֶר) From the Hebrew, meaning "my nation is my support."

Amihod (עֲמִיהוֹד) A variant form of Amihud. *See* Amihud.

Amihud (עֲמִיהוּד) From the Hebrew, meaning "my nation (people) is glorious." In the Bible (II Samuel 13:37), a member of the tribe of Simeon. Amichur and Amihod are variant forms.

Amikam (עֲמִיקָם) From the Hebrew, meaning "my nation has been resurrected."

Amikar (עֲמִיקָר) From the Hebrew, meaning "my nation is precious."

Amin (אָמִין) From the Hebrew and Arabic, meaning "trustworthy."

Aminadav (עֲמִּנָדָב) From the Hebrew, meaning "my nation is noble." In the Bible (Exodus 6:23), a leader of the tribe of Judah, the father-in-law of Aaron.

Aminon (אֲמִינוֹן) A variant form of Amnon. *See* Amnon.

Amior (עֲמִיאוֹר) From the Hebrew, meaning "my nation is a light, a beacon."

Amir (אָמִיר) From the Hebrew, meaning "mighty, strong." Also, from the Hebrew, meaning "sheaf of corn," and spelled עָמִיר.

Amiram (עֲמִירָם) From the Hebrew, meaning "my nation is mighty" or "my nation is exalted."

Amiran (עֲמִירָן) A variant form of Amiron. *See* Amiron.

Amiron (עֲמִירֹן) From the Hebrew, meaning "my nation is a song" or "my people sings." Amiran is a variant form.

Amishadai (עֲמִישַׁדָּי) From the Hebrew, meaning "my people is (belongs to) God." In the Bible (Numbers 1:12), a member of the tribe of Dan.

Amishai (עֲמִישַׁי)   From the Hebrew, meaning "the gift of my people."

Amishalom (עֲמִישָׁלוֹם)   From the Hebrew, meaning "my nation is peaceful."

Amishar (עֲמִישָׁר)   From the Hebrew, meaning "my people sings, rejoices."

Amishav (עֲמִישָׁב)   From the Hebrew, meaning "my people returns."

Amishoa, Amishoah (עֲמִישׁוֹעַ)   From the Hebrew, meaning "my people is destroyed."

Amit (עָמִית)   From the Hebrew, meaning "truth" or "friend." Akin to Amitai.

Amitai (אֲמִיתַּי)   From the Aramaic, meaning "truth" or "friend." In the Bible (Jonah 1:1), the father of the Prophet Jonah. Akin to Amit.

Amitan (אֲמִיתָן)   From the Hebrew, meaning "true, faithful friend."

Amiti (אֲמִיתִּי)   A variant form of Amit. From the Hebrew, meaning "my friend."

Amituv (עֲמִיטוֹב)   From the Hebrew, meaning "my nation is good."

Amitza (אֲמִיצָה)   From the Hebrew, meaning "strong." Also, a variant form of Amotz. Used also as a feminine name.

Amitzedek (עֲמִיצֶדֶק)   From the Hebrew, meaning "my nation is righteous."

Amitzur (עֲמִיצוּר)   From the Hebrew, meaning "my nation is my rock (support)."

Amizakai (עֲמִיזַכַּי)   From the Hebrew, meaning "my nation is pure, innocent."

Amizavad (עֲמִיזָבָד)   From the Hebrew, meaning "the gift of my nation." In the Bible (I Chronicles 27:6), a son of Benaiah, one of David's warriors.

Ammi   A variant spelling of Ami. See Ami.

Ammiel   A variant spelling of Amiel. See Amiel.

Amnon (אֲמְנוֹן)   From the Hebrew, meaning "faithful." In the Bible (II Samuel 3:2), the eldest son of King David. Aminon is a variant form.

Amok (עָמוֹק)   From the Hebrew, meaning "deep, unfathomable." In the Bible (Nehemiah 12:7), a High Priest who was among the Babylonian Exile returnees.

Amon (אָמוֹן)   From the Hebrew, meaning "hidden." In the Bible (II Kings 21:18), a king of Judah; also, the name of an Egyptian god; also, a son of David. Ammon is a variant spelling.

Amory   A variant spelling of Amery. See Amery.

Amos (עָמוֹס)   From the Hebrew, meaning "to be burdened, troubled." In the . Bible (Amos 1:1), one of the twelve Minor Prophets (eighth-century B.C.E.).

Amotz (אָמוֹץ)   From the Hebrew, meaning "strong." In the Bible (Isaiah 1:1), the father of Isaiah. Amoz is a variant spelling. Amitza and Amtzi are variant forms.

Amoz   A variant spelling of Amotz. *See* Amotz.

Amram (עַמְרָם)   From the Hebrew, meaning "mighty nation." Also, from the Arabic, meaning "life." In the Bible (Exodus 6:18), the father of Moses.

Amron (עַמְרוֹן)   A variant form of Omer. *See* Omer.

Amtzi (אַמְצִי)   A variant form of Amotz. From the Hebrew, meaning "my strength." In the Bible (I Chronicles 6:31), a descendant of Levi. Amzi is a variant spelling.

Amzi   A variant spelling of Amtzi. *See* Amtzi.

Ana (עֲנָה)   From the Hebrew, meaning "to sing, chant." In the Bible (Genesis 36:2), a descendant of Seir the Horite.

Anaia   A variant spelling of Anaya. *See* Anaya.

Anan (עָנָן)   From the Hebrew, meaning "cloud" or "soothsayer." In the Bible (Nehemiah 10:27), one of the Babylonian repatriates and a loyal follower of Nehemiah. In the Talmud (Bava Metzia 51b), a third-century Babylonian scholar. Anan ben David was founder of the Karaite sect in the eighth century. Aneni and Ananya are variant forms.

Anani (עֲנָנִי)   A variant form of Anan. *See* Anan. In the Bible (I Chronicles 3:24), a descendant of Zerubbabel. In the Talmud (Shabbat 64b), a third-century Palestinian scholar.

Anania   A variant spelling of Ananya. *See* Ananya.

Ananya (עֲנָנְיָה)   A variant form of Anan. *See* Anan. In the Bible (Nehemiah 3:23), a contemporary of Ezra and Nehemiah. Anania is a variant spelling.

Anastasius   From the Greek, meaning "resurrection."

Anat (עֲנָת)   From the Hebrew, meaning "oppression." In the Bible (Judges 3:31), the father of Shamgar the Judge.

Anatole   From the Greek, meaning "rising of the sun" or "from the east." Antal is a variant form.

Anav (עֲנָב)   From the Hebrew, meaning "grape."

Anavi (עֲנָבִי)   From the Hebrew, meaning "my grapes."

Anaya (עֲנָיָה)   From the Syriac and Arabic, meaning "to sing, to chant." In the Bible (Nehemiah 8:4), a loyal follower of Ezra and Nehemiah. Anaia is a variant spelling.

Ancel   From the Old German name Ansi, meaning "god."

Anchel, Anchelle   Variant spellings of Anshel. *See* Anshel.

Anders   A patronymic form of Andrew, meaning "son of Andrew." *See* Andrew. A popular name in Denmark. Akin to Andor.

Andor   A variant form of Andrew. *See* Andrew. Akin to Anders.

André A French form of Andrew. *See* Andrew.

Andreas A Latin form of Andrew. *See* Andrew.

Andres A Spanish form of Andrew. *See* Andrew.

Andrew From the Greek, meaning "manly, strong, courageous." Andy and Tandy are popular Scottish forms. Andor, André, Andreas, and Andres are variant forms. Andy is the favorite short form. Anders is a popular Danish form, as is its derivative surname Anderson.

Andy A pet form of Andrew. *See* Andrew.

Aner (עָנֵר) Origin unknown. In the Bible (Genesis 14:13), an ally of Abraham.

Angel, Angell From the Greek, meaning "messenger" or "saintly person." Angie is a pet form.

Angie A pet form of Angel. *See* Angel. Used also as a feminine form.

Angus From the Gaelic and Irish, meaning "exceptional, outstanding."

Aniam (אֲנִיעָם) From the Hebrew, meaning "I am the people" or "my nation." In the Bible (I Chronicles 7:19), a descendant of Manasseh.

Anschel A variant spelling of Anshel. *See* Anshel.

Ansel, Anselm From the Old German, meaning "divine helmet of God."

Anshel (אַנְשֶׁעל) A Yiddish form of Asher. *See* Asher. Anchel, Anchelle, and Anschel are variant spellings.

Anshil (אַנְשִׁיל) A Yiddish form of Asher. *See* Asher.

Anson, Ansonia From the Anglo-Saxon, meaning "the son of Ann" or "the son of Hans." *See* Hans.

Antal A form of Anatole. *See* Anatole.

Anthony A variant form of Antony. *See* Antony.

Anton, Antone, Antonin Variant forms of Antony. *See* Antony. Anton is used mostly by Germans, Scots, and Slavs.

Antony From the Greek, meaning "flourishing," and from the Latin, meaning "worthy of praise." Antonius is the original form. Anthony, Anton, Antone, and Antonin are variant forms.

Anuv (עָנוּב) From the Hebrew, meaning "bound, tied" or "modest." In the Bible (I Chronicles 4:8), a descendant of Judah.

Aphra A variant spelling of Ofra. *See* Ofra.

Aphri A variant spelling of Ofri. *See* Ofri.

Ara (אֲרָא) From the Hebrew, meaning "to pluck, to gather." In the Bible (I Chronicles 7:38), a descendant of Asher. Also, from the Latin, meaning "altar." Arah is a variant spelling.

Arach (עֲרָךְ) From the Hebrew, meaning "to prepare, to arrange." In the Talmud (Avot 2:8), the father of Elazar, a first-century Palestinian scholar.

Arad (עֲרָד) From the Hebrew, meaning "wild ox." In the Bible (I Chronicles 8:15), a descendant of Benjamin.

Arah A variant spelling of Ara. *See* Ara.

Aram (אֲרָם) From the Assyrian, meaning "high, heights." The ancient name of Syria, whose language was Aramaic. In the Bible (Genesis 10:23), the grandson of Noah.

Aran (אֲרָן) From the Assyrian and Arabic, meaning "chest, sarcophagus." In the Bible (Genesis 36:28), a son of Seir the Chorite.

Arba (אַרְבַּע) From the Hebrew, meaning "four." In the Bible (Joshua 14:15), a giant of a man, founder of Kiryat Arba, later known as Hebron.

Arbel (עַרְבֵּל) From the Hebrew, meaning "sieve."

Arbie Probably from the Old French, meaning "crossbow."

Arch A pet form of Archibald. Used also as an independent name.

Archibald From the Anglo-Saxon, meaning "bold," or "holy prince." Arch, Archie, Archy, and Arky are pet forms.

Archie, Archy Pet forms of Archibald. *See* Archibald.

Ard (אַרְדְּ) From the Hebrew, meaning "bronze" or "wild ox." In the Bible (Numbers 26:40), a member of the tribe of Benjamin. Also, a variant form of Adar. *See* Adar. Arda and Ardi are variant forms. Akin to Ardon.

Arda A variant form of Ard and Arden. May also be from Middle High German, meaning "heart, deer."

Arden From the Latin, meaning "to burn." Arda is a variant form.

Ardi (אַרְדִּי) From the Hebrew, meaning "bronze" or "wild ox." In the Bible (I Chronicles 2:18), a son of Caleb of the tribe of Judah. Akin to Ard.

Arel (אַרְאֵל) From the Hebrew, meaning "lion of God." Areli is a variant form. Akin to Ariel.

Areli (אַרְאֵלִי) A variant form of Arel. *See* Arel. In the Bible (Genesis 46:16), a son of Gad and a grandson of Jacob.

Arend Possibly a variant form of Aaron or Arnold. *See* Aaron *and* Arnold.

Argaman (אַרְגָּמָן) From the Hebrew, meaning "purple (reddish-purple)."

Argus From the Greek, meaning "bright." In Greek mythology, a giant with one hundred eyes.

Ari (אֲרִי) From the Hebrew, meaning "lion." A short form of Arye. *See* Arye. Also, a pet form of Aristotle. *See* Aristotle. Arie and Ary are variant spellings. Ario is a variant form. Akin to Arye.

Ariav (אֲרִיאָב) From the Hebrew, meaning "father is a lion," hence "strong."

Aric, Arick Early German forms of Richard. *See* Richard.

Aricha (אֲרִיכָא) From the Aramaic, meaning "long." Akin to Aryoch.

Arie   A variant spelling of Ari. *See* Ari.

Ariel (אֲרִיאֵל)   From the Hebrew, meaning "lion of God." In the Bible (Ezra 8:16), a leader who served under Ezra. Also, a symbolic name for Jerusalem, David's city (Isaiah 29:1). Akin to Arel. Used also as a feminine name. Aryel and Aryell are variant spellings.

Arig (אָרִיג)   From the Hebrew, meaning "weave, woven."

Arik (אָרִיק)   A pet form of Ariel and Aryeh. *See* Ariel and Aryeh.

Ario   A variant form of Ari. *See* Ari *and* Arion.

Arioch   A variant spelling of Aryoch. *See* Aryoch.

Arion   From the Italian *aria* and *arioso*, meaning "songlike, melodious." Ario is a variant form.

Aristo   From the Greek, meaning "the best." Aristotle is a variant form.

Aristotle   A variant form of Aristo. *See* Aristo. Ari is a pet form.

Arky   A pet form of Archibald. *See* Archibald. Used also as a short form of Arkansas.

Arland   A variant form of Arland. *See* Arland.

Arlando   A variant form of Orlando. *See* Orlando.

Arlee   A variant spelling of Arleigh. *See* Arleigh.

Arleigh   A variant form of Arles. *See* Arles. May also be a variant form of Harley. *See* Harley. Arlee, Arley, and Arlie are variant spellings.

Arlen   The Celtic form of Arles, meaning "pledge." *See* Arles. Arlin and Arlyn are variant spellings.

Arles   Originally a Hebrew word, *eravon*, meaning "pledge, promise to pay." Arrived at its present form via Latin, French, and Middle English. Also, the name of a French city. Arleigh, Arlen, and Arliss are variant forms.

Arley   A variant spelling of Arleigh. *See* Arleigh.

Arlie   A variant spelling of Arleigh. *See* Arleigh.

Arlin   A variant spelling of Arlen. *See* Arlen.

Arliss   A variant form of Arles. *See* Arles.

Arlo   Probably from the Old English, meaning "fortified hill."

Arlyn   A variant spelling of Arlin. *See* Arlin.

Armand   The French and Italian form of the Old German name Hermann, meaning "warrior." Armond is a variant spelling. Armen and Armin are variant forms.

Armen, Armin   Variant forms of Armand. *See* Armand.

Armon (אַרְמֹן)   From the Hebrew, meaning "castle, palace." When spelled with the Hebrew letter *ayin*, rather than *alef* (עַרְמֹן), the meaning is "a tree in the oak family." Armoni is a variant form.

Armond A variant spelling of Armand. *See* Armand.

Armoni (אַרְמוֹנִי) A variant form of Armon. *See* Armon. In the Bible (II Samuel 21:8), a son of King Saul.

Arnan (אַרְנָן) From the Arabic, meaning "lotus fruit," or from the Hebrew, meaning "roaring stream." In the Bible (I Chronicles 3:21), a descendant of Zerubbabel.

Arndt A variant form of Arnold. *See* Arnold.

Arne A short form of Adrian that was popular in the north of England in the Middle Ages. *See* Adrian.

Arni, Arnie Pet forms of Arnold. *See* Arnold.

Arno A pet form of Arnold. *See* Arnold.

Arnold From the Old German, meaning either "honorable, honest ruler" or "having the power of an eagle." Arnold was one of the most commonly used Christian names in northern Europe prior to the sixteenth century. Arno and Arny are pet forms.

Arnon (אַרְנוֹן) From the Hebrew, meaning "roaring stream." In the Bible (Numbers 21:13), a stream on the frontier of Moab that flowed into the Dead Sea. Arnoni is a variant form.

Arnoni (אַרְנוֹנִי) A variant form of Arnon. *See* Arnon.

Arny A pet form of Arnold. *See* Arnold.

Arod (אָרוֹד) From the Hebrew, meaning "bronze." In the Bible (Numbers 26:17), a son of Gad.

Arodi (אָרוֹדִי) From the Hebrew, meaning "bronze." In the Bible (Genesis 46:16), a son of Gad.

Aron A variant form of Aharon (Aaron). *See* Aharon.

Arsen From the Greek, meaning "manly, strong."

Art A pet form of Arthur. *See* Arthur.

Arthur From the Gaelic, meaning "rock," hence "noble, lofty hill." Or, from the Celtic, meaning "a bear." Also, from the Icelandic, meaning "follower of Tur (Thor)," the Norse god of war. Arthur was the legendary sixth-century king of Britain who led the knights of the Round Table. Art, Artie, and Arty are pet forms.

Artie A pet form of Arthur. *See* Arthur.

Arty A pet form of Arthur. *See* Arthur.

Artza (אַרְצָא) From the Aramaic, meaning "earth." In the Bible (I Kings 16:9), the chamberlain of King Zimri. Arza is a variant spelling.

Artzi (אַרְצִי) From the Hebrew, meaning "my land, my country." Arzi is a variant spelling.

Arval, Arvala From the Latin, meaning "cultivated land."

Arvid, Arvin From the Anglo-Saxon, meaning "man of the people" or "friend of the people."

Ary A variant spelling of Ari. *See* Ari.

Arye, Aryeh (אַרְיֵה) From the Hebrew, meaning "lion." In the Bible (II Kings 15:25), an officer in the army of Pekach. Akin to Ari. Arik is a pet form.

Aryel, Aryell Variant spellings of Ariel. *See* Ariel.

Aryoch (אַרְיוֹךְ) From the Aramaic, meaning "measurement" or "long." In the Bible (Genesis 14:1), a king of Elasar. Also, a Persian name which was conferred on the third-century Babylonian talmudic scholar Mar Samuel, who was fond of Persian customs. For the same reason, the name Shabur Malka (after King Shapur of Persia) was applied to him. Arioch is a variant spelling. Akin to Aricha.

Arza (אַרְזָא) From the Aramaic, meaning "cedar." Also, a variant spelling of Artza. *See* Artza. In the Talmud (Avoda Zara 58a), a third-century Palestinian scholar.

Arzi (אַרְזִי) From the Hebrew, meaning "my cedar." Also, a variant spelling of Artzi. *See* Artzi.

Asa (אָסָא) From the Aramaic and Arabic, meaning "to heal" or "healer." In the Bible (I Kings 15:8), a king of Judah.

Asael (עֲשָׂהאֵל) From the Hebrew, meaning "God has created." In the Bible (II Samuel 2:18), a brother of Yoav.

Asaf, Asaph (אָסָף) From the Hebrew, meaning "gather." In the Bible (II Kings 18:18), a Levite.

Asarel (אֲשַׂרְאֵל) From the Hebrew, meaning "prince of God." In the Bible (I Chronicles 4:16), a descendant of Caleb of the tribe of Judah. Asarela is a variant form.

Asarela (אֲשַׂרְאֵלָה) A variant form of Asarel (I Chronicles 25:2). *See* Asarel.

Asaya (עֲשָׂיָה) From the Hebrew, meaning "God's creation." In the Bible (II Kings 22:12), a servant of King Josiah.

Aser A variant spelling of Asser. *See* Asser.

Ash From the Old Norse and the Middle English, meaning "ash tree."

Ashbei (אַשְׁבֵּעַ) From the Hebrew, meaning "to swear, to take an oath." In the Bible (I Chronicles 4:21), a grandson of Judah.

Ashbel (אַשְׁבֵּל) From the Hebrew, meaning "the fire of (the god) Bel." In the Bible (Genesis 46:21), a son of Benjamin.

Ashchur (אַשְׁחוּר) From the Aramaic, meaning "black." In the Bible (I Chronicles 2:24), a member of the tribe of Judah.

Asher (אָשֵׁר) From the Hebrew, meaning "blessed, fortunate, happy." In the Bible (Genesis 30:13), a son of Jacob and Zilpah. Anshel, Anshil, and Asser are variant forms.

Ashi (אָשִׁי) Probably a short form of Yoshiyahu (Josiah). *See* Yoshiyahu. Also, a variant form of Assi. *See* Assi. In the Talmud (Kidushin 72b), a fifth-century Babylonian talmudic scholar. Also spelled אַשִּׁי.

Ashian A variant spelling of Ashyan. *See* Ashyan.

Ashir (עָשִׁיר) From the Hebrew, meaning "rich."

Ashkenaz (אַשְׁכְּנַז) Meaning uncertain. In modern times a reference to people of German descent. In the Bible (Genesis 10:3), the son of Gomer and great-grandson of Noah.

Ashvat (עָשְׁוָת) From the Hebrew, meaning "a heavenly constellation," probably the Great Bear. In the Bible (I Chronicles 7:33), a member of the tribe of Asher.

Ashyan (אַשְׁיָן) A variant form of Assi. *See* Assi. In the Talmud (Suka 42a), a third-century Palestinian scholar. Ashian is a variant spelling.

Asiel (עֲשִׂיאֵל) From the Hebrew, meaning "creation of God." In the Bible (I Chronicles 4:35), a descendant of Simeon.

Asif (אָסִיף) From the Hebrew, meaning "harvest." Also spelled Asiph.

Asiph A variant spelling of Asif. *See* Asif.

Asir (אָסִיר) From the Arabic and Aramaic, meaning "bound" or "imprisoned." In the Bible (Exodus 6:24), a son of Korach.

Asis (עָסִיס) From the Hebrew, meaning "fruit juice."

Asna, Asnah (אָסְנָה) From the Egyptian, meaning "unfortunate, luckless." Or, from the Hebrew and Aramaic, meaning "thornbush." In the Bible (Ezra 2:50), head of a family of Temple workers.

Asriel (אַשְׂרִיאֵל) From the Hebrew, meaning "prince of God." In the Bible (Numbers 26:31), a son of Gilead and a grandson of Manasseh.

Asser A variant form of Asher. *See* Asher. Aser is a variant spelling.

Assi (אַסִּי) From the Aramaic, meaning "doctor." In the Talmud (Kidushin 31b), a fourth-century Babylonian scholar who settled in Palestine. Among its many variant forms are Ashi, Ashyan, Asya, Issi, Josah, and Jose.

Asya (אַסְיָא) A variant form of Assi. *See* Assi.

Atai (עַתַּי) From the Aramaic, meaning "timely" or "ready." In the Bible (I Chronicles 2:35), one of King David's warriors from the tribe of Gad.

Atalya (עֲתַלְיָה) From the Aramaic, and Hebrew, meaning "God is great, God is exalted." In the Bible (I Chronicles 8:26), a member of the tribe of Benjamin. Used also in the Bible as a feminine name.

Atanya (אֲתַנְיָה) From the Aramaic and Hebrew, meaning "she-goat."

Atar (עָתַר) From the Hebrew, meaning "to pray."

Ataya (עֲתָיָה) From the Hebrew, meaning "timely, ready, prepared" or "future time." In the Bible (Nehemiah 11:4), a descendant of Judah. Akin to Atid.

Ater (אָטֵר) From the Hebrew, meaning "bind, close, shut up." In the Bible (Ezra 2:16), one of the sons of King Hezekiah.

Atid (עָתִיד) From the Hebrew, meaning "timely, prepared, ready" or "future time." Akin to Ataya.

Atir (עָטִיר) From the Hebrew, meaning "wreath, crown, ornament."

Atlai (עַתְלַי) From the Assyrian, meaning "to grow" or "to be exalted." In the Bible (Ezra 10:28), an Israelite who abandoned his foreign wife.

Atzalya (אֲצַלְיָה) A variant form of Atzel. See Atzel.

Atzalyahu (אֲצַלְיָהוּ) A variant form of Atzel. See Atzel. In the Bible (II Kings 22:3), the father of Shaphan, King Josiah's scribe.

Atzel (אָצֵל) From the Hebrew, meaning "to lay aside, reserve, withdraw, withhold." In the Bible (I Chronicles 8:37), a descendant of Benjamin. Atzalyahu is a variant form.

Atzmon (עַצְמוֹן) From the Hebrew, meaning "strength." An ancient town along the southern border of Canaan.

Aubrey From the Anglo-Saxon, meaning "elf ruler." The original form was Alberic. See Alberic. Avery is a variant form.

August A variant form of Augustus. See Augustus.

Augustus From the Latin, meaning "revered, exalted." Gus and Augie are pet forms. August, Austen, and Austin are variant forms.

Auriel From the Latin, meaning "gold, golden." Orel is a variant form.

Austen, Austin English variant forms of Augustus. See Augustus.

Autrey A masculine form of the feminine Audrey. See Audrey (feminine section).

Av (אָב) From the Hebrew, meaning "father." Also, a pet form of Averel. See Averel.

Avda (עַבְדָּא) From the Aramaic and Arabic, meaning "servant, worshipper." In the Bible (I Kings 4:6), a Levite. Abda is a variant spelling. Avdon is a variant form.

Avdan (אַבְדָּן) A variant form of Avidan. See Avidan. In the Talmud (Berachot 27b), a third-century Palestinian scholar also known as Avidan and Abba Yudan. Abdan is a variant spelling.

Avdel (עַבְדְּאֵל) From the Hebrew, meaning "servant of God." In the Bible (Jeremiah 36:26), one of the officers of King Jehoiakim's court. Abdel is a variant spelling.

Avdi (עַבְדִּי) From the Hebrew, meaning "my servant." In the Bible (I Chronicles 6:29), a Levite. Abdi is a variant spelling.

Avdiel (עַבְדִּיאֵל) From the Hebrew, meaning "servant of God." In the Bible (I Chronicles 5:15), a leader of the tribe of Gad. Abdiel is a variant spelling.

Avdima (אַבְדִימָא) From the Aramaic, meaning "destruction, loss." Abdima is a variant spelling. The name of a fourth-century Palestinian talmudic scholar who was also known as Avdimi.

Avdimei (אַבְדִּימֵי) A variant spelling of Avdimi. See Avdimi.

Avdimi (אַבְדִּימִי) A variant form of Avdima. See Avdima. Abdimi is a variant spelling. In the Talmud (Shabbat 88a), a third-century Palestinian scholar. Dimi is a pet form.

Avdon (עַבְדּוֹן) A variant form of Avda. See Avda. In the Bible (Judges 12:13), one of the Judges who ruled over Israel. Abdon is a variant spelling.

Averel, Averell From the Anglo-Saxon, meaning "to open." Associated with the month April, which marks the "opening" of the spring season. Av is a pet form. Averil and Averill are variant spellings.

Averil, Averill Variant spellings of Averel. See Averel.

Avery A variant form of Aubrey. See Aubrey.

Avgar (אַבְגָּר) From the Hebrew, meaning "dwelling of the father" or "father's house."

Avi (אָבִי) From the Hebrew, meaning "my father." Abba is a popular Aramaic form. In the Bible (II Kings 18:2), used as a feminine name. Abi and Abie are variant spellings.

Avia A variant spelling of Aviya. See Aviya.

Aviad (אֲבִיעָד) From the Hebrew, meaning "my father is witness" or "my father is eternal."

Aviah A variant spelling of Avia. See Avia.

Aviam (אֲבִיָּם) From the Hebrew, meaning "the father of a nation." In the Bible (I Kings 14:31), a son of Jeroboam.

Aviasaf (אֲבִיאָסָף) From the Hebrew, meaning "father of a multitude" or "my father has gathered." In the Bible (Exodus 6:24), a descendant of Korach. Abiasaph and Aviasaph are variant spellings.

Aviav (אֲבִיאָב) From the Hebrew, meaning "grandfather."

Aviaz (אֲבִיעָז) From the Hebrew, meaning "father of strength."

Avichai (אֲבִיחַי) From the Hebrew, meaning "my father lives" or "father of all living things."

Avichayil (אֲבִיחַיִל) From the Hebrew, meaning "father of strength" or "my father is strong." In the Bible (Esther 2:15), the father of Queen Esther.

Avichen (אֲבִיחֵן) From the Hebrew, meaning "father of grace."

Avida (אֲבִידָע) From the Hebrew, meaning "my father knows." In the Bible (Genesis 25:4), a grandson of Abraham and Ketura. Abida is a variant spelling.

Avidan (אֲבִידָן) From the Hebrew, meaning "my father is judge (or judgment)." In the Bible (Numbers 1:11), a leader of the tribe of Benjamin. Abdan is a variant spelling. *See also* Avdan.

Avidor (אֲבִידוֹר) From the Hebrew, meaning "father of a generation."

Avidror (אֲבִידְרוֹר) From the Hebrew, meaning "father of freedom."

Aviel (אֲבִיאֵל) From the Hebrew, meaning "my father is God." In the Bible (I Samuel 9:1), King Saul's grandfather. Abiel is a variant spelling. Abbe is a short form.

Aviezer (אֲבִיעֶזֶר) From the Hebrew, meaning "my father is salvation." In the Bible (Joshua 17:2), a member of the tribe of Manasseh. Abiezer is a variant spelling.

Aviezri (אֲבִיעֶזְרִי) From the Hebrew, meaning "my father is my help." Based on Judges 6:11, where Joash is called Avi Haezri.

Avifelet (אֲבְפָּלֶט) From the Hebrew, meaning "my father is my savior." Aviphelet is a variant spelling.

Avigal (אֲבִיגַל) From the Hebrew, meaning "father of waves (the sea)" or "father of joy," both referring to God. Avigayil is a feminine variant form.

Avigdor (אֲבִיגְדוֹר) From the Hebrew, meaning "father protector." Created in the Middle Ages based upon I Chronicles 4:18. The Talmud (Megilla 13a) relates this name to Moses.

Avihu (אֲבִיהוּא) From the Hebrew, meaning "he is my father." In the Bible (Exodus 6:23), the second son of Aaron and Elisheva, and nephew of Moses. Abihu is a variant spelling.

Avihud (אֲבִיהוּד) From the Hebrew, meaning "my father is majestic." In the Bible (I Chronicles 8:3), a son of Bela, and a grandson of Benjamin. Abihud is a variant spelling.

Avikam (אֲבִיקָם) From the Hebrew, meaning "my father is resurrection."

Avikar (אֲבִיקָר) From the Hebrew, meaning "my father is precious."

Avimaatz (אֲבִימַעָץ) From the Hebrew, meaning "my father is wrath" or "father of anger."

Avimael (אֲבִימָאֵל) From the Hebrew, meaning "God is my father." In the Bible (Genesis 10:28), a descendant of Shem, Noah's son.

Avimei (אֲבִימֵי) A variant spelling of Avimi. *See* Avimi.

Avimelech (אֲבִמֶלֶךְ) From the Hebrew, meaning "father of the king" or "my father is the king." In the Bible (Judges 9:1), a son of Gideon, one of Israel's Judges. Abimelech is a variant spelling.

Avimi (אֲבִימִי) A contraction of *avi immi*, meaning "grandfather." In the Talmud (Ketubot 53a), a third-century Babylonian talmudic scholar. Abimi and Avimei are variant spellings.

Avin (אֲבִין) The Aramaic form of Av, meaning "father." In the Talmud (Shabbat 23b), a fourth-century Babylonian scholar, the father of Chiya. Also, a short form of Avina. Abin is a variant spelling.

Avina (אֲבִינָא) From the Aramaic, meaning "father." A variant form of Avin. In the Talmud (Gittin 66a), a fourth-century Babylonian scholar. Abina is a variant spelling. Avin is a short form. Avuna is a variant form.

Avinadav (אֲבִינָדָב) From the Hebrew, meaning "father of a prince" or "princely father." In the Bible (I Samuel 16:8), the second son of Jesse and a brother of David. Also, a son of King Saul and brother of Jonathan (I Samuel 31:2). Abinadab is a variant spelling.

Avinaim (אֲבִינְעִים) A variant form of Avinoam. See Avinoam.

Avinatan (אֲבִינָתָן) From the Hebrew, meaning "my father has given."

Aviner (אֲבִינֵר) From the Hebrew, meaning "my father is a lamp." In the Bible (I Samuel 14:50), a variant form of Avner, Saul's uncle and chief-of-staff.

Avinoam (אֲבִינֹעַם) From the Hebrew, meaning "father of delight." In the Bible (Judges 4:6), the father of Barak of the tribe of Naftali. Abinoam is a variant spelling. Avinaim is a variant form.

Avior (אֲבִיאוֹר) From the Hebrew, meaning "father of light." Akin to Aviur.

Aviphelet A variant spelling of Avifelet. See Avifelet.

Avira (אֲוִירָא) From the Aramaic, meaning "air, atmosphere, spirit." The father of a third-century Babylonian talmudic scholar.

Aviram (אֲבִירָם) From the Hebrew, meaning "my father is mighty." In the Bible (Numbers 16:1), a co-conspirator with his brother Dathan against Moses. Abiram is a variant spelling.

Avisar (אֲבִישָׂר) From the Hebrew, meaning "my father is a prince."

Avisha (אֲבִישָׁה) A variant form of Avishai. See Avishai.

Avishachar (אֲבִישַׁחַר) From the Hebrew, meaning "father of dawn."

Avishai (אֲבִישַׁי) From the Aramaic, meaning "my father is my gift" or "gift of God." In the Bible (I Samuel 26:6), a grandson of Jesse, a brother of Joab. Avisha and Avshai are variant forms. Abishai is a variant spelling.

Avishalom (אֲבִישָׁלוֹם) From the Hebrew, meaning "my father is peace" or "father of peace." In the Bible (I Kings 15:2), Maacha, the daughter of Avishalom, was the mother of Aviyam, king of Judah. Avshalom is a variant form.

Avishama (אֲבִישָׁמָע) From the Hebrew, meaning "my father hears."

Avishar (אֲבִישָׁר) From the Hebrew, meaning "my father is song."

Avishua (אֲבִישׁוּעַ) From the Hebrew, meaning "my father is salvation." In the Bible (Ezra 7:5), a son of Phineas. Abishua is a variant spelling.

Avishur (אֲבִישׁוּר) From the Hebrew, meaning "my father is upright" or "my father is a wall (strong, dependable)." In the Bible (I Chronicles 2:28), a member of the tribe of Judah. Abishur is a variant spelling.

Avitagar (אֲבִתַּגָּר) From the Hebrew, meaning "my father is a merchant."

Avital (אֲבִיטָל) From the Hebrew, meaning "father of dew." Used also as a feminine name. In the Bible (I Chronicles 3:3), one of the six sons of David born in Hebron. Abital is a variant spelling. Used also as a feminine name. Avitul and Avtalyon are variant forms.

Avitul (אֲבִיטוּל) A variant form of Avital. See Avital. In the Talmud (Moed Katan 18a), the name of a third-century Babylonian scholar.

Avitus From the Latin, meaning "bird."

Avituv (אֲבִיטוּב) From the Hebrew, meaning "father of goodness." In the Bible (I Chronicles 8:11), a member of the tribe of Benjamin. Abituv is a variant spelling.

Avitzedek (אֲבִיצֶדֶק) From the Hebrew, meaning "my father is my rock (strength)." Avizur is a variant spelling.

Aviur (אֲבִיאוּר) From the Hebrew, meaning "father of light (fire)." Akin to Avior.

Aviv (אָבִיב) From the Hebrew, meaning "spring."

Avivi (אֲבִיבִי) From the Hebrew, meaning "springlike" or "springtime."

Aviya (אֲבִיָּה) From the Hebrew, meaning "God is my father." In the Bible, a member of the tribe of Benjamin (I Chronicles 7:8), a son of Samuel (I Samuel 8:2), and a king of Judah (I Chronicles 13:1). Used also as a feminine name in the Bible (I Chronicles 2:24). The father of a fifth-century Babylonian talmudic scholar. Abia, Abiah, Avia, and Aviah are variant spellings.

Aviyam (אֲבִיָּם) From the Hebrew, meaning "father of the sea." In the Bible (I Kings 14:31), a king of Judah, also known as Aviya.

Avizemer (אֲבִיזֶמֶר) From the Hebrew, meaning "my father is song."

Avizur A variant spelling of Avitzur. See Avitzur.

Avner (אֲבְנֵר) From the Hebrew, meaning "father of light" or "father's candle," connoting strength and inspiration. In the Bible (I Samuel 17:55), Avner ben Ner was the uncle of King Saul and commander of his army. Abner is an Anglicized spelling. Aviner is a variant form.

Avniel (אֲבְנִיאֵל) From the Hebrew, meaning "God is my rock (strength)."

Avraham (אַבְרָהָם) From the Hebrew, meaning "father of a mighty nation" or "father of a multitude." In the Bible (Genesis 11:26), the first Hebrew. His name was originally Avram, which was later changed to Avraham (Genesis 17:5). The Hebrew letter "H," the symbol for God, was added (thereby changing Avram to Avraham), symbolizing his acceptance of one God. In the post-talmudic period (after the year 500), the name Avraham became popular. Prior to that time it was not used. Not one rabbi in the entire Talmud is named Avraham, although one scholar is named Avram.

Abraham is the Anglicized form of Avraham. Early Christians refrained from using the name because of its association with Judaism. Later, however, this bias disappeared, and after the Reformation (sixteenth century) we find the name adopted more and more by the Christian community. Among

English Jewry of the eleventh and twelfth centuries it ranked third in popularity. The Arabic form of Abraham is Ibrahim. In England and among the Dutch, Bram was often used as a variant form. In seventeenth-century England Abra gained popularity as a feminine form of Abraham. Avrom, Avrum, and Avrumke are Yiddish forms.

Avram (אַבְרָם) In the Bible (Genesis 17:5), Avraham's original name. *See* Avraham. In the Talmud, only one scholar is known by the name Avram: the Babylonian Avram of Hozae; Abraham is not used at all. Abram is a variant spelling.

Avrech (אַבְרֵךְ) From the Hebrew, meaning "young man." In the Bible (Genesis 41:43), a salutation by which Joseph was addressed.

Avrom (אַבְרָם) A variant Yiddish form of Avraham. *See* Avraham.

Avron (אַבְרֹן) From the Hebrew, meaning "father of song."

Avrum (אַבְרוּם) A variant Yiddish form of Avraham. *See* Avraham.

Avrumel (אַבְרוּמֶעל) A pet form of Avrum. *See* Avrum.

Avrumke (אַבְרָמְקֶע) A Yiddish pet form of Avraham. *See* Avraham.

Avshai (אַבְשַׁי) A variant form of Avishai. *See* Avishai.

Avshal (אַבְשָׁל) A pet form of Avshalom. *See* Avshalom.

Avshalom (אַבְשָׁלוֹם) A variant form of Avishalom. *See* Avishalom. In the Bible (II Samuel 14:25), the rebellious third son of King David. Absalom is a variant spelling. Avshal is a pet form.

Avtalyon (אַבְטַלְיוֹן) From the Hebrew, meaning "father of dew." In the Talmud (Mishna Avot 1:10), a first-century B.C. scholar. Avital is a variant form. Abtalyon is a variant spelling.

Avuha (אֲבוּהּ) From the Aramaic, meaning "father." In the Talmud (Gittin 53a), a third-century Babylonian scholar. Abuha is a variant spelling.

Avuna (אֲבוּנָא) A variant form of Avina. *See* Avina. Abuna is a variant spelling.

Avuya (אֲבוּיָה) From the Aramaic, meaning "God is our father." In the Talmud (Chagiga 14b), the father of Elisha, a second-century Palestinian scholar who was reputed to be weak in his faith.

Axel, Axtel Swedish names of Germanic origin, meaning "divine source of life."

Aya (אַיָּה) From the Hebrew, meaning "vulture." In the Bible (II Samuel 3:7), the father of Rizpah, who was King Saul's concubine. Also (Job 28:7), the name of a bird. Used also as a feminine name.

Ayal (אַיָּל) From the Hebrew, meaning "deer" or "ram." Ayalon is a variant form.

Ayalon (אַיָּלוֹן) A variant form of Ayal. *See* Ayal.

Az (עַז) From the Hebrew, meaning "strong." Akin to Azai and Azaz.

Azai (עַזַאי)   From the Aramaic, meaning "strength." Azzai is a variant spelling. In the Talmud (Mishna Avot 4:2), a Palestinian scholar. *See also* Ben Azzai. Akin to Az and Azaz.

Azan (עָזָן)   From the Hebrew, meaning "strength." In the Bible (Numbers 34:26), one of the leaders of the tribe of Issachar.

Azania, Azaniah   Variant spellings of Azanya. *See* Azanya.

Azanya (אֲזַנְיָה)   From the Hebrew, meaning "the hearing of God." In the Bible (Nehemiah 10:10), the father of Jeshua the Levite who was loyal to Ezra and Nehemiah. Azania and Azaniah are variant spellings. Azanyahu is a variant form.

Azanyahu (אֲזַנְיָהוּ)   A variant form of Azanya. *See* Azanya.

Azarel (עֲזַרְאֵל)   From the Hebrew, meaning "the help of the Lord." In the Bible (I Chronicles 12:7), one of King David's warriors.

Azaria, Azariah   Variant spellings of Azarya. *See* Azarya.

Azariahu   A variant spelling of Azaryahu. *See* Azaryahu.

Azarya (עֲזַרְיָה)   From the Hebrew, meaning "the help of God." In the Bible (II Kings 14:21), a king of Judah. Used in England and America by the Puritans. Azaria and Azariah are variant spellings. Azaryahu is a variant form.

Azaryahu (עֲזַרְיָהוּ)   A variant form of Azarya. *See* Azarya. In the Bible (II Kings 15:6), the name of a king of Judah. Azariahu is a variant spelling.

Azaz (עָזָז)   From the Hebrew, meaning "strength." In the Bible (I Chronicles 5:8), a descendant of Benjamin. Akin to Az.

Azazyahu (עֲזַזְיָהוּ)   From the Hebrew, meaning "God's strength." In the Bible (I Chronicles 15:21), a Levite in the time of King David.

Azi (עָזִי)   From the Hebrew, meaning "strength." Akin to Az.

Aziel (עֲזִיאֵל)   From the Hebrew, meaning "God is my strength." A variant form of Yaaziel (I Chronicles 15:18).

Aziz (עָזִיז)   From the Hebrew, meaning "strength."

Aziza (עֲזִיזָא)   From the Hebrew, meaning "strength." In the Bible (Ezra 10:27), a contemporary of Ezra.

Azriel (עֲזְרִיאֵל)   From the Hebrew, meaning "God is my help." In the Bible (I Chronicles 27:19), the father of a leader of the tribe of Naftali.

Azrikam (עֲזְרִיקָם)   From the Hebrew, meaning "my help (succor) is established." In the Bible (I Chronicles 3:23), a descendant of Zerubbabel.

Azzai   A variant spelling of Azai. *See* Azai.

Baal (בַּעַל) From the Hebrew, meaning "master." In the Bible (I Chronicles 5:5), a member of the tribe of Reuben.

Baana (בַּעֲנָה) From the Aramaic, meaning "son of distress." In the Bible (II Samuel 23:29), one of King David's warriors. Also one of King Solomon's officials (I Kings 4:12), spelled בַּעֲנָא.

Baba A variant spelling of Bava. See Bava.

Bachan (בַּחַן) From the Egyptian, meaning "observation tower."

Bachir (בָּכִיר) From the Hebrew, meaning "the eldest son."

Bachur (בָּחוּר) From the Hebrew, meaning "boy" or "young man."

Bachya (בַּחְיָא) From the Aramaic, meaning "life."

Bahat (בַּהַט) From the Hebrew, meaning "ivory" or "alabaster." Used also as a feminine name.

Bahir (בָּהִיר) From the Hebrew, meaning "bright, light." Also, a variant spelling of Bachir. See Bachir.

Bakbuk (בַּקְבּוּק) From the Hebrew, meaning "bottle." In the Bible (Ezra 2:51), an ancestor of a family of Babylonian Exile returnees.

Bakbukia, Bakbukiah Variant spellings of Bakbukya. See Bakbukya.

Bakbukya (בַּקְבּוּקְיָה) From the Hebrew, meaning "bottle." In the Bible (Nehemiah 11:17), one of the Levites who was among the Babylonian Exile returnees.

Balak (בָּלָק) From the Hebrew, meaning "to destroy." In the Bible (Numbers 22:2), the son of Tzipor, king of Moab.

Balder From the Old Norse, meaning "bold, dangerous." In Norse mythology, the god of sun and summer, light and peace.

Baldwin From the Middle High German name Baldewin, meaning "bold friend." Baldwin I was King of Jerusalem in the twelfth century. Ball is a pet form.

Balfor A variant spelling of Balfour. See Balfour.

Balfour (בַּלְפוּר) From the Old English, meaning "a hill along the way." Balfouria is a feminine form. Adopted as a personal name in Israel after 1917, when the Balfour Declaration was issued (November 12, 1917) by British Foreign Secretary Lord Arthur James Balfour (1848-1930), who was greatly impressed by Chaim Weizmann. The Balfour Declaration announced the favorable attitude of England towards the establishment of a Jewish State in Palestine.

Ball From the Middle English, meaning "a ball," or from the Old French, meaning "to dance." Also, a pet form of Baldwin. See Baldwin.

Ballard From the Middle English and Old French, meaning "a dancing song."

Balor From the Old French and the Old High German, meaning "one who makes bales or packages."

Bancroft From the Anglo-Saxon, meaning "bean field." Banfield is a variant form.

Banet A short form of Barnett and Benedict. *See* Barnet *and* Benedict.

Banfield From the Anglo-Saxon, meaning "bean field." Bancroft is a variant form.

Bani (בָּנִי) From the Aramaic, meaning "son" or "build." In the Bible (Ezra 10:29), an ancestor of a family of Babylonian Exile returnees. Also (II Samuel 22:36), one of King David's warriors, a member of the tribe of Gad.

Barachel (בָּרַכְאֵל) From the Hebrew, meaning "blessed of the Lord." In the Bible (Job 32:6), the father of Elihu, one of Job's three friends.

Barak (בָּרָק) From the Hebrew, meaning "flash of light." In the Bible (Judges 4:6), an army officer during Deborah's rule over Israel.

Baram (בַּרְעָם) From the Aramaic, meaning "son of the nation."

Barami (בַּרְעַמִי) From the Aramaic, meaning "son of my people."

Bard From the Gaelic and Irish, meaning "minstrel" or "poet."

Bareket (בָּרֶקֶת) From the Hebrew, meaning "lightning" or "emerald."

Baretta Probably from the French, meaning "cap, beret."

Bari A variant spelling of Barrie. *See* Barrie. Also, from the Old English, meaning "gate, fence."

Bariach (בָּרִיחַ) From the Hebrew and Arabic, meaning "to flee, withdraw." In the Bible (I Chronicles 3:22), a descendant of King David.

Bar-Ilan (בַּר-אִילָן) From the Aramaic, meaning "fruit of the tree."

Barkai (בַּרְקָאי) An Aramaic form of Barak. *See* Barak.

Barker From the Old English, meaning "a logger of birch trees." An English occupational name. Birk is a Scottish form.

Bar-Kochba A variant spelling of Bar-Kochva. *See* Bar-Kochva.

Bar-Kochva (בַּר-כּוֹכְבָא) From the Aramaic, meaning "son of a star." In Jewish history, a second-century military leader who was believed by some (including Rabbi Akiba) to be the Messiah.

Barkos (בַּרְקוֹס) Meaning unknown. In the Bible (Ezra 2:53), a Temple porter who was among the Babylonian Exile returnees.

Barnabas From the Latin, Greek, and Aramaic, meaning "son of exhortation" or "a plea, a sermon." A disciple of Paul in the New Testament. Barney is a pet form. Barnaby is a variant form.

Barnaby A variant form of Barnabas. *See* Barnabas.

Barnard The French form of Bernard. *See* Bernard.

Barnes From the Old English, meaning "a bear."

Barnet, Barnett Variant forms of Bernard. *See* Bernard. Banet is an abbreviated form.

Barney A pet form of Bernard or Barnaby. *See* Bernard *and* Barnaby.

Barnum From the German, meaning "storage place" or "barn."

Barr, Barre A short form of Bernard and Barnard. *See* Bernard *and* Barnard.

Barret, Barrett A short form of Barnet. *See* Barnet.

Barri, Barrie Variant spellings of Barry. *See* Barry.

Barron From the Old High German, meaning "man, person of nobility."

Barry A Welsh patronymic form of Harry (from Ap-Harry and Ab-Harry), meaning "son of Harry." *See* Harry. May also be an Old Celtic name, meaning "spear" or "marksman." Bari, Barri, and Barrie are variant spellings.

Bart A pet form of Barton and Bartholomew. *See* Barton *and* Bartholomew. May also be a variant spelling of Bard. *See* Bard.

Barth A variant spelling of Bart. *See* Bart. Also, from the Anglo-Saxon, meaning "shelter."

Bartholomew (בַּרְתַּלְמָי) From the Aramaic and Hebrew, meaning "hill, furrow." A patronymic form, meaning "son of Talmai." *See* Talmai.

Bartlet, Bartlett Variant forms of Bartholomew. *See* Bartholomew.

Bartley From the Anglo-Saxon, meaning "Bart's (Bartholomew's) town" or "barley town." Also, from the Old English, meaning "bear town."

Baruch (בָּרוּךְ) From the Hebrew, meaning "blessed." In the Bible (Jeremiah 32:12), the friend, disciple, and scribe of the prophet Jeremiah. Barrie and Barry are pet forms.

Barur (בָּרוּר) From the Hebrew, meaning "clear, pure."

Bar-Yochai (בַּר-יוֹחָאִי) A patronymic form of Yochai. *See* Yochai.

Barzilai (בַּרְזִלַּי) From the Aramaic, meaning "man of iron." In the Bible (II Samuel 21:8), the father of Edriel, the husband of Michal, King Saul's daughter.

Basha (בַּעְשָׁא) From the Aramaic, meaning "act of God." Probably a distorted form of the name Baaseiah (I Chronicles 6:25), akin to Maaseiah. In the Bible (I Kings 15:16), the third king of Israel.

Basil From the Greek, meaning "royal, kingly."

Basti, Bastian Old German forms of Sebastian. *See* Sebastian.

Bat An English variant form of Bartholomew. *See* Bartholomew.

Batzlit A variant form of Batzlut (Nehemiah 7:54). *See* Batzlut.

Batzlut (בַּצְלוּת) From the Ethiopic, meaning "to strip off," and from the Hebrew, meaning "onion." In the Bible (Ezra 2:52), the head of a family of Babylonian Exile returnees. Batzlit is a variant form.

Bava (בָּבָא)   From the Aramaic, meaning "gate." In the Talmud (Keritut 6:3), a talmudic scholar, the son of Buta. Baba is a variant spelling.

Bavai (בַּוָּי)   From the Aramaic, meaning "to cut, to cleave," or from the Hebrew, meaning "to despise, to hate." In the Bible (Nehemiah 3:18), a Levite who helped rebuild the walls of Jerusalem.

Baxter   From the Old English, meaning "baker."

Bayard   From the Old French, meaning "bay horse," normally reddish-brown in color.

Bayless   From the Old French, meaning "one who leases out a bay." Akin to Bayard.

Baylor   From the Anglo-Saxon, meaning "one who trains horses."

Bazak (בָּזָק)   From the Hebrew, meaning "flash of light."

Bazuka (בַּזוּקָה)   From the Dutch, meaning "trumpet." A military trumpet-shaped weapon, so-named by U.S. comedian Bob Burns. Used as a modern Israeli name.

Beattie   A variant form of Beatrice. *See* Beatrice (feminine section).

Beau   From the Latin and French, meaning "pretty, handsome."

Beaumont   From the French, meaning "beautiful mountain."

Beauregard   From the French, meaning "to be well regarded."

Becher (בֶּכֶר)   From the Hebrew, meaning "firstborn, elder," or from the Arabic, meaning "young camel." In the Bible (Genesis 46:21), a son of Benjamin and a grandson of Jacob and Rachel.

Bechiel (בְּכִיאֵל)   From the Hebrew, meaning "(I swear) by the life of God."

Bechor (בְּכוֹר)   From the Hebrew, meaning "firstborn, elder." Akin to Becher. Popular for first-born sons in Sefardi families.

Bechorat (בְּכוֹרַת)   From the Hebrew, meaning "eldest son" or "first fruits." In the Bible (I Samuel 9:1), an ancestor of King Saul. Akin to Bechor and Becher.

Beck   From the Middle English and Old Norse, meaning "brook."

Bede   From the Middle English, meaning "prayer."

Bedell   From the Old French, meaning "messenger."

Beebe   From the Anglo-Saxon, meaning "one who lives on a bee farm."

Beivar (בֵּינָר)   From the Hebrew, meaning "zoo."

Bela (בֶּלַע)   From the Hebrew, meaning "to swallow, engulf." In the Bible (Genesis 46:21), a son of Benjamin and grandson of Jacob. *See also* Bela (feminine section).

Belden   From the Anglo-Saxon, meaning "beautiful pasture land."

Bell   From the Latin and French, meaning "beautiful."

Bellamy   From the Latin and French, meaning "beautiful friend."

Belton   From the French, meaning "beautiful town."

Ben (בֶּן)   From the Hebrew, meaning "son." In the Bible, (I Chronicles 15:18), the name of a Levite. Used occasionally as an independent name, but most often as the pet form of names whose first syllable is "ben."

Ben-Ad (בֶּן־עַד)   From the Hebrew, meaning "eternal, forever."

Ben-Ami (בֶּן־עַמִי)   From the Hebrew, meaning "son of my people." In the Bible (Genesis 19:38), the son of one of Lot's daughters.

Ben-Asor (בֶּן־עָשׂוֹר)   From the Hebrew, meaning "one of ten" or "tenth son" in the family.

Benaya (בְּנָיָה)   A variant form of Benayahu. *See* Benayahu.

Benayahu (בְּנָיָהוּ)   From the Hebrew, meaning "God has built." In the Bible (II Samuel 8:18), the captain of David's guard. Benaya is a variant form.

Ben-Azai, Ben-Azzai (בֶּן־עֲזַאי)   From the Hebrew, and Aramaic, meaning "man of strength." In the Talmud (Mishna Yoma 2:3), a second-century Palestinian scholar.

Ben-Baruch (בֶּן־בָּרוּךְ)   From the Hebrew, meaning "son of Baruch."

Ben-Carmi   A variant spelling of Ben-Karmi. *See* Ben-Karmi.

Ben-Chanan (בֶּן־חָנָן)   From the Hebrew, meaning "son of grace, gracious." In the Bible (I Chronicles 4:20), a member of the tribe of Judah. Ben-Hanan is a variant spelling.

Ben-Chayil (בֶּן־חַיִל)   From the Hebrew, meaning "son (man) of strength" or "son of valor." In the Bible (II Chronicles 17:7), one of the leaders of the tribe of Judah.

Ben-Chen (בֶּן־חֵן)   From the Hebrew, meaning "son (man) of grace, gracious."

Ben-Chesed (בֶּן־חֶסֶד)   From the Hebrew, meaning "merciful" or "subject of mercy." In the Bible (I Kings 4:10), one of King Solomon's twelve supply officers.

Ben-Chur (בֶּן־חוּר)   A patronymic form, meaning "son of Chur." *See* Chur. In the Bible (I Kings 4:8), one of King Solomon's officials.

Bendit (בֶּנְדִיט)   A Yiddish form of Baruch. *See* Baruch.

Benedict   From the Latin, meaning "blessed" or "well thought of." Berachya, the Hebrew form of Benedict, was extremely popular among twelfth-century Jewry. Berachya Nakdan, a great Jewish literary figure, became known as Benedict Le Puncteur. Benesh and Bennet are variant forms.

Benesh (בֶּענעש)   The Yiddish form of Benedict. *See* Benedict.

Ben-Ezra (בֶּן־עֶזְרָא)   From the Hebrew, meaning "son of salvation." Also a patronymic form of Ezra. *See* Ezra. Also spelled בֶּן־עֶזְרָה (I Chronicles 4:17).

Ben-Gever (בֶּן־גֶּבֶר)   From the Hebrew, meaning "son of man" or "man of strength." In the Bible (I Kings 4:13), one of King Solomon's twelve supply officers.

Ben-Gurion (בֶּן־גּוּרִיוֹן)   From the Hebrew, meaning "son of the lion" or "son of might."

Ben-Hanan   A variant spelling of Ben-Chanan. *See* Ben-Chanan.

Ben-Hayil   A variant spelling of Ben-Chayil. *See* Ben-Chayil.

Ben-Hesed   A variant spelling of Ben-Chesed. *See* Ben-Chesed.

Beni (בְּנִי)   From the Hebrew, meaning "my son." Akin to Ben.

Benish (בֶּעֲנִישׁ)   A Yiddish form of Benedict. *See* Benedict.

Benjamin   A variant spelling of Binyamin. *See* Binyamin. Ben, Benji, Benjie, Benjy, and Bennie are pet forms. Benno is a variant form.

Ben-Karmi (בֶּן־כַּרְמִי)   From the Hebrew, meaning "produce from my vineyard."

Bennet, Bennett   Variant English forms of the Latin name Benedict. *See* Benedict.

Bennie   A pet form of Benjamin. *See* Benjamin.

Benno   A variant form of Benjamin. *See* Benjamin.

Benny   A pet form of Benjamin. *See* Benjamin.

Beno (בְּנוֹ)   From the Hebrew, meaning "his son." In the Bible (I Chronicles 24:26), a Levite of the Merari family. Also from the Latin, French, and Italian, meaning "well, good."

Benoit   A yellow-flowered plant of the rose family. Also, the French form of Bennett. *See* Bennet.

Ben-Oni (בֶּן־אוֹנִי)   From the Hebrew, meaning "son of sorrow." In the Bible (Genesis 35:18), the name of Rachel's second son. After her death, Jacob (Rachel's husband) called him Benjamin, meaning "son of the right hand."

Benroy   From the Gaelic and French, meaning "royal mountain."

Ben-Shachar (בֶּן־שַׁחַר)   From the Hebrew, meaning "son of the dawn."

Ben-Shem (בֶּן־שֵׁם)   A patronymic form, meaning "son of Shem" or "a highly respected person." *See* Shem.

Benson   Either a patronymic form, meaning "son of Ben (or Benjamin)." Or, a form of Ben Zion. *See* Benjamin *and* Ben Zion.

Bentley   From the Old English, meaning " meadow of ben (grass)."

Benton   From the Old English, meaning "Ben's town." *See* Ben.

Ben-Tov (בֶּן־טוֹב)   From the Hebrew, meaning "good son." Ben Tovim is a variant form.

Ben-Tovim (בֶּן־טוֹבִים)   From the Hebrew, meaning "son of goodness" or "a member of a highly esteemed family."

Bentzi (בֶּנְצִי) A pet form of Ben-Tziyon or Binyamin. *See* Ben-Tziyon *and* Binyamin.

Ben-Tziyon (בֶּן־צִיוֹן) From the Hebrew, meaning "excellence" or "son of Zion." Ben-Zion is a variant spelling.

Ben-Tzvi (בֶּן־צְבִי) From the Hebrew, meaning "son of Tzevi." *See* Tzevi.

Benyamin A variant spelling of Binyamin. *See* Binyamin.

Ben-Yishai (בֶּן־יִשַׁי) From the Hebrew, meaning "son of Yishai." *See* Yishai.

Benzecry A patronymic form, meaning "son of Zechariah." *See* Zechariah.

Benzi A variant spelling of Bentzi. *See* Bentzi.

Ben-Zion A variant spelling of Ben-Tziyon. *See* Ben-Tziyon. Benzi is a pet form in vogue in Israel.

Ber (בֶּער) A Yiddish name from the German *Baer*, meaning "bear." Also, from the Anglo-Saxon, meaning "boundary."

Beracha (בְּרָכָה) From the Hebrew, meaning "blessed." In the Bible (I Chronicles 12:3), one of David's warriors from the tribe of Benjamin. Used more commonly as a modern feminine form.

Berachia, Berachiah Variant spellings of Berachya. *See* Berachya.

Berachya (בְּרָכְיָה) From the Hebrew, meaning "blessed of the Lord." Akin to Beracha. Berechya is a variant form.

Berechya (בֶּרֶכְיָה) From the Hebrew, meaning "blessed of the Lord." In the Bible (I Chronicles 3:20), a Levite, the father of Asaph, a leading singer during the reign of King David. Also, the father of the Prophet Zechariah (Zechariah 1:1). Berachia and Berachiah are variant spellings. Berechyahu is a variant form.

Berechyahu (בֶּרֶכְיָהוּ) A variant form of Berechya. *See* Berechya.

Bered (בֶּרֶד) From the Aramaic, meaning "cold" or "hail." In the Bible (I Chronicles 7:20), a son of Ephraim and grandson of Joseph.

Berg From the German, meaning "mountain."

Bergen From the German, meaning "one who lives on a hill or mountain."

Berger A variant form of Burgess. *See* Burgess. Also, a form of Bergen. *See* Bergen.

B'era (בְּאֶרָה) From the Hebrew, meaning "well." In the Bible (I Chronicles 7:37), a leader of the tribe of Asher.

B'eri (בְּאֵרִי) From the Hebrew, meaning "my well." In the Bible, the father of the Prophet Hosea (Hosea 1:1) and the father of Judith, one of Esau's wives (Genesis 26:34).

Beria, Beriah (בְּרִיעָה) From the Hebrew, meaning "evil." In the Bible (I Chronicles 7:23), a son of Asher. Bria is a variant spelling.

Beril   A variant spelling of Beryl. *See* Beryl.

Berkeley, Berkley, Berkly   From the Anglo-Saxon, meaning "from the birch meadow." Barclay is a variant form.

Berlin, Berlyn   From the German, meaning "boundary line."

Bern, Berna   From the German, meaning "bear." Berne is a variant spelling.

Bernard   From the Old High German, meaning "bold as a bear." Barnard is the French form. Barnet, Bernis, and Bernt are variant forms. Berni and Bernie are pet forms.

Bernarr   A variant form of Bernard. *See* Bernard.

Bernd, Berndt   Variant forms of Bernard. *See* Bernard.

Berne   A variant spelling of Bern. *See* Bern.

Bernhard, Bernhardt   Variant German forms of Bernard. *See* Bernard.

Berni, Bernie   Pet forms of Bernard. *See* Bernard.

Bernis   A variant form of Bernard. *See* Bernard.

Bernt   A variant form of Bernard. *See* Bernard.

Beros   From the Hebrew, meaning "a tree of the cedar family."

Berry   From the Old English, meaning "berry, grape."

Bert, Bertie   Pet forms of Albert, Berthold, Bertol, and Bertram.

Berthold   From the German, meaning "bright." Bertol, Bertold, Bertolt, and Berton are variant forms. Bert and Bertie are pet forms.

Bertin   A variant form of Bertram. *See* Bertram.

Bertol, Bertold, Bertolt   Variant forms of Berthold. *See* Berthold.

Berton   A variant form of Berthold. *See* Berthold.

Bertram   From the Old High German, meaning "bright, illustrious one." Bertin, Bertran, Bertrand, and Bertrem are variants. Bert and Bertie are pet forms.

Bertran   A variant form of Bertram. *See* Bertram.

Bertrand   A variant form of Bertram. *See* Bertram.

Bertrem   A variant spelling of Bertram. *See* Bertram.

Berwin   From the Anglo-Saxon, meaning "powerful friend."

Beryl (בֶּעְרִיל)   From the Greek, meaning "a sea-green precious stone." Or, a Yiddish form of Bernard. *See* Bernard. Also considered an acronym for Ben Rabbi Yehuda Leib, meaning "the son of Rabbi Yehuda Leib." Beril is a variant spelling.

Betach (בֶּטַח)   From the Hebrew, meaning "secure, quiet, restful."

Beteira (בְּתֵירָא)   From the Aramaic, meaning "the last, latest." In the Talmud (Peah 4:6), the father of the second-century Palestinian scholar Judah.

Bethel (בֵּית־אֵל) From the Hebrew, meaning "house of God." In the Bible, a city north of Jerusalem.

Bethuel A variant spelling of Betuel. *See* Betuel.

Betuel (בְּתוּאֵל) From the Hebrew, meaning "house of God" or "daughter of God." In the Bible (Genesis 22:23), the father of Rebecca and a nephew of Abraham.

Betzalel (בְּצַלְאֵל) From the Hebrew, meaning "shadow of God," signifying God's protection. In the Bible (Exodus 31:2), the builder of the Tabernacle. Zalel is a pet form. Bezalel is a variant spelling.

Betzer (בֶּצֶר) From the Hebrew, meaning "enclosure" or "protection."

Bevai A variant spelling of Bivai. *See* Bivai. Also, from the Aramaic *bava*, meaning "gate."

Bevan A Celtic patronymic form of Evan, meaning "son of Evan." *See* Evan.

Bevar A variant spelling of Beivar. *See* Beivar.

Beverley, Beverly From the Old English, meaning "beaver meadow" or "field." Used most often as a feminine form.

Bevin A variant spelling of Bevan. *See* Bevan.

Bevis A patronymic form of Evan, meaning "son of Evan." Also, from the French, meaning "bull, beef."

Bezalel A variant spelling of Betzalel. *See* Betzalel.

Bezek (בֶּזֶק) From the Hebrew, meaning "lightning" or "a flash of lightning."

Bichri (בִּכְרִי) From the Hebrew, meaning "my eldest son" or "youthful." In the Bible (II Samuel 20:1), the father of Sheba of the tribe of Benjamin.

Bidkar (בִּדְקַר) From the Aramaic, meaning "to explore" or "to repair." In the Bible (II Kings 9:25), an officer of King Jehu of Israel.

Bigvai (בִּגְוַי) Possibly from the Sanskrit, meaning "happy." In the B. 'ᵊ (Ezra 2:2), one of the Babylonian Exile returnees.

Bildad (בִּלְדָד) From the Hebrew, meaning "Baal has loved." In the Bible (Job 8:1), one of the three friends of Job.

Bilga, Bilgah (בִּלְגָּה) From the Hebrew, meaning "joy, cheer." In the Bible (I Chronicles 24:14), a Priest during the reign of King David.

Bilgai (בִּלְגַּי) From the Arabic and Aramaic, meaning "joy, cheerfulness." In the Bible (Nehemiah 10:9), a Priest who was a loyal follower of Ezra and Nehemiah. Bilguy is a variant spelling.

Bilguy A variant spelling of Bilgai. *See* Bilgai.

Bilhan (בִּלְהָן) From the Hebrew, meaning "calamity" or "intellectual weakness." In the Bible (Genesis 36:27), a descendant of Esau.

Bill, Billie, Billy, Billye Pet forms of William. *See* William.

Bilshan (בִּלְשָׁן)   From the Hebrew, meaning "linguist."

Bilu (בִּילוּ)   An acronym from the Hebrew words *Bet Yisrael, lechu v'neilcha*, meaning "House of Israel, come, let us walk" (Isaiah 2:5). The motto of early settlers in Palestine.

Bin   A masculine form of Binnie. *See* Binnie (feminine section).

Bina (בִּינָה)   From the Hebrew, meaning "knowledge, intelligence." Used also as a feminine name. Akin to Buna.

Binyamin (בִּנְיָמִין)   From the Hebrew, meaning "son of my right hand," having the connotation of strength. In the Bible (Genesis 35:18), the youngest of Jacob's twelve sons. Benjamin did not become popular until the Middle Ages. Benjamin of Tudela, the famous world traveler of the twelfth century, is the first well-known Benjamin. Among Christians, the name Benjamin came into use after the sixteenth century. *See also* Ben-Oni.

Binyamin-Ze'ev (בִּנְיָמִין־זְאֵב)   A hybrid of Binyamin and Ze'ev (Zev). *See* Binyamin *and* Ze'ev. The Hebrew name of Theodor Herzl (1860-1904), founder of political Zionism.

Bird   From the English and Anglo-Saxon *bridd*, which by metathesis became "bird" with its present common meaning. Used also as a feminine name.

Birdie   A pet form of Bird. *See* Bird.

Birk   A variant form of Barker. *See* Barker. Burke is a variant spelling.

Bitan (בִּיתָן)   From the Hebrew, meaning "house" or "palace."

Bitzaron (בִּצָרוֹן)   From the Hebrew, meaning "enclosure" or "protection."

Bivai (בִּיבָי)   From the Aramaic, meaning "Babylonian." Bevai is a variant spelling.

Bivi (בִּיבִי)   A variant form of Bivai. *See* Bivai. In the Talmud (Sanhedrin 66b), a fifth-century Babylonian scholar, the son of Abaye.

Blaine   From the Old English, meaning "the source of a river."

Blair   From the Celtic, meaning "place."

Blake   From the Anglo-Saxon, meaning "to white, to bleach." Blanchard is a variant form.

Blanchard   A variant form of Blake. *See* Blake.

Bland   From the Latin and Old French, meaning "mild."

Blandon, Blanton   Variant forms of Bland. *See* Bland. Also, from the Old English, meaning "the town near the river source." Akin to Blaine.

Blas, Blase   From the Greek and Latin, meaning "flatfooted." Blas is a Spanish form. Blaze is a variant spelling.

Blaze   A variant spelling of Blase. *See* Blase.

Blythe   From the Anglo-Saxon, meaning "spirited, joyful." Used also as a feminine name.

Bo   A pet form of Bogart. *See* Bogart.

Boaz (בֹּעַז)   From the Hebrew, meaning "strength" or "swiftness." In the Bible (Ruth 2:1), the second husband of Ruth.

Bob, Bobbie, Bobby   Pet forms of Robert. *See* Robert.

Bocher (בּוֹחֵר)   From the Hebrew, meaning "choose."

Bogart   From the Gaelic and the Irish, meaning "soft, marshy ground."

Bonesh (בּוֹנֶעש)   From the Yiddish, meaning "good."

Bonet   A variant spelling of Banet. *See* Banet. Used in the Middle Ages as a substitute name for Yomtov, meaning "holiday."

Boni   From the Italian, meaning "good." Akin to Boniface. *See* Boniface.

Boniface   From the Latin, meaning "well-doer."

Booker   From the Anglo-Saxon, meaning "beech tree." An occupational name for one who copies books, since paper for books was made from the beech tree.

Boone   From the Latin and the Old French, meaning "good."

Booth   From the Old Norse, meaning "temporary dwelling."

Borden   From the Old French, meaning "cottage," or from the Anglo-Saxon, meaning "den of boars."

Borg   From the Old Norse, meaning "castle." Also, a variant form of the German *Berg*, meaning "a mountain."

Boris   From the Russian, meaning "to fight" or "warrior."

Bosem (בֹּשֶׂם)   From the Hebrew, meaning "fragrance" or "perfume."

Boswell   From the Old English, meaning "thicket of willow trees."

Bourn, Bourne   From the French and Latin, meaning "boundary." Also, from the Anglo-Saxon, meaning "stream, brook."

Bowen   A Celtic patronymic form, meaning "the son (or descendant) of Owen." Bowie is a pet form.

Bowie   A pet form of Bowen. *See* Bowen.

Boyd   From the Slavic, meaning "fighting warrior," or from the Celtic, meaning "yellow."

Brad   A pet form of Braden. *See* Braden.

Braden   From the Old English, meaning "broad."

Bradford   From the Anglo-Saxon, meaning "broad ford."

Bradley   From the Old English, meaning "broad lea, meadow."

Brady   From the Anglo-Saxon, meaning "broad island."

Bram   A short form of Abraham and Abram. *See* Abraham *and* Abram. Also, from the Old English, meaning "brushwood."

Bran From the Irish, meaning "a raven." In Celtic mythology, the god of the netherworld. Brand is a variant form.

Branch From the Late Latin, meaning "paw, claw," or "an extension from a tree trunk."

Brand A variant form of Bran. *See* Bran. Or, from the Anglo-Saxon, meaning "sword." Brandi, Brandon, Brandt, and Brendan are variant forms.

Brandi A variant form of Brand. *See* Brand.

Brandon A variant form of Brand. *See* Brand.

Brandt A variant form of Brand. *See* Brand.

Brendan A variant form of Brandon. *See* Brandon.

Bret, Brett From the Celtic, meaning "Breton, a native of Brittany." *See* Brit.

Brevard From the Latin, meaning "short."

Brewster An occupational name. From the Middle English *breuen*, meaning "one who brews or makes beer."

Bria A variant spelling of Beria. *See* Beria.

Brian From the Celtic and Gaelic, meaning "strength." Also "one who is nobly born and eloquent." Bryan and Bryant are variant forms.

Briand From the French, meaning "castle."

Brice A patronymic form, meaning "son of Rice." Rice is the Anglo-Saxon form of the Middle English *riche*, meaning "rich, noble, powerful." Akin to Richard.

Brigham From the Old French and Italian, meaning "troop of soldiers."

Brindley From the Middle English, meaning "to burn." Brinley is a variant form.

Brinley A variant form of Brindley. *See* Brindley.

Bristol A variant form of Brice. *See* Brice.

Brit, Britt (בְּרִית) A short form of Briton. *See* Briton. An early name for Wales. Also, from the Hebrew, meaning "covenant." Used as variant forms of Bret. *See* Bret.

Brit-El, Britel (בְּרִית־אֵל) From the Hebrew, meaning "covenant of God."

Briton, Britton Early form for Britain (the British Isles). Also, a native or inhabitant of Great Britain.

Brock From the Anglo-Saxon and Gaelic, meaning "badger," an animal that steals grain and stores it. *See* Badger.

Broderick A name compounded from Brad and Richard, meaning "rich flat land."

Bromley From the Anglo-Saxon, meaning "meadow or field of brushwood."

Bromwell From the Old English, meaning "the well near the brushwood field." Akin to Bromley.

Bronson From the Old English, meaning "son of Brown."

Brook, Brooke From the Old English, meaning "stream." Used also as a feminine name.

Brooks A variant form of Brook. See Brook.

Bros From the Hebrew, meaning "cypress tree."

Brown From the Middle English, referring to the color brown, but originally meaning "bear" (most often colored brown).

Bruce A Scottish name of French origin, probably meaning "woods" or "thicket."

Bruchel (בְּרוּכָאֵל) From the Hebrew, meaning "blessed of the Lord."

Bruin A variant form of Bruno. See Bruno. In Danish legend, the brown bear (bruin) figures prominently.

Bruno From the Old German, meaning "brown or dark in appearance." Bruin and Bruns are variant forms.

Bruns A variant form of Bruno. See Bruno.

Bryan, Bryant Variant forms of Brian. See Brian.

Bryce A variant spelling of Brice. See Brice.

Bubba From the German, meaning "boy." The name of a tribal chief in ancient England.

Buck From the Anglo-Saxon and German, meaning "a male deer" or "a he-goat."

Buckner From the Anglo-Saxon, meaning "a dealer in bucks (deer or goats)." See also Buck.

Bucky A pet form of Buck. See Buck.

Bud From the Anglo-Saxon, meaning "beetle," or from the German, meaning "to swell up (as the bud on a branch)." Commonly used as a slang expression for a boy or man. Budd is a variant spelling.

Budd From the Old English, meaning "messenger," or from the Welsh, meaning "rich" or "victorious." Also, a variant spelling of Bud. See Bud.

Buddy A short form of Bud and Budd. See Bud and Budd. In an early British dialect, butty meant "companion."

Buell A variant form of the British bul, meaning "bull."

Buford, Bufford Compounded of the Old French boef, meaning "ox," and the Middle English ford, meaning "ford," hence "a stream (ford) where the oxen cross."

Buki (בֻּקִּי) From the Hebrew, meaning "bottle" or "tested, investigated." In the Bible (Numbers 34:22), a leader of the tribe of Dan.

Bukiya (בֻּקְיָה)   From the Hebrew, meaning "tested by the Lord." A variant form of Bukiyahu. *See* Bukiyahu.

Bukiyahu (בֻּקְיָהוּ)   A variant form of Bukiya. *See* Bukiya. In the Bible (I Chronicles 25:4), a Levite in the time of David.

Bun   An abbreviated form of Buna and Avuna (Abuna). *See* Buna *and* Avuna.

Buna (בּוּנָה)   From the Hebrew, meaning "knowledge, understanding." In the Bible (I Chronicles 2:25), a member of the tribe of Judah. Used also as a feminine name.

Buni, Bunni (בּוּנִי)   From the Hebrew, meaning "built." Also, a form of Ben, meaning "son." In the Bible (Nehemiah 11:15), a Levite in the time of Ezra and Nehemiah. In the Talmud (Sanhedrin 43a), mentioned as one of the disciples of Jesus.

Bunim (בּוּנִים)   From the Yiddish, meaning "good."

Burdette   From the Middle English, meaning "small bird." Akin to Bird.

Burgess   From the Middle English and Old French, meaning "shopkeeper," implying a "citizen" or a "free man." Berger is a variant form.

Burke   An Old English form of the German *Burg*, meaning "castle." Also, a variant spelling of Birk. *See* Birk.

Burl, Burle   From the Latin, meaning "coarse hair." Or, from the Middle English, meaning "a knot on a tree trunk."

Burleigh   From the Old English, meaning "a field with prickly, burr-covered plants." Burley is a variant spelling.

Burley   A variant spelling of Burleigh. *See* Burleigh.

Burr   From the Middle English, meaning "a prickly coating on a plant."

Burt, Burte   Either forms of Burton (*see* Burton) or from the Anglo-Saxon, meaning "bright, clear" or "excellent."

Burton   From the Old English, meaning "town on a hill" or "borough town."

Bustan (בֻּסְטָן)   From the Arabic, meaning "garden." Also spelled בֻּסְתָן.

Bustenai (בֻּסְתָנַאי)   From the Aramaic, meaning "gardener" or "farmer."

Buz (בּוּז)   From the Hebrew, meaning "contempt." In the Bible (Genesis 22:21), a son of Nachor.

Buzi (בּוּזִי)   A variant form of Buz. In the Bible (Ezekiel 1:13), the father of the Prophet Ezekiel.

Byrd   From the Anglo-Saxon, meaning "bird." Used also as a feminine name. Bird is a variant spelling.

Byron   From the German, meaning "cottage," or from the Old English, meaning "bear."

Cain (קַיִן) From the Hebrew, meaning "acquire" or "possess." In the Bible (Genesis 4:1), the son of Adam and Eve, and the brother of Abel. Kayin is a variant spelling.

Cal A pet form of Caleb, Calvert, and Calvin. See Caleb, Calvert, and Calvin.

Calbert A variant spelling of Calvert. See Calvert.

Calder From the Celtic, meaning "from the stony river."

Cale Possibly a pet form of Caleb. See Caleb.

Caleb A variant spelling of Kalev. See Kalev. Cal and possibly Cale are pet forms.

Calhoun From the Celtic, meaning "warrior."

Calvert An old English occupational name for a herdsman. Calbert is a variant spelling. Cal is a pet form.

Calvin From the Latin, meaning "bald."

Cameron From the Celtic, meaning "crooked nose."

Camillus From the Latin, meaning "attendant" or "messenger."

Capp A variant form of Chaplin. See Chaplin.

Carey From the Welsh or Cornish, meaning "rocky island." Cary is a variant spelling.

Carl A variant form of Charles. See Charles. Corliss is a variant form. Karl is a variant spelling.

Carleton A variant spelling of Carlton. See Carlton.

Carlisle From the Anglo-Saxon, meaning "Carl's island." Carlyle is a variant spelling. Corliss is a variant form.

Carlo, Carlos Italian and Spanish forms of Charles. See Charles.

Carlson A patronymic form, meaning "son of Carl." See Carl.

Carlton From the Old English, meaning "Carl's town." See Carl. Carleton is a variant spelling.

Carlyle A variant spelling of Carlisle. See Carlisle.

Carmel (כַּרְמֶל) From the Hebrew, meaning "vineyard" or "garden." Also spelled Karmel. Carmelo, Carmen, and Carmine are variant forms.

Carmeli (כַּרְמְלִי) From the Hebrew, meaning "my vineyard." Akin to Carmi. Also spelled Karmeli.

Carmelo A variant Italian form of Carmel. See Carmel.

Carmen The Spanish form of Carmel. Used also as a feminine form. See Carmen (feminine section).

Carmi (כַּרְמִי) From the Hebrew, meaning "my vineyard." Used also as a feminine name. Akin to Carmeli. In the Bible (Genesis 46:9), a son of Reuben and a grandson of Jacob. Karmi is a variant spelling.

Carmiel (כַּרְמִיאֵל)   From the Hebrew, meaning "the Lord is my vineyard."

Carmine   The Italian form of Carmen. *See* Carmel. Used also as a feminine form.

Carney   From the Celtic, meaning "fighter."

Carol   A variant form of Charles. *See* Charles. Used as a masculine name most often in the southern United States and in England. Carrol, Carroll, Karol, and Karole are variant spellings. *See* Caroline (feminine section).

Carr   From the Scandinavian and Old Norse, meaning "marshy land." Kerr is a variant spelling. Carson is a variant form.

Carrol, Carroll   Variant spellings of Carol. *See* Carol.

Carson   A patronymic form, meaning "son of Carr." *See* Carr.

Carter   An Old English occupational name, meaning "cart driver."

Carver   An Old English occupational name, meaning "wood carver, sculptor."

Cary   A variant spelling of Carey. *See* Carey.

Case   From the Old French, meaning "chest, box."

Casey   From the Celtic, meaning "valorous."

Cash   A short form of Cassius. *See* Cassius.

Casimir   From the Polish name Kazimier, meaning "proclamation of peace."

Caspar   From the German, meaning "imperial." Casper is a variant spelling.

Casper   A variant spelling of Caspar. *See* Caspar.

Cass   A short form of Cassius and Casimir. *See* Cassius *and* Casimir.

Cassius   From the Old Norman French and the Latin, meaning "box, sheath, protective cover." Cash and Cass are short forms. Cazzie is a pet form. Chaz is a variant form.

Cazzie   A pet form of Cassius. *See* Cassius.

Cecil   From the Latin, meaning "blind." Used also as a feminine name.

Cedric   A Welsh name meaning "bountiful" or "war chief."

Cerf   From the French, meaning "hart, deer."

Chachalia (חֲכַלְיָה)   From the Hebrew, meaning "red, ruddy (in appearance)" or possibly "waiting (for God)." In the Bible (Nehemiah 1:1), the father of Nehemiah.

Chacham (חָכָם)   From the Hebrew, meaning "wise man." Chachmon and Chachmoni are variant forms.

Chachmon (חַכְמוֹן)   A variant form of Chacham. *See* Chacham.

Chachmoni (חַכְמוֹנִי)   A variant form of Chacham. *See* Chacham. In the Bible

(I Chronicles 11:11), the father of a friend of one of King David's sons. Hachmoni is a variant spelling.

Chad From the Celtic, meaning "battle" or "warrior."

Chadad (חֲדַד) From the Hebrew, meaning "sharp." In the Bible (Genesis 25:15), the sixth son of Ishmael, and a grandson of Abraham. Also spelled Hadad.

Chadlai (חַדְלָי) From the Aramaic, meaning "to cease" or "to be negligent." In the Bible (II Chronicles 28:12), a descendant of Ephraim. Hadlai is a variant spelling.

Chafni A variant spelling of Chofni. See Chofni.

Chaga (חַגָּא) From the Aramaic, meaning "holiday." Akin to Chagai. See Chagai. Haga is a variant spelling.

Chagai (חַגַּי) From the Aramaic and Hebrew, meaning "my feast, festive." In the Bible (Haggai 1:1), one of the twelve Minor Prophets. In the Talmud (Yerushalmi Kidushin 3:2), a fourth-century Palestinian scholar. Hagai and Haggai are variant spellings. Chagi is a variant form.

Chagav (חָגָב) From the Hebrew, meaning "locust." In the Bible (Ezra 2:46), an ancestor of a family of Temple servants. Hagab is a variant spelling.

Chagi (חַגִּי) A variant form of Chagai. See Chagai. In the Bible (Genesis 46:16), a son of Gad and grandson of Jacob. Hagi is a variant spelling.

Chagia A variant spelling of Chagiya. See Chagiya.

Chagiya (חַגִּיָּה) From the Hebrew, meaning "festival of God." In the Bible (I Chronicles 6:15), a Levite. Chagia and Hagia are variant spellings.

Chai (חַי) From the Hebrew, meaning "life." Hai is a variant spelling.

Chaikel (חײקעל) A Yiddish form of Yechezkel. See Yechezkel.

Chaim A variant spelling of Chayim. See Chayim.

Chaklai (חַקְלָאי) From the Hebrew, meaning "farmer."

Chalafta (חֲלַפְתָּא) From the Aramaic, meaning "change, alter." In the Talmud (Rosh Hashana 27a), a second-century Babylonian scholar. Halafta is a variant spelling.

Chalamish (חַלָּמִישׁ) From the Hebrew, meaning "rock."

Chalfan (חַלְפָן) A variant form of Chalfon. See Chalfon.

Chalfon (חַלְפוֹן) From the Hebrew, meaning "change" or "pass away." Chalfan, Halfon, and Halphon are variant spellings.

Chalifa (חַלִיפָא) From the Aramaic, meaning "alter, change." The name of a fourth-century Palestinian talmudic scholar. Halifa is a variant spelling.

Chalil (חָלִיל) From the Hebrew, meaning "flute." Halil and Hallil are variant spellings.

Chalmer, Chalmers From the Old English, meaning "king of the household."

Chaltzon (חַלְצוֹן) A variant form of Cheletz. See Cheletz.

Chalutz (חָלוּץ) From the Hebrew, meaning "pioneer." Halutz is a variant spelling.

Chalutzel (חֲלוּצְאֵל) From the Hebrew, meaning "pioneer of the Lord." Halutzel is a variant spelling.

Cham (חָם) From the Hebrew, meaning "warm" or "swarthy, dark." In the Bible (Genesis 5:32), Noah's second son. Ham is a variant spelling. See Ham. Chama is a variant form.

Chama (חָמָא) A variant Aramaic form of Cham or Chamat. See Cham and Chamat. In the Talmud (Sanhedrin 17b), a fourth-century Babylonian scholar. Chami is a variant form. Hama is a variant spelling.

Chamadel (חֲמַדְאֵל) From the Hebrew, meaning "desired by God, loved by God."

Chamadia A variant spelling of Chamadya. See Chamadya.

Chamadya (חֲמַדְיָה) From the Hebrew, meaning "desired by God."

Chamat (חַמָת) Probably from the Hebrew, meaning "hot spring" or "fortress, sacred enclosure." In the Bible (I Chronicles 2:55), a member of the Rechabite family. Hamat is a variant spelling.

Chami (חָמִי) A variant form of Chama. See Chama. Hami is a variant spelling.

Champ From the Middle English and Old French, meaning "gladiator." Originally from the Latin *campus*, meaning "field, stadium where games are played." Champion is a variant form.

Champion A variant form of Champ. See Champ.

Chamran (חַמְרָן) From the Hebrew, meaning "red" or "red dye." In the Bible (I Chronicles 1:41), an Edomite. Chemdan is a variant form. Hamran is a variant spelling.

Chamud (חָמוּד) From the Hebrew, meaning "precious, cute." Hamud is a variant spelling.

Chamuel (חַמּוּאֵל) From the Hebrew, meaning "spared, saved by God." In the Bible (I Chronicles 4:26), a descendant of Simeon. Hamuel is a variant spelling.

Chamul (חָמוּל) From the Hebrew, meaning "spared, saved." In the Bible (Genesis 46:12), a son of Peretz and a grandson of Judah. Hamul is a variant spelling.

Chana (חָנָא) From the Hebrew, meaning "compassionate" or "gracious." In the Talmud (Shabbat 97a), a fourth-century Babylonian scholar. Used primarily as a feminine name. Hana is a variant spelling.

Chanamel (חֲנַמְאֵל) From the Hebrew, meaning "grace of God." In the Bible (Jeremiah 32:7), a contemporary of Jeremiah. Hanamel is a variant spelling.

Chanan (חָנָן) A variant form of Chanina. *See* Chanina. In the Bible (I Chronicles 8:23), a leader of the tribe of Benjamin. In the Talmud (Rosh Hashana 22a), a third-century Babylonian scholar. Hanan is a variant spelling.

Chananel (חֲנַנְאֵל) From the Hebrew, meaning "God is compassionate." In the Bible (Jeremiah 31:37), reference is made to the "tower of Chananel." In the Talmud (Pesachim 103a), a third-century Babylonian scholar. Hananel is a variant spelling.

Chanani (חֲנָנִי) From the Hebrew, meaning "gracious" or "compassionate." In the Bible (I Kings 16:1), the father of Jehu, a holy man who reproved King Asa of Judah. Hanani is a variant spelling.

Chanania, Chananiah Variant spellings of Chananya. *See* Chananya.

Chananya (חֲנַנְיָה) From the Hebrew, meaning "the compassion of God." In the Bible (Jeremiah 28:1), a Prophet during the reign of Zedekiah, king of Judah. In the Talmud (Yerushalmi Maaserot 3:1), a fourth-century Palestinian scholar. Chanania, Chananiah, Hanania, and Hananiah are variant spellings. Chananyahu, Chanina, and Chinena are variant forms.

Chananyahu (חֲנַנְיָהוּ) A variant form of Chananya. *See* Chananya. In the Bible (II Chronicles 26:11), an officer during the reign of King Uziah.

Chanaton (חֲנָתוֹן) From the Hebrew, meaning "gracious, compassionate." The name of a biblical city.

Chance An Americanized form of the Old English Chauncey. *See* Chauncey.

Chancellor From the Middle English and Old French, meaning "keeper of records" or "secretary."

Chandler From the French, meaning "maker or seller of candles."

Chaniel (חֲנִיאֵל) From the Hebrew, meaning "graciousness of the Lord." In the Bible (I Chronicles 7:39), a leader of the tribe of Asher. Haniel is a variant spelling.

Chanin (חָנִין) A short form of Chanina. *See* Chanina. In the Talmud (Yerushalmi Ketubot 9:10), a fourth-century Palestinian scholar. Chanan is a variant form.

Chanina (חֲנִינָא) From the Aramaic, meaning "gracious" or "compassionate." In the Talmud (Yerushalmi Peah 7:3), a third-century Palestinian scholar. Hanina is a variant spelling. Chanin is a short form. Chanan, Chaninai, Chinena, and Chunya are variant forms.

Chaninai (חֲנִינָאי) A variant form of Chanina. *See* Chanina. Chaninai Kahana was head (*gaon*) of the academy in Pumpedita, Babylonia, in the eighth century.

Chanita (חֲנִיתָה) From the Hebrew, meaning "compassionate, gracious." Used also as a feminine name. Hanita is a variant spelling. Akin to Chanina.

Channing From the Old French, meaning "canal."

Chanoch (חֲנוֹךְ) From the Hebrew, meaning "educated" or "dedicated." In the Bible (Genesis 5:18), the father of Metushelach. Hanoch and Hanokh are variant spellings. Chanuka is a variant form. Enoch is an Anglicized form.

Chanuka From the Hebrew, meaning "consecrated." A variant form of Chanoch. See Chanoch. Used primarily as a feminine name.

Chanun (חָנוּן) From the Hebrew, meaning "gracious" or "compassionate." In the Bible (II Samuel 10:1), the king of Ammon in the time of David. Hanun is a variant spelling.

Chapin A contracted form of the Old French, meaning "chaplain." Chopin is a variant form. Akin to Chaplin.

Chaplin From the Middle English, meaning "chaplain." Akin to Chapin.

Chapman From the Middle English, meaning "trader."

Charan From the Assyrian, meaning "road." In the Bible (I Chronicles 2:46), a son of Caleb.

Charef (חָרֶף) A variant form of Charif. See Charif. In the Bible (I Chronicles 2:51), a descendant of Caleb.

Charif (חָרִיף) From the Hebrew, meaning "sharp." Charef is a variant form.

Charim (חָרִים) From the Hebrew, meaning "consecrated, sacred." In the Bible (Nehemiah 10:6), a Priest in the time of Nehemiah. Charum is a variant form. Harim is a variant spelling.

Charle A variant spelling of Charley or Charlie. See Charley.

Charles A French form of the Anglo-Saxon, meaning "manly, strong" or, literally, "full-grown." Carl, Carleton, Carlo, Carlos, Carlson, Carlton, Carol, Charlton, and Karel are variant forms. Charle, Charley, Charlie, Chic, Chick, Chico, and Chuck are pet forms.

Charley, Charlie Pet forms of Charles. See Charles. Charle is a variant spelling.

Charlton A French-German form, meaning "Charles' farm" or "Charles' town." See Charles.

Charsom (חַרְסוֹם) From the Hebrew, meaning "sun." In the Talmud (Yoma 9a), the father of Eliezer, the High Priest. Harsom is a variant spelling.

Charum (חָרוּם) A variant form of Charim. See Charim.

Charutz (חָרוּץ) From the Hebrew, meaning "sharp" or "diligent." Also, from the Aramaic, meaning "trench, moat." Haruz is a variant spelling.

Chasadia, Chasadiah, Chasadya (חֲסַדְיָה) From the Hebrew, meaning "beloved of God" or "God is kind." In the Bible (I Chronicles 3:20), a son of Zerubavel, leader of the returnees from the Babylonian Exile. Hasadia and Hasadiah are variant spellings.

Chasdiel (חַסְדִּיאֵל) From the Hebrew, meaning "my God is gracious."

Chase From the Old French and Middle English, meaning "the hunt."

Chashavia, Chashaviah Variant spellings of Chashavya. *See* Chashavya.

Chashavya (חֲשַׁבְיָה) From the Hebrew, meaning "the reckoning of God" or "God has taken into account." A variant form of Chashuv. *See* Chashuv. In the Bible (Ezra 8:19), a Levite. Chashavia, Chashaviah, Hashavia, and Hashaviah are variant spellings. Chashavyahu is a variant form.

Chashavyahu (חֲשַׁבְיָהוּ) A variant form of Chashavya. *See* Chashavya.

Chashmon (חַשְׁמוֹן) From the Hebrew, meaning "prince" or "ambassador, messenger." Hashmon is a variant spelling. Chashmona'i is a variant form.

Chashmona'i (חַשְׁמוֹנָאִי) The Aramaic form of Chashmon. *See* Chashmon.

Chashuv (חָשׁוּב) From the Hebrew, meaning "important" or "accountable." In the Bible (Nehemiah 11:15), a Levite in the time of Nehemiah. Hashuv is a variant spelling. Chashavya is a variant form. *See* Chashavya.

Chashuva (חֲשׁוּבָה) A variant form of Chashuv. *See* Chashuv. Hashuva is a variant spelling. In the Bible (I Chronicles 3:20), one of the sons of Zerubavel. Used also as a feminine name.

Chasid (חָסִיד) From the Hebrew, meaning "pious, righteous." Chasud is a variant form.

Chasiel (חַסִיאֵל) From the Hebrew, meaning "refuge of the Lord." Hasiel is a variant spelling.

Chasin (חָסִין) From the Hebrew, meaning "strong." Hasin and Hassin are variant spellings.

Chaskel (חַאסְקעל) A Yiddish form of Yechezkel (Ezekiel). *See* Yechezkel *and* Haskel.

Chason (חָסוֹן) From the Hebrew, meaning "strong." Hason is a variant spelling.

Chasud (חָסוּד) A variant form of Chasid. *See* Chasid.

Chasun (חָסוּן) From the Hebrew, meaning "protected."

Chatat (חֲתַת) From the Akkadian, meaning "fear," or from the Aramaic, meaning "to dig." In the Bible (I Chronicles 4:13), a son of Othniel. Hatat is a variant spelling.

Chatifa (חֲטִיפָא) From the Hebrew, meaning "to catch, seize." In the Bible (Ezra 2:54), a Temple porter who was among the Babylonian Exile returnees. Hatifa is a variant spelling.

Chatil (חַטִיל) From the Aramaic, meaning "to be tall" or "lightning-quick." In the Bible (Ezra 2:57), a descendant of one of Solomon's servants. Hatil is a variant spelling.

Chatita (חֲטִיטָא) From the Aramaic, meaning "to make lines, to mark." In the Bible (Ezra 2:42), a Temple porter who was among the Babylonian Exile returnees. Hatita is a variant spelling.

Chatzkel (חַצְקֶעל)   A Yiddish form of Yechezkel (Ezekiel). *See* Yechezkel.

Chauncey, Chauncy   Pet forms of Chancellor. *See* Chancellor. Also, from the Old French, meaning "chance, luck." Chance is an Americanized form.

Chavaia, Chavaiah   Variant spellings of Chavaya. *See* Chavaya.

Chavakuk (חֲבַקּוּק)   From the Hebrew, meaning "to wrestle" or "to embrace." Also, an Assyrian garden plant. In the Bible (Habakuk 1:1), a Prophet in the kingdom of Judah. Habakuk and Habakkuk are variant spellings.

Chavatzinya (חֲבַצִּנְיָה)   From the Hebrew, meaning "crocus plant" (*chavatzelet*). In the Bible (Jeremiah 35:3), a member of the Rechabite family. *See also* Chavatzelet (feminine section).

Chavaya (חֲבָיָה)   From the Hebrew, meaning "to hide" or "to withdraw." In the Bible (Ezra 2:61), the head of a Priestly family. Havaia, Havaiah, Havaya, Chavaia, and Chavaiah are variant spellings.

Chavi (חֲבִי)   A pet form of Chaviva. *See* Chaviva. In the Talmud (Bava Kama 72a), a fifth-century Babylonian scholar.

Chavila (חֲוִילָה)   From the Hebrew, meaning "damp sand" or "soft mud," found near the river Pishon. In the Bible (Genesis 10:7), a grandson of Noah. Havila and Havilah are variant spellings.

Chaviv (חָבִיב)   From the Hebrew, meaning "beloved." Habib and Haviv are variant spellings. Akin to Chaviva.

Chaviva (חֲבִיבָה)   From the Hebrew, meaning "beloved." In the Talmud (Chulin 51a), a fifth-century Babylonian scholar. Akin to Chaviv. Habiba and Haviva are variant spellings. Chavi is a pet form.

Chavivam (חֲבִיבְעָם)   From the Hebrew, meaning "beloved by the nation." Akin to Chaviv.

Chavivel (חֲבִיבְאֵל)   From the Hebrew, meaning "beloved of God." Havivel is a variant spelling. Akin to Chaviv.

Chavivi (חֲבִיבִי)   From the Hebrew, meaning "my beloved" or "my friend." Akin to Chaviv. Habibi and Havivi are variant spellings.

Chaviviya (חֲבִיבִיָה)   A variant form of Chavivya. *See* Chavivya.

Chavivya (חֲבִיבְיָה)   From the Hebrew, meaning "beloved of God." Chaviviya is a variant form.

Chayil (חַיִל)   From the Hebrew, meaning "soldier" or "horseman," hence "strong."

Chayim, Chayyim, Chayym (חַיִּים)   From the Hebrew, meaning "life." Frequently bestowed upon a critically ill person in the hope that he will be restored to good health. Chaim, Haim, Hayyim, and Hayym are variant spellings.

Chaz   A variant form of Cassius. *See* Cassius.

Chazael (חֲזָאֵל)   From the Hebrew, meaning "God sees." In the Bible (II Kings

13:22), a king of Aram whose ascendancy to the throne was predicted by the Prophet Elisha. Hazael is a variant spelling.

Chazaya (חֲזָיָה) From the Hebrew, meaning "God has seen." In the Bible (Nehemiah 11:5), a member of the tribe of Judah. Hazaia and Hazaiah are variant spellings.

Chaziel (חֲזִיאֵל) From the Hebrew, meaning "vision of God." In the Bible (I Chronicles 23:9), a Levite in the time of King David. Haziel is a variant spelling.

Chazo (חֲזוֹ) From the Hebrew, meaning "breast (of an animal)." In the Bible (Genesis 22:22), a son of Nachor and a nephew of Abraham. Hazo is a variant spelling.

Chazon (חָזוֹן) From the Hebrew, meaning "seer." Hazon is a variant spelling.

Chedvi (חֶדְוִי) From the Hebrew, meaning "my joy." Hedvi is a variant spelling.

Chefer A variant spelling of Cheifer. *See* Cheifer.

Chefetz A variant spelling of Cheifetz. *See* Cheifetz.

Cheifer (חֵפֶר) From the Hebrew and Aramaic, meaning "to dig." In the Bible (Numbers 26:33), the father of Zelophehad, who had five daughters and no sons. Chefer, Hefer, and Hepher are variant spellings.

Cheifetz (חֵפֶץ) From the Hebrew, meaning "desire, delight." Chefetz is a variant spelling.

Cheilem (חֵלֶם) From the Hebrew, meaning "strength." In the Bible (Zechariah 6:14), one of the Babylonian Exile returnees. Chelem is a variant spelling.

Cheilev (חֵלֶב) From the Hebrew, meaning "fat." In the Bible (II Samuel 23:29), one of King David's warriors. Chelev is a variant spelling. Chelbo is a variant form.

Cheilon (חֵלֹן) From the Hebrew, meaning "rampart" or "fortress." In the Bible (Numbers 1:9), a member of the tribe of Zebulun. Chelon is a variant spelling.

Chelbo (חֶלְבּוֹ) From the Hebrew, meaning "crafty, clever." In the Talmud (Berachot 6b), a fourth-century Palestinian scholar. Helbo is a variant form.

Cheldai (חֶלְדָּי) The Aramaic form of Cheled. *See* Cheled. In the Bible (Zechariah 6:10), a Judean who returned from the Babylonian Exile. Heldai is a variant spelling.

Cheled (חֵלֶד) From the Hebrew, meaning "world." In the Bible (I Chronicles 11:30), a warrior in King David's army. Heled is a variant spelling. Cheldai is the Aramaic form.

Chelek (חֵלֶק) From the Hebrew, meaning "portion, share." In the Bible (Joshua 17:2), a son of Gilead and a grandson of Manasseh. Helek is a variant spelling. Akin to Chelkai.

Chelem   A variant spelling of Cheilem. *See* Cheilem.

Cheletz (חֶלֶץ)   From the Hebrew, meaning "to equip for war (strengthen)" hence, "lion." In the Bible (II Samuel 23:26), a warrior in King David's army. Helez is a variant spelling.

Chelev   A variant spelling of Cheilev. *See* Cheilev.

Chelkai (חֶלְקַי)   From the Aramaic, meaning "portion, share." In the Bible (Nehemiah 12:15), a Priest during the reign of King Jehoiakim. Helkai is a variant spelling. Akin to Chelek.

Chelon   A variant spelling of Cheilon. *See* Cheilon.

Chelton   A variant form of Chilton. *See* Chilton.

Chemdad (חֶמְדָד)   From the Hebrew, meaning "precious" or "beloved." Hemdad is a variant spelling.

Chemdan (חֶמְדָן)   From the Hebrew, meaning "precious, desirable." In the Bible (Genesis 36:26), a variant form of Chamran. *See* Chamran. Hemdan is a variant spelling. Akin to Chemed.

Chemed (חֶמֶד)   From the Hebrew, meaning "desirable, delightful" or "precious." Akin to Chemdan.

Chemya (חֶמְיָה)   A pet form of Nechemya. *See* Nechemya.

Chen (חֵן)   From the Hebrew, meaning "charm, grace." In the Bible (Zechariah 6:14), a Babylonian Exile returnee. Hen is a variant spelling.

Cheresh (חֶרֶשׁ)   From the Hebrew, meaning "magician" or "magic potion." In the Bible (I Chronicles 9:15), a Levite. Heresh is a variant spelling.

Chermon (חֶרְמוֹן)   From the Hebrew, meaning "consecrated" or "sacred." A mountain on the Israeli-Syrian border. Hermon is a variant spelling. Chermoni is a variant form.

Chermoni (חֶרְמוֹנִי)   A variant form of Chermon. *See* Chermon. Hermoni is a variant spelling.

Cherut (חֵרוּת)   From the Hebrew, meaning "freedom."

Chesed (חֶסֶד)   From the Hebrew, meaning "kindness, lovingkindness, goodness."

Chester   From the Latin, meaning "fortress" or "camp." Chet is a popular pet form.

Chet   A pet form of Chester. *See* Chester.

Chetzrai (חֶצְרַי)   From the Aramaic, meaning "enclosure" or "settlement." In the Bible (II Samuel 23:25), one of King David's warriors. Hezrai is a variant spelling. Chetzro is a variant form.

Chetzro (חֶצְרוֹ)   A variant form of Chetzrai. *See* Chetzrai. In the Bible (I Chronicles 11:37), one of King David's warriors. Hezro is a variant spelling.

Chetzron (חֶצְרוֹן)   From the Hebrew, meaning "an established settlement." In the Bible (Exodus 6:14), a son of Reuben and a grandson of Jacob. Hezron is a variant spelling.

Chever (חֶבֶר)   From the Hebrew, meaning "association" or "to unite, join." In the Bible (I Chronicles 7:32), a descendant of Asher. Chevron is a variant form. Hever is a variant spelling.

Chevron (חֶבְרוֹן)   A variant form of Chever. See Chever. In the Bible (Numbers 3:19), a Levite and also a place-name. Hevron and Hebron are variant spellings.

Chevy   From the British, meaning "hunt, chase." A name derived from the hunting cry "chivy," in the ballad *Chevy Chase.*

Chezyon (חֶזְיוֹן)   From the Hebrew, meaning "vision." In the Bible (I Kings 15:18), the grandfather of Ben-Hadad, king of Aram.

Chia   A variant spelling of Chiya. See Chiya.

Chic, Chick   Pet forms of Charles. See Charles.

Chico   A pet form of Charles. See Charles. Also, from the Spanish, meaning "small."

Chiel (חִיאֵל)   From the Hebrew, meaning "God lives." In the Bible (I Kings 16:34), one of the rebuilders of Jericho. A short form of Yechiel. Hiel is a variant spelling.

Chilkia, Chilkiah   Variant spellings of Chilkiya. See Chilkiya.

Chilkiya (חִלְקִיָה)   From the Hebrew, meaning "my portion is God." In the Bible (II Kings 22:8), the High Priest in the time of King Josiah. Chilkia, Chilkiah, and Hilkiah are variant spellings. Chilkiyahu is a variant form.

Chilkiyahu (חִלְקִיָהוּ)   A variant form of Chilkiya. See Chilkiya. In the Bible (Jeremiah 1:1), the father of Jeremiah.

Chilton   From the Anglo-Saxon, meaning "town by the river." Chelton is a variant form.

Chinan (חִנָּן)   From the Hebrew and Aramaic, meaning "gracious." Hinan is a variant spelling. Akin to Chinena.

Chinena (חִנְנָא)   From the Aramaic, meaning "grace, gracious." A variant form of Chanina and Chananya. See Chanina. In the Talmud (Pesachim 105a), a third-century Babylonian scholar. Hinena is a variant spelling. Akin to Chinan.

Chinton (חִנָתוֹן)   A variant form of Chanaton. See Chanaton.

Chiram (חִירָם)   From the Hebrew, meaning "lofty, exalted." A variant form of Achiram. In the Bible (I Kings 5:24), the Hebrew name of the king of Tyre who was very friendly with David. Hiram is a variant spelling. Chirom is a variant form.

Chirom (חִירוֹם)   A variant form of Chiram. See Chiram.

Chisda (חִסְדָּא)   From the Hebrew, meaning "gracious." In the Talmud

(Berachot 44a), a third-century Babylonian scholar. Hisda is a variant spelling. Akin to Chisdai.

Chisdai (חִסְדָּאי)   From the Aramaic, meaning "gracious." Akin to Chisda.

Chiya, Chiyah (חִיָּא)   From the Hebrew, meaning "life." In the Talmud (Shabbat 6b), a third-century Babylonian scholar. Chia, Hiya, and Hiyah are variant spellings.

Chizki (חִזְקִי)   From the Hebrew, meaning "my strength." In the Bible (I Chronicles 8:17), a leader of the tribe of Benjamin. Hizki is a variant spelling.

Chizkia, Chizkiah   Variant spellings of Chizkiya. See Chizkiya.

Chizkiya (חִזְקִיָּה)   From the Hebrew, meaning "God is my strength." In the Bible (II Kings 18:1), a king of Judah in the time of Isaiah. In the Talmud (Berachot 18b), a third-century Palestinian scholar. Chizkiyahu is a variant form. Hezekiah is an Anglicized form. Chizkia and Chizkiah are variant spellings.

Chizkiyahu (חִזְקִיָּהוּ)   A variant form of Chizkia. See Chizkia.

Chodesh (חֹדֶשׁ)   From the Hebrew, meaning "month." See also Chodesh (feminine section). Also spelled חוֹדֶשׁ.

Chofesh (חֹפֶשׁ)   From the Hebrew, meaning "freedom."

Chofni (חָפְנִי)   From the Hebrew, meaning "handful." In the Bible (I Samuel 1:13), the son of Eli the High Priest and a brother of Pinchas. Chofni HaKohen was the head of the academy (gaon) of Sura, Babylonia, in the ninth century. Chafni, Hophni, and Hofni are variant spellings.

Chonen (חוֹנֵן)   From the Hebrew, meaning "gracious." Honen is a variant spelling. Akin to Choni.

Choni (חוֹנִי)   From the Hebrew, meaning "gracious." Honi is a variant spelling. Akin to Chonen. In the Talmud (Taanit 23a), a miracle-performing Rip Van Winkle-type saintly character who slept for seventy years.

Chonio   A variant spelling of Chonyo. See Chonyo.

Chonyo (חוֹנְיוֹ)   From the Hebrew, meaning "gracious." Also spelled Honio. Chonio is a variant spelling.

Chopin   A variant form of Chapin. See Chapin.

Choreish (חֹרֵשׁ)   From the Hebrew, meaning "plower, farmer."

Choresh   A variant spelling of Choreish. See Choreish.

Chori (חוֹרִי)   From the Assyrian, meaning "to dig, bore, make a hole" or "cave-dweller." In the Bible (Numbers 13:5), the father of a leader of the tribe of Simeon. Hori is a variant spelling.

Chosa (חֹסָה)   From the Hebrew, meaning "protection" or "refuge." In the Bible (I Chronicles 16:30), a Levite who was a Tabernacle gatekeeper in the time of David. Hosa and Hosah are variant English spellings. Also spelled חוֹסָה.

Chosen (חֹסֶן)   From the Hebrew, meaning "strong."

Chotam (חוֹתָם) From the Hebrew, meaning "seal, signet ring." In the Bible (I Chronicles 7:32), a descendant of Asher. Hotam is a variant spelling.

Choter (חֹטֶר) From the Hebrew, meaning "branch."

Chovav (חֹבָב) From the Hebrew, meaning "beloved" or "friend." In the Bible (Judges 4:11), the father-in-law of Moses, who was better known as Jethro in the Book of Exodus. Hobab and Hovav are variant English spellings. Also spelled חוֹבָב.

Chovev (חוֹבֵב) From the Hebrew, meaning "friend" or "lover." Hovev and Hobeb are variant spellings.

Chozai (חוֹזַי) From the Aramaic, meaning "seer, prophet." In the Bible (II Chronicles 33:19), a scribe during the reign of Manasseh. Hozai is a variant spelling.

Chris A pet form of Christopher. *See* Christopher.

Chrissie A pet form of Christopher. *See* Christopher.

Christie A pet form of Christopher. *See* Christopher.

Christoff A variant form of Christopher. *See* Christopher.

Christophe A variant form of Christopher. *See* Christopher.

Christopher From the Greek and Latin, meaning "Christ-bearer." Akin to the Latin name Christian, meaning "a Christian." Chris, Chrissie, Christie, Christy, and Kit are pet forms. Christoff and Christophe are variant forms.

Christy A Scottish pet form of Christopher. *See* Christopher.

Chuba (חֻבָּה) From the Hebrew, meaning "beloved." In the Bible (I Chronicles 7:34), a member of the tribe of Asher. Huba is a variant spelling.

Chubb From the Old German, meaning "round, rounded." Chubby is a pet form.

Chubby A pet form of Chubb. *See* Chubb.

Chuck A pet form of Charles. *See* Charles.

Chug (חוּג) From the Hebrew, meaning "association" or "circle of people." Hug is a variant spelling.

Chugi (חוּגִי) A variant form of Chug. *See* Chug.

Chumi (חוּמִי) From the Yiddish, meaning "dark, black." Or a Yiddish form of Nachum. *See* Nachum. Humi is a variant spelling.

Chuna, Chunah (חוּנָא) Variant Yiddish forms of Nachum. *See* Nachum. Huna and Hunah are variant spellings.

Chunya (חוּנְיָא) A short form of Nechunya and a variant form of Chanina. *See* Chanina. In the Talmud (Yerushalmi Sheviit 9:1), a third-century scholar. Hunya is a variant spelling.

Chupa (חֻפָּה) From the Hebrew, meaning "canopy" or "enclosure." In the Bible (I Chronicles 24:13), the head of a family of Priests in the time of David. Hupa is a variant spelling.

Chupam (חֻפָּם) From the Hebrew, meaning "enclosure." In the Bible (Numbers 26:30), a son of Benjamin and grandson of Jacob. Hupam is a variant spelling. Chupim is a variant form.

Chupim (חֻפִּים) A variant form of Chupam. *See* Chupam. Hupim is a variant spelling.

Chur (חוּר) From the Akkadian, meaning "child." In the Bible (Exodus 31:2), the grandfather of Bezalel, the architect of the Tabernacle. Hur is a variant spelling. Churai is an Aramaic form.

Churai (חוּרָי) An Aramaic form of Chur. *See* Chur. In the Bible (I Chronicles 11:32), one of King David's warriors. Hurai is a variant spelling.

Churi (חוּרִי) From the Aramaic, meaning "white, to become white" and "white bread." In the Bible (II Chronicles 5:14), a descendant of Gad. Huri is a variant spelling.

Chusha (חֻשָׁה) From the Hebrew, meaning "feeling." In the Bible (I Chronicles 4:4), a son of Chur and also a place-name. Chushai, Chusham, and Chushim are variant forms.

Chushai (חוּשַׁי) The Aramaic form of Chusha. In the Bible (II Samuel 15:32), a friend of David. Hushai is a variant spelling.

Chusham (חֻשָׁם) A variant form of Chusha. *See* Chusha. In the Bible (Genesis 36:34), one of the kings of Edom.

Chushiam (חוּשִׁיָעָם) From the Hebrew, meaning "pulse (feeling) of the nation." *See also* Chusha.

Chushiel (חוּשִׁיאֵל) From the Hebrew, meaning "pulse (feeling) of God." *See also* Chusha.

Chushim (חֻשִׁים) A variant form of Chusha. *See* Chusha. In the Bible (Genesis 46:23), a member of the tribe of Dan. Used also as a feminine name.

Chutzpit (חֻצְפִּית) From the Hebrew, meaning "nerve, courage." In the Talmud (Berachot 27b), a second-century Babylonian scholar who was one of the Ten Martyrs who defied the Romans and was put to death after his tongue was cut out. This, and the fact that he was a great orator and interpreter of the law (*meturgeman*), may account for his name, "Chutzpit the Meturgeman." Huzpit is a variant spelling.

Cicero From the Latin, meaning "orator" or "guide" who explains the history of a place to sightseers.

Cid A Spanish name derived from the Arabic, meaning "lord, sir."

Cimon A variant form of Simon. *See* Simon.

Ciro A pet form of Cicero. *See* Cicero.

Claiborn, Claiborne Compounded from the German and French, meaning "boundary marked by clovers."

Clarence From the Latin, meaning "illustrious." Clair and Claire are short forms. Claron is a variant form.

Clark, Clarke From the Old English, meaning "clergyman" or "legend man." A clark, or clerk, was originally a member of a clerical order. The opportunity to study and become a scholar was originally confined, in the main, to members of the clergy.

Claron A variant form of Clarence. See Clarence.

Claud, Claude From the French and Latin, meaning "lame." Claudell is a pet form.

Claudell A pet form of Claude. See Claude.

Clay From the German and Indo-European, meaning "to stick together."

Clayton A variant form of Clay, meaning "town built upon clay." See Clay.

Clem A pet form of Clement. See Clement.

Clement From the Latin, meaning "merciful" or "gracious." Clem is a pet form. Clemon, Clemmons, Kalonymos, and Kalonymus are variant forms.

Clemmons A variant form of Clement. See Clement.

Clemon A variant form of Clement. See Clement.

Cleo A variant spelling of Clio. See Clio. Also, from the Old English, meaning "hill."

Cleon A variant form of clio. See Clio.

Cleve From the Old English, meaning "steep bank." Used also as a pet form of Cleveland. See Cleveland. Akin to Cliff.

Cleveland From the Old English, meaning "land near the steep bank." Cleve is a pet form.

Clever From the Old English, meaning "claw, hand."

Cliff, Cliffe From the Old English, meaning "steep bank." Also, a short form of Clifford or Clifton. Akin to Cleve.

Clifford An English local name, meaning "ford or crossing near the cliff." Cliff and Cliffe are short forms.

Clifton From the Old English, meaning "farm near the cliff." Cliff and Cliffe are short forms.

Clint A pet form of Clinton. See Clinton.

Clinton From the Anglo-Saxon, meaning "town on a hill." Clint is a pet form.

Clio From the Greek, meaning "to praise, to acclaim." In Greek mythology, the muse of history. Cleo is a variant spelling. See Cleo.

Clive From the Old English, meaning "steep bank." Originally a place-name in England. Akin to Cleve.

Clovis From the Anglo-Saxon and German, meaning "clover (a leguminous plant)."

Clyde From the Welsh, meaning "heard from afar." Clydell is a variant form.

Clydell A variant form of Clyde. *See* Clyde.

Coburn From the Middle English, meaning "where the streams come together." Coby is a pet form.

Coby A pet form of Coburn. *See* Coburn.

Cody From the Anglo-Saxon, meaning "cushion."

Colbert A French name from the Latin, meaning "neck," and the Old High German, meaning "bright," referring to a "good, bright passageway in a mountain range."

Colby From the Old English and Danish, meaning "coal town." Akin to Coleman. Cole is a pet form.

Cole A pet form of Colby or Coleman. *See* Colby *and* Coleman.

Coleman Of uncertain origin. Either from the Middle English, meaning "coal miner," or "a man who farms cabbage." Akin to Colby. Colman is a variant spelling. Cole is a pet form. *See also* Colvin.

Colin Usually taken as a pet form of Nicholas, meaning "victory." Also, from the Celtic, meaning "cub, whelp," the Gaelic and Latin, meaning "dove," and the Icelandic, meaning "headman." Collin is a variant spelling.

Collier From the Middle English, meaning "coal miner" or "ship for carrying coal." Collie is a pet form.

Collin A variant spelling of Colin. *See* Colin.

Colman A variant spelling of Coleman. *See* Coleman.

Colum From the Gaelic, meaning "dove," or from the Latin, meaning "hill." Akin to Columba. *See* Columba.

Columba From the Latin, meaning "dove." Akin to Colum. *See* Colum.

Colvin Compounded from the Middle English, meaning "coal," and the German, meaning "friend of." Colwyn is a variant form. Coleman is possibly a variant form.

Colwyn A variant form of Colvin. *See* Colvin.

Conan, Conant From the Middle English, meaning "to be able" or "to be knowledgeable." Also, from the Celtic, meaning "chief, king." Conn is a variant form. Connie is a pet form.

Conn A variant form of Conan. *See* Conan.

Connie A pet form of Constantine and Conan. *See* Constantine *and* Conan.

Conrad From the Old High German, meaning "able counsellor."

Constant A short form of Constantine. *See* Constantine.

Constantine From the Latin, meaning "constant, loyal, firm." Connie is a pet form. Constant is a short form.

Cook From the Latin, meaning "to cook." Cookie is a pet form.

Cookie A pet form of Cook. *See* Cook. Also, a term of endearment.

Coop A pet form of Cooper. *See* Cooper.

Cooper From the Latin, meaning "cask." An occupational name for persons who make and repair barrels. Coop is a pet form.

Corbet, Corbett From the Old French and the Middle English, meaning "raven" or "cow." Corbin is a variant form. Akin to Corwin.

Corbin A variant form of Corbet. *See* Corbet.

Cord A pet form of Cordell. *See* Cordell.

Cordell From the Latin and Old French, meaning "cord" or "rope." Cord is a pet form.

Corey A variant spelling of Cory. *See* Cory.

Corin From the Greek, meaning "maiden."

Corliss A variant form of Carl. *See* Carl. Also, a variant form of Carlisle. *See* Carlisle.

Cornel, Cornell Variant forms of Cornelius. *See* Cornelius.

Cornelius From the Norman-French, meaning "crow." Or from the Latin, meaning "horn of the sun (a symbol of kingship)" or "long life." Also, from the Greek, meaning "cornell tree." Cornel and Cornell are variant forms.

Corwan A variant spelling of Corwin. *See* Corwin.

Corwin, Corwyn From the Latin, meaning "raven." Akin to Corbet.

Cory From the Latin, meaning "helmet," or from the Anglo-Saxon, meaning "chosen one." Corey is a variant spelling.

Cosimo The Italian form of Cosmo. *See* Cosmo.

Cosmo From the Greek, meaning "universe, universal." Cosimo is the Italian form.

Cotton From the Middle English, referring to the cotton plant.

Courtland, Courtlandt From the Anglo-Saxon, meaning "land belonging to the king (court)."

Cowan From the Middle English and the Latin, meaning "hooded cloak," hence, a member of the clergy. Akin to Cohen, from the Hebrew, meaning "Priest."

Coy, Coye From the British, meaning "wood, a wooded area." Also, from the Old French, meaning "quiet, still."

Cozy From the Scottish and Norwegian, meaning "comfortable."

Craig From the Celtic and Gaelic, meaning "from the crag (rugged rocky mass)."

Cramer   From the Middle English, meaning "to cram in, squeeze in." Kramer is a variant spelling. Originally an occupational name for a peddler who traveled the country with a cram (pack) on his back.

Crandall   A variant spelling of Crandell. *See* Crandell.

Crandell   From the Old English, meaning "dale, valley of cranes." Crandall is a variant form.

Crane   From the Old English, meaning "to cry hoarsely."

Crawford   From the Old English, meaning "ford or stream where the crows flock."

Creighton   From the Old English, meaning "town near the creek."

Crockett   From the British, meaning "heap, hill."

Croft   From the Anglo-Saxon, meaning "field" or "appropriated land."

Cromwell   From the Welsh, meaning "bent," plus the Old English, meaning "well, water," hence "one who lives near the winding brook."

Crosby   From the Anglo-Saxon, meaning "crossroads near the town." Or, from the Middle English, meaning "cross in the town."

Crowell   From the Middle English and the German, meaning "to crow, call," hence "cry of victory."

Cullen   From the Celtic, meaning "cub, young animal."

Curt   A pet form of Curtis. *See* Curtis. Kurt is a variant spelling.

Curtis   From the Late Latin, meaning "enclosure, court." Or, from the Old French, meaning "courteous." Curt is a pet form.

Cy   A pet form of Cyrus. *See* Cyrus.

Cyril   From the Greek, meaning "lord, lordly."

Cyrus   From the Persian, meaning "sun." In the Bible (Ezra 1:1), a king of Persia (c. 600-529 B.C.E.) who defeated the Babylonians and permitted the Jews in exile to return to Palestine. Koresh (כֹּרֶשׁ) is the Hebrew spelling. Cy is a pet form.

Dab   A variant form of David. *See* David.

Dabbey, Dabby   A variant form of David. *See* David.

Dabney   A variant form of David. *See* David.

Dael (דְּעֵאֵל)   From the Hebrew, meaning "knowledge of God."

Daffy   A variant form of David. *See* David. Akin to Dabbey.

Dafna (דַּפְנָא)   From the Aramaic, meaning "wall."

Dag (דָּג) From the Danish and German, meaning "day." Also, from the Hebrew, meaning "fish." Dagget and Day are variant forms. Akin to Dailey, Dayman, Daymon, and Dalton.

Dagan (דָּגָן) From the Hebrew, meaning "grain." In Babylonian mythology, the god of the earth. Dagania is a feminine form.

Dagget An Anglo-Saxon form of Dag. *See* Dag.

Dago A variant form of Diego, the Spanish form of James. *See* James.

Dagul (דָּגוּל) From the Hebrew, meaning "banner, ensign."

Dailey From the Middle English, meaning "day." Akin to Dag. Daly is a variant spelling.

Dal A variant form of Dale. *See* Dale.

Dalbert From the German, meaning "bright, cheerful valley."

Dale From the Old English and the Old Norse, meaning "hollow, small valley" or "one who dwells in a vale between hills." Dal is a variant form.

Dalfon (דַּלְפוֹן) From the Hebrew, meaning "drop, drip" or "rainwater." In the Bible (Esther 9:7), one of the ten sons of Haman. Dalphon is a variant spelling.

Dall From the Old English, meaning "valley."

Dallas From the Old English, meaning "house in the valley."

Dallin From the Anglo-Saxon, meaning "from the dale."

Dalphon A variant spelling of Dalfon. *See* Dalfon.

Dalton From the Old English, meaning "town near the valley." Also, from the Middle English, meaning "bright, cheerful town." Akin to Dag. *See* Dag.

Dalva A variant form of Dale. *See* Dale.

Daly A variant spelling of Dailey. *See* Dailey.

Dama (דָּמָה) From the Hebrew and Aramaic, meaning "to resemble." Also spelled דְּמָא. In the Talmud (Menachot 99b), the father of Elazar, a second-century Palestinian scholar.

Damian A variant spelling of Damien. *See* Damien.

Damien From the Greek, meaning "divine power" or "fate." Damian is a variant spelling.

Damon From the Latin, meaning "spirit, demon." Also, from the Danish and the Anglo-Saxon, meaning "day." In Roman legend, Damon was the devoted friend of Pythias and has come to symbolize friendship.

Dan (דָּן) From the Hebrew, meaning "judge." In the Bible (Genesis 30:6), the fifth of the twelve sons of Jacob. Dana and Dani are variant forms.

Dana A variant form of Dan. *See* Dan. Used primarily as a feminine name.

Dandie, Dandy Pet forms of Andrew. *See* Andrew.

Dani (דָּנִי)   A variant form of Dan or Daniel. *See* Dan *and* Daniel.

Dani-Am (דָּנִי־עָם)   From the Hebrew, meaning "judgment of the people" or "the people (nation) is my judge."

Daniel (דָּנִיאֵל)   From the Hebrew, meaning "God is my judge." In the Bible (Daniel 1:6), a Hebrew official in the court of Nebuchadnezzar, king of Babylonia. The hero of the Book of Daniel, who was cast into the lions' den but was miraculously saved. In the Talmud (Taanit 9b), a fourth-century Babylonian scholar. Daniel and Danilo are variant forms. Dannie and Danny are pet forms.

Daniele   An Italian form of Daniel. *See* Daniel.

Danil, Danilo   Variant forms of Daniel. *See* Daniel. Danilo is an Italian form.

Dannie, Danny   Pet forms of Daniel. *See* Daniel. Used also as an independent name.

Dante   A pet form of the Italian name Durante, from the Latin, meaning "durable, lasting."

Dapi (דַּפִּי)   From the Hebrew, meaning "leaf, page, plank."

Dar (דַּר)   From the Hebrew, meaning "pearl, mother-of-pearl" or "marble." Also, from the British, meaning "oak."

Darby   From the British, meaning "home near the water." *See also* Derby.

Darda (דַּרְדַּע)   A variant form of Dar. *See* Dar. In the Bible (I Kings 5:11), a wise man in the time of Solomon.

Daren   A variant spelling of Darren. *See* Darren.

Daria   From the Persian, meaning "king." Akin to Darius. *See* Darius. Darian and Darien are variant forms.

Darian, Darien   Variant forms of Daria. *See* Daria.

Darin   A variant spelling of Darren. *See* Darren.

Darius (דָּרְיָשׁ)   From the Persian, meaning "king" or "one who is wealthy." In the Bible (Ezra 6:1), king of Persia (581-486 B.C.E.), who confirmed the permission granted the Jews who had returned to Palestine to rebuild the Temple. Daryavesh is the Hebrew form. Akin to Daria.

Darkon (דַּרְקוֹן)   From the Hebrew, meaning "to walk quickly." In the Bible (Ezra 2:56), one of the Babylonian Exile returnees.

Darlin   From the British, meaning "grove of oak trees." Darling, Darold, Darrol, Darroll, Darryl, Derel, Derell, Derrel, Derrell, Derril, and Derrill are variant forms.

Darling   A variant form of Darlin. *See* Darlin.

Daro   A variant spelling of Darrow. *See* Darrow.

Darold   A variant form of Darrell and Darlin. *See* Darrell *and* Darlin.

Darom (דָּרוֹם)   From the Hebrew, meaning "south."

Darrell From the Anglo-Saxon, meaning "dear, darling." Also, a variant form of Darlin. See Darlin. Daryl and Daryle are variant spellings.

Darren From the British, meaning "small rocky hill." Daren and Darin are variant spellings.

Darrol, Darroll Variant forms of Darlin. See Darlin.

Darrow From the Old English, meaning "spear." Daro is a variant spelling.

Darry A pet form of Darryl. See Darryl. Or, from the French, meaning "from Harry."

Darryl A variant form of Darlin. See Darlin. Darry is a pet form.

Darton From the British and Old English, meaning "town near the water."

Darwin From the British and Anglo-Saxon, meaning "lover of the sea."

Daryavesh (דָּרְיָוֶשׁ) The Hebrew form of Darius. See Darius.

Daryl, Daryle Variant spellings of Darrell. See Darrell.

Dashe, Dasheh (דֶּשֶׁא) From the Hebrew, meaning "grass."

Datan (דָּתָן) From the Hebrew, meaning "decree, law" or "religious usage." In the Bible (Numbers 16:25), a member of the tribe of Reuben who with his brother Aviram joined a conspiracy against Moses and Aaron.

Datiel (דָּתִיאֵל) From the Hebrew, meaning "knowledge of the Lord."

Daud The Arabic form of David. See David.

Dave A pet form of David. See David.

Daven A Scandinavian form of the British, meaning "two rivers." Davip is a variant form.

Davey A pet form of David. See David. Davy is a variant spelling.

Davi A pet form of David. See David. Used also as a feminine name.

David (דָּוִד) From the Hebrew, meaning "beloved." In the Bible (I Samuel 17:12), the son of Jesse and the second King of Israel; successor to King Saul and father of King Solomon. Strangely, not one rabbi in the Talmud is named David. Davyd is a variant spelling. Dab, Dabbey, Dabby, Dabney, Daffy, Daud, Davidson, Davidyne, Davis, Daw, Dawe, Dawes, Dawson, Delvin, and Dewey are variant forms. Dave, Davey, Davi, Davie, Davy, Tab, Taffy, and Tavi are pet forms.

Davidson A patronymic form of David, meaning "son of David." See David.

Davidyne A variant form of David. See David.

Davie A pet form of David. See David. Used also as an independent name.

Davip A variant form of Daven. See Daven.

Davis A patronymic form of David, meaning "son of David." See David.

Davy A pet form of David. See David.

Davyd A variant spelling of David. *See* David.

Daw, Dawe From the Old English, meaning "doe." Also, a variant form of David. *See* David. Dow and Dowe are variant spellings.

Dawes A patronymic form of David, meaning "son of David." *See* David.

Dawson A patronymic form of David, meaning "son of David." *See* David.

Day A variant form of Dag. *See* Dag. Akin to Dayman, Daymon, and Dalton.

Dayman, Daymon From the Anglo-Saxon, meaning "day." Akin to Day. *See* Day.

Dean, Deane From the Old French, meaning "head, leader." Also, from the Celtic and the Old English, meaning "hollow, small valley." Deno is a variant form. Dee is probably a short form.

Debs Probably a matronymic form of Deborah, meaning "son of Deborah." *See* Deborah (feminine section).

Decatur From the Greek, meaning "pure."

Dedan (דְּדָן) From the Hebrew, meaning "to move slowly." In the Bible (Genesis 25:3), a descendant of Abraham and Keturah.

Dee Probably a short form of Dean. *See* Dean.

Deems From the Middle English, meaning "to judge."

Dekel (דֶּקֶל) From the Arabic and Hebrew, meaning "palm (date) tree." Dikla is an Aramaic form.

Deker (דֶּקֶר) From the Hebrew, meaning "to pierce." In the Bible (I Kings 4:9), the son of Deker (Ben-Deker) is an officer of King Solomon.

Del A pet form of Delbert, Delmar, or Delmore. *See* Delbert *and* Delmar.

Delaia A variant spelling of Delaya. *See* Delaya.

Delano From the Old French, meaning "of the night." Or, from the Erse, meaning "a healthy, dark man."

Delaya (דְּלָיָה) From the Hebrew, meaning "God has drawn." In the Bible (I Chronicles 3:24), a descendant of Zerubbabel. Delaia is a variant spelling. Delayahu is a variant form.

Delayahu (דְּלָיָהוּ) A variant form of Delaya. *See* Delaya. In the Bible (Jeremiah 36:12), one of the officers of King Jehoiakim.

Delbert A variant form of Adelbert and Albert. *See* Adelbert *and* Albert.

Delmar, Delmer From the Latin, meaning "of the sea." Delmore is a variant form.

Delmore A variant form of Delmar. *See* Delmar.

Delvin From the Greek, meaning "dolphin."

Demetrius From the Greek, meaning "lover of the earth." In Greek mythology, Demeter is the goddess of agriculture and fertility. Dimitry is a variant form.

Demond   A short form of Desmond. *See* Desmond.

Denis   The French form of the Latin and Greek name Dionysius. In Greek mythology, the god of wine and revelry. Dennis and Denys are variant spellings. Dennit and Denman are variant forms.

Denman   A variant form of Denis, meaning "servant of Denis (Denys)." Or, from the Anglo-Saxon, meaning "resident of the valley (den)."

Dennis   A variant spelling of Denis. *See* Denis.

Dennit   A variant form of Denis. *See* Denis. Also, a variant form of Denton. *See* Denton.

Deno   An Italian form of Dean. *See* Dean.

Denton   A variant form of Dean, meaning "Dean's town." *See* Dean. Dennit is a variant form.

Denys   A variant spelling of Denis. *See* Denis.

Derby   From the Old English, meaning "the place where the deer live." Or, a variant form of Darby. *See* Darby.

Derek   An English form of the Old High German name Hrodrich, meaning "famous ruler." Derek, Derrick, and Derrik are variant spellings.

Derel   A variant form of Darlin. *See* Darlin.

Dero, Deron   From the British, meaning "water."

Deror (דְּרוֹר)   From the Hebrew, meaning "a bird (swallow)" or "free, free flowing." Dror is a variant spelling. Derori and Drori are variant forms.

Derori (דְּרוֹרִי)   A variant form of Deror. *See* Deror.

Derrek, Derrick, Derrik   Variant forms of Darlin. *See* Darlin.

Derril, Derrill   Variant forms of Darlin. *See* Darlin.

Derry   From the British, meaning "oak tree."

Derwin, Derwyn   From the British, meaning "water" or "friend (lover) of water."

Desi   A pet form of Desiderio. *See* Desiderio. Also, a pet form of Desmond.

Desiderio   From the Latin, meaning "desire." Popular in Italy. Desi is a pet form.

Desmond   From the French and Latin, meaning "world, society." Demond is a short form. Desi is a pet form.

Deuel (דְּעוּאֵל)   From the Hebrew, meaning "knowledge of God." In the Bible (Numbers 1:14), a member of the tribe of Gad. In the Bible, also spelled as Reuel, meaning "friend of God."

Devash (דְּבַשׁ) From the Hebrew, meaning "honey." Used also as a feminine name.

Devir (דְּבִיר) From the Hebrew, meaning "innermost room" or "sanctuary, holy place." In the Bible (Joshua 10:3), the king of Eglon in the time of Joshua. Dvir is a variant spelling. Divri is a variant form.

Devlin An Irish form of David. *See* David.

Dewey A Welsh form of David. *See* David.

Diamond From the Latin and Greek, meaning "precious stone."

Dibri A variant spelling of Divri. *See* Divri.

Dick, Dickey, Dickie, Dicky Pet forms of Richard. *See* Richard. Dix is a patronymic form.

Didi (דִּידִי) From the Hebrew, meaning "beloved." A pet form of Yedidya (Jedidiah).

Diego A Spanish form of James. *See* James. Dago is a variant form.

Dieter A variant form of Dietrich. *See* Dietrich. Also, possibly a variant form of Peter. *See* Peter.

Dietrich From the German, meaning "a rich people." Dieter is a variant form.

Difat (דִּיפַת) A variant form of Rifat (Genesis 10:3). *See* Rifat. In the Bible (I Chronicles 1:6), a son of Gomer and a grandson of Japheth.

Diglai (דִּגְלַי) From the Aramaic, meaning "banner, flag." In the Talmud (Tamid 3:8), the father of Eliezer, a first-century scholar.

Dikla (דִּקְלָה) From the Aramaic, meaning "a palm (date) tree." In the Bible (Genesis 10:27), a descendant of Shem. Dekel is the Hebrew form.

Dimai (דִּמַי) A variant form of Dimi. *See* Dimi.

Dimi (דִּימִי) A pet form of Avdimi and Dimitry. *See* Avdimi *and* Dimitry. In the Talmud (Chulin 124a), a fourth-century Babylonian scholar. Also known as Avudma.

Dimitry A variant form of Demetrius. *See* Demetrius.

Dinai (דִּינָאִי) From the Aramaic, meaning "law." In the Talmud (Sota 9:9), the father of Elazar, one of the Zealots toward the end of Second Temple days.

Dino A pet form of the Italian name Aldobrandino. From the German, meaning "little old sword."

Dion A short form of Dionysius. *See* Dionysius.

Dionysius, Dionysus In Greek mythology, the god of wine and revelry. Denis is a variant form. Dion is a short form.

Dirk An English form of the Old High German name Hrodrich, meaning "famous." Durk is a variant spelling.

Dishan (דִּישָׁן) A variant form of Dishon. *See* Dishon.

Dishon (דִּישׁוֹן) From the Hebrew, meaning "tread upon, threshed, threshing." In the Bible (Genesis 36:21), a son of Seir. Dishan is a variant form.

Diskin A metathesized form of Dixon. See Dixon.

Ditz (דִּיץ) From the Hebrew, meaning "joy."

Divlayim (דִּבְלַיִם) From the Hebrew, meaning "a lump (or cake) of pressed figs." In the Bible (Hosea 1:3), the father of Gomer, the wife of Hosea.

Divon (דִּיבוֹן) From the Hebrew, meaning "to walk gently." Akin to Dov. In the Bible (Nehemiah 11:25), a place in the territory of the tribe of Judah.

Divri (דִּבְרִי) From the Hebrew, meaning "orator." Also, a variant form of Devir. See Devir. In the Bible (Leviticus 24:11), a man whose daughter married an Egyptian. Dibri is a variant spelling.

Dix A patronymic form of Dick, meaning "Dick's son." A pet form of Richard. See Richard.

Dixie, Dixy Variant forms of Dix. See Dix.

Dixon A patronymic form of Richard, meaning "Richard's (Dick's) son." See Richard. Diskin is a metathesized form.

Doane From the Celtic, meaning "dweller on the sand dune."

Dob A variant form of Robert. See Robert. Dobs and Dobbs are patronymic forms.

Dobs, Dobbs Patronymic forms of Dob, meaning "son of Dob." See Dob.

Dodai (דּוֹדַי) From the Hebrew and Aramaic, meaning "mandrake" or "love." In the Bible (II Samuel 23:9), the father of one of David's warriors. Akin to Dodi and Dodo.

Dodi (דּוֹדִי) From the Hebrew, meaning "my beloved" or "my uncle."

Dodo (דּוֹדוֹ) From the Hebrew, meaning "his beloved" or "his uncle." In the Bible (Judges 10:1), a member of the tribe of Issachar.

Doeg (דֹּאֵג) From the Hebrew, meaning "anxious, concerned." In the Bible (I Samuel 21:8), an Edomite who was overseer of King Saul's herds.

Dofi (דֹּפִי) From the Hebrew, meaning "blemish."

Dolev (דּוֹלֵב) A tree common to Upper Galilee in Israel.

Dolph A short form of Adolph. See Adolph. Dolf is a variant spelling.

Dolphin (דּוֹלְפִין) A large water-dwelling mammal reputed to be the most intelligent of all fish. Used as a modern Israeli name.

Dom A pet form of Dominic. See Dominic.

Dominic, Dominick From the Latin, meaning "belonging to, pertaining to God." Dom is a pet form.

Don A pet form of Donald. See Donald. Also, from the Spanish and Latin, meaning "master." Donn and Donne are variant spellings.

Donal A variant form of Donald. *See* Donald.

Donald From the Irish, meaning "brown stranger." Also, from the Celtic and Scottish, meaning "proud ruler." Donald is a variant form. Don, Donnie, and Donny are pet forms.

Donn, Donne Variant spellings of Don. *See* Don.

Donnie, Donny Pet forms of Donald. *See* Donald.

Dor (דּוֹר) From the Hebrew, meaning "generation." Also, a French name derived from the Latin, meaning "of gold." Dori is a variant form.

Doran (דּוֹרָן) From the Hebrew and Greek, meaning "gift." Dorran is a variant spelling. Dorian and Doron are variant forms.

Dore From the Greek, meaning "gift." Often used as a pet form of Isidore. Akin to Doran. Dorian is a variant form.

Dori (דּוֹרִי) A variant form of Dor, meaning "my generation."

Dorian A variant form of Dore and Doran. *See* Dore *and* Doran. Also, from the Greek, meaning "from the town of Doris," where one group of ancient Greeks lived.

Dorne From the Gaelic, meaning "hand."

Doron (דּוֹרוֹן) A variant form of Doran. *See* Doran. Doroni is a variant form.

Doroni (דּוֹרוֹנִי) A variant form of Doron. *See* Doron.

Dorran A variant spelling of Doran. *See* Doran.

Dorris The masculine form of the feminine Doris. *See* Doris (feminine section).

Dosa (דּוֹסָא) An abbreviated form of Dosetai and Dositheus. *See* Dosetai *and* Dositheus. In the Talmud (Yerushalmi Peah 1:1), a fourth-century Palestinian scholar.

Dosetai (דּוֹסְתַּאי) From the Greek, meaning "gift of God." In the Talmud (Eruvin 45a), a second-century Palestinian and Babylonian scholar. Dositheus is a variant form. *See* Dositheus.

Dositheus From the Greek, meaning "gift of God." A favorite name in both Palestine and Alexandria (Egypt) during the talmudic period. Dosetai was the more common form of Dositheus. *See* Dosetai.

Doston A metathesis of Dotson. *See* Dotson.

Dotson A matronymic form of Dorothy, meaning "son of Dot or Dottie (Dorothy)." *See* Dorothy (feminine section). Doston is a metathesized form.

Doug A pet form of Douglas. *See* Douglas.

Dougal A variant form of Douglas. *See* Douglas.

Douglas From the Celtic, meaning "gray." Also, from the Gaelic, meaning "black stream." Dougal is a variant form. Doug is a pet form.

Dov (דּוֹב) From the Hebrew, meaning "bear." Also spelled דֹב.

Dove From the British, meaning "stream near the valley." Also, from the Middle English, meaning "a bird of the pigeon family." Dovey is a variant form.

Dovev (דּוֹבֵב) From the Hebrew, meaning "to speak, whisper."

Dovey A variant form of Dove. See Dove.

Dow, Dowe Variant spellings of Daw. See Daw.

Drake From the Latin, meaning "dragon." Or, from the Old High German, meaning "a male duck."

Drew A pet form of Andrew. See Andrew. Dru is a variant spelling.

Dror A variant spelling of Deror. See Deror.

Drori A variant spelling of Derori. See Derori.

Dru A variant spelling of Drew. See Drew.

Duane A variant form of Wayne. See Wayne. Dwaine and Dwayne are variant spellings.

Duard A variant form of Edward. See Edward.

Dubi (דֻּבִּי) From the Hebrew, meaning "my bear."

Dudai (דּוּדַי) From the Hebrew, meaning "mandrake," a love-producing plant mentioned in Genesis 30:14.

Dudley From the Old English, meaning "Dodd's meadow (lea)" or "Duda's meadow."

Duff From the Celtic, meaning "dark or black-faced." Or, from the Middle English, meaning "dough," hence "a baker."

Duke From the Latin, meaning "leader."

Duma (דּוּמָה) From the Hebrew, meaning "silence." In the Bible (Genesis 25:14), a son of Ishmael. Also, a nickname for Edom (I Chronicles 1:30).

Duncan From the Celtic, meaning "a warrior with dark skin."

Dunn, Dunne From the Old English, meaning "brown."

Dunstan From the Old English, meaning "brown rock quarry."

Dur (דּוּר) From the Hebrew, meaning "to heap, pile up" or "to circle." Also, from the Old English, meaning "wild animal, deer." Duriel is a variant form.

Durand The French form of the Latin, meaning "enduring, lasting." Durant and Durante are variant forms.

Durant, Durante Variant Italian forms of Durand. See Durand. Dante is a pet form.

Duriel (דּוּרִיאָל) From the Hebrew, meaning "God is my dwelling place."

Durk A variant spelling of Dirk. See Dirk.

Durwald From the Old English, meaning "forest of wild animals." Durwood is a variant form.

Durward From the Persian, meaning "porter, doorkeeper, guardian." Or, from the Old English, meaning "enclosure."

Durwood A variant form of Durwald. *See* Durwald.

Duryea From the Latin, meaning "enduring, lasting, eternal."

Dustin A variant form of Dunstan. *See* Dunstan.

Dusty A pet form of Dustin. *See* Dustin.

Dutton From the Celtic and Old English, meaning "fortified hill."

Dvir A variant spelling of Devir. *See* Devir.

Dwaine, Dwayne Variant spellings of Duane. *See* Duane.

Dwight From the Anglo-Saxon, meaning "white, fair."

Dylan From the Welsh, meaning "sea."

Dyne From the British, meaning "house."

Eamon An Irish form of the Old English name Eadmund, meaning "fortunate, happy warrior." Emmon is a variant spelling.

Earl, Earle From the Middle English, meaning "nobleman, count." Or, from the Anglo-Saxon, meaning "warrior, brave man."

Earlyd From the Middle English, meaning "the earl's lee (shelter)."

Earnest A variant spelling of Ernest. *See* Ernest.

Eaton From the Anglo-Saxon, meaning "the town near the river."

Eban A variant form of Even. *See* Even.

Ebed A variant spelling of Eved. *See* Eved.

Eben A variant form of Even. *See* Even.

Ebenezer A variant spelling of Evenezer. *See* Evenezer. Eben is a short form.

Eber A variant spelling of Ever. *See* Ever.

Eberhard, Eberhart From the Old French and High German, meaning "strong, wild boar." Ebert is a short form.

Eberle From the High German, meaning "wild boar."

Eberman (עֶבֶּערְמאַן) The Yiddish form of Abraham. *See* Abraham.

Ebert A short form of Eberhart. *See* Eberhart.

Ebin   A variant form of Even. *See* Even.

Echi   A variant spelling of Eichi. *See* Eichi.

Echud (אֱחוּד)   From the Hebrew, meaning "unity, togetherness." Akin to Eichi.

Ed   A pet form of Edward. *See* Edward.

Edan   From the Celtic, meaning "fire, flame." Also, a variant form of Eden. *See* Eden.

Edd   A pet form of Edward. *See* Edward.

Eddie   A pet form of Edward. *See* Edward.

Eddy   From the Middle English, meaning "whirlpool" or "unresting, energetic." Also, a pet form of Edward. *See* Edward. Edy is a variant spelling.

Eden (עֵדֶן)   From the Hebrew, meaning "delight, luxuriate." In the Bible (II Chronicles 31:15), a Levite in the time of King Hezekiah. Also, the name of the garden inhabited by Adam and Eve (Genesis 2:8), also known as Paradise. Edan is a variant form.

Eder (עֵדֶר)   From the Hebrew, meaning "herd, flock." In the Bible (I Chronicles 8:15), a member of the tribe of Benjamin.

Edgar   From the Anglo-Saxon, meaning "happy or blessed warrior."

Edi   A variant spelling of Eidi. *See* Eidi.

Edison   A patronymic form, meaning "son of Ed (Edward)." *See* Edward.

Edlow   From the Old English, meaning "fruitful hill."

Edmar   From the Anglo-Saxon, meaning "rich sea."

Edmond   From the Anglo-Saxon, meaning "rich, fortunate, happy warrior or protector." Akin to Edward. Edmund is a variant spelling.

Edmund   A variant spelling of Edmond. *See* Edmond.

Edom (אֱדוֹם)   From the Hebrew, probably meaning "red." In the Bible (Genesis 25:30), a name applied to Esau and his descendants. Edom is the name of an ancient kingdom south of the Dead Sea. Iduma is the Greek form.

Edouard   A French form of Edward. *See* Edward.

Edri (עֶדְרִי)   From the Hebrew, meaning "my flock."

Edric   From the Anglo-Saxon, meaning "rich ruler."

Edsel   From the Anglo-Saxon, meaning "rich."

Edson   A patronymic form, meaning "son of Ed (Edward)." *See* Edward.

Eduard   The German form of Edward. *See* Edward.

Eduardo   The Italian and Spanish form of Edward. *See* Edward. Edwardo is a variant spelling.

Edvard   The Scandinavian form of Edward. *See* Edward.

Edward From the Anglo-Saxon, meaning "blessed or happy guardian of prosperity." Ed, Edd, Eddie, Eddy, and Ned are pet forms. Edouard, Eduard, Eduardo, Edward, and Edwards are variant forms.

Edwardo A variant spelling of Eduardo. *See* Eduardo.

Edwin From the Anglo-Saxon, meaning "happy or blessed friend."

Edy A variant spelling of Eddy. *See* Eddy.

Efa, Efah Variant spellings of Eifa and Eifah. *See* Eifa and Eifah.

Efer (עֵפֶר) From the Hebrew, meaning "young mountain goat" or "stag, deer." In the Bible (Genesis 25:4), a son of Midian and grandson of Abraham and Keturah. Epher is a variant spelling. Efron is a variant form.

Efes (אֶפֶס) From the Hebrew, meaning "nothing, emptiness" or "end, boundary." The name of a third-century Palestinian talmudic scholar also called Pes or Pas.

Efim Origin uncertain. Possibly a variant form of Efrem (Efraim). *See* Efraim.

Eflal (אֶפְלָל) From the Hebrew, meaning "judge." In the Bible (I Chronicles 2:37), an Egyptian slave. Ephlal is a variant spelling.

Efod (אֵפוֹד) From the Hebrew, meaning "vest." In the Bible (Numbers 34:23), the father of a leader of the tribe of Manasseh. Ephod is a variant spelling.

Efraim A variant spelling of Efrayim. *See* Efrayim.

Efrat (אֶפְרָת) From the Hebrew, meaning "honored, distinguished." In the Bible (I Chronicles 2:50), the son of Caleb, a member of the tribe of Ephraim. Ephrath and Ephrat are variant spellings.

Efrayim (אֶפְרַיִם) From the Hebrew, meaning "fruitful." In the Bible (Genesis 41:52), the second son of Joseph and a grandson of Jacob. Efraim and Ephraim are variant spellings. Efrem is a variant form.

Efrem A variant form of Efrayim. *See* Efrayim.

Efron (עֶפְרוֹן) From the Hebrew, meaning "bird." Also, a variant form of Efer. *See* Efer. In the Bible (Genesis 23:8), a Hittite who sold Abraham a burial plot. Ephron is a variant spelling.

Egan From the Anglo-Saxon, meaning "formidable, strong." Egon is a variant spelling.

Egbert From the Anglo-Saxon, meaning "bright sword."

Egeton From the Middle English and the German, meaning "edge, corner of the town."

Egil From the Old French, meaning "sting, prickle."

Eglon (עֶגְלוֹן) From the Hebrew, meaning "wagon." In the Bible (Judges 3:12), a king of Moab in the time of Judge Ehud.

Egmont From the Middle English, meaning "corner (edge) of the mountain."

Egon A variant spelling of Egan. *See* Egan.

Ehren From the German, meaning "honored."

Ehud (אֵהוּד) From the Hebrew, meaning "love." In the Bible (Judges 3:15), a descendant of Benjamin and one of the Judges of Israel. Udi is a pet form.

Eichi (אֵחִי) From the Hebrew, meaning "my brother." In the Bible (Genesis 46:21), a son of Benjamin.

Eidi (עֵדִי) From the Hebrew, meaning "my witness." Edi is a variant spelling.

Eifa, Eifah (עֵיפָה) From the Hebrew, meaning "dark, darkness." In the Bible (I Chronicles 2:47), a son of Midian and a grandson of Abraham and Keturah. Efa, Efah, Epha, and Ephah are variant spellings. The name of a fourth-century Babylonian talmudic scholar (Shabbat 60b). Hefa is a variant form.

Eifai (עֵיפַי) From the Hebrew, meaning "darkness, gloominess." In the Bible (Jeremiah 40:8), the father of men who were military leaders in the time of Gedalia, governor of Judah. Ephai is a variant spelling.

Eila (אֵלָא) From the Hebrew, meaning "oak." In the Bible (I Kings 4:18), the father of one of King Solomon's officers. Also spelled אֵלָה (II Kings 16:8), the name of the son of Basha, king of Israel. Ela and Elah are variant spellings.

Eilam (עֵילָם) From the Hebrew, meaning "eternal." In the Bible (Genesis 10:22), the eldest of Shem's five sons and a grandson of Noah. Elam is a variant spelling.

Eili A variant spelling of Eli. See Eli.

Eilon (אֵלּוֹן) From the Hebrew, meaning "oak tree." In the Bible (Genesis 46:14), a son of Zebulun and a grandson of Jacob. Elon is a variant spelling. Also spelled אֵילוֹן (Judges 12:11), a Judge from the tribe of Zebulun.

Einan (עֵינָן) From the Hebrew, meaning "eyes." In the Bible (Numbers 1:15), a leader of the tribe of Naftali. Enan is a variant spelling.

Eini From the Hebrew, meaning "my eyes." Eni is a variant spelling.

Eisig (אֵייזִיג) A Yiddish form of Isaac (Yitzchak). See Yitzchak.

Eitan (אֵיתָן) From the Hebrew meaning "strong." In the Bible (I Chronicles 2:6), a son of Zerach and a grandson of Judah. Etan, Ethan, and Eytan are variant spellings.

Eizer (עֵזֶר) A variant spelling of Ezer. See Ezer. In the Bible (Nehemiah 3:19), an officer in the time of Nehemiah. Also, a Yiddish form of Eliezer. See Eliezer.

Eizik (אֵייזִיק) A Yiddish form of Isaac (Yitzchak). See Yitzchak.

Eker (עֵקֶר) From the Hebrew, meaning "barren" or "an offspring." In the Bible (I Chronicles 2:27), a leader of the tribe of Judah. Ekron is a variant form.

Ekron (עֶקְרוֹן) A variant form of Eker. See Eker.

Ela A variant spelling of Eila. See Eila.

Elad (אֶלְעָד)   From the Hebrew, meaning "God is eternal" or "God is witness." In the Bible (I Chronicles 7:21), a descendant of Ephraim. Elada is a variant form.

Elada (אֶלְעָדָה)   A variant form of Elad. See Elad. In the Bible (I Chronicles 7:20), a member of the tribe of Ephraim.

Elah   A variant spelling of Eila. See Eila.

Elam   A variant spelling of Eilam. See Eilam.

Elami (אֶלְעָמִי)   From the Hebrew, meaning "to my people."

Elan (אִילָן)   From the Hebrew, meaning "tree." Or, from the British, meaning "young deer."

Elasa (אֶלְעָשָׂה)   From the Hebrew, meaning "God has created." In the Bible (I Chronicles 8:37), a descendant of Jonathan, son of Saul.

Elazar (אֶלְעָזָר)   From the Hebrew, meaning "God has helped." In the Bible (Exodus 6:23), a son of Aaron the High Priest. Lazarus is the Greek form used in the New Testament. Eliezer is a variant form. Lazar is a pet form.

Elbert   A variant form of Albert. See Albert. Elbie is a pet form.

Elbie   A pet form of Elbert. See Elbert. Also, derived from the river Elbe, which flows through Germany and Czechoslovakia.

Elbridge   From the Old English, meaning "old bridge."

Elchai (אֶלְחַי)   From the Hebrew, meaning "God lives."

Elchanan (אֶלְחָנָן)   From the Hebrew, meaning "God is gracious." In the Bible (II Samuel 23:23), a warrior in King David's army. Elhanan is a variant spelling.

Eldaa (אֶלְדָּעָה)   From the Hebrew, meaning "God knows" or "God is all-knowing." In the Bible (Genesis 25:4), a descendant of Abraham and Keturah.

Eldad (אֶלְדָּד)   From the Hebrew, meaning "beloved of God" or "friend of God." In the Bible (Numbers 11:26), one of the two Israelites about whose prophecies Joshua complained to Moses.

Eldar (אֶלְדָּר)   From the Hebrew, meaning "habitation of God."

Elden   From the Anglo-Saxon, meaning "older."

Elder   From the Old English, meaning "old, older." Eldor is a variant form.

Eldon   From the Middle English, meaning "old age, antiquity."

Eldor   A variant form of Elder and Alder. See Elder and Alder.

Eldred   From the Old English, meaning "old, wise counsel."

Eldridge   From the Old English, meaning "old range" or "old fortification." Aldridge is a variant form.

Eldson   From the Old English, meaning "elder son."

Eldwin   From the Old English, meaning "noble friend" or "old friend."

Eleazar   A variant spelling of Eliezer. *See* Eliezer.

Eletz (עֶלֶץ)   From the Hebrew, meaning "joy."

Elex   A variant form of Alex. *See* Alex.

Elez (עֶלֶז)   From the Hebrew, meaning "joy."

Elezri (אֶלְעָזְרִי)   From the Hebrew, meaning "God is help." Akin to Elazar.

Elford   From the Old English, meaning "the old ford (river crossing)."

Elgar, Elger   From the Anglo-Saxon, meaning "noble spear (protector)."

Elgavish (אֶלְגָּבִישׁ)   From the Hebrew, meaning "meteor."

Elgin   From the Old English, meaning "true nobility."

Elhanan   A variant spelling of Elchanan. *See* Elchanan.

Eli (עֵלִי)   From the Hebrew, meaning "ascend" or "uplifted." In the Bible (I Samuel 1:14), a High Priest and the last of the Judges in the days of Samuel. Akin to Ali. Not to be confused with Elijah or Elisha. Eili is a variant spelling.

Elia   A variant form of Elijah. *See* Elijah.

Eliab   A variant spelling of Eliav. *See* Eliav.

Eliad (אֱלִיעַד)   From the Hebrew, meaning "My God is eternal."

Eliada   A variant spelling of Elyada. *See* Elyada.

Eliakim   A variant spelling of Elyakim. *See* Elyakim.

Eliakum   A variant spelling of Elyakum. *See* Elyakum.

Eliam (אֱלִיעָם)   From the Hebrew, meaning "God is my people." In the Bible (II Samuel 11:3), the father of Bathsheba, King David's wife.

Elias   The Greek form of Elijah. *See* Elijah.

Eliasaf   A variant spelling of Elyasaf. *See* Elyasaf.

Elisaph   A variant spelling of Elyasaf. *See* Elyasaf.

Eliashiv   A variant spelling of Elyashiv. *See* Elyashiv.

Eliashuv   A variant spelling of Elyashuv. *See* Elyashuv.

Eliata (אֱלִיאָתָה)   From the Hebrew, meaning "my God has come." In the Bible (I Chronicles 25:4), a Levite in the time of David.

Eliav (אֱלִיאָב)   From the Hebrew, meaning "my God is Father." In the Bible (Numbers 1:9), a leader of the tribe of Zebulun. Eliab is a variant spelling.

Eliaz (אֱלִיעָז)   From the Hebrew, meaning "my God is strong."

Elichai (אֱלִיחַי)   From the Hebrew, meaning "my God lives."

Eli-Choref (אֱלִיחֹרֶף)   From the Hebrew, meaning "my God is wintertime." In the Bible (I Kings 4:3), one of King Solomon's officers.

Elidad (אֱלִידָד)   From the Hebrew, meaning "my God is a friend." In the Bible (Numbers 34:21), a leader of the tribe of Benjamin.

Elied (אֱלִיעֵד)   From the Hebrew, meaning "my God is witness."

Eli-Einai (אֱלִיעֵינַי)   From the Hebrew, meaning "God is my eyes." In the Bible (I Chronicles 8:20), a member of the tribe of Benjamin.

Eliel (אֱלִיאֵל)   From the Hebrew, meaning "the Lord is God." In the Bible (I Chronicles 5:24), a leader of the tribe of Manasseh.

Eliezer (אֱלִיעֶזֶר)   A variant form of Elazar. From the Hebrew, meaning "my God has helped." In the Bible (Genesis 15:2), Abraham's servant. Also, a son of Moses (Exodus 18:4). A popular name among talmudic scholars. Eleazar is a variant spelling.

Elifal (אֱלִיפָל)   From the Hebrew, meaning "my God is judgment" or "my God is prayer." In the Bible (I Chronicles 11:35), a warrior in King David's army. Also known as Elifelet. Eliphal is a variant spelling.

Elifaz (אֱלִיפַז)   From the Hebrew, meaning "my God is pure gold." In the Bible (Job 2:11), the eldest of Job's three friends. Eliphaz is a variant spelling.

Elifelet (אֱלִיפָלֶט)   From the Hebrew, meaning "my God is deliverance." In the Bible (II Samuel 5:16), one of King David's sons. Eliphelet is a variant spelling.

Eligaal (אֱלִיגָאֵל)   From the Hebrew, meaning "my God redeems."

Elihu (אֱלִיהוּא)   From the Hebrew, meaning "He is my God." In the Bible (Job 34:1), one of Job's three friends. Akin to Eliyahu. See Eliyahu. Also spelled אֱלִיהוּ (Job 32:4).

Elihud (אֱלִיהוּד)   From the Hebrew, meaning "my God is majestic."

Elijah   The Anglicized form of Eliyahu. See Eliyahu. Elia, Elio, and Eliot are variant forms. Elias is the Greek form. Elly is a pet form.

Elika (אֱלִיקָא)   A variant form of Elyakim. See Elyakim. In the Bible (II Samuel 23:25), one of King David's warriors.

Elimelech (אֱלִימֶלֶךְ)   From the Hebrew, meaning "my God is King." In the Bible (Ruth 1:2), the husband of Naomi and father-in-law of Ruth.

Elinatan (אֱלִינָתָן)   From the Hebrew, meaning "my God has given." In the Talmud (Eduyot 6:2), the father of Nechunya, a second-century talmudic scholar.

Elinoar (אֱלִינֹעַר)   From the Hebrew, meaning "my God is young."

Elio   A Spanish form of Elijah. See Elijah.

Elior (אֱלִיאֹור)   From the Hebrew, meaning "my God is light."

Eliot   A variant form of Elijah. Also, a pet form of Elijah. See Elijah. Elliot and Elliott are variant spellings.

Eliphal   A variant spelling of Elifal. See Elifal.

Eliphaz   A variant spelling of Elifaz. See Elifaz.

Eliphelet   A variant spelling of Elifelet. See Elifelet.

Eliram (אֱלִירָם)   From the Hebrew, meaning "my God is mighty."

Eliran (אֱלִירָן) From the Hebrew, meaning "my God is joy" or "my God is song." Eliron is a variant spelling.

Eliron A variant spelling of Eliran. See Eliran.

Elisha (אֱלִישָׁע) From the Hebrew, meaning "my God is salvation." In the Bible (I Kings 19:16), a Prophet, a disciple of Elijah. Ellis and Ellas are variant forms.

Elishafat (אֱלִישָׁפָט) From the Hebrew, meaning "my God judges." In the Bible (II Chronicles 23:1), a Judean officer who was among those who executed Queen Athaliah. Elishaphat is a variant spelling.

Elishama (אֱלִישָׁמָע) From the Hebrew, meaning "my God hears." In the Bible (Numbers 1:10), a son of Amihud and the grandfather of Joshua.

Elishaphat A variant spelling of Elishafat. See Elishafat.

Elishua (אֱלִישׁוּעַ) From the Hebrew, meaning "my God is savior." In the Bible (II Samuel 5:15), a son of King David.

Elison A variant spelling of Ellison. See Ellison.

Elituv (אֱלִיטוּב) From the Hebrew, meaning "my God is goodness."

Elitzafan (אֱלִיצָפָן) In Numbers 3:30, a variant form of Eltzafan. See Eltzafan.

Elitzav (אֱלִיצָו) From the Hebrew, meaning "my God has commanded" or "commandment of God." Elizav is a variant spelling.

Elitzedek (אֱלִיצֶדֶק) From the Hebrew, meaning "my God is just."

Elitzur (אֱלִיצוּר) From the Hebrew, meaning "my God is a rock (strong)." In the Bible (Numbers 1:5), a man appointed by Moses to conduct the census among the tribe of Reuben. Elizur is a variant spelling.

Eliya A short form of Eliyahu. See Eliyahu.

Eli-Yada (אֱלִי־יָדָע) From the Hebrew, meaning "my God is knowledge" or "my God knows."

Eliyahu (אֱלִיָּהוּ) From the Hebrew, meaning "the Lord is my God." In the Bible (I Kings 17:1), one of the earliest of the Hebrew Prophets. The new Testament spelling is Elias. Elijah is the Anglicized form. Akin to Elihu. See Elihu. Ely is a pet form. Elya is a Yiddish form. Eliya is a short form.

Elizaphan A variant spelling of Elitzafan. See Elitzafan.

Elizav A variant spelling of Elitzav. See Elitzav.

Elizur A variant spelling of Elitzur. See Elitzur.

Elkan (עֶלְקָן) A Yiddish form of Elkanah. See Elkanah.

Elkana, Elkanah (אֶלְקָנָה) From the Hebrew, meaning "God bought" or "God is jealous." In the Bible (Exodus 6:24), one of the sons of Korach of the tribe of Levi. Also, the father of the Prophet Samuel (I Samuel 1:1). Elkan and Elkin are Yiddish forms.

Elkayam (אֶלְקָיָם) From the Hebrew, meaning "God lives."

Elkin (אֶלְקִין) A Yiddish form of Elkana. *See* Elkana.

Ellard From the Old English, meaning "the hardy alder tree."

Ellas A variant spelling of Ellis. *See* Ellis.

Ellery From the Old English, meaning the "alder tree."

Elliot, Elliott A variant spelling of Eliot. *See* Eliot.

Ellis A variant form of Elisha. *See* Elisha. Ellas is a variant spelling.

Ellison A patronymic form, meaning "son of Elijah." *See* Elijah. Elison is a variant form.

Ellsworth From the Anglo-Saxon, meaning "Ellis's homestead." *See* Ellis.

Ellwood From the Old English, meaning "the woods (land) of Ellis." *See* Ellis.

Elly A pet form of Elijah. *See* Elijah.

Elma From the Old English, meaning "elm tree." Also, a variant form of Elmer. *See* Elmer.

Elman From the Anglo-Saxon, meaning "noble man" or "noble servant."

Elmer From the Old English, meaning "noble, famous." Elma, Elmo, Elmor, and Elmore are variant forms.

Elmo A variant form of Elmer. *See* Elmer.

Elmor, Elmore Variant forms of Elmer. *See* Elmer.

Elnaam (אֶלְנַעַם) From the Hebrew, meaning "God is pleasant." In the Bible (I Chronicles 11:46), the father of two of King David's warriors.

Elnadav (אֶלְנָדָב) From the Hebrew, meaning "God is gracious."

Elnakam (אֶלְנָקָם) From the Hebrew, meaning "God will avenge."

Elnatan (אֶלְנָתָן) From the Hebrew, meaning "gift of God." In the Bible (II Kings 24:8), the father-in-law of King Jehoiakim.

Elois Probably a variant form of Louis. *See* Louis.

Elon A variant spelling of Eilon. *See* Eilon.

Elpaal (אֶלְפָּעַל) From the Hebrew, meaning "God has wrought." In the Bible (I Chronicles 8:11), a member of the tribe of Benjamin.

Elrad (אֶלְרָד) From the Hebrew, meaning "God is the ruler." Also, from the Old English and German, meaning "noble counsel." Elrod is a variant spelling.

Elra'i A variant form of Elro'i. *See* Elro'i.

Elrod A variant spelling of Elrad. *See* Elrad.

Elro'i (אֶלְרֹאִי) From the Hebrew, meaning "God sees." The name is based on Genesis 16:18. Elra'i is a variant form. Also spelled אֶלְרָאִי.

Elroy From the Latin, meaning "royal, king." Leroy is the French form. El Roy is a variant form.

El Roy A variant form of Elroy. *See* Elroy.

Elsen A patronymic form, meaning "son of Ellis" or "son of Elias." *See* Ellis *and* Elias.

Eltzafan (אֶלְצָפָן) From the Hebrew, meaning "God has hidden (protected)." In the Bible (Leviticus 10:4), Aaron's uncle. Elitzafan is a variant form.

Eltzedek (אֶלְצֶדֶק) From the Hebrew, meaning "God is righteousness."

Elul (אֱלוּל) The sixth month of the Jewish calendar, usually falling in August.

Eluzai (אֶלְעוּזַי) From the Hebrew, meaning "God is my strength." In the Bible (I Chronicle 12:5), a warrior from the tribe of Benjamin.

Eluzi (אֶלְעוּזִי) From the Hebrew, meaning "God is my strength."

Elvin From the Anglo-Saxon, meaning "godly friend." Elwyn is a variant spelling.

Elwyn A variant spelling of Elvin. *See* Elvin.

Ely A pet form of Eliyahu. *See* Eli.

Elya (עֶלְיָא) A Yiddish form of Eliyahu. *See* Eliyahu.

Elyada (אֶלְיָדָע) From the Hebrew, meaning "God knows." In the Bible (II Samuel 5:16), one of the sons of King David. Eliada is a variant spelling.

Elyakim (אֶלְיָקִים) From the Hebrew, meaning "God will establish." In the Bible (II Kings 18:18), the steward of King Hezekiah's palace; also (II Kings 23:34), the son of King Josiah, whose name was later changed to Jehoiakim. Elika and Elyakum are variant forms. Eliakim is a variant spelling.

Elyakum (אֶלְיָקוּם) A variant form of Elyakim. *See* Elyakim. In the Talmud (Avoda Zara 58a), a Babylonian scholar. Eliakum is a variant spelling.

Elyasaf (אֶלְיָסָף) From the Hebrew, meaning "God will increase" or "God will gather in." In the Bible (Numbers 1:14), a leader of the tribe of Gad. Eliasaf and Eliasaph are variant spellings.

Elyashiv (אֶלְיָשִׁיב) From the Hebrew, meaning "God will respond." In the Bible (Nehemiah 3:1), a High Priest in the days of Nehemiah. Eliashiv and Eliashib are variant spellings. Akin to Elyashuv.

Elyashuv (אֶלְיָשׁוּב) From the Hebrew, meaning "God will return." In the Talmud (Moed Katan 25b), a Babylonian scholar. Eliashuv is a variant spelling. Akin to Elyashiv.

Elzavad (אֶלְזָבָד) From the Hebrew, meaning "gift of God." In the Bible (I Chronicles 12:13), a warrior of the tribe of Gad who supported David. Elzabad is a variant spelling.

Emanuel (עִמָּנוּאֵל) From the Hebrew, meaning "God is with us, God is our protector." Emmanuel, Imanuel, and Immanuel are variant spellings. *See* Imanuel. In the Bible (Isaiah 7:14), a son of Isaiah.

Emek (עֵמֶק) From the Hebrew, meaning "valley."

Emerson A patronymic form, meaning "son of Emery." *See* Emery.

Emery   From the Old High German, meaning "rich in work, industrious." Emmory and Emory are variant spellings.

Emil   From the Latin, meaning "to emulate, to be industrious."

Emile   A French form of Emil. *See* Emil.

Emilio   An Italian form of Emil. *See* Emil.

Emir   From the Arabic, meaning "commander."

Emmanuel   A variant spelling of Emanuel. *See* Emanuel.

Emmet, Emmett   From the Hebrew, meaning "truth." Or, from the Anglo-Saxon, meaning "ant." Emmitt is a variant spelling.

Emmitt   A variant spelling of Emmett. *See* Emmett.

Emmon   A variant spelling of Eamon. *See* Eamon.

Emmons   A patronymic form of Eamon. *See* Eamon.

Emmory   A variant spelling of Emery. *See* Emery.

Emory   A variant spelling of Emery. *See* Emery.

Enan   A variant spelling of Einan. *See* Einan.

Enav   From the Hebrew, meaning "grapes."

Eni   A variant spelling of Eini. *See* Eini.

Ennis   A short form of Denis. *See* Denis.

Enoch   An Anglicized form of the Hebrew, Chanoch, meaning "educated" or "dedicated." In the Bible (Genesis 4:17), the eldest son of Cain and a grandson of Adam and Eve.

Enosh (אֱנוֹשׁ)   From the Hebrew, meaning "man." In the Bible (Genesis 4:26), a son of Seth, the third son of Adam.

Enzio   An Italian form of Henry. *See* Henry.

Ephai   A variant spelling of Eifai. *See* Eifai.

Epher   A variant spelling of Efer. *See* Efer.

Ephlal   A variant spelling of Eflal. *See* Eflal.

Ephod   A variant spelling of Efod. *See* Efod.

Ephraim   A variant spelling of Efraim. *See* Efraim.

Ephrat, Ephrath   Variant spellings of Efrat. *See* Efrat.

Ephron   A variant spelling of Efron. *See* Efron.

Er (עֵר)   From the Hebrew, meaning "awake" or "guardian." In the Bible (Genesis 38:3), a son of Judah. Eri is a variant form.

Eran (עֵרָן)   From the Hebrew, meaning "industrious" or "awake." In the Bible (Numbers 26:36), a grandson of Efraim and a leader of the tribe.

Erel (אֲרְאֵל)   From the Hebrew, meaning "I will see God."

Erez (אֶרֶז)   From the Hebrew, meaning "cedar."

Erez-Yisrael (אֶרֶז־יִשְׂרָאֵל)   From the Hebrew, meaning "cedar of Israel."

Eri (עֵרִי)   From the Hebrew, meaning "my guardian." In the Bible (Genesis 46:16), a son of Gad. A variant form of Er.

Eric   From the Old Norse, meaning "honorable ruler," and from the Anglo-Saxon, meaning "brave king." Erich, Erik, and Eryk are variant spellings.

Erich   A variant spelling of Eric. *See* Eric.

Erik   A variant spelling of Eric. *See* Eric.

Erland   From the German, meaning "honorable country."

Ernest   From the Old High German, meaning "resolute, earnest, sincere." Earnest is a variant spelling. Ernesto, Erno, and Ernst are variant forms. Ernie is a pet form.

Ernesto   The Spanish and Italian form of Ernest. *See* Ernest.

Ernie   A pet form of Ernest. *See* Ernest.

Erno   An Hungarian form of Ernest. *See* Ernest.

Ernst   A variant form of Ernest. *See* Ernest.

Errol   From the Latin, meaning "to wander." Eryle is a variant spelling.

Erv   A variant spelling of Irv (Irving). *See* Irving. Or, a pet form of Ervin. *See* Ervin.

Erve   A short form of Herve. *See* Herve. Or, a variant spelling of Erv. *See* Erv.

Ervin   A variant form of Irvin. *See* Irvin. Erwin is a variant form. Erv is a pet form.

Erwin   A variant form of Ervin. *See* Ervin.

Eryk   A variant spelling of Eric. *See* Eric.

Eryle   A variant spelling of Errol. *See* Errol.

Esau (עֵשָׂו)   From the Hebrew, meaning "hairy." In the Bible (Genesis 25:25), the son of Isaac and Rebekah, and twin brother of Jacob.

Esh (אֵשׁ)   From the Hebrew, meaning "fire."

Eshbaal (אֶשְׁבַּעַל)   In the Bible (I Chronicles 8:33), a variant form of Ish-Baal. See Ish-Baal.

Eshban (אֶשְׁבָּן)   From the Hebrew, meaning "galley." In the Bible (Genesis 36:26), a son of Dishon.

Eshchad (אֶשְׁחָד)   A type of bush that grows in Israel.

Eshed (אֶשֶׁד)   From the Hebrew, meaning "waterfall" or "foundation."

Eshek (עֵשֶׁק)   From the Hebrew, meaning "theft" or "oppression." In the Bible

(I Chronicles 8:39), a member of the tribe of Benjamin and a descendant of King Saul.

Eshel (אֶשֶׁל)   From the Hebrew, meaning "tamarisk tree."

Eshkol (אֶשְׁכּוֹל)   From the Hebrew, meaning "cluster of grapes." In the Bible (Genesis 14:13), a man with whom Abraham made a covenant. In Hebrew literature it signifies a group of outstanding scholars.

Eshton (אֶשְׁתּוֹן)   From the Hebrew, possibly meaning "womanly" or "effeminate." In the Bible (I Chronicles 4:11), a leader of the tribe of Judah.

Esmond   From the Anglo-Saxon, meaning "gracious protector." Esmund is a variant spelling.

Esmund   A variant spelling of Esmond. See Esmond.

Estes   A Spanish form of the Latin *aestus*, meaning "tide," hence "an inlet from the sea."

Etan   A variant spelling of Eitan. See Eitan.

Etel (אֶתְאֵל)   From the Hebrew, meaning "with God."

Eter (עֶטֶר)   From the Hebrew, meaning "crown, wreath" or "ornament."

Ethan   An Anglicized spelling of Eitan (Etan). See Eitan.

Ethnan   A variant spelling of Etnan. See Etnan.

Ethelbert   From the Old English, meaning "noble" and "bright." A variant form of Adelbert.

Ethni   A variant spelling of Etni. See Etni.

Etnan (אֶתְנָן)   From the Hebrew, meaning "gift" or "reward." In the Bible (I Chronicles 4:7), a leader of the tribe of Judah. Ethnan is a variant spelling. Etni is a variant form.

Etni (אֶתְנִי)   A variant form of Etnan. See Etnan. In the Bible (I Chronicles 6:12), a Levite who was an ancestor of King David's musician, Asaf. Ethni is a variant spelling.

Etzbonit (עֶצְבּוֹנִית)   From the Hebrew, meaning "wild rosebush."

Etzer (אֵצֶר)   From the Hebrew, meaning "wealth, treasure."

Etzion   A variant spelling of Etzyon. See Etzyon.

Etzioni   A variant spelling of Etzyoni. See Etzyoni.

Etz-Shaked (עֵץ־שָׁקֵד)   From the Hebrew, meaning "almond tree."

Etzyon (עֶצְיוֹן)   From the Hebrew, meaning "tree." Etzyon Gever was a biblical city on the Red Sea near Eilat (Numbers 33:35). In 1935, S. Z. Holzmann established a kibbutz in the Hebron hills and named it Kfar Etzyon, a translation of his own surname.

Etzyoni (עֶצְיוֹנִי)   A variant form of Etzyon. See Etzyon. Etzioni is a variant spelling.

Eugen   A variant form of Eugene. *See* Eugene.

Eugene   From the Greek, meaning "well-born, born lucky" or "one of noble descent." Eugen and Eugenio are variant forms.

Eugenio   A Spanish, Portuguese, and Italian form of Eugene. *See* Eugene.

Eulis   From the Greek, meaning "sweet-speaking."

Eumir   From the Greek, meaning "sweet-smelling."

Eurydemos, Eurydemus   From the Greek, meaning "the population at large, the wide spectrum of people." The name of a third-century talmudic scholar.

Eustace   From the Greek, meaning "rich in corn" or "fruitful."

Eval   From the Arabic, meaning "bulky, stout, fat."

Evan   A Welsh form of John. *See* John. Also, from the Celtic, meaning "young warrior." Owen is a variant form. Evander and Evans are variant forms.

Evander   A variant form of Evan. *See* Evan.

Evans   A patronymic form of Evan, meaning "son of Evan." *See* Evan.

Eved (עֶבֶד)   From the Hebrew, meaning "servant." In the Bible (I Chronicles 8:22), a member of the tribe of Benjamin. Ebed is a variant spelling.

Evel   A variant form of Evelyn. *See* Evelyn.

Evelyn   Used occasionally as a masculine name, as in the case of author Evelyn Waugh and polar explorer Richard Evelyn Byrd. First used as a masculine name by Evelyn Pierrepont, Duke of Kingston (born in 1665); Evelyn was his mother's maiden name. *See* Evelyn (feminine section). Evel is a variant form.

Even (אֶבֶן)   From the Hebrew, meaning "stone." Eban, Eben, and Ebin are variant forms.

Even-Ezer, Evenezer (אֶבֶן־עֶזֶר)   From the Hebrew, meaning "foundation stone." Ebenezer is a variant spelling.

Ever (עֵבֶר)   From the Hebrew, meaning "pass over" or "the other side (of the Euphrates River)." In the Bible (Genesis 10:21), a descendant of Shem, son of Noah. Eber is a variant spelling. Akin to Ivri.

Everett, Everette   From the Anglo-Saxon, meaning "boar." Also, from the Norse, meaning "warrior."

Everley   From the Old English, meaning "Ever's (Everett's) lea (field)."

Evi (אֱוִי)   From the Hebrew, meaning "desire." In the Bible (Numbers 31:8), one of the five kings of Midian.

Eviasaf   A variant spelling of Evyasaf. *See* Evyasaf.

Evo   An Italian form of Ivo, derived from the French Yves. Akin to Ivan. A form of John. *See* John.

Evon   A variant form of Ivan. *See* Ivan.

Evril (אַבְרִיל)   A Yiddish form of Abraham. *See* Abraham.

Evron (עֶבְרֹן) From the Hebrew, meaning "overflowing" or "anger, fury." A biblical place-name (Joshua 19:28). Evrona is the feminine form.

Evyasaf (אֶבְיָסָף) From the Hebrew, meaning "my father has gathered." Aviasaf is a variant form (Exodus 6:24). Eviasaf is a variant spelling. In the Bible (I Chronicles 6:8), a Levite of the Korach family.

Evyatar (אֶבְיָתָר) From the Hebrew, meaning "Father (God) is great." In the Bible (I Samuel 22:20), a Priest, the son of Achimelech.

Ewen Probably a variant form of Evan, the Welsh form of John. *See* Evan *and* John. Also, a variant form of Owen. *See* Owen.

Eyal A variant form of Ayal. *See* Ayal.

Eytan A variant spelling of Eitan. *See* Eitan.

Ezar A short form of Elazar. *See* Elazar.

Ezbai (אֶזְבַּי) From the Hebrew, meaning "hyssop." In the Bible (I Chronicles 11:37), the father of one of King David's warriors.

Ezekiel (יְחֶזְקֵאל) From the Hebrew, meaning "God will strengthen." In the Bible, one of the later Prophets. Zeke is a pet form. Yechezkel is the original Hebrew form.

Ezer (עֵזֶר) From the Hebrew, meaning "help." In the Bible (I Chronicles 7:21), a member of the tribe of Ephraim. Eizer, spelled עֵזֶר, is a variant spelling. *See* Eizer.

Ezio A short form of Enzio. *See* Enzio.

Ezra (עֶזְרָא) From the Hebrew, meaning "help." In the Bible (Nehemiah 12:1), a Priest who returned to Judah after the Babylonian Exile and with Nehemiah led the Jews in rebuilding their lives and their country. Yemenites have refused to name their sons Ezra, claiming that when he helped the exiled Jews of Babylonia return to Palestine, he did not help the Yemenites. Ezzard and Ezzret are possibly variant forms. Also spelled עֶזְרָה (I Chronicles 4:17), a member of the tribe of Judah. Used also as a feminine name.

Ezrach (אֶזְרָח) From the Hebrew, meaning "well-rooted plant" or "citizen." Ezrachi is a variant form.

Ezrachi (אֶזְרָחִי) A variant form of Ezrach. *See* Ezrach.

Ezri (עֶזְרִי) From the Hebrew, meaning "my help." In the Bible (I Chronicles 27:26), one of the overseers of King David's royal estate.

Ezzard Possibly a variant form of Ezra. *See* Ezra.

Ezzret Possibly a variant form of Ezra. *See* Ezra.

Fabian From the Latin, meaning "bean farmer." Akin to Fabius. *See* Fabius.

Fabius From the Latin, meaning "bean, member of the pea family of plants." In ancient Rome, members of the Fabia family were wealthy bean growers. Akin to Fabian.

Fairleigh, Fairley, Farley From the Anglo-Saxon, meaning "good, beautiful meadow."

Fait From the Old French, meaning "maker, creator."

Farrar From the Old French, meaning "worker with iron, blacksmith."

Farrel, Farrell From the Celtic, meaning "valorous one."

Feibush (פֵייבּוּשׁ) A variant form of Feivel. *See* Feivel.

Feivel (פֵייבֶּעל) The Yiddish form of Phoebus, from the Latin and Greek, meaning "bright one." In Greek mythology, Phoebus is the goddess of light. Feiwel is a variant spelling. Feibush is a variant form. Also spelled פֵייוֶל.

Feiwel A variant spelling of Feivel. *See* Feivel.

Felipe The Spanish form of Philip. *See* Philip.

Felix From the Latin, meaning "happy, fortunate, prosperous."

Fell From the Old Danish, meaning "field" or "hill."

Felton From the Old English, meaning "town in the garden."

Fenton From the Old English, meaning "town near the fen or marsh."

Ferd, Ferde A short form of Ferdinand. *See* Ferdinand. Also, from the German, meaning "horse." Ferdie and Ferdy are pet forms.

Ferdie A pet form of Ferd. *See* Ferd.

Ferdinand From the German, meaning "to be bold, courageous." Ferd and Ferde are short forms. Fernand, Fernandas, and Fernando are Spanish forms.

Ferdy A pet form of Ferd. *See* Ferd.

Fergus From the Irish and Gaelic, meaning "manly."

Fermin From the Latin, meaning "wild, savage." Firmin and Furman are variant spellings.

Fern A pet form of Ferdinand. *See* Ferdinand. Also, from the Old English, meaning "leafy plant."

Fernand, Fernandas, Fernando Spanish forms of Ferdinand. *See* Ferdinand.

Ferrin A variant form of Ferris. *See* Ferris.

Ferris From the Latin, meaning "iron." Ferrin is a variant form.

Ferrol From the Old French, meaning "iron ring on a staff."

Festus From the Latin, meaning "festive, joyous."

Fibber From the seventeenth-century word *fible*, meaning "fable, lie."

Fichel, Fishel (פִישֶׁעל) From the Yiddish, meaning "fish." Derived from Ephraim, meaning "fruitful" or "prolific," like a fish.

Fico From the Italian, meaning "fig."

Fidel From the Latin, meaning "faithful."

Field, Fielding From the Middle English, meaning "field."

Firmin A variant spelling of Fermin. *See* Fermin.

Firpo From the Middle English, meaning "fir tree."

Fish From the German, meaning "fish." Fishel, Fishkin, and Fishlin are pet forms.

Fishel (פִישֶׁעל) A Yiddish pet form of Fish. *See* Fish.

Fishke (פִישׁקֶע) A Yiddish name derived from the Old German, meaning "fish."

Fishkin A pet form of Fish. *See* Fish.

Fishlin A pet form of Fish. *See* Fish.

Fisk, Fiske From the Scandinavian, meaning "fish."

Flan, Flann From the Old English, meaning "arrow."

Flavian From the Latin, meaning "yellow, blonde." Used for people with flaxen or blonde hair. Flavio and Flavius are variant forms.

Flavio A variant form of Flavian. *See* Flavian.

Flavius A variant form of Flavian. *See* Flavian.

Flem A pet form of Fleming. *See* Fleming.

Fleming From the Middle Dutch, meaning "native of Flanders." Flem is a pet form.

Fletcher From the Old French, meaning "arrow."

Flint From the Old English and Norwegian, meaning "stone splinter."

Florence From the Latin, meaning "blooming." Primarily a feminine name. *See* Florence (feminine section). Florentz and Florenz are variant spellings. Florentino is a diminutive form.

Florentino A diminutive form of Florence. *See* Florence.

Florentz, Florenz Variant spellings of Florence. *See* Florence.

Florian From the Latin, meaning "flowering, blooming."

Floyd A corrupt form of Lloyd. *See* Lloyd.

Fob From the German, meaning "pocket for carrying a watch."

Fon A short form of Fonda. *See* Fonda.

Fonda From the French, meaning "to melt." Used most often as a feminine form. *See* Fonda (feminine section). Fon is a short form.

Forbes   From the Greek, meaning "fodder (a broad-leaved flowering plant)."

Forester   An Old French occupational name, meaning "one in charge of a forest." Forrester is a variant spelling.

Forrest   From the Latin meaning "out-of-doors, woods."

Forrester   A variant spelling of Forester. *See* Forester.

Fortney   From the Latin, meaning "strong."

Fortune   From the Latin, meaning "chance."

Foster   A variant form of Forester or Forrest. *See* Forester *and* Forrest.

Fowler   From the Old English and the German, meaning "one who traps fowl (birds)."

Fox   From the German, meaning "fox."

Foy   From the Middle Dutch, meaning "journey." Later, a Scottish name, meaning "feast in honor of one going on a journey."

Francesco, Francisco   Variant forms of Francis. *See* Francis.

Franchot   A French form of Francis. *See* Francis.

Francis   From the Middle English, meaning "a free man." Francesco, Franchot, Francisco, and Franz are variant forms. Frank is a pet form.

Frank   A pet form of Francis and Franklin. *See* Francis *and* Franklin.

Frankie   A pet form of Frank. *See* Frank.

Franklin   From the Old English, meaning "free-holder." *See* Frank *and* Francis. Franklyn is a variant spelling.

Franklyn   A variant spelling of Franklin. *See* Franklin.

Franz   The German form of Francis. *See* Francis.

Fraser   An occupational name, from the French, meaning "one who makes charcoal." Frazer and Frazier are variant spellings.

Frazer, Frazier   Variant spellings of Fraser. *See* Fraser.

Fred, Freddie, Freddy   Pet forms of Frederick. *See* Frederick.

Frederic   A variant spelling of Frederick. *See* Frederick.

Frederick   From the Latin and Old High German, meaning "peaceful ruler." Frederic, Fredric, and Fredrick are variant spellings. Freed is a variant form. Fred, Freddie, and Freddy are pet forms.

Fredric, Fredrick   Variant spellings of Frederick. *See* Frederick.

Freed   A variant form of Frederick. *See* Frederick.

Freeman   From the Anglo-Saxon, meaning "one born free." *See* Francis.

Fremont   From the French, meaning "freedom mountain."

Frits   A variant spelling of Fritz. *See* Fritz.

Fritz   A German form of Frederick. *See* Frederick.

Fromel, Frommel (פְרָאמֶעל)   A Yiddish pet form of Avraham. *See* Avraham. Also, a Yiddish pet form of Efrayim. *See* Efrayim.

Fry, Frye   From the Middle English and the Old Norse, meaning "seed" or "offspring."

Fulton   From the Anglo-Saxon, meaning "field near the town."

Furman   A variant spelling of Fermin. *See* Fermin.

Fuzzy   A variant form of the Dutch, meaning "spongy, covered with down."

Gaal (גַּעַל)   From the Hebrew, meaning "to loathe, abhor." In the Bible (Judges 9:26), a Canaanite, son of Eved.

Gab   A pet form of Gabriel. *See* Gabriel.

Gabai, Gabbai (גַּבָּי)   From the Aramaic, meaning "collector of taxes" or "synagogue attendant." In the Bible (Nehemiah 11:8), a leader of the tribe of Benjamin who was among the Babylonian Exile returnees.

Gabby   A pet form of Gabriel. *See* Gabriel. Gabi is a variant spelling.

Gabe   A pet form of Gabriel. *See* Gabriel.

Gabi (גַּבִּי)   A pet form of Gabriel. Gabby is a variant spelling.

Gabirol   A variant form of Gavirol. *See* Gavirol.

Gabriel (גַּבְרִיאֵל)   From the Hebrew, meaning "God is my strength." Gavriel is the exact Hebrew form. *See* Gavriel. Gab, Gabby, Gabe, and Gabi are pet forms.

Gacham (גַּחַם)   From the Hebrew, meaning "to kindle, burn," hence "a flame." In the Bible (Genesis 22:24), Abraham's nephew. Gaham is a variant spelling.

Gachar (גַּחַר)   From the Hebrew, meaning "to retreat, retire." In the Bible (Ezra 2:47), the father of Babylonian Exile returnees. Gahar is a variant spelling.

Gad (גָּד)   From the Hebrew and Arabic, meaning "happy, lucky, fortunate" or "a warrior." Akin to an old British word, meaning "a battle." In the Bible (Genesis 35:26), one of the sons of Jacob from his wife Zilpah. Gadi, Gaddi, and Gadiel are variant forms.

Gada (גָּדָא)   From the Hebrew, meaning "bank (of a river)." Or, from the Aramaic, meaning "wall." In the Talmud (Eruvin 11b), a fourth-century Babylonian scholar. Used also as a feminine form. *See* Gada (feminine section).

Gadi, Gaddi (גַּדִּי) Variant forms of Gad. *See* Gad. In the Bible (Numbers 13:11), a leader of the tribe of Manasseh, one of the twelve scouts sent by Moses to explore the Promised Land. Spelled גָּדִי in II Kings 15:14.

Gadiel (גַּדִּיאֵל) From the Hebrew, meaning "God is my fortune, my blessing." A variant form of Gad. *See* Gad. In the Bible (Numbers 13:10), a member of the tribe of Zebulun, one of the twelve scouts sent by Moses to explore the Promised Land.

Gadish (גָּדִישׁ) From the Arabic, meaning "tomb." The name of the father of a second-century talmudic scholar (Eruvin 27a).

Gadol (גָּדוֹל) From the Hebrew, meaning "great, large."

Gafni (גַּפְנִי) From the Hebrew, meaning "my vineyard."

Gage From the Middle English and Old French, meaning "pledge, pawn."

Gaham A variant spelling of Gacham. *See* Gacham.

Gahar A variant spelling of Gachar. *See* Gachar.

Gai (גַּיְא) From the Hebrew, meaning "valley." Guy is a variant English spelling, and גַּי and גַּיְא are variant Hebrew spellings.

Gail A short form of Gaylord. *See* Gaylord. Gale is a variant spelling. Used also as feminine name.

Gaines From the Middle English and French, meaning "to increase in wealth." Gayne is a variant form.

Gal (גַּל) From the Hebrew, meaning "wave" or "heap, mound." Used also as a feminine name. Galal is a variant form.

Galal (גָּלָל) A variant form of Gal. *See* Gal. In the Bible (Nehemiah 11:17), a Levite.

Gale From the German, meaning "hardy shrub." Or, from the Greek, meaning "weasel." Also, a variant spelling of Gail. *See* Gail.

Galen From the Greek, meaning "still, tranquil." Gaylon is a variant form.

Gali (גַּלִּי) From the Hebrew, meaning "my wave."

Galia, Galiah Variant spellings of Galya. *See* Galya.

Galil (גָּלִיל) From the Hebrew, meaning "boundary" or "cylinder." Also, from the Hebrew and Aramaic, meaning "rolling hills." The hilly country of northern Israel is known as the Galil or Galilee. Gallil is a variant spelling. Gilean is a variant form.

Galili A variant spelling of Gelili. *See* Gelili.

Gallagher From the Celtic, meaning "eager helper."

Gallil A variant spelling of Galil. *See* Galil.

Galt From the British, meaning "a steep, wooded area."

Galway From the Old Norse, meaning "blast of wind."

Galya (גַּלְיָה)   From the Hebrew, meaning "the hill (mound) of the Lord." Galia and Galiah are variant spellings.

Galyat   A variant spelling of Golyat. *See* Golyat.

Gamad (גָּמָד)   From the Aramaic and Arabic, meaning "to congeal" or "to contract," hence "a dwarf."

Gamada (גַּמְדָּא)   A variant form of Gamad. *See* Gamad. In the Talmud (Ketuvot 63b), a fourth-century Babylonian scholar.

Gamal (גָּמָל)   From the Arabic and Hebrew, meaning "camel." Gimal is a variant form.

Gamala   A variant spelling of Gamla. *See* Gamla.

Gamaliel   A variant spelling of Gamliel. *See* Gamliel.

Gamel   From the Old Norse and the Old English, meaning "old." Gemmel is a Scottish form.

Gamla (גַּמְלָא)   The Aramaic form of Gamal. *See* Gamal. In the Talmud (Yoma 3:9), the father of Joshua, a talmudic scholar of the first century. Gamala is a variant spelling.

Gamliel (גַּמְלִיאֵל)   From the Hebrew, meaning "God is my reward." In the Bible (Numbers 1:10), a leader of the tribe of Manasseh. A popular name among the Puritans. In the Talmud (Berachot 1:1), the nephew of Hillel and the name of many talmudic scholars. Gamaliel is a variant spelling.

Gamul (גָּמוּל)   From the Hebrew, meaning "reward" or "recompense." In the Bible (I Chronicles 24:17), a Levite who served in the time of King David.

Gan (גַּן)   From the Hebrew, meaning "garden."

Gani (גַּנִּי)   From the Hebrew, meaning "my garden."

Gaon (גָּאוֹן)   From the Hebrew, meaning "proud" or "majestic." A prestigious title for outstanding scholars.

Gardell   From the Old High German, meaning "guard, protector."

Garden   From the Old High German and Danish, meaning "enclosure, garden." Gardener is a variant form.

Gardener   An occupational name. A variant form of Garden. *See* Garden. Gardiner and Gardner are variant spellings.

Gardi (גַּרְדִּי)   From the Greek, meaning "weaver."

Gardiner, Gardner   Variant spellings of Gardener. *See* Gardener.

Gareth   A variant form of Garth. *See* Garth.

Garev (גָּרֵב)   From the Aramaic and Arabic, meaning "a scab." In the Bible (II Samuel 23:38), one of King David's warriors.

Garfield   From the Old English, meaning "promontory."

Garland   From the Old French and Italian, meaning "wreath of flowers." Garlon is probably a variant form.

Garlon   Probably a variant form of Garland. *See* Garland.

Garner   From the Middle English and the Latin, meaning "granary."

Garnet, Garnett   From the Latin, meaning "grain." The dark red seed of the pomegranate resembled the precious jewel in color and shape, hence the name garnet for the deep red-colored jewel.

Garon (גָּרוֹן)   From the Hebrew, meaning "a threshing-floor" for grain. Also, from the Hebrew, meaning "throat." Guryon is a variant form. *See* Guryon. The father of a talmudic scholar.

Garrard   A variant form of the German name Gerhard, akin to the Old French name Gerard. *See* Gerard.

Garret   From the Old French, meaning "to watch." Akin to Garth. *See* Garth. Gary is a pet form. Garrett is a variant spelling. Garreth and Geritt are variant forms.

Garreth   A variant form of Garret. *See* Garret.

Garrett   A variant spelling of Garret. *See* Garret.

Garrick   From the Anglo-Saxon, meaning "oak spear."

Garrison   From the Old French, meaning "garrison, troops stationed at a fort." Garson is a variant form.

Garson   A short form of Garrison. *See* Garrison.

Garth   From the Old Norse, meaning "enclosure, field, garden." Gareth, Garton, and Garvey are variant forms.

Garton   From the Anglo-Saxon, meaning "town near the field." A variant form of Garth.

Garvey   From the Anglo-Saxon, meaning "spearbearer, warrior." Also, a form of Garth. *See* Garth. Garvie is a variant spelling. Gary and Garry are variant forms.

Garvie   A variant spelling of Garvey. *See* Garvey.

Garvin   From the Anglo-Saxon, meaning "war friend." Akin to Garvey.

Gary, Garry   Variant forms of Garvey. *See* Garvey. Also, pet forms of Garret. *See* Garret.

Gaspar, Gasper   From the Persian, meaning "treasure-holder." May also be variant spellings of Caspar and Casper. *See* Caspar *and* Casper.

Gavan, Gavin   From the Welsh, meaning "little hawk."

Gavirol (גְּבִירוֹל)   A Sephardic form of Gavriel. *See* Gavriel.

Gavrel (גַאבְרֶעל)   A variant Yiddish form of Gavriel. *See* Gavriel.

Gavri (גַּבְרִי)   A variant form of Gavriel. *See* Gavriel.

Gavriel (גַּבְרִיאֵל)   From the Hebrew, meaning "God is my strength." Gabriel is a variant spelling. In the Bible (Daniel 8:16), the angel seen by Daniel in a vision. Gavirol, Gavrel, and Gavri are variant forms.

Gay From the Old French, meaning "joyous, merry." Gaylord might be a variant form.

Gayle A pet form of Gaylord. *See* Gaylord.

Gaylon A variant form of Galen. *See* Galen.

Gaylord From the Old French, meaning "brave." Probably also a variant form of Gay. *See* Gay. Gaylard is a variant spelling. Gail and Gayle are short forms.

Gayne A variant form of Gaines. *See* Gaines.

Gaynor From the Irish, meaning "son of the white-haired man" or "son of the light-complexioned man."

Gazam (גַּזָּם) From the Hebrew, meaning "locust." In the Bible (Ezra 2:48), one of the Babylonian Exile returnees.

Gazaz (גָּזָז) A variant form of Gazez. *See* Gazez.

Gazez (גָּזֵז) From the Aramaic and Arabic, meaning "to shear, fleece." In the Bible (I Chronicles 2:46), a son of Caleb. Gazaz is a variant form. Akin to Giza.

Gealia, Gealiah Variant spellings of Gealya. *See* Gealya.

Gealya (גְּאַלְיָה) From the Hebrew, meaning "God redeems."

Geber A variant spelling of Gever. *See* Gever.

Gechazi (גֵּיחֲזִי) From the Hebrew, meaning "valley of vision." In the Bible (II Kings 4:12), the servant of the Prophet Elisha. Gehazi is a variant spelling.

Gedalia, Gedaliah Variant spellings of Gedalya. *See* Gedalya.

Gedaliahu A variant form of Gedalya. *See* Gedalya.

Gedalya (גְּדַלְיָה) From the Hebrew, meaning "God is great." In the Bible (Zephaniah 1:1), the governor of Judah appointed by Nebuchadnezzar, king of Babylonia. Gedalia and Gedaliah are variant spellings. Gedalyahu and Gedaliahu are variant forms. Gedil is a pet form.

Gedalyahu (גְּדַלְיָהוּ) A variant form of Gedalya (II Kings 25:22). *See* Gedalya.

Geddes From the Anglo-Saxon, meaning "javelin."

Gedil (גְּדִיל) A pet form of Gedalya. *See* Gedalya.

Gedor (גְּדוֹר) From the Hebrew, meaning "enclosure."

Gedula (גְּדוּלָה) From the Hebrew, meaning "greatness." In the Talmud (Yerushalmi Yevamot 4:11), a third-century Palestinian scholar.

Gefania, Gefaniah Variant spellings of Gefanya. *See* Gefanya.

Gefanya (גְּפַנְיָה) From the Hebrew, meaning "vineyard of the Lord." Gefania, Gefaniah, Gephania, and Gephaniah are variant spellings.

Gefen (גֶּפֶן) From the Hebrew, meaning "vine."

Gehazi A variant spelling of Gechazi. *See* Gechazi.

Gelili (גְּלִילִי) From the Hebrew, meaning "man from Galilee." Galili is a variant spelling.

Gemala (גְּמָלָא) From the Aramaic, meaning "reward." The name of an ancient city in Upper Galilee. The father of Joshua, a High Priest in the first century B.C.E. Also spelled גַּמְלָא.

Gemali (גְּמָלִי) From the Hebrew, meaning "my reward." Also, from the Arabic and Hebrew, meaning "my camel." In the Bible (Numbers 13:12), a member of the tribe of Dan.

Gemaliel A variant form of Gamliel. See Gamliel.

Gemaria, Gemariah Variant spellings of Gemarya. See Gemarya.

Gemarya (גְּמַרְיָה) From the Hebrew, meaning "acts of the Lord" or "accomplishments of the Lord." In the Bible (Jeremiah 29:3), a messenger of King Hezekiah. Gemaria and Gemariah are variant spellings. Gemaryahu is a variant form.

Gemaryahu (גְּמַרְיָהוּ) A variant form of Gemarya. See Gemarya. In the Bible (Jeremiah 36:10), the scribe of King Jehoiakim.

Gemmel A variant form of Gamel. See Gamel.

Gene A pet form of Eugene. See Eugene.

Geno An Italian and Greek form of John. See John.

Geoff A pet form of Geoffrey. See Geoffrey.

Geoffrey From the Anglo-Saxon, meaning "gift of peace" or "God's peace." Geoff is a pet form. Jeffrey is a variant spelling.

Geordie A variant Scottish form of George. See George.

George From the Greek, meaning "farmer" or "tiller of the soil." Geordie is a variant form.

Georgie A pet form of George. See George.

Gephania, Gephaniah Variant spellings of Gefanya. See Gefanya.

Gera, Gerah (גֵּרָא) From the Hebrew, meaning "combat" or "disputation." In the Bible (Genesis 46:21), one of the sons of Benjamin and a grandson of Jacob.

Gerald An Old French and Old High German form of Gerard. See Gerard. Gerry and Jerry are pet forms.

Gerard From the Anglo-Saxon, meaning "spear" or "spearbearer, warrior." Garrard, Gerald, Gerhard, Gerhardt, Gerhart, Girault, and Giraut are variant forms. Girard is a variant spelling.

Gerhard A variant form of Gerard. See Gerard.

Gerhardt, Gerhart Variant forms of Gerard. See Gerard.

Geri (גֵּרִי) From the Hebrew, meaning "my stranger."

Geritt A variant form of Garret. See Garret.

Germain The Middle English form of the Latin, meaning "sprout, bud."

Gerome From the Greek, meaning "holy fame" or "sacred name." Jerome is a variant spelling. Gerry is a pet form.

Gerrett A variant form of Garrett. See Garrett.

Gerry A pet form of Gerome. See Gerome.

Gershom (גֵּרְשֹׁם) From the Hebrew, meaning "stranger." In the Bible (Exodus 2:22), a son of Moses. Often interchangeable with Gershon.

Gershon (גֵּרְשׁוֹן) A variant form of Gershom. See Gershom. In the Bible (Genesis 46:11), a son of Levi and a grandson of Jacob. Gerson is a variant form.

Gerson A variant form of Gershon. See Gershon.

Gervais From the Old German, meaning "spear." Gervis is a variant form. Akin to Garvey. See Garvey.

Gervis A variant form of Gervais. See Gervais. Akin to Jarvis. See Jarvis.

Geshan (גִּישָׁן) From the Hebrew, meaning "hard (hands), calloused."

Geshem (גֶּשֶׁם) From the Hebrew, meaning "rain." In the Bible (Nehemiah 2:19), an opponent of Nehemiah.

Geshur (גְּשׁוּר) From the Hebrew, meaning "bridge."

Geter (גֶּתֶר) Meaning uncertain. In Genesis 10:23, an Aramean; in I Chronicles 1:17, a grandson of Noah.

Getz (גֶץ) A Yiddish name. An acronym formed from the Hebrew words *ger tzedek*, meaning "righteous proselyte," or *gabbai tzedaka*, meaning "dispensers of charitable funds." Goetz is a variant spelling. Getzel is a pet form.

Getzel (גֶּעצֶעל) A pet form of Getz. See Getz.

Geuel (גְּאוּאֵל) From the Hebrew, meaning "majesty of God" or "redeemed by God." In the Bible (Numbers 13:15), the member of the tribe of Gad who was one of the twelve scouts who explored the Promised Land.

Geula (גְּאוּלָה) From the Hebrew, meaning "redemption." Primarily a feminine name.

Geva (גֶּבַע) From the Hebrew, meaning "hill." In the Bible, a place-name.

Gevaram (גִּבְרְעָם) From the Hebrew, meaning "strength of a nation."

Gevaria, Gevariah Variant spellings of Gevarya. See Gevarya.

Gevarya, Gevaryah (גְּבַרְיָה) From the Hebrew, meaning "the might of the Lord." Gevaria and Gevariah are variant spellings. Gevaryahu is a variant form.

Gevaryahu (גְּבַרְיָהוּ) A variant form of Gevarya. See Gevarya.

Gever (גֶּבֶר) From the Hebrew, meaning "man." Or, from the Aramaic and Arabic, meaning "to be strong." In the Bible (I Kings 4:19), one of the twelve men who supervised the household of King Solomon. Geber is a variant spelling.

Giacomo An Italian form of Jacob. *See* Jacob.

Gib A pet form of Gilbert. *See* Gilbert.

Gibar, Gibbar (גִּבָּר) From the Hebrew, meaning "strong." In the Bible (Ezra 2:20), one of the Babylonian Exile returnees.

Gibby A pet form of Gilbert. *See* Gilbert.

Gibeon A variant form of Givon. *See* Givon.

Gibor, Gibbor (גִּיבּוֹר) From the Hebrew, meaning "strong person."

Gidal (גִּידָל) A variant form of Gidel. *See* Gidel. The name of a third-century Babylonian talmudic scholar (Eruvin 17a).

Gidalti (גִּדַּלְתִּי) From the Hebrew, meaning "I have raised." In the Bible (I Chronicles 25:4), a son of Heman the Levite.

Gidel, Giddel (גִּדֵּל) From the Hebrew, meaning "to raise, bring up (children)." In the Bible (Ezra 2:47), the father of one of the Babylonian Exile returnees. Gidal is a variant form.

Gideon A variant spelling of Gidon. *See* Gidon.

Gideoni A variant spelling of Gidoni. *See* Gidoni.

Gidi A pet form of Gidon. *See* Gidon.

Gidon (גִּדְעוֹן) From the Hebrew, meaning either "maimed" or "a mighty warrior." In the Bible (Judges 6:11), one of the Judges of Israel, the warrior-hero who defeated the Midianites. Also known as Yerubaal. Gideon is an Anglicized spelling. Gidi is a pet form.

Gidoni (גִּדְעוֹנִי) A variant form of Gidon. *See* Gidon. In the Bible (Numbers 1:11), a leader of the tribe of Benjamin. Gideoni is a variant spelling.

Gidron (גִּדְרוֹן) From the Hebrew, meaning "an enclosure (for sheep)."

Gifford From the Middle English, meaning "worthy gift."

Gig From the Middle English, meaning "horse-drawn carriage."

Gil (גִּיל) From the Hebrew, meaning "joy." Also, a pet form of Gilbert. *See* Gilbert. Gill is a variant spelling.

Gil-Ad (גִּיל־עָד) From the Hebrew, meaning "eternal joy."

Gilad (גִּלְעָד) From the Hebrew, meaning "mound (hill) of testimony." In the Bible, a mountainous area east of the Jordan River. Gilead is an Anglicized spelling. *See also* Giladi.

Giladi (גִּלְעָדִי) From the Hebrew, meaning "man from Gilad." *See also* Gilad.

Gilalai (גִּלֲלַי) From the Hebrew, meaning "to roll away." In the Bible (Nehemiah 12:36), a Levite who was a musician in the time of Ezra.

Gilam (גִּיל־עָם) From the Hebrew, meaning "joy of a people."

Gilbert From the Anglo-Saxon, meaning either "light of many, bright promise" or "sword." Gib, Gibby, and Gil are pet forms.

Gilboa (גִּלְבֹּעַ) Meaning unknown. A mountain ridge at the southeastern corner of the plain of Jezreel where Saul and Jonathan were killed (I Samuel 31:1).

Gilead An Anglicized spelling of Gilad. See Gilad.

Gilean A variant form of Galil, meaning "a man from Galilee." See Galil. Gileon is a variant spelling.

Gileon A variant spelling of Gilean. See Gilean.

Giles From the Greek, meaning "goatskin," hence "a shield that protects." In Greek mythology, a shield or breastplate used by Zeus. Gilles and Gyles are variant spellings. Gillian is a variant form.

Gilford From the Old English, meaning "a ford near the wooded ravine."

Gili (גִּילִי) From the Hebrew, meaning "my joy." Gilli and Gil-li are variant spellings. Also spelled גִּיל־לִי.

Gill A variant spelling of Gil. See Gil.

Gilles A variant spelling of Giles. See Giles.

Gilli A variant spelling of Gili. See Gili.

Gil-Li (גִּיל־לִי) A variant form of Gili. See Gili.

Gillian A variant form of Giles. See Giles.

Gilmore From the Celtic, meaning "glen near the sea."

Gil-On (גִּיל־אוֹן) From the Hebrew, meaning "age of strength."

Gilon (גִּילוֹן) From the Hebrew, meaning "joy."

Gilroy From the Latin, meaning "the king's faithful servant." Also, from the Old Norse and Gaelic, meaning "a ravine with a reddish hue."

Gimal A variant form of Gamal. See Gamal.

Gimpel (גִּימְפֶּעל) The Yiddish form of the German name Gumprecht.

Gina (גִּנָה) From the Hebrew, meaning "garden."

Ginat (גִּינַת) From the Hebrew, meaning "garden." In the Bible (I Kings 16:21), the father of Tibni, who sought the throne of Israel after the death of King Zimri. Ginath is a variant spelling.

Ginath A variant spelling of Ginat. See Ginat.

Gino The Italian pet form of John. See John.

Ginson A variant spelling of Ginton. See Ginton.

Gintoi (גִּנְתוֹי) A variant form of Ginton. See Ginton. In the Bible (Nehemiah 12:4), a Priest in the time of Ezra.

Ginton (גִּנְתוֹן) From the Hebrew, meaning "garden, orchard." In the Bible

(Nehemiah 10:6), a Priest who returned to Palestine after the Babylonian Exile. Ginnethon and Ginson are variant spellings.

Giora (גִּיּוֹרָא) From the Aramaic, meaning "stranger" or "convert." Simon bar Giora was a first-century Jewish leader in the war against Rome. Also spelled גִּיּוֹרָה.

Girard A variant spelling of Gerard. *See* Gerard.

Girault, Giraut Variant French forms of Gerard. *See* Gerard.

Gitai (גִּתַּי) From the Aramaic, meaning "one who presses grapes." Akin to Giti.

Giti (גִּתִּי) A variant form of Gitai. *See* Gitai.

Giva (גִּבְעָא) From the Aramaic and Hebrew, meaning "hill." In the Bible (I Chronicles 2:49), a son of Caleb of the tribe of Judah.

Givol (גִּבְעוֹל) From the Hebrew, meaning "budding, in bloom."

Givon (גִּבְעוֹן) From the Hebrew, meaning "hill, heights." Also, a biblical place-name. Gibeon is a variant spelling.

Givton (גִּבְתוֹן) From the Hebrew, meaning "hill." Akin to Givon.

Giza (גִּזָּה) From the Aramaic and Arabic, meaning "fleece." Akin to Gazez. The name of the father of a fourth-century Babylonian talmudic scholar (Avoda Zara 69a).

Glade From the Anglo-Saxon, meaning "to be glad" and "to bring light." Glat is a Scottish form.

Glat A Scottish form of Glade. *See* Glade.

Glen, Glenn From the Celtic, meaning "glen, dale, a secluded woody valley." Glyn and Glynn are Welsh forms.

Glover From the Middle English, meaning "glove, paw."

Glyn, Glynn Welsh forms of Glen. *See* Glen.

Goddard From the Old English, meaning "good in counsel."

Godfrey A variant form of Gottfried. *See* Gottfried.

Godwin From the Anglo-Saxon, meaning "friend of God." Goodwin is a variant form. Akin to Edwin.

Goel (גּוֹאֵל) From the Hebrew, meaning "redeemer."

Goetz A variant spelling of Getz. *See* Getz.

Gog (גּוֹג) Meaning unknown. In the Bible (I Chronicles 5:4), a member of the tribe of Reuben. Also (Ezekiel 38:2), the king or prince of the land called Magog.

Golan (גּוֹלָן) From the Hebrew, meaning "refuge."

Gold From the Old English, meaning "to shine," hence "yellow." Golden, Goldman, and Goldsmith are variant forms.

Golden A variant form of Gold. *See* Gold.

Goldman An occupational name for a person dealing in gold. *See* Gold. Akin to Goldsmith.

Goldsmith An occupational name for an artisan who fabricates ornaments of gold. Akin to Goldman. *See* Gold.

Goldwin, Goldwyn From the Anglo-Saxon, meaning "lover of gold."

Goliath (גָּלְיַח) Derivation uncertain. Possibly from the Hebrew, meaning "one who was exiled, a stranger," hence one who is conspicuous. In the Bible (I Samuel 17:4), the Philistine giant killed by David with a slingshot. Galyat and Golyat are original Hebrew forms.

Golyat (גָּלְיַח) The Hebraic form of Goliath. *See* Goliath.

Gomer (גֹּמֶר) From the Hebrew, meaning "to end, complete." In the Bible (Genesis 10:2), son of Japhet. Also, a feminine name in the Bible; the wife of the Prophet Hosea (Hosea 1:3).

Gonen (גּוֹנֵן) From the Hebrew, meaning "protector."

Goodman From the Anglo-Saxon, meaning "good man" or "good servant."

Goodwin A variant form of Godwin. *See* Godwin.

Goral (גּוֹרָל) From the Hebrew, meaning "lottery, chance."

Goran From the British, meaning "choir" or "cathedral."

Gordon From the Old English, meaning "dung pasture." Or, from the Gaelic, meaning "hero, strongman."

Gore A short form of either Goran or Gordon. *See* Goran *and* Gordon.

Gorham From the Old English, meaning "a hamlet built on or near the dung pasture" or "cathedral town."

Gorion A variant form of Guryon. *See* Guryon.

Gorman From the British, meaning "member of a choir."

Gottfried From the Old English and Old German, meaning "God's peace" or "divinely peaceful." Godfrey is a variant form.

Gottlieb From the German, meaning "God loves."

Gover (גּוֹבֵר) From the Hebrew, meaning "victorious." Also, an Anglo-Saxon occupational name, meaning "one who stores corn in a barn."

Gowell From the Old Norse, meaning "gold."

Gozal (גּוֹזָל) From the Hebrew, meaning "young bird."

Gozan (גּוֹזָן) From the Arabic, meaning "to encircle." A biblical place-name.

Grady From the Latin, meaning "grade, rank."

Graham From the Old English, meaning "from the gray home or dwelling."

Graig A variant spelling of Craig. *See* Craig.

Gram From the Latin, meaning "grain."

Granger   From the Old French, meaning "farm steward."

Grant   From the Old French, meaning "to give, grant, or assure."

Grantland   From the Old English, meaning "deeded land." Grantley is a variant form.

Grantley   A variant form of Grantland. *See* Grantland.

Granville   From the French, meaning "big town." Grenville is a variant form.

Gray   From the Old English, meaning "to shine."

Grayson   From the Anglo-Saxon, meaning "son of a *greve* (earl)." Or, a patronymic form of Gray. *See* Gray.

Grayston   From the Anglo-Saxon, meaning "Gray's town." *See* Gray.

Greeley, Greely   Abbreviated forms of the Anglo-Saxon *greenlea*, meaning "green meadow." Akin to Grimsley.

Green   From the Old English, referring to the color of growing grass. Used also as a feminine name.

Greg, Gregg   From the Anglo-Saxon, meaning "to shine." Also, pet forms of Gregory. *See* Gregory.

Gregor   The German and Scandinavian form of Gregory. *See* Gregory.

Gregory   From the Greek, meaning "vigilant watchman." Gregor is a variant form. Greg and Gregg are pet forms.

Grenville   A variant form of Granville. *See* Granville.

Gridley   From the Anglo-Saxon, meaning "flat meadow."

Griffin   From the Welsh, meaning "strong in faith." A mythological animal with the body and hind legs of a lion and the head and wings of an eagle. Griffith is a variant form.

Griffith   A Welsh form of Griffin. *See* Griffin.

Grimbald   From the Old English, meaning "fierce" or "bold."

Grimsley   From the Anglo-Saxon, meaning "green meadow." Akin to Greeley.

Griswald   Compounded from the French, meaning "gray," and the German, meaning "forest."

Grove   From the Old English, meaning "thicket, group of cultivated trees."

Grover   From the Anglo-Saxon, meaning "one who grows or tends trees."

Guido   From the Italian, meaning "guide."

Guni (גּוּנִי)   From the Hebrew, meaning "tinge of color" or "reddish-black." In the Bible (Genesis 46:24), a member of the tribe of Gad.

Gunn   From the Middle English and Old Norse, meaning "war."

Gunnar   From the Old Norse, meaning "war."

Gunter   A variant form of Gunther. *See* Gunther.

Gunther   From the Old German, meaning "war." Gunter is a variant form.

Gur (גּוּר)   From the Hebrew, meaning "young lion." In the Bible (Genesis 49:9), a word by which Jacob characterized his son Judah. Gurion is a variant form.

Gur-Ari (גּוּר־אָרִי)   A variant form of Gur-Arye. *See* Gur-Arye.

Gur-Arye, Gur-Aryeh (גּוּר־אַרְיֵה)   From the Hebrew, meaning "young lion, cub." In the Bible (Genesis 49:9), Judah is characterized as a young lion. In the Talmud (Pesachim 113b), the father of a first-century Babylonian scholar.

Guri (גּוּרִי)   From the Hebrew, meaning "my young lion."

Guria (גּוּרְיָא)   An Aramaic form of Gur. *See* Gur. The name of a second-century talmudic scholar. (Kiddushin 4:14).

Guriel (גּוּרִיאֵל)   From the Hebrew, meaning "God is my lion" or "God is my refuge or protection."

Gurion   The popular spelling of Guryon. *See* Guryon. David Ben-Gurion became the new name of David Green (Gruen) after he settled in Palestine. *See also* Gur.

Guryon (גּוּרְיוֹן)   From the Hebrew, meaning "lion," hence "strength." In the Talmud (Shabbat 1:4), the grandfather of Chananya ben Chizkiya, a second-century scholar. Garon and Gorion are variant forms. Gurion is a popular variant spelling.

Gus   A pet form of Gustavus. *See* Gustavus.

Gustaf   The Swedish form of Gustavus. *See* Gustavus.

Gustav, Gustave   German forms of Gustavus. *See* Gustavus.

Gustavo   The Italian and Spanish form of Gustavus. *See* Gustavus.

Gustavus   From the German and Swedish, meaning "the staff of the Goths." The staff, pole or club, often used as a weapon, was also a symbol of authority and power. Gustaf, Gustav, Gustave, and Gustavo are variant forms. Gus is a pet form.

Guthrie   From the Celtic, meaning "war serpent" or "war hero."

Gutkin, Gutkind   From the German, meaning "good child."

Gutman, Gutmann   From the German, meaning "good man."

Guy   From the Old French, meaning "a guide" or "a rope that guides." Also, a variant spelling of Gai. *See* Gai.

Gwynn, Gwynne   From the Welsh, meaning "fair, white." Used also as a feminine name.

Gyles   A variant spelling of Giles. *See* Giles.

Habakuk, Habakkuk (חֲבַקּוּק)   From the Hebrew, meaning "to embrace." In the Bible, a seventh-century B.C.E. Prophet. *See also* Chavakuk.

Habib   A variant spelling of Chaviv. *See* Chaviv.

Habiba   A variant form of Chaviva. *See* Chaviva.

Habibi   A variant spelling of Chavivi. *See* Chavivi.

Hadad (הֲדַד)   A variant form of Hadar. *See* Hadar.

Hadar (הֲדָר)   From the Hebrew, meaning "beautiful" or "ornamented" or "honored." In the Bible (Genesis 36:39), a king of Edom, also known as Hadad (I Chronicles 1:50). Also spelled הֲדַר.

Hadaram (הֲדַרְעָם)   From the Hebrew, meaning "glory, honor, splendor of the people."

Hadarezer (הֲדַרְעֶזֶר)   From the Hebrew, meaning "glorious help."

Hadas (הֲדַס)   From the Aramaic, meaning "myrtle (tree)."

Hadden   From the Old English, meaning "health, wasteland." Haddon is a variant spelling.

Haddon   A variant spelling of Hadden. *See* Hadden.

Hadlai   A variant spelling of Hadley. *See* Hadley. Also, a variant spelling of Chadlai. *See* Chadlai.

Hadley   From the Old English, meaning "the meadow near the wasteland (heath)." Hadlai is a variant spelling.

Hadoram (הֲדֹרָם)   A variant form of Adoram. *See* Adoram. In the Bible (II Chronicles 10:18), an official of King Rehoboam.

Hadrian   From the Greek, meaning "rich." Adrian is a variant form.

Hadriel (הַדְרִיאֵל)   From the Hebrew, meaning "splendor of the Lord."

Hadur (הָדוּר)   From the Hebrew, meaning "adorned."

Haga   A variant spelling of Chaga. *See* Chaga.

Hagab   A variant spelling of Chagav. *See* Chagav.

Hagai, Haggai   Variant spellings of Chagai. *See* Chagai.

Hagi   A variant spelling of Chagi. *See* Chagi.

Hagia   A variant spelling of Chagiya. *See* Chagiya.

Hai (הַאי)   A variant form and spelling of Chai. *See* Chai. Hai Gaon was the tenth-century head (*gaon*) of the academy in Pumbedita, Babylonia, and the son of Sherira Gaon. Also spelled הַי.

Haig   From the Middle English, meaning "to cut, chop."

Haim   A variant spelling of Chaim. *See* Chaim.

Haimes   A variant spelling of Hames.

Haines   A variant form of the German name Johannes, which is a form of John.

See John. Also, from the Anglo-Saxon, meaning "hedge, enclosure." **Hanes** and Haynes are variant spellings.

Hal   A pet form of Harold or Haley. *See* Harold *and* Haley.

Halafta   A variant spelling of Chalafta. *See* Chalafta.

Hale   A pet form of Haley. *See* Haley.

Haley   From the Old English, meaning "healthy, whole" or "holy." Halley and Hallie are variant spellings. Hollis is a variant form. Hal and Hale are pet forms.

Halford   From the Old English, meaning "Hal's (Harold's) ford (river crossing)."

Halifa   A variant spelling of Chalifa. *See* Chalifa.

Halil, Hallil   Variant spellings of Chalil. *See* Chalil.

Hall   From the Middle English, meaning "to cover, conceal."

Halley, Hallie   Variant spellings of Haley. *See* Haley.

Halutz   A variant spelling of Chalutz. *See* Chalutz.

Halutzel   A variant spelling of Chalutzel. *See* Chalutzel.

Ham   A variant spelling of Cham. *See* Cham. Used also as a pet form of Hamilton.

Hama   A variant spelling of Chama. *See* Chama.

Haman (הָמָן)   Probably from the Persian, meaning "to rage, to be turbulent." In the Bible (Esther 7:10), the wicked prime minister of King Ahasueros of Persia.

Hamat   A variant spelling of Chamat. *See* Chamat.

Hames   From the Old Norse and Scottish, meaning "home." Haimes is a variant spelling. Hamlet is a variant form.

Hami   A variant spelling of Chami. *See* Chami.

Hamilton   A variant form of Hamlet and Hamlin. *See* Hamlet *and* Hamlin. Ham is a pet form.

Hamish   A variant form of the Gaelic name Seumas, which is a form of James. *See* James. Also, from the Scottish, meaning "home." Akin to Hames.

Hamlet   From the Low German, meaning "enclosed area." Or, from the Old German, meaning "home." Also, a variant form of Hames and Hamilton.

Hamlin   From the Old English, meaning "brook near the home." Hamilton is a variant form.

Hammond   From the Old English, meaning "home" or "village."

Hamnuna (הַמְנוּנָא)   From the Aramaic and Greek, meaning "hymn, song." In the Talmud (Bova Kama 106a), a third-century Babylonian scholar.

Hampden   From the Old English, meaning "home in the valley."

Hampton   From the Old English, meaning "town" or "village."

Hamran   A variant spelling of Chamran. *See* Chamran.

Hamud   A variant spelling of Chamud. *See* Chamud.

Hamuel   A variant spelling of Chamuel. *See* Chamuel.

Hamul   A variant spelling of Chamul. *See* Chamul.

Hanamel   A variant spelling of Chanamel. *See* Chanamel.

Hanan   A variant spelling of Chanan. *See* Chanan. Also, a short form of Johanan (Yochanan), from which John is derived.

Hanani   A variant spelling of Chanani. *See* Chanani.

Hanania, Hananiah   Variant spellings of Chananya. *See* Chananya.

Handley   A variant form of Hanley. *See* Hanley.

Hanes   A variant spelling of Haines. *See* Haines.

Haniel   A variant spelling of Chaniel. *See* Chaniel.

Hanina   A variant spelling of Chanina. *See* Chanina.

Hanita   A variant spelling of Chanita. *See* Chanita.

Hanley   From the Old English, meaning "field or meadow belonging to Hans or Hanes." Handley and Henlee are variant forms.

Hannibal   From the British, meaning "steep hill."

Hanns   A variant spelling of Hans. *See* Hans.

Hanoch, Hanokh   Variant spellings of Chanoch. *See* Chanoch.

Hanry   A variant spelling of Henry. *See* Henry.

Hans   A short form of the German Johannes, a Dutch, German and Swedish form of John. *See* John. Haines, Hanes, Hansel, Hanson, Heinz, and Honus are variant forms. Hanns is a variant spelling.

Hansel   A Bavarian form of Hans. *See* John.

Hansen   A variant spelling of Hanson. *See* Hanson.

Hanson   A patronymic form of Hans. *See* Hans.

Hanun   A variant spelling of Chanun. *See* Chanun.

Haran (הָרָן)   A variant spelling of Charan. *See* Charan. Also, from the Hebrew, meaning "mountaineer" or "mountain-people." In the Bible (Genesis 11:26), the brother of Abraham.

Harden   A variant form of Hardy. *See* Hardy.

Hardin   A variant form of Hardy. *See* Hardy.

Harding   A variant form of Hardy. *See* Hardy.

Hardley   From the Old English, meaning "a hardy green meadow."

Hardy   From the Middle English and Old French, meaning "bold, robust." Harden, Hardin, and Harding are variant forms.

Harel (הַרְאֵל)   From the Hebrew, meaning "mountain of God." In the Bible, a place-name. Harrell is a variant spelling.

Harim   A variant spelling of Charim. *See* Charim.

Harl   A short form of Harlan. *See* Harlan.

Harlan   From the Middle English and the Low German, meaning "a strand of hemp or flax," or from the Old English, meaning "a warrior." Harlin is a variant spelling. Harl is a short form. Akin to Harley.

Harley   From the Old English, meaning "a field of plants yielding a hemplike fiber." Akin to Harlan.

Harlin   A variant spelling of Harlan. *See* Harlan.

Harlow   From the Old Norse, meaning "army leader."

Harm   A short form of Harman. *See* Harman.

Harman   A form of the Anglo-Saxon name Herenan, meaning "army man, soldier." Akin to Herman. Or, from the Old English, meaning "keeper of hares or deer." Harm is a short form.

Harmon   From the Greek, meaning "peace, harmony."

Harold   From the Old English name Hereweald and the Germanic name Hariwald, meaning "leader of the army" or "warrior." Herald is a variant form. Hal and Harry are pet forms.

Harper   From the Old Norse, meaning "one who uses a javelin to spear whales."

Harrell   A variant spelling of Harel. *See* Harel.

Harris   A patronymic form, meaning "Harry's son." *See* Harry.

Harrison   A patronymic form, meaning "Harry's son." *See* Harry.

Harry   From the Middle English name Herry, a form of Henry. *See* Henry. English Kings named Henry were called Harry by their subjects. Also, a pet form of Harold. *See* Harold. Harris and Harrison are patronymic forms. Harriet is a feminine form.

Harsom   A variant spelling of Charsom. *See* Charsom.

Hart, Harte   From the Middle English, meaning "hart, deer, stag." Hartman and Hartwell are variant forms.

Hartley   From the Old English, meaning "a field in which the deer roam." Akin to Hartwig.

Hartman   A variant form of Hart, meaning "a man who traps or deals with deer." *See* Hart.

Hartwell   A variant form of Hart, meaning "a well at which the deer drink." *See* Hart.

Hartwig From the Old English, meaning "the way of the deer, the deer path." Akin to Hartley.

Harum A variant spelling of Charum. *See* Charum.

Haruz A variant spelling of Charutz. *See* Charutz.

Harve A short form of Harvey. *See* Harvey.

Harvey From the Old High German, meaning "army battle." Or, from the Celtic, meaning "progressive, liberal." Harve is a short form.

Hasadia, Hasadiah Variant spellings of Chasadya. *See* Chasadya.

Hashavia, Hashaviah Variant spellings of Chashavya. *See* Chashavya.

Hashmon A variant spelling of Chashmon. *See* Chashmon.

Hashuv A variant spelling of Chashuv. *See* Chashuv.

Hashuva A variant spelling of Chashuva. *See* Chashuva.

Hasiel A variant spelling of Chasiel. *See* Chasiel.

Hasin, Hassin Variant spellings of Chasin. *See* Chasin.

Haskel, Haskell (הַשְׂכֵּל) From the Hebrew, meaning "wise, wisdom." Also, from the Anglo-Saxon, meaning "ash tree." (The aspirated *h* was added to ash.) Also, a Yiddish form of the Hebrew Yechezkel (Ezekiel), meaning "God is my strength," and spelled הַאסקעל. Chaskel is a variant spelling. Heskel is a variant form.

Hason A variant spelling of Chason. *See* Chason.

Hassan From the Arabic, meaning "nice, good."

Hasting, Hastings From the Latin, meaning "spear." Also, from the Old English and Old Norse, meaning "house council."

Hatat A variant spelling of Chatat. *See* Chatat.

Hatchen From the Old English *haeth*, meaning "small wasteland."

Hatifa A variant spelling of Chatifa. *See* Chatifa.

Hatil A variant spelling of Chatil. *See* Chatil.

Hatita A variant spelling of Chatita. *See* Chatita.

Havaia, Havaiah, Havaya Variant spellings of Chavaya. *See* Chavaya.

Havelock From the surname of Sir Henry Havelock (1795-1857), an English general serving in India who introduced a light cloth (havelock) to cover the military cap for protection against the sun. Also, from the Anglo-Saxon, meaning "haven by the lake."

Haven From the Middle Dutch and Old English, meaning "harbor, port." Hazen and Hogan are variant forms.

Havila, Havilah Variant spellings of Chavila. *See* Chavila.

Haviv A variant spelling of Chaviv. *See* Chaviv.

Haviva   A variant spelling of Chaviva. *See* Chaviva.

Havivel   A variant spelling of Chavivel. *See* Chavivel.

Havivi   A variant spelling of Chavivi. *See* Chavivi.

Hawthorne   From the Old English, meaning "hedge of thorns." Refers primarily to thorny shrubs of the rose family.

Hayden   From the Anglo-Saxon, meaning "hay pasture." Haydn is a variant spelling.

Haydn   A variant spelling of Hayden. *See* Hayden.

Hayes   From the Old English, meaning "one who grows hay, a farmer." Hays is a variant spelling.

Haym   A variant spelling of Chaim. *See* Chaim.

Haynes   A variant spelling of Haines. *See* Haines.

Hays   A variant spelling of Hayes. *See* Hayes.

Hayward   From the Middle English, meaning "hedge" or "guardian." Akin to Haywood.

Haywood   From the Old English, meaning "hay field." Akin to Hayward.

Hayyim, Hayym   Variant spellings of Chaim. *See* Chaim.

Hazael   A variant spelling of Chazael. *See* Chazael.

Hazaia, Hazaiah   Variant spellings of Chazaya. *See* Chazaya.

Hazen   A variant form of Haven. *See* Haven.

Haziel   A variant spelling of Chaziel. *See* Chaziel.

Hazo   A variant spelling of Chazo. *See* Chazo.

Hazon   A variant spelling of Chazon. *See* Chazon.

Heath   From the Middle English, meaning "wasteland."

Heber   A variant form of Herbert. *See* Herbert.

Hebert   A variant form of Herbert. *See* Herbert.

Hebron   A variant spelling of Chevron. *See* Chevron.

Hector   From the Greek, meaning "anchor."

Hed (הַד)   From the Hebrew, meaning "echo."

Heder (הֶדֶר)   From the Hebrew, meaning "splendor, adornment."

Hedley   From the Old English, meaning "covering" or "covered meadow."

Hedric, Hedrick   From the Old English, meaning "the ruler's or rich man's house." Hendric, Hendrick, and Hendrik are variant forms.

Hedvi   A variant spelling of Chedvi. *See* Chedvi.

Hefer   A variant spelling of Chefer. *See* Chefer.

Heiman (הֵימָן) From the Hebrew, meaning "faithful." In the Bible (II Chronicles 5:12), a Levite musician in the time of King David. Heman is a variant spelling.

Heine, Heinie Variant forms of Henry. See Henry.

Heinrich The German form of Henry. See Henry. Heinz is a pet form. Henach is a Yiddish form.

Heinz A variant form of Hans. Also, a pet form of Heinrich. See Hans *and* Heinrich.

Helbo A variant spelling of Chelbo. See Chelbo.

Heldai A variant spelling of Cheldai. See Cheldai.

Heled A variant spelling of Cheled. See Cheled.

Helek A variant spelling of Chelek. See Chelek.

Helem (הֵלֶם) From the Hebrew, meaning "hammer." In the Bible (I Chronicles 7:35), a member of the tribe of Asher. הָלֶם is a variant spelling.

Helez A variant spelling of Cheletz. See Cheletz.

Helgi Possibly a form of Hel, who in Norse mythology is the goddess of the underworld and death.

Heli From the Greek, meaning "sun." In the Bible (Luke), the father of Joseph (Mary's husband).

Helkai A variant spelling of Chelkai. See Chelkai.

Heller An Old High German form of the Latin, meaning "sun."

Hellmut, Helmut From the Anglo-Saxon name Helmaer, meaning "helmet."

Helm From the Old English, meaning "elm tree." The *h* is aspirated. Or, a form of Helmut. See Helmut.

Heman A variant spelling of Heiman. See Heiman.

Hemdad A variant spelling of Chemdad. See Chemdad.

Hemdan A variant spelling of Chemdan. See Chemdan.

Hen A variant spelling of Chen. See Chen.

Henderson A variant form of Anderson, a patronymic of Andrew. See Andrew.

Hendric, Hendrick, Hendrik Variant forms of Hedric. See Hedric. Hendrik is the Dutch form. Henrik is the Swedish form.

Henech (הֶענֶעך) A Yiddish form of Heinrich. See Heinrich.

Henlee A variant form of Hanley. See Hanley.

Henri The French form of Henry. See Henry.

Henrik A variant Swedish form of Hendrik, the Dutch form of Henry. See Henry.

Henry From the Anglo-Saxon, meaning "ruler of the home, rich lord." In France the name was Henri, and it came to be pronounced Harry. All English kings named Henry were called Harry. Heinrich is a German form of Henry. Hank and Heriot are pet forms. Henson is a patronymic form. Henty is a variant form.

Henson A patronymic form, meaning "son of Henry." *See* Henry.

Henty A variant form of Henry. *See* Henry. Or, from the Old English, meaning "to hunt."

Hepher A variant spelling of Chefer. *See* Chefer.

Herald A variant form of Harold. *See* Harold.

Herbert From the Old High German, meaning "bright in mind and spirit" or "excellent ruler or soldier." Hubert is a variant form.

Heresh A variant spelling of Cheresh. *See* Cheresh.

Heriot A pet form of Henry. *See* Henry. Herriot is a variant spelling.

Herman From the Old High German name Hariman, meaning "army man" or "soldier." Akin to Harman. Hermann is a variant spelling.

Hermann A variant German spelling of Herman. *See* Herman.

Hermon A variant spelling of Chermon. *See* Chermon.

Hermoni A variant form of Chermoni. *See* Chermoni.

Herod (הוֹרדוֹס) From the Greek, meaning "to watch over, protect." Herodotus was a fifth-century B.C.E. Greek historian. Herod the Great was a first-century B.C.E. king of Judea. Herodias is a feminine form.

Herriot A variant spelling of Heriot. *See* Heriot.

Hersch, Herschel Variant spellings of Hersh and Hershel. *See* Hersh *and* Hershel.

Hersh (הֶערש) From the Yiddish, meaning "deer." Hersch, Hirsch, Hirsh, Herschel, Hertz, Herz, Herzl, Heschel, Hesh, and Heshel are variant forms.

Hershel (הֶערשׁעל) A pet form of Hersh. *See* Hersh.

Hertz A variant form of Hersh. *See* Hersh. Herz is a variant spelling.

Hertzel A variant spelling of Herzl. *See* Herzl.

Herve, Hervey French forms of Harvey. *See* Harvey.

Herz A variant spelling of Hertz. *See* Hertz.

Herzl (הֶרצֶל) A pet form of Hersh. *See* Hersh. The name became popular as a result of the activity of Theodor Herzl (1860-1904), who worked for the establishment of a Jewish state. Hertzel is a variant spelling.

Heschel (הֶעשׁעל) A variant form of Hershel. *See* Hershel. Heshel is a variant spelling.

Hesh (הֶעש) A Yiddish pet form of Hersh. *See* Hersh.

Heshel A variant spelling of Heschel. *See* Heschel.

Heskel (הֶעסְקֶעל) A variant form of Haskel. *See* Haskel.

Hesketh Probably a variant form of Hezekia. *See* Hezekia.

Heskiah A variant spelling of Hezkia. *See* Hezkia.

Hevel (הֶבֶל) From the Hebrew, meaning "breath, vapor," or from the Assyrian, meaning "son." In the Bible (Genesis 4), the son of Adam and Eve. Abel is the Anglicized form.

Hever A variant spelling of Chever. *See* Chever.

Hevron A variant spelling of Chevron. *See* Chevron.

Hew A pet form of Hewlett or a variant spelling of Hugh. *See* Hewlett *and* Hugh.

Hewlett From the British, meaning "the fountainhead of a stream." Hew is a pet form.

Heywood From the Old English, meaning "hay field" or "dark forest."

Hezeki A variant form of Hezekia. *See* Hezekia.

Hezekia, Hezekiah Variant spellings of Chizkiya. *See* Chizkiya. Hezeki and probably Hesketh are variant forms.

Hezrai A variant spelling of Chetzrai. *See* Chetzrai.

Hezro A variant spelling of Chetzro. *See* Chetzro.

Hezron A variant spelling of Chetzron. *See* Chetzron.

Hi A pet form for a variety of names, including Hilary, Hiram, and Hyman. Used also as an independent name. High is a variant spelling.

Hicks A patronymic form of Richard, meaning "Richard's son." Evolved from Dick and Dix. May also be a variant form of Isaac, with the aspirated *h* added. Hickson is a variant form.

Hickson A patronymic form of Hicks. *See* Hicks.

Hiel A variant spelling of Chiel. *See* Chiel.

High From the Old English, meaning "high, a hillsite." Also, a variant spelling of Hi. *See* Hi.

Hila (הִלָּא) From the Hebrew, meaning "praise." An abbreviated form of the word *tehila*. Also, a variant form of Hillel. In the Talmud (Yerushalmi Pesachim 8:8), a fourth-century Palestinian scholar also known as Ila. Akin to Hillel. Also spelled הִלָּה.

Hilai (הִלָּאִי) A variant form of Hila. *See* Hila. The name of a seventh-century head (*gaon*) of the academy in Sura, Babylonia.

Hilan (הִלָּן) A variant form of Hila. *See* Hila.

Hilary From the Greek and Latin, meaning "cheerful." Also, from the Anglo-

Saxon, meaning "guardian in war, protector." Used also as a feminine name. Hi is a pet form. *See also* Hillary.

Hili (הִילִי)   A pet form of Hillel. *See* Hillel.

Hilkia, Hilkiah   Variant spellings of Chilkia and Chilkiah.

Hill   From the Anglo-Saxon, meaning "hill, high place." Hillard, Hilliard, Hillary, and Hilton are variant forms. Hilly is a pet form.

Hillard   A variant form of Hill. *See* Hill.

Hillary   A variant spelling of Hilary. Also, a variant form of Hill. *See* Hilary *and* Hill.

Hillel (הִלֵּל)   From the Hebrew, meaning "the shining one" or "praised, famous." In the Bible (Judges 12:13), the father of one of the Judges of Israel. Popularized as a result of the career of the great first-century B.C.E. talmudic scholar Hillel the Great, who was born in Babylonia. Hila, Hilai, and Ila'i are variant forms. Hili and Hilly are pet forms.

Hilliard   A variant form of Hill. *See* Hill.

Hilly   A pet form of Hill and Hillel. *See* Hill *and* Hillel.

Hilmer   From the Old English, meaning "town on the hill." A variant form of Hill. *See* Hill.

Hilton   From the Old English, meaning "town on the hill." A variant form of Hill. *See* Hill.

Hinena   A variant spelling of Chinena. *See* Chinena.

Hiram   A variant spelling of Chiram. *See* Chiram.

Hirsch   A variant spelling of Hersh. *See* Hersh.

Hirsh, Hirshel   Variant spellings of Hersh and Hershel. *See* Hersh.

Hisda   A variant spelling of Chisda. *See* Chisda.

Hitzilyahu (הִצְלִיָהוּ)   From the Hebrew, meaning "God has saved."

Hiya, Hiyah   Variant spellings of Chiya. *See* Chiya.

Hizki   A variant spelling of Chizki. *See* Chizki.

Hob   A variant Middle English form of Rob, Robin, and Robert. *See* Robert. Hopkins is a pet form. Hobs and Hobbs are variant forms.

Hobab   A variant spelling of Chovav. *See* Chovav.

Hobart   From the Danish, meaning "Bart's hill." Hobert is a variant form.

Hobbs   A variant spelling of Hobs. *See* Hobs.

Hobeb   A variant spelling of Chovev. *See* Chovev.

Hobert   A variant form of Hobart. *See* Hobart.

Hobs   A variant form of Hob. *See* Hob. Hobbs is a variant spelling.

Hobson A patronymic form of Robert, meaning "Robert's son." Hob is a variant form of Rob, a nickname for Robert. *See* Hob *and* Robert.

Hockley From the Old English, meaning "meadow (lea) in the highlands."

Hod (הוֹד) From the Hebrew, meaning "splendor, vigor." In the Bible (I Chronicles 7:37), a leader of the tribe of Asher.

Hodding From the Middle Dutch, meaning "bricklayer." Or, from the Anglo-Saxon, meaning "a heath near water."

Hodge, Hodges A variant form of Roger and Rogers, from the Old High German name Hrodger, meaning "famous spear." *See also* Roger.

Hodia, Hodiah Variant spellings of Hodiya. *See* Hodiya.

Hodiya (הוֹדִיָּה) A biblical name derived from the Hebrew, meaning "God is my splendor." Used as a masculine and feminine name in Israel. In the Bible (I Chronicles 4:19), a member of the tribe of Judah. Hodia and Hodiah are variant spellings.

Hoffman From the German, meaning "man at court."

Hogan An Irish form of Haven. *See* Haven.

Hogarth From the Old Norse, meaning "garden on the hill."

Holbrook From the Old English, meaning "brook in the valley."

Holden From the Old English, meaning "valley."

Hollis A variant form of Haley. *See* Haley.

Holm From the Old Norse, meaning "island." Holmes is a variant form.

Holmes A variant form of Holm. *See* Holm.

Holt From the Old English and the German, meaning "wood" or "wooded area."

Homer From the Greek and Latin, meaning "hostage, one who is being led," hence "one who is blind."

Honen A variant spelling of Chonen. *See* Chonen.

Honi A variant spelling of Choni. *See* Choni.

Honio A variant spelling of Chonyo. *See* Chonyo.

Honor, Honore From the Middle English and the Latin, meaning "dignity, esteem." Also, from the Old French, meaning "lord, nobleman."

Honus A variant form of Hans and a short form of Johannes. *See* Johannes. Also, from the Latin, meaning "honor, dignity."

Hopkins A pet form of Hob and Hobs, which are pet forms of Robert. *See* Robert.

Horace From the Greek, meaning "to see, to behold." Horatio is a variant form.

Horatio The Italian form of Horace. *See* Horace.

Hori   A variant spelling of Chori. *See* Chori.

Hornsby   From the Anglo-Saxon, meaning "the place where the heron live."

Horst   From the German, meaning "thicket."

Horton   From the Latin, meaning "garden."

Hosa, Hosah   A variant spelling of Chosa. *See* Chosa.

Hosea   The Anglicized form of Hosheia. *See* Hosheia.

Hoshama (הוֹשָׁמָע)   From the Hebrew, meaning "God hears." In the Bible (I Chronicles 3:18), a son of Yechanya.

Hoshaya (הוֹשַׁעְיָה)   From the Hebrew, meaning "God saves" or "God is salvation. In the Bible (Jeremiah 43:1), the father of a leader in the time of Jeremiah. Also spelled הוֹשַׁעְיָא.   In the Talmud (Eruvin 53a), a Babylonian scholar.

Hosheia (הוֹשֵׁעַ)   From the Hebrew, meaning "salvation." In the Bible (Hosea 1:1), an eighth-century B.C.E. Prophet who prophesied in the Kingdom of Israel during the reign of King Jeroboam. Joshua's original name was Hosheia (Numbers 13:8). Hosea is the Anglicized form.

Hotam   A variant spelling of Chotam. *See* Chotam.

Hothir   A variant spelling of Hotir. *See* Hotir.

Hotir (הוֹתִיר)   From the Hebrew, meaning "wealth" or "abundance." In the Bible (I Chronicles 25:4), a son of Heman, one of King David's musicians. Hothir is a variant spelling.

Hovav   A variant spelling of Chovav. *See* Chovav.

Hovev   A variant spelling of Chovev. *See* Chovev.

Howard   From the Anglo-Saxon, meaning "watchman" or "protector, guardian of the army." Howie is a pet form.

Howe   From the Anglo-Saxon, meaning "hill."

Howel, Howell   From the Old English, meaning "well on the hill."

Howie   A pet form of Howard. *See* Howard.

Hoyt   From the Middle English, meaning "vessel, sloop."

Hozai   A variant spelling of Chozai. *See* Chozai.

Huba   A variant spelling of Chuba. *See* Chuba.

Hubert   A variant form of Herbert. *See* Herbert. Hubie, Huey, Hugh, and Hugo are pet forms.

Hubie   A pet form of Hubert. *See* Hubert.

Hudd, Hudde   Pet forms of Richard common in the thirteenth and fourteenth centuries. *See* Richard.

Hudson   A patronymic form, meaning "son of Hudd." *See* Hudd.

Huey   A pet form of Hubert. *See* Hubert.

Hug, Hugi   Variant spellings of Chug and Chugi. *See* Chug.

Hugh   A pet form of Hubert. *See* Hubert. Used also as an independent name. Hew is a variant spelling. Hulett is a variant form.

Hugo   A pet form of Hubert. *See* Hubert.

Hulett   From the Old English, meaning "hill." Also, a variant form of Hugh. *See* Hugh.

Humbert   From the Old German, meaning "bright home," or from the Old English, meaning "home on a hill."

Humi   A variant spelling of Chumi. *See* Chumi.

Humphrey, Humphry   From the Anglo-Saxon, meaning "protector of the home," or from the Old German, meaning "man of peace."

Huna, Hunah (הוּנָא)   Variant spellings of Chuna and Chunah. *See* Chuna. Also, from the Aramaic, meaning "wealth." In the Talmud (Ketubot 105a), a leading third-century Babylonian scholar. Hunya is a variant form.

Hunt   From the Old English, meaning "to search, hunt."

Hunter   From the Old English, meaning "one who hunts." Akin to Hunt.

Huntington   From the Old English, meaning "town where the hunters gather." Akin to Hunt and Hunter.

Hunya   A variant spelling of Chunya. *See* Chunya.

Hupa   A variant spelling of Chupa. *See* Chupa.

Hupam   A variant spelling of Chupam. *See* Chupam.

Hupim   A variant spelling of Chupim. *See* Chupim.

Hur   A variant spelling of Chur. *See* Chur.

Hurai   A variant spelling of Churai. *See* Churai.

Huri   A variant spelling of Churi. *See* Churi.

Hushai   A variant spelling of Chushai. *See* Chushai.

Huxley   From the Anglo-Saxon, meaning "field of ash trees."

Hy   A pet form of Hyman and Hyland. *See* Hyman *and* Hyland. *See also* Hi.

Hyland   From the Anglo-Saxon, meaning "one who lives on high land." Hy is a pet form.

Hyman   From the Anglo-Saxon, meaning "one who lives in a high place, or on a mountaintop." Also, a variant spelling of Hymen. Not related to Hayim. Hy is a pet form.

Hymen   From Hymenaeus, the Greek god of marriage. Hyman is a variant spelling.

Hyrkanos (הוּרקָנוֹס)   A Greek name of uncertain origin. First used by the Jerusalem-born collector of royal revenues in Egypt in the third century B.C.E.

Also, the surname of John, son and successor of Simon the Hasmonean (135-104 B.C.E.). In the Talmud (Avot 2:8), the father of the Palestinian scholar Eliezer.

Iain   A variant Scottish spelling of Ian. *See* Ian.

Ian   The Scotch form of John. *See* John. Iain is a variant spelling.

Ib   An Old English form of the Hebrew *ab (av)*, meaning, "father."

Iben   A variant form of John. *See* John.

Ibn   From the Aramaic, meaning "son of."

Ichabod   A variant spelling of Ikavod. *See* Ikavod.

Idan (עִידָן)   From the Aramaic, meaning "time, era." Also, a variant form of Eden. *See* Eden.

Idi (אִדִּי)   A variant form of Ido. *See* Ido. In the Talmud (Shabbat 23b), a fourth-century Babylonian scholar.

Ido, Iddo (אִדּוֹ)   From the Hebrew and Aramaic, meaning "to rise up (like a cloud)" or "to reckon time." In the Bible (Ezra 8:17), one of the leaders of the tribe of Judah. Also, from the Arabic, meaning "to be destructive (strong)" or "to count." In the Bible (I Kings 4:14), the father of an officer of King Solomon's court, spelled עֲדֹא. Also, the name of a Levite (I Chronicles 6:6), spelled עִדּוֹ and the grandfather of the Prophet Zechariah (1:1), spelled עִדּוֹא. Idi is a variant form.

Iezer (אִיעֶזֶר)   A contracted form of Aviezer. *See* Aviezer. In the Bible (Numbers 26:30), one of the sons of Gilad.

Igal   A variant spelling of Yigal. *See* Yigal.

Ignatius   From the Greek and Latin, meaning "the fiery or lively one."

Igor   From the Scandinavian, meaning "hero."

Igron (אַגְרוֹן)   A variant form of Agron. *See* Agron.

Ikavod (אִי־כָבוֹד)   From the Hebrew, meaning "without glory" or "without honor." In the Bible (I Samuel 4:21), a son of Pinchas (Phineas) and a grandson of Eli. Ichabod is a variant spelling.

Ike   A pet form of Isaac. *See* Isaac.

Ikesh (עִקֵּשׁ)   From the Hebrew, meaning "crooked, perverted" or "stubborn." In the Bible (II Samuel 23:26), one of King David's warriors. In the Talmud (Berachot 35a), a first-century Babylonian scholar.

Ila (אִלָּעָא)   From the Aramaic, meaning "exalted," and the Arabic, meaning "noble cause." In the Talmud (Sota 49a), a fourth-century scholar. A variant form of Hillel.

Ilai (עִילַי)   From the Hebrew and Aramaic, meaning "superior." In the Bible (I Chronicles 11:29), one of David's warriors.

Ilan (אִילָן)   From the Hebrew, meaning "tree."

Ilan-Tov (אִילָן־טוֹב)   From the Hebrew, meaning "good tree."

Ilbert   From the Old German, meaning "brilliant warrior."

Ilie   A variant form of Elijah or Elisha. *See* Elijah *and* Elisha. Elie is a variant spelling.

Ilija   A variant Slavic form of Elijah. *See* Elijah. Ilya is a variant spelling.

Ilya   A variant spelling of Ilija. *See* Ilija.

Imanuel, Immanuel (עִמָנוּ־אֵל)   From the Hebrew, meaning "God is with us." In the Bible (Isaiah 7:14), a symbolic name given by Isaiah to the child he foretold would be born to the royal family of Judah. Also spelled עִמָנוּאֵל.

Imer (אִמֵר)   A variant form of Imra. *See* Imra. In the Bible (I Chronicles 24:14), a Priest during the time of David.

Imishai (אִמִישַׁי)   From the Hebrew, meaning "my mother is a gift" or "my mother's gift."

Imra (אָמְרָה)   From the Hebrew, meaning "utterance, speech, word." Imer is a variant form.

Imray   A variant form of Amory or Emery. *See* Amory *and* Emery.

Imre   A variant spelling of Imri. *See* Imri.

Imri, Imrie (אִמְרִי)   From the Hebrew, meaning "my utterance." In the Bible (I Cronicles 9:4), a member of the tribe of Judah. Akin to Imra and Imer. Imre is a variant spelling.

Inge   From the Middle English, derived from the Gaelic, meaning "island."

Ingmar   From the Old English, meaning "meadow near the sea."

Ingram   From the British, meaning "angel."

Inman   An Old English occupational name, meaning "innkeeper."

Inness   From the British, meaning "island." Innis is a Cornish form.

Innis   A variant form of Inness. *See* Inness.

Iob   A variant spelling of Yov. *See* Yov. A son of Issachar (Genesis 46:13).

Iona   The Hawaiian form of Jonah. *See* Jonah.

Iosif   A Russian form of Joseph. *See* Joseph.

Ir (עִיר)   From the Hebrew, meaning "city, town." In the Bible (I Chronicles 7:12), a member of the tribe of Benjamin.

Ira (עִירָא)   From the Arabic, meaning "to escape (by being swift)," hence "a young ass." In the Bible (II Samuel 23:26), one of David's soldiers. Irad, Iram, Iran, and Iri are variant forms.

Irad (עִירָד) A variant form of Ira. *See* Ira. In the Bible (Genesis 4:18), a grandson of Cain.

Iram (עִירָם) A variant form of Ira. *See* Ira. In the Bible (Genesis 36:43), one of the princes in Esau's family.

Iran (עִירָן) A variant form of Ira. *See* Ira.

Iri (עִירִי) A variant form of Ira. *See* Ira. In the Bible (I Chronicles 7:7), a son of Bela and a grandson of Benjamin.

Iris (אִירִיס) A member of a family of plants. Used in Israel as a masculine and a feminine name.

Iru (עִירוּ) A variant form of Ira. *See* Ira. In the Bible (I Chronicles 4:15), a son of Caleb.

Irvin From the Gaelic, meaning "beautiful, handsome, fair." Ervin, Irvine, Irving, Irwin, and Irwyn are variant forms.

Irvine A variant form of Irvin. *See* Irvin.

Irving A variant form of Irvin. *See* Irvin. Also, from the Anglo-Saxon, meaning "sea friend." Akin to Marvin and Mervin.

Irwin, Irwyn Variant spellings of Irvin. *See* Irvin.

Is A short form of Isaiah. *See* Isaiah. Also, from the Old British, meaning "lower than" or "below (the woods or village)." Also, a pet form of Isidor. *See* Isidor. Akin to Iz and Izzy.

Isa, Issa Short forms of Isaiah and Isaac. *See* Isaiah *and* Isaac.

Isaac (יִצְחָק) From the Hebrew, meaning "he will laugh." In the Bible (Genesis 21:3), Isaac was the second of the three Patriarchs. In the Talmud (Bava Kama 60b), a third-century Palestinian scholar. One of the most frequently used biblical names in the Talmud. Abraham was not acceptable to the early Christians, but Isaac left a deep impression, and the name was commonly used. Among English jewry of the twelfth-century Isaac was the most popular name. Yitzchak is the exact Hebrew form. Ike is a pet form. Isa and Issa are pet forms.

Isador, Isadore Variant spellings of Isidor. *See* Isidor.

Isaiah From the Hebrew, meaning "God is salvation." The Anglicized form of Yeshaya (יְשַׁעְיָה) and Yeshayahu (יְשַׁעְיָהוּ). One of the most famous of the Hebrew Prophets, Isaiah was born in Jerusalem and began a prophetic career in 740 B.C.E., a career that lasted for forty years. Not used as a talmudic name, it first appears as the name of the eighth-century head *(gaon)* of the academy in Pumbedita, Babylonia. Is, Isa, and Issa are short forms.

Isak A variant spelling of Isaac. *See* Isaac.

Iser A variant spelling of Isser. *See* Isser.

Ish-Baal (אִישׁ־בַּעַל) A variant form of Ish-Boshet. *See* Ish-Boshet.

Ish-Boshet (אִישׁ־בֹּשֶׁת)   From the Hebrew, meaning "man of Baal" or "man of shame." In the Bible (II Samuel 2:8), a son of King Saul. Eshball and Ish-Baal are variant forms.

Ish-Chayil (אִישׁ־חַיִל)   From the Arabic, meaning "horseman," or from the Hebrew, meaning "man of strength, man of war."

Ish-Hod (אִישׁ־הוֹד)   From the Hebrew, meaning "glory, majesty." In the Bible (I Chronicles 7:18), a member of the tribe of Manasseh.

Ishi   A variant spelling of Yishi. See Yishi.

Ishma   A variant spelling of Yishma. See Yishma.

Ishmael (יִשְׁמָעֵאל)   The Anglicized form of the Hebrew, meaning "God will hear." In the Bible (Genesis 16:11), the son of Abraham and the brother of Isaac. Yishmael is the exact Hebrew equivalent. In the Talmud (Gittin 58a), a second-century scholar. Strangely, Abraham is not used in the Talmud, but Ishmael is a common name.

Isho   A variant spelling of Yisho. See Yisho.

Ish-Sechel (אִישׁ־שֶׂכֶל)   From the Hebrew, meaning "man of understanding, intelligent person." In the Bible (Ezra 8:18), a Levite in Ezra's time.

Ish-Shalom (אִישׁ־שָׁלוֹם)   From the Hebrew, meaning "man of peace."

Ish-Tov (אִישׁ־טוֹב)   From the Hebrew, meaning "good man." In the Bible (II Samuel 10:6), an enemy of King David. Also spelled Ishtov.

Isidor, Isidore   From the Greek, meaning "gift of Isis." Isis was the Egyptian moon goddess. Isador and Isadore are later spellings. Is, Iz, Izzie, and Izzy are pet forms.

Ismar   A variant form of Itamar. See Itamar.

Israel (יִשְׂרָאֵל)   The Anglicized form of the Hebrew, meaning either "prince of God" or "wrestled with God." The name was given to Jacob, the third of the three Patriarchs, after wrestling with the angel of God (Genesis 32:28). Adopted as a synonym for the Jewish nation and as a place-name for the northern part of Palestine, where the ten tribes of Israel lived. Yisrael is the exact Hebrew form. See Yisrael. Strangely, Yisrael is not used as a talmudic name. It first appears as the name of the eleventh-century head (gaon) of the academy in Sura, Babylonia.

Issachar (יִשָּׂשׂכָר)   From the Hebrew, meaning "there is a reward." In the Bible (Genesis 30:18), a son of Jacob and Leah, head of one of the twelve tribes of Israel.

Isser (אִיסֶר)   A Yiddish form of Yisrael (Israel). See Yisrael and Israel. Issi is a pet form. Isur and Issur are variant spellings.

Issi (אִיסִי)   A pet form of Isser. See Isser. Also, a pet form of Yosef (Joseph). See Yosef. In the Talmud (Moed Katan 20b), the father of a third-century Babylonian scholar. Assa, Yosa, and Yosi are variant forms.

Isur, Issur   Variant spellings of Isser. See Isser.

Itai (אִתַּי)   From the Hebrew, meaning "friendly, compassionate," or, literally, "God is with me." In the Bible (II Samuel 23:29), one of King David's warriors. Ittai is a variant spelling.

Itamar (אִיתָמָר)   From the Hebrew, meaning "island of palms." In the Bible (Exodus 6:23), the youngest son of Aaron and a nephew of Moses. Ismar is a variant form. Ithamar and Ittamar are variant spellings.

Itche   A Yiddish form of Yitzchak. See Yitzchak (Israel).

Ithamar   A variant spelling of Itamar. See Itamar.

Ithiel   A variant spelling of Itiel. See Itiel.

Iti (אִתִּי)   From the Hebrew, meaning "with me." Akin to Itai. A short form of Itiel. See Itiel.

Itiel (אִיתִיאֵל)   From the Hebrew, meaning "God is with me." In the Bible (Nehemiah 11:7), a member of the tribe of Benjamin. Iti is a short form.

Ittai   A variant spelling of Itai. See Itai.

Ittamar   A variant spelling of Itamar. See Itamar.

Itzig (אִיצִיג)   A variant form of Itzik. See Itzik.

Itzik (אִיצִיק)   A Yiddish form of Yitzchak (Isaac). See Yitzchak.

Ivair   A variant form of Ivar. See Ivar.

Ival   A variant form of Ewald. See Ewald.

Ivan   The Russian form of John, meaning "grace." See John. Yvan is a variant spelling. Yvon is a variant form.

Ivar   A variant spelling of Ivor. See Ivor. Ivair is a variant form.

Ive   From the Middle English, meaning "climbing vine." Irving, Iver, and Ivy are variant forms.

Iver   A variant form of Ive. See Ive.

Ives   A variant spelling of Yves. See Yves.

Iving   A variant form of Ive. See Ive.

Ivol   A variant form of Ewald. See Ewald.

Ivor   From the Latin, meaning "ivory," and the Egyptian, meaning "elephant ivory."

Ivri (עִבְרִי)   From the Hebrew, meaning "Hebrew." In the Bible (I Chronicles 24:27), a Levite of the family of Merari. Abraham was called Ivri because he came from the "other side (ever)" of the Euphrates River. See also Ever.

Ivtzan (אִבְצָן)   From the Hebrew, meaning "coated with zinc."

Ivy   A variant form of Ive. See Ive.

Iyar (אִיָּר, אִיָּיר)   Probably the Assyrian form of the Hebrew or, meaning "light." The name of the second month in the Jewish religious calendar. Also known in the Bible (I Kings 6:11) as the month of *Ziv*, meaning "brightness of flowers." Taurus is the zodiacal sign of Iyar. Iyari is a variant form.

Iyari   A variant form of Iyar. *See* Iyar.

Iyov (אִיּוֹב)   The Hebrew form of Job. *See* Job.

Iz   A pet form of Isidor. *See* Isidor.

Izhar   A variant spelling of Yitzhar. *See* Yitzhar.

Izri   A variant spelling of Yitzri. *See* Yitzri.

Izzie, Izzy   Pet forms of Isidor. *See* Isidor.

Jaala   A variant spelling of Yaala. *See* Yaala.

Jabal   A variant spelling of Yaval. *See* Yaval.

Jabesh   A variant spelling of Yavesh. *See* Yavesh.

Jabez   A variant spelling of Yabetz. *See* Yabetz.

Jacinto   A Spanish pet form of Jacob. *See* Jacob.

Jack   A pet form of Jacob. *See* Jacob. Also used as a nickname for John. *See* John. Jackson is a patronymic form.

Jackie   A pet form of Jack. *See* Jack.

Jackman   A variant form of Jack and Jacob, meaning "servant of Jack." *See* Jack.

Jackson   A patronymic form, meaning "son of Jack" or "son of Jacob." *See* Jack *and* Jacob.

Jacob (יַעֲקֹב)   The Anglicized form of Yaakov. Jakob is a variant spelling. From the Hebrew, meaning "held by the heel, supplanted, or protected." The third of the three Patriarchs and the father of the twelve sons who were founders of the tribes of Israel. The Book of Genesis (32:28) describes Jacob's encounter with an angel and how he was given the name. Among the many variations of the name that have developed over the centuries, James and Jacques are the most popular. Jake, Jack, and Jackie are popular pet forms. Jackson and Jakon are patronymic forms.

Jacobo   A Spanish form of Jacob. *See* Jacob.

Jacopo   An Italian form of Jacob. *See* Jacob.

Jacque, Jacques   French forms of Jacob. *See* Jacob.

Jada   A variant spelling of Yada. *See* Yada.

Jadin   A variant spelling of Yadin. *See* Yadin.

Jadon   A variant spelling of Yadon. *See* Yadon.

Jadua   A variant spelling of Yadua. *See* Yadua.

Jaeson   A variant spelling of Jason. *See* Jason.

Jaime   A Spanish pet form of James. *See* James.

Jaimie   A pet form of James. *See* James. Commonly used as a feminine name. Jamie is a variant spelling.

Jair   A variant spelling of Yair. *See* Yair.

Jake   A pet form of Jacob. *See* Jacob.

Jakim   A variant spelling of Yakim. *See* Yakim.

Jakob   A variant spelling of Jacob. *See* Jacob.

Jakon   A patronymic form of the Hebrew name Jacob, meaning "Jack's son." *See* Jack *and* Jacob.

Jalon   A variant spelling of Yalon. *See* Yalon.

James (יַעֲקֹב)   The English form of the Hebrew Jacob (Yaakov). *See* Jacob. Jamie, Jan, Jim, Jimm, Jimmie, and Jimmy are popular pet forms.

Jamie   A Scottish pet form of James. *See* James.

Jamin   A variant spelling of Yamin. *See* Yamin.

Jan   A form of John. *See* John. Also, a pet form of James. *See* James. *See also* Yancy.

Janai, Jannai   Variant spellings of Yanai. *See* Yanai.

Jannie   A variant form of John used in South Africa. *See* John.

Janny   A variant form of John. *See* John.

Janus   From the Latin, meaning "gate, arched passageway."

Japhet, Japheth   Variant spellings of Yefet. *See* Yefet.

Japhia   A variant spelling of Yafia. *See* Yafia.

Jardine   From the Anglo-Saxon and French, meaning "garden."

Jareb   A variant spelling of Yarev. *See* Yarev.

Jared   A variant spelling of Yared. *See* Yared. Jarrod is a variant spelling.

Jarib   A variant spelling of Yariv. *See* Yariv.

Jaron   A variant spelling of Yaron. *See* Yaron.

Jarrell   A variant form of Gerald. *See* Gerald. Jarrel is a variant form.

Jarrett   A variant form of Garret. *See* Garret.

Jarrod   A variant spelling of Jared. *See* Jared.

Jarvis   From the Old English, meaning "battle spear" or "conqueror." Gary is a variant form. Jary is a pet form. Jervis is a variant form.

Jary   A pet form of Jarvis. *See* Jarvis.

Jascha   A Russian form of James and Jacob. *See* James *and* Jacob.

Jason   From the Greek, meaning "healer." Jaeson is a variant spelling. Jason, whose name was also Joshua, was a famous High Priest in the second century B.C.E.

Jaspar, Jasper   From the Greek, meaning "semiprecious stone." Also, from the Persian, meaning "treasured secret." Kaspar is a variant German form.

Jay   From the Old French and Latin, referring to a bird in the crow family. Gaius is a variant form. Also, from the Anglo-Saxon, meaning "happy."

Jaziz   A variant spelling of Yaziz. *See* Yaziz.

Jean   The French form of John. *See* John.

Jeb   Probably a pet form of Jacob. *See* Jacob.

Jed   From the Arabic, meaning "hand." Also, a short form of Jared and Jedidia. *See* Jared *and* Jedidia.

Jedaia, Jedaiah   Variant spellings of Yedaya. *See* Yedaya.

Jedidia, Jedidiah   Variant spellings of Yedidya. *See* Yedidya.

Jedo   A variant spelling of Yido. *See* Yido.

Jef, Jeff   Short forms of Jeffery and Geoffrey. *See* Jeffery *and* Geoffrey.

Jefferies   A patronymic form, meaning "son of Jeffery." *See* Jeffery.

Jefferson   A patronymic form, meaning "son of Jeffers or Jeffery."

Jeffery, Jefferey   Variant spellings of Geoffrey. *See* Geoffrey. Jeffrey is a variant spelling. Jef and Jeff are short forms. Jefferies and Jefferson are patronymic forms.

Jeffie   A pet form of Jeffery. *See* Jeffery.

Jeffrey   A variant spelling of Jeffery. *See* Jeffery.

Jeffries   A variant spelling of Jefferies. *See* Jefferies.

Jeffry   A variant spelling of Jeffery. *See* Jeffery.

Jehiel   A variant spelling of Yechiel. *See* Yechiel.

Jehoash   A variant spelling of Yehoash. *See* Yehoash.

Jehoiachin   A variant spelling of Yehoyachin. *See* Yehoyachin.

Jehoiakim   A variant spelling of Yehoyakim. *See* Yehoyakim.

Jehoram   A variant spelling of Yehoram. *See* Yehoram.

Jehu   A variant spelling of Yehu. *See* Yehu.

Jekutiel, Jekuthiel   Variant spellings of Yekutiel. *See* Yekutiel.

Jephta, Jephthah   Anglicized forms of Yiftach. *See* Yiftach.

Jerald   A variant spelling of Gerald. *See* Gerald.

Jere   A variant spelling of Jerry. *See* Jerry. Also, a short form of Jeremiah. *See* Jeremiah.

Jered   A variant spelling of Yered. *See* Yered.

Jeremai   A variant spelling of Yeremai. *See* Yeremai.

Jeremiah (יִרְמְיָהוּ)   From the Hebrew, meaning "God will loosen (the bonds)" or "God will uplift." Jeremiah is one of the six Hebrew Prophets whose name is mentioned as a personal name in the Talmud. He belonged to a family of Priests living near Jerusalem, and began to prophesy in 625 B.C.E. The Greek New Testament records Jeremiah as Jeremias. Jeremy is a pet form. Yirmeyahu is the exact Hebrew form. Jere is a short form.

Jeremias   The Greek form of Jeremiah. *See* Jeremiah.

Jeremy   A pet form of Jeremiah. *See* Jeremiah.

Jeria, Jeriah   Variant spellings of Yeriah. *See* Yeriah.

Jeriel   A variant spelling of Yeriel. *See* Yeriel.

Jeroboam   A variant spelling of Yeravam. *See* Yeravam.

Jerold   A variant spelling of Gerald. *See* Gerald. Jerrald and Jerrold are variant spellings. Jere, Jerre, and Jerry are pet forms.

Jerome   A variant spelling of Gerome, meaning "of holy fame" or "sacred name." Jerram is a variant form. Jere, Jerre, and Jerry are pet forms.

Jerrald   A variant spelling of Jerold. *See* Jerold.

Jerram   A variant form of Jerome. *See* Jerome.

Jerre   A variant spelling of Jerry used in Sicily. *See* Jerry. *See also* Jere.

Jerrel   A variant form of Jarrell and Gerald. *See* Jarrell *and* Gerald.

Jerrold   A variant spelling of Jerold. *See* Jerold.

Jerry   A pet form of Jerold, Jerome, or Jeremiah. *See* Jerold, Jerome, *and* Jeremiah. Jere is a variant spelling.

Jervis   A variant form of Jarvis. *See* Jarvis.

Jesher   A variant spelling of Yesher. *See* Yesher.

Jess   A short form of Jesse. *See* Jesse.

Jessamine   A variant form of Jesse. *See* Jesse.

Jesse (יִשַׁי)   From the Hebrew, meaning "wealthy" or "gift." Yishai is the exact Hebrew equivalent. *See* Yishai. Jessamine is a variant form. Jess is a short form.

Jesus   A variant form of the Hebrew name Yehoshua (Joshua). *See* Joshua *and* Yeshu.

Jether   A variant spelling of Yeter. *See* Yeter.

Jethro (יִתְרוֹ)   From the Hebrew, meaning "abundance, riches." Yitro is the exact Hebrew equivalent. *See* Yitro. Jett is a pet form.

Jett   A pet form of Jethro. *See* Jethro.

Jido   A variant spelling of Yido. *See* Yido.

Jim, Jimm   Pet forms of James which evolved by shortening the long *a* sound. *See* James.

Jimbo   A pet form of James, probably a short form of Jimboy. *See* James.

Jimmie, Jimmy   Pet forms of James. *See* James.

Joab   A variant spelling of Yoav. *See* Yoav.

Joachim   A variant form of Yehoyakim. *See* Yehoyakim.

Joakim   A variant form of Yehoyakim. *See* Yehoyakim.

Joaquin   A Spanish form of Yehoyachin. *See* Yehoyachin.

Joash   A variant spelling of Yoash. *See* Yoash.

Job (אִיּוֹב)   From the Hebrew, meaning "hated, oppressed." The Anglicized form of Iyov. *See* Iyov.

Joce   A variant form of Joseph. *See* Joseph.

Jody   A pet form of Joseph. *See* Joseph.

Joe, Joey   Pet forms of Joseph. *See* Joseph.

Joel   From the Hebrew, meaning "God is willing." Yoel is the exact Hebrew form. *See* Yoel.

Joela, Joelah   Variant spellings of Yoela. *See* Yoela. Used also as feminine names.

Joezer   A variant spelling of Yoezer. *See* Yoezer.

Joffre   The French form of Geoffrey. *See* Geoffrey.

Johanan   A variant spelling of Yochanan. *See* Yochanan.

Johannes   A Middle Latin form of John. *See* John.

John (יוֹחָנָן)   The Anglicized form of Yochanan. *See* Yochanan. John is a contraction of Johanan. Variant forms of John appear in many languages: Hans, Ian, Ivan, Jan, Jean, and Sean are among the most popular. Jack is a popular nickname for John. Johnnie, Johnny, and Jon are popular pet forms.

Johnnie, Johnny   Pet forms of John. *See* John.

Jojo   A pet form of Joseph. *See* Joseph.

Jokim   A variant spelling of Yokim. *See* Yokim.

Jon   A pet form of John or Jonathan. *See* John *and* Jonathan.

Jona, Jonah (יוֹנָה)   From the Hebrew, meaning "dove." Yona is the exact Hebrew form. *See* Yona. Iona is the Hawaiian form.

Jonas   The Greek form of Jonah, also used in the Latin (Vulgate) translation of the Bible. *See* Jonah.

Jonathan (יוֹנָתָן)   From the Hebrew, meaning "God has given" or "gift of God." The exact Hebrew form is Yehonatan, and Yonatan is a short form. *See* Yehonatan. Jonathon is a variant spelling. Jon, Jondi, Jonji, Jon-Jon, Jonni, Jonnie, and Jonny are pet forms.

Jonathon A variant spelling of Jonathan. *See* Jonathan.

Jonji A pet form of Jonathan. *See* Jonathan.

Jon-Jon A pet form of Jonathan. *See* Jonathan.

Jonni, Jonnie, Jonny Pet forms of Jonathan. *See* Jonathan.

Jophrey A variant form of Geoffrey. *See* Geoffrey.

Jora A variant spelling of Yora. *See* Yora.

Jorai A variant spelling of Yorai. *See* Yorai.

Joram A variant spelling of Yoram. *See* Yoram.

Jordan (יַרְדֵן) The exact Hebrew form is Yarden. *See* Yarden. Jordy, Jori, and Jory are pet forms.

Jordy A pet form of Jordan. *See* Jordan.

Jorge A Spanish form of George. *See* George.

Jori, Jory Pet forms of Jordan. *See* Jordan.

Jose (יוֹסִי) An Aramaic form of Joseph popular in talmudic times (from the second to the sixth centuries). Also popular today in Spanish-speaking countries. *See* Joseph.

Joseph (יוֹסֵף) From the Hebrew, meaning "He (God) will add or increase." Yosef is the exact Hebrew form. *See* Yosef. Iosif, Joca, Jose, Josephus, and Josephy are variant forms. Jody, Joe Joey, and Jojo are pet forms.

Josephus (יוֹסְפוּס) The Latin form of Joseph. *See* Joseph. Flavius Josephus is the name of a famous Jewish soldier and historian who lived in the first century *(circa* 30-100). In Hebrew he was known as Yosef ben Matityahu ha-Kohen.

Josephy A variant form of Joseph. *See* Joseph.

Josh A pet form of Joshua. *See* Joshua.

Joshafat A variant spelling of Yoshafat. *See* Yoshafat.

Joshua (יְהוֹשֻׁעַ) From the Hebrew, meaning "the Lord is my salvation." In the post-biblical period Joshua was one of the most commonly used biblical names. During the Greek period, Jews in the upper strata of society whose Hebrew name was Joshua used the secular name Jason. Joshua was the name of many High Priests. The name Jesus is a variant form of Joshua. Josh is a popular pet form.

Josiah (יֹאשִׁיָהוּ) From the Hebrew, meaning "fire of the Lord." In the Bible, Josiah was a king of Judah (637-608 B.C.E.) who ascended the throne at the age of eight, upon the murder of his father, Amon. Yoshiyahu is the exact Hebrew form. *See* Yoshiyahu.

Josiphia, Josiphiah Variant spellings of Yosifya. *See* Yosifya.

Joslyn A variant form of the Latin name Justus. *See* Justus.

Jotham   A variant spelling of Yotam. *See* Yotam.

Jovett   A French pet form, meaning "beloved God."

Joyce   From the Latin name Jocosa, meaning "merry." Used mostly as a feminine name.

Joyner   From the Old French, meaning "to join together." An occupational name for a carpenter who finishes and joins wood planks.

Jozavad   A variant form of Yehozavad. *See* Yehozavad.

Jubal   A variant spelling of Yuval. *See* Yuval.

Jud   A variant spelling of Judd. *See* Judd.

Judah (יְהוּדָה)   From the Hebrew, meaning "praise." An Anglicized form of Yehuda. *See* Yehuda. Jud, Judd, Judas, Jude, Judea, and Judson are variant forms.

Judas   The Latin form of Judah. *See* Judah. In the New Testament, Judas is a disciple who betrayed Jesus. Judas Maccabaeus was the hero of the Hasmonean revolt against the Syrian-Greeks who ruled Palestine in the second century B.C.E.

Judd   A variant form of Judah. *See* Judah. Jud is a variant spelling.

Jude   A variant form of Judah. *See* Judah. The name of an apostle in the New Testament.

Judea   A variant form of Judah. *See* Judah. *See also* Yehuda *and* Yehudi.

Judson   A patronymic form of Judah, meaning "Judah's (or Judd's) son." *See* Judah.

Jule, Jules   Variant forms of Julian or Julius. *See* Julian *and* Julius.

Julian   From the Greek, meaning "soft-haired, mossy-bearded," having the symbolic meaning of "youth." Jule, Jules, and Julio are variant forms.

Julio   The Spanish form of Julian and Julius. *See* Julian *and* Julius.

Julius   A variant form of Julian. *See* Julian. Popularized by the Romans, who named the month in which Julius Caesar was born (July). The Julian calendar was named after him.

Junior   A contracted form of the Latin *juvenior*, meaning "young." Possibly a variant form of Junius.

Junius   From the Latin, meaning "young lion." Junior may be a variant form of Junius.

Jurgen   A Germanic form of George. *See* George. Akin to the Danish name Jorgen.

Justin   A variant form of Justus. *See* Justus. Jut is a short form.

Justino   An Italian form of Justus. *See* Justus.

Justus From the Latin, meaning "just, honest." Joslyn, Justin, Justino, and Yustus are variant forms. Jut is a short form.

Jut A short form of Justus and Justin. *See* Justus *and* Justin.

Kadi (כַּדִי) From the Hebrew, meaning "my pitcher." In the Talmud (Horayot 8a), a talmudic scholar of the third century.

Kadish, Kaddish (קַדִּישׁ) From the Hebrew, meaning "sanctification, holy." Akin to Kadosh.

Kadmiel (קַדְמִיאֵל) From the Hebrew, meaning "God is my east" or "God is ancient." In the Bible (Ezra 2:40), the head of a Levite family who returned with Zerubbabel to Judah from the Babylonian Exile.

Kadosh (קָדוֹשׁ) From the Hebrew, meaning "holy, holy person." Akin to Kadish.

Kadur (כַּדּוּר) From the Hebrew, meaning "ball."

Kaduri (כַּדּוּרִי) From the Hebrew, meaning "my ball."

Kahana (כַּהֲנָא) From the Aramaic, meaning "Priest." In the Talmud (Yevamot 102a), a third-century Babylonian scholar.

Kailil (כַּיְילִיל) A variant form of Kalil. *See* Kalil. In the Talmud (Zevachim 118b), the father of Abaye, the noted scholar.

Kalai (קָלָי) From the Aramaic, meaning "curse." In the Bible (Nehemiah 12:20), a Priest during the reign of King Jehoiakim.

Kalev (כָּלֵב) From the Hebrew, meaning "dog" or "heart." Also, from the Assyrian, meaning "messenger" or "Priest," and from the Arabic, meaning "bold, brave." In the Bible (Numbers 13:6), Kalev ben Yefuneh was one of the twelve scouts sent out by Moses to explore the Promised Land. He became the leader of Israel after the death of Moses. Caleb is the Anglicized spelling.

Kalil (כָּלִיל) From the Greek, meaning "beautiful." Also, from the Hebrew, meaning "crown, wreath." Kailil and Kallie are variant forms. Kalila is a feminine form.

Kallie A variant form of Kalil. *See* Kalil.

Kalman (קַלְמָן) A short form of Kalonymos. *See* Kalonymos.

Kalonymos, Kalonymus (קָלוֹנִימוֹס) Variant forms of the Latin name Clement, meaning "merciful" or "gracious." Also, from the Greek, meaning "beautiful name." Klonimos is a variant spelling. In the Talmud (Avoda Zara 11a), the father of Onkelos, who converted to Judaism. Also, the name of a ninth-century poet. A popular name after the fourteenth century, following the death of the famous author and translator Kalonymos ben Kalonymos, who lived in France and Italy and translated many Arabic works into Hebrew and Latin for King Robert of Naples. According to the historian Graetz, Kalonymos is a corrupted form of Clemens, and the proselyte Onkelos was Flavius Clemens.

Kalton From the Greek, meaning "beautiful town."

Kalul (כָּלוּל) From the Hebrew, meaning "whole, perfect."

Kamus (כָּמוּס) From the Hebrew, meaning "hidden."

Kane A variant form of Keene. See Keene. Kayne is a variant spelling.

Kaneyahu (כָּנְיָהוּ) From the Hebrew, meaning "established by God." A variant form of Jehoiachin (Jeremiah 22:24).

Kani A variant form of Keene. See Keene. Or, a pet form of Kaniel. See Kaniel.

Kaniel (קָנִיאֵל) From the Hebrew, meaning "God is my reed (support)." Also, from the Arabic, meaning "spear." Kani is a pet form.

Kapara (קַפָּרָא) From the Aramaic, meaning "atonement." In the Talmud (Yevamot 32a), a first-century Palestinian scholar.

Karcha (קַרְחָה) An Aramaic form of Kareach. See Kareach. In the Talmud (Berachot 2b), the father of Joshua, a prominent first-century Palestinian scholar.

Kareach (קָרֵחַ) From the Hebrew, meaning "bald." In the Bible (II Kings 25:23), the father of an army commander in the time of Gedaliah, governor of Judah. Kareah is a variant spelling.

Kareem From the Arabic, meaning "noble, exalted." Karim is a variant spelling.

Karel A variant form of Carol and Charles. See Charles.

Karim A variant spelling of Kareem. See Kareem.

Karin (קָרִין) From the Aramaic, meaning "horn."

Kariv (קָרִיב) From the Aramaic, meaning "near, nearness" or "relative."

Karkom (כַּרְכֹּם) From the Hebrew, meaning "saffron."

Karl A variant spelling for Carl. See Carl.

Karmel (כַּרְמֶל) From the Hebrew, meaning "vineyard." Also spelled Carmel.

Karmeli (כַּרְמְלִי) From the Hebrew, meaning "my vineyard." Also spelled Carmeli.

Karmi (כַּרְמִי) From the Hebrew, meaning "my garden, my vineyard." In the Bible (Genesis 46:9), a son of Reuben and a grandson of Jacob. Also spelled Carmi.

Karmiel (כַּרְמִיאֵל) From the Hebrew, meaning "God is my vineyard" or "God is my protection." Also spelled Carmiel.

Karna (קַרְנָא) From the Aramaic, meaning "horn." In the Talmud (Kidushin 44b), a third-century Babylonian scholar.

Karni (קַרְנִי) From the Hebrew, meaning "my horn."

Karniel (קַרְנִיאֵל) From the Hebrew, meaning "God is my horn."

Karol, Karole Variant spellings of Carol. See Carol.

Kashti (קַשְׁתִּי) From the Hebrew, meaning "my bow" or "my rainbow."

Kasriel A variant spelling of Katriel. See Katriel.

Katan (קָטָן) From the Hebrew, meaning "small." In the Bible (Ezra 8:12), one of the Babylonian Exile returnees was named Hakatan, meaning "little one." The name of American clergyman Cotton Mather (1663-1728) is probably derived from the Hebrew word *katan*. His father's name was Increase Mather.

Kati (כַּתִּי) A pet form of Katriel used in Israel. See Katriel.

Katriel (כַּתְרִיאֵל) From the Hebrew, meaning "God is my crown." Kasriel is a variant pronunciation. Kati is a pet form.

Katzir (קָצִיר) From the Hebrew, meaning "harvest."

Kaufman, Kaufmann From the German, meaning "buyer." Also, a short form of Yaakovman (Yaakofman). See Yaakov.

Kavika The Hawaiian form of David. See David.

Kavud (כָּבוּד) From the Hebrew, meaning "honored."

Kay From the Greek, meaning "rejoicing," or from the Anglo-Saxon, meaning "fortified place" or "warden, keeper." Kay may also be derived from the Latin, meaning "gay." Popularized by the Welsh, who converted it into Kai. Caius (or Gaius) was the first name, the praenomen, of Julius Caesar.

Kayam (קַיָם) From the Hebrew, meaning "established."

Kayin (קַיִן) The Hebrew form of Cain. See Cain.

Kayne A variant spelling of Kane. See Kane.

Kaz A pet form of Cassius. See Cassius. Chaz is a variant spelling.

Kean, Keane Variant forms of Keene. See Keene.

Kedar (קֵדָר) From the Hebrew, meaning "black, swarthy" or "dark." In the Bible (Genesis 25:13), a son of Ishmael and a grandson of Abraham.

Kedem (קֶדֶם) From the Hebrew, meaning "east."

Kedma (קֵדְמָה) From the Hebrew, meaning "eastward." In the Bible (Genesis 25:15), a son of Ishmael and a grandson of Abraham.

Keefe An Irish form of the Arabic, meaning "well-being, peacefulness (induced by smoking narcotics)." Keever is a variant form.

Keena A variant form of Keene. See Keene.

Keenan A variant form of Keene. See Keene.

Keene   From the Old English, meaning "wise, learned," and the German, meaning "bold." Kane, Kani, Kean, Keane, Keena, and Keenan are variant forms.

Keever   A variant form of Keefe. See Keefe.

Kefir (כְּפִיר)   From the Hebrew, meaning "cub, young lion."

Kehat (קְהָת)   From the Hebrew, meaning "faint, weak." Also, a variant form of Kohelet. See Kohelet. In the Bible (Genesis 46:11), a son of Levi and a grandson of Jacob. Kehath is a variant spelling. Kohath is a variant form.

Kehath   A variant spelling of Kehat. See Kehat.

Keith   Akin to the Old Gaelic word for wood, although some authorities claim it means "wind." A popular name in Scotland.

Kelaya (קְלָיָה)   From the Aramaic, meaning "parched grain." In the Bible (Ezra 10:23), a Levite. Also, a variant form of Kelita. See Kelita.

Kelcey   A variant spelling of Kelsey. See Kelsey.

Kelita (קְלִיטָא)   From the Aramaic, meaning "to be stunted, drawn in" or "to harbor." In the Bible (Nehemiah 8:7), a Levite who was a contemporary of Ezra. Also known as Kelaya (Ezra 10:23).

Kellog, Kellogg   Variant forms of Kelly. See Kelly.

Kellow   A variant form of Kelly. See Kelly.

Kelly   From the Old English, meaning "keel, ship." Also, from the Dutch and the Old Norse, meaning "stream, river, inlet." Kellog, Kellogg, and Kellow are variant forms

Kelsey   A variant form of Kelson. See Kelson. Kelcey is a variant spelling.

Kelson   From the Middle Dutch, meaning "boat." Kelsey is a variant form.

Kelton   From the Old English, meaning "keel town" or "the town where ships are built."

Keluv (כְּלוּב)   From the Hebrew, meaning "basket, cage." In the Bible (1 Chronicles 27:26), the father of King David's prefect in charge of agriculture.

Keluvai (כְּלוּבַי)   From the Aramaic, meaning "basket, cage." In the Bible (I Chronicles 2:9), a member of the tribe of Judah.

Kelvin, Kelwin, Kelwyn   From the Anglo-Saxon, meaning "friend or lover of ships."

Kemp   From the Anglo-Saxon, meaning "Saxon lord" or "royalty."

Kemuel (קְמוּאֵל)   From the Hebrew, meaning "to stand up for God." In the Bible (Genesis 22:21), a son of Nachor, Abraham's brother.

Ken   A pet form of Kenneth. See Kenneth. Also, an independent name derived from the Scotch and meaning either "to know" or "chief, champion."

Kenan (קֵינָן)   From the Hebrew, meaning "acquire, possess." In the Bible (Genesis 5:9), a son of Enosh and a great-grandson of Adam.

Kenanya (כְּנַנְיָה) From the Hebrew, meaning "upright, honest" or "God's establishment." In the Bible (I Chronicles 15:27), a Levite in charge of the Temple choir.

Kenaz (קְנַז) From the Hebrew, meaning "reed," or from the Arabic, meaning "spear" or "to hunt." In the Bible (Genesis 36:11), a son of Elifaz and a grandson of Esau.

Kendal, Kendall From the Celtic, meaning "ruler of the valley." Also, the name of a green wool cloth woven in Kendal, England.

Kendig A variant form of Kendrick. See Kendrick.

Kendrick From the Anglo-Saxon, meaning "royal." Kendig is a variant form.

Kene A variant spelling of Kenny, the pet form of Kenneth. See Kenneth. Also, from the the Old English, meaning "brave." Akin to Keene.

Kenley From the Anglo-Saxon, meaning "ruler of the meadow."

Kenman From the Old English, meaning "leadman, ruler."

Kenn A pet form of Kenneth. See Kenneth.

Kennard A variant form of Kennedy. See Kennedy.

Kennedy From the Old English, meaning "royal." Kennard is a variant form.

Kenneth From the Celtic and Scotch, meaning "comely, handsome." Kent, Kenton, and Kenyon are variant forms. Ken, Kenn, and Kenny are pet forms.

Kenny A pet form of Kenneth. See Kenneth. Kenne is a variant spelling.

Kenric, Kenrick From the British and the Anglo-Saxon, meaning "royal."

Kent A variant form of Kenneth. See Kenneth. Kenton is a variant form.

Kenton A variant form of Kent and Kenneth. See Kenneth.

Kenward From the Old English, meaning "brave guard."

Kenyon A variant form of Kenneth. See Kenneth.

Kerby A variant spelling of Kirby. See Kirby.

Kerem (כֶּרֶם) From the Hebrew, meaning "vineyard."

Keren (קֶרֶן) From the Hebrew, meaning "horn."

Kermit From the Dutch, meaning "church."

Kern From the Old Irish, meaning "band of soldiers."

Kerr From the Norse, meaning "marshland." Carr is a variant spelling. Kerry is a variant form.

Kerry A variant form of Kerr. See Kerr.

Kerwin From the Old English, meaning "friend of the marshlands."

Keskel (קֶעסקֶעל) A Yiddish variant form of Yechezkel (Ezekiel). See Yechezkel.

Kester   A variant English form of Christopher. *See* Christopher.

Keter (כֶּתֶר)   From the Hebrew, meaning "crown."

Ketina (קְטִינָא)   From the Hebrew and Aramaic, meaning "small, minor." In the Talmud (Menachot 41a), a third-century Babylonian scholar.

Ketti   A variant form of the Old English surnames Kettle and Kittle, meaning "cauldron (of the gods)."

Keven   A variant spelling of Kevin. *See* Kevin.

Kevin   From the Gaelic, meaning "handsome, beautiful." Keven is a variant spelling.

Key   From the Old English, meaning "key," hence "protected palace." Keys is a variant form.

Keys   A variant form of Key. *See* Key.

Kibby   From the British, meaning "cottage by the water."

Kidd   From the British, meaning "strong."

Kildaire   Compounded from the Dutch, meaning "stream, creek," and the Old English, meaning "courageous, bold," hence "powerful stream."

Kile   A variant spelling of Kyle. *See* Kyle.

Kilgore   Compounded from the Dutch, meaning "stream, creek," and "warm, hot (blood of an animal)," hence "warm stream."

Kilian, Killian   From the British, meaning "cell, retreat." Akin to Kilmer.

Kilmer   From the Dutch and French, meaning "inlet to the sea," or "retreat near the sea." Akin to Kilian.

Kim   A pet form of Kimball or Kimberly. *See* Kimball *and* Kimberly.

Kimball   Probably from the Greek, meaning "hollow vessel." Kim is a pet form.

Kimberly   Used most often as a feminine name. *See* Kimberly (feminine section). Kim is a pet form.

Kimchi (קִמְחִי)   From the Hebrew, meaning "my flour."

Kimo   The Hawaiian form of James. *See* James.

Kimui (קִמוּי)   From the Aramaic, meaning "establishment." The head *(gaon)* of the academy in Pumpedita, Babylonia, in 898. Also spelled Kimoi.

Kimum (קָמוּם)   From the Hebrew, meaning "establishment."

Kin   A pet form of Kingsley and Kingston. *See* Kingsley *and* Kingston.

Kinchen   From the Old English and the Old Norse, meaning "related to, family, kin." Chen is a diminutive German form, hence the meaning "little relative."

King   From the Anglo-Saxon, meaning "ruler."

Kingsley   From the Anglo-Saxon, meaning "from the king's meadow."

Kingston   From the Old English, meaning "king's town."

Kini (קְנִי)   From the Hebrew, meaning "my reed, my stalk."

Kinnaird   From the Old English, meaning "king."

Kinsey   From the British, meaning "royal."

Kinta   An American Indian name, meaning "beaver." Also, an African name of uncertain meaning.

Kip   A pet form of Kipling. *See* Kipling.

Kipling   From the Middle English, meaning "kippered (cured) herring or salmon." Kip is a pet form.

Kirby   From the Old English and the Middle English, meaning "church." Or, from the British, meaning "cottage by the water." Kerby is a variant spelling.

Kiril   A variant spelling of Cyril, meaning "church." Kyril is another variant spelling.

Kirk   From the Old Norse and Old English, meaning "church."

Kirkland   From the Old English, meaning "church's land." Kirtland is a variant form.

Kirtland   A variant form of Kirkland. *See* Kirkland.

Kish (קִישׁ)   From the Hebrew, meaning "bow" or "noise." In the Bible (I Samuel 9:1), the father of King Saul. Kishoni is a variant form.

Kishi (קִישִׁי)   A variant form of Kushayahu. *See* Kushayahu. In the Bible (Zephaniah 1:1), the father of the Prophet Zephaniah. A variant form of Kushayahu (I Chronicles 6:29).

Kishoni (קִישׁוֹנִי)   A variant form of Kish. *See* Kish.

Kislon (כִּסְלוֹן)   From the Aramaic and Arabic, meaning "to be sluggish" or "stupid." Also, from the Hebrew, meaning "loins."

Kit   A pet form of Christopher. *See* Christopher.

Kitron (קִטְרוֹן)   From the Hebrew, meaning "crown."

Kiva (קִיבָה)   A pet form of Akiva. *See* Akiva.

Kivi (קִיבִי)   A pet form of Akiva or Yaakov (Jacob). *See* Akiva *and* Yaakov.

Klaas, Klaus   Short forms of Nicolaus. *See* Nicolaus.

Klemens   A variant form of Clement. *See* Clement.

Klonimos   A variant spelling of Kalonymos. *See* Kalonymos.

Knut, Knute   From the Swedish, meaning "knot."

Koby (קוֹבִּי)   A pet form of Yaakov (Jacob). *See* Yaakov.

Kochav (כּוֹכָב)   From the Hebrew, meaning "star." Akin to Kochva.

Kochva (כּוֹכְבָא)   From the Aramaic, meaning "star." Kochba is a variant spelling. Akin to Kochav.

Kohath   A variant form of Kehat. *See* Kehat.

Kohelet (קֹהֶלֶת)   From the Hebrew, meaning "preacher, speaker" or "collector of sentences." Also, from the Hebrew, meaning "assembly of people." In the Bible (Ecclesiastes 12:8), a name ascribed to King Solomon, who according to tradition was the author of the Book of Kohelet (Ecclesiastes). Also spelled קוֹהֶלֶת.

Kohen (כֹּהֵן)   From the Hebrew, meaning "Priest."

Kolaia, Kolaiah   Variant spellings of Kolaya. *See* Kolaya.

Kolaya (קוֹלָיָה)   From the Hebrew, meaning "voice of God." In the Bible (Jeremiah 29:21), the father of the Prophet Ahab. Kolaia and Kolaiah are variant spellings. Koliya and Kolya are variant forms.

Kolet   From the Hebrew, meaning "to be stunted" or "to harbor."

Kolia   A variant spelling of Kolya. *See* Kolya.

Koliya   A variant spelling of Kolaya. *See* Kolaya.

Kolya (קוֹלְיָה)   A variant form of Kolaya. *See* Kolaya. Kolia is a variant spelling.

Komem (קוֹמֵם)   From the Hebrew, meaning "to establish."

Konania, Konaniah   Variant spellings of Konanya. *See* Konanya.

Konanya (כּוֹנַנְיָה)   From the Hebrew, meaning "the establishment of the Lord." Konania and Konaniah are variant spellings.

Konen (כּוֹנֵן)   From the Hebrew, meaning "to acquire."

Konrad   A variant spelling of Conrad. *See* Conrad.

Koppel (קאָפֶּעל)   A Yiddish form of Yaakov (Jacob). *See* Yaakov.

Korach (קֹרַח)   From the Hebrew, meaning "bald." In the Bible (Numbers 16:3), a Levite who led a rebellion against the leadership of Moses and Aaron, but failed when the earth opened up and swallowed him and his group of 250 rebels. Korah is a variant spelling. Korcha is a variant form.

Korah   A variant spelling of Korach. *See* Korach.

Korcha   A variant form of Korach. *See* Korach.

Kore, Korei (קוֹרֵא)   From the Hebrew, meaning "quail" or "to call." In the Bible (I Chronicles 9:19), a Levite who was a descendant of Korach.

Koresh (כּוֹרֶשׁ)   From the Hebrew, meaning "to dig" or "sun." The Hebrew form of Cyrus, the Persian conqueror of Babylonia who was friendly toward the Jews (Ezra 1:7). *See* Cyrus. Also spelled כֹּרֶשׁ.

Kotz (קוֹץ)   From the Hebrew, meaning "thorn." In the Bible (I Chronicles 4:8), a leader of the tribe of Judah. Koz is a variant spelling.

Kovi (קוֹבִי)   A pet form of Yaakov (Jacob). *See* Yaakov.

Koz   A variant spelling of Kotz. *See* Kotz.

Kraig   A variant spelling of Craig. *See* Craig.

Kramer   A variant spelling of Cramer. *See* Cramer.

Kris   A variant form of Christian and Christopher. *See* Christian *and* Christopher.

Kristian   A variant spelling of Christian. *See* Christian.

Kurt   A pet form of Konrad. *See* Konrad. Also, a variant spelling of Curt. *See* Curt.

Kusi   A pet form of Kusiel (Kutiel). *See* Kusiel.

Kush (כּוּשׁ)   From the Hebrew, meaning "dark" or "black." Also, from the Hebrew, meaning "to lay bait, lure."

Kushayahu (קוּשָׁיָהוּ)   From the Hebrew, meaning "lure of the Lord." In the Bible (I Chronicles 15:17), a Levite.

Kusiel   A variant spelling of Kutiel. *See* Kutiel. Kus is a pet form.

Kuti (קוּתִּי)   A pet form of Yekutiel. *See* Yekutiel.

Kutiel (קוּתִיאֵל)   A short form of Yekutiel. *See* Yekutiel.

Kyle   A Gaelic form of the Old English name Kyloe, meaning "hill where the cattle graze." Kile is a variant spelling.

Kyril   A variant spelling of Cyril. *See* Cyril *and* Kiril.

Laban   A variant spelling of Lavan. *See* Lavan.

Label (לייבְּל)   A pet form of the Yiddish name Leib, meaning "lion." Also spelled לייבֶּעל.

Labert   A French form of the Anglo-Saxon name Bert, meaning "bright." *See* Bert.

LaBron   From the French, meaning "brown." A variant form of Bruno. LeBron is a variant spelling.

Lachlan   From the Old English, meaning "enclosure, prison."

Lachma (לַחְמָא)   From the Aramaic, meaning "food, bread." In the Talmud (Rosh Hashana 29b), the father of a third-century Palestinian scholar.

Lachmi (לַחְמִי)   From the Hebrew, meaning "my bread, my food." In the Bible (I Chronicles 20:5), a brother of Goliath.

Lada, Ladah (לַעְדָּה)   From the Hebrew, meaning "witness." In the Bible (I Chronicles 4:21), a member of the tribe of Judah. Akin to Ladan.

Ladan (לַעְדָּן)   From the Hebrew, meaning "witness." In the Bible (I Chronicles 7:26), a member of the tribe of Ephraim. Akin to Lada.

Ladd From the Middle English, meaning "boy."

Laddie, Laddy Pet forms of Ladd. *See* Ladd.

Lael (לָאֵל) From the Hebrew, meaning "belonging to God." In the Bible (Numbers 3:24), a Levite and a leader of the Gershon family.

Lafayette From the Old French, meaning "faith."

Lahad (לַהַד) Derivation unknown. In the Bible (I Chronicles 4:2), a descendant of Judah.

Lahav (לַהַב) From the Hebrew, meaning "flame, fire."

Laish A variant spelling of Layish. *See* Layish.

Lakish (לָקִישׁ) From the Hebrew, meaning "aftergrowth." In the Talmud (Shabbat 32b), the father of Simeon, a second-century scholar.

Lale, Lalo From the Latin *lallare*, meaning "to sing a lullaby."

Lamar, Lamarr From the Latin and French, meaning "of the sea." Lemar is a variant form. Lammie and Lammy are pet forms.

Lambert From the German and French, meaning "brightness of the land." Lammie and Lammy are pet forms.

Lamech (לָמֶךְ) A variant form of Lemech. *See* Lemech.

Lammie, Lammy A pet form of either Lambert or Lamar. *See* Lambert *and* Lamar.

La Mont, Lamont From the Latin, French, and Spanish, meaning "the mountain."

Lance From the Latin, meaning "light spear" or "servant." Lancelot is a variant form.

Lancelot A variant form of Lance. *See* Lance.

Landan From the Anglo-Saxon, meaning "open, grassy area; lawn." Landis, Landon, and Landor are variant forms.

Landis A variant form of Landan. *See* Landan.

Landon A variant form of Landan. *See* Landan.

Landor A variant form of Landan. *See* Landan.

Landry From the Old English, meaning "rough land." Langtry is a variant form.

Lane From the Old English, meaning "to move, go on," hence "a path."

Lang From the German, meaning "long, tall."

Langdon From the Old English, meaning "long valley." *See also* Lang.

Langer From the German, meaning "tall one."

Langford From the Old English, meaning "long river crossing."

Langley From the Old English, meaning "long meadow."

Langston From the English, meaning "long, narrow town."

Langtry A variant form of Landry. *See* Landry.

Lapid (לַפִּיד) From the Hebrew, meaning "flame, torch."

Lapidos A variant form of Lapidot. *See* Lapidot.

Lapidot (לַפִּידוֹת) From the Hebrew, meaning "flame, torch." In the Bible (Judges 4:4), the husband of Deborah, the Judge and Prophet. Lapidos is a variant form.

Larns A pet form of Laurence. *See* Laurence. Larson is a patronymic form.

Larron From the French, meaning "thief."

Larry A pet form of Laurence. *See* Laurence.

Lars A Swedish pet form of Laurence. *See* Laurence. Larson is a patronymic form.

Larson A patronymic form of Larns and Lars. *See* Larns *and* Lars.

Latham From the Old English, meaning "division, district." Akin to Lather.

Lather From the Old English, meaning "division, district." Akin to Latham.

Latif (לָטִיף) From the Hebrew and Arabic, meaning "friendly, kindly, comforting."

Latimer From the Old English, meaning "district near the sea."

Laurence From the Latin, meaning "laurel, crown." Lawrence is a variant spelling. Lauriston, Lauro, Lorenzo, Loring, Lorn, and Lorne are variant forms. Larns, Lars, and Laurie are pet forms. Lorence and Lorentz are variant spellings.

Laurie A pet form of Laurence. *See* Laurence. Lorry is a variant spelling.

Lauriston A variant form of Laurence, meaning "Laurie's town." *See* Laurence.

Lauro An Italian form of Laurence. *See* Laurence.

Lavan (לָבָן) From the Hebrew, meaning "white." In the Bible (Genesis 24:29), a resident of Aram Naharaim, the brother of Rebekah and father of Leah and Rachel. In Jewish folklore Laban, the Aramean, is synonymous with "deceiver." Laban is the Anglicized form.

Lavern, Laverne, La Verne From the Latin, meaning "belonging to spring," and the French, meaning "green." Vernon is a variant form. Used also as a feminine name. Luvern is a variant spelling.

Lavey A variant spelling of Levi. *See* Levi.

Lavi (לָבִיא) From the Hebrew, meaning "lion." Also, a variant spelling of Levi. *See* Levi.

Lawrence A variant spelling of Laurence. *See* Laurence.

Lawton   From the Old English, meaning "town on the hill."

Layish (לַיִשׁ)   From the Hebrew, meaning "lion-like (strong)." In the Bible (I Samuel 25:44), the father of Palti, to whom King Saul gave his daughter Michal in marriage. Laish is a variant spelling.

Lazar (לָאזַאר)   A short form of Lazarus. See Lazarus. Also a Yiddish form of Elazar.

Lazaro   The Italian form of Lazarus. See Lazarus.

Lazarus   The Greek form of Elazar and Eliezer. See Elazar and Eliezer. Lazar is a short form. Lazaro is the Italian form.

Lazer (לִייזֶער)   A Yiddish form of Eliezer. See Eliezer. Lesser is a variant form. Also spelled לייזר.

Lebert   A variant form of Lever. See Lever.

LeBron   A variant spelling of LaBron. See LaBron.

Lebush   A variant spelling of Leibush. See Leibush.

Lee   A pet form of Leo, Leon, or Leslie. Or, from the Anglo-Saxon, meaning "field, meadow." Also, a short form of LeRoy. See LeRoy. Also, a variant spelling of Li. See Li. Leigh and Lie are variant spellings.

Leek   From the Old Norse and the Old English, meaning "to bind."

Leeland   From the Old English and the German, meaning "shelter, protected area." Leland, Leighland, and Leyland are variant spellings.

Leib (לײב)   A Yiddish form of the German name Loeb, meaning "lion." Akin to Leo. Label and Leibel are pet forms. Lebush and Leibush are variant forms.

Leibel (לײבָּל)   A pet form of Leib. See Leib. Also spelled לײבֶּעל.

Leibush (לײבּוש)   A variant form of Leib. See Leib.

Leif   From the Old Norse, meaning "beloved." Akin to Lief. See Lief.

Leigh   A variant spelling of Lee. See Lee.

Leighland   A variant form of Leeland. See Leeland.

Leland   A variant spelling of Leeland. See Leeland.

Lem   A pet form of Lemuel. See Lemuel.

Lemar   A variant form of Lamar. See Lamar.

Lemech (לֶמֶך)   Origin and meaning uncertain. Probably a short Hebrew form of an Akkadian name. Arabic etymologists explain it as meaning "mighty, strong youth." In the Bible (Genesis 4:19), a descendant of Cain. Lamech is a variant form.

Lemel (לֶעמְל)   From the Yiddish, meaning "little lamb" or "meek."

Lemuel (לְמוּאֵל)   From the Hebrew, meaning "belonging to God." In the Bible (Proverbs 31:1), an alternate name for Solomon. Lem is a pet form.

Len   A pet form of Leonard. *See* Leonard. Also, from the Old English, meaning "tenant house on a farm."

Lendal   From the Old English, meaning "river near the alder tree."

Lendon   From the Old English, meaning "river near the tenant farmer's house."

Leni   A variant spelling of Lennie. *See* Lennie.

Lenis   From the Latin, meaning "gentle, mild."

Lenn   A variant spelling of Len. *See* Len.

Lennard, Lennart   Variant forms of Leonard. *See* Leonard.

Lennie   A pet form of Leonard. *See* Leonard. Leni is a variant spelling.

Lennon   From the Old English, meaning "river near the tenant farmer's house."

Lennox   From the Old English and French, meaning "tenant house near the town."

Lenvil   From the Old English and French, meaning "tenant house near the town."

Lenwood   From the Old English, meaning "tenant house in the woods."

Leo   From the Latin, meaning "lion" or "of the lion's nature." Leib, Leibel, and Label are variant Yiddish forms. Lee is a pet form. Leodis, Leon, Leona, Leonid, Leonidas, Leonis, and Lion are variant forms. *See* Leonard.

Leodis   A variant form of Leo. *See* Leo.

Leon   The Greek form of Leo, meaning "lion." *See* Leo. To the Greeks the lion was king of the beasts. Lee is a pet form. Lion is a variant form.

Leonala   The Hawaiian form of Leonard. *See* Leonard.

Leonard   A French form of the Old High German, meaning "strong as a lion." Lennard, Lennart, Leonardo, and Leonhard are variant forms. Len, Leni, Lenn, and Lennie are pet forms. *See also* Leo.

Leonardo   An Italian variant form of Leonard. *See* Leonard.

Leone   The Hawaiian form of Leo. *See* Leo.

Leonhard   A Germanic form of Leonard. *See* Leonard.

Leonid   A Russian form of Leo. *See* Leo.

Leonidas   A variant form of Leo. *See* Leo.

Leonis   A variant Old English form of Leon, meaning "Leon's house." *See* Leon.

Leopold   From the Old High German and the Old English, meaning "bold, free man" and "defender of people."

Leor (לְאוֹר)   From the Hebrew, meaning "light."

Leron, Lerone   From the French, meaning "round." Also, variant spellings of Liron. *See* Liron.

Lerond A variant form of Leron. *See* Leron.

LeRoy A French form of the Latin, meaning "the king" or "royalty." Le Roy is a variant spelling. Lee is a short form.

Les A pet form of Lester and Leslie. *See* Lester *and* Leslie.

Leshem (לֶשֶׁם) From the Hebrew, meaning "precious stone." In the Bible, a precious stone (amber) that the High Priest wore in his breastplate.

Lesley A variant spelling of Leslie. *See* Leslie.

Leslie From the Anglo-Saxon, meaning "meadowlands." Used also as a feminine name. Lesley is a variant spelling. Lee and Les are pet forms.

Lesser A variant form of the Yiddish Lazer. *See* Lazer.

Lester Originally Leicester, a place-name in England. From the Latin and the Old English, meaning "camp, protected area." Chester is a variant form. Les is a pet form. *See also* Letcher.

Letcher An early English form of Leicester and Lester. *See* Lester. Also, a short form of Fletcher, from the Old French, meaning "arrow."

Leumi (לְאוּמִי) From the Hebrew, meaning "national, nationalist."

Lev (לֵב) Either from the Hebrew, meaning "heart," or from the Yiddish, meaning "lion." Also, a pet form of Levi.

Levana (לְבָנָה) From the Hebrew, meaning "white" or "moon." In the Bible (Ezra 2:45), the head of a family who returned to Judah from the Babylonian Exile. Used also as a modern feminine name.

Levander A variant form of Levant, meaning "man from the East." *See* Levant.

Levanon (לְבָנוֹן) From the Hebrew, meaning "white" or "moon, month." A place-name in the Bible (Lebanon). In the Midrash (Sifri 117), a substitute name for the Temple.

Levant A Spanish and French form of the Latin, meaning "to rise" or "rising of the sun." A name applied to Eastern countries. Levander and Lever are variant forms.

Le Var A French variant form of the Old English, meaning "bear."

Lever A variant French form of Levant. *See* Levant. Also, possibly a form of the Anglo-Saxon, meaning "love." Lebert and Leverett are variant forms.

Leverett A variant form of Lever. *See* Lever.

Levi (לֵוִי) From the Hebrew, meaning "joined to" or "attendant upon." In the Bible (Genesis 29:34), the son of Jacob and Leah. The descendants of Levi were the Priests and Levites who served in the Temple of Jerusalem. In the Talmud (Yerushalmi Suka 5:1), a fourth-century Palestinian scholar. Lavey and Lavi are variant spellings. Levai, Levitas, and Lewi are variant forms. Lev is a pet form.

Leviathan The Anglicized form of Livyatan. *See* Livyatan.

Levitas (לְוִיטַס)   A variant form of Levi. *See* Levi. In the Talmud (Avot 4:4), a second-century Palestinian scholar.

Lew   A pet form of Lewis. *See* Lewis.

Lewes   A variant spelling of Lewis. *See* Lewis.

Lewi   The Hawaiian form of Levi. *See* Levi.

Lewis   An English form of the French name Louis. *See* Louis. Also, a variant form of the Welsh name Llewellyn. *See* Llewellyn. Lewes is a variant spelling. Lew is a pet form.

Lex   From the Greek, meaning "word, vocabulary." Lexington is a variant form.

Leyland   A variant spelling of Leeland. *See* Leeland.

Lezer (לְייזֶר)   A Yiddish form of Eliezer. *See* Eliezer.

Li (לִי)   From the Hebrew, meaning "me" or "to me." Lee is a variant spelling.

Liad (לִי־עַד)   From the Hebrew, meaning "eternity is mine."

Liam (לִי־עָם)   From the Hebrew, meaning "my people, my nation." Also, a variant form of Lian. *See* Lian. Popular in Hawaii. Lyam is a variant spelling.

Lian   From the French, meaning "to bind, tie." Liam is a variant form.

Li-Av, Liav (לִי־אָב)   From the Hebrew, meaning "I have a father" or "my father," possibly referring to God. Also spelled לִיאָב.

Liba   A variant spelling of Lieber. *See* Lieber.

Liber   A variant spelling of Lieber. *See* Lieber.

Libni   A variant spelling of Livni. *See* Livni.

Liddon   From the Old English, meaning "to hide."

Lie   A variant spelling of Lee. *See* Lee.

Lieb   A short form of Lieber. *See* Lieber.

Lieber (לִיבֶּער)   A Yiddish form of the German, meaning "beloved." Liba and Liber are variant spellings. Akin to Lief. *See* Lief.

Lief   From the Middle English and the Old English, meaning "beloved, dear." Akin to Leif and Lieb. *See* Leif *and* Lieb.

Liezer   A short form of Eliezer. *See* Eliezer.

Li-Hu, Lihu (לִיהוּא)   From the Hebrew, meaning "he is mine" or "I belong to him." Also a pet form of Elihu. *See* Elihu.

Likchi (לִקְחִי)   From the Hebrew, meaning "my teaching" or "my lesson." In the Bible (I Chronicles 7:19), a member of the tribe of Manasseh. Likhi is a variant spelling.

Likhi   A variant spelling of Likchi. *See* Likchi.

Limon (לִימוֹן)   A modern Israeli name. The Hebrew word for lemon.

Lin   A variant spelling of Lynn. *See* Lynn.

Lincoln   From the Old English and the German, meaning "lithe, bending, flexible," referring to the trees of the linden family. Or, from the Old English and Latin, meaning "camp near the stream." Akin to Lindsey. *See also* Lind.

Lind, Linde   From the Old English and the German, meaning "lithe, supple, flexible." *See also* Lincoln. Lynd and Lynde are variant spellings. Lindal, Lindall, Lindel, Lindell, Linden, Lindon, Lynden, and Lyndon are variant forms.

Lindal, Lindall   Variant forms of Lind. *See* Lind. Lyndal and Lyndall are variant spellings.

Lindbergh   From the German, meaning "mountain of linden trees." Akin to Lind. Lindbert is a variant form.

Lindbert   A variant form of Lindbergh. *See* Lindbergh.

Lindel, Lindell   A variant form of Lind. *See* Lind.

Linden   A variant form of Lind. *See* Lind. Lindon, Lynden, and Lyndon are variant spellings.

Lindley Lindly   From the Old English, meaning "meadow near the linden trees."

Lindon   A variant spelling of Linden. *See* Linden.

Lindsay   A variant form of Lindsey. *See* Lindsey.

Lindsey   From the Old English, meaning "linden trees near the water (sea)." Akin to Lincoln. Lindsay, Lindsy, Linsey, Linsy, and Linzy are variant forms. Lindy is a pet form.

Lindsy   A variant spelling of Lindsey. *See* Lindsey.

Lindy   A pet form of Lindsey. *See* Lindsey.

Link   From the Old English, meaning "enclosure."

Linley   From the Old English, meaning "meadow near the brook." Lynley is a variant spelling.

Linn, Linnie   Variant forms of Lynn. *See* Lynn.

Lino   From the French, meaning "linen."

Linsey, Linsy   Variant spellings of Lindsey. *See* Lindsey.

Linton   From the Old English, meaning "town near the brook." Lynton is a variant spelling.

Linus   From the Latin, meaning "linen-colored, flaxen-colored," after the linnet, a colored songbird of the finch family.

Linwood   From the Old English, meaning "forest near the brook." Lynwood is a variant spelling.

Linzy   A variant spelling of Lindsey. *See* Lindsey.

Lion (לִי־אָון)   A variant spelling of Leon. Also, from the Hebrew, meaning "I have strength." Lionel, Lionello, Lyon, Lyonell, and Lyons are variant forms.

Lionel   A variant form of Lion. *See* Lion.

Lionello   An Italian form of Lion. *See* Lion.

Li-Or, Lior (לְאוֹר)   From the Hebrew, meaning "light is mine" or "I have light." Also spelled לִי־אוֹר. Used also as a feminine name.

Lipe (לִיפֶּע)   A short form of Lipman. *See* Lipman.

Lipman, Lipmann (לִיפְּמָן)   A Yiddish form of the German name Liebman, meaning "lover of man."

Liron (לִירוֹן)   From the Hebrew, meaning "song is mine." Lyron is a variant spelling.

Lisle   From the Spanish, meaning "strong cotton thread." Derived from the French city of Lisle, now spelled Lille, where the thread is manufactured.

Lital   From the Hebrew, meaning "I have dew."

Li-Tov, Litov (לִי־טוֹב)   From the Hebrew, meaning "goodness is mine" or "I have good fortune."

Litton   From the Old English, meaning "little town."

Livingston   An Anglicized form of the Anglo-Saxon, meaning "Lever's town, Leif's town." *See* Lever *and* Leif.

Livnat (לִבְנַת)   A variant form of Livne. *See* Livne.

Livnati (לִבְנָתִי)   From the Hebrew, meaning "man from Lebanon." In the Talmud (Yerushalmi Yevamot 9:8), a fourth-century Palestinian scholar.

Livne, Livneh (לִבְנֶה)   From the Hebrew, meaning "poplar tree," which in biblical times (Hosea 4:13) marked the site of idolatrous incense-burning. Livnat is a variant form.

Livni (לִבְנִי)   From the Hebrew, meaning "white" or "frankincense (because of its white color)." In the Bible (Exodus 6:17), a Levite and a son of Gershom. Libni is a variant spelling.

Livyatan (לִוְיָתָן)   From the Hebrew, meaning "sea monster." Leviathan is the Anglicized form.

Llewellyn   From the Welsh, meaning "in the likeness of a lion." Lewis is a variant form.

Lloyd   From the Celtic or Welsh, meaning "grey or brown" or "a person with a dark complexion." Floyd is a variant form.

Lo-Ami (לֹא־עַמִּי)   From the Hebrew, meaning "not my people." In the Bible (Hosea 1:9), a symbolic name given by Hosea to one of his sons.

Lochesh (לוֹחֵשׁ)   From the Hebrew, meaning "whisper." In the Bible (Nehemiah 3:12), one of the Babylonian Exile returnees.

Locke   From the German, meaning "hole," or from the Old English, meaning "enclosure." An occupational name for locksmiths.

Lod (לוֹד)   A place in Israel between Tel Aviv and Jerusalem. In the Bible (Ezra 2:33), the head of a family of Babylonian Exile returnees.

Lodge   From the Middle English, meaning "hut."

Loeb (לֵיבּ)   From the German, meaning "lion." Common as a Yiddish form. Jews use it as a middle name with Judah (Judah Loeb) because of the biblical comparison of Judah to a lion (Genesis 49:9). Loewy and Lowe are variant forms.

Loewy   A variant form of Loeb. See Loeb.

Logan   From the Middle English and the Old Norse, meaning "felled tree."

Lon, Lonnie, Lonny   Pet forms of Alphonso, from the Old German, meaning "of noble family." See Alphonso.

Lopez   From the Spanish, meaning "wolf." A name associated with Binyamin (Benjamin), who in the Bible (Genesis 49:27) is compared to a wolf. Lupez is a variant form. Akin to Lupo.

Loral   From the Old English, meaning "learning, teaching."

Loren   A short form of Lorence. See Lorence. Lorin is a variant spelling.

Lorence   A variant spelling of Laurence. See Laurence. Loren is a short form.

Lorentz   A variant spelling of Laurence. See Laurence.

Lorenzo   An Italian form of Laurence. See Laurence.

Lorimer   From the Latin, meaning "harness maker."

Lorin   A variant spelling of Loren. See Loren.

Loring   A variant form of Laurence. See Laurence.

Loris   From the Dutch, meaning "clown."

Lorn, Lorne   Variant forms of Laurence. See Laurence.

Lorry   A variant spelling of Laurie, and a pet form of Laurence. See Laurie.

Lot (לוֹט)   From the Hebrew, meaning "hidden, covered, wrapped up." In the Bible (Genesis 11:27), a nephew of Abraham. See Lotan.

Lotam (לוֹטָם)   From the Hebrew, referring to "golden-yellow vegetation" indigenous to Israel. Lotem is a variant form.

Lotan (לוֹטָן)   From the Hebrew, meaning to "envelop." Lot is the original form. In the Bible (Genesis 36:20), a son of Seir the Horite. See Lot.

Lotem (לוֹטֶם)   A variant form of Lotam. See Lotam.

Lothar   From the Anglo-Saxon, meaning "noted warrior, renowned soldier" or "hero of the people." The name of a Saxon king. Lother and Lothario are variant forms.

Lothario   An English form of Lothar. See Lothar.

Lother   A variant spelling of Lothar. See Lothar.

Lothur A variant spelling of Lothar. *See* Lothar.

Louis From the Old French and the Old High German, meaning "famous in battle" or "refuge of the people." Lewis is the original spelling. *See* Lewis. Ludwig, Lui, and Luis are variant forms.

Lovell A variant form of Lowell. *See* Lowell.

Lowe A variant form of the German name Loeb. *See* Loeb.

Lowell From the Old English, meaning "beloved." Also, from the Old English, meaning "hill." Lovell is a variant form.

Loy A pet form of Loyal. *See* Loyal.

Loyal From the Old French and the Latin, meaning "faithful, true." Loy is a pet form.

Lu A pet form of Lucas or Lucius. *See* Lucius.

Luc A pet form of Lucas. *See* Lucas. Also, a name derived from the Old English, meaning "enclosure."

Lucas A variant form of Lucius. *See* Lucius. Lu and Luc are pet forms.

Lucian A variant form of Lucius. *See* Lucius.

Luciano An Italian form of Lucius. *See* Lucius.

Lucien A French form of Lucius. *See* Lucius.

Lucio An Italian form of Lucius. *See* Lucius.

Lucius From the Latin, meaning "light." Lu is a pet form. Lucian, Luciano, Lucien, Lucio, Luke, and Luka are variant forms.

Lud (לוּד) The name of a people in northeast Africa. Akin to Lydia. *See* Lydia (feminine section). In the Bible (Genesis 10:22), a son of Shem and a grandson of Noah.

Ludwig A German form of Louis. *See* Louis.

Lui The Hawaiian form of Louis. *See* Louis.

Luis A Spanish form of Louis. *See* Louis.

Luka The Hawaiian form of Lucius. *See* Lucius.

Luke The English form of Lucius. *See* Lucius.

Lupez A variant form of Lopez. *See* Lopez.

Lupo From the Latin, meaning "wolf." Lupus is a variant form. Akin to Lopez.

Lupus A variant form of Lupo. *See* Lupo.

Luther A variant form of Lothar. *See* Lothar.

Luvern A variant spelling of Lavern. *See* Lavern.

Luz (לוּז) From the Hebrew, meaning "almond tree."

Lyall A variant form of Lyle. *See* Lyle.

Lyam A variant spelling of Liam. *See* Liam.

Lyde From the Old English and the Middle English, meaning "hill," referring to "hilly pastureland." Lydell is a variant form.

Lydell A variant form of Lyde. *See* Lyde.

Lyell A variant form of Lyle. *See* Lyle.

Lyle A French form of the Latin, meaning "from the island." Also, a Scotch name, meaning "little." Lyall and Lyell are variant forms.

Lyman An occupational name, meaning "one who works lime, plasterer, bricklayer." *See* Lyme.

Lyme From the Old English, meaning "lime or mud." *See* Lyman.

Lyn A variant spelling of Lynn. *See* Lynn.

Lynd, Lynde Variant spellings of Lind. *See* Lind.

Lyndal, Lyndall Variant spellings of Lindal. *See* Lindal.

Lynden A variant spelling of Linden. *See* Linden.

Lyndon A variant spelling of Linden. *See* Linden.

Lynford From the Old English, meaning "the crossing (ford) over the brook."

Lynley A variant spelling of Linley. *See* Linley.

Lynn From the Old English and Welsh, meaning "cataract, lake, brook." Lin and Lyn are variant spellings. Linn and Linnie are variant forms.

Lynton A variant spelling of Linton. *See* Linton.

Lynwood A variant spelling of Linwood. *See* Linwood.

Lyon The French form of Lion. *See* Lion.

Lyonell A variant form of Lyon. *See* Lyon.

Lyons The English form of Lyon. *See* Lyon.

Lyron A variant spelling of Liron. *See* Liron.

Lytel From the Anglo-Saxon, meaning "little, less."

Maacha (מַעֲכָה) From the Hebrew, meaning "to press, squeeze." Also, from the Arabic, meaning "to rub." In the Bible (Genesis 22:24), a son of Nachor and a nephew of Abraham. Used also as a feminine name.

Maadai (מַעֲדַי) From the Aramaic, meaning "delight." In the Bible (Ezra 10:34), a Babylonian Exile returnee.

Maadia, Maadiah Variant spellings of Maadya. *See* Maadya.

Maadya (מַעַדְיָה) From the Hebrew, meaning "delight of God." In the Bible (Nehemiah 12:5), a Priest who was among the Babylonian Exile returnees. Maadia and Maadiah are variant spellings.

Maarav (מַעֲרָב) From the Hebrew, meaning "west, western."

Maaseiya (מַעֲשֵׂיָה) From the Hebrew, meaning "God's creations." In the Bible (Jeremiah 21:1), the father of Zephaniah the Priest. Masai is a variant form.

Maaseiyahu (מַעֲשֵׂיָהוּ) A variant form of Maaseiya. See Maaseiya.

Maatz (מַעַץ) From the Hebrew, meaning "anger." In the Bible (I Chronicles 2:27), a leader of the tribe of Judah. Maaz is a variant spelling.

Maayan (מַעֲיָן) From the Hebrew, meaning "water well, spring."

Maaz A variant spelling of Maatz. See Maatz.

Maazia, Maaziah Variant spellings of Maazya. See Maazya.

Maazya (מַעַזְיָה) From the Hebrew, meaning "strength of the Lord." In the Bible (Nehemiah 10:9), a Priest during King David's reign. Maazia and Maaziah are variant spellings.

Maazyahu (מַעַזְיָהוּ) A variant form of Maazya. See Maazya.

Mac From the Gaelic, meaning "son of." Mc and Mac are used as Gaelic and Irish prefixes to personal names, thus forming patronymics. Mack is a variant spelling.

Macabee, Maccabee (מַכַּבִּי) From the Hebrew, meaning "hammer." Makabi is a variant spelling.

Mace An English form of the Old French, meaning "club," a symbol of authority. Macey is a variant form.

Macey A variant form of Mace. See Mace. Also, a pet form of Matthew. See Matthew. Macy is a variant spelling.

Machaseh (מַחְסֶה) From the Hebrew, meaning "protection" or "cover, shelter."

Machat (מַחַת) From the Hebrew, meaning "shovel, pan" or "incense bowl." In the Bible (I Chronicles 6:20), a son of Kehat.

Machi (מָכִי) Possibly from the Aramaic and Arabic, meaning "to suck out, consume, diminish." In the Bible (Numbers 13:15), a member of the tribe of Gad and one of the twelve scouts sent by Moses to explore the Promised Land.

Machir (מָכִיר) From the Hebrew, meaning "merchandise." In the Bible (Genesis 50:23), a son of Manasseh and a grandson of Jacob.

Machli (מַחְלִי) A variant form of Machlon. See Machlon. In the Bible (Exodus 6:19), the eldest son of Merari and a grandson of Levi.

Machlon (מַחְלוֹן) From the Hebrew, meaning "fat." In the Bible (Ruth 1:2), the son of Elimelech and Naomi, and the first husband of Ruth. Mahlon is a variant spelling. Machli is a variant form.

Machol (מָחוֹל)   From the Hebrew, meaning "dance" or "sickly." In the Bible (I Kings 5:11), the father of three wise men.

Machseiya (מַחְסֵיָה)   From the Hebrew, meaning "the protection of God." In the Bible (Jeremiah 32:12), the grandfather of Baruch, Jeremiah's scribe.

Mack   A variant spelling of Mac. See Mac. Also, from the Middle English and German, meaning "to make." Mackey is a variant form.

Mackey   A variant form of Mack. See Mack.

Macon   From the Middle English and German, meaning "to make."

Macy   A variant spelling of Macey. See Macey.

Madai (מָדַי)   From the Hebrew, meaning "strife, war." In the Bible (Genesis 10:2), a son of Japhet and a grandson of Noah.

Madison   A patronymic form, meaning "son of Maude." Also, from the British, meaning "good."

Madoc   An Old Welsh name, meaning "fortunate."

Magdiel (מַגְדִּיאֵל)   From the Hebrew, meaning "goodness, sweetness, excellence of the Lord." In the Bible (Genesis 36:43), a descendant of Esau.

Magen (מָגֵן)   From the Hebrew, meaning "protection" or "protector."

Magen Deror (מָגֵן דְּרוֹר)   From the Hebrew, meaning "protector of freedom" or "freedom fighter."

Magnus   From the Latin, meaning "great." Manus is a variant form used in Ireland. Akin to Major and Mayer.

Magus   From the Latin, meaning "magician, sorcerer."

Mahalalel (מַהֲלַלְאֵל)   From the Hebrew, meaning "praise." In the Bible (Genesis 5:12), a son of Kenan and a grandson of Enosh. In the Talmud (Sanhedrin 87b), the father of Akavia, a first-century Palestinian scholar. Akin to Mehulal.

Maharai (מַהֲרַי)   From the Aramaic, meaning "haste, speed." In the Bible (II Samuel 23:28), one of King David's warriors.

Mahari (מַהֲרִי)   From the Hebrew, meaning "hurry." Akin to Maher.

Maher (מַהֵר)   From the Hebrew, meaning "quick, hurry." Akin to Mahari and Mahir.

Maher-Shalal-Chash-Baz (מַהֵר־שָׁלָל־חָשׁ־בַּז)   From the Hebrew, meaning "swift spoil and easy prey," a symbolic name imposed by Isaiah upon his son (Isaiah 8:3) to forewarn Israel that the Assyrian armies would crush them. A name sometimes used by Puritans.

Mahir (מָהִיר)   From the Hebrew, meaning "industrious, excellent, expert." Akin to Maher.

Mahlon   A variant spelling of Machlon. See Machlon.

Maimon (מַימוֹן)   From the Arabic, meaning "luck, good fortune." Moses ben

Maimon (also called Maimonides) was a Jewish philosopher who lived from 1135 to 1204. Maimun is a variant spelling.

Maimun A variant spelling of Maimon. *See* Maimon.

Maitland From the Old English, meaning "meadowland."

Major From the Latin, meaning "great." Akin to Magnus.

Makabi A variant spelling of Macabee. *See* Macabee.

Maks A variant spelling of Max. *See* Max.

Maksim (מַקְסִים) From the Hebrew, meaning "enchanting, attractive."

Malach (מַלְאָךְ) From the Hebrew, meaning "messenger" or "angel."

Malachai A variant form of Malachi. *See* Malachi.

Malachi (מַלְאָכִי) From the Hebrew, meaning "my messenger, my minister," or "my servant." Malachi was the last of the Hebrew Prophets. His period of most intense activity was 460-450 B.C.E. Malachai and Malachy are Anglicized forms.

Malachy A variant form of Malachi. *See* Malachi.

Malbin (מַלְבִּין) From the Hebrew, meaning "to whiten" or "to embarrass."

Malcam A variant spelling of Malkam. *See* Malkam.

Malcolm From the Arabic, meaning "dove," or from the Gaelic, meaning "servant of St. Columba." Until recent times, a popular name in Scotland.

Malden, Maldon From the Old English, meaning "meeting place in the pasture." Malton is a variant form.

Malka (מַלְכָּה) From the Aramaic, meaning "king." The name of a head of the academy *(gaon)* in Sura, Babylonia. Used more often as a feminine name. *See* Malka (feminine section). Akin to Maluch and Melech.

Malkam (מַלְכָּם) From the Hebrew, meaning "God is their King." In the Bible (I Chronicles 8:9), a member of the tribe of Benjamin. Malcam is a variant spelling.

Malki (מַלְכִּי) From the Hebrew, meaning "my king."

Malkia, Malkiah A variant spelling of Malkiya. *See* Malkiya.

Malkiel (מַלְכִּיאֵל) From the Hebrew, meaning "my King is God" or "God is my King." In the Bible (Genesis 46:17), a son of Beriah and a grandson of Asher.

Malkiram (מַלְכִּירָם) From the Hebrew, meaning "God is mighty." In the Bible (I Chronicles 3:18), a son of Jehoiakim, the last king of Judah. Also spelled מַלְכִּי־רָם.

Malkishua (מַלְכִּישׁוּעַ) From the Hebrew, meaning "my King (God), is salvation." In the Bible (I Samuel 31:2), the third son of King Saul and his wife Achinoam.

Malki-Tzedek (מַלְכִּי־צֶדֶק) From the Hebrew, meaning "my king is right-eousness." In the Bible (Genesis 14:18), the king of Salem, a contemporary of Abraham.

Malkiya (מַלְכִּיָה) From the Hebrew, meaning "God is my King." In the Bible (Jeremiah 21:1), the father of a Priest during the reign of King Zedekiah. In the Talmud (Makot 21a), a third-century Babylonian scholar. Malkia and Malkiah are variant spellings. Malkiyahu is a variant form.

Malkiyahu (מַלְכִּיָהוּ) A variant form of Malkiya. See Malkiya. In the Bible (Jeremiah 38:6), a son of King Hezekiah.

Malkosh (מַלְקוֹשׁ) From the Hebrew, meaning "last rain (of the year)."

Malon (מָלוֹן) From the Hebrew, meaning "lodge, place to rest."

Maloti (מַלּוֹתִי) From the Aramaic, meaning "I have spoken." In the Bible (I Chronicles 25:4), a son of Heman the Levite.

Malton A variant form of Maldon. See Maldon.

Maluch (מַלּוּךְ) From the Aramaic, meaning "king" or "ruler." In the Bible (Ezra 10:29), a Levite of the Merari family. In the Talmud (Yerushalmi Suka 3:1), a third-century Palestinian scholar. Maluchi is a variant form. Akin to Malka and Melech.

Maluchi (מַלּוּכִי) In the Bible (Nehemiah 18:14), a variant form of Maluch. See Maluch.

Malvern From the British and Welsh, meaning "bare hill."

Malvin A variant spelling of Melvin. See Melvin.

Mana (מָנָה) A short form of Manasseh. See Manasseh. In the Talmud (Yeru-shalmi Yoma 4:1), a third-century Palestinian scholar.

Manashi A variant spelling of Menashi. See Menashi.

Manasseh (מְנַשֶׁה) An Anglicized form of Menashe. See Menashe. Mana is a short form. Mani is a pet form.

Mandel From the Old French and the Middle Latin, meaning "almond."

Mandy A pet form of Manfred. See Manfred.

Manford From the Anglo-Saxon, meaning "small crossing over a brook."

Manfred From the German, meaning "man of peace." Mandy, Mani, Manni, Manny, and Mannye are pet forms.

Manheim From the German, meaning "the servant's home."

Mani (מָנִי) A pet form of Emanuel, Manasseh, Manfred, and Manuel. See Emanuel, Manasseh, Manfred, and Manuel. In the Talmud (Taanit 23b), a Palestinian scholar, the son of Rabbi Jonah. Manni, Manny, and Mannye are variant spellings. Also spelled מַאנִי.

Manin A variant form of Mann. See Mann.

Manish (מֶאֲנִיש) A Yiddish form of Mann. *See* Mann. Also a short form of Menashe and Menachem. *See* Menashe *and* Menachem.

Manley, Manly From the Old English, meaning "protected field."

Mann From the German, meaning "man." Also, a variant form of Menachem. *See* Menachem. Manin, Manish, and Mannes are variant forms.

Mannes (מֶאֲנֶעס) A variant Yiddish form of Mann. *See* Mann.

Manni A variant spelling of Mani and Manny. *See* Mani *and* Manny.

Manning From the Old English, meaning "to man (a garrison), to protect."

Manny, Mannye Pet forms of Emanuel, Manasseh, Manfred, and Manuel. *See* Emanuel, Manasseh, Manfred, *and* Manuel. Mani and Manni are variant spellings.

Mano A Spanish form of Manuel and Emanuel. *See* Emanuel.

Manoa, Manoah Variant spellings of Manoach. *See* Manoach.

Manoach (מָנוֹחַ) From the Hebrew, meaning "rest, resting place." In the Bible (Judges 13:2), the father of Samson. In the Talmud (Bava Metzia 71b), the father of Huna, a fifth-century scholar. Manoa and Manoah are variant spellings.

Mante A variant form of Monte. *See* Monte.

Manu A pet form of Manuel. *See* Manuel.

Manuel A short form of Emanuel. *See* Emanuel. Mani, Manni, Manny, Mannye, and Manu are pet forms. Mano and Manuela are variant forms.

Manuela The Hawaiian form of Manuel. *See* Manuel.

Manus A variant form of Magnus. *See* Magnus. A popular Irish name.

Manvel A variant form of Manville. *See* Manville.

Manville From the Old English, meaning "village of the workers." Manvel is a variant form.

Manyomi (מָנְיוֹמִי) A variant spelling of Minyomei. *See* Minyomei.

Maon (מָעוֹן) From the Hebrew, meaning "dwelling." In the Bible (I Chronicles 2:45), a descendant of Judah.

Maor (מָאוֹר) From the Hebrew, meaning "light."

Maoz (מָעוֹז) From the Hebrew, meaning "strength" or "fortress, stronghold."

Maozia A variant spelling of Maoziya. *See* Maoziya.

Maoziya (מָעוֹזְיָה) From the Hebrew, meaning "strength of the Lord" or "God's protection."

Mar (מַר) From the Aramaic, meaning "master" or "lord." Used among Babylonian talmudic scholars as a title of respect. The equivalent form in the

Palestinian academies was Mari and Rabi (Rabbi). Used also as an independent name. *See also* Mari.

Marc   A short form of Marcus. *See* Marcus. Mark is a variant spelling.

Marceau   A French form of Marcus. *See* Marcus.

Marcel   A popular French pet form of Marcus. *See* Marcus. Marcelino, Marcellino, and Marcello are Italian forms.

Marcelino, Marcellino, Marcello   Italian pet forms of Marcel. *See* Marcel.

March   A variant form of Marcus. *See* Marcus.

Marchall   A variant spelling of Marshall. *See* Marshall.

Marcus   From the Latin name Mars, meaning "warlike." In Roman mythology, the god of war. Marc is a short form. Marceau, Marcel, March, Marcy, Marilo, Mario, Marius, and Marshe are variant forms. *See* Marcel. Akin to Martin.

Marcy   A variant form of Marcus. *See* Marcus. Or, from the Old English, meaning "pool, lake."

Marden   From the British, meaning "field near the water." Mardyth is a variant form.

Mardut (מַרְדוּת)   From the Hebrew, meaning "rebellion."

Mardyth   A variant form of Marden. *See* Marden.

Maresha (מָרֵשָׁה)   From the Hebrew, meaning "hilltop." In the Bible (I Chronicles 2:42), a son of Caleb of the tribe of Judah.

Margia (מַרְגִּיעַ)   From the Hebrew, meaning "peace, rest."

Margoa (מַרְגּוֹעַ)   From the Hebrew, meaning "peace, rest."

Mari (מָרִי)   A pet form of Marius. *See* Marius. Also, a variant form of Mar. *See* Mar. In the Talmud (Bava Metzia 103a), a third-century Babylonian scholar and the son of Mar Samuel's daughter. Since he was fathered by a Gentile (who had converted to Judaism by the time Mari was born), he was named Mari ben Ashi, after his maternal grandfather, not after his father.

Marian   A variant English form of Mary, once popular in England. *See* Mary (feminine section). Marion is a variant spelling. Mario is a variant form.

Marilo   A Spanish form of Marcus. *See* Marcus.

Marin   From the Latin, meaning "small harbor."

Marinos   A variant form of Marinus. *See* Marinus.

Marinus (מָרִינוֹס)   From the Latin, meaning "sea." In the Talmud (Yerushalmi Berachot 6:5), a third-century Palestinian scholar. Marinos and Merinus are variant forms.

Mario   A variant form of Marian or Marcus. *See* Marcus *and* Marian.

Marion   A variant spelling of Marian. *See* Marian.

Maris   From the Old English and French, meaning "sea, lake."

Marius   A variant form of Marcus. *See* Marcus. Mari is a pet form.

Mariyon (מָרְיוֹן)   A variant form of Mari. *See* Mari. In the Talmud (Bava Batra 26b), a Babylonian scholar.

Mark   A variant spelling of Marc. *See* Marc.

Marlin   From the Latin, Old English, and French, meaning "sea." Also, from the Middle English and Old French, meaning "sand pit." Marlon is a variant spelling. Marlis, Marlo, Marlow, and Marlowe are variant forms.

Marlis   A variant form of Marlin. *See* Marlin.

Marlo   A variant form of Marlin. *See* Marlin. Used also as a feminine form.

Marlon   A variant spelling of Marlin. *See* Marlin.

Marlow, Marlowe   A variant form of Marlin. *See* Marlin.

Marne   From the Latin, Old English, and French, meaning "sea." *See also* Marin. Or, from the Latin, meaning "master."

Marnin (מַרְנִין)   From the Hebrew, meaning "one who creates joy" or "one who sings."

Marom (מָרוֹם)   From the Hebrew, meaning "lofty, exalted."

Maron (מָרוֹן)   From the Hebrew, meaning "flock of sheep."

Marpe, Marpei (מַרְפֵּא)   From the Hebrew, meaning "healing" or "medicine."

Marron   From the French, meaning "chestnut."

Marsden   From the Old English, meaning "pastureland near the sea."

Marshal, Marshall   From the Old English, meaning "horse," hence "one who grooms a horse," later "one who masters a horse," and finally "an officer in charge of military matters." Marchall is a variant spelling. Marshe is a variant form.

Marshe   A variant form of Marcus and Marshal. *See* Marcus *and* Marshal.

Marston   From the Anglo-Saxon, meaning "town near the sea."

Martin   A French form of the Latin name Martinus. Akin to Marcus, meaning "warlike." *See* Marcus. Martine is a variant form.

Martine   A variant form of Martin. *See* Martin.

Martzin   A variant form of Meretz. *See* Meretz.

Marvel, Marvell   From the Latin, meaning "to wonder, to marvel."

Marvin   From the Old English, meaning "friend of the sea" or "friendly sea." Also, from the Celtic, meaning "white sea," or from the Gaelic, meaning "mountainous area." Marwin, Mervin, Mervyn, Merwin, and Merwyn are variant forms.

Marwin   A variant form of Marvin. *See* Marvin.

Masa (מָשָׂא) From the Hebrew, meaning "burden." In the Bible (I Chronicles 1:30), a son of Ishmael and a grandson of Isaac.

Masai (מַעֲשַׂי) A variant form of Maaseiya. *See* Maaseiya. In the Bible (I Chronicles 9:12), a Priest.

Mashel (מאַשעל) A Yiddish form of Asher. *See* Asher.

Mashen (מִשְׁעָן) From the Hebrew, meaning "support, staff."

Mashiach (מָשִׁיחַ) From the Hebrew, meaning "messiah, anointed one." Mashiah is a variant spelling.

Mashiah A variant spelling of Mashiach. *See* Mashiach.

Maskil (מַשְׂכִּיל) From the Hebrew, meaning "enlightened, educated."

Mason From the Anglo-Saxon, meaning "mason, worker in stone."

Masos (מָשׂוֹשׂ) From the Hebrew, meaning "joy."

Mat A pet form of Matthew. *See* Matthew.

Matan (מַתָּן) From the Hebrew, meaning "gift." Akin to Matnai. In the Bible (Jeremiah 38:1), the father of Shefatya, who imprisoned Jeremiah. Matena, Matteno, Matnam, Maton, and Mattun are variant forms. Mattan is a variant spelling.

Matania, Mataniah Variant spellings of Matanya. *See* Matanya.

Mataniahu A variant spelling of Matanyahu. *See* Matanyahu.

Matanya (מַתַּנְיָה) From the Hebrew, meaning "gift of God." In the Bible (II Kings 24:17), the earlier name of King Zedekiah. Matania and Mataniah are variant spellings. Matanyahu is a variant form.

Matanyahu (מַתַּנְיָהוּ) A variant form of Matanya. *See* Matanya. In the Bible (I Chronicles 25:4), a son of Heman, one of King David's musicians.

Matena, Mattena (מַתְּנָה) Variant forms of Matan. *See* Matan. In the Talmud (Eruvin 6b), a third-century Babylonian scholar. Matna is a variant spelling.

Mateo A Spanish form of Matthew. *See* Matthew.

Mathias A variant form of Mattathias. *See* Mattathias.

Mathon A variant spelling of Maton. *See* Maton.

Mati (מַתִּי) A pet form of Mattathias and Matthew. *See* Mattathias *and* Matthew.

Matia, Matiah Variant spellings of Matya. *See* Matya.

Matisya A variant pronunciation of Matitya. *See* Matitya.

Matisyahu A variant pronunciation of Matityahu. *See* Matityahu.

Matitia, Matitiah Variant spellings of Matitya. *See* Matitya.

Matitya, Matityah (מַתִּתְיָה) From the Hebrew, meaning "gift of God." Mattathias is a Greek form. *See also* Mattathias. In the Bible (Ezra 10:43,

Nehemiah 8:4), contemporaries of Ezra and Nehemiah. Matisya, Matitia, and Matitiah are variant spellings. Matityahu is a variant form. Matya is a short form.

Matityahu (מַתִּתְיָהוּ) A variant form of Matitya. *See* Matitya.

Matmon (מַטְמוֹן) From the Hebrew, meaning "treasure, wealth."

Matna A variant spelling of Matena. *See* Matena.

Matnai (מַתְּנַי) From the Aramaic, meaning "gift." Akin to Matan. In the Bible (Ezra 10:33), a Priest in the time of Ezra.

Matnan (מַתְּנָן) A variant form of Matan. *See* Matan.

Maton A variant form of Matan. *See* Matan.

Matok (מָתוֹק) From the Hebrew, meaning "sweet."

Matri (מַטְרִי) From the Hebrew, meaning "rain, my rain." In the Bible (I Samuel 10:21), an ancestor of King Saul.

Matt A pet form of Matthew. *See* Matthew.

Mattan A variant spelling of Matan. *See* Matan.

Mattathias (מַתִּתְיָהוּ) A Greek form of the Hebrew name Matityahu, meaning "gift of God." The first Mattathias was a Jewish patriot and Priest who died about 167 B.C.E. He was the father of the five Hasmonean brothers, Judah the Maccabee being the most famous. Mathias, Matthew, and Matthias are variant forms. Mati is a pet form. *See also* Matthew *and* Matitya.

Matteo An Italian form of Matthew. *See* Matthew.

Matthew A variant form of Mattathias. *See* Mattathias. Mateo, Matteo, and Mayo are variant forms. Macey, Macy, Mat, Matt, Mati, Mattie, Matty, and Mattye are pet forms.

Matthias A variant form of Mattathias. *See* Mattathias.

Mattie, Matty, Mattye Pet forms of Matthew. *See* Matthew.

Mattun (מָתּוּן) A variant form of Matan. *See* Matan. In the Talmud (Bava Kama 96a), a third-century Palestinian scholar.

Matya (מַתְיָא) A short form of Matitya. *See* Matitya. Also, from the Aramaic, meaning "place, town." In the Talmud (Sanhedrin 32b), a scholar who established an academy of learning and a Bet Din (court) in Rome. Matia and Matiah are variant spellings. Also spelled מַתְיָה.

Matzliach (מַצְלִיחַ) From the Hebrew, meaning "victorious, successful."

Maurey A pet form of Maurice. *See* Maurice.

Maurice From the Greek, Latin, and Middle English, meaning "moorish, dark-skinned." Also, from the Old English and the Middle English, meaning "marshy, swampy wasteland." Akin to Murray. *See* Murray. Moritz, Morris, and Morse are variant forms. Maurey, Maurie, Maury, and Morey are pet forms.

Maurie A pet form of Maurice. *See* Maurice.

Maury   A pet form of Maurice. *See* Maurice.

Max   A short form of Maximilian. *See* Maximilian. Maks is a variant spelling.

Maxim, Maxime   Short forms of Maximilian. *See* Maximilian.

Maximilian   From the Latin, meaning "great" or "famous." Maxwell is an English form. Max, Maxim, and Maxime are short forms.

Maxwell   An English form of Maximilian. *See* Maximilian.

Mayer   From the Latin, meaning "great." Akin to Magnus. Also, a variant spelling of Meir. *See* Meir.

Mayes, Mays   From the British, meaning "field." Mayo is a variant form.

Maynard   From the Old High German, meaning "powerful, strong." Or, from the Latin and the French, meaning "hand."

Mayo   A variant form of Mayes or Matthew. *See* Mayes *and* Matthew.

Mazal (מָזָל)   From the Hebrew, meaning "star" or "luck."

Mazal-Tov (מָזָל־טוֹב)   From the Hebrew, meaning "good star, lucky star." Popular among Jews in the Middle Ages, particularly in Mediterranean countries.

Mechir (מְחִיר)   From the Hebrew, meaning "price" or "value." In the Bible (I Chronicles 4:11), a member of the tribe of Judah.

Mechonan (מְחוֹנָן)   From the Hebrew, meaning "talented, gifted." Mechonen is a variant form.

Mechonen (מְחוֹנָן)   A variant form of Mechonan. *See* Mechonan.

Mechubad (מְכֻבָּד)   From the Hebrew, meaning "honored."

Medad (מֵידָד)   From the Hebrew, meaning "friend." In the Bible (Numbers 11:26), a leader in the time of Moses who began prophesying when Israel was in the wilderness.

Medan (מְדָן)   From the Hebrew, meaning "strife, contention, war." In the Bible (Genesis 25:2), a son of Abraham and Keturah.

Medford   From the Old English, meaning "ford (brook crossing) in the meadow."

Meged (מֶגֶד)   From the Hebrew, meaning "goodness, sweetness, excellence."

Megen   A variant spelling of Meigein. *See* Meigein.

Mehader (מְהַדֵּר)   From the Hebrew, meaning "pleasant" or "excellent." Mehudar is a variant form.

Meharsheia (מְהַרְשֵׁיָא)   An Aramaic form of Moshe. *See* Moshe. Moses (Meharsheia) Kahane ben Jacob served as the head of the academy in Sura, Babylonia, in 825.

Mehudar (מְהֻדָּר)   A variant form of Mehader. *See* Mehader.

Mehulal (מְהֻלָל) From the Hebrew, meaning "praised, adored." Akin to Mahalalel.

Meigein (מָגֵן) From the Hebrew, meaning "to protect, protector." Megen is a variant spelling. Akin to Magen.

Meir (מֵאִיר) From the Hebrew, meaning "one who brightens or shines." In the Talmud (Yevamot 62b), a leading second-century scholar, the most brilliant of Rabbi Akiba's students. He came from a family of proselytes related to the Roman emperors. According to some authorities his real name was Miasa or Moise. Mayer, Meyer, and Myer are variant spellings. Meiri is a variant form. Muki is a pet form.

Meiri (מְאִירִי) A variant form of Meir. *See* Meir.

Mei-Zahav (מֵי־זָהָב) From the Hebrew, meaning "golden water." In the Bible (Genesis 36:39), an Edomite.

Mel, Mell Pet forms of Melvin. *See* Melvin.

Melabev (מְלַבֵּב) From the Hebrew, meaning "endearing."

Melatya (מְלַטְיָה) From the Hebrew, meaning "saved by God." In the Bible (Nehemiah 3:7), one of the Babylonian Exile returnees.

Melbourne From the Old English, meaning "brook near the mill."

Melchior A variant form of the Modern Latin name Melchita. Derived from the Hebrew *melech*, meaning "king."

Meldon From the Old English, meaning "master of the mill." Or, from the German, meaning "to proclaim, to announce."

Melech (מֶלֶךְ) From the Hebrew, meaning "king." In the Bible (I Chronicles 8:35), a member of the tribe of Benjamin and a descendant of King Saul. Akin to Maluch and Malka.

Melford From the Old English, meaning "ford near the mill."

Melitz (מֵלִיץ) From the Hebrew, meaning "advocate, advisor, interpreter."

Melton A variant form of Milton. *See* Milton.

Melville From the Old English, meaning "village near the mill."

Melvin From the Celtic, meaning "leader" or "chief." Also, from the Anglo-Saxon, meaning "friendly toiler" or "famous friend." Malvin and Melvyn are variant spellings. Mel and Mell are pet forms.

Melvyn A variant spelling of Melvin. *See* Melvin.

Melwood From the Old English, meaning "mill near the woods."

Menachem (מְנַחֵם) From the Hebrew, meaning "comforter." In the Bible (II Kings 15:14), a king of Israel notorious for his cruelty. In the Talmud (Yerushalmi Peah 6:4), a fourth-century Palestinian scholar. Menelaus, the Greek form of Menachem, was commonly used by the upper strata of society, including some High Priests. Among Italian Jews it was common to translate Menachem into Tranquillus. During the Middle Ages children born on the ninth of Av (a day of fasting and mourning for the destruction of the Temple) were named Menachem. Menahem is a variant spelling. At one point Menachem was shortened to Men, to which the diminutive suffix *del* was later added, forming the name Mendel. Menachem Mendel are often used together. Mann is a variant form.

Menahem A variant spelling of Menachem. *See* Menachem.

Menashe (מְנַשֶּׁה) From the Hebrew, meaning "causing to forget." In the Bible (Genesis 41:51), the eldest son of Joseph and the brother of Ephraim. Manasseh is an Anglicized form. Menashi and Menashya are variant forms.

Menashi (מְנַשִּׁי) A variant form of Menashe. *See* Menashe. In the Talmud (Avoda Zara 30b), a third-century Babylonian scholar.

Menashia, Menashiah Variant spellings of Menashya. *See* Menashya.

Menashya (מְנַשְׁיָא) An Aramaic form of Menashe. *See* Menashe. In the Talmud (Shavuot 45b), the son of Zevid and a third-century Babylonian scholar. Menashia and Menashiah are variant spellings.

Mendel (מֶנְדְל) From the Middle English *menden*, meaning "to repair, to amend." Probably an occupational name for one who does general repairs. Also, a Yiddish name derived from Menachem. *See* Menachem. Also spelled מֶענדְעל.

Mene A pet form of Menelaus. *See* Menelaus.

Menelaus In Greek legend, a king of Sparta, brother of Agamemnon. A variant form of Menachem. *See* Menachem. Mene is a pet form.

Menka (מֶנְקָא) A Yiddish form of Abraham. *See* Abraham.

Menucha (מְנוּחָה) From the Hebrew, meaning "rest, peace."

Merald From the Anglo-Saxon, meaning "old pool of water."

Merari (מְרָרִי) From the Hebrew, meaning "bitter." In the Bible (Exodus 6:19), a son of Levi and a grandson of Jacob.

Meraya (מְרָיָה) From the Hebrew, meaning "bitter" or "contentious." In the Bible (Nehemiah 12:12), a Priest in the time of Jehoiakim.

Mercer From the Old French, meaning "goods," hence "a dealer in textiles."

Mered (מֶרֶד) From the Hebrew, meaning "rebellion." In the Bible (I Chronicles 4:17), a member of the tribe of Judah, a descendant of Caleb.

Meredith From the Anglo-Saxon, meaning "sea-dew" or "sea defender." Also, of Welsh origin, meaning "great chief" or "defender."

Meretz (מֶרֶץ) From the Hebrew, meaning "energetic, alert" or "industrious." Martzin is a variant form.

Merinus A variant form of Marinus. *See* Marinus.

Merle From the Latin and the French, meaning "blackbird." Used also as a feminine name.

Merom (מֵרוֹם) From the Hebrew, meaning "heights." In the Bible (Joshua 11:5), the site of one of Joshua's military victories.

Meron (מֵרוֹן) From the Hebrew, meaning "troops, soldiers." An ancient town in northern Israel where the tomb of Rabbi Simeon bar Yochai is located.

Merrick From the Old English, meaning "ruler of the sea."

Merrill From the Old English, meaning "sea, pool, river, body of water." Also, from the Old English, meaning "famous." Myril is a variant form.

Merrit, Merritt From the Latin, meaning "valuable."

Merton From the Anglo-Saxon, meaning "from the farm by the sea." Myrton is a variant spelling.

Mervin A Welsh form of Marvin. *See* Marvin. Mervyn is a variant spelling.

Mervyn A variant spelling of Mervin. *See* Mervin.

Merwin, Merwyn Variant forms of Marvin. *See* Marvin.

Mesha (מֵישָׁא) From the Hebrew, meaning "freed, saved." In the Bible (I Chronicles 8:9), a leader of the tribe of Benjamin. Also in the Bible (II Kings 3:4), a king of Moab spelled מֵישַׁע, and (I Chronicles 2:42), a son of Caleb spelled מֵישָׁע.

Meshar (מֵישָׁר) From the Hebrew, meaning "upright, righteous, honorable."

Meshelemya (מְשֶׁלֶמְיָה) From the Hebrew, meaning "God's place" or "God's perfection." In the Bible (I Chronicles 9:21), a Levite.

Meshech (מֶשֶׁךְ) From the Hebrew, meaning "to draw." In the Bible (Genesis 10:2), a son of Japhet.

Meshi (מֶשִׁי) From the Hebrew, meaning "silk."

Meshovav (מְשׁוֹבָב) From the Hebrew, meaning "backslider, apostate." In the Bible (I Chronicles 4:34), a member of the tribe of Simeon.

Meshubach (מְשֻׁבָּח) From the Hebrew, meaning "excellent, superior." Mishbach is a variant form. Also spelled מְשׁוּבָּח.

Meshulam (מְשֻׁלָּם) From the Hebrew, meaning "complete, whole" or "peace." Mishlam is a variant form. In the Bible (II Kings 22:3), a scribe during the reign of King Josiah of Judah. Also spelled מְשׁוּלָם.

Mesushelach A variant pronunciation of Metushelach. *See* Metushelach.

Metav (מֵיטָב) A variant form of Metiv. *See* Metiv.

Methuselah The Anglicized spelling of Metushelach. *See* Metushelach.

Metushael (מְתוּשָׁאֵל) From the Hebrew, meaning "man who was asked." In the Bible (Genesis 4:12), a descendant of Cain.

Metiv (מֵיטִיב) From the Hebrew, meaning "good" or "improved." Metav is a variant form.

Metushelach (מְתוּשֶׁלַח) From the Hebrew, meaning "man who was sent, messenger." In the Bible (Genesis 5:21), the man who lived longer than anyone else (969 years). Methuselah is the Anglicized spelling.

Meudan (מְעֻדָּן) From the Hebrew, meaning "adorned."

Meushar (מְאֻשָּׁר) From the Hebrew, meaning "blessed, fortunate."

Meutar (מְעֻטָּר) From the Hebrew, meaning "crowned" or "adorned."

Mevaser (מְבַשֵּׂר) From the Hebrew, meaning "messenger." From 916 to 925, Mevaser was head (gaon) of the academy in Pumbedita, Babylonia.

Mevaser-Tov (מְבַשֵּׂר־טוֹב) From the Hebrew, meaning "bringer of good tidings."

Mevorach (מְבוֹרָךְ) From the Hebrew, meaning "blessed." The name of a tenth-century poet.

Mevorar (מְבוֹרָר) From the Hebrew, meaning "clear, pure."

Meyer A variant spelling of Meir. See Meir.

Meyuchas (מְיֻחָס) From the Hebrew, meaning "special, pedigreed."

Mibhar A variant spelling of Mivchar. See Mivchar.

Mibsam A variant spelling of Mivsam. See Mivsam.

Mibzar A variant spelling of Mivtzar. See Mivtzar.

Mica, Micah Anglicized forms of Micha. See Micha.

Micha (מִיכָה) From the Hebrew, meaning "Who is like God?" A short form of Michael. In the Bible (Micah 1:1), one of the twelve Minor Prophets who prophesied in the latter part of the eighth century B.C.E. Mica and Micah are Anglicized forms. Michaya and Michayahu are variant forms. Mika is a variant spelling.

Michael (מִיכָאֵל) From the Hebrew, meaning "Who is like God?" In the Bible (Numbers 13:13), a member of the tribe of Asher. In the Book of Daniel (12:1), the prince of the Angels—the archangel closest to God—and the chief divine messenger who carries out God's judgments. A popular name in England in the twelfth century, having been imported from France, where it was spelled Michel. Michon was another form used in France. Mitchel and Mitchell are variant English forms. In Italy Michele was a popular form, and in Spanish-speaking countries Miguel was common. Mikhail and Misha are Russian forms. Micah is like a short form. Mychal is a variant spelling. See Micha. Mickey, Mickie, Micky, Mike, Mikel, and Miki are pet forms.

Michal (מִיכָל) A short form of Michael. A popular feminine name.

Michaya (מִיכָיָה) A variant form of Micah. See Micah. In the Bible (Nehemiah 12:35), a Priest in the time of Nehemiah.

Michayahu (מִיכָיָהוּ) A variant form of Micah. See Micah. In the Bible (II Chronicles 7:17), an officer in King Jehoshaphat's court.

Michel A variant form of Michael. See Michael.

Michelangelo   Compounded of Michel (Michael) and Angelo. *See* Michael *and* Angelo.

Michele   A variant form of Michael. *See* Michael.

Michlal (מִכְלָל)   From the Hebrew, meaning "perfect, perfection."

Michlol (מִכְלוֹל)   From the Hebrew, meaning "glory, majesty."

Michman (מִכְמָן)   From the Hebrew, meaning "treasure" or "something hidden."

Michon (מִיכוֹן)   A variant spelling of Michael. *See* Michael.

Michri (מִכְרִי)   From the Hebrew, meaning "my merchandise." In the Bible (I Chronicles 9:8), a member of the tribe of Benjamin.

Mickey, Mickie, Micky   Pet forms of Michael. *See* Michael.

Midge   A variant form of Mitch. *See* Mitch.

Midian (מִדְיָן)   From the Hebrew, meaning "strife, war, contention." In the Bible (Genesis 25:2), a son of Abraham and Keturah.

Mifrach (מִפְרָח)   From the Hebrew, meaning "flower" or "flight."

Migdal (מִגְדָּל)   From the Hebrew, meaning "tower" or "protection."

Miguel   The Spanish and Portuguese form of Michael. *See* Michael.

Mika   A variant spelling of Micah. *See* Micah.

Mike   A pet form of Michael. *See* Michael.

Mikel   A pet form of Michael. *See* Michael.

Mikhail   A Russian form of Michael. *See* Michael.

Miki   A pet form of Michael. *See* Michael.

Miklot (מִקְלוֹת)   From the Hebrew, meaning "rod" or "sprout." Also, from the Hebrew, meaning "palm tree." In the Bible (I Chronicles 8:32), a leader of the tribe of Benjamin.

Mikneiyahu (מִקְנֵיָהוּ)   From the Hebrew, meaning "property of the Lord." In the Bible (I Chronicles 15:18), a Levite.

Milalai (מִלְלַי)   From the Aramaic, meaning "speak." In the Bible (Nehemiah 12:36), a Priest.

Miles   From the Greek and Latin, meaning "warrior, soldier." In England used as a short form of Michael. *See* Michael. Some authorities consider Miles to be derived from the Old German, meaning "beloved." Milo is a variant form. Myles is a variant spelling.

Milford   From the Latin, meaning "warrior, soldier." Akin to Miles.

Millard   From the Latin, meaning "millet."

Miller   An Old English occupational name, meaning "one who grinds or mills grain." Akin to Mills.

Mills   From the Old English *miln*, meaning "mill." Akin to Miller.

Milo   A variant form of Miles. *See* Miles.

Milton   From the Old English, meaning "from the mill, farmstead, or mill town." Melton is a variant form.

Minor   From the Middle English, meaning "one of lesser rank."

Minyamin (מִנְיָמִין)   A variant form of Binyamin (Benjamin). In the Bible (II Chronicles 31:15), a Priest in the time of King Hezekiah. In the Talmud (Sota 9a), a second-century scholar who was originally from Egypt. Minyomei is a variant form.

Minyomei (מִנְיוֹמֵי)   A variant form of Minyamin. *See* Minyamin. In the Talmud (Menachot 32b), a third-century Babylonian scholar. Minyomi is a variant spelling.

Minyomi   A variant spelling of Minyomei. *See* Minyomei.

Mirma, Mirmah (מִרְמָה)   From the Hebrew, meaning "deceit, trickery." In the Bible (I Chronicles 8:10), a descendant of Benjamin.

Misha   A Russian form of Michael. *See* Michael.

Mishael (מִישָׁאֵל)   From the Hebrew, meaning "borrowed." In the Bible (Exodus 6:22), an uncle of Moses and Aaron.

Misham (מִשְׁעָם)   From the Assyrian, meaning "to wash, cleanse." In the Bible (I Chronicles 8:12), a member of the tribe of Benjamin.

Mishan (מִשְׁעָן)   From the Hebrew, meaning "support" or "protection."

Mishbach (מִשְׁבָּח)   A variant form of Meshubach. *See* Meshubach.

Mishlam (מִשְׁלָם)   A variant form of Meshulam. *See* Meshulam.

Mishma (מִשְׁמָע)   From the Hebrew, meaning "hear, hearing" or "news." In the Bible (Genesis 25:14), a son of Ishmael and a grandson of Abraham.

Mishmana (מִשְׁמַנָּה)   From the Hebrew, meaning "delicacy" or "fertile land." In the Bible (I Chronicles 12:1), one of King David's warriors.

Mishmar (מִשְׁמָר)   From the Hebrew, meaning "guard" or "prison."

Miska   A Slovakian form of Michael. *See* Michael.

Mispar (מִסְפָּר)   From the Hebrew, meaning "number." In the Bible (Ezra 2:2), a leader of Judah who was among the Babylonian Exile returnees. Also called Misperet (Nehemiah 7:7).

Misperet (מִסְפֶּרֶת)   A variant form of Mispar. *See* Mispar.

Mitch   A pet form of Mitchell. *See* Mitchell. Midge is a variant form.

Mitchel, Mitchell   Variant forms of Michael. *See* Michael. Or, from the Old English, meaning "great." Mitch is a pet form.

Mitford   From the Middle English, meaning "small river crossing."

Mitzhal (מִצְהָל) From the Hebrew, meaning "joy." Mizhal is a variant spelling.

Mivchar (מִבְחָר) From the Hebrew, meaning "choice." In the Bible (I Chronicles 11:38), one of King David's warriors. Mivhar and Mibhar are variant spellings.

Mivhar A variant spelling of Mivchar. *See* Mivchar.

Mivsam (מִבְשָׂם) From the Hebrew, meaning "perfumed" or "spiced." In the Bible (I Chronicles 4:25), a son of Ishmael and a grandson of Abraham. Mibsam is a variant spelling.

Mivtach (מִבְטָח) From the Hebrew, meaning "secure place."

Mivtachyahu (מִבְטַחְיָהוּ) From the Hebrew, meaning "security of God."

Mivtzar (מִבְצָר) From the Hebrew, meaning "secure place." In the Bible (Genesis 36:42), a descendant of Esau. Mibzar is a variant spelling.

Miza, Mizah (מִזָּה) From the Hebrew, meaning "to suck out, empty." In the Bible (Genesis 36:17), a grandson of Esau.

Mizell From the Old High German, meaning "tiny gnat."

Mizhal A variant spelling of Mitzhal. *See* Mitzhal.

Mo A pet form of Morris. *See* Morris.

Moadia, Moadiah Variant spellings of Moadya. *See* Moadya.

Moadya (מוֹעַדְיָה) From the Hebrew, meaning "assembly of God." In the Bible (Nehemiah 12:17), a Priest who was among the Babylonian Exile returnees. Moadia and Moadiah are variant spellings.

Modi A nickname for Mordechai. *See* Mordechai.

Moe A pet form of Moses. *See* Moses.

Mohar (מֹהַר) From the Hebrew, meaning "gift" or "dowry."

Moise A French form of Moses. *See* Moses.

Moke The Hawaiian form of Moses. *See* Moses.

Mokir (מוֹקִיר) From the Hebrew, meaning "honor" or "respect."

Molada (מוֹלָדָה) From the Hebrew, meaning "homeland, birthplace." In the Talmud (Sanhedrin 70a), the father of a third-century Babylonian scholar. Used in modern times as a feminine name.

Molid (מוֹלִיד) From the Hebrew, meaning "progenitor propagator." In the Bible (I Chronicles 2:29), a member of the tribe of Judah.

Mona A variant form of Muna. *See* Muna. In the Talmud (Shabbat 108b), a second-century Palestinian scholar.

Monford From the British, meaning "mountain ford (crossing)."

Monroe From the Latin, French, and Scottish, meaning "a wheeler, one who rolls objects on a wheel." Also, from the Celtic, meaning "red marsh." Munroe is a variant form.

Montague   The French form of the Latin, meaning "from the pointed mountain." Montgomery is an English variant form. Monte and Monty are pet forms.

Monte   A pet form of Montague and Montgomery. *See* Montague *and* Montgomery. Monty is a variant spelling.

Montgomery   The English variant of the French name Montague. *See* Montague.

Monty   A variant spelling of Monte. *See* Monte.

Moon   From the Old English, meaning "month."

Mor (מֹר)   From the Hebrew, meaning "spice." Also spelled מוֹר.

Morag (מוֹרַג)   From the Hebrew, meaning "threshing board."

Moran (מוֹרָן)   From the Hebrew, meaning "teacher." Used also as a feminine name.

Morash (מוֹרָשׁ)   From the Hebrew, meaning "inheritance, legacy."

Mordche (מָאִרְדְכֶע)   A Yiddish form of Mordechai. *See* Mordechai.

Mordecai   The Anglicized form of Mordechai. *See* Mordechai.

Mordechai (מָרְדְּכַי)   From the Persian and Babylonian, meaning "warrior, warlike." A variant form of Marduk. In Babylonian mythology Marduk was the god of war. In the Bible (Esther 2:5), Mordechai was the cousin of Queen Esther, who saved the Jews of Persia from Haman's plot to exterminate them. The Purim holiday celebrates this victory. In the Middle Ages, Jewish boys born on Purim were often named Mordechai. Mordecai is the Anglicized form. Mordche is the Yiddish form. Modi, Mordy, Motche, Moti, Motti, and Motke are pet forms.

Mordy   A pet form of Mordechai. *See* Mordechai.

Morenu (מוֹרֵנוּ)   From the Hebrew, meaning "our teacher."

Moreton   A variant spelling of Morton. *See* Morton.

Morey   A pet form of Maurice. *See* Maurice. Mori, Morie, Morrey, Morrie, and Mory are variant spellings.

Morgan   From the Celtic, meaning "one who lives near the sea."

Mori, Morie (מוֹרִי)   From the Hebrew, meaning "my teacher." Also, variant spellings of Morey. *See* Morey.

Moriel (מוֹרִיאֵל)   From the Hebrew, meaning "God is my guide" or "God is my teacher."

Moritz   A variant form of Maurice. *See* Maurice.

Morrey   A variant spelling of Morey. *See* Morey.

Morrie A variant spelling of Morey. *See* Morey.

Morris A variant form of Maurice. *See* Maurice. Also, from the Gaelic, meaning "great warrior." Morrison is a patronymic form. Mo is a pet form.

Morrison A patronymic form, meaning "son of Morris." *See* Morris.

Morry A variant spelling of Morey. *See* Morey.

Morse A variant form of Maurice. *See* Maurice. In Roman mythology, death personified as a god. Akin to Thanatos, the god of death in Greek mythology.

Mortimer From the Anglo-French, meaning "one who lives near the sea" or "one who dwells near still water."

Morton From the Old English, meaning "town near the sea" or "farm on the moor." Moreton is a variant spelling. Morty is a pet form.

Morty A pet form of Morton. *See* Morton.

Mose A pet form of Moses. Also, the Hawaiian form of Moses. *See* Moses.

Moses The Anglicized form of Moshe. *See* Moshe. Moise, Moke, Mose, Moss, Moy, and Moyse are variant forms. Moe is a pet form.

Mosha (מוֹשַׁע) From the Hebrew, meaning "salvation." Akin to Joshua. Moshaa is a variant form.

Moshaa A variant form of Mosha. *See* Mosha.

Moshe (מֹשֶׁה) From the Hebrew, meaning "drawn out (of the water)." Or, from the Egyptian, meaning "son, child." In the Bible (Exodus 2:10), the leader who brought the Israelites out of bondage in Egypt and led them to the Promised Land. In the Talmud (Bava Batra 174b and repeated in Arachin 23a), a person by the name of Moshe bar Etzri is mentioned. He appears to be a layman, the father-in-law of a scholar named Huna. The Talmud (Megilla 13a) says that two names, Yered and Gedor, mentioned in I Chronicles 4:18 are nicknames for the biblical Moshe.

Moshel (מוֹשֵׁל) From the Hebrew, meaning "ruler."

Moss An English variant form of Moses. *See* Moses.

Motche A pet form of Mordecai. *See* Mordecai.

Motel A pet form of Mordechai. *See* Mordechai.

Moti, Motti (מוֹטִי) Nicknames for Mordechai. *See* Mordechai.

Motke (מוֹטְקֶע) A pet form of Mordechai. *See* Mordechai. Also spelled מאַטְקֶע.

Motza (מוֹצָא) From the Hebrew, meaning "to go forth, to exit." In the Bible (I Chronicles 2:46), a son of Caleb and his concubine Efa.

Moy, Moyse Variant English forms of Moses. *See* Moses.

Muki (מוּקִי) A pet form of Meir. *See* Meir.

Mull From the Middle English, meaning "to grind." Akin to Mills. *See* Mills.

Mumi (מוּמִי) A pet form of Shlomo (Solomon). *See* Shlomo.

Muna (מוּנָא) From the Aramaic, meaning "counted, numbered." In the Talmud (Megila 18b), a second-century Babylonian scholar. Mona is a variant form.

Munroe A variant form of Monroe. *See* Monroe.

Murray From the Celtic and Welsh, meaning "sea" or "seaman." Akin to Maurice. *See* Maurice. Murry is a variant spelling.

Murry A variant spelling of Murray. *See* Murray.

Mushi (מוּשִׁי) From the Hebrew, meaning "feel, touch" or "remove." In the Bible (Exodus 6:19), the younger son of Merari and a grandson of Levi.

Mychal A variant spelling of Michael. *See* Michael.

Myer A variant spelling of Mayer. *See* Mayer.

Myles A variant spelling of Miles. *See* Miles.

Myril A variant form of Merrill. *See* Merrill. Myrl is a variant spelling.

Myrl A variant spelling of Myril. *See* Myril.

Myron From the Greek, meaning "fragrant, sweet, pleasant."

Myrton A variant spelling of Merton. *See* Merton.

Naam (נַעַם) From the Hebrew, meaning "sweet, pleasant." In the Bible (I Chronicles 4:15), a son of Caleb. Akin to Naaman.

Naaman (נַעֲמָן) From the Hebrew, meaning "sweet, beautiful, pleasant, good." In the Bible (II Kings 5:1), the general of the army of Aram (circa ninth century B.C.E. who visited the Prophet Elisha to be cured of leprosy. Akin to Naam. Naon and Noam are variant forms.

Naarai (נַעֲרַי) From the Aramaic, meaning "boy." In the Bible (I Chronicles 11:37), a warrior in the army of King David. Paarai is a variant form (II Samuel 23:35).

Naari (נַעֲרִי) From the Hebrew, meaning "my boy."

Naaria A variant spelling of Naarya. *See* Naarya.

Naarya (נַעַרְיָה) From the Hebrew, meaning "child of God." In the Bible (I Chronicles 3:23), a descendant of King David. Naaria is a variant spelling.

Nabal A variant spelling of Naval. *See* Naval.

Naboth A variant spelling of Navot. *See* Navot.

Nacham (נַחַם) From the Hebrew, meaning "consolation, comfort." In the Bible (I Chronicles 4:19), a member of the tribe of Judah. Naham is a variant spelling.

Nachash (נָחָשׁ) From the Hebrew, meaning "serpent." In the Bible (II Samuel 17:25), a man who supported King David. Nachshon is a variant form. Nahash is a variant spelling.

Nachat (נַחַת) From the Aramaic, meaning "to go down, descend." In the Bible (II Chronicles 31:13), an overseer in the time of King Hezekiah.

Nachbi (נַחְבִּי) From the Hebrew, meaning "to hide, withdraw." In the Bible (Numbers 13:14), one of the twelve scouts sent out by Moses to explore the Promised Land.

Nachliel (נַחְלִיאֵל) From the Hebrew, meaning "God is my possession." In the Bible (Numbers 21:19), a place-name in the wilderness.

Nachman (נַחְמָן) From the Hebrew, meaning "comforter." Akin to Nachmani. In the Talmud (Betza 29b), a Babylonian scholar.

Nachmani (נַחְמָנִי) From the Hebrew, meaning "comfort." In the Bible (Nehemiah 7:7), a leader of Judah who was among the Babylonian Exile returnees. In the Talmud (Horayot 14a), Nachmani is the nickname of Abaye. Nahamani is a variant spelling. Akin to Nachman.

Nachmiel (נַחְמִיאֵל) From the Hebrew, meaning "God is my comfort."

Nachon (נָכוֹן) From the Hebrew, meaning "right, honest, proper" or "firm, enduring." In the Bible (II Samuel 6:6), the owner of a threshing floor.

Nachor (נָחוֹר) From the Assyrian and Arabic, meaning "nostril" or "to snort." In the Bible (Genesis 11:26), the son of Terach and the brother of Abraham. Nahor is a variant spelling.

Nachshon (נַחְשׁוֹן) From the Hebrew, meaning "diviner." In the Bible (Exodus 6:23),a brother-in-law of Aaron. Nahshon is a variant spelling.

Nachum (נַחוּם) From the Hebrew, meaning "comfort." In the Bible (Nahum 1:1), a minor Prophet of the seventh century B.C.E. who foretold the fall of Nineveh. In the Talmud (Berachot 22a), a second-century Palestinian scholar known as Nachum Ish Gamzu was Rabbi Akiba's teacher. Nahum is a variant spelling.

Nadab A variant spelling of Nadav. *See* Nadav.

Nadav (נָדָב) From the Hebrew, meaning "generous" or "noble." In the Bible (Exodus 6:23), the eldest son of Aaron, the High Priest. Nadiv is a variant form. Nadab is a variant spelling.

Nadir (נָדִיר) From the Hebrew, meaning "oath."

Nadiv (נָדִיב) A variant form of Nadav. *See* Nadav.

Naeh (נָאֶה) From the Hebrew, meaning "beautiful."

Naf (נַף) A pet form of Naftali. *See* Naftali.

Nafish (נָפִישׁ) From the Syriac and Hebrew, meaning "to breathe" or "to refresh oneself." In the Bible (Genesis 25:15), a son of Ishmael and a grandson of Abraham. Naphish is a variant spelling.

Naftali, Naftalie (נַפְתָּלִי) From the Hebrew, meaning "to wrestle," "to be crafty." Also, from the Hebrew, meaning "likeness, comparison." In the Bible (Genesis 30:8), the sixth son of Jacob; the second with his wife Bilhah. Naf is a pet form. Naphtali and Naphthali are variant spellings.

Nagid (נָגִיד) From the Hebrew, meaning "ruler, prince."

Nagiv (נָגִיב) From the Hebrew, meaning "pertaining to the south." Akin to Negev.

Naham A variant spelling of Nacham. See Nacham.

Nahamani A variant spelling of Nachmani. See Nachmani.

Nahash A variant spelling of Nachash. See Nachash.

Nahir (נָהִיר) A variant form of Nahor. See Nahor.

Nahor (נָהוֹר) From the Aramaic, meaning "light." Nehor is a variant spelling. Nahir, Nahur, and Nehorai are variant forms. Also, a variant spelling of Nachor. See Nachor.

Nahshon A variant spelling of Nachshon. See Nachshon.

Nahum A variant spelling of Nachum. See Nachum.

Nahur (נָהוּר) A variant form of Nahor. See Nahor.

Naim (נָעִים) From the Hebrew, meaning "splendid, sweet."

Nakdimon (נַקְדִּימוֹן) From the Hebrew, meaning "one who sheds light." In the Talmud (Ketubot 66b), son of Guryon, one of the three esteemed members of the Jerusalem community in the last years of the Second Temple. According to the Talmud (Taanit 20a), his proper name was Boni.

Namer (נָמֵר) From the Hebrew, meaning "leopard."

Namir (נָמִיר) From the Hebrew, meaning "leopard." Akin to Namer.

Nanas (נַנָּס) A variant spelling of Nanos. See Nanos.

Nanos (נַנּוֹס) From the Aramaic and Hebrew, meaning "short, a dwarf." In the Talmud (Mishna Menachot 4:3), the father of a second-century Palestinian scholar. Nanas is a variant spelling.

Nansen A Scandinavian matronymic form, meaning "son of Nancy."

Naom (נָעוֹם) A variant form of Naaman. See Naaman. The masculine form of Naomi. Akin to Noam.

Naor (נָאוֹר) From the Hebrew, meaning "light" or "enlightened." Akin to Ner.

Naot (נָאוֹת) From the Hebrew, meaning "fit, proper, beautiful." Akin to Naeh.

Naphish A variant spelling of Nafish. See Nafish.

Naphtali, Naphthali   Variant spellings of Naftali. *See* Naftali.

Napoleon   From the Greek name Neapolis, meaning "new town." Napoli is the Italian form of Naples.

Nardimon (נַרְדִּימוֹן)   A variant form of Nerd. *See* Nerd.

Narkis (נַרְקִיס)   A plant name of the amaryllis family, which includes daffodils and jonquils. Related to Narcissus, a beautiful youth in Greek mythology.

Nash, Nashe   From the Old English, meaning "protruding cliff."

Nasi (נָשִׂיא)   From the Hebrew, meaning "prince."

Nat   A pet form of Nathan. *See* Nathan.

Natan (נָתָן)   From the Hebrew, meaning "gift." In the Bible (II Samuel 5:15), the Prophet who pronounced that the dynasty of King David would be perpetually established. He reprimanded David for his unfair treatment of Uriah the Hittite. In the Talmud (Suka 19b), a second-century Babylonian scholar. Nat and Nate are pet forms. Nathan is a variant spelling.

Nate   A pet form of Nathan. *See* Nathan.

Nathan   A variant spelling of Natan. *See* Natan.

Nathanel, Nathaniel   Variant spellings of Netanel. *See* Netanel.

Nativ (נָתִיב)   From the Hebrew, meaning "path, road."

Natron (נַטְרוֹן)   A variant form of Natronai. *See* Natronai.

Natronai (נַטְרוֹנָאי)   From the Aramaic, meaning "gift" or "keepsake." The name of a ninth-century talmudic scholar *(gaon)*, the head of the academy in Sura, Babylonia. Natron and Nitron are variant forms.

Naval (נָבָל)   From the Hebrew, meaning "foolish, senseless" or "depraved." In the Bible (I Samuel 25:3), a wealthy sheepherder whose wife, Abigail, later married King David. Nabal is a variant spelling.

Naveh (נָאוֶה)   From the Hebrew, meaning "beautiful."

Navon (נָבוֹן)   From the Hebrew, meaning "wise."

Navot (נָבוֹת)   From the Hebrew, meaning "to see, prophesy." Related to the Babylonian god Nebo. In the Bible (I Kings 21:2), the owner of a vineyard coveted by Queen Jezebel. Naboth is a variant spelling.

Neal, Neale   From the Middle English and the Gaelic, meaning "champion, courageous person" or "dark-complexioned one." Neely and Nyle are variant forms. Neil and Niel are variant spellings. Neilson, Nelson, Niles, and Nils are patronymic forms.

Nechemia, Nechemiah   Variant spellings of Nechemya. *See* Nechemya.

Nechemya (נְחֶמְיָה)   From the Hebrew, meaning "comforted of the Lord." In the Bible (Ezra 2:2), a governor of Judah. He had previously been cupbearer to the Persian king, Ataxerxes I. Nechemia, Nechemiah, and Nehemiah are variant spellings.

Nechmad (נֶחְמָד) From the Hebrew, meaning "beautiful, desirable."

Nechum (נָחוּם) From the Hebrew, meaning "comfort." In the Bible (Nehemiah 7:7), a leader of the Babylonian Exile returnees. Nehum is a variant spelling.

Nechunia A variant spelling of Nechunya. *See* Nechunya.

Nechunya (נְחוּנְיָה) From the Aramaic, meaning "comfort." In the Talmud (Eduyot 86b), the son of Elinatan. Also spelled נְחוּנְיָא. Nechunia is a variant spelling.

Ned A pet form of Edmond and Edward. *See* Edmond *and* Edward.

Nedavia, Nedaviah Variant spellings of Nedavya. *See* Nedavya.

Nedavya (נְדַבְיָה) From the Hebrew, meaning "generosity of the Lord" or "God's gift." In the Bible (I Chronicles 3:18), a descendant of Solomon. Nedavia and Nedaviah are variant spellings.

Neddy A pet form of Edmond and Edward. *See* Edmond *and* Edward.

Ne'edar (נֶאְדָּר) From the Hebrew, meaning "glorified, exalted, esteemed."

Neely A variant form of Neal. *See* Neal.

Ne'eman (נֶאֱמָן) From the Hebrew, meaning "loyal, honest, trustworthy."

Ne'etzal (נֶאֱצָל) From the Hebrew, meaning "ennobled" or "influenced."

Nefeg (נֶפֶג) From the Hebrew, meaning "casualty, wounded." In the Bible (Exodus 6:21), a Levite, the son of Yitzhar.

Negev (נֶגֶב) From the Hebrew, meaning "south, southerly." Akin to Nagiv.

Nehedar (נֶהְדָּר) From the Hebrew, meaning "glorious, magnificent, splendid."

Nehemia, Nehemiah Variant spellings of Nechemya. *See* Nechemya. Nemiah is a variant form.

Nehor A variant spelling of Nahor. *See* Nahor.

Nehorai (נְהוֹרַאי) A variant form of Nahor. *See* Nahor. In the Talmud (Nazir 5a), a second-century Babylonian scholar.

Nehum A variant spelling of Nechum. *See* Nechum.

Neil A variant spelling of Neal. *See* Neal. Also, a pet form of Nathaniel.

Neilson A patronymic form of Neil, meaning "son of Neil." *See* Neil.

Nelson A patronymic form of Neal, meaning "son of Neal." *See* Neal.

Nemalia A variant form of Nemuel. *See* Nemuel.

Nemesh (נֶמֶשׁ) From the Hebrew, meaning "gleaners" or "gold, golden." Nimshi is a variant form.

Nemiah A variant form of Nehemiah. *See* Nehemiah.

Nemo Probably an Old English contraction of Nehemiah. *See* Nehemiah.

Nemuel (נְמוּאֵל) From the Hebrew, meaning "ant," hence "industrious." Also, from the Hebrew, meaning "harbor." In the Bible (Numbers 26:9), a leader of the tribe of Reuben. Nemalia and Nimli are variant forms.

Neora (נְאוֹרָה) From the Hebrew, meaning "enlightened, cultured." Neorai is an Aramaic form.

Neorai (נְאוֹרַאי) An Aramaic form of Neora. See Neora.

Ner (נֵר) From the Hebrew, meaning "light." In the Bible (I Samuel 14:3), the father of Abner, King Saul's army general.

Nerd (נֵרְדְּ) From the Sanskrit and Persian, meaning "nard, spikenard," a fragrant spice used in ancient times. Nardimon is a variant form.

Neri (נֵרִי) From the Hebrew, meaning "my light."

Neria, Neriah Variant spellings of Neriya. See Neriya.

Neriahu A variant spelling of Neriyahu. See Neriyahu.

Neriya (נֵרִיָה) From the Hebrew, meaning "light of the Lord." In the Bible (Jeremiah 32:12), the father of Baruch, Jeremiah's scribe. Neria and Neriah are variant spellings. Neriyahu is a variant form.

Neriyahu (נֵרִיָהוּ) A variant form of Neriya. See Neriya.

Nerli (נֵרְלִי) From the Hebrew, meaning "I have (a) light."

Nes, Ness (נֵס) From the Hebrew, meaning "miracle."

Neta (נֶטַע) From the Hebrew, meaning "plant, growth" or "flower."

Netanel (נְתַנְאֵל) From the Hebrew, meaning "gift of God." In the Bible (I Chronicles 2:14), the fourth son of Jesse, a brother of King David. Nathanel, Nathaniel, Nethanel, and Nethaniel are Anglicized forms.

Netania, Netaniah Variant spellings of Netanya. See Netanya.

Netaniahu A variant spelling of Netanyahu. See Netanyahu.

Netanya (נְתַנְיָה) From the Hebrew, meaning "gift of God." In the Bible (II Kings 25:23), the father of the murderer of Gedaliah. Netania and Netaniah are variant spellings. Netanyahu is a variant form.

Netanyahu (נְתַנְיָהוּ) A variant form of Netanya. See Netanya.

Nethanel A variant spelling of Netanel. See Netanel.

Nethaniel A variant spelling of Netanel. See Netanel.

Netia, Netiah Variant spellings of Netiya. See Netiya.

Netiya (נְטִיַע) From the Hebrew, meaning "plant" or "sapling." Netia and Netiah are variant spellings.

Netzach (נֶצַח) From the Hebrew, meaning "victory." Akin to Netziach.

Netzer (נֵצֶר) From the Hebrew, meaning "shoot, branch."

Netziach (נְצִיחַ) From the Hebrew, meaning "victory." In the Bible (Ezra

2:54), one of the Temple porters. Netziah is a variant spelling. Akin to Netzach.

Netziah A variant spelling of Netziach. *See* Netziach.

Nevat (נְבָט) From the Hebrew, meaning "behold, look, see." In the Bible (I Kings 11:26), the father of King Jeroboam. Nevayot is a variant form.

Nevayot (נְבָיוֹת) A variant form of Nevat. *See* Nevat. In the Bible (Genesis 25:13), the elder son of Ishmael.

Neven From the Old English, meaning "middle" or "hub of a wheel." Nevin and Nevins are variant forms.

Nevil, Nevile, Nevill, Neville From the French, meaning "new town."

Nevin, Nevins Variant forms of Neven. *See* Neven.

Newbold From the Old English, meaning "new town beside the tree."

Newell An English form of the Latin, meaning "something new, unusual." Nowell is a variant form.

Newman From the Anglo-Saxon, meaning "new man."

Newton From the Old English, meaning "from the new estate or farmstead" or "new town." Akin to Newbold.

Nichbad (נִכְבָּד) From the Hebrew, meaning "honored."

Nicholas From the Greek, meaning "victory of the people." Nicol and Colin are pet forms. Nicolas is a variant spelling. Niel is a variant form.

Nicolas A variant spelling of Nicholas. *See* Nicholas.

Nidri (נִדְרִי) From the Hebrew, meaning "my oath."

Niel A variant Norse form of Nicholas. *See* Nicholas. Also, a variant spelling of Neal. *See* Neal.

Nike From the Greek, meaning "victory."

Nilbav (נִלְבָּב) From the Hebrew, meaning "good-natured" or "beloved."

Niles A patronymic form of Neal, meaning "son of Neal." *See* Neal. Akin to Nils.

Nili (נִילִי) An acronym of the Hebrew words from I Samuel 15:29: "The glory [or eternity] of Israel will not lie." Nili was the name of a pro-British and anti-Turkish Jewish underground organization in Palestine during World War I. Used also as a feminine name.

Nils A patronymic form of Neal, meaning "son of Neal." *See* Neal. Akin to Niles.

Nimli (נִמְלִי) A variant form of Nemuel. *See* Nemuel.

Nimrod (נִמְרוֹד) From the Hebrew, meaning "rebel." In the Bible (Genesis 10:8), the son of Kish and a grandson of Ham.

Nimshi (נִמְשִׁי)   A variant form of Nemesh. *See* Nemesh. In the Bible (I Kings 19:16), the grandfather of Jehu, a king of Israel.

Nin (נִין)   From the Hebrew, meaning "grandson."

Nir (נִיר)   From the Hebrew, meaning "to plough" or "to cultivate a field." Used also as a feminine name.

Niram (נִירְעָם)   From the Hebrew, meaning "cultivated fields of the people."

Nirel (נִירְאֵל)   From the Hebrew, meaning "cultivated field of the Lord." Niriel, Niriya, and Nirya are variant forms.

Niria, Niriah   Variant spellings of Nirya. *See* Nirya.

Niriel (נִירִיאֵל)   A variant form of Nirel. *See* Nirel.

Nirya (נִירְיָה)   A variant form of Nirel. *See* Nirel. Niria and Niriah are variant spellings.

Nisan   A variant spelling of Nissan. *See* Nissan.

Niriya (נִירִיָּה)   From the Hebrew, meaning "cultivated land of the Lord." Niria and Niriah are variant spellings. Akin to Nirel. *See* Nirel.

Nisi (נִסִי)   From the Hebrew, meaning "my sign" or "my miracle." Nissan and Nissim are variant forms. Nissi is a variant spelling

Nissan (נִיסָן)   From the Hebrew, meaning "banner, emblem" or "miracle." Also, the name of the Hebrew month in which the Passover holiday occurs. The first month of spring. Nisan is a variant spelling. Akin to Nissim.

Nissi   A variant spelling of Nisi. *See* Nisi.

Nissim (נִסִים)   From the Hebrew, meaning "signs" or "miracles." Akin to Nissan. *See* Nissan.

Nitai (נִתַּאי)   From the Hebrew, meaning "seedling, plant." In the Talmud (Avot 1:7), Nitai Haarbeli was one of the early scholars during the Hasmonean period.

Nitron (נִטְרוֹן)   A variant form of Natronai. *See* Natronai.

Nitzan (נִצָּן)   From the Hebrew, meaning "bud." Also spelled נִיצָן.

Nitzchan (נִצְחָן)   From the Hebrew, meaning "victory, winner." Akin to Nitzchi.

Nitzchi (נִצְחִי)   From the Hebrew, meaning "my victory." Akin to Nitzchan.

Niv (נִיב)   From the Aramaic and Arabic, meaning "speech, expression."

Nivai (נִיבָי)   A variant form of Niv. In the Bible (Nehemiah 10:20), a supporter of Nehemiah.

Nivchar (נִבְחָר)   From the Hebrew, meaning "chosen."

Noach (נֹחַ)   From the Hebrew, meaning "rest, quiet, peace." In the Bible (Genesis 5:29), the main character in the story of the flood. Noah is the Anglicized form. Akin to Nocha.

Noad (נוֹעָד)   From the Hebrew, meaning "assembled" or "prepared."

Noadia, Noadiah   Variant spellings of Noadya. *See* Noadya.

Noadya (נוֹעַדְיָה)   From the Hebrew, meaning "assembly of God." In the Bible (Ezra 8:33), a Levite. Noadia and Noadiah are variant spellings.

Noah   The Anglicized form of Noach. *See* Noach.

Noam (נוֹעַם)   From the Hebrew, meaning "sweetness" or "friendship." A variant form of Naaman. *See* Naaman.

Noaz (נוֹעַז)   From the Hebrew, meaning "daring, bold."

Noble   From the Latin, meaning "well-known, famous."

Nocha (נוֹחָה)   From the Hebrew, meaning "rest, calm." Akin to Noach. In the Bible (I Chronicles 8:5), a son of Benjamin.

Nocham (נוֹחָם)   From the Hebrew, meaning "comfort, consolation."

Noda (נוֹדָע)   From the Hebrew, meaning "famous, well-known."

Noel   An Old French form of the Latin, meaning "to be born" or "birthday." Children born on Christmas are often named Noel. Nowell is a variant form.

Nofech (נֹפֶךְ)   From the Hebrew, meaning "precious stone (turquoise)."

Noga (נֹגַה)   From the Hebrew, meaning "light" or "bright." In the Bible (I Chronicles 3:7), a son of King David. Used also as a feminine name.

Noi   A variant spelling of Noy. *See* Noy.

Nolan   From the Celtic, meaning "noble" or "famous." Nolen is a variant spelling. Noland is a variant form.

Noland   A variant form of Nolan. *See* Nolan.

Nolen   A variant spelling of Nolan. *See* Nolan.

Norbert   From the German, meaning "divine brightness."

Norman   From the Anglo-Saxon, meaning "man from the North." Refers to the Northmen, who conquered Normandy in the tenth century. Normann is a variant spelling. Normand is a variant form.

Normand   A French form of Norman. *See* Norman.

Normann   A variant spelling of Norman. *See* Norman.

Norris   From the Anglo-Saxon, meaning "house of a man from the North." Also, from the French and Latin, meaning "caretaker."

North   From the Anglo-Saxon, meaning "man from the North."

Norton   From the Anglo-Saxon, meaning "town in the North." It refers specifically to the northern town of Yorkshire. *See* Norman.

Norwood   From the Old English, meaning "woods in the North."

Notea (נוֹטֵעַ)   From the Hebrew, meaning "to plant."

Noter (נוֹטֵר)   From the Hebrew, meaning "guard, protector."

Notzar (נוֹצָר)   From the Hebrew, meaning "guarded, protected."

Notzer (נוֹצֵר)   From the Hebrew, meaning "guard, guardian."

Nowell   A variant form of Noel and Newell. *See* Noel *and* Newell.

Noy (נוֹי)   From the Hebrew, meaning "beauty." Noi is a variant spelling.

Nufar (נוּפָר)   From the Hebrew, referring to a variety of water plant. Nuphar is a variant spelling.

Nugent   Possibly from the Old English and Middle Low German, meaning "to nudge, shove."

Nun (נוּן)   From the Hebrew, meaning "son, offspring" or "to sprout, grow." In the Bible (Exodus 33:11), the father of Joshua, successor to Moses.

Nuphar   A variant spelling of Nufar. *See* Nufar.

Nur (נוּר)   From the Aramaic, meaning "fire."

Nuri (נוּרִי)   From the Hebrew and Aramaic, meaning "my fire." In the Talmud (Eruvin 45b), the father of Yochanan, a first-century scholar.

Nuria, Nuriah   Variant spellings of Nuriya. *See* Nuriya.

Nuriel (נוּרִיאֵל)   From the Aramaic and Hebrew, meaning "fire of the Lord." Akin to Nuriya.

Nuriya (נוּרִיָה)   From the Aramaic and Hebrew, meaning "fire of the Lord." Nuria and Nuriah are variant spellings. Nurya is a variant form. Akin to Nuriel.

Nurya (נוּרִיָה)   A variant form of Nuriya. *See* Nuriya.

Nyle   A variant Irish form of Neal. *See* Neal. Also, from the Old English, meaning "island."

Oak   A pet form of Oakley. *See* Oakley.

Oakes   From the Old English, meaning "one who sells oak trees."

Oakleigh   A variant spelling of Oakley. *See* Oakley.

Oakley   From the Old English, meaning "field of oak trees." Oakleigh is a variant spelling.

Obadiah   The Anglicized form of Ovadya. *See* Ovadya. Obe is a pet form.

Obe A pet form of Obadiah. *See* Obadiah.

Obed A variant spelling of Oved. *See* Oved.

Obil A variant spelling of Ovil. *See* Ovil.

Odam From the Middle English, meaning "son-in-law."

Oded (עֹדֵד) From the Hebrew, meaning "to restore." In the Bible (II Chronicles 28:9), a Prophet in the time of King Ahaz.

Odell An Irish form of the Danish, meaning "otter." Also, from the Greek, meaning "ode, melody."

Odo From the Old German and the Old English, meaning "rich." Otto is a variant form.

Ofar (עוֹפָר) From the Hebrew, meaning "young deer." Ophar is a variant spelling. Ofir and Ophir are variant forms.

Ofer (עֹפֶר) From the Hebrew, meaning "young mountain goat" or "young deer." Opher is a variant spelling.

Ofir (אוֹפִיר) From the Hebrew, meaning "gold." In the Bible (Genesis 10:29), a son of Yaktan. *See* Ofar.

Ofra (עָפְרָה) From the Hebrew, meaning "young mountain" or "young deer." In the Bible (I Chronicles 4:14), a descendant of Judah. Afra, Aphra, and Ophra are variant spellings.

Ofri (עָפְרִי) From the Hebrew, meaning "my goat" or "my deer." Afri, Aphri, and Ophri are variant spellings.

Ogden From the Anglo-Saxon, meaning "from the oak valley."

Ogen (אֹגֶן) From the Hebrew, meaning "to imprison" or "to anchor." Aguna and Ogenya are feminine forms. Agnon is a variant form.

Ohad (אֹהַד) From the Hebrew, meaning "love, beloved." In the Bible (Genesis 46:10), the third son of Simeon and a grandson of Jacob. Ohed is a variant form.

Ohed (אֹהֵד) From the Hebrew, meaning "love" or "beloved." Ohad is a variant form.

Ohel (אֹהֶל) From the Hebrew, meaning "tent." In the Bible (I Chronicles 3:20), a descendant of King Solomon.

Ohev (אוֹהֵב) From the Hebrew, meaning "lover."

Oholi (אָהֳלִי) From the Hebrew, meaning "my tent."

Oholiav (אָהֳלִיאָב) From the Hebrew, meaning "father (God) is my tent." In the Bible (Exodus 31:6), a helper of Betzalel.

Olaf From the Norse and Danish, meaning "ancestor." Olof is a variant form.

Oleg From the Norse, meaning "holy."

Olin From the Old English and the Middle English, meaning "holly." Olney is a variant form.

Oliver From the Latin, meaning "man of peace." Derived from the olive tree, the symbol of peace. Olivier is a French form introduced in the Middle Ages. Some authorities maintain that Havelock is a Welsh form of Oliver. Ollie is a pet form.

Olivier The French form of Oliver. *See* Oliver.

Ollie A pet form of Oliver. *See* Oliver.

Olney A variant form of Olin. *See* Olin.

Olof A variant form of Olaf. *See* Olaf.

Omar (אוֹמָר) From the Hebrew, meaning "to praise, revere." In the Bible (Genesis 36:11), a descendant of Esau. Omer is a variant form. Also, from the Arabic, meaning "to command, order."

Omen (אוֹמֶן) From the Hebrew, meaning "faithful."

Omer (עֹמֶר) From the Hebrew, meaning "sheaf."

Ometz (אוֹמָץ) From the Hebrew, meaning "strength." Omez is a variant spelling.

Omez A variant spelling of Ometz. *See* Ometz.

Omri (עָמְרִי) From the Hebrew, meaning "my sheaf." Akin to Omer. In the Bible (I Kings 16:16), a king of Israel (887-876 B.C.E.).

On (אוֹן) From the Hebrew, meaning "strength" or "wealth." Onam and Onan are variant forms. In the Bible (Numbers 16:1), a leader of the Korach group.

Ona From the British, meaning "ash tree."

Onam (אוֹנָם) A variant form of On. *See* On. In the Bible (Genesis 36:23), a descendant of Esau.

Onan (אוֹנָן) From the Hebrew, meaning "pain" or "iniquity." In the Bible (Genesis 38:4), the second son of Judah and a grandson of Jacob. Also, a variant form of On. *See* On.

Onkelos From the Greek, meaning "crooked." A first-century talmudic scholar who was a proselyte. According to legend, he was the son of the sister of Titus the Roman.

Ophar A variant spelling of Ofar. *See* Ofar.

Opher A variant spelling of Ofer. *See* Ofer.

Ophra A variant spelling of Ofra. *See* Ofra.

Ophri A variant spelling of Ofri. *See* Ofri.

Or (אוֹר) From the Hebrew, meaning "light."

Oral From the Latin, meaning "mouth," hence "the spoken word (oral)."

Oran (אוֹרָן) From the Aramaic, meaning "light." Also, the name of a star.

Orban From the French and the Latin, meaning "circle, globe, sphere."

Or-Chayim (אוֹר־חַיִּים) From the Hebrew, meaning "light of life."

Orde   From the Latin, meaning "order," and the Old English, meaning "beginning." Ordell is a variant form.

Ordell   A variant form of Orde. *See* Orde.

Oreg (אוֹרֵג)   From the Hebrew, meaning "weaver."

Orel   An English variant form of Auriel. *See* Auriel.

Oren (אֹרֶן)   From the Hebrew, meaning "a tree (cedar or fir)." In the Bible (I Chronicles 2:25), Oren was a descendant of Judah. Orin, Orrin, and Oron are variant forms.

Orev (עוֹרֵב)   From the Hebrew, meaning "raven." In the Bible (Judges 7:25), a leader of the Midianites.

Ori (אוֹרִי)   From the Hebrew, meaning "my light."

Orie   A variant form of Orien. *See* Orien. Also, a variant spelling of Ori. *See* Ori.

Orien   A French form of the Latin name Oriens, meaning "the Orient, the East (where the sun rises)."

Orin, Orrin   Variant forms of Oren. *See* Oren.

Orion   A variant form of Orien. *See* Orien.

Oris   A variant form of Orien. *See* Orien.

Orland   A variant form of Roland and Rolando by metathesis. *See* Roland. Or, from the Latin, meaning "golden, yellow," hence "land of gold (sunshine)." Orlando is a variant form. Arland is a variant form.

Orlando   A variant form of Orland. *See* Orland. Arlando is a variant form.

Orleans   From the Latin, meaning "golden." Orley, Orlin, and Orlo are variant forms.

Orley   A variant form of Orleans. *See* Orleans.

Orlin   A variant form of Orleans. *See* Orleans.

Orlo   A variant form of Orleans. *See* Orleans.

Orman   From the Norse, meaning "serpent, worm."

Ormand   A variant form of Orman. *See* Orman.

Ormond   A variant form of Ormand. *See* Ormand.

Oron (אוֹרוֹן)   From the Hebrew, meaning "light." Also, a variant form of Oren. *See* Oren.

Orono   A variant form of Oron. *See* Oron.

Orson   From the Latin, meaning "bear."

Or-Tal (אוֹר־טַל)   From the Hebrew, meaning "morning dew."

Or-Tziyon (אוֹר־צִיוֹן)   From the Hebrew, meaning "light of Zion."

Orval   A variant form of Orville. *See* Orville.

Orville   From the French, meaning "golden city." Orval is a variant form.

Oryan (אוֹרְיָן)   From the Hebrew, meaning "light." A name often ascribed to a scholar. Uryan is a variant form.

Or-Yesh (אוֹר־יֵשׁ)   From the Hebrew, meaning "there is light."

Osaias   From the Greek, meaning "salvation." Akin to Oshaya and Hosea.

Osbert   From the Anglo-Saxon and the German, meaning "famous (bright) god."

Osborn, Osborne   From the Anglo-Saxon, meaning "divinely strong."

Oscar   From the Anglo-Saxon, meaning "divine spear" or "divine strength." Also, from the Celtic, meaning "leaping warrior." Oskar is a variant spelling.

Osgood   From the Anglo-Saxon, meaning "a god."

Oshaya (אוֹשַׁעְיָא)   From the Hebrew, meaning "helped by God." In the Talmud (Bava Metzia 43b), a fourth-century Babylonian scholar.

Osher (עֹשֶׁר)   From the Hebrew, meaning "wealth" or "happiness."

Oshia   A variant spelling of Oshiya. See Oshiya.

Oshiya (אוֹשִׁיָא)   From the Hebrew, meaning "salvation" or "Please, God, save!" Oshia is a variant spelling.

Oshri (אָשְׁרִי)   From the Hebrew, meaning "my good fortune." A variant form of Asher.

Osias   A variant form of Hosea. See Hosea.

Osip   A Russian form of Joseph. See Joseph.

Oskar   A variant spelling of Oscar. See Oscar.

Osman   From the Anglo-Saxon, meaning "servant of God" or "protected by God." Osmand, Osmond, and Osmund are variant forms.

Osmand   A variant form of Osman. See Osman.

Osmond   A variant spelling of Osmand. See Osmand.

Osmund   A variant spelling of Osmond. See Osmond.

Ossie   A pet form of Oswald or Oscar. See Oswald and Oscar.

Osvald   A variant spelling of Oswald. See Oswald.

Oswald   From the Old English, meaning "god of the forest" or "house steward." Ossie and Ozzie are pet forms. Osvald is a variant spelling.

Oswin   From the Old English, meaning "friend of God."

Othni   A variant spelling of Otni. See Otni.

Othniel   A variant spelling of Otniel. See Otniel.

Otis   From the Greek, meaning "one who hears well."

Otni (עָתְנִי)   From the Hebrew, meaning "my strength." Othni is a variant spelling. In the Bible (I Chronicles 26:7), a Levite in the time of King David.

Otniel (עָתְנִיאֵל) From the Hebrew, meaning "strength of God" or "God is my strength." In the Bible (Joshua 15:17), the son of Kenaz, the brother of Caleb." Othniel is a variant spelling. Otni is a pet form.

Otto From the Old High German, meaning "prosperous, wealthy." Odo is a variant form.

Otzar (אוֹצָר) From the Hebrew, meaning "treasure." Ozar is a variant spelling.

Otzem (עֹצֶם) From the Hebrew, meaning "strength" or "anger." In the Bible (I Chronicles 2:15), a brother of King David. Ozem is a variant spelling.

Ov (עֹב) From the Hebrew, meaning "beam, rafter."

Ovad (עוֹבָד) From the Hebrew, meaning "servant."

Ovadia, Ovadiah Variant spellings of Ovadya. See Ovadya.

Ovadya (עוֹבַדְיָה) From the Hebrew, meaning "servant of God." In the Bible (Obadiah 1:1), one of the twelve Minor Prophets. Obadiah is a variant spelling.

Oved (עוֹבֵד) From the Hebrew, meaning "servant, worker." In the Bible (Ruth 4:17), a son of Naomi and the father of Jesse.

Ovid From the Latin, meaning "egg, egg-shaped" or "obedient."

Ovil (אוֹבִיל) From the Hebrew, meaning "I will carry" or "I will lead." In the Bible (I Chronicles 27:30), a servant of King David. Obil is a variant spelling.

Owen From the Welsh, meaning "young" or "young warrior."

Oz (עֹז) From the Hebrew, meaning "strength."

Ozar A variant spelling of Otzar. See Otzar.

Ozem A variant spelling of Otzem. See Otzem.

Ozer (עוֹזֵר) From the Hebrew, meaning "strength" or "helper."

Ozni (אָזְנִי) From the Hebrew, meaning "my ear" or "my hearing." In the Bible (Numbers 26:16), a son of Gad and a grandson of Jacob. Oz is a pet form.

Oz-Tziyon (עֹז־צִיּוֹן) From the Hebrew, meaning "the might of Zion (Israel)."

Ozzie A pet form of Oswald. See Oswald.

Oz-Zion A variant spelling of Oz-Tziyon.

Paarai (פַּעֲרַי) In the Bible (II Samuel 23:35), a variant form of Naarai. *See* Naarai.

Pablo A Spanish form of Paul. *See* Paul.

Padon (פָּדוֹן) From the Hebrew, meaning "a plough." In the Bible (Ezra 2:44), one of the Babylonian Exile returnees.

Page From the Italian, meaning "boy attendant, servant." Used also as a feminine name.

Pagiel (פַּגְעִיאֵל) From the Hebrew, meaning "to pray, to entreat God." In the Bible (Numbers 1:13), a leader of the tribe of Asher.

Palal (פָּלָל) Form the Aramaic, meaning "to pray" or "to judge." In the Bible (Nehemiah 3:25), a supporter of Nehemiah.

Palmer From the Middle English, meaning "a pilgrim who carried a palm leaf (as a sign that he had been to the Holy Land)."

Paltai (פַּלְטַי) A variant form of Palti. *See* Palti.

Palti (פַּלְטִי) From the Hebrew, meaning "my escape, my deliverance." In the Bible (I Samuel 25:44), the second husband of Michal. Paltai, Paltiel, Pelet, and Piltai are variant forms.

Paltiel (פַּלְטִיאֵל) From the Hebrew, meaning "God is my savior." Akin to Palti. *See* Palti. In the Bible (Numbers 34:26), a leader of the tribe of Issachar.

Paltoi (פַּלְטוֹי) A variant Aramaic form of Pelet. *See* Pelet. The name of a ninth-century head of the academy (*gaon*) in Pumbedita, Babylonia.

Palu (פַּלּוּא) From the Aramaic, meaning "miracle." In the Bible (Numbers 26:8), Reuben's second son and a grandson of Jacob.

Pancho A Spanish form of the Old Italian, meaning "tuft, plume," symbolic or a carefree spirit.

Paolo The Italian form of Paul. *See* Paul.

Papa (פָּפָּא) From the Greek and Latin, meaning "father." In the Talmud (Berachot 57a), a third-century Babylonian scholar. Papai is a variant form. Pappa is a variant spelling.

Papai (פָּפָּי) A variant form of Papa. *See* Papa. In the Talmud (Shabbat 93a), a fifth-century Babylonian scholar.

Papos (פָּפּוֹס) A variant form of Papa. *See* Papa. In the Talmud (Berachot 41b), a contemporary of Rabbi Akiba.

Pappa A variant spelling of Papa. *See* Papa.

Pappos A variant spelling of Papos. *See* Papos.

Pardes (פַּרְדֵּס) From the Hebrew, meaning "vineyard" or "citrus grove."

Park, Parke From the Middle English, meaning "enclosed parcel of land."

Parker An occupational name, meaning "one who tends a park." *See* Park.

Parnas (פַּרְנָס) From the Hebrew, meaning "supporter."

Parnell A variant form of Peter. *See* Peter. Pernell is a variant form.

Parpar (פַּרְפַּר) From the Hebrew, meaning "butterfly."

Parry A patronymic form from the Welsh apHarry, meaning "son of Harry."

Partha From the Greek, meaning "maiden, virgin." Or, from the Latin, meaning "to part with, sell, divide."

Paruach (פָּרוּחַ) From the Hebrew, meaning "bird" or "to fly away." In the Bible (I Kings 4:17), a father of one of King Solomon's prefects.

Pascal The Latin form of the Hebrew *pesach*, meaning "paschal lamb sacrifice," offered on Passover.

Paseach (פָּסֵחַ) A variant form of Pesach. *See* Pesach. In the Bible (Nehemiah 3:6), one of Ezra's supporters.

Pashchur (פַּשְׁחוּר) From the Aramaic, meaning "to tear to pieces." In the Bible (Jeremiah 20:1), a Priest.

Pat A pet form of Patrick. *See* Patrick.

Patish (פַּטִּישׁ) From the Hebrew, meaning "hammer." In the Talmud (Pesachim 66b), a third-century Palestinian scholar.

Patrick From the Latin, meaning "patrician, one of noble descent." Pat is a popular pet form. Paxton and Payton are variant forms.

Paul From the Latin, meaning "small." First used in the New Testament by Saul of Tarsus, who dropped his Old Testament name to symbolize his rejection of Judaism. Paolo, Pauley, and Paulos are variant forms. Paulinas is a pet form.

Paulos The Greek form of Paul. *See* Paul.

Pauley A variant form of Paul. *See* Paul.

Paxton From the Latin, meaning "town of peace." Also, a variant form of Patrick. *See* Patrick.

Payton The Scottish form of Patrick. *See* Patrick. Paxton is a variant form. *See* Paxton. Peyton is a variant spelling.

Paz (פָּז) From the Hebrew, meaning "gold, golden, sparkling." Used also as a feminine name.

Pazi (פָּזִי) From the Hebrew, meaning "my gold." In the Talmud (Yerushalmi Ketuvot 9:4), the father of the scholar Hillel.

Pedael (פְּדַהְאֵל) From the Hebrew, meaning "God's redemption." In the Bible (Numbers 34:28), a leader of the tribe of Naftali. Akin to Pedaya.

Pedaia A variant spelling of Pedaya. *See* Pedaya.

Pedat (פְּדָת) From the Hebrew, meaning "redemption." In the Talmud (Berachot 11b), a third-century Palestinian scholar.

Pedatzur (פְּדָהְצוּר) From the Hebrew, meaning "the Rock (God) has redeemed." In the Bible (Numbers 1:10), the father of Gamliel, a leader of the tribe of Manasseh.

Pedaya (פְּדָיָה) From the Hebrew, meaning "redemption" or "ransom of the Lord." In the Bible (II Kings 23:26), the father-in-law of King Josiah. In the Talmud (Me'ila 4b), the father of Judah, a third-century Babylonian scholar. Pedaia is a variant spelling. Akin to Pedael. Pedayahu is a variant form.

Pedayahu (פְּדָיָהוּ) A variant form of Pedaya. See Pedaya. In the Bible (I Chronicles 27:20), a leader of the tribe of Manasseh.

Pedro A Spanish and Portuguese form of Peter. See Peter.

Pe'er (פְּאֵר) From the Hebrew, meaning "beauty" or "glory."

Peka (פֶּקַע) From the Hebrew, meaning "flower bud."

Pekach (פֶּקַח) From the Hebrew, meaning "to blossom, to flower." In the Bible (II Kings 15:25), a king of Israel. Pekachya is a variant form.

Pekachia, Pekachiah Variant spellings of Pekachya. See Pekachya.

Pekachya (פְּקַחְיָה) From the Hebrew, meaning "flowering of the Lord." In the Bible (II Kings 15:22), a king of Israel. A variant form of Pekach. Pekahiah, Pekachia, and Pekachiah are variant spellings.

Pekah A variant spelling of Pekach. See Pekach.

Pekahiah A variant spelling of Pekachya. See Pekachya.

Pelaia, Pelaiah Variant spellings of Pelaya. See Pelaya.

Pelalia, Pelaliah Variant spellings of Pelalya. See Pelalya.

Pelalya (פְּלַלְיָה) From the Aramaic, meaning "to beseech the Lord." In the Bible (Nehemiah 11:12), a Priest. Pelalia and Pelaliah are variant spellings.

Pelatia, Pelatiah Variant spellings of Pelatya. See Pelatya.

Pelatya (פְּלַטְיָה) From the Hebrew, meaning "the deliverance (salvation) of the Lord." In the Bible (I Chronicles 4:22), a descendant of Simeon.

Pelatyahu (פְּלַטְיָהוּ) A variant form of Pelatya. See Pelatya. In the Bible (Ezekiel 11:1), an official in the time of Ezekiel.

Pelaya (פְּלָיָה) From the Aramaic, meaning "miracle of the Lord." In the Bible (I Chronicles 3:24), a descendant of Zerubbabel, and also a Levite in the time of Ezra, spelled פְּלָאיָה (Nehemiah 8:7). Pelaia and Pelaiah are variant spellings.

Pele, Peleh (פֶּלֶא) From the Hebrew, meaning "miracle."

Peled (פֶּלֶד) From the Hebrew, meaning "iron."

Peleg (פֶּלֶג) From the Hebrew, meaning "canal, channel." In the Bible (Genesis 10:25), a son of Ever.

Pelet (פֶּלֶט) From the Hebrew, meaning "escape" or "deliverance." In the Bible (Numbers 16:1), a son of Reuben and a grandson of Jacob. Palti and Piltai are variant forms. See Palti.

Peniel (פְּנִיאֵל) A variant form of Penuel. *See* Penuel.

Penini (פְּנִינִי) From the Hebrew, meaning "pearl" or "precious stone."

Penn From the Latin, meaning "pen, quill."

Penuel (פְּנוּאֵל) From the Hebrew, meaning "face of God" or "sight of God." In the Bible (I Chronicles 4:4), a descendant of Benjamin. Penuel is a variant form.

Pepe An Italian form of Pip, a pet form of Philip. *See* Philip.

Pepper From the Latin, meaning "condiment derived from a plant." Used also as a feminine form.

Per A Swedish form of Peter. Akin to the English Piers. *See* Piers.

Perach (פֶּרַח) From the Hebrew, meaning "flower." Perah is a variant spelling.

Perachia, Perachiah Variant spellings of Perachya. *See* Perachya.

Perachya (פְּרַחְיָה) From the Hebrew, meaning "flower of the Lord." Perachia and Perachiah are variant spellings. In the Talmud (Avot 1:6), the father of Joshua, a second-century B.C.E. president of the Sanhedrin.

Perceval, Percival From the French, meaning "valley piercer." Percival is a later spelling. Percy is a pet form.

Percy A pet form of Percival. *See* Percival.

Peregrine From the Latin, meaning "wanderer, traveler."

Peresh (פֶּרֶשׁ) From the Hebrew, meaning "horse" or "one who breaks ground." In the Bible (I Chronicles 7:16), a son of Machir and a grandson of Manasseh.

Peretz (פֶּרֶץ) From the Hebrew, meaning "burst forth." In the Bible (Genesis 38:29), a son of Judah and Tamar. Perez is a variant spelling.

Perez A variant spelling of Peretz. *See* Peretz.

Perida (פְּרִידָא) From the Hebrew, meaning "to divide, division." Also, from the Syriac, meaning "berry." In the Bible (Nehemiah 7:57), a servant of King Solomon. In the Talmud, the father of Jose, a second-century scholar. Peruda is a variant form.

Periel (פְּרִיאֵל) From the Hebrew, meaning "fruit of the Lord."

Pernell A variant form of Parnell. *See* Parnell.

Perry The French form of Peter. *See* Peter.

Peruda (פְּרוּדָא) A variant form of Perida. *See* Perida.

Pesach (פֶּסַח) Form the Hebrew, meaning "to pass over" or "to limp." The Hebrew name of the Passover (freedom) holiday, when the houses of the Israelites were "passed over" and the firstborn were spared the tenth plague meted out to the Egyptians. Pesah is a variant spelling. Paseach is a variant form.

Pesachia, Pesachiah Variant spellings of Pesachya. *See* Pesachya.

Pesachya (פְּסַחְיָה) From the Hebrew, meaning "the *pesach* (freedom sacrifice) of the Lord." *See also* Pesach. Pesachia and Pesachiah are variant spellings.

Pesah A variant spelling of Pesach. *See* Pesach.

Petachia, Petachiah Variant spellings of Petachya. *See* Petachya.

Petachya (פְּתַחְיָה) From the Hebrew, meaning "opening or entrance to the Lord." In the Bible (I Chronicles 24:16), a Priest. Petachia and Petachiah are variant spellings.

Pete A pet form of Peter. *See* Peter.

Peter From the Greek and the Latin, meaning "rock." Parnell, Per, Pernell, Perry, and Piers are variant forms. Pete is a pet form.

Petit From the French, meaning "small." Petite is a feminine form.

Petuel (פְּתוּאֵל) From the Aramaic, meaning "spacious, abundant," or from the Arabic, meaning "youthful, young." In the Bible (Joel 1:1), the father of the Prophet Joel.

Peyton A variant spelling of Payton. *See* Payton.

Phelps A variant form of Philip. *See* Philip.

Philbert, Philibert From the Anglo-Saxon, meaning "bright" or "illustrious."

Philip A variant spelling of Phillip. *See* Phillip.

Phillip, Phillipe From the Greek, meaning "lover of horses." Dickens, in his *Great Expectations*, was probably the first to use Pip as a pet form of Philip. Phillipp is a Scotch spelling.

Phillipp A Scotch spelling of Phillip. *See* Phillip.

Philmore From the Greek and the Welsh, meaning "lover of the sea."

Philo From the Greek, meaning "loving." The first Philo in history was Philo Judaeus, a first-century Jewish philosopher, born in Alexandria, Egypt.

Phineas The Anglicized form of Pinchas. *See* Pinchas.

Phinehas An Anglicized form of Pinchas. *See* Pinchas.

Phoebus In Greek mythology, the god of light and sun. Pheobe is the feminine counterpart.

Pierce A form of Peter, meaning "rock." *See* Peter.

Piers An English variant form of Peter. *See* Peter. Akin to the Swedish Per.

Pildash (פִּלְדָּשׁ) From the Hebrew, meaning "iron." In the Bible (Genesis 22:22), a brother of Abraham.

Piltai (פִּלְטַי) From the Aramaic, meaning "my salvation." In the Bible (Nehemiah 12:17), a Priest during the reign of Jehoiakim. Palti, Paltiel, Paltai, and Pelet are variant forms.

Pinchas (פִּנְחָס) From the Egyptian, meaning "Negro, dark-complexioned," or from the Hebrew, meaning "mouth of a snake." In the Bible (Exodus 6:25), a High Priest, the grandson of Aaron. In the Talmud (Yerushalmi Pesachim 5:3), a fourth-century Palestinian scholar, also known as Rabbi Pinchas ben Chama the Priest. Pinchos and Pinhas are variant spellings. Phineas and Phinehas are Anglicized forms. Pincus, Pinkas, and Pinkus are variant forms. Pini, Pinia, and Pinky are pet forms. פִּנְחָס is a variant Hebrew spelling.

Pinchos   A variant spelling of Pinchas. See Pinchas.

Pincus   A variant form of Pinchas. See Pinchas.

Pineh (פִּנֶע)   A Yiddish form of Pinchas. See Pinchas.

Pinhas   A variant spelling of Pinchas. See Pinchas.

Pini (פִּינִי)   A pet form of Pinchas. See Pinchas.

Pinia   A pet form of Pinchas. See Pinchas.

Pink   A pet form of Pinkerton. See Pinkerton.

Pinkas   A variant form of Pinchas. See Pinchas.

Pinkeh (פִּינְקֶע)   A Yiddish pet form of Pineh. See Pineh.

Pinkerton   From the Old English, meaning "to prick, to perforate." Pink and Pinky are pet forms.

Pinkus   A variant spelling of Pincus. See Pincus.

Pinky   A pet form of Pinkerton or Pincus. See Pinkerton and Pincus.

Pip   A pet form of Philip. See Philip. Pepe is a variant form.

Pirchai (פִּרְחָאִי)   From the Aramaic, meaning "flower."

Pitkin   From the Latin, meaning "little pious one."

Piton (פִּיתוֹן)   From the Hebrew, meaning "python."

Pius   From the Latin, meaning "pious, devoted."

Placid   From the Latin, meaning "to please" or "to be tranquil, undisturbed, at peace."

Placido   From the Latin, meaning "to appease, to quiet."

Plato   From the Greek, meaning "broad, flat."

Poco   From the Italian, meaning "little, little by little."

Porat (פֹּרָת)   From the Hebrew and Ethiopic, meaning "to bear fruit, be fruitful." In the Bible (Genesis 49:22), Joseph is so characterized by his father, Jacob.

Poriel (פּוֹרִיאֵל)   From the Hebrew, meaning "the Lord is my fruitfulness" or "God is my fulfillment."

Porter   From the Latin, meaning "to carry."

Potifar (פּוֹטִיפַר)   From the Egyptian, meaning "servant of the (sun) god." In the Bible (Genesis 39:1), a prefect in Pharaoh's court who purchased Joseph as a slave. Potifera is a variant form. Potiphar is a variant spelling.

Potifera (פּוֹטִי־פֶרַע)   A variant form of Potifar. *See* Potifar. In the Bible (Genesis 46:20), the Priest of On, Joseph's father-in-law.

Potiphar   A variant spelling of Potifar. *See* Potifar.

Potter   From the Old English, meaning "one who makes pots."

Poul   A variant spelling of Paul. *See* Paul.

Powell   A patronymic Welsh form of apHowell, meaning "son of Howell." *See* Howell.

Prentice   From the Middle English, meaning "beginner, learner." Prentiss is a variant spelling.

Prentiss   A variant spelling of Prentice. *See* Prentice.

Preston   An Old English name, meaning "priest's town."

Price   From the Middle English and Old French, meaning "price, value."

Priestley   From the Middle English and the Anglo-Saxon, meaning "elder (particulary of the church)."

Prime   From the Latin, meaning "first." Primo is a variant form.

Primo   An Italian form of Prime. *See* Prime.

Prince   From the Latin, meaning "first, chief."

Prior   From the Latin, meaning "first, a superior."

Pua, Puah (פּוּאָה)   From the Hebrew, meaning "mouth." In the Bible (Judges 10:1), the father of Tola, a Judge of Israel.

Pura, Purah (פּוּרָה)   From the Hebrew, meaning "fruitful." In the Bible (Judges 7:10), a servant of Gideon.

Purnal   From the Old English, meaning "pear tree."

Purvis   From the Anglo-French, meaning "to provide food."

Put (פּוּת)   From the Aramaic, meaning "spacious." Akin to Puti. In the Bible (I Chronicles 2:53), a member of the tribe of Judah.

Puti (פּוּתִי)   A variant form of Put. *See* Put.

Putiel (פּוּטִיאֵל)   From the Egyptian, meaning "servant of God." In the Bible (Exodus 6:25), the father-in-law of Elazar, son of Aaron.

Putnam   From the Latin, meaning "to prune," hence, "a gardener." Or, from the Anglo-Saxon, meaning "pitman, miner."

Quentin   From the Latin, meaning "fifth." This name was sometimes given in Roman times to the fifth son in a family, just as the seventh was called Septimus and the eighth, Octavius. Quenton is a variant spelling. Quincy, Quinn, and Quintin are variant forms.

Quenton   A variant spelling of Quentin. *See* Quentin.

Quincy   A variant form of Quentin. *See* Quentin.

Quinn   A variant form of Quentin. *See* Quentin. Also, possibly from the Old English, meaning "queen" or "companion."

Quintin   A variant form of Quentin. *See* Quentin.

Raam (רַעַם)   From the Hebrew, meaning "thunder."

Raamia, Raamiah   Variant spellings of Raamya. *See* Raamya.

Raamya (רַעַמְיָה)   From the Hebrew, meaning "God's thunder." Raamia and Raamiah are variant spellings. In the Bible (Nehemiah 7:7), one of the Babylonian Exile returnees.

Raanan (רַעֲנָן)   From the Hebrew, meaning "fresh, luxuriant, beautiful." Ranan is a variant spelling.

Rab   A variant spelling of Rav. *See* Rav.

Raba, Rabba, Rabbah (רַבָּה)   Variant forms of Rava. *See* Rava. In the Talmud (Rosh Hashana 18a), a Babylonian scholar.

Rabban (רַבָּן)   From the Hebrew, meaning "teacher." A title reserved for Hillel's descendants who held the office of *Nasi* (President) of the Sanhedrin for over 400 years.

Rabbit   From the Middle English, referring to a member of the coney family of animals. Used occasionally as a form of Robert. *See* Robert.

Rabi (רַבִּי)   From the Hebrew, meaning "my teacher." Ravi is a variant form.

Rabin (רַבִּין)   A contracted form of Rabbi Abin. In the Talmud (Pesachim 34a), the father of Abaye, a fourth-century Babylonian scholar. *See* Abin.

Rabina   A variant spelling of Ravina. *See* Ravina.

Racham (רָחָם)   From the Hebrew, meaning "compassion." In the Bible (I Chronicles 2:44), a descendant of Judah. Raham is a variant spelling.

Rachaman (רַחֲמָן)   From the Hebrew, meaning "compassionate one (God)."

Rachamim (רַחֲמִים)   From the Hebrew, meaning "compassion, mercy." Rahamim is a variant spelling. A popular name among Oriental Jews.

Rachim (רַחִים)   From the Aramaic, meaning "compassion." Rahim is a variant spelling.

Rachmiel (רַחְמִיאֵל) From the Hebrew, meaning "compassion of the Lord" or "God is my comforter." A short form of Yerachmiel.

Rachum (רָחוּם) From the Hebrew, meaning "compassionate." Rechum, Rechumei, and Rechumi are variant forms.

Radai (רַדַּי) From the Hebrew, meaning "to beat down, spread out." In the Bible (I Chronicles 2:14), the fifth of Jesse's seven sons.

Rafa (רָפָא) From the Hebrew, meaning "heal." In the Bible (I Chronicles 8:2), a descendant of Benjamin. Rapha is a variant English spelling. Also spelled רָפָה.

Rafael A Spanish form of Refael. See Refael.

Raffaello An Italian form of Refael. See Refael.

Rafi (רָפִי) A pet form of Refael and its variant forms. See Refael.

Rafu (רְפוּא) From the Aramaic and Hebrew, meaning "to heal." In the Bible (Numbers 13:9), a member of the tribe of Benjamin. Raphu is a variant spelling.

Ragnar From the Old English, meaning "rugged, rocky."

Raham A variant spelling of Racham. See Racham.

Rahamim A variant spelling of Rachamim. See Rachamim.

Rahim A variant spelling of Rachim. See Rachim.

Raimund A variant spelling of Raymond. See Raymond.

Rain Probably from the British *rhen*, meaning "lord," or *ragin*, meaning "wise." Raines and Rains are variant forms.

Raines, Rains Variant forms of Rain. See Rain.

Raleigh From the Old French, meaning "field of wading birds," or from the Old English, meaning "deer meadow." Rawly is a variant spelling.

Ralph From the Old Norse and Anglo-Saxon, meaning "courageous advice" or "fearless advisor." *See also* Randal *and* Randolph. Raoul is a French form. Rawly is a variant form.

Ralston From the Old English, meaning "Ralph's town."

Ram (רָם) From the Hebrew, meaning "high, exalted" or "mighty." In the Bible (I Chronicles 2:25), a descendant of Judah. Rama, Rami, Ramia, and Ramya are variant forms.

Rama (רַעְמָה) From the Hebrew, meaning "mane (of an animal), crest." In the Bible (Genesis 10:7), a son of Kush and a grandson of Noah.

Rami (רָמִי) A variant form of Ram. See Ram. In the Talmud (Eruvin 10a), a fourth-century Babylonian scholar. Also, a contracted form of Rabbi Ami. Also spelled רָמֵי.

Ramia A variant spelling of Ramya. See Ramya.

Ramon A Spanish form of Raymond. See Raymond.

Ramsay   A variant spelling of Ramsey. *See* Ramsey.

Ramsey   From the Old English, meaning "ram's island."

Ramya (רַמְיָה)   A variant form of Ram. *See* Ram. From the Hebrew, meaning "God has exalted" or "God has freed." In the Bible (Ezra 10:25), a contemporary of Ezra. Ramia is a variant spelling.

Ranald   A variant spelling of Ronald. *See* Ronald.

Ranan   A variant spelling of Raanan. *See* Raanan.

Randal, Randall   From the Anglo-Saxon, meaning "superior protection." Randell and Randle are variant spellings. Randy is a pet form.

Randee   A variant spelling of Randy. *See* Randy.

Randell   A variant spelling of Randall. *See* Randall.

Rander   From the Middle English, meaning "border, strip." Originally, an occupational name for shoemakers, derived from the leather strip on which the heel of a shoe is fastened.

Randi   A variant spelling of Randy. *See* Randy.

Randle   A variant spelling of Randal. *See* Randal.

Randolph   From the Anglo-Saxon, meaning "good counsel." Akin to Ralph and Randal. Randy is a pet form. Raoul is a French form. Rawlings is a variant form.

Randy   A pet form of Randal or Randolph. *See* Randal *and* Randolph. Randee and Randi are variant spellings.

Ranen (רָנֶן)   From the Hebrew, meaning "to sing, to be joyous." Ranon is a variant form.

Ranger   From the Middle English, meaning "wanderer." An occupational name for "one who guards the forest."

Rani (רָנִי)   From the Hebrew, meaning "my joy" or "my song."

Ranon (רָנוֹן)   A variant form of Ranen. *See* Ranen.

Ransom   From the Latin, meaning "to redeem."

Raoul   A French form of Ralph and Randolph. *See* Ralph *and* Randolph. Raul is a variant spelling.

Rapha   A variant spelling of Rafa. *See* Rafa.

Raphael   The Anglicized form of Refael. *See* Refael.

Raphu   A variant spelling of Rafu. *See* Rafu.

Ratz (רָץ)   From the Hebrew, meaning "to run."

Ratzon (רָצוֹן)   From the Hebrew, meaning "will" or "desire." Razon is a variant spelling.

Raul   A variant spelling of Raoul. *See* Raoul.

Rav (רַב) From the Hebrew, meaning "great" or "teacher." Rava is a variant form. Rab is a variant spelling.

Rava (רָבָא) A variant form of Rav. See Rav. Raba, Rabba, and Rabbah are variant spellings. In the Talmud (Bava Batra 12b), a fouth-century Babylonian scholar whose full name was Abba ben Rav Chama.

Raven From the Old English, meaning "raven (a bird of the crow family)."

Ravi (רָבִי) From the Hebrew, meaning "my teacher." Also, from the Hindi, meaning "sun."

Ravia A variant spelling of Ravya. See Ravya.

Ravid (רָבִיד) From the Hebrew, meaning "ornament, jewelry."

Ravina (רָבִינָא) A contracted form of Rav Avin. See Avin (Abin). In the Talmud (Pesachim 12b), a fourth-century Babylonian scholar. Rabina is a variant English spelling. Also spelled רָבִינָא.

Raviv (רָבִיב) From the Hebrew, meaning "rain" or "dew."

Raviya (רָבִיעַ) From the Hebrew and Aramaic, meaning "four, fourth." Ravia is a variant spelling.

Rawlings A variant form of Randolph. See Randolph.

Rawly A variant of Ralph or Raleigh. See Ralph and Raleigh.

Ray From the Old English, meaning "stream," or from the Celtic, meaning "grace." Also, a pet form of Raymond. See Raymond. Ray is a variant spelling.

Raya (רָעַ) From the Hebrew, meaning "friend." Reia is a variant spelling.

Rayfield From the Old English, meaning "stream in the field."

Rayford From the Old English, meaning "the ford (shallow spot) in the stream." See also Ray.

Rayi (רֵעִי) From the Hebrew, meaning "my friend, my companion." Rei'i is a variant spelling. In the Bible (I Kings 1:8), one of King David's officers.

Raymond From the Old French, meaning "mighty protector," or from the German, meaning "quiet, peaceful." Raimund and Raymund are variant spellings. Ray is a pet form.

Raymund A variant spelling of Raymond. See Raymond.

Raynard A variant spelling of Reynard. See Reynard.

Rayner An English spelling of Reyner. See Reyner.

Raz (רָז) From the Aramaic, meaning "secret." Used also as a feminine name.

Razi (רָזִי) From the Aramaic, meaning "my secret."

Raziel (רָזִיאֵל) From the Aramaic, meaning "God is my secret" or "secret of the Lord."

Razon A variant spelling of Ratzon. *See* Ratzon.

Read, Reade From the Old English, meaning "reed." Reed and Reid are variant spellings.

Reamer From the Old English, meaning "to enlarge (a hole), to make roomy."

Re'aya (רְאָיָה) From the Hebrew, meaning "to see." In the Bible (I Chronicles 5:5), a descendant of Reuben.

Rechab A variant spelling of Reichav. *See* Reichav.

Rechan A variant spelling of Reichan. *See* Reichan. Reichan is a variant spelling.

Rechav A variant spelling of Reichav. *See* Reichav.

Rechavam (רְחַבְעָם) From the Hebrew, meaning "expanse of the people," symbolizing "freedom." In the Bible (I Kings 11:43), Solomon's son, who succeeded him as king of Israel. Rehavam is a variant spelling. Rehoboam is the Anglicized form.

Rechavia, Rechaviah A variant spelling of Rechavya. *See* Rechavya.

Rechavya (רְחַבְיָה) From the Hebrew, meaning "expanse of the Lord," symbolizing "freedom." In the Bible (I Chronicles 23:17), the son of Eliezer and grandson of Moses. Rechavia, and Rehaviah are variant spellings. Rechavyahu is a variant form.

Rechavyahu (רְחַבְיָהוּ) A variant form of Rechavya. *See* Rechavya.

Rechev (רֶכֶב) From the Hebrew, meaning "horseman."

Rechov (רְחוֹב) From the Hebrew, meaning "path, road." In the Bible (Nehemiah 10:12), a contemporary of Nehemiah.

Rechum (רְחוּם) A variant form of Rachum. *See* Rachum. In the Bible (Ezra 2:2), one of the Babylonian Exile returnees. Rehum is a variant spelling.

Rechumei (רְחוּמֵי) A variant form of Rechumi. *See* Rechumi.

Rechumi (רְחוּמִי) A variant form of Rechum. *See* Rechum. In the Talmud (Nazir 13a), a third-century Babylonian scholar.

Redd From the Old English, meaning "reed." Akin to Rhett.

Redding From the Old English, meaning "reed meadow."

Redifa (רְדִיפָה) From the Hebrew, meaning "to pursue" or "pursuit." In the Talmud (Yerushalmi Peah 4:5), a fourth-century Palestinian scholar. Redipha is a variant spelling.

Redipha A variant spelling of Redifa. *See* Redifa.

Redmond, Redmund From the Old English, meaning "mount of reeds" or "protected by reeds."

Reece A Welsh form of the Old English, meaning "stream." Reese is a variant spelling. Rice and Royce are variant forms.

Reed   A variant spelling of Read. *See* Read.

Reelia   A variant spelling of Re'elya. *See* Re'elya.

Re'elya (רְעֶלְיָה)   From the Hebrew, meaning "God's veil." In the Bible (Ezra 2:2), one of the Babylonian Exile returnees.

Re'em (רְאֵם)   From the Hebrew, meaning "antelope" or "reindeer."

Reese   A variant spelling of Reece. *See* Reece.

Reeve   A variant form of Reeves. *See* Reeves.

Reeves   An Old English occupational name, meaning "steward, one in charge of a manor." Reeve is a variant form.

Refael (רְפָאֵל)   From the Hebrew, meaning "God has healed." Raphael is the archangel and divine messenger mentioned in the apocryphal books of Enoch and Tobit. In the Bible (I Chronicles 26:7), a Levite who was one of the Temple doorkeepers. Rephael is a variant spelling and Raphael is the Anglicized form. Rafael and Rafaello are variant forms. Rafi and Refi are pet forms.

Refaya (רְפָיָה)   From the Hebrew, meaning "God has healed." In the Bible (I Chronicles 3:21), a descendant of Solomon. Rephaia and Rephaiah are variant spellings.

Refi (רְפִי)   A pet form of Refael. *See* Refael. Rephi is a variant spelling.

Regan   From the Old High German, meaning "wise." Also, possibly from the Latin, meaning "king."

Regem (רֶגֶם)   From the Hebrew, meaning "to stone." In the Bible (I Chronicles 2:47), a descendant of the tribe of Judah.

Regev (רֶגֶב)   From the Hebrew, meaning "clod of earth."

Reg, Reggie   Pet forms of Reginald. *See* Reginald.

Reginald   From the Old High German, meaning "wise, judicious" or "powerful ruler." Reggie is a pet form. Reinhold, Reynold, and Ronald are variant forms.

Regis   From the Latin, meaning "kingly, regal."

Rehabiah   A variant spelling of Rechavya. *See* Rechavya.

Rehavam   A variant spelling of Rechavam. *See* Rechavam.

Rehavia, Rehaviah   Variant spellings of Rechavya. *See* Rechavya.

Rehoboam   The Anglicized form of Rechavam. *See* Rechavam.

Rehum   A variant spelling of Rechum. *See* Rechum.

Reia   A variant spelling of Raya. *See* Raya.

Reichan (רֵיחָן)   From the Aramaic, meaning "spice." Rechan is a variant spelling.

Reichav (רֵכָב)   From the Hebrew, meaning "horseman." In the Bible (II Kings 10:15), the father of Yehonadav in the time of King Jehu. Rechav and Rechab are variant spellings.

Reid   A variant spelling of Read. *See* Read.

Rei'i   A variant spelling of Rayi. *See* Rayi.

Reinhard, Reinhart   Variant forms of Reynard. *See* Reynard.

Reinhold   A German form of Reginald. *See* Reginald.

Rekach (רֶקַח)   From the Hebrew, meaning "spice" or "ointment."

Rekem (רֶקֶם)   From the Hebrew, meaning "weaving, embroidery." In the Bible (Joshua 13:21), a king of Midian.

Remalia, Remaliah   Variant spellings of Remalya. *See* Remalya.

Remalya (רְמַלְיָה)   A variant form of Remalyahu. *See* Remalyahu.

Remalyahu (רְמַלְיָהוּ)   From the Hebrew, meaning "adornment of the Lord." In the Bible (II Kings 15:25), the father of Pekach, captain of King Pekachya's army. Remalya is a variant form.

Remez (רֶמֶז)   From the Hebrew, meaning "sign" or "signal."

Renaud   A variant form of Reynard. *See* Reynard.

Rene   A French name from the Latin, meaning "to be reborn, renew." Reno is probably a variant form.

Renfred   From the Old German, meaning "peaceful counsel."

Reno   Probably a variant form of Rene. *See* Rene.

Reo   A variant form of the Old English *rae*, meaning "stream." Rio is a variant spelling.

Rephael   A variant spelling of Refael. *See* Refael.

Rephaia, Rephaiah   Variant spellings of Refaya. *See* Refaya.

Rephi   A variant spelling of Refi. *See* Refi.

Reshef (רֶשֶׁף)   From the Hebrew, meaning "flame, fire." In the Bible (I Chronicles 7:25), a descendant of Ephraim, the son of Jacob. Resheph is a variant spelling.

Resheph   A variant spelling of Reshef. *See* Reshef.

Retzin (רְצִין)   Possibly from the Hebrew, meaning "to be pleased." In the Bible (II Kings 15:37), a king of Aram in the time of King Ahaz. Rezin is a variant spelling.

R'eu (רְעוּ)   From the Hebrew, meaning "friend, companion." In the Bible (Genesis 11:18), a son of Peleg.

Reuben, Reubin   Variant forms of Reuven. *See* Reuven. Ruben and Rubin are variant spellings. Rube and Ruby are pet forms. Rubens is a patronymic form.

Reuel (רְעוּאֵל)   From the Hebrew, meaning "friend of God." In the Bible (Exodus 2:18), another name for Jethro, the father-in-law of Moses. Ruel is a variant spelling.

Reuven, Re'uven (רְאוּבֵן) From the Hebrew, meaning "behold, a son!" In the Bible (Genesis 29:32), Jacob's firstborn son from his wife Leah. Reuben, Reubin, Ruben, Rubin, and Ruvane are variants. Revie is a pet form.

Revie A pet form of Reuven and its variants. See Reuven.

Rex From the Latin, meaning "king." Also, a pet form of Reynold.

Rexford From the Latin and Old English, meaning "a crossing on the king's estate."

Rey A variant spelling of Ray. See Ray.

Reynard From the Old High German name Reginhart, compounded from the Germanic, meaning "wise," and "bold, courageous." Raynard is a variant spelling. Reinhard, Reinhart, Renaud, Reynaud, and Reyner are variant forms.

Reynaud A variant French form of Reynard. See Reynard.

Reyner A variant form of Reynard. See Reynard.

Reynold A variant French form of Reginald. In Scotland it took the form of Ronald. Rex, Reg, and Reggie are pet forms. See Reginald. Reynolds is a patronymic form.

Reynolds A patronymic form of Reynold, meaning "son of Reynold."

Rezin A variant spelling of Retzin. See Retzin.

Rezon (רְזוֹן) A variant form of Retzin. See Retzin. In the Bible (I Kings 11:23), king of Damascus in Solomon's time.

Rhett A variant form of the Old English ret, meaning "small stream." Akin to Redd.

Rhodric From the Greek, meaning "rose," and from the Middle English, meaning "rich, regal," hence "rich in roses."

Ribbans A variant form of Rubens. See Rubens.

Ric A pet form of Richard. See Richard.

Ricardo, Riccardo Spanish and Italian forms of Richard. See Richard.

Ricco A pet form of Richard. See Richard.

Rice A variant form of Reece. See Reece.

Rich A pet form of Richard. See Richard.

Richard A French form of the Old High German name Richart, meaning "powerful, rich ruler" or "valiant rider." Dix, Dixon, Ricardo, Riccardo, and Richardo are variant forms. Dick, Dickey, Dickie, Dicky, Hudd, Hudde, Ric, Ricco, Rich, Rici, Ricci, Richie, Ricki, Rickie, Ricky, Rico, Rik, and Rocco are pet forms.

Richardo A Spanish form of Richard. See Richard. Rici and Ricci are pet forms.

Rici, Ricci Pet forms of Richard and Richardo. See Richard.

Richie   A pet form of Richard. *See* Richard.

Ricki, Rickie, Ricky   Pet forms of Richard. *See* Richard.

Rico   A pet form of Richard. *See* Richard.

Rid   A variant form of Rider. *See* Rider.

Rider   From the Middle English, meaning "to clear land." An occupational name for "one who clears land, a farmer." Rid is a variant form.

Rifat (רִיפַת)   Of doubtful origin. Probably a form of grain or fruit. In the Bible (Genesis 10:3), a son of Gomer.

Rigo   A short form of the Italian Arrigo, a pet form of Harry. *See* Harry.

Rik   A short form of Heinrich, Hendrick, or Richard. *See* Heinrich, Hendrick, *and* Richard.

Rimon, Rimmon (רִימוֹן)   From the Hebrew, meaning "pomegranate." In the Bible (II Samuel 4:2), the father of two of King Saul's officers. Used also as a feminine name.

Rimzi (רִמְזִי)   From the Hebrew, meaning "my sign" or "my signal."

Rina (רִנָּה)   From the Hebrew, meaning "joy." Used primarily as a feminine name. In the Bible (I Chronicles 4:20), a descendant of Judah. Rinna and Rinnah are variant spellings. Also used as a feminine name.

Ring   From the Greek *kirkos*, meaning "ring," and from which is derived "circus," which takes place in a circular enclosure. Ringo is a variant form.

Ringo   The Italian form of Ring. *See* Ring.

Rinna, Rinnah   Variant spellings of Rina. *See* Rina.

Rio   A variant spelling of Reo. *See* Reo.

Rip   From the Latin, meaning "river bank."

Rishon (רִאשׁוֹן)   From the Hebrew, meaning "first."

Ritter   From the Low German, meaning "judge."

Rivai (רִיבַי)   From the Hebrew, meaning "strife, contention." In the Bible (I Chronicles 11:31), a member of the tribe of Benjamin.

Roald   A short form of Ronald. *See* Ronald.

Rob   A pet form of Robert. *See* Robert.

Roban   A variant spelling of Robin. *See* Robin.

Robard, Robart   Variant French forms of Robert. *See* Robert.

Robben   A variant spelling of Robin. *See* Robin. Also, a form of Reuben. *See* Reuben.

Robert   From the Anglo-Saxon, meaning "bright, wise counsel." Dob, Hob, Hobs, Hobson, Rabbit, Robard, Robart, Robson, and Rupert are variant forms. Rob, Roban, Robben, Robin, and Robyn are pet forms.

Robin   A pet form of Robert popular in France. *See* Robert. Roban, Robben, and Robyn are variant spellings.

Robson   A patronymic form, meaning "son of Rob (Robert)." *See* Robert.

Robyn   A variant spelling of Robin. *See* Robin.

Rocco   A pet form of Richard or Rockne. *See* Richard *and* Rockne.

Rock   From the Old English, meaning "rock."

Rockne   From the Old English, meaning "rock." Rocco and Rocky are pet forms.

Rockwell   From the Old English, meaning "the well near the rock." Rocky is a pet form.

Rocky   A pet form of Rockne and Rockwell. *See* Rockne *and* Rockwell.

Rod, Rodd   From the British, meaning "open or cleared land."

Roddy   A pet form of Rod or Rodman. *See* Rod *and* Rodman.

Roderic, Roderick   From the Old German, meaning "famous ruler." Rory is an Irish form.

Rodger   A variant spelling of Roger. *See* Roger.

Rodgers   A patronymic form of Roger. *See* Roger.

Rodman   An occupational name. From the Old English, meaning "one who clears the land, a farmer." Roddy is a pet form.

Rodney   From the Old English, meaning "cleared land near the water" or "one who carries a leveling rod," hence "a surveyor."

Roeh (רֹאֶה)   From the Hebrew, meaning "seer" or "Prophet." In the Bible (I Chronicles 2:52), a descendant of Judah.

Roger   From the Old French and the Anglo-Saxon, meaning "famous, noble warrior" or "honorable man." Rodger is a variant spelling. Rodgers is a patronymic form.

Rohn   From the Greek, meaning "rose."

Ro'i (רוֹעִי)   From the Hebrew, meaning "my shepherd," or from a Hebrew root meaning "my seer" and spelled רֹאִי.

Roland   A French form of the Old High German, meaning "fame of the land." Rolland is a variant spelling. Rolando, Rolla, Rollan, Rollen, Rollin, Rollo, and Rowland are variant forms.

Rolando   An Italian and Portuguese form of Roland. *See* Roland.

Rolf, Rolfe   Pet forms of Rudolph. *See* Rudolph.

Rolla, Rollan   Variant forms of Roland. *See* Roland.

Rolland   A variant spelling of Roland. *See* Roland.

Rollen, Rollin   Variant forms of Roland. *See* Roland.

Rollo   A variant form of Roland and Rudolph introduced into France by the early Normans. *See* Roland *and* Rudolph.

Rom (רוֹם)   From the Hebrew, meaning "high" or "exalted." Romem is a variant form.

Roman   From the Latin name Romanus, meaning "a person from Rome."

Romanus   A variant form of Roman. *See* Roman. In the Talmud (Nedarim 38a), a third-century Palestinian scholar and a member of Judah the Prince's household.

Romem (רוֹמֵם)   A variant form of Rom. *See* Rom.

Romi, Romie (רוֹמִי)   From the Hebrew, meaning "heights" or "nobility."

Ron (רוֹן)   From the Hebrew, meaning "joy" or "song." Also, a pet form of Ronald. *See* Ronald. Used as a feminine name as well. Also spelled רֹן.

Ronald   The Scottish form of Reginald. *See* Reginald. Ranald is a variant spelling. Roald is a short form. Ron, Ronel, Ronello, Ronnie, and Ronny are pet forms.

Ronel (רוֹנְאֵל)   From the Hebrew, meaning "song of the Lord" or "joy of the Lord." Also, a pet form of Ronald. *See* Ronald.

Ronello   A pet form of Ronald. *See* Ronald.

Roni (רוֹנִי)   From the Hebrew, meaning "my song" or "my joy." Used also as a feminine name. Ronli is a variant form. Also spelled רֹנִי.

Ronli (רוֹנְלִי)   From the Hebrew, meaning "song is mine." Akin to Roni.

Ronnie, Ronny   Pet forms of Ronald. *See* Ronald.

Roric   A pet form of Rory. *See* Rory.

Rory   An Irish form of Roderick. *See* Roderick. Also, from the Celtic, meaning "ruddy one." Roric is a pet form.

Roscoe   A variant form of Ross. *See* Ross. Also, from the Old English, meaning "swift horse."

Rosh (רֹאשׁ)   From the Hebrew, meaning "chief, head" or "bitter." In the Bible (Genesis 46:21), a son of Benjamin and a grandson of Jacob.

Ross   From the Anglo-Saxon, meaning "woods, meadow." Also, from the Norse, meaning "headland," or from the Latin, meaning "rose." Roscoe is a variant form.

Roswald   From the Old English, meaning "field of roses."

Rotam (רוֹתָם)   From the Hebrew, meaning "harness." Also, a variant form of Rotem. *See* Rotem.

Rotem (רוֹתֶם)   From the Hebrew, meaning "broom." Also, a plant-name.

Roul   A variant French form of Rudolph. *See* Rudolph. Akin to Raoul.

Rowe   A short form of Rowland. *See* Rowland.

Rowland   From the Old English, meaning "rugged land." Also, a variant form of Roland. *See* Roland.

Rowle   A variant form of Ralph. *See* Ralph.

Roy   From the Old French, meaning "king." Akin to Royal. Also, from the Gaelic, meaning "red." Roye is a variant spelling.

Royal   From the Middle English and the Latin, meaning "king." Akin to Roy. Royle is a variant form.

Royce   A variant form of Reece. *See* Reece. Also, a variant form of Rose introduced into England by the Normans. *See* Rose (feminine section).

Royden   From the Middle English, meaning "the king's land."

Roye   A variant spelling of Roy. *See* Roy.

Royle   A variant form of Royal. *See* Royal.

Rozen (רוֹזֵן)   From the Hebrew, meaning "prince" or "ruler."

Rube   A pet form of Reuben. *See* Reuben.

Ruben   A variant spelling of Reuben. *See* Reuben.

Rubens   A patronymic form of Reuben, meaning "son of Reuben." *See* Reuben. Ribbans is a variant form.

Rubin   A variant spelling of Reuben. *See* Reuben.

Ruby   A pet form of Reuben. *See* Reuben. Or, a French form of the Latin, meaning "red," usually referring to the precious ruby. Used also as a feminine name.

Rudd   From the Anglo-Saxon, meaning "red."

Rudel   From the Anglo-Saxon, meaning "red."

Rudolph   A variant form of Randolph and Ralph. *See* Randolph *and* Ralph. Rudulph is a variant spelling. Rollo and Roul are variant forms. Rolf and Rolfe are pet forms.

Rudulph   A variant spelling of Rudolph. *See* Rudolph.

Rudyard   From the Anglo-Saxon, meaning "red pole."

Ruel   A variant spelling of Reuel. *See* Reuel.

Rufus   From the Latin, meaning "red, red-haired."

Rupert   A variant English, French, and German form of Robert. *See* Robert.

Rush   From the Old English, meaning "grassy plant with a hollow stem (which grows in marshy places)."

Rusk   From the Spanish *rosca*, meaning "twisted roll, bread, cake."

Russ   A pet form of Russell. *See* Russell.

Russel, Russell   French forms of the Latin, meaning "rusty-haired." Also, from the Anglo-Saxon, meaning "horse." In medieval England a red fox was known as a russel. Russ and Rusty are popular pet forms.

Rusty A pet form of Russel. *See* Russel.

Ruvane A variant spelling of Reuven. *See* Reuven.

Ruvel (רוּבֶעל) A Yiddish pet form of Ruvane. *See* Ruvane.

Saad (סַעַד) From the Aramaic, meaning "support."

Saadia, Saadiah Variant spellings of Saadya. *See* Saadya.

Saadya, Saadyah (סַעַדְיָה) From the Hebrew and Aramaic, meaning "the help of God." Saadia and Saadiah are variant spellings. Saadya ben Joseph (882-942) was an Egyptian-born Jewish scholar and author. Also spelled סְעַדְיָה.

Saar (סַעַר) From the Hebrew, meaning "storm, tempest."

Saba (סָבָא) From the Aramaic, meaning "old" or "grandfather." *See also* Sava. Used also as a feminine name.

Sabath, Sabbath Variant forms of Shabat. *See* Shabat.

Sabato A variant form of Shabat. *See* Shabat.

Sabin From the Old French and the Latin, meaning "juniper tree." Savin is a variant form.

Sabra (סַבְּרָא) From the Aramaic, meaning "cactus" or "prickly pear." סַבְרָה is a variant Hebrew spelling.

Sabta A variant spelling of Savta. *See* Savta.

Sacha A Russian pet form of Alexander. *See* Alexander.

Sachar (שָׂכָר) A short form of Yisachar (Issachar). *See* Yisachar. Also, from the Hebrew, meaning "reward." In the Bible (I Chronicles 11:35), one of King David's warriors.

Sadir (סָדִיר) From the Aramaic, meaning "order."

Saer A variant spelling of Sayer. *See* Sayer.

Saf (סַף) From the Hebrew, meaning "threshold." In the Bible (II Samuel 21:18), a strongman in the time of King David. Saph is a variant spelling.

Safra From the Aramaic, meaning "writer, author." In the Talmud (Chulin 55b), a first-century scholar.

Sagei A variant spelling of Sagi. *See* Sagi.

Sagi (שַׂגִּי) From the Aramaic and Hebrew, meaning "sufficient" or "strong, mighty." Sagei is a variant spelling.

Sagiv (סָגִיב) From the Aramaic and Hebrew, meaning "tall, noble" or "strong, mighty."

Sal From the Latin, meaning "salt." Or, from the Old English, meaning "willow." Also, a pet form of Salvador. Sale is a variant form.

Salai (סַלָּי) From the Aramaic, meaning "basket." In the Bible (Nehemiah 12:20), a member of the tribe of Benjamin.

Sale A variant form of Sal. See Sal.

Salem The English form of the Hebrew, meaning "peace." In the Bible, a locality over which Melchizedek ruled. Akin to Salim.

Sali (סַלִּי) From the Hebrew, meaning "my basket."

Salim From the Aramaic, meaning "complete, whole." Akin to Salem.

Salma (שַׂלְמָה) From the Hebrew, meaning "garment." In the Bible (Ruth 4:20), the father of Boaz, who was also called Salmon. Also spelled שַׂלְמָא (I Chronicles 2:51), a son of Caleb.

Salmai (שַׂלְמָי) From the Aramaic, meaning "garment." In the Bible (Ezra 2:46), one of the Babylonian Exile returnees.

Salman A variant spelling of Salmon. See Salmon.

Salmon (שַׂלְמוֹן) From the Aramaic, meaning "garment." In the Bible (Ruth 4:21), the father of Boaz, also known as Salma. Salman is a variant spelling.

Salo A short form of Saloman. See Saloman.

Saloman, Salomon Variant forms of Solomon. See Solomon. Salo is a short form.

Salu (סַלּוּא) From the Aramaic, meaning "basket." In the Bible (Numbers 25:14), the father of Zimri, a leader of the tribe of Simeon. Also spelled סַלַּאי (Nehemiah 11:7), a Priest who was among the Babylonian Exile returnees.

Salvador, Salvatore From the Latin, meaning "to be saved." Sal is a pet form. See Sal.

Sam A pet form of Samuel. See Samuel. Samm is a variant spelling.

Samal (סֶמֶל) From the Aramaic, meaning "sign, symbol."

Sami From the Aramaic, meaning "high, lofty, exalted."

Samir From the Aramaic, meaning "entertainer."

Samla (שַׂמְלָה) From the Hebrew, meaning "garment" or "left-handed." In the Bible (Genesis 36:36), a king of Edom. Samlai is a variant form.

Samlai (שַׂמְלָאי) The Aramaic form of Samla. See Samla.

Samm A variant spelling of Sam. See Sam.

Sammy A pet form of Samuel. See Samuel.

Sampson A variant spelling of Samson. See Samson.

Samson (שִׁמְשׁוֹן) From the Hebrew, meaning "seen" or "service, ministry." In the Bible, a Judge in Israel. Shimshon is the exact Hebrew form. *See* Shimshon. Sampson is a variant spelling.

Samuel (שְׁמוּאֵל) From the Hebrew, meaning "His name is God." In the Bible (I Samuel 1:20), an eleventh-century B.C.E. Prophet and Judge who anointed Saul as first king of Israel. Shmuel is the exact Hebrew equivalent. Sam, Sammy, and Samy are pet forms.

Samy A pet form of Samuel. *See* Samuel.

Sander (סֶנְדֶּר) A short form of Alexander. *See* Alexander. Sanders is a variant patronymic form. Sandor, Sender, and Zander are variant forms.

Sanders A patronymic form, meaning "son of Sander." *See* Sander. Saunders is a variant spelling.

Sandol From the Latin, meaning "sandals, footwear."

Sandor A variant spelling of Sander, a pet form of Alexander. *See* Alexander.

Sandy A pet form of Alexander and Sanford. *See* Alexander *and* Sanford.

Sanford From the Old English, meaning "sandy river crossing" or "peaceful crossing." Sandy is a pet form.

Santo, Santos From the Spanish and Latin, meaning "saint."

Saph A variant spelling of Saf. *See* Saf.

Saphir From the Greek and the Hebrew, meaning "sapphire," a blue-colored precious stone. Sapir is a variant form. *See* Sapir.

Sapir (סַפִּיר) A variant form of Saphir. *See* Saphir. Used also as a feminine name.

Sar (שַׂר) From the Hebrew, meaning "prince."

Saraf (שָׂרָף) From the Hebrew, meaning "serpent." In the Bible (I Chronicles 4:22), a descendant of Judah. Also, from the Hebrew, meaning "to burn." Saraph is a variant spelling. *See also* Seraf.

Saraph A variant spelling of Saraf. *See* Saraf.

Sardis From the Latin, meaning "hard, precious stone."

Sargent From the Latin, meaning "military man." Seargent is a variant spelling.

Sarid (שָׂרִיד) From the Hebrew, meaning "remainder" or "refugee."

Sarig (שָׂרִיג) From the Hebrew, meaning "branch." Also from the Hebrew, meaning "lattice, grill," and spelled סָרִיג.

Sar-Shalom (שַׂר-שָׁלוֹם) From the Hebrew, meaning "prince of peace." In the Bible (Isaiah 9:5), a symbolic name.

Sarto The Italian form of the Latin, meaning "to patch (material)." An occupational name for tailors.

Sasha A Russian pet form of Alexander. *See* Alexander.

Sason, Sasson (שָׂשׂוֹן)   From the Hebrew, meaning "joy."

Saul (שָׁאוּל)   From the Hebrew, meaning "asked" or "borrowed." In the Bible, the first king to rule over Israel (eleventh-century B.C.E.) was the son of Kish from the tribe of Benjamin. Samuel, the Prophet, anointed him king only because of the clamor of the populace, and despite his own better judgment. Saul of Tarsus in the New Testament adopted the name Paul after his conversion to Christianity. Shaul is the original Hebrew form. See Shaul. Saulo is a Spanish form.

Saulo   A Spanish form of Saul. See Saul.

Saunders   A variant spelling of Sanders. See Sanders.

Sava (סָבָא)   From the Aramaic and Arabic, meaning "wine imbibers." Also, from the Aramaic, meaning "old" or "grandfather." Saba is a variant spelling. See Saba.

Savin   A variant form of Sabin. See Sabin.

Savta (סָבְתָא)   From the Aramaic, meaning "old" or "grandfather." In the Bible (Genesis 10:7), a son of Kush (Cush). Sabta is a variant spelling. סָבְתָה is a variant Hebrew spelling. Also used as a feminine name.

Savyon (סָבְיוֹן)   From the Hebrew, referring to a plant in the groundsel or yellow-weed family.

Sawney   A Scottish pet name for Alexander. See Alexander.

Sawyer   From the Middle English, meaning "one who works with a saw." An occupational name used by woodcutters and cabinetmakers.

Saxon   From the Old High German, meaning "sword, knife."

Sayer   From the Old German, meaning "victory of the people."

Scott   From the Late Latin form for "Scotchman," meaning "tattooed one." Scottie and Scotty are pet forms.

Scottie, Scotty   Pet forms of Scott. See Scott.

Seabern   From the Anglo-Saxon, meaning "sea warrior." Or, from the Norse, meaning "sea bear."

Seabrook   From the Old English, meaning "brook running into the sea."

Seadya   A variant spelling of Saadya. See Saadya.

Seaman   From the Old English, meaning "sailor."

Seamus   A variant form of the Gaelic name Seumuis, derived from Jacob and James. See Jacob and James.

Sean   A popular Gaelic form of John. See John. Shane and Shoon are variant forms. Shaun and Shawn are variant spellings.

Sear   From the Old English, meaning "battle." Searl, Searle, and Sears are variant forms.

Seargent   A variant spelling of Sargent. See Sargent.

Searl, Searle A variant form of Sear. *See* Sear.

Sears A patronymic form, meaning "son of Sear." *See* Sear.

Sebastian From the Greek, meaning "venerable."

Sebert From the Anglo-Saxon, meaning "bright victory." Akin to Sebold.

Sebold From the Anglo-Saxon, meaning "bold victory." Akin to Sebert.

Sechora (סְחוֹרָה) From the Hebrew, meaning "merchandise." In the Talmud (Berachot 5a), a fourth-century Babylonian scholar.

Sedgewick, Sedgwick From the Middle English, meaning "village with the trees that have leaves with saw-shaped edges."

Seff (סֶעֶף) A Yiddish form of Zev, meaning "wolf." *See* Zev. Sif is a variant form. Also, a pet form of Yosef (Joseph). *See* Yosef.

Sefi A pet form of Yosef (Joseph). *See* Yosef.

Segel (סֶגֶל) From the Hebrew, meaning "treasure." In the Bible, Israel is referred to as "a treasured people." Also, the name of a flower (pansy or violet). Commonly used as a surname in the forms Segal, Siegal, and Siegel.

Segev (שֶׂגֶב) From the Hebrew, meaning "glory, majesty, exalted."

Seguv (שְׂגוּב) From the Hebrew, meaning "exalted." In the Bible (I Chronicles 2:21), a member of the tribe of Judah.

Sela (סֶלַע) From the Hebrew, meaning "rock" or "cliff."

Selby A variant form of Shelby. *See* Shelby.

Selden, Seldon From the Middle English, meaning "rare, strange."

Seled (סֶלֶד) From the Hebrew, meaning "leap for joy" or "praise." In the Bible (I Chronicles 2:30), a member of the tribe of Judah.

Selig (סֶעליג) From the German and Old English, meaning "blessed, holy." A Yiddish name common among Jews of the eighteenth and nineteenth centuries. Zelig is a variant spelling.

Sellman, Selman, Selmann From the Old English, meaning "one who sells." An occupational name used by peddlers.

Selva The Spanish and Portuguese form of Silvanus. *See* Silvanus.

Selwyn From the Anglo-Saxon, meaning "holy place" or "friend at court."

Semach (שֶׂמַח) A variant form of Simcha. *See* Simcha.

Semachiahu A variant spelling of Semachyahu. *See* Semachyahu.

Semachyahu (סְמַכְיָהוּ) From the Hebrew, meaning "God supports, God sustains." In the Bible (I Chronicles 26:7), a Levite. Semachiahu is a variant spelling.

Sender (סֶנְדֶר) A Yiddish form of Sander (Alexander). *See* Alexander.

Seneh (סֶנֶה) A variant form of Sneh. *See* Sneh. In the Bible (I Samuel 14:4), the name of a rocky crag.

Senior   From the Latin, meaning "elder." Shneur is a Yiddish variant form.

Seraf   A variant spelling of Saraf. *See* Saraf. In the Bible, the serafim are fiery angels who guard the throne of God. Seraph is a variant spelling. Serafino is a variant form. Serafina is a feminine form.

Serafino   A variant form of Seraf. *See* Seraf.

Seraia, Seraiah   Variant spellings of Seraya. *See* Seraya.

Serali (שְׂרָלִי)   A pet form of Yisrael. *See* Yisrael.

Seraph   A variant spelling of Seraf. *See* Seraf.

Seraya (שְׂרָיָה)   From the Turkish and Persian, meaning "inn" or "palace." Also, from the Hebrew and Arabic, meaning "to persist." In the Bible (II Samuel 8:17), one of King David's scribes. Serayahu is a variant form. Seraia and Seraiah are variant spellings.

Serayahu (שְׂרָיָהוּ)   A variant form of Seraya.   *See* Seraya. In the Bible (Jeremiah 36:26), an officer of King Jehoiakim.

Sered (סֶרֶד)   From the Hebrew, meaning "frightened, fearful." In the Bible (Genesis 46:14), one of the sons of Zebulun and a grandson of Jacob.

Serge   From the Old French and the Latin, meaning "to serve." Sergei, Sergi, and Sergio are variant forms.

Sergei, Sergi, Sergio   Variant forms of Serge. *See* Serge.

Seriel (שְׂרִיאֵל)   From the Hebrew, meaning "prince of God." A pet form of Yisrael (Israel). Sriel is a variant spelling.

Serug (שְׂרוּג)   From the Hebrew, meaning "twig" or "intertwine." In the Bible (Genesis 11:20), a descendant of Shem, son of Noah.

Setav (סְתָו)   From the Hebrew, meaning "autumn."

Seth (שֵׁת)   The Anglicized form of Shet, the son of Adam. *See* Shet.

Seton   From the Anglo-Saxon, meaning "town near the sea."

Seumas, Seumus   Variant forms of Seamus, the Irish form of James.   *See* James. Akin to Shamua.

Seva (סְבָא)   From the Aramaic, meaning "imbibers of wine." In the Bible (Genesis 10:7), the eldest son of Kush (Cush).

Seviram (סְבִירָם)   From the Aramaic, meaning "to think" or "to have an opinion."

Seward   From the Anglo-Saxon, meaning "defender of the sea coast."

Sewell   From the Old English, meaning "well near the sea."

Seymore   A variant spelling of Seymour. *See* Seymour.

Seymour   From the Old English, meaning "marshy land near the sea." Seymore is a variant spelling. Akin to Maurice. *See* Maurice. Sy is a pet form.

Shaaria, Shaariah   Variant spellings of Shaarya. *See* Shaarya.

Shaarya (שַׁעַרְיָה)   From the Hebrew, meaning "the gate of the Lord." Shaaria and Shaariah are variant spellings.

Shabat, Shabbat (שַׁבָּת)   From the Hebrew, meaning "rest, Sabbath." Sabath, Sabato, and Sabbath are variant forms. Akin to Shabtai.

Shabetai, Shabbetai, Shabbethai   Variant spellings of Shabtai. See Shabtai.

Shabtai, Shabbtai (שַׁבְּתַי)   From the Aramaic, meaning "rest, Sabbath." In the Bible (Ezra 10:15), a Levite in the time of Ezra. In the Talmud (Bava Metzia 163a), a third-century Palestinian scholar. Shabetai, Shabbetai, and Shabbethai are variant spellings. Akin to Shabat and Shabbat.

Shachaf (שַׁחַף)   The Hebrew name for "seagull."

Shachafit (שַׁחֲפִית)   A variant form of Shachaf. See Shachaf.

Shachar (שַׁחַר)   From the Hebrew, meaning "dawn" or "light."

Shacharayim (שַׁחֲרַיִם)   From the Hebrew, meaning "dawn."

Shachna (שַׁכְנָא)   From the Aramaic, meaning "neighbor, neighborhood." A short form of Shechanya.

Shachor (שָׁחוֹר)   From the Hebrew, meaning "black." Shahor is a variant spelling.

Shadmon (שַׁדְמוֹן)   From the Hebrew, meaning "farm" or "vineyard."

Shafan (שָׁפָן)   From the Hebrew, meaning "badger." In the Bible (II Kings 22:3), the scribe of King Josiah. Shaphan is a variant spelling.

Shafat (שָׁפָט)   From the Hebrew, meaning "judge." In the Bible (I Kings 19:16), the father of the Prophet Elisha.

Shafer (שָׁפֶר)   From the Aramaic, meaning "good, beautiful." Shapir is a variant form.

Shafrir (שַׁפְרִיר)   From the Hebrew, meaning "canopy."

Shahor   A variant spelling of Shachor. See Shachor.

Shai (שַׁי)   From the Hebrew and Aramaic, meaning "gift." Also, a pet form of Yeshaya (Isaiah). See Yeshaya.

Shaked (שָׁקֵד)   From the Hebrew, meaning "almond" or "to be alert, awake."

Shakmon (שַׁקְמוֹן)   A variant form of Shikmon. See Shikmon.

Shaldon (שַׁלְדוֹן)   From the Hebrew, meaning "skeleton."

Shalem (שָׁלֵם)   From the Hebrew, meaning "whole." Akin to Shalmai.

Shalev (שָׁלֵו)   From the Hebrew, meaning "peaceful, calm, secure."

Shalmai (שַׁלְמַי)   From the Aramaic, meaning "peace." Akin to Shalem.

Shalman (שַׁלְמָן)   From the Assyrian, meaning "to be complete" or "to be rewarded." In the Bible (Hosea 10:14), a king of Moab. In the Talmud (Baba Batra 13b), a fourth-century Babylonian scholar.

Shalmia   A variant spelling of Shalmiya. See Shalmiya.

Shalmiya (שְׁלְמְיָה) From the Aramaic, meaning "peace." In the Talmud (Shabbat 46b), the father of Yemar, a third-century Babylonian scholar. Shelemya is a variant form. Shalmia is a variant spelling.

Shalmon (שַׁלְמוֹן) The Hebrew name of a plant in the *Cephalaria* family (Syrian *Scabious*). Shalmoni is a variant form. Also akin to Shelomo.

Shalmoni (שַׁלְמוֹנִי) A variant form of Shalmon. *See* Shalmon. The name of a talmudic scholar mentioned in *Bereshit Rabba* 68.

Shalom (שָׁלוֹם) From the Hebrew, meaning "peace." In the Talmud (Yerushalmi Demai 12:4), a fourth-century Palestinian scholar. Sholom is a variant spelling. *See also* Shlomi, Shlomo, Shlumiel.

Shaltiel A variant spelling of Shealtiel. *See* Shealtiel.

Shalum, Shallum (שַׁלּוּם) From the Hebrew, meaning "whole, complete, peace" or "reward, retribution." In the Bible (II Kings 15:10), a king of Israel; also (Jeremiah 2:11), a king of Judah. Akin to Shalem.

Shama (שָׁמָע) From the Aramaic, meaning "to hear." In the Bible (I Chronicles 11:44), one of King David's warriors.

Shamai A variant spelling of Shammai. *See* Shammai.

Shamash (שָׁמָשׁ) From the Aramaic and Hebrew, meaning "sun god" or "servant."

Shamir (שָׁמִיר) From the Aramaic and Hebrew, meaning "diamond" or "flint." In the Bible (I Chronicles 24:24), a Levite during the reign of King David. According to talmudic legend, a strong, rocklike substance capable of cutting through metal was created on Sabbath Eve, at twilight. Solomon used it to cut the huge stones required for the building of the Temple. Shamur is a variant form.

Shammai (שַׁמַּאי) From the Hebrew and Aramaic, meaning "name." A first-century B.C.E. Palestinian talmudic scholar noted for his disputes with Hillel. Shamai is a variant spelling.

Shamua (שַׁמּוּעַ) From the Hebrew, meaning "he that heard" or "he that obeyed." In the Bible (II Samuel 5:14), a son of King David. In the Talmud (Ethics of the Fathers 1:15), the father of Eliezer, a first-century scholar who war martyred by the Romans.

Shamur (שָׁמוּר) A variant form of Shamir. *See* Shamir.

Shamus, Shammus Irish forms of James. *See* James. Akin to Seumas and Seumus.

Shanan (שָׁנָן) From the Hebrew, meaning "peaceful, secure." Also, a variant spelling of Shannon. *See* Shannon.

Shane A variant form of Sean used prominently in Ireland. *See* Sean.

Shanen A variant spelling of Shannon. *See* Shannon.

Shani (שָׁנִי) From the Hebrew, meaning "scarlet, crimson."

Shannon, Shanon   Variant forms of Sean. *See* Sean.

Shap   From the Old English, meaning "sheep."

Shaphan   A variant spelling of Shafan. *See* Shafan.

Shapir (שָׁפִּיר)   From the Aramaic, meaning "beautiful." Shapira is a variant form.

Shapira (שַׁפִּירָא)   A variant Aramaic form of Shapir. *See* Shapir.

Shapley   A variant form of Shepley. *See* Shepley.

Sharar (שָׁרָר)   From the Aramaic, meaning "firm, hard" or "truthful." In the Bible (II Samuel 23:33), the father of one of King David's warriors.

Sharir (שָׁרִיר)   From the Aramaic, meaning "strong." Akin to Sherira.

Sharon (שָׁרוֹן)   Used primarily as a feminine name. *See* Sharon (feminine section). Sharoni is a variant form.

Sharoni (שָׁרוֹנִי)   A variant form of Sharon. *See* Sharon.

Shashai (שֵׁשַׁי)   From the Hebrew, meaning "to lead, to lead one." In the Bible (Ezra 10:40), a contemporary of Ezra.

Shatil (שָׁתִיל)   From the Hebrew, meaning "sprout." Akin to Shatul.

Shatul (שָׁתוּל)   From the Aramaic and Arabic, meaning "to plant (a shoot)" or "to transplant." Akin to Shatil.

Shatzi (שָׁאצִי)   A Yiddish pet name from the German, meaning "deer."

Shaul (שָׁאוּל)   From the Hebrew, meaning "asked" or "borrowed." In the Bible (I Samuel 9:2), the first king of Israel. Saul is the Anglicized form. *See* Saul.

Shaun   A variant spelling of Sean. *See* Sean.

Shavit (שָׁבִיט)   From the Hebrew, meaning "comet."

Shaw   From the Old English, meaning "thicket, grove."

Shawn   A variant spelling of Sean. *See* Sean.

Shay, Shaya (שַׁעְיָה)   Short forms of Yeshaya (Isaiah). *See* Yeshaya.

Shealtiel (שְׁאַלְתִּיאֵל)   From the Hebrew, meaning "borrowed from God." In the Bible (Haggai 1:1), the father of Zerubbabel. Shaltiel is a variant spelling.

Shearia   A variant spelling of Shearya. *See* Shearya.

Shear-Jashub   A variant spelling of Shear-Yashuv. *See* Shear-Yashuv.

Shearman   From the Old English, meaning "one who shears sheep."

Shearya (שְׁעַרְיָה)   From the Hebrew, meaning "gate of God." In the Bible (I Chronicles 8:38), a member of the tribe of Benjamin. Shearia is a variant spelling.

Shear Yashuv (שְׁאָר יָשׁוּב)   From the Hebrew, meaning "a remnant will return." In the Bible (Isaiah 7:3), a symbolic name given by the Prophet Isaiah to his son to indicate that although Judah and Israel would be destroyed, a remnant would return to Judah. Shear-Jashub is a variant spelling.

Sheba   A variant spelling of Sheva. *See* Sheva. Used also as a feminine name.

Shebsel (שֶׁעבְּסָעל)   From the Yiddish, meaning "sheep." Shepsel is a variant spelling.

Shechania, Shechaniah   Variant spellings of Shechanya. *See* Shechanya.

Shechanya (שְׁכַנְיָה)   From the Hebrew, meaning "God's abode." In the Bible (I Chronicles 3:21), a descendant of King Jehoiakim. Shechania and Shechaniah are variant spellings. Shechanyahu is a variant form. Shachna is a short form.

Shechanyahu (שְׁכַנְיָהוּ)   A variant form of Shechanya. *See* Shechanya.

Shecharia, Shechariah   A variant spelling of Shecharya. *See* Shecharya.

Shecharya (שְׁחַרְיָה)   From the Hebrew, meaning "dawn, morning" or "light." In the Bible (I Chronicles 8:26), a descendant of Benjamin. Shecharia and Shechariah are variant spellings.

Shechem (שְׁכֶם)   From the Hebrew, meaning "shoulder." In the Bible (Genesis 34:2), the son of Chamor (Hamor), who planned to marry Dinah, daughter of Jacob. Also, a biblical place-name (Nablus).

Shedeur (שְׁדֵיאוּר)   From the Aramaic and Hebrew, meaning "flame." In the Bible (Numbers 1:5), a member of the tribe of Reuben.

Shefa (שֶׁפַע)   From the Syriac and Hebrew, meaning "abundance, overflowing" or "multitude." Shifi is a variant form.

Shefatia, Shefatiah   Variant spellings of Shefatya. *See* Shefatya.

Shefatya, Shefatyah (שְׁפַטְיָה)   From the Hebrew, meaning "judgment of the Lord" or "God is my judge." In the Bible (II Samuel 3:4), a son of King David. Shefatia and Shefatiah are variant spellings.

Shefer (שֶׁפֶר)   From the Hebrew, meaning "pleasant, beautiful." Derived from the same root as the name Shapir.

Shefi (שְׁפִי)   From the Hebrew, meaning "bare, barren." Shefo is a variant form.

Shefifon (שְׁפִיפוֹן)   From the Hebrew, meaning "snake."

Shefo (שְׁפוֹ)   A variant form of Shefi. *See* Shefi. In the Bible (Genesis 36:23), a descendant of Seir the Horite. Shefi is a variant form.

Sheishai (שֵׁשַׁי)   From the Aramaic, meaning "ivory." In the Bible (Numbers 13:22), a descendant of Anak the giant. Sheshai is a variant spelling. Sheishan and Sheshan are variant forms.

Sheishan (שֵׁישָׁן)   A variant form of Sheishai. *See* Sheishai. In the Bible (I Chronicles 2:31), a member of the tribe of Judah. Sheshan is a variant spelling.

Shel   A pet form of Shelley or Shelby. *See* Shelley *and* Shelby.

Shela (שֵׁלָה) From the Hebrew, meaning "peaceful." In the Bible (Genesis 38:5), the youngest son of Judah.

Shelach (שֶׁלַח) From the Hebrew, meaning "missile, weapon" or "sprout." In the Bible (Genesis 10:24), the father of Ever (Eber). Shelah is a variant spelling.

Shelah A variant spelling of Shelach. See Shelach.

Shelby From the Anglo-Saxon, meaning "sheltered town." Selby is a variant form.

Sheldon From the Old English, meaning "shepherd's hut" or "hut on a hill" or "protected hill." Probably akin to Skelton. See Skelton.

Shelef (שֶׁלֶף) From the Hebrew, meaning "to draw (a sword)" or "to plunder." In the Bible (Genesis 10:26), a son of Yoktan.

Shelemia, Shelemiah Variant spellings of Shelemya. See Shelemya.

Shelemya (שֶׁלֶמְיָה) From the Hebrew and Aramaic, meaning "peace of God." In the Bible (Jeremiah 37:3), the father of one of King Zedekiah's officers. Shelemia and Shelemiah are variant spellings. Shalmiya and Shelemyahu are variant forms.

Shelemyahu (שֶׁלֶמְיָהוּ) A variant form of Shelemya. See Shelemya.

Shelesh (שֶׁלֶשׁ) From the Hebrew, meaning "three" or "a third child (in a family)." In the Bible (I Chronicles 7:35), a leader of the tribe of Asher.

Shelley From the Old English, meaning "island of shells." Shelly is a variant spelling.

Shelly A variant spelling of Shelley. See Shelley.

Shelomi A variant spelling of Shlomi. See Shlomi.

Shelomit Used commonly as a feminine name. See Shelomit (feminine section).

Shelomo A variant spelling of Shlomo. See Shlomo.

Shelton From the Old English, meaning "protected town."

Shelumiel A variant spelling of Shlumiel. See Shlumiel.

Shem (שֵׁם) From the Hebrew, meaning "name" and connoting "reputation." In the Bible (Genesis 5:32), the eldest of Noah's three sons.

Shema (שְׁמַע) From the Hebrew, meaning "to hear" or "a sound." In the Bible (I Chronicles 2:44), a descendant of Judah. See also Shemaya.

Shemaia, Shemaiah Variant spellings of Shemaya. See Shemaya.

Shemaram (שִׁמְרָעָם) From the Hebrew, meaning "guardian of the people."

Shemaria, Shemariah Variant spellings of Shemarya. See Shemarya.

Shemarya (שְׁמַרְיָה) From the Hebrew, meaning "protection of the Lord." In the Bible (II Chronicles 11:19), a son of King Rehoboam. Shemaryahu is a variant form. Shmerel is a Yiddish form. Shemaria, Shemariah, and Shmarya are variant spellings.

Shemaryahu (שְׁמַרְיָהוּ)   A variant form of Shemarya. *See* Shemarya.

Shemaya (שְׁמַעְיָה)   From the Aramaic, meaning "to hear." In the Bible (I Kings 12:22), a Prophet during the reign of King Rehoboam. In the Talmud, one of the members of the Great Bet Din during the reign of King Herod and the President of the Sanhedrin in the first century B.C.E. Shemaia and Shemaiah are variant spellings. *See also* Shema.

Shemayahu (שְׁמַעְיָהוּ)   A variant form of Shemaya. *See* Shemaya.

Shemer (שֶׁמֶר)   From the Hebrew, meaning "to guard, watch" or "preserve." In the Bible (I Kings 16:24), a contemporary of King Omri of Israel.

Shemi (שְׁמִי)   From the Hebrew, meaning "my name" or "my reputation."

Shem-Tov (שֶׁם־טוֹב)   From the Hebrew, meaning "good name" or "good reputation."

Shemuel   A variant spelling of Shmuel. *See* Shmuel.

Shep   A variant form of Shap. *See* Shap.

Shepard   From the Anglo-Saxon, meaning "shepherd."

Shephatia, Shephatiah   Variant spellings of Shefatya. *See* Shefatya.

Shepherd   From the Old English, meaning "one who tends sheep."

Shephi   A variant spelling of Shefi. *See* Shefi.

Shepho   A variant spelling of Shefo. *See* Shefo.

Shepley   From the Old English, meaning "sheep meadow." Shapley is a variant form.

Sheppard   A variant spelling of Shepherd. *See* Shepherd.

Shepsel (שֶׁעפְּסָעל)   From the Yiddish, meaning "sheep." Shebsel is a variant spelling.

Sheraga, Sheragai (שְׁרָגָא)   From the Aramaic, meaning "light." In Yiddish, the hybrid name Shraga-Feivel is commonly used, Feivel being a variant form of Phoebus, the goddess of light in Greek mythology. Shraga and Shragai are variant spellings.

Sheresh (שֶׁרֶשׁ)   From the Hebrew, meaning "root" or "foundation." In the Bible (I Chronicles 7:16), a grandson of Manasseh.

Sherira (שְׁרִירָא)   From the Aramaic, meaning "firm, hard, strong." The first important personage to have this name was a Babylonian scholar (*gaon*), the head of an academy in Pumbedita in the tenth century. Akin to Sharir.

Sherman   From the Old English, meaning "servant (or resident) of the shire (district)" or "one who shears (cuts)."

Sherry   A pet form of Sherman. *See* Sherman.

Sherwin   From the Anglo-Saxon, meaning "one who shears the wind." Also from the Old English, meaning "shining friend."

Sherwood From the Anglo-Saxon, meaning "forest, wooded area."

Sheshack (שֵׁשַׁךְ) A disguised name for Bavel (Babylonia) in Jeremiah 51:41, arrived at by a special rearrangement of the Hebrew letters in which the *shin* is substituted for the *bet* and the *kaf* is substituted for the *lamed.*

Sheshai A variant spelling of Sheishai. *See* Sheishai.

Sheshan A variant spelling of Sheishan. *See* Sheishan.

Sheshet (שֵׁשֶׁת) From the Hebrew, meaning "six, sixth." In the Talmud (Nedarim 78a), a fourth-century Babylonian scholar.

Shet (שֵׁת) From the Hebrew, meaning "garment" or "appointed," or from the Syriac, meaning "appearance." In the Bible (Genesis 5:3), the son of Adam born to him after the death of Abel. Adam called him Shet, for he said, "God hath appointed me another seed instead of Abel." Seth is an Anglicized form.

Shetach (שֶׁטַח) From the Hebrew, meaning "expanse." Shetah is a variant spelling.

Shetah A variant spelling of Shetach. *See* Shetach.

Shetil (שְׁתִיל) From the Hebrew, meaning "plant" or "sprout."

Sheva (שֶׁבַע) From the Hebrew, meaning "oath." In the Bible (II Samuel 20:1), a member of the tribe of Benjamin. Sheba is a variant spelling.

Shevach (שֶׁבַח) From the Hebrew, meaning "praise" or "fame." Shevah is a variant spelling.

Shevah A variant spelling of Shevach. *See* Shevach.

Shevanya (שְׁבַנְיָה) A variant form of Shevna. *See* Shevna.

Shevaya (שְׁבָיָה) From the Hebrew, meaning "captivity."

Shever (שֶׁבֶר) From the Hebrew, meaning "break, breach" or "food grain." In the Bible (I Chronicles 2:48), a member of the tribe of Judah.

Shevi (שְׁבִי) From the Hebrew, meaning "return, repatriation."

Shevna (שֶׁבְנָא) From the Aramaic, meaning "return, repatriation" or "resting place." In the Bible (Isaiah 22;15), a secretary and major-domo of King Hezekiah.

Shevuel (שְׁבוּאֵל) From the Hebrew, meaning "return to God." In the Bible (I Chronicles 23:16), a son of Gershom and a grandson of Moses. Shvuel is a variant spelling.

Shifi (שִׁפְעִי) A variant form of Shefa. *See* Shefa. In the Bible (I Chronicles 4:37), a member of the tribe of Simeon. Shiphi is a variant spelling.

Shifron (שִׁפְרוֹן) From the Hebrew, meaning "beautiful" or "pleasant."

Shiftan (שִׁפְטָן) From the Aramaic, meaning "judge." In the Bible (Numbers 34:24), a leader of the tribe of Ephraim. Shiphtan is a variant spelling.

Shikmon (שִׁקְמוֹן) From the Hebrew, meaning "sycamore tree." Shakmon is a variant form.

Shila (שִׁילָא)   A variant form of Shilya. *See* Shilya. Also, a variant spelling of Shilo. *See* Shilo. In the Talmud (Shabbat 7a), the father of Abba, a third-century Babylonian scholar.

Shilchi (שִׁלְחִי)   From the Hebrew, meaning "sprout, shoot" or "missile, weapon." In the Bible (I Kings 22:42), the father-in-law of Asa, king of Judah.

Shilem, Shillem (שִׁלֵּם)   From the Hebrew, meaning "peace" or "reward, recompense." In the Bible (Genesis 46:24), a son of Naftali and a grandson of Jacob.

Shilo, Shiloh (שִׁילֹה)   From the Hebrew, taken as a contraction of *shai lo*, meaning "the gift is His (God's)," or *shello*, meaning "his," but the precise meaning is uncertain. In the Bible (Genesis 49:10), a place-name and also a reference to the Messiah.

Shilsha (שִׁלְשָׁה)   From the Hebrew, meaning "three, a triad." In the Bible (I Chronicles 7:37), a member of the tribe of Asher.

Shilya (שִׁלְיָא)   An acrostic of *sheyichyeh l'orech yamin amen*, meaning "May he live long. Amen!" Shila is a variant form.

Shima (שִׁמְעָה)   From the Hebrew, meaning "to hear" or "reputation." In the Bible (II Samuel 21:21), a brother of King David.

Shimel, Shimmel (שִׁימְעֶל)   Yiddish pet forms of Shimon. *See* Shimon.

Shimi (שִׁמְעִי)   From the Hebrew, meaning "my name" or "reputation." In the Bible (II Samuel 16:5), a member of the tribe of Benjamin. Also, the grandfather of Mordecai (Esther 2:5).

Shimon (שִׁמְעוֹן)   From the Hebrew, meaning "to hear" or "to be heard" or "reputation." In the Bible (Genesis 29:33), the second son of Jacob and Leah. Simon is a Greek form. Simeon is an Anglicized form.

Shimrai (שִׁמְרַי)   From the Aramaic, meaning "guard."

Shimrat (שִׁמְרָת)   From the Aramaic, meaning "guard, protector." In the Bible (I Chronicles 8:21), a member of the tribe of Benjamin.

Shimri (שִׁמְרִי)   From the Hebrew, meaning "my guard." In the Bible (I Chronicles 4:37), a member of the tribe of Simeon.

Shimron (שִׁמְרוֹן)   From the Hebrew, meaning "guard, guardian." Akin to Shomer. In the Bible (Genesis 46:13), a son of Issachar.

Shimshai (שִׁמְשַׁי)   From the Aramaic, meaning "servant." In the Bible (Ezra 4:8), a scribe in the time of Artaxerxes, king of Persia.

Shimshon (שִׁמְשׁוֹן)   From the Hebrew, meaning "sun." In the Bible (Judges 13:24), a Judge from the tribe of Dan noted for his strength and courage, and his success in battling the Philistines, until he was betrayed by Delilah. Samson is the Anglicized form.

Ship   A pet form of Shipley. *See* Shipley.

Shiphi   A variant spelling of Shifi. *See* Shifi.

Shiphtan A variant spelling of Shifton. *See* Shifton.

Shipley A variant form of Shepley. *See* Shepley.

Shir (שִׁיר) From the Hebrew, meaning "song." Used also as a feminine name.

Shirian A variant spelling of Shiryan. *See* Shiryan.

Shirion A variant spelling of Shiryon. *See* Shiryon.

Shirley Used occasionally as a masculine name. *See* Shirley (feminine section).

Shiron (שִׁירוֹן) From the Hebrew, meaning "song, songfest."

Shiryan (שִׁירְיָן) A variant form of Shiron. *See* Shiron.

Shiryon (שִׁרְיוֹן) From the Hebrew, meaning "armor, armor-plate."

Shisha (שִׁישָׁא) From the Hebrew, meaning "alabaster." In the Bible (I Kings 4:3), a scribe during the reign of King Solomon. In the Talmud (Taanit 13a), a fourth-century Babylonian scholar, the son of Idi bar Abin.

Shitrai (שִׁטְרַי) From the Assyrian, meaning "to write," and from the Aramaic, meaning "official" or "guard." In the Bible (I Chronicles 27:29), one of King David's officers.

Shlomi (שְׁלוֹמִי) From the Hebrew, meaning "my peace." In the Bible (Number 34:27), the father of a leader of the tribe of Asher. Shelomi is a variant spelling. Akin to Shalom, Shlomo, and Shlumiel.

Shlomo (שְׁלֹמֹה) From the Hebrew, meaning "his peace." The Hebrew form of Solomon. *See* Solomon. Akin to Shalom, Shlomi, and Shlumiel. Shelomo is a variant spelling.

Shlomot (שְׁלוֹמוֹת) A variant form of Shlomo. In the Bible (I Chronicles 24:22), a Levite.

Shlumiel (שְׁלוּמִיאֵל) From the Aramaic, meaning "God is my ace" or "God is my reward." Shelumiel is a variant spelling. In the Bible (Numbers 1:6), a member of the tribe of Simeon. Akin to Shalom, Shlomi, Shlomo.

Shmaram (שְׁמָרְעָם) From the Aramaic, meaning "guard, watchman" or "protector of the people." Shemaram is a variant spelling.

Shmarya (שְׁמַרְיָה) A variant spelling of Shemarya. *See* Shemarya.

Shmelke A Yiddish pet form of Shmuel. *See* Shmuel.

Shmerel (שְׁמֶערְעל) A Yiddish form of Shemarya. *See* Shemarya.

Shmiel (שְׁמִיל) A pet form of Shemuel (Samuel). *See* Samuel.

Shmuel (שְׁמוּאֵל) From the Hebrew, meaning "his name is God." Samuel is the Anglicized form. *See* Samuel. Shmiel, Shmelke, and Shmulka are Yiddish pet forms. Shemuel is a variant spelling.

Shmulke (שְׁמוּלְקֶע) A Yiddish pet form of Shmuel. *See* Shmuel.

Shneur (שְׁנִיאוּר) A Yiddish variant form of Senior. *See* Senior.

Shofar (שׁוֹפָר) From the Hebrew, meaning "horn" or "trumpet."

Shofet (שׁוֹפֵט)   From the Hebrew, meaning "judge."

Shoham (שׁהַם)   From the Hebrew, meaning "precious stone (onyx)." In the Bible (I Chronicles 24:27), a Levite.

Sholom   A variant spelling of Shalom. See Shalom.

Shomer (שׁוֹמֵר)   From the Hebrew, meaning "guard, guardian." In the Bible (II Kings 12:21), the father of one of King Joash's murderers.

Shoni (שׁוֹנִי)   From the Hebrew, meaning "change, difference."

Shoon   A variant Irish form of Sean. See Sean.

Shoshan (שׁוֹשָׁן)   From the Hebrew, meaning "lily." Also from the Egyptian and Coptic, meaning "lotus." In ancient times the lotus, which was common in Egypt, also grew in the Jordan Valley. Used also as a feminine name. Shushan is a variant form. Shoshana is a feminine form.

Shoter (שׁוֹטֵר)   From the Hebrew, meaning "guard, guardian."

Shovai (שׁבָי)   From the Aramaic. The name of a precious stone. In the Bible (Ezra 2:42), one of the Babylonian Exile returnees.

Shoval (שׁוֹבָל)   From the Hebrew, meaning "way, path." In the Bible (I Chronicles 4:1), the youngest son of Judah and a grandson of Jacob.

Shovav (שׁוֹבָב)   From the Hebrew, meaning "recalcitrant" or "apostate." In the Bible (II Samuel 5:14), a son of King David.

Shovek (שׁוֹבֵק)   From the Aramaic, meaning "to leave, pass away." In the Bible (Nehemiah 10:25), a follower of Nehemiah.

Shovi (שׁבִי)   From the Hebrew, meaning "return, repatriation." In the Bible (II Samuel 17:27), an Ammonite prince.

Shraga   A variant spelling of Sheraga. See Sheraga.

Shragai   A variant spelling of Sheragai. See Sheragai.

Shua (שׁוּעַ)   From the Hebrew, meaning "salvation" or "victory." In the Bible (Genesis 38:2), the father-in-law of Judah. Used also as a feminine name.

Shuach (שׁוּחַ)   From the Hebrew, meaning "to walk." In the Bible (Genesis 25:2), the son of Abraham and Keturah.

Shual (שׁוּעָל)   From the Hebrew, meaning "fox." In the Bible (I Chronicles 7:36), a member of the tribe of Asher.

Shucha (שׁוּחָה)   From the Hebrew, meaning "pit" or "depth." In the Bible (I Chronicles 4:11), a member of the tribe of Judah.

Shuma (שׁוּמָה)   From the Hebrew, meaning "assessment" or "assessor." In the Bible (I Chronicles 2:53), a member of the tribe of Judah.

Shuni (שׁוּנִי)   From the Hebrew, meaning "harbor" or "seashore." Also, from the Aramaic, meaning "rock." In the Bible (Genesis 46:16), a son of Gad and a grandson of Jacob. Used also as a feminine name.

Shur (שׁוּר)   From the Aramaic, meaning "wall."

Shushan (שׁוּשָׁן) A variant form of Shoshan. *See* Shoshan. In the Bible (Esther 1:2), the capital city of Persia. Shoshan is a variant form.

Shvuel A variant spelling of Shevuel. *See* Shevuel.

Si A pet form of Seymour, Simon, and Simeon. *See* Seymour, Simon, *and* Simeon.

Siach (שִׂיחַ) From the Hebrew, meaning "to speak, talk, meditate." Akin to Suach.

Sidney A contracted form of Saint Denys. The original form of Denys or Denis was Dionysius, the Greek god of wine, drama, and fruitfulness. Also, from the Phoenician, meaning "charming" or "enchanter." Sydney is a variant spelling.

Sidra (סִדְרָה) From the Hebrew, meaning "order" or "school." Used also as a feminine name.

Siegfried From the German, meaning "victorious peace."

Siegmond, Siegmund From the German, meaning "victory" and "protection."

Siel (שִׂיאָל) A short form of Asiel. *See* Asiel.

Sif A variant form of Seff. *See* Seff.

Sigmond, Sigmund Variant spellings of Siegmond and Siegmund. *See* Siegmond *and* Siegmund.

Signe From the Latin, meaning "sign, mark, seal."

Silas A Latin form of the Aramaic and Hebrew, meaning "to ask, borrow." Also, a short form of Silvanus. *See* Silvanus.

Silon From the Greek, meaning "conduit carrying water" or "stream." Silona and Silonit are variant forms.

Silvan, Silvano Variant forms of Silvanus.

Silvanus From the Latin, meaning "forest." In Roman mythology, the god of the woods and fields. Sylvanus is a variant spelling. Selva, Silvan, Silvano, Silvio, and Sylvan are variant forms. Silas is a short form.

Silver From the German, meaning "silver."

Silvester A variant spelling of Sylvester. *See* Sylvester.

Silvio An Italian form of Silvanus. *See* Silvanus.

Sim A pet form of Simon and Simeon. *See* Simon *and* Simeon.

Sima (סִימָה) From the Aramaic, meaning "treasure." Simai is a variant form. Used also as a feminine name.

Simai (סִימָאי) A variant form of Sima. *See* Sima. In the Talmud (Yevamot 83b), a third-century scholar.

Siman-Tov (סִימָן־טוֹב) From the Hebrew, meaning "good star" or "lucky star," hence "good luck."

Simcha (שִׂמְחָה) From the Hebrew, meaning "joy." Semach, Simchon, and Simchoni are variant forms. Simha is a variant spelling.

Simchai (שִׂמְחַאי) An Aramaic form of Simcha. See Simcha.

Simchon (שִׂמְחוֹן) A variant form of Simcha. From the Hebrew, meaning "a celebration." Simchoni is a variant form.

Simchoni (שִׂמְחוֹנִי) A variant form of Simchon. See Simchon.

Simeon An Anglicized form of Shimon. See Shimon. Sim, Simi, Simie, and Simmie are pet forms.

Simha A variant spelling of Simcha. See Simcha.

Simi, Simie, Simmie Pet forms of Simeon and Simon. See Simeon and Simon. In the Talmud (Gitin 60b), a fourth-century Babylonian scholar.

Simla (שִׂמְלָה) From the Hebrew, meaning "garment."

Simlai (שִׂמְלָאי) The Aramaic form of Simla. See Simla. In the Talmud (Rosh Hashana 20b), a third-century Palestinian scholar.

Simon A Greek form of Shimon. See Shimon. Simone is a variant form. Simi, Simie, and Simmie are pet forms. Sims is a patronymic form.

Simone (סִימוֹן) A variant form of Simon. See Simon. Also, a third-century Palestinian scholar and the father of Rabbi Judah, noted as a master of the *Agada*. Used also as a feminine name.

Simp A pet form of Simpson. See Simpson.

Simpson A patronymic form, meaning "son of Simon." See Simon. Simp is a pet form.

Sims A patronymic form, meaning "son of Simon." See Simon.

Sinai (סִינַי) From the Hebrew, used figuratively as a designation for a great scholar. In the Bible, the mountain on which Moses received the Ten Commandments. In the Talmud (Chulin 18b), a nickname for Joseph bar Chiya, a fourth-century Babylonian scholar whose memory was compared to Mt. Sinai, the source of all wisdom.

Sinclair From the Latin, meaning "shining" or "sanctified." Also, a contracted form of St. Claire. See Claire.

Sion A variant form of Zion. See Zion.

Sira (סִירָה) From the Aramaic and Hebrew, meaning "boat."

Sirya (סִרְיָה) From the Aramaic, meaning "spear."

Siryon (סִרְיוֹן) A variant form of Sirya. See Sirya.

Sisera (סִיסְרָא) From the Hebrew, meaning "horse." In the Bible (Judges 4:2), the captain of the army of Jabin, king of Canaan.

Sisi (שִׁישִׁי) From the Hebrew, meaning "my joy." Sisi is a variant spelling.

Sissi A variant spelling of Sisi. *See* Sisi.

Sitri (סִתְרִי) From the Hebrew, meaning "my secret" or "my hidden place." In the Bible (Exodus 6:22), a Levite of the Kehat family.

Sivan (סִיוָן) An Assyrian-Babylonian word of uncertain meaning. The ninth month in the Jewish calendar, corresponding to May-June. In the zodiac, its sign is Gemini ("twins"). Used also as a feminine name.

Skelton From the Greek, meaning "dried up." Also, possibly from the Modern Dutch, meaning "town where the shells are." Also, possibly a variant form of Sheldon. *See* Sheldon.

Skipper From the Middle Dutch, meaning "one who captains a ship.'

Slade From the Anglo-Saxon, meaning "slide."

Sloan From the Celtic, meaning "warrior."

Sneh (סְנֶה) From the Hebrew, meaning "bush." Seneh is a variant form.

Sna'i (סְנָאִי) From the Hebrew, meaning "squirrel." Senai is a variant spelling.

Snapir (סְנַפִּיר) From the Hebrew, meaning "fin."

Sodi (סוֹדִי) From the Hebrew, meaning "my secret." In the Bible (Numbers 13:10), the father of Gadiel, the scout of the tribe of Zebulun who explored the Promised Land.

Soed (סוֹעֵד) From the Hebrew, meaning "support."

Sofer (סוֹפֵר) From the Hebrew, meaning "scribe" or "writer."

Sol A pet form of Solomon. *See* Solomon. Also, from the Latin, meaning "sun." The sun god, Apollo, is often referred to as Sol. *See also* Solon.

Solel (סוֹלֵל) From the Hebrew, meaning "to pave" or "to beat a path."

Solomon (שְׁלֹמֹה) From the Hebrew, meaning "peace." In the Bible, the king of Israel, son of King David and Bathsheba (II Samuel 12:24). Salman, Saloman, and Salomon are variant forms. Sol is a short form. Zalman, Zalmen, Zalmon, and Zelman are variant Yiddish forms. Zalkin is a Yiddish pet form.

Solon From the Latin, meaning "sun." *See also* Sol.

Somech (סוֹמֵךְ) From the Hebrew, meaning "support."

Sonny A popular nickname, meaning "son" or "boy."

Sorrel, Sorrell From the Old French, meaning "light reddish brown," often referring to a horse because of its color.

Sotai (סוֹטַי) From the Hebrew, meaning "faithless (wife)." In the Bible (Ezra 2:55), one of the sons of Solomon's slaves.

Spark, Sparky From the Old English, meaning "flash of light."

Speed From the Old English, meaning "wealth, power, success."

Speer From the Middle English and Old English, meaning "spearlike weapon."

Spencer From the Anglo-Saxon, meaning "steward, administrator, guardian."

Spike From the Middle English and the Latin, meaning "ear of grain."

Spiro From the Latin, meaning "to breathe."

Squire From the Old French, meaning "young man of high birth serving as an attendant to nobility."

Sriel (שְׂרִיאֵל) A pet form of Yisrael. *See* Yisrael. Seriel is a variant spelling.

Srol (שְׂרוֹל) A Yiddish form of Yisrael. *See* Yisrael.

Srul, Srule (שְׂרוּל) Yiddish forms of Israel (Yisrael). *See* Yisrael.

Srully (שְׂרוּלִי) A pet form of Israel (Yisrael). *See* Israel.

Stacey, Stacy From the Latin, meaning "firmly established."

Stafford From the Old English, meaning "a pole with which to ford (cross) a river."

Stan A pet form of Stanley. *See* Stanley.

Stanford From the Old English, meaning "from the stone or paved ford."

Stanhope From the Old English, meaning "hop stone (on which one stood to see afar)."

Stanislav From the Slavic, meaning "glory of the camp."

Stanley From the Old English, meaning "from the stony field." Stan is a pet form.

Stansfield From the Old English, meaning "field of stone."

Stanton From the Old English, meaning "town near the stony field."

Stanwood From the Old English, meaning "stony wooded area."

Stefan A variant spelling of the German Stephan. *See* Stephan.

Stefano The Italian form of Stephen. *See* Stephen.

Stephan The German form of Stephen. *See* Stephen.

Stephen From the Greek, meaning "crown." Stefan, Stefano, Stephan, and Steven are variant forms.

Sterling From the Middle English, meaning "silver penny." Also, possibly from the Old English, meaning "starling (bird)."

Stevan A variant form of Stephen. *See* Stephen.

Steven A variant form of Stephen. *See* Stephen.

Stew A pet form of Stewart. *See* Stewart.

Stewart From the Anglo-Saxon, meaning "administrator, guardian, or keeper of the estate." Stuart is a variant form. Stew is a pet form.

Stillman From the Old English, meaning "stall, station," hence "a man (servant) assigned to a station."

Stirling A variant spelling of Sterling. *See* Sterling.

Storm From the Old English, meaning "storm."

Strom From the Greek, meaning "bed, mattress."

Struther From the Latin, meaning "ostrich."

Stu A pet form of Stuart. *See* Stuart.

Stuart A variant form of Stewart. *See* Stewart.

Studs From the Old English, meaning "post, pillar" or "house."

Suach (סוּחַ) From the Hebrew, meaning "speech, to speak." In the Bible (I Chronicles 7:36), a member of the tribe of Asher. Siach is a variant form.

Sumner From the French and Latin, meaning "one who summons, a messenger."

Sunny From the Old English, meaning "sun." A popular nickname.

Susi (סוּסִי) From the Hebrew, meaning "my horse." In the Bible (Numbers 13:11), the father of the scout from the tribe of Manasseh who explored the Promised Land.

Sy A pet form of Seymour and Sylvan. *See* Seymour *and* Sylvan. Akin to Si.

Sydney A variant spelling of Sidney. *See* Sidney. Used also as a feminine name.

Sylvan A variant form of Silvanus. *See* Silvanus.

Sylvanus A variant spelling of Silvanus. *See* Silvanus.

Sylvester A variant form of Silvanus. *See* Silvanus. Silvester is a variant spelling.

Syshe (סִישֶׁע) A Yiddish form of the German, meaning "sweet."

Tab A pet form of David. *See* David. Taffy is a variant form. Also, a short form of Tabbai. *See* Tabbai.

Tabaot (טַבָּעוֹת) From the Hebrew, meaning "rings." In the Bible (Ezra 2:43), one of the Babylonian Exile returnees.

Tabai, Tabbai (טַבַּאי) From the Aramaic, meaning "good." In the Talmud (Chagiga 2:2), the father of Judah, a first-century scholar.

Tabor From the Persian, meaning "drum." *See also* Tavor.

Tachan (תַּחַן) From the Hebrew, meaning "prayer, supplication." In the Bible (I Chronicles 7:25), one of the sons of Ephraim.

Tachash (תַּחַשׁ) From the Hebrew, meaning "dolphin" or "seal" or "badger." In the Bible (Genesis 22:24), the son of Nachor and a nephew of Abraham.

Tachat (תַּחַת) From the Hebrew, meaning "substitute" or "under, below." In the the Bible (I Chronicles 7:20), one of the sons of Ephraim.

Tachkemoni (תַּחְכְּמוֹנִי) From the Hebrew, meaning "change." In the Talmud (Megilla 23b), a Babylonian scholar.

Tachlifa (תַּחְלִיפָא) From the Aramaic, meaning "change." In the Talmud (Megilla 23b), a Babylonian scholar.

Tad A pet form of Thadeus. *See* Thadeus.

Tadmor (תַּדְמוֹר) The name of a city built by King Solomon (II Chronicles 8:4), possibly Palmyra.

Taffy From the British, meaning "river." Akin to Taft. Also, the Welsh nickname for David (Davy), which is pronounced Taffy. *See also* Tab.

Taft From the British, meaning "river." Akin to Taffy.

Taga (תָּגָא) From the Aramaic, meaning "crown" or "wreath." Also from the Latin, meaning "robe."

Tal (טַל) From the Hebrew, meaning "dew." Used also as a feminine name.

Talbot From the Old English, meaning "Botolph's river." Tolbert is a variant form.

Tali (טַלִי) From the Hebrew, meaning "my dew."

Talia, Taliah Variant spellings of Talya. *See* Talya.

Talmai (תַּלְמַי) From the Aramaic, meaning "mound" or "hill." In the Bible (II Samuel 3:3), the king of Geshur, father-in-law of King David. Akin to Talmi.

Talmi (תַּלְמִי) From the Hebrew, meaning "my mound, hill." Akin to Talmai.

Talmon (טַלְמוֹן) From the Aramaic, meaning "to oppress, injure." In the Bible (Ezra 2:42), a Levite, one of the Temple porters.

Tal-Or (טַל-אוֹר) From the Hebrew, meaning "dew of the light (morning)." Also spelled טלור and טלאור. Akin to Tal-Shachar.

Tal-Shachar (טַל-שַׁחַר) From the Hebrew, meaning "morning dew."

Talya (טַלְיָא) From the Aramaic, meaning "young lamb." Used also as a feminine name. Talia and Taliah are variant spellings.

Tam (תָּם) From the Hebrew, meaning "complete, whole" or "honest."

Tamach (תֶּמַח) From the Hebrew, probably meaning "large pot." In the Bible (Ezra 2:53), the head of a family of Temple servants. Temach is a variant spelling.

Tamir (תָּמִיר) From the Hebrew, meaning "tall, stately, like the palm tree." Also, from the Hebrew, meaning "hidden" or "sacred vessel" and spelled טמיר. Tamur is a variant spelling.

Tammuz (תַּמּוּז) A Babylonian deity in charge of springtime. Also, the name of a month in the Jewish calendar.

Tamsen   A Scandinavian patronymic form of Thomas, meaning "son of Thomas." *See* Thomas.

Tamson   A patronymic form of Thomas, meaning "son of Thomas." *See* Thomas.

Tamur (תָּמוּר)   A variant form of Tamir. *See* Tamir.

Tanchum (תַּנְחוּם)   From the Hebrew, meaning "comfort, consolation." In the Talmud (Moed Katan 25b), a third-century Babylonian scholar. Tanhum is a variant spelling.

Tanchuma (תַּנְחוּמָא)   From the Aramaic, meaning "comfort." Akin to Tanchum. In the Talmud (Yerushalmi Shekalim 6:1), a fourth-century Palestinian scholar. Tanhuma is a variant spelling.

Tanhum   A variant spelling of Tanchum. *See* Tanchum.

Tanhuma   A variant spelling of Tanchuma. *See* Tanchuma.

Tanna (תַּנָּא)   From the Aramaic, meaning "teacher." The title of Palestinian and Babylonian scholars of the early centuries of the Common Era.

Tarfon (טַרְפוֹן)   From the Hebrew, meaning "torn (a torn animal)" or "predatory, cruel," hence a nonkosher animal. A name given to a prominent first-century Palestinian talmudic scholar because he erroneously ruled that an animal was nonkosher (*treifa*) when it was actually kosher. Tarphon is a variant spelling.

Tarphon   A variant spelling of Tarfon. *See* Tarfon.

Tarshish (תַּרְשִׁישׁ)   From the Hebrew, meaning "precious stone." Also, a place-name in the Book of Jonah (1:3).

Tarver   From the Old English, meaning "tower, hill" or "leader."

Tate   From the Old English, meaning "tenth, tithing" or "to be cheerful."

Taval (טָבְאָל)   From the Hebrew, meaning "good for nothing." In the Bible (Isaiah 7:6), a contemporary of King Achaz.

Tavas (טַוָּס)   From the Hebrew, meaning "peacock."

Tavi (טָבִי)   From the Aramaic, meaning "good." In the Talmud (Berachot 15b), a third-century Babylonian scholar. Also spelled טָבִי. Tavot is a variant form. Also, a pet name for David. *See* David.

Tavla (טַבְלָא)   From the Aramaic, meaning "board" or "plateau." In the Talmud (Eruvin 12a), a fourth-century Babylonian scholar.

Tavlai (טַבְלַי)   A variant form of Tavla. *See* Tavla.

Tavor (תָּבוֹר)   From the Aramaic, meaning "fracture" or "misfortune." A mountain in northern Israel. Tabor is a variant spelling.

Tavot   A variant form of Tavi. *See* Tavi.

Taylor   From the Old English, meaning "tailor."

Taz   From the Arabic, meaning "a shallow, ornamental cup."

Teague From the Celtic, meaning "poet." Also, an Irish form of Thadeus. *See* Thadeus. Teige is a variant spelling.

Tebi A variant form of Tev. *See* Tev.

Techina (תְּחִנָה) From the Hebrew, meaning "prayer, petition." In the Bible (I Chronicles 4:12), a member of the tribe of Judah.

Ted, Teddy Pet forms of Theodor. *See* Theodor.

Teige A variant spelling of Teague. *See* Teague.

Tel (תֵּל) A variant form of Telem. *See* Telem.

Tel-Chai (תֵּל-חַי) From the Hebrew, meaning "mound (hill) of the living." Also, a settlement in Upper Galilee (founded in 1917) that was attacked by Arabs in 1920; Joseph Trumpeldor lost his life in its defense.

Telem (תֶּלֶם) From the Hebrew, meaning "mound" or "furrow." Also from the Aramaic, meaning "oppress, injure" and spelled טְלַם. In the Bible (Ezra 10:24), a Levite.

Telli, Telly Pet forms of Theodosius (Theodor), popular with Greek-speaking people. *See* Theodosius *and* Theodor.

Telmo Possibly from the Old English, meaning "to till, cultivate."

Tema, Temah (תֵּימָא) From the Hebrew and Aramaic, meaning "astonishment, wonder." In the Talmud (Avot 5:23), the father of a second-century scholar.

Temach (תֶּמַח) A variant spelling of Tamach. *See* Tamach.

Teman (תֵּימָן) From the Hebrew, meaning "right side," denoting the south. (The south is to the right of a person as he faces east, towards Jerusalem.) Used in Israel primarily by new settlers who came from Yemen (Teman). In the Bible (Genesis 36:11), a descendant of Esau.

Temani (תֵּימָנִי) From the Hebrew, meaning "one who is from Teman (the south)." *See also* Teman. In the Bible (I Chronicles 4:6), a member of the tribe of Judah.

Temple From the Latin, meaning "sanctuary."

Templeton From the Old English, meaning "a town in which a sanctuary is situated."

Teneh (טֶנֶא) From the Hebrew, meaning "basket."

Tennyson A patronymic form, meaning "son of Tenny (Dennis)." *See* Dennis.

Tera A variant spelling of Terach. *See* Terach.

Terach (תֶּרַח) From the Hebrew, meaning "wild goat, ibex." In the Bible (Genesis 11:25), a descendant of Shem and the father of Abraham. Tera and Terah are variant spellings.

Teradyon (תְּרַדְיוֹן) Possibly from the Aramaic, meaning "sleep, slumber. In the Talmud (Avot 3:2), the father of Rabbi Chanina, a first-century Palestinian scholar.

Terah   A variant spelling of Terach. *See* Terach.

Terence, Terrance, Terrence   From the Latin, meaning "tender, good, gracious." Terri and Terry are pet forms. Torrance and Torrence are variant forms.

Terri, Terry   A pet form of Terence. *See* Terence.

Tesher (תֶּשֶׁר)   From the Hebrew, meaning "gift."

Tevach (טֶבַח)   From the Hebrew, meaning "slaughter." In the Bible (Genesis 22:24), a son of Nachor.

Tevi   An Aramaic form of Tzevi. *See* Tzevi.

Thad   A pet form of Thadeus. *See* Thadeus.

Thadeus, Thaddeus (תּוֹדִיּוֹס)   From the Greek, meaning "gift of God." Akin to Theodor, Theodosius, and Timothy. Tad and Thad are pet forms. In the Talmud (Pesachim 53a), Thaddeus of Rome is a second century scholar. variant form.

Thalmus   From the Greek, meaning "young shoot, sprout."

Than   From the Greek, meaning "death." A pet form of Thanatos.

Thanatos   In Greek mythology, death personified. Than is a pet form.

Tharon   A variant spelling of Theron. *See* Theron.

Thel   From the Old English, meaning "upper story."

Theo   A pet form of Theobald and Theodore. *See* Theobald *and* Theodore.

Theobald, Theobold   From the Old German, meaning "brave people." Theo is a pet form.

Theodor, Theodore   From the Greek, meaning "divine gift." Ted, Teddy, and Theo are popular pet forms. Akin to Thadeus, Theodosius, and Timothy.

Theodoric   A variant form of Theodric. *See* Theodric.

Theodosius (תּוֹדִוֹס)   From the Greek, meaning "gift of God." Akin to Thadeus, Theodor, and Timothy. In the Talmud (Betza 23a), a scholar of the second century also known as Thadeus. Theuda is a variant form. Telli and Telly are pet forms.

Theodric   From the Old German, meaning "ruler of the people." Theodoric is a variant form.

Theophillus, Theophilus   From the Greek, meaning "beloved of God." In the New Testament, the person to whom St. Luke's Gospel was addressed.

Theron   From the Greek, meaning "hunter." Tharon is a variant spelling.

Theuda   A variant form of Theodosius. *See* Theodosius.

Thom   A pet form of Thomas. *See* Thomas.

Thomas (תְּאוֹם) From the Hebrew and Aramaic, meaning "twin." Also, from the Phoenician, meaning "sun god." Tomas is a variant form. Thom, Tom, Tomie, and Tommy are pet forms. Tamsen, Tamson, and Thompson are patronymic forms.

Thompson A patronymic form, meaning "son of Thomas." *See* Thomas.

Thor In Norse mythology, the god of thunder and war. Thor was the eldest son of Odin, creator of the world. Thork, Thorold, and Thorwald are variant forms. *See also* Thunderbird, Thurgood, Thurlow, Thurman, and Thurstan.

Thork A Gaelic form of Thor. *See* Thor.

Thorndike From the Old English, meaning "hedge thorn," hence "dike near the hawthorn tree."

Thornton From the Anglo-Saxon, meaning "from the thorny place (town)."

Thorold A variant form of Thor. *See* Thor.

Thorpe From the Old English, meaning "farmhouse."

Thorwald From the Old English, meaning "Thor's forest." *See* Thor.

Thron From the Greek, meaning "seat of royalty, throne."

Thruston A variant form of Thurstan. *See* Thurstan.

Thunderbird From the Old English, meaning "bird of Thor." *See* Thor.

Thurgood From the Old English, meaning "Thor is good." *See* Thor.

Thurlow A hybrid of Thor and *loe*, meaning "hill," hence "Thor's sanctuary." *See* Thor.

Thurman, Thurmon From the Norse and Old English, meaning "servant of Thor." *See* Thor.

Thurstan, Thurston From the Scandinavian, a hybrid of Thor and *stan*, meaning "stone," hence "Thor's stone or jewel." Thruston is a variant form.

Tibon, Tibbon Variant spellings of Tivon. *See* Tivon. The Ibn Tibbon family were outstanding Spanish and French Jewish scholars of the twelfth and thirteenth centuries who contributed significantly to the development of the Hebrew language and literature.

Tidhar (תִּדְהָר) From the Hebrew, meaning "plane tree," referred to in Isaiah 41:19.

Tiger From the Greek, Latin, and Old French, meaning "tiger."

Tikva, Tikvah (תִּקְוָה) From the Hebrew, meaning "hope." In the Bible (II Kings 22:14), a contemporary of King Josiah. Used also as a feminine name.

Tilden From the Anglo-Saxon, meaning "tilled or fertile valley." Tilly is a pet form.

Tilghman From the Old English, meaning "station."

Tilly A pet form of Tilden. *See* Tilden.

Tilon (תִּילוֹן) From the Hebrew, meaning "small mound." In the Bible (I Chronicles 4:20), a descendant of Judah.

Tim A pet form of Timothy. *See* Timothy.

Timna (תִּמְנָע) From the Hebrew, meaning "withhold." In the Bible (I Chronicles 1:36), a son of Eliphaz. Used also as a feminine name.

Timo A short form of Timothy. *See* Timothy.

Timothy From the Greek, meaning "to honor (or fear) God." Akin to Thadeus, Theodor, and Theodosius. Timo is a short form. Tim is a pet form.

Timur (תִּמוּר) From the Hebrew, meaning "tall, stately" or "to rise up." Akin to Tamir and the feminine Tamar.

Tino An Italian suffix meaning "small." Also, a pet form of Tony. *See* Tony.

Tinsley From the Old English, meaning "the fortification in (or near) the meadow."

Tip A nickname for Thomas. *See* Thomas.

Tirya (תִּרְיָא) From the Aramaic, meaning "to be awake." In the Bible (I Chronicles 4:16), a member of the tribe of Judah.

Tito A variant form of Titos. *See* Titos.

Titos From the Greek name Titan, meaning "a person or thing of great size and power." Tito and Titus are variant forms.

Titus The Latin form of Titos. *See* Titos.

Tiv (טִיב) From the Hebrew and Aramaic, meaning "good, goodness." Tivon is a variant form.

Tivon (טִבְעוֹן) From the Hebrew, meaning "natural." Tibon and Tibbon are variant spellings.

Tobey A variant spelling of Toby. *See* Toby.

Tobi A variant spelling of Tovi. *See* Tovi.

Tobiah A variant spelling of Tuviya. *See* Tuviya.

Tobias The Greek form of Tobiah. *See* Tobiah.

Tobin A variant spelling of Tobyn. *See* Tobyn.

Toby A pet form of Tobiah. *See* Tobiah. Tobey and Tobi are variant spellings.

Tobyn A pet form of Tobiah, popular in Ireland. *See* Tobiah. Tobin is a variant spelling.

Tod From the Old English, meaning "thicket." Also, from the Scottish and Norse, meaning "fox." Todd is a variant spelling.

Toda, Todah (תּוֹדָה) From the Hebrew, meaning "thanks, thankfulness." Mentioned in the Talmud (Sanhedrin 43a) as one of the disciples of Jesus.

Todd A variant spelling of Tod. *See* Tod.

Todos (תּוֹדוֹס) The Hebrew equivalent of Thaddeus and Theodosius. *See* Thaddeus *and* Theodosius.

Todros (טוֹדְרוֹס) From the Greek, meaning "gift." Adopted as a Hebrew name in Israel.

Tola (תּוֹלָע) From the Hebrew, meaning "worm" or "scarlet material." In the Bible (Genesis 46:13), one of the sons of Issachar and also one of Israel's Judges (Judges 11:1).

Tolbert A variant form of Talbot. *See* Talbot.

Toller From the Old English, meaning "one who levies or collects taxes."

Tom A pet form of Thomas. *See* Thomas.

T'om (תְּאוֹם) From the Hebrew, meaning "twin." *See also* Thomas.

Tomas A variant form of Thomas. *See* Thomas.

Tomer (תּוֹמֶר) From the Hebrew, meaning "tall, stately."

T'omi (תְּאוֹמִי) From the Hebrew, meaning "my twin."

Tomie A pet form of Thomas. *See* Thomas.

Tommy A pet form of Thomas. *See* Thomas.

Toney A variant spelling of Tony. *See* Tony.

Toni, Tony Pet forms of Anthony. *See* Anthony. Tino is a pet form. Toney is a variant spelling.

Topo From the Spanish, meaning "mole, gopher."

Topper From the British, meaning "hill."

Tor (תּוֹר) From the Hebrew, meaning "turn, appointed time" or "dove."

Torbert From the Anglo-Saxon, meaning "bright (prominent) hill."

Torn A pet form of Torrance. *See* Torrance.

Torrance, Torrence Irish forms of Terence. *See* Terence. Torn and Torrey are pet forms.

Torrey A pet form of Torrance. *See* Torrance. Tory is a variant spelling.

Tory A variant spelling of Torrey. *See* Torrey.

Tov (טוֹב) From the Hebrew, meaning "good." In the Bible (II Chronicles 17:8), a Levite in the time of King Jehoshaphat.

Tovi (טוֹבִי) A variant form of Tov. *See* Tov. From the Hebrew, meaning "my good, my goodness." In the Talmud (Bava Kama 36b), a third-century Babylonian scholar.

Tovia, Toviah Variant spellings of Toviya. *See* Toviya.

Toviel (טוֹבִיאֵל) From the Hebrew, meaning "my God is goodness." Akin to Toviya.

Tovim (טוֹבִים) From the Hebrew, meaning "good, goodness."

Tovi-Shilem (טוֹבִי־שָׁלֵם) From the Hebrew, meaning "my goodness (good fortune) is complete."

Toviya (טוֹבִיָה) From the Hebrew, meaning "goodness of God." In the Bible (Ezra 12:60), one of the Babylonian Exile returnees. A Palestinian scholar who is quoted in the Midrash (Bereshit Rabba 41:4). Toviyahu is a variant form.

Toviyahu (טוֹבִיָהוּ) A variant form of Toviya. See Toviya.

Tov-Shilem (טוֹב־שָׁלֵם) From the Hebrew, meaning "well rewarded."

Townsend From the Anglo-Saxon, meaning "end of town."

Tracey, Tracy From the Old French, meaning "path" or "road."

Travers A variant form of Travis. See Travis.

Travis From the Latin and French, meaning "crossroads." Travers is a variant form.

Trent From the French, meaning "thirty."

Trenton A variant form of Trent. See Trent.

Trevor From the Celtic, meaning "prudent."

Trini From the Latin, meaning "three, trinity."

Tristam From the Celtic, meaning "tumult, noise."

Tristan An Old French form of Tristam. See Tristam.

Truett From the Middle English, meaning "true."

Truman From the Anglo-Saxon, meaning "true, loyal man."

Trygve From the British, meaning "town by the water."

Tsali A variant spelling of Tzali. See Tzali.

Tug From the Old Norse, meaning "to draw, to pull."

Turner From the Latin, meaning "worker with a lathe."

Tuval The name of a nation in Asia Minor. In the Bible (Isaiah 66:19), a son of Japhet.

Tuvia, Tuviah Variant spellings of Tuviya. See Tuviya.

Tuviya (טוּבִיָה) From the Hebrew, meaning "God is good" or "goodness of God." Tobiah, Tuvia and Tuviah are variant spellings. Tobias is a Greek form. Toby and Tobyn are pet forms. In the Bible (Zechariah 6:10), one of the Babylonian Exile returnees.

Tuviyahu (טוּבִיָהוּ) A variant form of Tuviya. In the Bible (II Chronicles 17:8), a Levite during the reign of Jehoshaphat.

Ty From the British, meaning "house." Tyson is a patronymic form.

Tyler From the British, possibly meaning "house builder."

Tyron, Tyrone   From the Greek, meaning "lord, ruler." Also, from the Latin, meaning "young soldier."

Tyson   A patronymic form, meaning "son of Ty." *See* Ty.

Tzabar (צַבָּר)   From the Arabic, meaning "cactus." A folk-name for native-born Israelis. Zabar is a variant spelling.

Tzach (צַח)   From the Hebrew, meaning "clear, pure." Tzachai is a variant form.

Tzachai (צְבָאי)   A variant form of Tzach. *See* Tzach.

Tzachar (צָחַר)   From the Hebrew, meaning "white, whiteness."

Tzachi (צָחִי)   A pet form of Yitzchack (Isaac). *See* Yitzchack.

Tzadik (צָדִיק)   From the Hebrew, meaning "righteous person." Tzadok is a variant form. Zadik and Zaddik are variant spellings.

Tzadkiel (צָדְקִיאֵל)   From the Hebrew, meaning "God is my righteousness, my justification." Zadkiel is a variant spelling.

Tzadok (צָדוֹק)   From the Hebrew, meaning "just" or "righteous." Zadok is a variant spelling.

Tzafrir (צַפְרִיר)   From the Hebrew, meaning "morning" or "morning breeze." Tzafriri and Tzafrit are variant forms. Zafrir is a variant spelling.

Tzafriri (צַפְרִירִי)   A variant form of Tzafrir. *See* Tzafrir. Zafriri is a variant spelling.

Tzafrit (צַפְרִית)   A variant form of Tzafrir. *See* Tzafrir. Zafrit is a variant spelling.

Tzahal (צָהַל)   From the Hebrew, meaning "joy, a shout or expression of joy." Also, an acronym formed from the Hebrew words *Tzeva Hagana l'Yisrael,* meaning "Israel Defense Forces." Zahal is a variant spelling. Tzahalon is a variant form.

Tzahalon (צָהֲלוֹן)   A variant form of Tzahal. *See* Tzahal. Zahalon is a variant spelling.

Tzahuv (צָהוּב)   From the Hebrew, meaning "turning yellow" or "angry, hostile."

Tzalaf (צָלָף)   From the Hebrew, meaning "common caperbush." In the Bible (Nehemiah 3:30), one of Nehemiah's supporters.

Tzalel (צָלְאֵל)   A short form of Betzalel. *See* Betzalel. Zalel is a variant spelling.

Tzali (צָלִי)   A pet form of Betzalel. *See* Betzalel.

Tzalmon (צַלְמוֹן)   From the Hebrew, meaning "darkness." In the Bible (II Samuel 23:28), one of King David's warriors. Zalmon is a variant spelling.

Tzalul (צָלוּל)   From the Hebrew, meaning "clear, lucid." Zalul is a variant spelling. Tzelil and Zelil are variant forms.

Tzameret (צָמֶרֶת) From the Hebrew, meaning "tree top," because of its feathery, woolly appearance. Akin to Tzemari. Zameret is a variant spelling.

Tzecharya (צְחַרְיָה) From the Hebrew, meaning "white" or "the purity of God."

Tzechi (צְחִי) A pet form of Yitzchak (Isaac). *See* Yitzchak.

Tzedef (צֶדֶף) From the Hebrew, meaning "mother of pearl."

Tze'el (צָאֵל) From the Hebrew, meaning "jujube."

Tzefanya (צְפַנְיָה) From the Hebrew, meaning "hidden by God" or "protected by God." Zefania and Zefaniah are variant spellings. Tzefanyahu is a variant form.

Tzefanyahu (צְפַנְיָהוּ) A variant form of Tzefanya. *See* Tzefanya.

Tzefi (צְפִי) From the Hebrew, meaning "overseer, guardian" or "spectator."

Tzefo (צְפוֹ) A variant form of Tzefi. *See* Tzefi.

Tzelafchad (צְלָפְחָד) From the Hebrew, probably meaning "protection from fear." In the Bible (Numbers 26:33), a member of the tribe of Manasseh who had five daughters and no sons. Zelophehad is a variant spelling.

Tzelek (צֶלֶק) From the Hebrew, meaning "scar."

Tzelil (צְלִיל) From the Hebrew, meaning "cookie" or "musical tone." Zelil is a variant spelling. Also, a variant form of Tzalul. *See* Tzalul.

Tzemach (צֶמַח) From the Hebrew, meaning "plant." In the Bible (Zechariah 3:8), a man named in Zechariah's prophecy. Tzemah and Zemach are variant spellings.

Tzemari (צְמָרִי) From the Hebrew, meaning "wool, woolly." Zemari is a variant spelling. Akin to Tzameret. Tzomri is a variant form.

Tzeri (צְרִי) From the Hebrew, meaning "my wreath, my crown" or "spice, balsam." Zeri and Zri are variant forms.

Tzeror (צְרוֹר) From the Hebrew, meaning "rock." In the Bible (I Samuel 9:1), a member of the tribe of Benjamin, an ancestor of King Saul. Zeror is a variant spelling.

Tzevi (צְבִי) From the Hebrew, meaning "deer, gazelle." Tzvi, Zevi, and Zvi are variant spellings. Tzivya and Tzivyon are variant forms.

Tzeviel (צְבִיאֵל) From the Hebrew, meaning "gazelle of the Lord." Zeviel is a variant spelling.

Tzevieli (צְבִיאֵלִי) From the Hebrew, meaning "God is my gazelle." A variant form of Tzeviel. Zevieli is a variant spelling.

Tzi (צִי) From the Hebrew, meaning "ship" or "navy." Also, a pet form of Tziyon. *See* Tziyon. Zi is a variant spelling.

Tzidkiya (צִדְקִיָה) From the Hebrew, meaning "righteousness of the Lord" or "God is righteousness." In the Bible (II Kings 24:17), the last king of Judah

(597-586 B.C.E.). His original name was Mattaniah, but he adopted the name Tzidkiya when he was appointed king by Nebuchadnezzar of Babylonia to succeed the exiled Jehoiakin. Zedekia and Zedekiah are Anglicized spellings. Tzidkiyahu is a variant form.

Tzidkiyahu (צִדְקִיָהוּ) A variant form of Tzidkiya. *See* Tzidkiya.

Tzif (צִיף) A variant form of Tzuf. *See* Tzuf. Zif is a variant spelling.

Tzifyon (צְפִיוֹן) From the Hebrew, meaning "watchtower." In the Bible (Genesis 46:16), a son of Gad and a grandson of Jacob. Ziphion is a variant spelling.

Tziltai (צִלְתָי) From the Aramaic, meaning "black," or from the Hebrew, meaning "shaded, protected." In the Bible (I Chronicles 8:20), a descendant of Benjamin. Ziltai is a variant spelling.

Tzipor, Tzippor (צִפּוֹר) From the Hebrew, meaning "bird." In the Bible (Numbers 22:2), the father of Balak. Zipor and Zippor are variant spellings.

Tzivya (צִבְיָה) The Aramaic form of Tzevi. *See* Tzevi. Zivia is a variant spelling.

Tzivyon (צִבְיוֹן) From the Hebrew, meaning "beauty" or "honor." Zivion is a variant spelling.

Tziyon (צִיוֹן) From the Hebrew, meaning "excellent" or "a sign." In the Bible, Zion is used as the name of a place as well as the appellation for the Hebrew people. Zion is the Anglicized form.

Tzochar (צֹחַר) From the Hebrew, meaning "tan, reddish-gray." In the Bible (Genesis 46:10), a son of Simeon and a grandson of Jacob. Zochar and Zohar are variant spellings.

Tzofai (צֹפַי) From the Aramaic, meaning "scouts, spies."

Tzofar (צֹפַר) From the Hebrew, meaning "he-goat" or "to leap, jump." In the Bible (Job 11:1), one of Job's three friends. Zofar, Zophar, and Tzophar are variant spellings.

Tzomri (צָמְרִי) A variant form of Tzemari. *See* Tzemari.

Tzophar A variant spelling of Tzofar. *See* Tzofar.

Tzoveva (צֹבֵבָה) From the Hebrew, meaning "to cleave" or "low covered wagon." In the Bible (I Chronicles 4:8), a member of the tribe of Judah. Zoveva is a variant spelling.

Tzuar (צוּעָר) From the Hebrew, meaning "small." In the Bible (Numbers 1:8), a leader of the tribe of Issachar. Zuar is a variant spelling.

Tzuf (צוּף) From the Hebrew, meaning "flow, overflow." In the Bible (I Samuel 1:1), an ancestor of Elkanah and Samuel. Zuf and Zuph are variant spellings. Tzif is a variant form.

Tzur (צוּר) From the Hebrew, meaning "rock" or "cliff." In the Bible (I Chronicles 8:30), a descendant of Benjamin. Zur is a variant spelling.

Tzuri (צוּרִי)   A variant form of Tzur. From the Hebrew, meaning "my rock." Zuri is a variant spelling.

Tzuriel (צוּרִיאֵל)   From the Hebrew, meaning "God is my rock." In the Bible (Numbers 3:35), a leader of the Merari family. Zuriel is a variant spelling. Akin to Tzurishadai and Tzuriya.

Tzurishadai (צוּרִישַׁדָּי)   From the Hebrew, meaning "God is my rock." In the Bible (Numbers 1:6), the father of a leader of the tribe of Simeon. Zurishadai is a variant spelling. Akin to Tzuriel and Tzuriya.

Tzuriya (צוּרִיָה)   From the Hebrew, meaning "God is my rock." Akin to Tzuriel and Tzurishadai.

Tzvi   A variant spelling of Tzevi. See Tzevi. Zevi is a variant spelling.

Ud (אוּד)   From the Hebrew, meaning "firebrand." Udi and Udiel are variant forms.

Udi (אוּדִי)   From the Hebrew, meaning "firebrand." A variant form of Ud. Also, a nickname of Ehud.

Udiel (אוּדִיאֵל)   From the Hebrew, meaning "torch of the Lord." A variant form of Ud.

Uel   A short form of Samuel. See Samuel.

Ukba   A variant spelling of Ukva. See Ukva.

Ukva (עֻקְבָא)   A variant Aramaic form of Yaakov. See Yaakov. In the Talmud (Kidushin 44b), a third-century Babylonian scholar was known as Mar Ukva. Ukba is a variant spelling.

Ula (עוּלָא)   From the Aramaic and Hebrew, meaning "yoke." In the Talmud (Berachot 38b), a third-century Babylonian and Palestinian scholar. In the Bible (I Chronicles 7:39), a member of the tribe of Asher.

Ull   A variant form of Ulric. See Ulric.

Ulric, Ulrich, Ulrick   From the Danish, meaning "wolf." Ull is a variant form.

Uni (עֻנִּי)   From the Hebrew, meaning "to sing, chant." In the Bible (I Chronicles 15:18), a Levite.

Upaz (אוּפָּז)   From the Hebrew, meaning "gold." Akin to Paz.

Ur (אוּר)   From the Hebrew, meaning "flame." In the Bible (I Chronicles 11:35), the father of one of King David's warriors. In the Bible (Genesis 11:28), a place-name, the birthplace of Abraham. Uri and Uriah are variant forms.

Urban, Urbane   From the Latin, meaning "city."

Uri (אוּרִי)   A variant form of Ur. From the Hebrew, meaning "my flame" or "my light." Also, a short form of Uriah. See Uriah. In the Bible (Exodus 31:2), a leader of the tribe of Judah. Urie is a variant spelling.

Uria, Uriah   Variant spellings of Uriya. See Uriya.

Uriahu   A variant spelling of Uriyahu. See Uriyahu.

Urian   A variant spelling of Uryan. See Uryan.

Urie   A variant spelling of Uri. See Uri.

Uriel (אוּרִיאֵל)   From the Hebrew, meaning "God is my light" or "God is my flame." Akin to Uriah. In the Bible (I Chronicles 6:9), a Levite of the Kohat family. In Jewish legend, one of four angels who minister in God's presence.

Urion   A variant spelling of Uryon. See Uryon.

Uriya (אוּרִיָה)   A variant form of Ur. From the Hebrew, meaning "God is my flame." In the Bible (II Samuel 11:3), the husband of Bathsheba, who later became King David's wife. Uria and Uriah are variant spellings. Uri is a short form. Uriyahu is a variant form. Akin to Uriel.

Uriyahu (אוּרִיָהוּ)   A variant form of Uriya. See Uriya. In the Bible (Jeremiah 26:20), a Prophet slain by King Jehoiakim.

Ur-Malki (אוּר־מַלְכִּי)   From the Hebrew, meaning "my king is light."

Ursel   From the Latin, meaning "bear." Ursula is a feminine form. Urshell is a variant form.

Urshell   A variant form of Ursel. See Ursel.

Uryan (אוּרְיָן)   From the Aramaic, meaning "light," an appellation often assigned to a great luminary or scholar. Urian is a variant spelling. Orvan is a variant form. Akin to Uryon.

Uryon (אוּרְיוֹן)   From the Hebrew, meaning "flame" or "light." Orion is a variant spelling. Akin to Uryan.

Utai (עוּתַי)   From the Hebrew, meaning "aid, help." In the Bible (I Chronicles 9:4), a descendant of Judah.

Utz (עוּץ)   From the Hebrew, meaning "advice, wisdom" or "to make haste." In the Bible (Genesis 10:23), a grandson of Shem. Uz is a variant spelling.

Uz (עֵץ)   A variant spelling of Utz. See Utz. Also, from the Hebrew, meaning "strength." In the Bible (Genesis 10:23), a grandson of Shem. Uza, Uzi, Uziel, and Uziya are variant forms.

Uza (עֻזָּה)   A variant form of Uz. From the Hebrew, meaning "strength." In the Bible (I Chronicles 6:14), a descendant of Levi of the Merari family. Also the name of a bird. Uzza is a variant English spelling. עֻזָּא is a variant Hebrew spelling.

Uzal (אוּזָל)   From the Hebrew, meaning "to leave, depart" or "to be exhausted." In the Bible (Genesis 10:27), a descendant of Shem.

Uzi (עֻזִּי) From the Hebrew, meaning "my strength." In the Bible (II Kings 15:30), a king of Judah also known as Azariah. Uzzi is a variant spelling.

Uzia, Uziah Variant spellings of Uziya. See Uziya.

Uziahu A variant spelling of Uziyahu. See Uziyahu.

Uziel (עֻזִּיאֵל) From the Hebrew, meaning "God is my strength." In the Bible (Exodus 6:18), a son of Kohat and a grandson of Levi. Akin to Uziya.

Uziya (עֻזִּיָה) From the Hebrew, meaning "God is my strength." In the Bible (II Kings 15:13), a king of Judah. Also, the name of a bird. Uzia, Uziah, and Uzziah are variant spellings. Uziyahu is a variant form. עֻזִּיָא is a variant Hebrew spelling.

Uziyahu (עֻזִּיָהוּ) A variant form of Uziya. See Uziya. Uziahu is a variant spelling.

Uzza A variant spelling of Uza. See Uza.

Uzzi A variant spelling of Uzi. See Uzi.

Uzziah A variant spelling of Uziya. See Uziya.

Vachel A French occupational name, meaning "one who raises cows." Also, possibly from the British, meaning "little ash tree."

Vada From the Latin, meaning "shallow place, ford."

Vail From the Latin, meaning "valley." Vale is a variant spelling. Val is a French form.

Val A French form of Vail. Also, a pet form of Valentine and Valery. See Valentine *and* Valery.

Vale A variant spelling of Vail. See Vail.

Valentine From the Latin, meaning "strong, valorous." Akin to Valery. Val, Vali, and Vallie are pet forms.

Valery The French form of the Latin, meaning "strong." Akin to Valentine. Val, Vali, and Vallie are pet forms.

Vali In Norse mythology, a son of Odin, creator of the world. Also, a pet form of Valentine and Valery. See Valentine *and* Valery. Valle is a variant form.

Valle A variant French form of Vali. See Vali.

Vallie A pet form of Valentine and Valery. See Valentine *and* Valery.

Van The Dutch form of the German *von*, meaning "from (a particular city)." Akin to the French *de*. Vane and Vanne are variant forms.

Vance   A form of the British name Vans, meaning "high, high places."

Vander   Probably from the Dutch, meaning "of the" or "from the," a prefix to many place-names.

Vane, Vanne   Variant forms of Van. *See* Van.

Vardimon (וַרְדִּימוֹן)   From the Hebrew, meaning "the essence of rose" or "rose oil." Vardinon is a variant form.

Vardinon (וַרְדִּינוֹן)   A variant form of Vardimon. *See* Vardimon.

Varner   Probably a variant form of Werner. *See* Werner. Also, a variant form of Vernon. *See* Vernon. Varney is a variant form.

Varney   A variant form of Varner or Vernon. *See* Varner *and* Vernon.

Vaughan, Vaughn   From the Celtic, meaning "small."

Vedie   Probably from the Latin, meaning "to see."

Velvel (וֶעלוֶל)   A pet form of the Yiddish Volf (Wolf). *See* Volf. Also spelled וֶעלוָעל.

Venn   From the British, meaning "fair, beautiful."

Verda   From the Old French, meaning "green." Akin to Verdi. Verdo is a variant form.

Verdi   From the Old French, meaning "green, springlike." Akin to Verda.

Verdo   A variant form of Verda. *See* Verda.

Vere   A French form of the Latin, meaning "true." Vera is the feminine form.

Vered (וֶרֶד)   From the Hebrew, meaning "rose." Used also as a feminine name.

Verion   From the Latin, meaning "spring." *See also* Verlin.

Verle   A variant form of Verlin. *See* Verlin.

Verlin   From the Latin, meaning "spring," hence "flourishing." Verlon is a variant spelling. Verle is a variant form. Akin to Verion.

Verlon   A variant spelling of Verlin. *See* Verlin.

Vern   From the British, meaning "alder tree." Or, a pet form of Vernon. *See* Vernon. Verne is a variant spelling.

Vernal   From the Latin, meaning "belonging to spring."

Verne   A variant spelling of Vern. *See* Vern.

Vernice   A variant form of Vern. *See* Vern.

Vernon   From the Latin, meaning "belonging to spring." Akin to Vernal. Also, from the British, meaning "alder tree." Varner, Varney, and Vernice are variant forms. Vern and Verne are pet forms.

Vester   A pet form of Sylvester. *See* Sylvester.

Vibert   From the French, meaning "full of good cheer, vivacious."

Vic, Vickie   Pet forms of Victor. *See* Victor.

Victor   From the Latin, meaning "victor, conqueror." Vittorio is a variant form. Vic and Vickie are pet forms.

Vida   A variant form of Vitas. *See* Vitas. Used also as a form of Davida. *See* Davida (feminine section). Vidal is a variant form.

Vidal   A variant form of Vida. *See* Vida.

Vin   A pet form of Vincent. *See* Vincent.

Vince   A pet form of Vincent. *See* Vincent.

Vincent   From the Latin, meaning "victor" or "conqueror." Vincente is a variant spelling. Vin, Vince, Vine, and Vinnie are pet forms. Vinson is a patronymic form.

Vincente   A variant spelling of Vincent. *See* Vincent.

Vine   A pet form of Vincent. *See* Vincent.

Vinnie   A pet form of Vincent. *See* Vincent.

Vinson   A patronymic form, meaning "son of Vincent." *See* Vincent.

Virgil   From the Latin, meaning "strong, flourishing."

Viron   From the Latin, meaning "spring."

Vitalis   From the Latin, meaning "alive, vital."

Vitas   From the Latin, meaning "life." Vida is a variant form.

Vito   A pet form of Vittorio. *See* Vittorio.

Vittorio   The Italian form of Victor. Vito is a pet form.

Vivian, Vivien   Used only occasionally as masculine names. *See* Vivian (feminine section). Vyvyan is a variant spelling.

Vladimir, Vladmir   From the Slavic, meaning "world prince."

Vofsi (וָפְסִי)   Meaning unknown. In the Bible (Numbers 13:4), a member of the tribe of Naphtali. Vophsi is a variant spelling.

Volf (וָאלף)   From the Yiddish, meaning "wolf." Velvel is a pet form.

Von   The German form of Van. *See* Van.

Vophsi   A variant spelling of Vofsi. *See* Vofsi.

Vyvyan   A variant spelling of Vivian. *See* Vivian.

Wade   From the Old English, meaning "to wade." Wadell is a variant form.

Wadell   A variant form of Wade. *See* Wade.

Waite   From the Old English, meaning "road."

Wal   A short form of Wallace and Walter. *See* Wallace *and* Walter.

Walbert   From the Old English, meaning "secure fortification." Wilber and Wilbert are variant forms.

Walcott   From the Old English, meaning "a worker with cloth."

Walden   From the Old English, meaning "woods."

Waldo   From the Old English, meaning "ruler."

Walker   From the Old English, meaning "one who cleans and thickens cloth."

Wallace   From the Anglo-French and the Middle English, meaning "foreigner, stranger." Wallis is a variant spelling. Walsh is a variant form. Wal is a short form.

Wallie   A pet form of Walter. *See* Walter.

Wallis   A variant spelling of Wallace. *See* Wallace.

Wally   A pet form of Walter and Wallace. *See* Walter *and* Wallace.

Walsh   A variant form of Wallace. *See* Wallace.

Walt   A short form of Walter. *See* Walter. Wilt is a variant form.

Walter   From the Old English, meaning "woods" or "master of the woods." Also, from the Old French, meaning "army leader, general." Wal and Walt are short forms. Wallie, Wally, Wolli, and Wolly are pet forms. Walther is a variant form.

Walther   A variant form of Walter. *See* Walter.

Walton   From the Old English, meaning "wall, fortification, fortified town."

Ward   From the Old English, meaning "guard, guardian."

Warner   A variant form of Warren. *See* Warren.

Warren   From the Middle English and the Old French, meaning "to preserve" or "enclosure, park." Warner and Werner are variant forms.

Warrick   A variant form of Warwick. *See* Warwick.

Warwick   From the British, meaning "hero." Or, from the Norse, meaning "village." Warrick is a variant form.

Wayne   From the British, meaning "meadow." Or, from the Old English, meaning "way" or "maker of wagons." Wene is the Hawaiian form.

Weaver   From the Old English, meaning "path by the water." Also, a variant form of Webster. *See* Webster.

Webb   A pet form of Webster. *See* Webster. Weeb is a variant form.

Webster From the Old English, meaning "weaver." Webb is a pet form. Weaver is a variant form.

Weeb A variant form of Webb. *See* Webb.

Welby From the Old English, meaning "village near the willow tree."

Weldon A variant form of Welton. *See* Welton.

Wellesley A variant form of Wesley. *See* Wesley.

Wells From the Old English, meaning "well" or "willow tree."

Welsh From the Old English, meaning "stranger."

Welthy From the Old English, meaning "house near the willow tree."

Welton From the Old English, meaning "town near the willow tree." Weldon is a variant form.

Wendel, Wendell From the British, meaning "good dale or valley," or from the Old English, meaning "wanderer, stranger."

Wendelin From the British, meaning "fair."

Wene The Hawaiian form of Wayne. *See* Wayne.

Werner A variant form of Warren. *See* Warren. *See also* Varner. Wernher is a German form.

Wernher A German form of Werner. *See* Werner.

Wesley From the Old English, meaning "west meadow." Wellesley is a variant form.

Westbrook From the Old English, meaning "brook in the western field."

Westcott From the Old English, meaning "cottage in the western field."

Weston From the Old English, meaning "house built on wasteland" or "west town, the town to the west."

Wharton From the Old English, meaning "path by the water."

Wheeler An English occupational name for a "driver of a vehicle."

Whitelaw From the Early Modern English, meaning "small hill."

Whitey A nickname for a light-complexioned person.

Whitfield From the Early Modern English, meaning "small field."

Whitley From the Early Modern English, meaning "small field."

Whitney From the Old English, meaning "small piece of land near the water" or "white palace."

Whittaker From the Early Modern English, meaning "small parcel of land."

Wid From the Old English, meaning "wide."

Wilber, Wilbert Variant forms of Walbert. *See* Walbert. Or, from the Old English, meaning "bright willows." Wilbur and Wilburn are variant forms.

Wilbur, Wilburn   Variant forms of Wilber. *See* Wilber.

Wilder   From the Old English, meaning "person from the wilds, wilderness."

Wilem   A variant spelling of Willem. *See* Willem.

Wiley   From the Old English, meaning "meadow of willows."

Wilf   A variant form of Wolf. *See* Wolf.

Wilford   From the Old English, meaning "willow tree near the ford." *See also* Wilfred.

Wilfred, Wilfrid, Wilfried   From the Old English, meaning "hope for peace." Also, variant forms of Wilford. *See* Wilford.

Wilhelm   The German form of William. *See* William.

Will   A pet form of William. *See* William. Wille is a variant spelling.

Willard   From the Old English, meaning "yard full of willows." Also, a variant form of William. *See* William.

Wille   A variant spelling of Will. *See* Will.

Willem   A Dutch form of William. *See* William. Wilem is a variant spelling.

Willi   A pet form of William. *See* William.

William   A variant form of the Old French name Willaume and the Old High German Willehelm, meaning "resolute protector." Wilhelm, Willard, Willem, Williamson, Willis, Wilmot, and Wilson are variant forms. Will, Willi, Willie, and Willy are pet forms.

Williamson   A patronymic form, meaning "son of William." *See* William. Popular as a Welsh surname.

Willie   A pet form of William. *See* William.

Willis   A patronymic form, meaning "son of William." *See* William. Akin to Wilson.

Willoughby   From the Dutch, meaning "house near the willow trees."

Willy   A pet form of William. *See* William.

Wilmar, Wilmer, Willmer   From the Old English, meaning "willows near the sea."

Wilmot   A variant form of William. *See* William.

Wilson   A patronymic form, meaning "son of William." *See* William. Akin to Willis.

Wilt   A variant form of Walt (Walter). *See* Walter. Or, a pet form of Wilton. *See* Wilton.

Wilton   From the Old English, meaning "from the farmstead by the spring." Wilt is a pet form.

Win   From the Old English, meaning "victory."

Winfield From the Old English, meaning "field with good produce."

Winford A variant form of Winfred. *See* Winfred.

Winfred, Winfrid From the Old English, meaning "friend of peace" or "peaceful friend." Winford is a variant form.

Wingate From the Old English, meaning "victory gate."

Winslow From the Old English, meaning "victory hill."

Winston From the Old English, meaning "victory town" or "a friend firm like a stone." Winton is a variant form.

Winthrop From the Old English, meaning "victory at the crossroads" or "friendly village."

Winton A variant form of Winston. *See* Winston.

Wirt From the Old English, meaning "estate, manor."

Witt, Witter From the Old English, meaning "white, fair."

Wolcott From the Old English, meaning "cottage in the field."

Wolf, Wolfe From the Anglo-Saxon, meaning "wolf." Wilf and Volf are variant forms.

Wolli, Wolly Pet forms of Walter. *See* Walter.

Wood From the Anglo-Saxon, meaning "from the wooded area or forest."

Woodie A pet form of Woodrow. *See* Woodrow.

Woodrow From the Anglo-Saxon, meaning "wooded hedge." Woodie and Woody are pet forms.

Woody A pet form of Woodrow. *See* Woodrow.

Worley From the Old English, meaning "a piece of uncultivated land."

Worthy From the Old English, meaning "estate, manor."

Wray Possibly from the Old English, meaning "crooked."

Wright From the Old English, meaning "artisan, worker."

Wyatt, Wyatte From the British, meaning "water." Wyeth is a variant form.

Wyck From the Old Norse, meaning "village." Wycliffe is a variant form.

Wycliffe A variant form of Wyck, meaning "village near the cliff."

Wyeth A variant form of Wyatt. *See* Wyatt.

Wylie From the Old English, meaning "deceitful, beguiling, coquettish."

Wyman From the British, meaning "a person who works on the water, a sailor."

Wyndham From the Scotch, meaning "village near the winding road."

Wynn From the British, meaning "white, fair."

Xander   A short form of Alexander. *See* Alexander.

Xanthus   From the Greek, meaning "yellow."

Xavier   From the Latin, meaning "savior, one who saves." A Christian name first used by St. Francis (1506-52), a Jesuit missionary.

Xerxes   From the Persian, meaning "king."

Yaacov   A variant spelling of Yaakov. *See* Yaakov.

Yaakov (יַעֲקֹב)   From the Hebrew, meaning "supplanted" or "held by the heel." In the Bible (Genesis 25:26), a son of Isaac and Rebekah, and the twin brother of Esau. In the Talmud (Kidushin 53b), a fourth-century Babylonian scholar. Jacob is the Anglicized form. *See* Jacob. Akiva is a variant form. *See* Akiva. Yaaqov is a variant spelling. Yankel is a Yiddish form. Yaki and Yuki are pet forms.

Yaakova (יַעֲקֹבָה)   A variant form of Yaakov. *See* Yaakov. In the Bible (I Chronicles 4:36), a member of the tribe of Benjamin. Used also as a feminine name.

Yaal (יַעַל)   From the Hebrew, meaning "to ascend."

Yaala (יַעֲלָה)   A variant form of Yala. *See* Yala. Also spelled יַעְלָא. Jaala is a variant spelling.

Yaaqov   A variant spelling of Yaakov. *See* Yaakov.

Yaar (יַעַר)   From the Hebrew, meaning "forest." Yaari is a variant form.

Yaari (יַעְרִי)   A variant form of Yaar. From the Hebrew, meaning "my forest."

Yaasai (יַעֲשַׂי)   From the Aramaic, meaning "to do, create." In the Bible (Ezra 10:37), a contemporary of Ezra.

Yaasiel (יַעֲשִׂיאֵל)   From the Hebrew, meaning "creation of God" or "God will create." In the Bible (I Chronicles 11:47), a distinguished warrior in King David's army.

Yaazanya (יַאֲזַנְיָה)   From the Hebrew, meaning "God will listen." In the Bible (Jeremiah 35:3), the leader of the Rechabites. Yaazania and Yaazaniah are variant spellings.

Yaazanyahu (יַאֲזַנְיָהוּ)   A variant form of Yaazanya. *See* Yaazanya. In the Bible (II Kings 25:23), an officer in the time of Jeremiah.

Yaaziahu   A variant spelling of Yaaziyahu. *See* Yaaziyahu.

Yaaziel (יַעֲזִיאֵל)   From the Hebrew, meaning "God is my strength." In the Bible (I Chronicles 15:18), a Levite.

Yaaziyahu (יְעֲזִיָּהוּ) From the Hebrew, meaning "God is my strength." In the Bible (I Chronicles 24:26), a Levite. Yaaziahu is a variant spelling.

Yabetz (יַעְבֵּץ) From the Hebrew, meaning "pain." In the Bible (I Chronicles 4:9), a member of Caleb's family. Also, a biblical place-name (I Chronicles 2:55). Jabez is a variant spelling. Yavetz is a variant form.

Yachad (יַחַד) From the Hebrew, meaning "together, togetherness, unity" or "joy."

Yachat (יַחַת) From the Hebrew, meaning "snatch up." In the Bible (I Chronicles 4:2), a grandson of Judah.

Yachaziel (יַחֲזִיאֵל) From the Hebrew, meaning "God sees." In the Bible (I Chronicles 16:6), a Priest in the time of David.

Yachdiel (יַחְדִּיאֵל) From the Hebrew, meaning "God is my joy." In the Bible (I Chronicles 5:24), a warrior of the tribe of Manasseh.

Yachdo (יַחְדוֹ) A variant form of Yachad. In the Bible (I Chronicles 5:14), one of the sons of Gad.

Yachel (יָחֵל) From the Hebrew, meaning "hope, trust" or "to wait."

Yachid (יָחִיד) From the Hebrew and Arabic, meaning "one" or "alone."

Yachil (יָחִיל) From the Hebrew, meaning "hope."

Yachin (יָכִין) From the Hebrew, meaning "He (God) will establish." In the Bible (Genesis 46:10), a son of Simeon and a grandson of Jacob. A short form of Yehoyachin. See Yehoyachin.

Yachl'el (יַחְלְאֵל) From the Hebrew, meaning "waiting for God" or "faith in God." In the Bible (Genesis 46:14), a member of the tribe of Zebulun. Yachl'eli is a variant form.

Yachl'eli (יַחְלְאֵלִי) A variant form of Yachl'el. See Yachl'el.

Yachmai (יַחְמַי) From the Aramaic, meaning "May he protect!" In the Bible (I Chronicles 7:2), a son of Tola and a grandson of Issachar.

Yachon (יָחוֹן) From the Hebrew, meaning "May He (God) have compassion!"

Yada (יָדָע) From the Hebrew, meaning "to know." In the Bible (I Chronicles 2:32), a member of the tribe of Judah. Jada is a variant spelling.

Yadai (יַדַי) A variant form of Yedidya. See Yedidya. Akin to Yido.

Yadid (יָדִיד) From the Hebrew, meaning "beloved" or "friend." Yedid is a variant form.

Yadin (יָדִין) A variant form of Yadon. See Yadon. Jadin is a variant spelling.

Yadon (יָדוֹן) From the Hebrew, meaning "he will judge." In the Bible (Nehemiah 3:7), a supporter of Nehemiah who helped rebuild the walls of Jerusalem. Yadin is a variant form. Jadon is a variant spelling.

Yadua (יַדּוּעַ) From the Hebrew, meaning "knowledge." In the Bible

(Nehemiah 12:11), a Levite who was one of the Babylonian Exile returnees. Jadua is a variant spelling.

Yadun (יָדוּן) ᐧ From the Hebrew, meaning "to judge."

Yael (יָעֵל) From the Hebrew, meaning "mountain goat." Used primarily as a feminine name.

Yaen (יָעֵן) From the Hebrew, meaning "ostrich." Used also as a feminine name.

Yafe, Yaffe (יָפֶה) From the Hebrew, meaning "beautiful."

Yafet A variant spelling of Yefet. See Yefet.

Yafia (יָפִיעַ) From the Hebrew, meaning "to shine forth," hence "to glorify." In the Bible (II Samuel 5:15), a son of King David. Japhia is a variant spelling.

Yafim (יָפִים) From the Hebrew, meaning "beautiful."

Yaflet (יַפְלֵט) From the Hebrew, meaning "God will save, God will deliver." In the Bible (I Chronicles 7:33), a descendant of Asher.

Yagel (יָגֵל) From the Hebrew, meaning "he will rejoice."

Yagev (יָגֵב) From the Hebrew, meaning "cultivated land, farmland."

Yagil (יָגִיל) From the Hebrew, meaning "to rejoice." Akin to Yagel.

Yagli A variant spelling of Yogli. See Yogli.

Yahali (יַהֲלִי) A variant form of Yahel. See Yahel.

Yahalom (יַהֲלֹם) From the Hebrew, meaning "precious stone, diamond."

Yahav (יָהַב) From the Hebrew, meaning "to give" or "gift." Yahev is a variant form.

Yahel (יָהֵל) From the Hebrew, meaning "tent," hence "protection." Also, the name of a sweet-smelling plant. Yahali is a variant form.

Yahev (יָהֵב) A variant form of Yahav. See Yahav.

Yair (יָאִיר) From the Hebrew, meaning "to light up" or "to enlighten." In the Bible (Deuteronomy 3:14), a son of Manasseh and a grandson of Joseph. Also, from the Hebrew, meaning "reveal, uncover" and spelled יָעִיר. In the Bible (I Chronicles 20:5), the father of Elchanan, one of King David's warriors. Jair is a variant spelling.

Yaish (יָעִישׁ) From the Hebrew, meaning "constellation of stars," also referred to as "Big Bear."

Yakar (יָקָר) From the Hebrew, meaning "precious, dear" or "beloved, honorable." Yakir is a variant form.

Yaki (יָקִי) A pet form of Yaakov. See Yaakov.

Yakim (יָקִים) A short form of Yehoyakim (Jehoiakim). See Yehoyakim. In the Bible (I Chronicles 24:12), a Priest in the time of King David. In the

Talmud (Mishna Eduyot 7:5), a second-century Palestinian scholar. Jakim is a variant spelling. Akin to Yakum.

Yakir (יָקִיר) A variant form of Yakar. *See* Yakar.

Yaktan A variant spelling of Yoktan. *See* Yoktan.

Yakum (יָקוּם) A variant form of Yakim. *See* Yakim.

Yala (יַעְלָה) From the Hebrew and Aramaic, meaning "wild goat." In the Bible (Ezra 2:56), a descendant of a servant of King Solomon. Yaala is a variant form.

Yale From the Anglo-Saxon, meaning "one who pays or yields."

Yalon (יָלוֹן) From the Hebrew, meaning "he will sleep, rest" or "he will murmur, complain." In the Bible (I Chronicles 4:17), a descendant of Caleb of the tribe of Judah. Jalon is a variant spelling. Yalun is a variant form.

Yalun (יָלוּן) A variant form of Yalon. *See* Yalon.

Yamin (יָמִין) From the Hebrew, meaning "right-handed." In the Bible (Genesis 46:10), a son of Simeon and a grandson of Jacob. Jamin is a variant spelling.

Yamir (יָמִיר) From the Hebrew, meaning "to change."

Yamlech (יַמְלֵךְ) From the Hebrew, meaning "he will rule." In the Bible (I Chronicles 4:34), a descendant of Simeon and a grandson of Jacob.

Yan, Yana (יַן) Variant forms of John. *See* John. Also, short forms of Yanai. *See* Yanai. Yanni is a variant form.

Yanai (יַנַּאי) From the Hebrew and Aramaic, meaning "to shake, wave" or "to answer." In the Bible (I Chronicles 5:12), a descendant of Gad, spelled יַעְנַי. A king of Israel in the first century B.C.E., the husband of Queen Salome. In the Talmud (Yerushalmi Berachot 3:1), a fourth-century Palestinian scholar who was of a Priestly family. Janai, Jannai, and Yannai are variant spellings. Yan and Yanna are short forms.

Yancy A corruption of the French word for "Englishman," which later became "Yankee," and was applied to Americans. Or, a variant form of the Danish Jan, which is a form of John. *See* John. Yank is a variant form.

Yanir (יָנִיר) From the Hebrew, meaning "he will plough (the soil)."

Yaniv (יָנִיב) From the Hebrew, meaning "he will speak."

Yank A variant form of Yancy. *See* Yancy.

Yankel (יַאנְקֵל) A Yiddish form of Yaakov. *See* Yaakov. Yekel is a variant form. Also spelled יַאנְקֶעל.

Yannai A variant spelling of Yanai. *See* Yanai.

Yanni (יַנִּי) A variant form of Yan. *See* Yan.

Yanoach (יָנוֹחַ) From the Hebrew, meaning "to rest."

Yanuv (יָנוּב) From the Hebrew, meaning "he will cause to grow." Also a variant form of Yaniv. *See* Yaniv.

Yaoz (יָעוֹז) From the Hebrew, meaning "he will be strong."

Yaphet A variant spelling of Yafet. *See* Yafet.

Yara (יַעְרָה) From the Hebrew, meaning "forest." In the Bible (I Chronicles 9:52), a descendant of King Saul.

Yarchinai (יַרְכִינָאִי) From the Aramaic, meaning "month, monthly." A nickname of the talmudic scholar Samuel bar Abba, also known as Mar Samuel.

Yarden (יַרְדֵּן) From the Hebrew, meaning "to flow down, descend," hence the connotation of "descendant." Also, the name of a river (Jordan).

Yarden-Li (יַרְדֵּן־לִי) From the Hebrew, meaning "the Jordan (river) is mine."

Yardley From the Old English, meaning "enclosure, yard."

Yared (יֶרֶד) From the Hebrew, meaning "to descend" or "descendant." In the Bible (Genesis 5:15), the grandfather of Methuselah. Akin to Yarden. Jared is a variant spelling

Yarev (יָרֵב) A variant form of Yariv. *See* Yariv. In the Bible (Hosea 5:13), an Assyrian king. Jareb is a variant spelling.

Yariv (יָרִיב) From the Hebrew, meaning "quarrel, he will quarrel." In the Bible (Ezra 8:16), a leader of Judah in the time of Nehemiah. Jarib is a variant spelling. Yarev is a variant form.

Yarkon (יַרְקוֹן) From the Hebrew, meaning "green." The name of a bird of greenish-yellow color that inhabits Israel in the summertime and migrates to Egypt in the fall. Also, the name of a river in Israel.

Yaroach (יָרוֹחַ) From the Hebrew, meaning "moon." In the Bible (I Chronicles 5:14), a descendant of Gad.

Yarom (יָרוֹם) From the Hebrew, meaning "he will raise up." Yarum is a variant form.

Yaron (יָרוֹן) From the Hebrew, meaning "he will sing, cry out." Jaron is a variant spelling.

Yarum (יָרוּם) A variant form of Yarom. *See* Yarom.

Yascha, Yasha Russian forms of James and Jacob. *See* James *and* Jacob.

Yashar (יָשָׁר) A variant form of Yesher. *See* Yesher.

Yashavam (יָשָׁבְעָם) From the Hebrew, meaning "dwelling place of the people" or "the nation will be repatriated." In the Bible (I Chronicles 11:11), one of King David's warriors. Yeshavam is a variant spelling.

Yashen (יָשֵׁן) From the Hebrew, meaning "sleeping." In the Bible (II Samuel 23:32), the father of one of King David's warriors.

Yashir (יָשִׁיר) From the Hebrew, meaning "he will sing."

Yashish (יָשִׁישׁ) From the Hebrew, meaning "old."

Yashiv (יָשִׁיב) A variant form of Yashuv. *See* Yashuv.

Yashuv (יָשׁוּב) From the Hebrew, meaning "he will return, he will be repatriated." In the Bible (I Chronicles 7:1), a contemporary of Ezra. Yashiv and Yov are variant forms. Jashub is a variant spelling.

Yasis (יָשִׁישׁ) From the Hebrew, meaning "he will rejoice."

Yasmin (יַסְמִין) From the Persian, meaning "jasmine." Used also as a feminine name.

Yasniel A variant form of Yatniel. See Yatniel.

Yates From the British, meaning "gate."

Yatniel (יַתְנִיאֵל) From the Hebrew, meaning "gift of God." In the Bible (I Chronicles 26:2), a Levite. Yasniel is a variant form.

Yatva (יָטְבָה) From the Aramaic, meaning "to be good, pleasing."

Yatzliach (יַצְלִיחַ) A variant form of Yitzlach. See Yitzlach.

Yaush (יָאוּשׁ) From the Hebrew, meaning "to regret" or "to lose hope."

Yaval (יָבָל) From the Hebrew, meaning "stream." In the Bible (Genesis 4:20), a son of Lemach and his wife Adah. Jabal is a variant spelling.

Yavesh (יָבֵשׁ) From the Hebrew, meaning "dried up, withered." In the Bible (II Kings 15:10), the father of Shalum, king of Israel. Jabesh is a variant spelling.

Yavetz (יַעְבֵּץ) A variant form of Yabetz. See Yabetz. Also, an acronym of Rabbi Yaakov Emden ben Tzevi, an eminent eighteenth-century rabbinic scholar. Jabez is a variant spelling.

Yavin (יָבִין) From the Hebrew, meaning "one who is intelligent." In the Bible (Joshua 11:1), a Canaanite king in the days of Deborah. Jabin is a variant spelling.

Yavne'el (יַבְנְאֵל) From the Hebrew, meaning "God builds." In the Bible (Joshua 15:11), a place-name.

Yavniel (יַבְנִיאֵל) A variant form of Yavne'el. See Yavne'el.

Yazer (יַעְזֵר) From the Hebrew, meaning "to spread, scatter." Also from the Hebrew, meaning "help" and spelled יַעְזֻר.

Yaziz (יָזִיז) From the Assyrian and Hebrew, meaning "to move, rise up" or "to be agitated, angry." In the Bible (I Chronicles 27:31), one of King David's ministers. Jaziz is a variant spelling.

Yechania, Yechaniah Variant spellings of Yechanya. See Yechanya.

Yechanya, Yechanyah (יְכָנְיָה) From the Hebrew, meaning "God will prepare" or "God will establish." Yechanyahu is a variant form. Yehoiachim is a variant form.

Yechanyahu (יְכָנְיָהוּ) A variant form of Yechanya. See Yechanya.

Yechezkel (יְחֶזְקֵאל) From the Hebrew, meaning "God will strengthen." In the Bible (Ezekiel 1:3), one of the Prophets of the sixth century B.C.E. **(end of**

First Temple). Chaskel and Chatzkel are Yiddish forms. Ezekiel is the Anglicized form.

Yechia, Yechiah   Variant spellings of Yechiya. *See* Yechiya.

Yechiach (יְחִיאָח)   From the Hebrew, meaning "May my brother live!"

Yechiam (יְחִיעָם)   From the Hebrew, meaning "May the nation live!"

Yechiav (יְחִיאָב)   From the Hebrew, meaning "May my father live!"

Yechiel (יְחִיאֵל)   From the Hebrew, meaning "May God live!" In the Bible (Ezra 8:9), one of King David's chief musicians. Jehiel and Yehiel are variant spellings. Yechieli is a variant form. Akin to Yechiya.

Yechieli (יְחִיאֵלִי)   From the Hebrew, meaning "May my God live!" In the Bible (I Chronicles 26:21), an ancestor of Gershon, a Levite in the time of King David. Yehieli is a variant spelling.

Yechi-Shalom (יְחִי־שָׁלוֹם)   From the Hebrew, meaning "long live peace."

Yechiya (יְחִיָּה)   From the Hebrew, meaning "May God live!" In the Bible (I Chronicles 15:24), one of the two gatekeepers for the Ark in the time of King David. Yechia and Yechiah are variant spellings. Akin to Yechiel.

Yechizkiya (יְחִזְקִיָּה)   From the Hebrew, meaning "May God strengthen!" A variant form of Chizkiya. *See* Chizkiya. In the Bible (Ezra 2:16), the head of a family of Babylonian Exile returnees. Yechizkiyahu is a variant form.

Yechizkiyahu (יְחִזְקִיָּהוּ)   A variant form of Yechizkiya. *See* Yechizkiya. In the Bible (II Chronicles 28:12), a member of the tribe of Ephraim. Akin to Chizkiyahu.

Yedaya (יְדָיָה)   From the Hebrew, meaning "hand of God," or from a second root, meaning "knowledge of God" and spelled יְדָעְיָה. In the Bible (I Chronicles 4:37), a member of the tribe of Simeon. Jedaiah is a variant spelling.

Yediael (יְדִיעָאֵל)   From the Hebrew, meaning "knowledge of the Lord." In the Bible (I Chronicles 7:6), a son of Benjamin. Yediel is a variant form.

Yedid (יְדִיד)   A variant form of Yadid. *See* Yadid.

Yedidia, Yedidiah   Variant spellings of Yedidya. *See* Yedidya.

Yedidya (יְדִידְיָה)   From the Hebrew, meaning "friend of God" or "beloved of God." In the Bible (II Samuel 12:25), a name by which King Solomon was known. Used also as a feminine name. Jedidia, Jedidiah, Yedidia, and Yedidiah are variant spellings. Didi is a pet form. Yadai and Yido are variant forms.

Yediel (יְדִיעֵל)   A variant form of Yediael. *See* Yediael.

Yedutun (יְדוּתוּן)   From the Hebrew, referring to a musical instrument mentioned in Psalms 77:1. In I Chronicles 16:42, one of the Levite choristers.

Yefet (יֶפֶת)   From the Hebrew, meaning "beautiful," or from the Aramaic, meaning "abundant, spacious." In the Bible (Genesis 5:32), the youngest of Noah's three sons. Yaphet, Japhet, and Japheth are variant spellings.

Yefune, Yefuneh (יְפֻנֶּה)   From the Hebrew, meaning "to face" or "to turn." In the Bible (Numbers 13:6), the father of Caleb and a leader of the tribe of Judah. Jephuneh is a variant spelling.

Yehalalel   A variant spelling of Yehalelel. See Yehalelel.

Yehalelel (יְהַלֶּלְאֵל)   From the Hebrew, meaning "he will praise God." In the Bible (I Chronicles 4:16), a member of the tribe of Judah. Yehalalel is a variant spelling.

Yehiel   A variant spelling of Yechiel. See Yechiel.

Yehieli   A variant spelling of Yechieli. See Yechieli.

Yehoachaz (יְהוֹאָחָז)   From the Hebrew, meaning "God will hold" or "God will support." In the Bible (II Kings 10:35), the eleventh king of Israel and successor to his father, King Yehu (Jehu). Yoachaz is a variant form. Jehoahaz is a variant spelling.

Yehoash (יְהוֹאָשׁ)   From the Hebrew, meaning "God is strong." A variant form of Yoash. In the Bible (II Kings 13:10), the king of Israel when Yoash was king of Judah.

Yehochanan (יְהוֹחָנָן)   From the Hebrew, meaning "God is gracious." In the Bible (Ezra 10:6), the High Priest in the time of Ezra. Yochanan is a short form. See Yochanan. Jehohanan is a variant spelling.

Yehoiachin   A variant spelling of Yehoyachin. See Yehoyachin.

Yehoiada   A variant spelling of Yehoyada. See Yehoyada.

Yehoiakim   A variant spelling of Yehoyakim. See Yehoyakim.

Yehonadav (יְהוֹנָדָב)   From the Hebrew, meaning "God is noble." In the Bible (II Samuel 13:5), a nephew of King David. Yonadav is a short form.

Yehonatan (יְהוֹנָתָן)   From the Hebrew, meaning "God has given; gift of God." In the Bible (I Samuel 14:6), the son of King Saul and the very close friend of David. Yonatan is a variant form. See Yonatan. Jonathan is the Anglicized form.

Yehoram (יְהוֹרָם)   From the Hebrew, meaning "God is exalted." In the Bible (II Kings 1:17), the son of King Ahab and the successor of his brother Achazya (Ahaziah) to the throne of Israel. Jehoram is a variant spelling. Joram and Yoram are short forms.

Yehosef (יְהוֹסֵף)   A variant form of Yosef. See Yosef. Yehoseph is a variant spelling.

Yehoseph   A variant spelling of Yehosef. See Yehosef.

Yehoshafat (יְהוֹשָׁפָט)   From the Hebrew, meaning "God will judge." Jehoshafat is the Anglicized spelling. In the Bible, a king of Judah (I Kings 15:24) and the father of Yehu (Jehu), king of Israel (II Kings 9:2). Jehoshaphat is a variant spelling. Yoshafat is a short form.

Yehoshua (יְהוֹשֻׁעַ)   From the Hebrew, meaning "God is salvation." In the Bible (Exodus 16:9), the leader of the Israelites after the death of Moses, who led the Children of Israel into the Promised Land. Yeshua is a variant form. Joshua is the Anglicized form. Hoshea was the original Hebrew name to which the letter *yad* was later prefixed. *See also* Joshua.

Yehotzadak (יְהוֹצָדָק) From the Hebrew, meaning "God is righteous." In the Bible (Haggai 1:1), the father of Joshua the High Priest. Yotzadak is a short form.

Yehoyachin (יְהוֹיָכִין) From the Hebrew, meaning "God will appoint" or God will establish." In the Bible (II Kings 24:6), a king of Judah and the son of King Yehoyakim of Judah. Jehoiachin and Yehoiachin are variant spellings. Joaquin is a variant form. Yachin and Yoyachin are short forms.

Yehoyada (יְהוֹיָדָע) From the Hebrew, meaning "God knows." In the Bible (II Kings 11:9), a High Priest in the time of King Achazya. Jehoiada and Yehoiada are variant spellings. Yoyada is a variant form.

Yehoyakim (יְהוֹיָקִים) From the Hebrew, meaning "God will establish." In the Bible (II Kings 23:36), a king of Judah who was defeated by the Babylonians. Akim, Yakim, and Yokim are short forms. Joachim, Joakim, and Yoyakim are variant forms. Jehoiakim and Yehoiakim are variant spellings.

Yehoyariv (יְהוֹיָרִיב) From the Hebrew, meaning "God will contend." In the Bible (I Chronicles 9:10), a Priest during the reigns of Saul and David.

Yehozavad (יְהוֹזָבָד) From the Hebrew, meaning "God has bestowed" or "gift of God." In the Bible (II Kings 12:22), the murderer of King Joash. Jehozabad is a variant spelling. Jozavad is a variant form.

Yehu (יֵהוּא) From the Hebrew, meaning "God lives." In the Bible (I Kings 19:16), the tenth king of Israel, the son of Ahab. Also, the name of a Prophet (I Kings 16:1). Jehu is a variant spelling.

Yehuda, Yehudah (יְהוּדָה) From the Hebrew, meaning "praise." Judah is an Anglicized spelling. In the Bible (Genesis 29:35), the fourth son of Jacob and Leah and the founder of one of the twelve tribes. After the division of King David's dynasty, that part of the Jewish nation that lived in the South became known as Judah, and a citizen of Judah (Yehuda) was called a Yehudi. Eventually the northern kingdom, consisting of the ten tribes, disappeared, and all Jews in subsequent generations became known by the appellation Yehudi. *See* Yehudi *and* Yudel.

Yehudi (יְהוּדִי) From the Hebrew, meaning "praise." In the Bible (Jeremiah 36:14), a man in the service of King Jehoiakim. Used also as a generic name to refer to a person from the part of Palestine called Judah (Yehuda). *See* Yehuda.

Yekamam (יְקַמְעָם) From the Hebrew, meaning "the nation will be established." In the Bible (I Chronicles 24:23), a Levite.

Yekamya (יְקַמְיָה) From the Hebrew, meaning "God will establish." In the Bible (I Chronicles 3:18), the son of Yechanya, king of Judah.

Yekel (יֶעְקֶעל) A variant form of Yankel. *See* Yankel.

Yekusiel The Ashkenazic form of Yekutiel. *See* Yekutiel. Kus and Kusiel are pet forms.

Yekutiel (יְקוּתִאֵל) From the Hebrew, meaning "God will nourish." Jekutiel and Jekuthiel are variant spellings. Yekusiel is the Ashkenazic form. Kuti is a pet form. In the Bible (I Chronicles 4:18), a descendant of Caleb.

Yemin (יְמִין) From the Hebrew, meaning "right, right-handed." A short form of Binyamin (Benjamin). See Binyamin.

Yemuel (יְמוּאֵל) From the Hebrew, meaning "day of the Lord." In the Bible (Genesis 46:10), a son of Simeon and a grandson of Jacob. Jemuel is a variant spelling.

Yeor (יְאוֹר) From the Hebrew, meaning "river." Yeori is a variant form.

Yeori (יְאוֹרִי) A variant form of Yeor. From the Hebrew, meaning "my river."

Yerach (יֶרַח) From the Hebrew, meaning "moon" or "month." In the Bible (Genesis 10:26), one of the sons of Yaktan and a descendant of Shem.

Yerachm'el, Yerachmeel (יְרַחְמְאֵל) From the Hebrew, meaning "mercy of God." In the Bible (Jeremiah 36:26), a son of Jehoiakim, king of Judah. Yerachmiel is a variant form.

Yerachmiel (יְרַחְמִיאֵל) A variant form of Yerachm'el. See Yerachm'el.

Yeravam (יְרָבְעָם) From the Hebrew, meaning "the nation will contend." In the Bible (I Kings 11:28), the first king of Israel after the death of Solomon. Jeroboam is the Anglicized form.

Yered (יֶרֶד) From the Hebrew, meaning "descend." In the Bible (Genesis 5:15), the father of Chanoch. Jered is a variant spelling.

Yereimai (יְרֵמַי) An Aramaic form of Yirmiyahu (Jeremiah). See Yirmiyahu. In the Bible (Ezra 10:33), a contemporary of Ezra. Jeremai is a variant spelling.

Yeriel (יְרִיאֵל) From the Hebrew, meaning "God has established" or "God has taught." In the Bible (I Chronicles 7:2), a son of Tola and a grandson of Issachar. Jeriel is a variant spelling.

Yeriya (יְרִיָה) From the Hebrew, meaning "God has established" or "God has taught." In the Bible (I Chronicles 26:31), the eldest son of Chevron the Levite. Jeria, Jeriah, and Jerijah are variant spellings. Yeriyahu is a variant form. Akin to Yeriel.

Yeriyahu (יְרִיָהוּ) A variant form of Yeriya. See Yeriya.

Yerocham (יְרֹחָם) From the Hebrew, meaning "may he be compassionate." In the Bible (I Samuel 1:1), the father of Elkana and grandfather of Samuel.

Yerubaal (יְרוּבַּעַל) A name of Gideon (Judges 6:25). See Gideon.

Yerucham (יְרוּחָם) A variant form of Yerocham. See Yerocham.

Yerushalayim (יְרוּשָׁלַיִם) Most often used as a feminine name. See feminine section.

Yesarel (יְשָׂרְאֵל) A variant form of Yisrael. See Yisrael.

Yesarela (יְשָׂרְאֵלָה) A variant form of Yisrael. In the Bible (I Chronicles 28:14), one of the Levites in the time of King David.

Yeshaia, Yeshaiah   Variant spellings of Yeshaya. *See* Yeshaya.

Yeshaiahu   A variant spelling of Yeshayahu. *See* Yeshayahu.

Yeshavam   A variant spelling of Yashavam. *See* Yashavam.

Yeshaya (יְשַׁעְיָה)   A variant form of Yeshayahu. *See* Yeshayahu. Shay and Shaya are pet forms. Yeshaia and Yeshaiah are variant spellings.

Yeshayahu (יְשַׁעְיָהוּ)   From the Hebrew, meaning "God is salvation." In the Bible (Isaiah 1:1), the great eighth-century Prophet in the kingdom of Judah who was born in Jerusalem in 765 B.C.E. Isaiah is the Anglicized form. Yeshaya is a short form. Yeshaiahu is a variant spelling.

Yesher (יֵשֶׁר)   From the Hebrew, meaning "upright, honest." In the Bible (I Chronicles 2:18), a son of Caleb. Yeshar is a variant form. Jesher is a variant spelling.

Yeshevav (יֵשֶׁבְאָב)   From the Hebrew, meaning "dwelling place of the father." In the Bible (I Chronicles 24:13), a Levite. Also spelled יֵשֶׁבָב.

Yeshish (יְשִׁישׁ)   A variant form of Yeshishai. *See* Yeshishai.

Yeshishai (יְשִׁישַׁי)   From the Aramaic, meaning "old." In the Bible (I Chronicles 5:14), a descendant of Gad. Yeshish is a variant form.

Yeshu (יֵשׁוּ)   A variant form of Yeshua. *See* Yeshua. The Hebrew name of Jesus. Also spelled יֵשׁוּעַ.

Yeshua (יְשׁוּעָה)   From the Hebrew, meaning "salvation." Akin to Yehoshua. *See* Yehoshua. In the Bible (Nehemiah 8:7), another name for Joshua, and also the name of a High Priest in the time of Zerubbabel (Ezra 3:2).

Yeshurun (יְשֻׁרוּן)   From the Hebrew, meaning "upright." In the Bible (Deuteronomy 32:15 and Isaiah 44:2), a poetic and honorable nickname for the people of Israel. Also spelled יְשׁוּרוּן.

Yeshuvam (יְשָׁבְעָם)   From the Hebrew, meaning "the nation will return."

Yeter (יֶתֶר)   From the Hebrew, meaning "abundance." In the Bible (Exodus 4:18), a nickname of Yitro (Jethro), the father-in-law of Moses. Jether is a variant spelling.

Yetur (יְטוּר)   From the Hebrew, meaning "row." In the Bible (Genesis 25:15), a son of Ishmael.

Yetzer (יֵצֶר)   From the Hebrew, meaning "desire" or "inclination." In the Bible (Genesis 46:24), a son of Naftali and a grandson of Jacob.

Ye'utz (יְעוּץ)   From the Hebrew, meaning "advice, counsel." In the Bible (I Chronicles 8:10), a leader of the tribe of Benjamin.

Yeverechya (יְבֶרֶכְיָה)   From the Hebrew, meaning "God's blessing."

Yeverechyahu (יְבֶרֶכְיָהוּ)   A variant form of Yeverechya. *See* Yeverechya. In the Bible (Isaiah 8:2), a contemporary of Isaiah.

Yevorach (יְבוֹרָךְ)   From the Hebrew, meaning "May he be blessed!"

Yeziel (יְזִיאֵל)   Possibly from the Hebrew, meaning "God will sprinkle."

Yeziya (יְזִיָה)   From the Hebrew, meaning "to sprinkle."

Yichya (יִחְיָא)   A variant form of Yichye. *See* Yichye. A popular name among Yemenites.

Yichye (יִחְיֶה)   From the Hebrew, meaning "May he live!"

Yidbash (יִדְבָּשׁ)   From the Hebrew, meaning "honey." In the Bible (I Chronicles 4:3), a member of the tribe of Judah.

Yidel (יְדָעֵל)   A variant form of Yudel. *See* Yudel. Also spelled יְדֵל.

Yido (יִדּוֹ)   A variant form of Yedidya. *See* Yedidya. In the Bible (I Chronicles 27:21), a leader of the tribe of Manasseh. Yadai is a variant form. Ido, Iddo, Jedo, and Jido are variant spellings.

Yifdeya (יִפְדְּיָה)   From the Hebrew, meaning "redemption of God" or "God will redeem." In the Bible (I Chronicles 8:25), a member of the tribe of Benjamin.

Yifrach (יִפְרָח)   From the Hebrew, meaning "May he grow!"

Yifracham (יִפְרַחְעָם)   From the Hebrew, meaning "May the nation grow!"

Yiftach (יִפְתָּח)   From the Hebrew, meaning "he will open." In the Bible (Judges 11:1), one of the Judges of Israel. Jephthah and Jephta are variant forms.

Yiftach-El (יִפְתַּח־אֵל)   From the Hebrew, meaning "God will open."

Yigael (יִגְאָל)   From the Hebrew, meaning "he will redeem." Akin to Yagel and Yigal.

Yigal (יִגְאָל)   From the Hebrew, meaning "he will redeem." In the Bible (Numbers 13:7), one of the twelve scouts sent by Moses to explore the Promised Land. Igal is a variant spelling. Akin to Yagel and Yigael.

Yigdal (יִגְדָּל)   From the Hebrew, meaning "he will grow" or "he will be exalted." Yigdalyahu is a variant form.

Yigdalyahu (יִגְדַּלְיָהוּ)   A variant form of Yigdal. From the Hebrew, meaning "God will raise up" or "God will exalt." In the Bible (Jeremiah 35:4), a Priest who was also a Prophet.

Yimla (יִמְלָה)   From the Hebrew, meaning "he will fill (reward)." In the Bible (I Kings 22:8), the father of the Prophet Michayahu.

Yimna (יִמְנָה)   From the Hebrew, meaning "good fortune" or "right side." In the Bible (Genesis 46:17), a son of Asher and a grandson of Jacob. Also from the Hebrew, meaning "deny, withhold," and spelled יִמְנָע. In the Bible (I Chronicles 7:35), a member of the tribe of Asher. Used also as a feminine name.

Yiriya (יִרְאִיָּה)   From the Hebrew, meaning "God sees." In the Bible (Jeremiah 37:13), an officer during the reign of King Zedekiah.

Yirmeya (יִרְמְיָה)   A variant form of Yirmeyahu. *See* Yirmeyahu. In the Bible (I Chronicles 5:24), a member of the tribe of Manasseh.

Yirmeyahu (יִרְמְיָהוּ) From the Hebrew, meaning "God will raise up." In the Bible (Jeremiah 1:1), the Prophet who along with Isaiah was a giant among the Prophets of Israel. Jeremiah is the Anglicized form. *See* Jeremiah. Yeremai and Yirmeya are variant forms.

Yisachar (יִשָּׂשכָר) From the Hebrew, meaning "there is reward." In the Bible (Genesis 30:18), a son of Jacob. Yisaschar is a variant form. Issachar is the English equivalent.

Yisaschar (יִשָּׂשׂכָר) A variant form of Yisachar. *See* Yisachar.

Yischak (יִשְׂחָק) A variant form of Yitzchak. *See* Yitzchak.

Yishai (יִשַׁי) From the Hebrew, meaning "gift." In the Bible (I Samuel 16:1), the father of King David. Jesse is an Anglicized form.

Yishbach (יִשְׁבָּח) From the Hebrew, meaning "he will praise." In the Bible (I Chronicles 4:17), one of the sons of Caleb.

Yishbak (יִשְׁבָּק) From the Aramaic, meaning "to let go." In the Bible (Genesis 25:2), a son of Abraham and Keturah.

Yishi (יִשְׁעִי) From the Hebrew, meaning "my deliverer, savior." In the Bible (I Chronicles 4:20), a member of the tribe of Judah. Ishi is a variant spelling.

Yishma (יִשְׁמָא) From the Hebrew, meaning "He (God) will lay waste." In the Bible (I Chronicles 4:3), a member of the tribe of Judah. Ishma is a variant spelling.

Yishmael (יִשְׁמָעֵאל) From the Hebrew, meaning "God will hear." In the Bible (Genesis 16:11), a son of Abraham and brother of Isaac. Ishmael is the Anglicized form.

Yishmaya (יִשְׁמַעְיָה) From the Hebrew, meaning "God will hear." In the Bible (I Chronicles 12:4), one of King David's warriors.

Yishmayahu (יִשְׁמַעְיָהוּ) A variant form of Yishmaya. *See* Yishmaya. In the Bible (I Chronicles 27:19), one of King David's officers.

Yisho (יִשׁוֹ) From the Hebrew, meaning "his deliverer, savior." Isho is a variant spelling.

Yishpa (יִשְׁפָּה) From the Hebrew, meaning "barren." In the Bible (I Chronicles 8:16), a descendant of Benjamin.

Yishpan (יִשְׁפָּן) From the Hebrew, meaning "rock-badger, coney." In the Bible (I Chronicles 8:22), a descendant of Benjamin.

Yishva (יִשְׁוָה) From the Hebrew, meaning "even, smooth" or "agreeable." In the Bible (Genesis 46:17), a son of Asher and a grandson of Jacob. Yishvi is a variant form.

Yishvi (יִשְׁוִי) A variant form of Yishva. *See* Yishva.

Yismachya (יִסְמַכְיָה) A variant form of Yismachyahu. *See* Yismachyahu.

Yismachyahu (יִסְמַכְיָהוּ) From the Hebrew, meaning "God will support." In the Bible (I Chronicles 31:13), a Levite.

Yisrael (יִשְׂרָאֵל) From the Hebrew, meaning "prince of God" or "to contend, fight" or "to rule." In the Bible (Genesis 32:29), a son of Isaac whose primary name is Yaakov (Jacob). Israel is the Anglicized form. Iser and Isser are Yiddish forms. *See* Israel. Yesarel is a variant form.

Yitma (יִתְמָה) From the Hebrew, meaning "orphaned." In the Bible (I Chronicles 11:46), one of King David's warriors.

Yitra (יִתְרָא) From the Aramaic, meaning "abundance." In the Bible (II Samuel 17:25), the father of Amasa.

Yitran (יִתְרָן) A variant form of Yitro. *See* Yitro. In the Bible (I Chronicles 7:37), a member of the tribe of Asher.

Yitro (יִתְרוֹ) From the Hebrew, meaning "abundance, riches" or "excellence." In the Bible (Exodus 3:1), the father-in-law of Moses; also known as Yeter. Yitran is a variant form. Jethro is the Anglicized spelling.

Yitzchak (יִצְחָק) From the Hebrew, meaning "he will laugh." In the Bible (Genesis 21:5), the son born to Abraham and Sara in their old age. Yitzhak and Yizhak are variant spellings. Isaac is the Anglicized form. Yischak is a variant form. Itzik is a Yiddish form.

Yitzhak A variant spelling of Yitzchak. *See* Yitzchak.

Yitzhal (יִצְהָל) From the Hebrew, meaning "he will be joyous."

Yitzhar (יִצְהָר) From the Hebrew, meaning "fresh oil" or "he will shine." In the Bible (Exodus 6:21), a son of Korach and a grandson of Levi. Izhar is a variant spelling. Yizhar is a variant form.

Yitzlach (יִצְלָח) From the Hebrew, meaning "he will succeed, he will be victorious." Yatzliach is a variant form.

Yitzmach (יִצְמָח) From the Hebrew, meaning "he will grow."

Yitzri (יִצְרִי) From the Hebrew, meaning "my desire, my inclination." Izri is a variant spelling.

Yivchar (יִבְחָר) From the Hebrew, meaning "he will choose." In the Bible (II Samuel 5:15), a son of King David.

Yivneya (יִבְנְיָה) From the Hebrew, meaning "God will build." In the Bible (I Chronicles 9:8), one of the sons of Benjamin. Also spelled יִבְנִיָּה.

Yivsam (יִבְשָׂם) From the Hebrew, meaning "perfumed, spiced." In the Bible (I Chronicles 7:2), the son of Tola and grandson of Issachar.

Yizhak A variant spelling of Yitzchak. *See* Yitzchak.

Yizhar (יִזְהָר) From the Hebrew, meaning "shine, brightness." Akin to Yitzhar.

Yizrach (יִזְרָח) From the Hebrew, meaning "shine, he will shine." In the Bible (I Chronicles 27:8), one of King David's officers.

Yizrachia A variant spelling of Yizrachya. *See* Yizrachya. In the Bible (Nehemiah 12:42), an officer in Nehemiah's time.

Yizrachya (יִזְרַכְיָה)   From the Hebrew, meaning "God will shine." Yizrachia is a variant spelling.

Yizrael (יִזְרַעֵאל)   A variant form of Yizr'el. *See* Yizr'el.

Yizre'el   A variant spelling of Yizr'el. *See* Yizr'el.

Yizr'el (יִזְרְעֵאל)   From the Hebrew, meaning "God will plant." In the Bible (I Chronicles 4:3), a descendant of Judah. Also, a symbolic name given by the Prophet Hosea to his son (Hosea 1:4). Yizre'el is a variant spelling. Yizrael is a variant form.

Yoach (יוֹאָח)   From the Hebrew, meaning "God is brother." Yocha is possibly a variant form. In the Bible (II Kings 18:18), King Hezekiah's secretary.

Yoachaz (יוֹאָחָז)   A short form of Yehoachaz (II Kings 14:1). *See* Yehoachaz.

Yoad (יוֹעָד)   From the Hebrew, meaning "God is witness."

Yoash (יוֹאָשׁ)   From the Hebrew, meaning "God is strong." In the Bible (Judges 6:11), the father of Gideon. Also (II Kings 13:1), the eighth king of Judah, successor to his father, Achazya (Ahaziah). Jehoash and Yehoash are variant forms. Joash is a variant spelling. Also from the Hebrew, meaning "moth," hence "to lay waste," spelled יוֹעָשׁ. In the Bible (I Chronicles 7:8), a member of the tribe of Benjamin.

Yoav (יוֹאָב)   From the Hebrew, meaning "God is father" or "God is willing." In the Bible (II Samuel 2:13), King David's nephew and captain of his army. Joab is a variant spelling.

Yoaz (יוֹעָז)   From the Hebrew, meaning "strength."

Yocha (יוֹחָא)   Meaning uncertain, but possibly a variant form of Yoach. *See* Yoach. In the Bible (I Chronicles 8:16), a member of the tribe of Benjamin.

Yocha'i (יוֹחָאִי)   From the Hebrew and Aramaic, meaning "life" or "God lives." In the Talmud (Avot 6:8), the father of Simeon, a second-century Palestinian talmudic scholar. Yochai is a variant form.

Yochai (יוֹחָאִי)   A variant form of Yocha'i. *See* Yocha'i. Yochie is a variant form.

Yochanan (יוֹחָנָן)   A short form of Yehochanan. *See* Yehochanan. From the Hebrew, meaning "God is gracious." In the Bible (II Kings 25:23), the eldest son of Josiah, king of Judah. John is the Anglicized form. Johanan and Yohanan are variant spellings. A popular name in talmudic times. In the Talmud, more than fifty different Palestinian and Babylonian scholars are named Yochanan.

Yochie   A variant form of Yochai. *See* Yochai.

Yoed (יוֹעֵד)   From the Hebrew, meaning "God is witness." In the Bible (Nehemiah 11:7), a descendant of Benjamin.

Yoel (יוֹאֵל)   From the Hebrew, meaning "God is willing" or "the Lord is God." In the Bible (Joel 1:1), one of the Minor Prophets. Joel is a variant spelling.

Yoela (יוֹעֵאלָה)   A variant form of Yoel. In the Bible (I Chronicles 12:8), one of

King David's warriors. Used primarily as a modern feminine name. Joela and Joelah are variant spellings.

Yoetz (יוֹעֵץ)   From the Hebrew, meaning "advisor, counselor."

Yoezer (יוֹעֶזֶר)   From the Hebrew, meaning "God will help." In the Bible (I Chronicles 12:7), a Levite and one of David's warriors. Joezer is a variant spelling.

Yogev (יוֹגֵב)   From the Hebrew, meaning "farmer."

Yogli (יָגְלִי)   From the Hebrew, meaning "exile." Also, a variant form of Yagil. See Yagil. In the Bible (I Chronicles 34:22), the father of a leader of the tribe of Dan. Yagli is a variant spelling.

Yohanan   A variant spelling of Yochanan. See Yochanan.

Yokim (יוֹקִים)   A short form of Yehoyakim. See Yehoyakim. In the Bible (I Chronicles 4:22), a descendant of Judah. Jokim is a variant spelling.

Yoktan (יָקְטָן)   From the Hebrew, meaning "small." Yaktan is a variant form. In the Bible (Genesis 10:25), a descendant of Shem.

Yom-Tov (יוֹם־טוֹב)   From the Hebrew, meaning "good day, holiday."

Yon (יוֹן)   A variant form of Yona or Yonatan. See Yona and Yonatan.

Yona, Yonah (יוֹנָה)   From the Hebrew, meaning "dove." In the Bible (Jonah 1:1), one of the Minor Prophets, noted for being swallowed by a big fish and emerging unscathed. In the Talmud (Yerushalmi Sanhedrin 6:10), a fourth-century Palestinian scholar. Jona and Jonah are variant spellings.

Yonadav (יוֹנָדָב)   A short form of Yehonadav. See Yehonadav.

Yonatan (יוֹנָתָן)   A short and more commonly used form of Yehonatan. See Yehonatan. In the Talmud (Menachot 57b), a second-century Palestinian scholar. Jonathan is a variant form.

Yora (יוֹרָה)   From the Hebrew, meaning "to teach" or "to shoot." In the Bible (Ezra 2:18), one of the Babylonian Exile returnees. Jora is a variant spelling.

Yorai (יוֹרַי)   From the Hebrew, meaning "my teaching" or "early rain." In the Bible (I Chronicles 5:13), a member of the tribe of Gad. Jorai is a variant spelling.

Yoram (יוֹרָם)   From the Hebrew, meaning "God is exalted." A short form of Yehoram. Joram and Jehoram are Anglicized spellings. In the Bible (II Samuel 8:10), the son of Toi, king of Chamat (Hamath); also (II Kings 8:23), the king of Judah.

Yoran (יוֹרָן)   From the Hebrew, meaning "to sing."

Yore, Yoreh (יוֹרֶה)   From the Hebrew, meaning "to teach."

Yorick   Probably a Danish variant form of George. See George. York is a variant form.

York   A variant form of Yorick. See Yorick.

Yos (יאָס)   A Yiddish pet form of Yosef. *See* Yosef.

Yosa   A variant form of Yosi. *See* Yosi.

Yosef (יוֹסֵף)   From the Hebrew, meaning "God will add, increase." In the Bible (Genesis 30:24), one of the twelve sons of Jacob; one of the two sons of Jacob and Rachel. Joseph and Yoseif are variant spellings. Yehosef, Yosifiel, Yosifus (Josephus), and Yosifya are a few of the variant forms. Issi, Seff, Sefi, Yosei, Yosel, Yosi, Zif, and Ziff are pet forms.

Yosei (יוֹסִי)   A variant form of Yosi. *See* Yosi. Thirty-nine Palestinian and Babylonian scholars are named Yosei, Yosei Hagalili (Moed Katan 28) being one of the most prominent. Jose is a variant spelling.

Yoseif   A variant spelling of Yosef. *See* Yosef.

Yosel (יאָסֶעל)   A Yiddish pet form of Yosef. *See* Yosef. Yossel is a variant spelling.

Yosha (יוֹשָׁה)   From the Hebrew, meaning "wisdom." In the Bible (I Chronicles 4:34), a descendant of Simeon.

Yoshafat (יוֹשָׁפָט)   A short form of Yehoshafat. *See* Yehoshafat. In the Bible (I Chronicles 11:43), one of King David's warriors.

Yoshavya (יוֹשַׁוְיָה)   From the Hebrew, meaning "fitting, appropriate" or "equal." In the Bible (I Chronicles 11:15), one of King David's warriors.

Yosher (יוֹשֶׁר)   From the Hebrew, meaning "straight" or "justice."

Yoshia, Yoshiah   Variant spellings of Yoshiya. *See* Yoshiya.

Yoshivya (יוֹשִׁבְיָה)   From the Hebrew, meaning "God will return." In the Bible (I Chronicles 4:35), a member of the tribe of Simeon.

Yoshiya (יאשִׁיָה)   A variant form of Yoshiyahu. *See* Yoshiyahu. Josiah is the Anglicized form. Yoshia and Yoshiah are variant spellings.

Yoshiyahu (יאשִׁיָהוּ)   From the Hebrew, meaning "God will save." In the Bible (I Kings 13:2), the sixteenth king of Judah. Yoshia is a variant form. Josiah is an Anglicized form.

Yosi (יוֹסִי)   A pet form of Yosef. *See* Yosef. Yosei is a variant form. Yossi is a variant spelling. Assa, Issi, and Yosa are variant forms.

Yosiel (יוֹסִיאֵל)   From the Hebrew, meaning "God will add." Akin to Yosifel. *See* Yosifel.

Yosifel (יוֹסְפְאֵל)   From the Hebrew, meaning "God will increase."

Yosifus (יוֹסְפוּס)   A variant form of Yosef. *See* Yosef. *See also* Josephus.

Yosifya (יוֹסִיפְיָה)   From the Hebrew, meaning "may God increase." In the Bible (Ezra 8:10), an ancestor of some of the Babylonian Exile returnees. Josiphia and Josiphiah are variant spellings.

Yossel   A variant spelling of Yosel. *See* Yosel. Yossele is a diminutive form.

Yossele (יאָסֶעלֶע)   A diminutive form of Yossel. *See* Yossel.

Yossi   A variant spelling of Yosi. *See* Yosi. Akin to Yossel.

Yossil (יָאסִיל) A Yiddish pet form of Yosef. *See* Yosef.

Yotam (יוֹתָם) From the Hebrew, meaning "God is perfect" or "orphan." In the Bible (Judges 9:5), the youngest of Judge Gideon's seventy sons. Also (II Kings 15:7), the king of Judah from 751 to 735 B.C.E. His father was King Uzia. Jotham is the Anglicized spelling.

Yotzadak (יוֹצְדָק) From the Hebrew, meaning "God is righteous." A short form of Yehotzadak. In the Bible (Ezra 3:8), the father of Joshua, the High Priest at the time of the Babylonian Exile.

Yov (יוֹב) A variant form of Yashuv. *See* Yashuv. In the Bible (Genesis 46:13), a son of Issachar and a grandson of Jacob. Iob is a variant spelling.

Yoval (יוֹבָל) A variant form of Yuval. *See* Yuval.

Yovav (יוֹבָב) From the Hebrew, meaning "to lament, cry." In the Bible (Genesis 10:29), a son of Yoktan.

Yovel (יוֹבֵל) From the Hebrew, meaning "jubilee, jubilee year" or "ram's horn."

Yoyachin (יוֹיָכִין) A short form of Yehoyachin. *See* Yehoyachin.

Yoyada (יוֹיָדָע) A variant form of Yehoyada. *See* Yehodaya. In the Bible (Nehemiah 3:6), a supporter of Nehemiah.

Yoyakim (יוֹיָקִים) A variant form of Yehoyakim. *See* Yehoyakim. In the Bible (Nehemiah 12:10), a High Priest.

Yozavad (יוֹזָבָד) A short form of Yehozavad. *See* Yehozavad.

Yuchal (יוּכָל) From the Hebrew, meaning "to be able" or "God is able." In the Bible (Jeremiah 38:1), a contemporary of Jeremiah.

Yudan (יוּדָן) From the Hebrew, meaning "will be judged." In the Talmud (Yerushalmi Yoma 8:5), a second-century Palestinian scholar.

Yudel (יוּדְעל) From the Yiddish, meaning "Jew." A variant form of Yehuda. *See* Yehuda. Yidel is a variant form.

Yuki (יוּקִי) A pet form of Yaakov. *See* Yaakov.

Yul, Yule From the Old English, meaning "jolly; the Christmas season." The original word for yuletide.

Yuri (יוּרִי) A pet form of Uriah. *See* Uriah.

Yustus (יוּסטוּס) A Hebrew form of the Latin Justus. *See* Justus. In Second Temple days, one of the Zealots who lived in Tiberias.

Yuval (יוּבָל) From the Hebrew, meaning "stream." In the Bible (Genesis 4:21), a son of Lamech. Jubal is a variant spelling.

Yvan A variant spelling of Ivan. *See* Ivan.

Yves From the Scandinavian, meaning "archer." Ives is a variant spelling.

Yvon A variant form of Ivan. *See* Ivan.

Zabad A variant spelling of Zavad. *See* Zavad.

Zabar A variant spelling of Tzabar. *See* Tzabar.

Zabdi A variant spelling of Zavdi. *See* Zavdi.

Zabdiel A variant spelling of Zavdiel. *See* Zavdiel.

Zaccur A variant spelling of Zakur.

Zach (זַך) From the Hebrew, meaning "pure, clean." Also, a pet form of Yitzchak (Isaac) and Zachary. *See* Yitzchak *and* Zachary.

Zachariah A variant spelling of Zecharya. *See* Zecharya.

Zacharias The Greek form of Zecharya. *See* Zecharya. Zecharias is a variant spelling.

Zachary A variant form of Zecharya. *See* Zecharya. Zach and Zak are pet forms.

Zachi (זַכִי) A pet form of Zecharya. *See* Zecharya. Zakai is a variant form.

Zadik, Zaddik Variant spellings of Tzadik. *See* Tzadik.

Zadkiel A variant spelling of Tzadkiel. *See* Tzadkiel.

Zadok A variant spelling of Tzadok. *See* Tzadok.

Zafrir A variant spelling of Tzafrir. *See* Tzafrir.

Zafriri A variant spelling of Tzafriri. *See* Tzafriri.

Zafrit A variant spelling of Tzafrit. *See* Tzafrit.

Zahal A variant spelling of Tzahal. *See* Tzahal.

Zahalon A variant spelling of Tzahalon. *See* Tzahalon.

Zahavi (זְהָבִי) From the Hebrew, meaning "gold." Zehavi is a variant form.

Zahir (זָהִיר) From the Hebrew, meaning "bright" or "shining." Zahur is a variant form.

Zahur (זָהוּר) A variant form of Zahir. *See* Zahir.

Zahuv (זָהוּב) From the Hebrew, meaning "yellow-haired, blonde."

Zaide A variant spelling of Zeide. *See* Zeide.

Zak (זַק) A pet form of Yitzchak and Zachary. *See* Yitzchak *and* Zachary. Also, an acronym for the Hebrew words *zera kodesh*, meaning "holy seed" or "Priestly family."

Zakai (זַכַּי) From the Hebrew, meaning "pure, clean, innocent." In the Bible (Ezra 2:9), the head of a family of Babylonian Exile returnees. Also from the Aramaic, spelled זַכַּאי, the father of Rabbi Yochanan, a second-century leading talmudic scholar (Avot 2:8). Zakkai is a variant spelling.

Zaken (זָקֵן) From the Hebrew, meaning "old, ancient."

Zakif (זָקִיף) From the Hebrew, meaning "upright." Zakuf is a variant form.

Zakkai   A variant spelling of Zakai. *See* Zakai.

Zakuf (זָקוּף)   A variant form of Zakif. *See* Zakif.

Zakur (זַכּוּר)   From the Hebrew, meaning "male." In the Bible (Numbers 13:4), the father of one of the twelve scouts who explored the Promised Land. Zaccur is a variant spelling.

Zalel   A variant spelling of Tzalel. *See* Tzalel.

Zales   From the Old English, meaning "to sell" or "salaried." Derived from the Latin *sal*, meaning "salt," originally used as currency.

Zalkin (זַאלְקִין)   Yiddish pet forms of Solomon. *See* Solomon.

Zalman, Zalmen, Zalmon   Yiddish short forms of Solomon. *See* Solomon. Zelman is a variant form. Zalmon is also a variant spelling of Tzalmon. *See* Tzalmon.

Zalul   A variant spelling of Tzalul. *See* Tzalul.

Zameret   A variant spelling of Tzameret. *See* Tzameret.

Zamir (זָמִיר)   From the Hebrew, meaning "song, singing." Also, the name of a bird (nightingale).

Zan (זָן)   From the Hebrew, meaning "nourished, fed," or a kind of plant (II Chronicles 16:14). Also, from the Italian, meaning "clown." Zane is a variant form.

Zander   A variant spelling of Sander (Alexander). *See* Alexander.

Zane   A variant form of Zan. *See* Zan. A Yiddish form of Shmuel (Samuel). *See* Shmuel. Akin to Zanvel and Zanvil.

Zangwill (זַאנגְוִויל)   A Yiddish form of Shmuel (Samuel). *See* Shmuel. Akin to Zanvel and Zanvil.

Zanvel (זַאנְוֶועל)   A Yiddish form of Shmuel (Samuel). *See* Shmuel. Zavel and Zavil are variant forms.

Zanvil (זַאנְוִיל)   A variant form of Zanvel. *See* Zanvel.

Zarchi (זַרְחִי)   A variant form of Zerach. *See* Zerach.

Zavad (זָבָד)   From the Hebrew, meaning "gift, portion, dowry." In the Bible (I Chronicles 11:41), one of King David's warriors. Zabad is a variant spelling. Zavdi, Zavdiel, and Zavud are variant forms.

Zavdi (זַבְדִי)   A variant form of Zavad. From the Hebrew, meaning "my gift." In the Bible (I Chronicles 8:19), a descendant of Benjamin. In the Talmud (Yerushalmi Avoda Zara 3:1), a third-century Palestinian scholar. Zabdi is a variant spelling.

Zavdiel (זַבְדִיאֵל)   A variant form of Zavad. From the Hebrew, meaning "God is my gift." In the Bible (I Chronicles 8:19), a descendant of Benjamin. Zabdiel is a variant spelling.

Zavel (זַאוֶועל)   A variant form of Zanvel. *See* Zanvel.

Zavil (זָאוִיל) A variant form of Zanvil. *See* Zanvil.

Zavud (זָבוּד) A variant form of Zavad. *See* Zavad. In the Bible (I Kings 4:5), a friend of King Solomon.

Zayit (זַיִת) From the Hebrew, meaning "olive."

Zaza (זָזָא) From the Aramaic, meaning "money, a silver coin (valued in early times at one-quarter of a shekel)." Also, from the Hebrew, meaning "movement."

Zeb A pet form of Zebulun. *See* Zebulun.

Zebedee (זַבְדִּי) From the Hebrew, meaning "gift of God." In the New Testament, the father of James and John.

Zebul A variant spelling of Zevul. *See* Zevul.

Zebulon, Zebulun Variant spellings of Zevulun. *See* Zevulun. Zeb is a pet form. Zubin is a variant form.

Zecharia, Zechariah Variant spellings of Zecharya. *See* Zecharya.

Zecharias A variant spelling of Zacharias. *See* Zacharias.

Zecharya (זְכַרְיָה) From the Hebrew, meaning "memory" or "remembrance of the Lord." One of the twelve Minor Prophets. Also, one of the kings of Israel, the son of Jeroboam (II Kings 14:29). Zachariah, Zecharia, and Zechariah are variant spellings. Zacharias, Zachary, and Zecharyahu are variant forms. Zachi is a pet form.

Zecharyahu (זְכַרְיָהוּ) A variant form of Zecharya. *See* Zecharya. In the Bible (II Kings 15:8), a king of Israel.

Zecher (זֶכֶר) From the Hebrew, meaning "memory" or "remembrance." In the Bible (I Chronicles 8:31), a member of the tribe of Benjamin.

Zed A pet form of Zedekia. *See* Zedekia.

Zedekia, Zedekiah Anglicized spellings of Tzidkiya. *See* Tzidkiya. Zed is a pet form.

Zeeb A variant spelling of Zev. In the Bible (Judges 7:25), a prince of Midian. *See* Zev.

Ze'eira A variant spelling of Z'eira. *See* Z'eira.

Ze'ev (זְאֵב) From the Hebrew, meaning "wolf." In the Bible (Genesis 49:27), when Benjamin is blessed by his father, Jacob, he is compared to a wolf. As a result, among Jews, Zev and Wolf are used as first and middle names. Zev is sometimes used as a pet form of Zevulun (Zebulun). Zev is a variant spelling. In Judges 7:25, the name of a Midianite military officer. Seff is a Yiddish form. Ze'evi, Zeff, and Zif are variant forms.

Ze'evi (זְאֵבִי) A variant form of Ze'ev. *See* Ze'ev.

Zefania, Zefaniah Variant spellings of Tzefanya. *See* Tzefanya.

Zeff (זֶעף)   A Yiddish form of Zev, or a short form of Joseph. *See* Zev *and* Joseph.

Zeharia, Zehariah   Variant spellings of Zeharya. *See* Zeharya.

Zeharya (זְהַרְיָה)   From the Hebrew, meaning "light of the Lord." Zeharia and Zehariah are variant spellings.

Zehavi (זְהָבִי)   From the Hebrew, meaning "gold." Used also as a feminine name. Zahavi is a variant form.

Zeide (זֵיידֶע)   From the Yiddish, meaning "grandfather" or "old man." Zaide is a variant spelling.

Z'eira (זְעִירָא)   From the Aramaic, meaning "small, junior" and also "boundary." In the Talmud (Berachot 39a), a third-century Babylonian scholar who settled in Palestine. Z'iri, Zera, *and* Zero are variant forms. Ze'eira and Zeira are variant spellings.

Ze'iri (זְעִירִי)   A variant form of Z'eira. In the Talmud (Yevamot 21a), a third-century Babylonian scholar. Zeiri is a variant spelling.

Zeke   A pet form of Zecharia. *See* Zecharia. Also, from the Aramaic, meaning "spark," Or, from the Arabic, meaning "shooting star." Zik is a variant spelling.

Zelick   A variant form of Zelig. *See* Zelig.

Zelig   A variant form of Selig. *See* Selig.

Zelil   A variant spelling of Tzelil. *See* Tzelil.

Zelman   A variant form of Zalman. *See* Zalman. Zelmo is probably a variant form.

Zelmo   Probably a variant form of Zelman. *See* Zelman.

Zelophehad   A variant spelling of Tzelafchad. *See* Tzelafchad.

Zemach   A variant spelling of Tzemach. *See* Tzemach.

Zemari   A variant spelling of Tzemari. *See* Tzemari.

Zemaria, Zemariah   Variant spellings of Zemarya. *See* Zemarya.

Zemarya (זְמַרְיָה)   From the Hebrew, meaning "song, melody of God. Zemaria and Zemariah are variant spellings.

Zemer (זֶמֶר)   From the Hebrew, meaning "song."

Zemira, Zemirah (זְמִירָה)   From the Hebrew, meaning "song" or "melody." In the Bible (I Chronicles 7:8), a member of the tribe of Benjamin. Used also as a feminine name.

Zeno   From the Greek, meaning "sign, symbol," and from the Latin, meaning "path, way."

Zephania, Zephaniah   Variant spellings of Zefania. *See* Zefania.

Zephyr   From the Greek, meaning "west wind."

Zer (זֵר)   From the Hebrew, meaning "wreath" or "crown."

Zera (זֶרַע)   From the Hebrew, meaning "seed." Also, a variant form of Z'eira, and spelled זֵירָא. *See* Z'eira.

Zerach (זֶרַח)   From the Hebrew, meaning "light" or "shine." In the Bible (Genesis 38:30), the son of Judah and Tamar. Zerah is a variant spelling. Zarchi is a variant form.

Zerachia, Zerachiah   Variant spellings of Zerachya. *See* Zerachya.

Zerachya (זְרַחְיָה)   From the Hebrew, meaning "light of the Lord." In the Bible (Ezra 7:4), a son of Pinchas. Zerachia and Zerachiah are variant spellings.

Zerah   A variant spelling of Zerach. *See* Zerach.

Zerem (זֶרֶם)   From the Hebrew, meaning "stream."

Zeri   A variant spelling of Tzeri. *See* Tzeri.

Zerika (זְרִיקָא)   From the Aramaic, meaning "sprinkling." In the Talmud (Yoma 4b), a fourth-century Palestinian scholar.

Zero   A French and Italian form of the Arabic, meaning "cipher." Also, a variant form of Z'eira. *See* Z'eira.

Zeror   A variant spelling of Tzeror. *See* Tzeror.

Zerubavel (זְרוּבָּבֶל)   From the Hebrew, meaning "Babylonian Exile" or "dispersion." In the Bible (Nehemiah 7:7), the leader of the first of the returning Babylonian exiles. Zerubbabel is a variant English spelling. Also spelled זְרֻבָּבֶל.

Zerubbabel   A variant spelling of Zerubavel. *See* Zerubavel.

Zetam (זֵתָם)   From the Hebrew, meaning "olive." In the Bible (I Chronicles 26:22), a Levite, a descendant of the family of Gershon.

Zetan (זֵיתָן)   From the Hebrew, meaning "olive tree." In the Bible (I Chronicles 7:10), a member of the tribe of Benjamin.

Zev   A variant spelling of Ze'ev. *See* Ze'ev.

Zevach (זֶבַח)   From the Hebrew, meaning "sacrifice." In the Bible (Judges 8:5), one of the Midianite kings. Zevah is a variant spelling.

Zevachia, Zevachiah   Variant spellings of Zevachya. *See* Zevachya.

Zevachya (זְבַחְיָה)   From the Hebrew, meaning "sacrifice of the Lord." Zevachia and Zevachiah are variant spellings.

Zevadia, Zevadiah   Variant spellings of Zevadya. *See* Zevadya.

Zevadya (זְבַדְיָה)   From the Hebrew, meaning "God has bestowed." In the Bible (I Chronicles 27:7), the son of Asael, who was the brother of Joab. Zevadia and Zevadiah are variant spellings. Zevadyahu is a variant form.

Zevadyahu (זְבַדְיָהוּ)   A variant form of Zevadya. In the Bible (I Chronicles 26:2), a Levite in the time of David.

Zevah   A variant spelling of Zevach. *See* Zevach.

Zevi   A variant spelling of Tzevi. *See* Tzevi.

Zevid (זְבִיד)   From the Hebrew, meaning "gift." In the Talmud (Berachot 46b), a fourth-century Babylonian scholar. Zevida is a variant form.

Zevida (זְבִידָא)   A variant form of Zevid. *See* Zevid. In the Talmud (Yerushalmi Bava Kama 9:7), a fourth-century scholar.

Zeviel   A variant spelling of Tzeviel. *See* Tzeviel.

Zevieli   A variant spelling of Tzevieli. *See* Tzevieli.

Zevina (זְבִינָא)   From the Aramaic, meaning "acquired, purchased." In the Bible (Ezra 10:43), a contemporary of Ezra.

Zevul (זְבוּל)   A short form of Zevulun. *See* Zevulun. In the Bible (Judges 9:30), a prefect of Avimelech, a Judge of Israel. Zebul is a variant spelling.

Zevulun (זְבוּלוּן)   From the Hebrew, meaning "to exalt, to honor" or "lofty house." In the Bible (Genesis 30:20), the sixth son of Jacob and Leah. Zebulon and Zebulun are variant spellings. Zubin is a variant form. Zev is a pet form. Zevul is a short form.

Zi   A variant spelling of Tzi. *See* Tzi.

Zia (זִיעַ)   From the Hebrew, meaning "to tremble" or "to move." In the Bible (I Chronicles 5:13), a member of the tribe of Gad.

Zichri (זִכְרִי)   From the Hebrew, meaning "my memory" or "my remembrance." In the Bible (Exodus 6:21), the grandson of Levi.

Zichrini (זִכְרִינִי)   From the Hebrew. A plant-name, probably a forget-me-not. Zichria is a feminine form.

Zichroni (זִכְרוֹנִי)   From the Hebrew, meaning "my remembrance."

Zif, Ziff (זִיף)   Variant Yiddish forms of Zev or short forms of Joseph. *See* Zev and Joseph. In the Bible (I Chronicles 4:16), a member of the tribe of Judah. Also, variant spellings of Tzif. *See* Tzif. Also, the early name of the Hebrew month Iyar. Zifa is a variant form.

Zifa (זִיפָה)   A variant form of Zif. *See* Zif. Also, from the Hebrew, meaning "bristle."

Zik (זִיק)   A Yiddish pet form of Itzik (Issac). *See* Isaac. Also, a variant spelling of Zeke. *See* Zeke.

Ziltai   A variant spelling of Tziltai. *See* Tziltai.

Zimra (זִמְרָה)   From the Aramaic, meaning "song, tune."

Zimran (זִמְרָן)   A variant form of Zimri. *See* Zimri. In the Bible (Genesis 25:2), the son of Abraham and Keturah.

Zimri (זִמְרִי)   From the Hebrew, meaning "mountain-sheep, goat." Also from the Hebrew, meaning "protected, sacred thing" or "my vine, my branch." In the Bible (I Chronicles 2:6), a member of the tribe of Simeon. Zimran is a variant form.

Zimroni (זִמְרוֹנִי) From the Hebrew, meaning "my song, my melody."

Zindel (זִינְדֶעל) From the Yiddish, meaning "son, sonny." Akin to Zundel.

Zion A variant spelling of Tziyon. *See* Tziyon.

Ziphion A variant spelling of Tzifyon. *See* Tzifyon.

Zipor, Zippor Variant spellings of Tzipor. *See* Tzipor.

Ziruz (זִירוּז) From the Hebrew, meaning "encouragement" or "acceleration."

Zisa (זִיסָע) From the Yiddish, meaning "sweet." Zisel is a pet form.

Zisel, Zissel (זִיסֶעל) Pet forms of Zisa. *See* Zisa.

Ziskind (זִיסְקִינְד) A Yiddish form of the German, meaning "sweet child."

Ziv (זִיו) From the Hebrew, meaning "to shine, brilliance" or "gazelle." Also, an early Hebrew synonym for the Hebrew month Iyar. Zivi and Zivan are variant forms. *See also* Zevi.

Zivan (זִיוָן) A variant form of Ziv. *See* Ziv.

Zivi (זִיוִי) A variant form of Ziv. *See* Ziv.

Zivia A variant spelling of Tzivya. *See* Tzivya.

Zivion A variant spelling of Tzivyon. *See* Tzivyon.

Ziza (זִיזָא) From the Hebrew, meaning "agitation" or "industrious." In the Bible (I Chronicles 4:37), a descendant of Reuben.

Zochar A variant spelling of Tzochar. *See* Tzochar.

Zofar A variant spelling of Tzofar. *See* Tzofar.

Zohar (זֹהַר) From the Hebrew, meaning "light, brilliance." Also spelled זוֹהַר. Used also as a feminine name.

Zoie From the Greek, meaning "life." When spelled Zoe, it is a feminine name.

Zola From the German, meaning "toll, duty, cost." Zollie is a pet form.

Zollie A pet form of Zola. *See* Zola.

Zoltan A variant form of the Arabic, meaning "ruler, prince."

Zoma (זוֹמָא) From the Hebrew, meaning "plotting, scheming." In the Talmud (Kidushin 49b), the father of Shimon, a second-century Palestinian scholar generally referred to as Ben Zoma.

Zomer A variant spelling of Zomeir. *See* Zomeir.

Zomeir (זוֹמֵר) From the Hebrew, meaning "one who prunes (vines)." Zomer is a variant spelling. Also spelled זָמֵר.

Zophar A variant spelling of Tzofar. *See* Tzofar.

Zorea A variant spelling of Zoreia. *See* Zoreia.

Zoreia (זוֹרֵעַ) From the Hebrew, meaning "one who plants, farmer."

Zoreiach (זוֹרֵחַ) From the Hebrew, meaning "shine."

Zoveva A variant spelling of Tzoveva. *See* Tzoveva.

Zri A variant spelling of Zeri. *See* Zeri.

Zuar A variant spelling of Tzuar. *See* Tzuar.

Zubin A variant form of Zevulun. *See* Zevulun.

Zuf A variant spelling of Tzuf. *See* Tzuf.

Zundel (זונדל) From the Yiddish, meaning "son, sonny." Akin to Zindel.

Zuph A variant spelling of Tzuf. *See* Tzuf.

Zur A variant spelling of Tzur. *See* Tzur.

Zuri A variant spelling of Tzuri. *See* Tzuri.

Zuriel A variant spelling of Tzuriel. *See* Tzuriel.

Zurishadai A variant spelling of Tzurishadai. *See* Tzurishadai.

Zusa (זוסא) From the Yiddish, meaning "sweet." Akin to Zisa.

Zuse (זוסֶע) A variant form of Zusa. *See* Zusa.

Zushe (זושֶע) A variant form of Zusa. *See* Zusa.

Zusman, Zusmann (זוסמאן) Yiddish forms of the German, meaning "sweet person" or "sweet man." Akin to Ziskind.

Zuta (זוטא) From the Aramaic, meaning "small" or "younger." Zutra is a variant form.

Zutai (זוטי) A variant form of Zuta. *See* Zuta. In the Talmud (Shabbat 157a), a fourth-century Babylonian scholar.

Zutei (זוטי) A variant form of Zutai. *See* Zutai.

Zutra (זוטרא) From the Aramaic, meaning "small" or "junior." In the Talmud (Berachot 43b), a third-century Babylonian scholar. Zuta is a variant form.

Zvi A variant spelling of Tzvi. *See* Tzvi.

FEMININE NAMES

Abbe A pet form of Abigail. *See* Abigail. Used also as a masculine name.

Abbey A pet form of Abigail. *See* Abigail.

Abbie A pet form of Abigail. *See* Abigail. Used also as a masculine name.

Abby A variant spelling of Abbey. *See* Abbey.

Abela From the Latin, meaning "beautiful."

Abibi A variant spelling of Avivi. *See* Avivi.

Abibit A variant spelling of Avivit. *See* Avivit.

Abiela, Abiella Variant spellings of Aviela. *See* Aviela.

Abigail A variant form of Avigayil. *See* Avigayil. Abbe, Abbey, Abbie, and Abby are pet forms. Gail is a short form.

Abihail A variant spelling of Avichayil. *See* Avichayil.

Abira (אַבִּירָה) From the Hebrew, meaning "strong."

Abirama A variant spelling of Avirama. *See* Avirama.

Abiri (אַבִּירִי) From the Hebrew, meaning "my strong one" or "my strength."

Abishag A variant spelling of Avishag. *See* Avishag.

Abital A variant spelling of Avital. *See* Avital.

Abra A short form of Abraham used in seventeenth-century England, where it attained a degree of popularity. *See* Abraham (masculine section).

Achava (אַחֲוָה) From the Hebrew, meaning "friendship."

Achinoam (אֲחִינֹעַם) From the Hebrew, meaning "my brother is good, pleasant." In the Bible, a wife of King Saul (I Samuel 14:20), and a wife of King David (I Samuel 25:43).

Achishalom (אֲחִישָׁלוֹם) From the Hebrew, meaning "my brother is peace."

Achsa (עַכְסָה) From the Hebrew and Aramaic, meaning "anklet." In the Bible (Joshua 15:16), the daughter of Caleb and wife of Othniel.

Achuza (אֲחֻוָּה) From the Hebrew, meaning "possession" or "territory."

Ada, Adah (עָדָה) From the Hebrew, meaning "adorned, beautiful." Also, from the Latin and German, meaning "of noble birth." In the Bible (Genesis

4:19), the wife of Lamech and a wife of Esau (Genesis 36:2). Adda is a variant spelling. Used also as a masculine name in the Talmud (Ketubot 8b).

Adabelle A hybrid name compounded of Ada and Belle. *See* Ada *and* Belle.

Adalia A variant form of Adelia. *See* Adelia.

Adaline A pet form of Adelaide. *See* Adelaide.

Adama (אֲדָמָה) From the Hebrew, meaning "earth." The feminine form of Adam.

Adamina A feminine pet form of Adam, coined in nineteenth century Scotland. *See* Adam (masculine section).

Adamma Used by the Ibo of Nigeria, meaning "child of beauty."

Adara (אֲדָרָה) The feminine form of Adar. *See* Adar (masculine section).

Adaya (עֲדָיָה) A variant form of Ada. *See* Ada.

Adda A variant spelling of Ada. *See* Ada.

Addie A pet form of Adelaide. *See* Adelaide. Also, a variant spelling of Adi. *See* Adi.

Adel (עֲדִיאֵל) A variant spelling of Adele. *See* Adele. Also, from the Hebrew, meaning "towards God."

Adela A variant form of Adelaide. *See* Adelaide.

Adelaide A French form of the German name Adelheid, meaning "of noble birth." Became popular in tenth-century Germany when Queen Adelaide ruled the country. Adela, Adele, Adelia, Adelina, Adeline, Adelle, Alice, Aline, Alisa, Arline, and Else are variants. *See also* Adi.

Adele A variant form of Adelaide. *See* Adelaide.

Adelia A variant form of Adelaide. *See* Adelaide. Adalia is a variant form.

Adelina A pet form of Adele and Adelaide. *See* Adelaide.

Adeline A pet form of Adelaide. *See* Adelaide.

Adella A variant form of Adelaide. *See* Adelaide.

Adelle A variant form of Adelaide. *See* Adelaide. Also a variant spelling of Adele. *See* Adele.

Adena (עֲדִינָה) From the Hebrew and Greek, meaning "noble" or "delicate." Adina is a variant spelling. Adene is a variant form.

Adene A variant form of Adena. *See* Adena.

Aderet (אַדֶּרֶת) From the Hebrew, meaning "cape, outergarment."

Adi (עֲדִי) From the Hebrew, meaning "ornament." Used also as a pet form of Adele, Adeline, or Adelaide. Addie and Adie are variant spellings. Used also as a masculine name.

Adia, Adiah Variant spellings of Adiya. *See* Adiya.

Adie A variant spelling of Adi. *See* Adi.

Adiel (עֲדִיאֵל) From the Hebrew, meaning "ornament of the Lord." Akin to Adie. Adiella is a variant form.

Adiella (עֲדִיאֵלָה) A variant form of Adiel. *See* Adiel.

Adifa (עֲדִיפָה) From the Hebrew, meaning "superior, preferred." Adipha is a variant spelling.

Adina A variant spelling of Adena. *See* Adena. Used also as a masculine name.

Adipha A variant spelling of Adifa. *See* Adifa.

Adira (אַדִּירָה) From the Hebrew, meaning "mighty, strong."

Adiva (אַדִּיבָה) From the Hebrew and Arabic, meaning "gracious, pleasant."

Adiya (עֲדִיָּה) From the Hebrew, meaning "God's treasure, God's ornament." Adia and Adiah are variant spellings.

Adonia, Adoniah Variant spellings of Adoniya. *See* Adoniya.

Adoniya The feminine form of the Greek name Adonis, meaning "beautiful lad." In the Bible, the same name is a masculine form meaning "my Lord is God."

Adora From the Latin, meaning "one who is adored or loved."

Adorna From the Anglo-Saxon, meaning "to adorn."

Adra (אַדְרָה) From the Aramaic, meaning "coat (made of animal skin)" or "glory, majesty." Also, a variant form of Idra. *See* Idra.

Adrea A variant spelling of Adria. *See* Adria.

Adria A variant form of Adrien. *See* Adrien. Adrea is a variant spelling.

Adrian Basically a masculine name, derived from Hadrian. *See* Adrian *and* Hadrian (masculine section). Also, a variant spelling of Adrien. *See* Adrien. Adriana is a variant form. Adriane and Adrianne are variant spellings.

Adriana A variant form of Adrian. *See* Adrian.

Adriane A variant spelling of Adrian. *See* Adrian.

Adrianne A variant spelling of Adrian. *See* Adrian.

Adrie A pet form of Adrien. *See* Adrien.

Adrien A French form derived from the Greek meaning "girl from Adria." Adrian and Adrienne are variant spellings. Adria is a variant form.

Adrienne A variant spelling of Adrien. *See* Adrien.

Aduka, Adukah (אֲדוּקָה) From the Hebrew, meaning "committed, observant."

Adva (אַדְוָה) From the Aramaic, meaning "wave, ripple."

Afa (עָפָה) From the Hebrew, meaning "she flies." Apha is a variant spelling.

Afeka (אֲפֵקָה) From the Hebrew, meaning "horizon" or "steam, water." In the Bible (Joshua 15:53), a place-name meaning "channel" or "fortress." Apheka is a variant spelling.

Afna A variant spelling of Ofna. See Ofna.

Afra A variant spelling of Ofra. See Ofra.

Afrat A variant spelling of Ofrat. See Ofrat.

Afrit A variant spelling of Ofrit. See Ofrit.

Agala (עֲגָלָה) From the Hebrew, meaning "wagon, cart."

Agatha From the Greek, meaning "good.' Aggie, Agy, and Aggy are pet forms.

Aggie A pet form of Agatha. See Agatha.

Agnes From the Greek and Latin, meaning "lamb," symbolizing purity and chastity. In the Middle Ages, Annis, Annice, and Annes were popular forms of Agnes. Inez is a Portuguese variant.

Agy, Aggy Pet forms of Agatha. See Agatha.

Ahada, Ahadah (אֲהָדָה) From the Hebrew, meaning "adoration."

Aharona (אַהֲרֹנָה) A feminine form of Aharon (Aaron). See Aharon (masculine section).

Aharonit (אַהֲרֹנִית) A feminine form of Aharon (Aaron). See Aharon (masculine section).

Ahava, Ahavah (אַהֲבָה) From the Hebrew, meaning "love." In the Talmud (Rosh Hashana 29a), a fourth-century Palestinian scholar.

Ahavat (אַהֲבַת) From the Hebrew, meaning "love."

Ahuda, Ahudah (אֲהוּדָה) From the Hebrew, meaning "adored."

Ahuva, Ahuvah (אֲהוּבָה) From the Hebrew, meaning "beloved."

Ahuvia, Ahuviah (אֲהוּבִיָה) From the Hebrew, meaning "beloved of God."

Aida From the Latin and Old French, meaning "to help."

Aidan A variant form of Aida. See Aida.

Aileen From the Greek, meaning "light." Akin to Helen. Ailina is a variant form. Ailene is a variant spelling.

Ailene A variant spelling of Aileen. See Aileen.

Aili, Ailie A Scotch form of Alice. See Alice.

Ailina The Hawaiian form of Aileen. See Aileen.

Aimee From the French and Latin, meaning "love, friendship." Ami, Amie, and Amy are variant spellings.

Ainslee A variant spelling of Ainsley. See Ainsley.

Ainsley From the Scotch, meaning "one's own meadow or land." Used also as a masculine name.

Alaina, Alaine Variant feminine forms of Alan. *See* Alan (masculine section).

Alameda A North American Indian name, meaning "cottonwood grove." Also, from the Spanish *alamo*, meaning "grove of poplar trees."

Alana, Alanna Variant forms of Alan. *See* Alan (masculine section).

Alathea A variant spelling of Althea. *See* Althea.

Alayne A variant spelling of Alaine. *See* Alaine.

Alba A pet form of Alberta. *See* Alberta.

Alberta The feminine form of Albert. *See* Albert (masculine section).

Albertina, Albertine Pet forms of Alberta. *See* Alberta.

Albina From the Latin, meaning "white." Albinia is a variant form.

Albinia A variant form of Albina. *See* Albina.

Alcina A pet form of Alice. *See* Alice.

Alda From the Old German, meaning "old" or "rich." Aldine and Aleda are variant forms.

Aldine A variant form of Alda. *See* Alda. Aldyne is a variant spelling.

Aldona From the Old German, meaning "old one."

Aldora From the Anglo-Saxon, meaning "noble gift."

Aldyne A variant spelling of Aldine. *See* Aldine.

Aleda A variant form of Alda. *See* Alda.

Aleeza (עֲלִיזָה) From the Hebrew, meaning "joy or joyous one." Aliza and Alizah are variant spellings.

Alei (עָלֶה) From the Hebrew, meaning "leaf."

Aleka A variant spelling of Alika. *See* Alika.

Alena A Russian form of Helen. *See* Helen.

Alene A variant form of Arlene and Eileen. *See* Arlene *and* Eileen.

Alessandra An Italian variant form of Alexandra. *See* Alexandra.

Alethea From the Greek, meaning "truth." Alethia is a variant spelling.

Alethia A variant spelling of Alethea. *See* Alethea.

Aletta From the Latin, meaning "winged one."

Alevia Probably a variant form of Alva. *See* Alva.

Alexa A variant form of Alexandra. *See* Alexandra.

Alexandra (אַלְכְּסַנְדְּרָה) A feminine form of the Greek Alexander, meaning "protector of man." Queen Salome-Alexandra, ruler of Judea from 76-67 B.C.E., was one of the earliest to use this name. Alessandra, Alexa, Alexandria, and Alexis are variant forms. Alexandrina, Alexina, and Alexine are pet forms. *See* also Alexander (masculine section).

Alexandria   A variant form of Alexandra. *See* Alexandra.

Alexandrina   A pet form of Alexandra. *See* Alexandra.

Alexina, Alexine   Pet forms of Alexandra. *See* Alexandra.

Alexis   A variant form of Alexandra. *See* Alexandra. Used also as a masculine name. Aliki is a variant form.

Alfreda   The feminine form of Alfred, meaning "all peace" or "wise counsellor." *See* Alfred (masculine section). Elfreda is a variant spelling.

Ali   A pet form of Alice and Alison. *See* Alice *and* Alison.

Alice   From the Middle English and the Old French, meaning "of noble birth." Aili, Ailie, Alicia, Alisa, Alison, Alissa, Alix, Allison, Allissa, and Alyssa are variant forms. Alyce, Alys, Alyse, and Alyss are variant spellings. Alcina, Ali, and Allie are pet forms.

Alicen   An early variant form of Alison. *See* Alison.

Alicia   A variant form of Alice. *See* Alice.

Alida   From the Greek, meaning "beautifully dressed." Derived from a city in ancient Asia-Minor, well known for its finely-dressed citizens. Alidia is a variant form.

Alidia   A variant form of Alida. *See* Alida.

Alika   An Hawaiian form of Alice. *See* Alice. Aleka is a variant spelling.

Aliki   A variant form of Alexis. *See* Alexis.

Alima (אַלִּימָה)   From the Hebrew, meaning "strong."

Alina, Aline   Pet forms of Adeline. May also be derived from the Celtic, meaning "fair, fair one." *See* Adeline *and* Alyna.

Alinor   A variant form of Eleanor. *See* Eleanor.

Alisa (עֲלִיסָה)   A variant form of Alice. *See* Alice. Also, from the Hebrew, meaning "joy."

Alison   A matronymic form, meaning "son of Alice." *See* Alice. Alyson is a variant spelling. Ali is a pet form.

Alissa   A variant form of Alice. *See* Alice.

Alistair   Used more commonly as a masculine name. *See* Alistair (masculine section).

Alita (עֲלִיתָה)   From the Hebrew, meaning "high, above" or "excellent."

Alitza, Alitzah (עֲלִיצָה)   From the Hebrew, meaning "joy, happiness."

Alix   A French form of Alice. *See* Alice.

Aliya, Aliyah (עֲלִיָּה)   From the Hebrew, meaning "to ascend, to go up."

Aliza, Alizah (עֲלִיזָה)   Variant spellings of Aleeza and Alitza. *See* Aleeza *and* Alitza.

Allana A feminine form of Alan. *See* Alan (masculine section).

Allegra From the Latin, meaning "brisk, cheerful."

Alley A pet form of Alice. *See* Alice.

Allianora An invented name probably compounded of Alice or Allison and Nora.

Allie A pet form of Alice or Allison. *See* Alice *and* Allison.

Allison A matronymic form, meaning "son of Alice." *See* Alice.

Allissa A variant form of Alice. *See* Alice.

Allonia A variant form of Alona. *See* Alona.

Allyn A feminine section of Allen. *See* Allen (masculine section).

Alma (עַלְמָה) From the Hebrew, meaning "maiden." May also be derived from the Latin, meaning "nourishing" or "bountiful," as in *alma mater* ("nourishing mother"). In Spanish, *alma* means "soul." Almah is a variant spelling.

Almah A variant spelling of Alma. *See* Alma.

Almira From the Arabic, meaning "princess" or "exalted one."

Almoga (אַלְמוֹגָה) From the Hebrew, meaning "coral."

Almuga (אַלְמֻגָּה) The Hebrew name of the sandalwood tree.

Alola The Hawaiian form of Aurora. *See* Aurora.

Alona (אַלּוֹנָה) From the Hebrew, meaning "oak tree." Alon is the masculine form. Allonia and Eilona are variant forms.

Alouise From the German, meaning "famous in battle." A feminine form of Louis. *See* Louis (masculine section).

Alpha From the Greek, meaning "first," being the first letter of the Greek alphabet.

Alta A Spanish form of the Latin *alta*, meaning "tall." Used also as a masculine name. Altai and Alto are variant forms.

Altai A variant form of Alta. *See* Alta.

Altair From the Arabic, meaning "bird."

Alte (אַלְטֶע) From the Yiddish, meaning "old" or "old woman."

Althea From the Greek and Latin, meaning "to heal" or "healer." Alathea is a variant spelling. Thea is a short form.

Alto A Spanish form of Alta. *See* Alta.

Alufa (אַלּוּפָה) From the Hebrew, meaning "leader" or "princess." The feminine form of Aluf. *See* Aluf (masculine section). Alupha is a variant spelling.

Aluma, Alumah (עֲלוּמָה) From the Hebrew, meaning "girl, maiden" or "hidden secret." Also, from the Latin, meaning "aluminum." Alumit is a variant form.

Alumit A variant form of Aluma. *See* Aluma.

Alupha A variant spelling of Alufa. *See* Alufa.

Alva, Alvah (עַלְוָה) From the Hebrew, meaning "sin, transgression." Also, from the Latin, meaning "white." A masculine name in the Bible (Genesis 36:40), a leader of the family of Esau. Alvan and Alvania are variant forms. Alevia is probably a variant form as well.

Alvan A variant form of Alva. *See* Alva.

Alvania A variant form of Alva. *See* Alva.

Alya (אַלְיָה) From the Aramaic and Hebrew, meaning "dirge, elegy" or "lobe of an ear" or "tail of a sheep."

Alyce A variant spelling of Alice. *See* Alice.

Alyna A Latin form of Aline. Popular from the twelfth to the fifteenth century. *See* Aline.

Alys, Alyse Variant spellings of Alice. *See* Alice.

Alyson A variant spelling of Alison. *See* Alison.

Alyss A variant spelling of Alice. *See* Alice.

Alyssa A variant form of Alice. *See* Alice.

Alzina A variant spelling of Alcina. *See* Alcina.

Amabel Compounded from the Latin *amor*, meaning "love," and the French *belle*, meaning "beautiful."

Amadis From the Spanish, meaning "love of God."

Amal (עָמָל) From the Hebrew, meaning "work, toil."

Amalia, Amaliah Variant spellings of Amalya. *See* Amalya.

Amalie A German variant form of Amelia. *See* Amelia.

Amalthea A variant form of Amalia. *See* Amalia. In Greek and Latin mythology, Amalthea is the goat that nursed Zeus (Jupiter), one of its horns being called cornucopia, or horn of plenty.

Amalya (עֲמַלְיָה) From the Hebrew, meaning "work of the Lord" or "industrious." Amalthea and Amelia are variant forms. Amalia and Amaliah are variant spellings. Akin to Amela. *See* Amalthea, Amela, *and* Amelia.

Amana (אֲמָנָה) From the Hebrew, meaning "faithful."

Amanda From the Latin, meaning "to love." Mandy is a pet form.

Amania A variant spelling of Amanya. *See* Amanya.

Amanya (אֲמַנְיָה) From the Hebrew, meaning "God's faithful one." Amania is a variant spelling.

Amarinda From the Greek and Latin, meaning "long-lived." In poetry, an imaginary flower that never fades or dies.

Amaryllis A shepherdess in the poems of poets Virgil and Theocritus. A synonym for shepherd. Also, the name of a flower of the lily family.

Amber From the Old French and Arabic, meaning "amber" or "brownish yellow." Amberlie is a variant form. Amby is a pet form.

Amberlie A variant form of Amber. *See* Amber.

Ambrosia From the Greek and Latin, meaning "immortal." In Greek and Roman mythology, a food delicacy of the gods and immortal beings. Ambrosina and Ambrosine are variant forms. Amby is a pet form.

Ambrosina, Ambrosine Variant forms of Ambrosia. *See* Ambrosia.

Amby A pet form of Amber and Ambrosia. *See* Amber *and* Ambrosia.

Amela (עֲמֵלָה) From the Hebrew, meaning "industrious." Akin to Amalia and Amelia. *See* Amalia *and* Amelia.

Amelia From the Latin, meaning "to work, to be industrious." Also, a variant form of Amalia. *See* Amalia. Emily is a popular pet form. Akin to Amela. *See* Amela.

Amethyst The name of a violet-blue jewel worn by ancient Greeks to prevent intoxication.

Ami (עַמִּי) A variant spelling of Amy. *See* Amy. Also, from the Hebrew, meaning "my nation, my people."

Amia (עַמְיָה) From the Latin *amor*, meaning "love." Akin to Aimee. *See* Aimee. Also, a variant spelling of Amya. *See* Amya.

Amice From the Latin and Old French, meaning "cloak" or "hood" usually worn by priests at mass.

Amida, Amidah (עֲמִידָה) From the Hebrew, meaning "standing" or "upright."

Amie A variant spelling of Aimee. *See* Aimee.

Amiela (עֲמִיאֵלָה) From the Hebrew, meaning "people of God."

Amina, Amine (אֲמִינָה) From the Hebrew and Arabic, meaning "trusted, faithful."

Aminta (אֲמִינְתָה) From the Latin, meaning "to protect." Arminta is probably a corrupt form. Also, from the Hebrew, meaning "truth, friendship," or derived from the name of a plant. Amisa and Amissa are variant forms.

Amira (אֲמִירָה) From the Hebrew, meaning "speech, utterance."

Amisa, Amissa Variant forms of Aminta. *See* Aminta.

Amit (עָמִית) From the Hebrew, meaning "friend."

Amita (אֲמִתָּה) From the Hebrew, meaning "upright, honest."

Amity   From the Latin, meaning "love, friendship."

Amitza, Amitzah (אַמִּיצָה)   From the Hebrew, meaning "strong, powerful." Used also as a masculine name.

Amitzia, Amitziah   Variant spellings of Amitzya. See Amitzya.

Amitzya (אֲמִיצְיָה)   From the Hebrew, meaning "God is strong" or "strength of God." Amitzia and Amitziah are variant spellings.

Amiza   A variant spelling of Amitza. See Amitza.

Amma (אָמָה)   From the Hebrew and Arabic, meaning "servant."

Amtza, Amtzah (אַמְצָה)   From the Hebrew, meaning "strength."

Amuma (עֲמוּמָה)   From the Hebrew, meaning "dull, weak."

Amy   A variant spelling of Aimee. See Aimee.

Amya (עַמְיָה)   From the Hebrew, meaning "people of God."

Ana   A Spanish and Hawaiian form of Anna. See Anna.

Anabela   A variant form of Annabel. See Annabel.

Anabeth   A hybrid name compounded of Anna and Elizabeth. See Anna and Elizabeth.

Anais   A variant English form of Anne. See Anne.

Ana-Maria   A hybrid name. See Ana and Maria.

Anastasia   From the Greek, meaning "resurrection." Anastasius is a masculine form. Nastasya is a Russian form. Stacey, Stacia, Stacie, and Stacy are pet forms.

Anat (עֲנָת)   From the Hebrew, meaning "to sing." In the Bible (Judges 3:31), a masculine name, the father of Shamgar, an Israelite Judge. Anath is a variant spelling.

Anath   A variant spelling of Anat. See Anat.

Anatola   From the Greek, meaning "from the East." Anatole is a masculine form.

Anatone   A variant form of Antonia. See Antonia.

Anava, Anavah (עֲנָבָה)   From the Hebrew, meaning "grape." Also from the Hebrew, meaning "poor, humble," and spelled עֲנָוָה.

Anchelle   A feminine form of Anshel. See Anshel (masculine section).

Andra   From the Old Norse, meaning "breath." Also, a short form of Andrea. See Andrea.

Andrea   The feminine form of the Greek name Andrew, meaning "valiant, strong, courageous." See Andrew (masculine section). Andra is a short form.

Ane   The Hawaiian form of Anne. See Anne.

Anefa, Anefah (עֲנֵפָה)   A variant form of Anufa. See Anufa. Anepha and Anephah are variant spellings.

Anemone From the Greek, meaning "breath." In Greek legend, Anemone was a nymph pursued by the wind and changed into a delicate flower.

Anena (עֲנִינָא) A variant form of Anina. See Anina.

Anepha, Anephah Variant spellings of Anefa. See Anefa.

Aneta A variant spelling of Anita. See Anita.

Anett A variant spelling of Annette. See Annette.

Angela From the Latin, meaning "angel," or from the Greek, meaning "messenger." Angele, Angeles, and Angelica are variant forms. Angeleta, Angelina, and Angeline are pet forms.

Angele, Angeles Variant forms of Angela. See Angela.

Angeleta A pet form of Angela. See Angela.

Angelica The Latin form of Angela. See Angela.

Angelina A pet form of Angela. See Angela.

Angeline A pet form of Angela. See Angela.

Ania A variant spelling of Aniya. See Aniya.

Anina (עֲנִינָא) A pet form of Anna. See Anna. Also, from the Aramaic, meaning "answer my prayer." Anena is a variant form. See Anena.

Anita A pet form of Anna. See Anna. Nita is a short form.

Aniya (אָנִיָּה) From the Hebrew, meaning "boat, ship." Ania is a variant spelling.

Anka A Slavic pet form of Anna. See Anna.

Ann A variant form of Anna. See Anna. Annis is a variant form.

Anna (חַנָה) The Greek form of the Hebrew name Chana, meaning "gracious" and usually rendered as Hannah in Jewish translations of the Bible. The name Anna was popular among German-speaking peoples and in Italy. It was later carried to Russia, where it became popular after the appearance of Leo Tolstoy's nineteenth-century novel *Anna Karenina.* See Hannah for more information. Ana, Ann, and Anne are variant forms. Anina, Anita, Anka, Annie, and Nanette are pet forms. Anya is a Russian form.

Annabel Either a hybrid of Anna and Bela, meaning "gracious and beautiful." Or, a variant form of the Latin name Amabel, meaning "lovable." Anabela, Annabella and Annabelle are variants.

Annabella, Annabelle Variant forms of Annabel. See Annabel.

Anne A French form of Hannah, meaning "gracious." See Anna and Hannah. Anais is a variant form. Nina is a Russian pet form.

Annette A French form of Anna. See Anna. Anett is a variant spelling. Nettie and Netty are pet forms.

Annice An Old English variant form of Ann. See Ann. A variant spelling of Annis.

Annie A pet form of Anna. *See* Anna.

Annis A form of Agnes popular in the Middle Ages. *See* Agnes. Also, an Old English variant form of Ann. *See* Ann. Annice is a variant spelling.

Anthea From the Greek, meaning "flowery." Popular among poets who wrote about nature.

Antoinette From the Greek and Latin, meaning "of high esteem, revered." Nettie, Netty, Toni and Tonia are pet forms. Antonia and Antonette are variant forms.

Antonette A variant form of Antoinette. *See* Antoinette.

Antonia The Italian and Swedish form of Antoinette. *See* Antoinette.

Anufa, Anufah (עֲנוּפָה) From the Hebrew, meaning "multi-branched tree." Anupha and Anuphah are variant spellings.

Anuga, Anugah (עֲנֻגָה) From the Hebrew, meaning "delicate, dainty."

Anupha, Anuphah Variant spellings of Anufa. *See* Anufa.

Anya A Russian form of Anna. *See* Anna.

Apha A variant spelling of Afa. *See* Afa.

Apheka A variant spelling of Afeka. *See* Afeka.

Aphna A variant spelling of Afna. *See* Afna.

Aphra A variant spelling of Afra. *See* Afra.

Aphrat A variant spelling of Afrat. *See* Afrat.

Aphrit A variant spelling of Afrit. *See* Afrit.

Aphrodit (אַפְרוֹדִית) Used in Israel as an Hebraicized form of Aphrodite. *See* Aphrodite.

Aphrodite From the Greek, meaning "foam." In Greek mythology, the goddess of love and beauty who is said to have sprung from the foam of the sea. Aphrodit is the modern Hebrew form.

April From the Latin, meaning "to open," symbolic of springtime. In the Roman calendar, April was the second month of the year (following March).

Arabel From the German *ara*, meaning "eagle," plus the Latin *bella*, meaning "beautiful." Arabela, Arabella, Arbel, Arbela, and Arbell are variant forms. Arabelle is a variant spelling.

Arabela, Arabella Variant form of Arabel. *See* Arabel.

Arabelle A variant spelling of Arabel. *See* Arabel.

Araminta A hybrid form of Arabel and Aminta. *See* Arabel *and* Aminta.

Araxie An ancient name of the Aras River that flows from Turkey to the Caspian Sea.

Arbel A variant form of Arabel. *See* Arabel.

Arbela   A variant form of Arabel. *See* Arabel.

Arbell   A variant form of Arabel. *See* Arabel.

Arda, Ardah (אַרְדָּה)   From the Hebrew, meaning "bronze, bronzed." Also, a variant form of the Hebrew month Adar by metathesis. Ardona is a variant form.

Ardelia   From the Latin, meaning "zealous." Ardis is a variant form.

Arden   From the Old French and the Latin, meaning "flame" or "passionate."

Ardis   A variant form of Ardelia. *See* Ardelia.

Ardith   A variant Anglo-Saxon form of Edith. *See* Edith. Also, possibly a combination of Arthur and Edith.

Ardona   A variant form of Arda. *See* Arda.

Ardra   From the Celtic, meaning "high, high one."

Arela, Arella (אַרְאֵלָה)   From the Hebrew, meaning "angel, messenger."

Aretha   A variant form of Arethusa. *See* Arethusa. Oretha is a variant spelling.

Arethusa   In Greek mythology, a woodland nymph who was changed into a stream by Artemis. Also, a variety of orchid. Aretha is a variant form.

Aria   From the Latin, meaning "air," hence "melody in an opera." Or, the feminine form of the Hebrew name Ari, meaning "lion."

Ariadne   In Greek legend, the daughter of King Midas. In Greek mythology the daughter of the sun god.

Ariana (אַרִיאָנָה)   From the Latin, meaning "song." Ariana was a princess in Greek mythology. Used as a modern Hebrew name.

Ariane   A variant form of Ariadne. *See* Ariadne. Arianna is a variant form.

Arianna   A variant form of Ariane. *See* Ariane.

Ariel (אַרִיאֵל)   From the Hebrew, meaning "lioness of God." Arielle is a variant spelling. Ariela and Ariella are variant forms. Used primarily as a masculine name.

Ariela, Ariella (אַרִיאֵלָה)   Variant forms of Ariel. *See* Ariel. Erela is a variant form.

Arielle   A variant spelling of Ariel. *See* Ariel.

Arilita   A Spanish form of Arlene. *See* Arlene.

Arista   From the Latin, meaning "beard," referring to the beardlike part of grain or grasses. May also be related to the Greek name Aristos, meaning "best."

Aritha   A variant form of Arethusa. *See* Arethusa.

Ariza (אֲרִיזָה)   From the Hebrew, meaning "cedar panels" and "to package."

Arla   A variant form of Arlene. Or, a short form of Carla. *See* Arlene *and* Carla.

Arlana A variant form of Arlene. *See* Arlene.

Arleen A variant spelling of Arlene. *See* Arlene.

Arlene A variant spelling of Arline. *See* Arline. Or, from the Celtic, meaning "pledge, oath." Arilita, Arla, and Arlana, are variant forms. Arlette and Arleta are pet forms. Arleen, Arleyne, and Arlyne are variant spellings.

Arleta A pet form of Arlene. *See* Arlene.

Arlette A pet form of Arlene. *See* Arlene.

Arleyne A variant spelling of Arlene. *See* Arlene.

Arline From the German, meaning "girl." Or, a form of Adeline. *See* Adeline *and* Arlene.

Arlise A variant spelling of Arlyss. *See* Arlyss.

Arlyne A variant spelling of Arline. *See* Arline.

Arlyss A variant form of the masculine Arliss. *See* Arliss (masculine section). Arlise is a variant spelling.

Arminta Probably a corrupt form of Aminta. *See* Aminta.

Armona (אַרְמֹנָה) From the Hebrew, meaning "castle, palace" or "fortress." Also, the name of a tree, possibly from the oak family, spelled עַרְמוֹנָה and mentioned in the Bible (Genesis 30:37). Armonit is a variant form.

Armonit (אַרְמֹנִית) A variant form of Armona. *See* Armona.

Arna A variant spelling of Orna. *See* Orna.

Arnat A variant spelling of Ornat. *See* Ornat.

Arni (אַרְנִי) A pet form of Aron and Aharon (Aaron). *See* Aharon (masculine section). Also, a variant spelling of Orni. *See* Orni. Arnit and Arninit are variant forms. Arnina is a pet form.

Arnina (אַרְנִינָה) A pet form of Arni. *See* Arni. Also, a variant spelling of Ornina. *See* Ornina.

Arninit (אַרְנִינִית) A variant form of Arni. *See* Arni.

Arnit (אַרְנִית) A variant form of Arni. *See* Arni.

Arnolde A feminine form of Arnold. *See* Arnold (masculine section).

Arnoldine A French variant of Arnold, meaning "eagle rule" and signifying power. Arnolde is a variant form.

Arnona (אַרְנוֹנָה) From the Hebrew, meaning "stream" or "roaring stream." Arnonit is a pet form.

Arnonit (אַרְנוֹנִית) A pet form of Arnona. *See* Arnona.

Arona A variant spelling of Aharona, the feminine form of Aharon (Aaron). *See* Aharona *and* Aharon (masculine section).

Artemis   In Greek mythology, the goddess of the moon, wild animals, and hunting. Identified with the Roman goddess Diana. Artemis is mentioned in the Bible in the Book of Acts. Used also as a masculine name.

Arusa (אֲרוּסָה)   From the Hebrew, meaning "betrothed."

Arva   From the Latin, meaning "from the coast." Or, from the Danish, meaning "eagle," signifying strength. Used also as a masculine name. Arvella and Arvelle are variant forms.

Arvella, Arvelle   Variant forms of Arva. *See* Arva.

Arza (אַרְזָה)   From the Hebrew, meaning "cedar beams or panels." Arzit is a variant form.

Arzit   A variant form of Arza. *See* Arza.

Asenath   A variant spelling of Asnat. *See* Asnat.

Ashdoda   From the Aramaic, meaning "waterfall." Ashdod is the masculine form.

Ashera (אֲשֵׁרָה)   From the Hebrew, meaning "blessed, fortunate," Also, the name of an idol for moon worship (Isaiah 17:8). Asherit, Ashria, Ashra, and Ashrat are variant forms. Asher is the masculine form.

Asherit (אֲשֵׁרִית)   A variant form of Ashera. *See* Ashera.

Ashira (עֲשִׁירָה)   From the Hebrew, meaning "wealthy." Akin to Ashera. *See* Ashera.

Ashra (אַשְׁרָה)   A variant form of Ashera. *See* Ashera.

Ashrat (אַשְׁרַת)   A variant form of Ashera. *See* Ashera.

Ashria (אַשְׁרִיָה)   A variant form of Ashera. *See* Ashera.

Asia   A variant spelling of Asya. *See* Asya.

Asisa (עֲסִיסָה)   From the Hebrew, meaning "juicy, ripe."

Asisia   A variant spelling of Asisya. *See* Asisya.

Asisya (עֲסִיסְיָה)   From the Hebrew, meaning "juice of the Lord" or "fruit of the Lord." Asisia is a variant spelling.

Asnat (אָסְנַת)   From the Egyptian, meaning "belonging to the goddess Neith," or from the Aramaic, meaning "thornbush." Also attributed to the Hebrew, meaning "luckless, unfortunate." In the Bible (Genesis 41:45), the wife of Joseph and the mother of Ephraim and Manasseh. Asenath and Osnat are variant spellings.

Assia   A variant spelling of Asya. *See* Asya.

Asta   From the Greek, meaning "star." Akin to the Persian Esther. *See* Astera.

Astera   From the Persian and Greek, meaning "star." Because of its star-shaped leaves, the aster flower has been called the "starflower." Asteria, Asteriya, Astred, Astrid, and Esther are variant forms.

Asteria   A variant form of Astera. *See* Astera.

Asteriya A variant form of Astera. *See* Astera.

Astred, Astrid Variant forms of Astera. *See* Astera. Or, from the Old Norse, meaning "divine strength."

Asya (אָסְיָא) From the Aramaic, meaning "doctor" or "action, performance." Asia and Assia are variant spellings.

Atalia, Ataliah Variant spellings of Atalya. *See* Atalya.

Atalya (עֲתַלְיָה) From the Assyrian, meaning "to grow, be great," or from the Hebrew, meaning "God is exalted." In the Bible (II Kings 8:26), the daughter of King Omri of Israel. Atalia, Ataliah, Athalia, and Athaliah are variant spellings. Used also as a biblical masculine name (Ezra 8:7). Atlit is a variant form.

Atara (עֲטָרָה) From the Hebrew, meaning "crown" or "wreath." In the Bible (I Chronicles 2:26), the wife of Yerachmiel. *See also* Ateret *and* Atira.

Ateret (עֲתֶרֶת) From the Hebrew, meaning "prayer." Also, from the Hebrew, meaning "crown" and spelled עֲטֶרֶת. Akin to Atara and Atira.

Athalee Probably a variant form of Athalia. *See* Athalia.

Athalia, Athaliah Variant spellings of Atalya. *See* Atalya. Athalee is probably a variant form.

Athena From the Greek, meaning "wisdom." In Greek mythology, the goddess of wisdom and warfare.

Atida, Atidah (עֲתִידָה) From the Hebrew, meaning "future."

Atira (עֲתִירָה) From the Hebrew, meaning "prayer." Akin to Atara and Ateret.

Atlit (עֲתְלִית) A variant form of Atalya. *See* Atalya.

Atura (עֲטוּרָה) From the Hebrew, meaning "ornamented, adorned with a crown or wreath." Akin to Atara.

Atzila, Atzilah (אֲצִילָה) From the Hebrew, meaning "honorable" or "noble." Azila and Azilah are variant spellings.

Atzma, Atzmah (עָצְמָה) From the Hebrew, meaning "strength."

Atzmona, Atzmonah (עַצְמוֹנָה) From the Hebrew, meaning "strength." Akin to Atzmoni. *See* Atzmoni.

Atzmoni (עַצְמוֹנִי) From the Hebrew, referring to a plant in the myrtle family.

Audra, Audre Variant forms of Audrey. *See* Audrey.

Audrey From the Old English, meaning "noble, noble strength." Audra and Audre are variant forms. Audrina is a pet form.

Audrina A pet form of Audrey. *See* Audrey.

Audris From the Old German, meaning "fortunate" or "wealthy."

Augusta From the Latin, meaning "revered, sacred." Augustina and Augustine. are variant forms. Gussie and Gussy are pet forms.

Augustina A German variant form of Augusta. *See* Augusta.

Augustine A French form of Augusta. *See* Augusta.

Aura From the Greek, meaning "air, atmosphere." May also be a variant form of Aurelia. *See* Aurelia.

Aurea A variant form of Aurelia. *See* Aurelia.

Aurelia A feminine form of the Latin name Aurelius, meaning "gold." Aurea and possibly Aura are variant forms. Aury is a pet form.

Aurora From the Latin, meaning "dawn." Zora and Zorana are Slavic variant forms. Alola is the Hawaiian form.

Aury A pet form of Aurelia. *See* Aurelia.

Ava From the Latin, meaning "bird," or from the Hebrew, meaning "to desire" or "to agree."

Avalon, Avallon A French form of the Middle Latin name Avallonis, meaning "island." In Celtic mythology, the Isle of the Dead, an island in paradise where King Arthur and other heroes lived after death.

Aveline From the French, meaning "hazelnut." *See also* Hazel. Avella is a pet form.

Avella A pet form of Aveline. *See* Aveline.

Averi From the Old French, meaning "to confirm."

Avi (אֲבִי) From the Assyrian and Hebrew, meaning "father." Sometimes taken to mean "head of the clan." In the Bible (II Kings 18:2), the mother of King Hezekiah of Judah. Aviya is a variant form.

Avia, Aviah Variant spellings of Aviya. *See* Aviya.

Avice A variant spelling of Avis. *See* Avis.

Avichayil (אֲבִיחַיִל) From the Hebrew, meaning "father of might" or "my father is strong." In the Bible (II Chronicles 11:18), the wife of Rechavam (Rehoboam), king of Judah. Abihail and Avihayil are variant spellings.

Avichen (אֲבִיחֵן) From the Hebrew, meaning "my father is gracious" or "father of grace."

Aviela, Aviella (אֲבִיאֵלָה) From the Hebrew, meaning "God is my father." Abiela and Abiella are variant spellings.

Avigal (אֲבִיגַל) A variant spelling of Avigayil (II Samuel 17:25). *See* Avigayil.

Avigayil (אֲבִיגַיִל) From the Hebrew, meaning "father's joy" or "my father is joy." In the Bible (I Samuel 25:3), the wife of King David whom he married after the death of her husband, Nabal. Abigail is a variant form.

Avigdora (אֲבִיגְדוֹרָה) The feminine form of the masculine Avigdor. *See* Avigdor (masculine section).

Avihayil A variant spelling of Avichayil. *See* Avichayil. Also, in the Bible (II Chronicles 11:18), the wife of Rechavam (Rehobaom), king of Judah.

Avima (אֲבִימָה) Origin uncertain. Possibly a hybrid name compounded of the Hebrew *av*, meaning "father," and *ima*, meaning "mother."

Avirama (אֲבִירָמָה) From the Hebrew, meaning "my father is strong." Aviram is the masculine form. Abirama is a variant spelling.

Avirit (אֲוִירִית) From the Hebrew, meaning "air, atmosphere" or "spirit."

Avis An Old German name, meaning "refuge in war" or "fortress." It may also be derived from the Latin, meaning "bird." Avice is a variant spelling.

Avishag (אֲבִישַׁג) From the Hebrew, meaning "my father is a wanderer" or "my father is a sinner." In the Bible (I Kings 1:3), a servant of King David. Abishag is a variant spelling.

Avital (אֲבִיטַל) From the Hebrew, meaning "father of dew," referring to God as a sustainer. In the Bible (II Samuel 3:4), one of King David's wives. Abital is a variant spelling.

Aviva, Avivah (אֲבִיבָה) From the Hebrew, meaning "springtime," connoting youthfulness, freshness. Akin to Avivi. Avivit is a variant form.

Avivi (אֲבִיבִי) From the Hebrew, meaning "springlike." Akin to Aviva. Abibi is a variant spelling.

Avivit (אֲבִיבִית) A variant form of Aviva. *See* Aviva. Abibit is a variant spelling.

Aviya (אֲבִיָּה) From the Hebrew, meaning "God is my father." In the Bible (II Chronicles 29:1), the mother of Hezekia, king of Judah; the Book of Kings (II Kings 18:2) refers to her as Avi. Avia and Aviah are variant spellings. *See also* Avi.

Avi-Yona (אֲבִי-יוֹנָה) From the Hebrew, meaning "dove," mentioned in the Bible (Ecclesiastes 12:5). Also, a plant (caperberry) indigenous to Middle Eastern countries.

Avna (אַבְנָה) From the Aramaic, meaning "rock." In the Bible (II Kings 5:12), the name of a lake or river in Syria.

Avrahamit (אַבְרָהָמִית) A feminine form of Avraham (Abraham). *See* Avraham (masculine section).

Avramit (אַבְרָמִית) A feminine form of Avram (Abram). *See* Avram (masculine section).

Avrona (עַבְרֹנָה) A variant form of Evrona. *See* Evrona. A biblical place-name (Numbers 33:34).

Avtalia A variant spelling of Avtalya. *See* Avtalya.

Avtalya (אַבְטַלְיָה) From the Aramaic and Hebrew, meaning "young lamb" or "deer." Avtalia is a variant spelling.

Avuka, Avukah (אֲבוּקָה) From the Hebrew, meaning "torch, flame."

Aya, Ayah (אַיָּה) From the Hebrew, meaning "to fly swiftly." The name of a bird of prey. In the Bible (Genesis 36:24), a descendant of Esau. A biblical masculine name.

Ayala, Ayalah (אַיָּלָה)   From the Hebrew, meaning "deer, gazelle." Akin to Ayelet. Also from the Hebrew, meaning "terebinth tree" or "oak tree." Yalta is the Aramaic form. *See* Yalta.

Ayelet (אַיֶּלֶת)   From the Hebrew, meaning "deer, gazelle." *See also* Ayelet-Hashachar.

Ayelet-Hashachar (אַיֶּלֶת־הַשַּׁחַר)   From the Hebrew, meaning "daybreak," or the name of a star. In the Bible (Psalms 22:1), a musical instrument.

Ayla   A variant spelling of Eila. *See* Eila.

Aza, Azah (עַזָּה)   From the Hebrew, meaning "strong, powerful."

Azalea   From the Greek, meaning "dry." The name of a flower, so called because it thrives in dry, sun-baked soil. Azalee and Azalia are variant forms.

Azalee   A variant form of Azalea. *See* Azalea.

Azalia   A variant form of Azalea. *See* Azalea.

Aziaz (עֲזִיעָז)   From the Hebrew, meaning "strong."

Azila, Azilah   Variant spellings of Atzila. *See* Atzila.

Aziza, Azizah (עֲזִיזָה)   From the Hebrew, meaning "strong."

Azora   A variant form of Azura. *See* Azura.

Azriela (עֲזְרִיאֵלָה)   From the Hebrew, meaning "God is my strength."

Azura   From the Persian, meaning "sky-blue." Azora is a variant form.

Azuva, Azuvah (עֲזוּבָה)   From the Hebrew, meaning "abandoned, forsaken." In the Bible (I Kings 22:42), the mother of Jehoshafat, king of Judah.

Baara (בַּעֲרָא)   From the Aramaic, meaning "to burn, consume." In the Bible (I Chronicles 8:8), the wife of one of Benjamin's sons.

Bab   A pet form of Elizabeth and Barbara. *See* Elizabeth *and* Barbara.

Baba   A variant form of Bava. *See* Bava.

Babette   A pet form of Barbara. *See* Barbara.

Babs   A short form of Babson. *See* Babson. Also, a variant form of Bab. *See* Bab.

Babson   A matronymic form of Barbara, meaning "Barbara's son." *See* Barbara.

Bahat (בַּהַט)   From the Hebrew, meaning "ivory" or "alabaster." Used also as a masculine name.

Baile (בֵּיילֶע)   Either a variant Yiddish form of the Hebrew Bilha, meaning "troubled, weak, old," or from the Slavic, meaning "white." Also, a Yiddish form of Bela. Beylah is a variant spelling. *See* Bela.

Bairn   From the Scottish, meaning "child."

Bakara (בְּקָרָה)   From the Hebrew, meaning "investigation" or "visitation."

Bakura (בְּכּוּרָה)   From the Hebrew, meaning "ripe," usually referring to a fig. Bikura is a variant form.

Balfora (בַּלְפוֹרָה)   A variant form of Balfouria. See Balfouria.

Balfouria (בַּלְפוּרִיָה)   The feminine form of Balfour. In 1917, Lord Arthur James Balfour, the British statesman and philosopher (1848-1930), issued the Balfour Declaration, paving the way for the establishment of the State of Israel. The name Balfour and its feminine counterpart, Balfouria, are used primarily in Israel.

Bambi   A pet form of the Italian name Bambalina, meaning "little doll."

Bara (בָּרָה)   From the Hebrew, meaning "to choose." Barra is a variant spelling.

Barbara   From the Greek, meaning "strange, stranger, foreign." The ancient Greeks applied the term *barbaros* to all foreigners. In the ancient world, anyone who was not Greek, Roman, or Christian was a stranger, hence a barbarian. Babson is a variant form. Bab, Babette, Babs, Barbi, Bob, and Bobbe are pet forms. Bunny is a nickname.

Barbi   A pet form of Barbara. See Barbara.

Bareket (בָּרֶקֶת)   From the Hebrew. The name of a precious stone (emerald).

Bari   A feminine form of Barrie. See Barrie (masculine section).

Barkait (בַּרְקָאִית)   From the Hebrew, meaning "star" or "morning star."

Barkat (בַּרְקַת)   A variant form of Barkait. See Barkait.

Barra   A variant spelling of Bara. See Bara.

Barrie   Used primarily as a masculine name. See Barrie (masculine section).

Basha (בַּאשָׁא)   A Yiddish form of Basya (Batya) and Bas-Sheva (Bat-Sheva). See Batya *and* Bat-Sheva. Bashe is a variant form.

Bashe (בַּאשֶׁע)   A variant form of Basha. See Basha. Peshe and Pessel are Yiddish forms.

Basilia, Basilie   Feminine forms of Basil. See Basil (masculine section).

Basma   A variant spelling of Bosma. See Bosma.

Basmat   A variant spelling of Bosmat. See Bosmat.

Bas-Sheva   The Ashkenazi pronunciation of Bat-Sheva. See Bat-Sheva.

Basya   The Ashkenazic form of Batya. See Batya.

Bat (בַּת)   From the Hebrew, meaning "daughter." Beth is an Anglicized form.

Bat-Ami (בַּת־עַמִּי)   From the Hebrew, meaning "daughter of my people."

Bat-Chen (בַּת־חֵן)   From the Hebrew, meaning "daughter of grace" or "charming girl."

Bat-El (בַּת־אָל)   From the Hebrew, meaning "daughter of God."

Batela (בַּתְאָלָה)   A variant form of Bat-El. See Bat-El.

Bat-Eli (בַּת־אֵלִי)   From the Hebrew, meaning "daughter of my God."

Bat-Galim (בַּת־גַּלִּים)   From the Hebrew, meaning "daughter of high places (hills)" or "daughter of the waves." In the Bible (Isaiah 10:30), a place north of Jerusalem.

Bathsheba (בַּת־שֶׁבַע)   From the Hebrew, meaning "daughter of an oath." In the Bible (II Samuel 11:27), Bathsheba was the wife of King David. In order to marry her, David arranged the death of her husband, Uriah the Hittite, by sending him off to the battlefront. The Prophet Nathan rebuked David severely for this offense. Solomon, who later became king, was the second son of David and Bathsheba. Bat-Sheva is the original Hebrew spelling.

Bathshua   A variant spelling of Bat-Shua. See Bat-Shua.

Bat-Shachar (בַּת־שַׁחַר)   From the Hebrew, meaning "daughter of the dawn."

Bat-Shem (בַּת־שֵׁם)   From the Hebrew, meaning "daughter of the Name (God)" or "reputable person."

Bat-Sheva (בַּת־שֶׁבַע)   From the Hebrew, meaning "daughter of an oath." In the Bible (II Samuel 11:3), the daughter of Eliam and wife of Uriah the Hittite. Popularly spelled Bathsheba. See Bathsheba. Bas-Sheva is the Ashkenazi form. Basha and Bashe are Yiddish forms.

Bat-Shir (בַּת־שִׁיר)   From the Hebrew, meaning "songbird."

Bat-Shua (בַּת־שׁוּעַ)   A biblical name generally taken as a variant spelling of Bat-Sheva (Bathsheba). Also, from the Hebrew, meaning "daughter of opulence" or "daughter of disaster." In the Bible (I Chronicles 35), Bat-Shua (Bathshua) is referred to as the wife of King David and the mother of King Solomon. It is, therefore, probable that Bathshua is a variant spelling of Bathsheba.

Bat-Tziyon (בַּת־צִיּוֹן)   From the Hebrew, meaning "daughter of Zion" or "daughter of excellence."

Batya (בַּתְיָה)   From the Hebrew, meaning "daughter of God." Basya is a variant pronunciation. Basha is a Yiddish form.

Bat-Yam (בַּת־יָם)   From the Hebrew, meaning "daughter of the sea."

Batzra (בָּצְרָה)   From the Hebrew, meaning "enclosure" or "fortress."

Bava (בָּבָא)   From the Aramaic and Arabic, meaning "gate." Some authorities associate the name with the prattling sound made by infants. Baba is a variant form. Also spelled בָּבָה.

Bayla (בֵּיילָא)   A Yiddish form of Bela. See Bela. Also spelled בֵּיילְא.

Bayle   A variant spelling of Bayla. See Bayla. Also spelled Baile. See Baile.

Bea, Beah   Pet forms of Beatrice. See Beatrice.

Beata   From the Latin, meaning "blessed." Derived from the expression *Beata Virgo Maria*, meaning "Blessed Virgin Mary."

Beate   A short form of Beatrice. See Beatrice.

Beatrice   From the Latin, meaning "one who brings happiness and blessing." Beatrix is the original Latin form. Beate is a short form. Bea and Trixie are pet forms.

Beatrix   The original form of Beatrice. *See* TBeatrice.

Bechira (בְּחִירָה)   From the Hebrew, meaning "chosen one."

Bechora (בְּכוֹרָה)   From the Hebrew, meaning "eldest daughter."

Bechura (בְּכוּרָה)   From the Hebrew, meaning "chosen one."

Beckie, Becky   Pet forms of Rebecca. *See* Rebecca.

Behira (בְּהִירָה)   From the Hebrew, meaning "light, clear, brilliant."

Bela   Either a form of Isabella, meaning "God's oath," or from the Hungarian, meaning "nobly bright." Also, from the Latin, meaning "beautiful one." Belle is a French form. Baile is a Yiddish form. Used also as a masculine name. *See* Bela (masculine section).

Belinda   An Old Germanic name derived from the Latin, meaning "beautiful serpent," having the connotation of wise, shrewd. Snakes were once regarded as sacred animals.

Bell   A pet form of Isabel used originally in the thirteenth century. *See* Isabel.

Bella   A short form of Isabella. *See* Isabella.

Belle   A variant form of Bella. *See* Bella.

Belva   From the Latin, meaning "beautiful view."

Belynda   A variant spelling of Belinda. *See* Belinda.

Bena   A variant spelling of Bina. *See* Bina.

Benedicta   A feminine form of Benedict, meaning "blessed" in the Latin. Dixie is a pet form. Benedictine, Benet, Benita, Bennet, Bennitt, and Benoite are variant forms.

Benedictine   A German form of Benedicta. *See* Benedicta.

Benet   A short form of Benedicta. *See* Benedicta.

Benita   A Spanish form of Benedicta. *See* Benedicta.

Benjamina (בְּנְיָמִינָה)   A feminine form of Benjamin. *See* Benjamin (masculine section). Binyamina is the exact Hebrew form.

Bennet   A variant form of Benedicta. *See* Benedicta.

Bennitt   A variant form of Benedicta. *See* Benedicta.

Benoite   The French form of Benedicta. *See* Benedicta.

B'era (בְּאֵרָה)   From the Hebrew, meaning "well." B'erit is a variant form.

Beracha (בְּרָכָה)   From the Hebrew, meaning "blessing" or "valley."

Berenice   From the Greek, meaning "bringer of victory." Bernita and Bunny are pet forms. Bernice and Berniece are variant forms.

B'erit (בְּאֵרִית)   From the Hebrew, meaning "well." A variant form of B'era.

Bernadette From the French and German, meaning "bold as a bear." Bernard is the masculine form. Bernadot, Bernadotte, Berneta, Bernetta, and Bernette are variant forms. Bernadina and Bernadine are pet forms.

Bernadina A pet form of Bernadette. See Bernadette.

Bernadine A pet form of Bernadette. See Bernadette.

Bernadot A Swedish and Norwegian form of Bernadette. See Bernadette.

Bernadotte A variant form of Bernadot. See Bernadot.

Berneta, Bernetta Variant forms of Bernadette. See Bernadette.

Bernette A variant form of Bernadette. See Bernadette.

Bernice A variant form of Berenice. See Berenice.

Berniece A variant form of Berenice. See Berenice.

Bernine A pet form of Bernice and Bernadette. See Bernice *and* Bernadette.

Bernita A pet form of Berenice. See Berenice.

Beronica (בֶּרוֹנִיקָה) A variant form of Berenice. See Berenice. The sister of Aggripa, king of Judah, in Second Temple times.

Berosa (בְּרוֹשָׁה) From the Hebrew, meaning "cedar tree."

Berta A variant spelling of Bertha. See Bertha.

Bertha From the Anglo-Saxon, meaning "bright" or "beautiful" or "famous." Berta is a variant spelling.

Berucha (בְּרוּכָה) From the Hebrew, meaning "blessed." Baruch is the masculine form.

Beruchiya (בְּרוּכִיָה) A variant form of Beruchya. See Beruchya.

Beruchya (בְּרוּכְיָה) From the Hebrew, meaning "blessed of the Lord." Beruchiya is a variant form.

Berura (בְּרוּרָה) From the Hebrew, meaning "pure, clean." Also, from the Aramaic, meaning "pious, kind, honest."

Berurit (בְּרוּרִית) A variant form of Berura. See Berura.

Beruriya (בְּרוּרִיָה) A variant form of Berura. See Berura.

Berurya (בְּרוּרְיָה) A variant form of Berura. See Berura. The wife of the noted second-century talmudic scholar Rabbi Meir, and a scholar in her own right (Pesachim 62b).

Beryl From the Greek and the Sanskrit, meaning "precious stone." Also, from the Persian and Arabic, meaning "crystal, crystal clear." Berylla is a variant form.

Berylla A variant form of Beryl. See Beryl.

Besora (בְּשׂוֹרָה) From the Hebrew, meaning "greeting." Akin to Besura.

Bess A popular pet form of Elizabeth. See Elizabeth.

Bessie A pet form of Elizabeth. See Elizabeth.

Besura (בְּשׂוּרָה) From the Hebrew, meaning "tidings" or "greetings." Akin to Besora.

Bet (בַּת) From the Hebrew, meaning "daughter." A variant form of Bat. Beth is a variant spelling.

Beta A Greek form of the Hebrew *bet*, meaning "house." The second letter of the Greek alphabet.

Beth (בַּת) A short form of Elizabeth. *See* Elizabeth. Bet is a variant spelling.

Bethany A Greek and Latin form of the Hebrew *bet t'eina*, meaning "house of figs." In the Bible, a town near Jerusalem.

Bethel, Beth-El (בֵּית־אֵל) From the Hebrew, meaning "house of God." In the Bible, a town near Jerusalem.

Bethuel A variant spelling of Betuel. *See* Betuel.

Bethula, Bethulah Variant spellings of Betula. *See* Betula.

Betsey, Betsy Pet forms of Elizabeth. *See* Elizabeth.

Bette A pet form of Elizabeth. *See* Elizabeth.

Bettina A pet form of Elizabeth. *See* Elizabeth.

Betty, Bettye Pet forms of Elizabeth. *See* Elizabeth.

Bettylou A hybrid name of Betty and Louise. *See* Betty *and* Louise.

Betuel (בְּתוּאֵל) From the Hebrew, meaning "daughter of God." Bethuel is a variant spelling.

Betula, Betulah (בְּתוּלָה) From the Hebrew, meaning "maiden, girl."

Beula, Beulah (בְּעוּלָה) From the Hebrew, meaning "married" or "possessed." In the Bible, allegorical reference to the Land of Israel. In Bunyon's *Pilgrim's Progress*, a peaceful country near the end of man's journey.

Bever-Leigh A variant spelling of Beverley. *See* Beverley.

Beverley, Beverly From the Old English, meaning "beaver's meadow." Used also as a masculine name.

Beylah A variant spelling of Baila. *See* Baila.

Bianca The Italian form of the Spanish *blanc*, meaning "white."

Bibi From the French, meaning "bauble, toy." Akin to Bubbles.

Biddie, Biddy Variant forms of Bridget. *See* Bridget.

Bika (בִּקְעָה) From the Hebrew, meaning "valley."

Bikura (בִּכּוּרָה) From the Hebrew, meaning "ripe," usually referring to a fig. A variant form of Bakura.

Bilha, Bilhah (בִּלְהָה) From the Hebrew, meaning "weak, troubled, old." In the Bible (Genesis 30:3), the maidservant of Jacob's wife, Rachel, and the mother of Dan and Naftali. Baile is a Yiddish form.

Billie   A feminine pet form of William. *See* William (masculine section).

Bina (בִּינָה)   From the Hebrew, meaning "understanding, intelligence, wisdom." Bena is a variant spelling. Akin to Buna.

Binnie   From the Celtic and Anglo-Saxon, meaning "bin, receptacle." Bin is a masculine form.

Binyamina (בִּנְיָמִינָה)   A feminine form of Binyamin (Benjamin). *See* Binyamin (masculine section). Benjamina is a variant form.

Bira (בִּירָה)   From the Hebrew, meaning "fortress" or "capital." Biranit and Biriya are variant forms.

Biranit (בִּירָנִית)   A variant form of Bira. *See* Bira.

Bird, Birdie   From the English, meaning "bird." Sometimes used as a pet form of Bertha. Byrd and Byrdie are variant spellings.

Birgit, Birgitta   Variant forms of Bridget. *See* Bridget.

Biria   A variant spelling of Biriya. *See* Biriya.

Biriya (בִּירִיָה)   A variant form of Bira. *See* Bira.

Bitaniya (בִּיתָנְיָה)   From the Hebrew, meaning "pavilion."

Bitcha (בִּטְחָה)   From the Hebrew, meaning "hope, confidence."

Bithia   A variant spelling of Bitya. *See* Bitya.

Bitia   A variant spelling of Bitya. *See* Bitya.

Bitya, Bityah (בִּתְיָה)   From the Hebrew, meaning "daughter of God." In the Bible (I Chronicles 4:18), a daughter of Pharaoh who married Mered, a member of the tribe of Judah. Bitia and Bithia are variant spellings.

Blair, Blaire   From the Gaelic, meaning "field" or "battle." Used also as masculine names.

Blanca   The Spanish form of the Old French *blanc*, meaning "white." In Old English *blanca* means "white steed," and in Late Latin, "pure, unstained." Blanch and Blanche are popular variant forms.

Blanch, Blanche   Variant forms of Blanca. *See* Blanca.

Blandina   A pet form of Blanche. *See* Blanche.

Blaze   From the Old English, meaning "flame" or "a mark made on a tree (to mark a trail in a forest)." Also, from the Middle English, meaning "to blow (a trumpet)," hence "to announce, proclaim."

Blenda   A short form of Belinda. *See* Belinda. Or, from the Old English and the Old Norse, meaning "to mix, blend."

Bliss   From the Anglo-Saxon, meaning "perfect joy."

Blossom   From the Old English, meaning "blooming flower."

Bluma (בְּלוּמָא)   From the German, meaning "flower." A popular Yiddish name. Blume is a variant form.

Blume (בְּלוּמֶע)   A variant form of Bluma. *See* Bluma.

Blythe   From the Anglo-Saxon, meaning "happy."

Bob   A pet form of Barbara and Roberta. *See* Barbara *and* Roberta.

Bobbe   A pet form of Barbara and Roberta. *See* Barbara *and* Roberta.

Bona (בּוֹנָה)   From the Hebrew, meaning "builder."

Bonita   A Spanish form of Bonnie. *See* Bonnie.

Bonna   A variant spelling of Bona. *See* Bona.

Bonnie, Bonny   From the Latin and the French, meaning "good" or "pretty."

Bosemet (בּוֹשְׂמֶת)   From the Hebrew, meaning "spiced, perfumed." Also spelled בּוֹסְמָת.

Bosma (בָּשְׂמָה)   From the Hebrew, meaning "perfume, perfumed." Basma is a variant spelling.

Bosmat (בָּשְׂמַת)   From the Aramaic, meaning "perfumed; sweet odor." In the Bible, a wife of Esau (Genesis 26:34) and a daughter of King Solomon (I Kings 4:15). Basmat is a variant spelling.

Bracha (בְּרָכָה)   From the Hebrew, meaning "blessing." Beracha and Brocha are variant spellings.

Bree   From the Middle English, meaning "broth, watery soup." Breyette is a pet form.

Breindel (בְּרײַנְדֹל)   A Yiddish form of the German *braune*, meaning "brown," or from Brunhild, meaning "fighter in armor." Also spelled בְּרײַנְצֶל.

Brenda   From the Celtic, meaning "dark-haired."

Brenna   Probably a variant form of Brenda. *See* Brenda.

Breyette   A pet form of Bree. *See* Bree.

Brian   From the Celtic or Gaelic, meaning "strength" or "nobly-born" or "one who is eloquent." Used also as a masculine name. Briny is a pet form.

Briane, Brianne   Variant forms of Brian. *See* Brian.

Brick   A variant form of the masculine Brice. *See* Brice (masculine section).

Bridget   From the Celtic, meaning "strong" or "lofty." Bridgit, Bridgitte, Briget, Brigid, Brigit, and Bridgitte are variants.

Bridgit, Bridgitte   Variant forms of Bridget. *See* Bridget.

Briget   A variant spelling of Bridget. *See* Bridget.

Brigid   A variant form of Bridget. *See* Bridget.

Brigit, Brigitte   Variant spellings of Bridget. *See* Bridget.

Brilliant   From the French and Italian, meaning "sparkle, whirl."

Brina (בְּרײַנָא)   From the Yiddish, meaning "brown." Also, from the Slavic, meaning "protector."

Brine (בְּרײַנֶע)   From the Yiddish, meaning "brown." Akin to Brune.

Briny   A pet form of Brian. *See* Brian.

Brit, Brita   Pet forms of Bridget. *See* Bridget.

Brocha   A variant spelling of Bracha. *See* Bracha.

Brook, Brooke   From the Old English and the Middle English, meaning "to break out," as a stream of water. May also be forms of Brock. *See* Brock (masculine section).

Brown   From the Middle English and German, meaning "brown-colored."

Brune (ברונע)   From the Yiddish, meaning "brown," or from the German name Brunhild, meaning "fighter in armor." *See also* Brina *and* Brine.

Brunhild, Brunhilda   From the Old High German, meaning "fighter in armor, warrior."

Brunhilde, Brunnhilde   Variant spellings of Brunhild. *See* Brunhild.

Bryn   Variant forms of Brian. *See* Brian.

Bryna (בְּרײַנֶע)   Variant form of Brune. *See* Brune. Akin to Brina.

Brynhild, Brynhilda, Brynhilde   Variants of Brunhild. *See* Brunhild.

Buba (בֻּבָּה)   From the Hebrew, meaning "doll."

Bubati (בֻּבָּתִי)   From the Hebrew, meaning "my doll."

Bubbles   From the Middle Dutch, meaning "thin spherical film of liquid." Or, from the Old French, meaning "toy, bauble."

Buna (בּוּנָה)   From the Hebrew, meaning "understanding, intelligence." In the Bible (I Chronicles 2:25), a member of the tribe of Judah. Akin to Bina. Used also as a masculine name.

Bunie   A variant form of Buna. *See* Buna.

Bunny   A nickname for Roberta or Barbara. *See* Roberta *and* Barbara.

Byrd   A variant spelling of Bird. *See* Bird.

Byrdie   A variant spelling of Birdie. *See* Birdie.

Caasi   A pet form of Catherine. *See* Catherine.

Cacilia   A variant spelling of Cecilia. *See* Cecilia.

Cadette   A pet form of the French name Cadice. *See* Cadice.

Cadice   From the French, meaning "chief." Cadette is a pet form.

Caesarina, Caesrina   Variant feminine forms of the Latin Caesar, hence these names mean "queen."

Caitlin   A variant Welsh form of Catherine. *See* Catherine.

Calandra   From the Greek, meaning "park."

Calista   From the Greek, meaning "most beautiful."

Cameo   The Italian form of the Latin, meaning "a carving." A two-layered gem with a figure carved into one layer.

Camilla, Camille   From the Latin, meaning "servant or helper (at a sacrifice)" or "virgin of unblemished character."

Candace   From the Greek, meaning "fire-white" or "incandescent." Or, from the Latin, meaning "pure, unsullied." Candice and Candyce are variant spellings. Candy is a pet form. Candance, Candida, and Candide are variant forms.

Candance   A variant form of Candace. *See* Candace.

Candice   A variant spelling of Candace. *See* Candace.

Candida, Candide   Variant forms of Candace. *See* Candace.

Candy   A pet form of Candace. *See* Candace. Kandi is a variant spelling.

Candyce   A variant spelling of Candace. *See* Candace.

Cara   A pet form of Charlotte and Caroline. *See* Charlotte *and* Caroline.

Caren   A pet form of Catherine. *See* Catherine. Carin, Caron, Karen, and Karin are variant spellings.

Carey   A pet form of Caroline. *See* Caroline. A variant spelling of Carrie. Used also as a masculine name.

Carin   A variant spelling of Caren. *See* Caren.

Carina   From the Latin, meaning "keel." One of the five stars in the constellation Orion, each of which bears the name of a part of a ship. Also, a pet form of Catherine. Karina is a variant spelling.

Carita   From the Latin, meaning "charity." Karita is a variant spelling.

Carla, Carlana   Feminine forms of Carl or Charles. Also, pet forms of Caroline. *See* Caroline. Karla is a variant spelling. Arla is a short form.

Carleen   A pet form of Caroline. *See* Caroline.

Carlen, Carlene   Pet forms of Caroline. *See* Caroline.

Carley   A pet form of Caroline. *See* Caroline. Carly is a variant spelling.

Carlia   A pet form of Caroline. *See* Caroline.

Carlin   A variant form of Caroline. *See* Caroline.

Carlita   An Italian pet form of Caroline. *See* Caroline.

Carlotta   The Italian form of Charlotte. *See* Charlotte.

Carly   A variant spelling of Carley. *See* Carley.

Carma (כַּרְמָה)   From the Aramaic, meaning "vineyard" or "park." Also, from the Arabic, meaning "field of fruit." Karma is a variant spelling. *See also* Carmel.

Carmaniya (בַּרְמָנִיָה) A variant form of Carma. *See* Carma.

Carmel (כַּרְמֶל) From the Hebrew, meaning "vineyard." Akin to Kerem. Used also as a masculine name. Karmel and Karmela are variant spellings. Carmania, Carmela, Carmelit, Carmen, Carmia, and Carmit are variant forms.

Carmela (כַּרְמֶלָה) A variant form of Carmel. *See* Carmel.

Carmeli (כַּרְמֶלִי) From the Hebrew, meaning "the Carmelite." Karmeli is a variant spelling. Akin to Carmel.

Carmelit (כַּרְמֶלִית) From the Hebrew, meaning "lawn, a grassy semi-public area." Karmelit is a variant spelling.

Carmen The Spanish form of Carmel. *See* Carmel. Carmine is a variant form.

Carmia A variant spelling of Carmiya. *See* Carmiya.

Carmiela (כַּרְמִיאֵלָה) A variant form of Carmia. *See* Carmia.

Carmine The Italian form of Carmen. *See* Carmen.

Carmit (כַּרְמִית) A variant Hebrew form of Carmel. *See* Carmel. Karmit is a variant spelling.

Carmiya (כַּרְמִיָה) From the Hebrew, meaning "vineyard of the Lord." Carmiela is a variant form. Carmia, Karmia, and Karmiya are variant spellings.

Carna (קַרְנָא) From the Aramaic, meaning "horn (of an animal)," symbolizing "strength." Karna is a variant spelling. Carni, Carnia, Carniela and Carnit are variant forms.

Carni (קַרְנִי) A variant form of Carna. From the Hebrew, meaning "my horn." Karni is a variant spelling.

Carnia (קַרְנִיָה) A variant form of Carna. From the Hebrew, meaning "horn of God." Karnia is a variant spelling.

Carniela, Carniella (קַרְנִיאֵלָה) A variant form of Carnia. From the Hebrew, meaning "horn of the Lord." Karniela and Karniella are variant spellings.

Carnit (קַרְנִית) A variant form of Carna. From the Hebrew, meaning "horn." *See* Carna. Karnit is a variant spelling.

Caro A pet form of Caroline. *See* Caroline.

Carol Either from the Gaelic, meaning "melody, song," or a pet form of Caroline. *See* Caroline. Carole, Carroll, Caryl, Karol, Karole, and Karyl are variant spellings. Carola is a variant form.

Carola A variant form of Carol. *See* Carol.

Carole A variant spelling of Carol. *See* Carol.

Caroleen A variant form of Caroline. *See* Caroline.

Carolina An Italian form of Caroline. *See* Caroline. Lina is a pet form.

Caroline From the French, meaning "strong, virile." Akin to the masculine Charles. Carolyn is a variant spelling. Carlin, Caroleen, and Carolina are variant forms. Cara, Carla, Carlana, Carleen, Carlen, Carlene, Carley, Carlia,

Carlita, Caro, Carol, Carrie, Carry, and Cary are pet forms. Karolyn is a variant spelling.

Carolyn   A variant spelling of Caroline. *See* Caroline.

Caron   A variant spelling of Caren. *See* Caren. Carona is a variant form.

Carona   A variant form of Caron. *See* Caron.

Carrie   A pet form of Caroline. *See* Caroline. Karri is a variant spelling.

Carroll   A variant spelling of Carol. *See* Carol. Used also as a masculine name.

Carry, Cary   Pet forms of Caroline. *See* Caroline.

Caryl   A variant spelling of Carol. *See* Carol.

Cashia   A variant form of Cassia. *See* Cassia.

Cass   A pet form of Cassandra. *See* Cassandra.

Cassandra   From the Greek, referring to "one whose warnings are ignored." Cass and Cassie are pet forms.

Cassia   From the Greek, meaning "a type of cinnamon." Cashia is a variant form.

Cassie   A pet form of Cassandra and Catherine. *See* Cassandra *and* Catherine. Casy is a variant spelling.

Casy   A variant spelling of Cassie. *See* Cassie.

Cathee   A variant spelling of Cathy. *See* Cathy.

Catherina   A variant form of Catherine. *See* Catherine.

Catherine   From the Greek, meaning "pure, unsullied." Cathleen is a variant form. Cathryn and Katherine are variant spellings. Caitlin, Cathleen, and Cathlin are variant forms. Caasi, Caren, Carina, Cassie, Casy, Cathy, and Cattie are pet forms. *See* Katherine.

Cathleen   A variant form of Catherine. *See* Catherine. Kathleen is a variant spelling.

Cathlin   An Irish form of Catherine. *See* Cathleen.

Cathryn   A variant spelling of Catherine. *See* Catherine.

Cathy   A pet form of Catherine and Cathleen. *See* Catherine *and* Cathleen. Cathee is a variant spelling.

Cattie   A pet form of Catherine. *See* Catherine.

Cecelia   From the Latin, meaning "blind" or "dim-sighted." The original form is Cecil, used primarily as a masculine name. In ancient Rome there was a famous family named Caecilii, whose founder was said to have been blind. Cacilia is a variant spelling. Cecely, Cecil, Cecile, Cecille, Cecily, Celia, Cicely, Cicily, Sheila, and Sheilah are variant forms. Cis, Ciss, Cissy, Ceil, and Cele are pet forms.

Cecely   A variant form of Cecelia. *See* Cecelia.

Cecil   A variant form of Cecilia. *See* Cecilia. Cecile and Cecille are variant spellings.

Cecile, Cecille Variant spellings of Cecil. *See* Cecil. Also variant forms of Cecelia. *See* Cecelia.

Cecily A variant form of Cecilia. *See* Cecilia.

Ceil A pet form of Cecelia. *See* Cecelia. Cele is a variant spelling.

Cele A variant spelling of Ceil. *See* Ceil.

Celeste From the Latin, meaning "heavenly." Celina is a variant form.

Celia A variant form of Cecilia. *See* Cecilia. Also, from the Latin, meaning "heavenly." Kayla and Kayle are variant forms.

Celina A variant form of Celeste. *See* Celeste. Salina is a variant spelling.

Celosia From the Greek, meaning "flame."

Cerena A variant spelling of Serena. *See* Serena.

Chachila (חֲכִילָה) From the Hebrew, meaning "dark" or "dull."

Chadasha (חֲדָשָׁה) From the Hebrew, meaning "new." Hadasha is a variant spelling. Akin to Chadusha.

Chadusha (חֲדוּשָׁה) From the Hebrew, meaning "ne w, renewed." Hadusha is a variant spelling. Akin to Chadasha.

Chafshia A variant spelling of Chafshiya. *See* Chafshiya.

Chafshiya (חָפְשִׁיָה) From the Hebrew, meaning "free." Chafshia and Hafshia are variant spellings.

Chagiga (חֲגִיגָה) From the Hebrew, meaning "holiday, celebration." Hagiga is a variant spelling.

Chagit (חַגִּית) From the Aramaic, meaning "feast, festival, festive celebration" or "born at a feast." In the Bible (II Samuel 3:4), one of King David's wives. Hagit is a variant spelling.

Chagiya (חַגִּיָה) From the Hebrew, meaning "God's festival." Hagiya and Hagia are variant spellings. Used as a masculine name in the Bible (I Chronicles 6:15).

Chaifa A variant spelling of Cheifa. *See* Cheifa. Haifa is a variant spelling.

Chali-La (חֲלִי־לָה) From the Hebrew, meaning "pray for her." Also spelled חֲלִילָה.

Chalutza (חֲלוּצָה) From the Hebrew, meaning "pioneer." Halutza is a variant spelling. Chalutz and Halutz are masculine forms.

Chamama (חַמְמָא) From the Aramaic, meaning "heat, warmth." Hamama is a variant spelling.

Chamania A variant spelling of Chamaniya. *See* Chamaniya.

Chamaniya (חֲמָנִיָה) From the Hebrew, meaning "sun" or "sunflower." Chamania and Hamania are variant spellings.

Chamital (חֲמִיטַל) From the Hebrew, meaning "den." In the Bible (II Kings 23:31), the wife of King Josiah and the mother of Zedekiah. Hamital is a variant spelling. Chamutal is a variant form.

Chamuda (חֲמוּדָה) From the Hebrew, meaning "desired, desirable, cute, precious." Hamuda is a variant spelling.

Chamutal (חֲמוּטַל) A variant form of Chamital. See Chamital. Hamutal is a variant spelling.

Chana, Chanah (חַנָּה) From the Hebrew, meaning "grace, gracious, merciful." In the Bible (I Samuel 1:2), the mother of the Prophet Samuel; the wife of Elkanah. Hana, Hanna, and Hannah are variant spellings. Ann and Anna are variant forms (the New Testament records Hana as Anna). Chani is a pet form. Heneh is a Yiddish form.

Chandelle From the French, meaning "candle."

Chandra From the Sanskrit, meaning "illustrious" or "eminent."

Chani A pet form of Chana. See Chana.

Chania A variant spelling of Chaniya. See Chaniya. Hania is a variant spelling.

Chanina (חֲנִינָא) From the Hebrew, meaning "gracious." Hanina is a variant spelling. Used also as a masculine name.

Chanit (חֲנִית) From the Hebrew, meaning "spear." Hanit is a variant spelling.

Chanita (חֲנִיתָה) From the Aramaic, meaning "spear." Hanita is a variant spelling.

Chaniya (חֲנִיָּה) From the Hebrew, meaning "resting place, encampment." Chania, Hania, and Haniya are variant spellings.

Chanuka (חֲנוּכָּה) From the Hebrew, meaning "dedicated, consecrated" or "trained, educated." Hanuka is a variant spelling. Used occasionally as a masculine name.

Chanuna (חֲנוּנָה) From the Aramaic, meaning "gracious." Hanuna is a variant spelling.

Chanya (חַנְיָה) From the Hebrew, meaning "grace of the Lord." Hanya is a variant spelling.

Char Probably a pet form of Charlotte and Charlene. See Charlotte and Charlene.

Charis From the Greek, meaning "grace, beauty, kindness." Charissa and Charito are variant forms.

Charissa A variant form of Charis. See Charis.

Charito An Italian form of Charis. See Charis.

Charity From the Latin, meaning "love, affection."

Charitza (חֲרִיצָה) From the Hebrew, meaning "slice, chunk." Also, a variant form of Charutza. See Charutza. Haritza is a variant spelling.

Charla A feminine form of Charles. See Charles (masculine section). Akin to Carla.

Charlayne   A variant form of Charlene. *See* Charlene.

Charleen   A variant spelling of Charlene. *See* Charlene.

Charlen   A variant form of Charlene. *See* Charlene.

Charlena   A variant form of Charlene. *See* Charlene.

Charlene   A variant form of Caroline, meaning "strong, valiant." Charleen and Sharleen are variant spellings. Charlayne, Charlen, Charlena, and Charlene are variant forms. Char is a pet form.

Charlet   A variant form of Charlotte. *See* Charlotte.

Charlot   A variant spelling of Charlotte. *See* Charlotte.

Charlotta   The Italian form of Charlotte. *See* Charlotte.

Charlotte   The feminine form of Charles, meaning "strong." *See* Charles (masculine section). Charlot is a variant spelling. Carlotta, Charlet, Charlotta, and Charo are variant forms. Cara, Char, Lotta, Lote, Lottie, and Tottie are pet forms.

Charmain, Charmaine   From the Latin, meaning "to sing."

Charmian   From the Greek, meaning "a bit of joy."

Charo   A variant form of Charlotte. *See* Charlotte.

Chartzit (חַרְצִית)   From the Hebrew, meaning "chrysanthemum." Hartzit and Harzit are variant spellings.

Charutza (חֲרוּצָה)   From the Hebrew, meaning "industrious, energetic," or from a second root, meaning "gold." Charitza is a variant form. Harutza is a variant spelling.

Chashmona (חַשְׁמוֹנָה)   From the Hebrew, meaning "princess" or "ambassador." Chashmonit is a variant form.

Chashmonit (חַשְׁמוֹנִית)   A variant form of Chashmona. *See* Chashmona.

Chashuva (חֲשׁוּבָה)   From the Hebrew, meaning "distinguished, important person."

Chasia   A variant spelling of Chasya. *See* Chasya.

Chasida (חֲסִידָה)   From the Hebrew, meaning "stork" and also "righteous." Hasida is a variant spelling.

Chasina (חֲסִינָה)   From the Aramaic, meaning "strong, powerful." Hasina is a variant spelling.

Chasna (חַסְנָא)   From the Aramaic, meaning "strong, powerful." Hasna is a variant spelling.

Chasuda (חֲסוּדָה)   from the Hebrew, meaning "gracious" or "pious." Hasuda is a variant spelling.

Chasya (חַסְיָה)   From the Hebrew, meaning "protected by God." Chasia, Hasia, and Hasya are variant spellings.

Chava (חַוָּה)   From the Hebrew, meaning "life." In the Bible (Genesis 2:23), the first woman, the wife of Adam. Hava is a variant spelling. Eve is an Anglicized form.

Chavatzelet (חֲבַצֶּלֶת)   From the Hebrew, meaning "lily," and from the Akkadian, meaning "meadow saffron" or "crocus." *See also* Sharon.

Chavatzelet-Hasharon (חֲבַצֶּלֶת־הַשָּׁרוֹן)   The name of a flower that grows in the Sharon Plain, the coastal plain between Mount Carmel and Jaffa. *See* Chavatzelet.

Chavatzinya (חֲבַצִּנְיָה)   A biblical masculine name used also for females. *See* Chavatzinya (masculine section).

Chaviva (חֲבִיבָה)   From the Hebrew, meaning "beloved." Haviva is a variant spelling.

Chavuka (חֲבוּקָה)   From the Hebrew, meaning "beloved." Havuka is a variant spelling.

Chavuva (חֲבוּבָה)   From the Hebrew, meaning "beloved." Havuva is a variant spelling.

Chaya (חַיָּה)   From the Hebrew, meaning "alive, living." Haya is a variant spelling.

Chayei-Sara (חַיֵּי־שָׂרָה)   From the Hebrew, meaning "life of Sarah" or "story of Sarah." The name of a section in the Book of Genesis (23-25).

Chayuta (חַיּוּתָה)   From the Aramaic, meaning "livelihood" or "life." Chiyuta is a variant form. Hayuta is a variant spelling.

Chazona (חֲזוֹנָה)   From the Hebrew, meaning "visionary, prophetess."

Chedva (חֶדְוָה)   From the Hebrew, meaning "joy." Hedva is a variant spelling.

Cheftzi (חֶפְצִי)   From the Hebrew, meaning "my desire."

Cheftzi-Ba (חֶפְצִי־בָּהּ)   From the Hebrew, meaning "she is my desire." In the Bible (II Kings 21:1), the mother of King Manasseh, the wife of King Hezekiah. Also (Isaiah 62:4), a nickname for Zion. Cheftzibah, Hephziba, and Hepziba are variant spellings.

Cheftziya (חֶפְצִיָּה)   From the Hebrew, meaning "God is my desire."

Cheifa (חֵיפָה)   From the Hebrew, meaning "harbor." Haifa, Heifa, and Chaifa are variant spellings.

Chel'a (חֶלְאָה)   From the Hebrew, meaning "depraved." In the Bible (I Chronicles 4:5), the wife of Ashchur, a descendant of Judah. Hela and Helah are variant spellings.

Chelkat (חֶלְקַת)   From the Hebrew, meaning "portion" or "place."

Chelly   A variant form of Shelley. *See* Shelley.

Chelmit (חֶלְמִית)   A variant form of Chelmonit. *See* Chelmonit. Helmit is a variant spelling.

Chelmonit (חֶלְמוֹנִית)   From the Hebrew. A flower of the *Narcissus* genus. Chelmit is a variant form.

Chemda (חֶמְדָּה) From the Hebrew, meaning "desire, charm" or "precious." Hemda is a variant spelling.

Chemdia, Chemdiah Variant spellings of Chemdiya. *See* Chemdiya.

Chemdiya (חֶמְדִּיָה) From the Hebrew, meaning "God is my desire." Chemdia, Chemdiah, Hemdia, and Hemdiah are variant spellings.

Chen (חֵן) From the Hebrew, meaning "grace." Hen is a variant spelling.

Chenetta From the Greek, meaning "goose," or from the French, meaning "oak tree."

Chenia A variant spelling of Chenya. *See* Chenya.

Chenya (חֶנְיָה) From the Hebrew, meaning "grace of the Lord." Chenia, Henia, and Henya are variant spellings.

Cher, Chere Pet forms of Cheryl. *See* Cheryl. Sher is a variant spelling.

Cheri, Cherie French pet forms of Cheryl. *See* Cheryl.

Cherilee, Cheri-Lee A hybrid of Cheri and Lee. *See* Cheri and Lee.

Cherlene A variant form of Charlene. *See* Charlene.

Chermona (חֶרְמוֹנָה) From the Hebrew, meaning "sacred mountain." Hermona is a variant spelling.

Cherri, Cherrie Pet forms of Cheryl. *See* Cheryl.

Cherry A pet form of Cheryl. *See* Cheryl.

Cherut (חֵרוּת) From the Hebrew, meaning "freedom." Herut is a variant spelling.

Cheruta (חֵרוּתָה) A variant form of Cherut. *See* Cherut. Heruta is a variant spelling.

Cheryl, Cheryle From the French, meaning "dear, beloved." Sheryl is a variant spelling. Cher, Chere, Cheri, Cherie, Cherri, Cherrie, Cherry, and Cherylie are pet forms.

Cherylie A pet form of Cheryl. *See* Cheryl.

Chesna From the Slavic, meaning "peaceful." Chessy is a pet form.

Chessy A pet form of Chesna. *See* Chesna.

Chetzrona (חֶצְרוֹנָה) From the Hebrew, meaning "groundskeeper." Hetzrona is a variant spelling.

Chiba (חִבָּה) From the Hebrew, meaning "love." Hiba is a variant spelling.

Chibat-Tziyon (חִבַּת־צִיּוֹן) From the Hebrew, meaning "love of Zion."

Chila (חִילָה) From the Hebrew, meaning "pain, anguish" or "army, warriors." Hila is a variant spelling.

China (חִנָּה) From the Aramaic, meaning "grace." Hina is a variant spelling.

Chinanit (חֲנָנִית) From the Hebrew, meaning "spear." Hinanit is a variant spelling.

Chinit (חֲנִית)   From the Hebrew, meaning "spear." Hinit is a variant spelling.

Chita (חִטָּה)   From the Hebrew, meaning "grain, wheat, food." Hita is a variant spelling. Also, from the Middle English, meaning "kitten."

Chiyuta (חִיּוּתָה)   A variant form of Chayuta. See Chayuta. Hiyuta is a variant spelling.

Chloe   From the Greek, meaning "blooming, verdant." Clea is a variant form. Cloe is a variant spelling.

Chlorine   From the Greek, meaning "blooming, verdant."

Chloris   From the Greek, meaning "blooming, verdant." Akin to Chloe and Chlorine. In Greek mythology, the goddess of flowers. Cloris is a variant spelling.

Chochit (חוֹחִית)   From the Hebrew, meaning "brier, thorn."

Chochma (חָכְמָה)   From the Hebrew, meaning "wisdom."

Chodesh (חֹדֶשׁ)   From the Hebrew, meaning "month." In the Bible (I Chronicles 8:9), the wife of one of Benjamin's sons. Hodesh is a variant spelling. Used also as a masculine name.

Chogla (חָגְלָה)   From the Hebrew, meaning "hop, hobble," hence "partridge" (which has those characteristics). In the Bible (Numbers 26:33), one of the five daughters of Zelophehad. Hogla and Hoglah are variant spellings.

Chosa (חוֹסָה)   From the Hebrew, meaning "protection" or "strength." Hosa is a variant spelling.

Chriselda   A variant form of Griselda. See Griselda.

Chrissie   A pet form of Christina. See Christina.

Christa   A short form of Christina. See Christina.

Christiana   The feminine form of Christianus, meaning "a Christian." Christina is a popular variant form. See Christina.

Christina   A variant form of Christiana, meaning "Christian, a believer in Jesus as the anointed one." A name often used without regard to its meaning. Christine, Kristian, Kristin, and Kristine are variant forms. Christa is a short form. Chris, Chrissie, Christy, and Crissie are pet forms. See also Kristin.

Christine   A variant form of Christina. See Christina.

Christy   A pet form of Christina. See Christina.

Chrystal   A variant spelling of Crystal. See Crystal.

Chufshit (חוּפְשִׁית)   From the Hebrew, meaning "freedom."

Chula (חוּלָה)   From the Hebrew, meaning "to play (an instrument)." Hula is a variant spelling.

Chulda (חוּלְדָה)   From the Hebrew and Aramaic, meaning "to dig" or "to creep, crawl," hence "a weasel." In the Bible (II Kings 22:14), a Prophetess in the time of King Josiah. Hulda and Huldah are variant spellings. Also spelled חלדה.

Chuma (חוּמָה) From the Aramaic, meaning "warmth" or "hot springs." Huma is a variant spelling. Chumi is a variant form. In the Talmud (Yevamot 64a), the wife of the prominent scholar Abaye.

Chumi (חוּמִי) A variant form of Chuma. See Chuma. Humi is a variant spelling.

Churshit (חוּרְשִׁית) From the Hebrew, meaning "to engrave" or "to plough."

Chushim (חוּשִׁים) From the Hebrew, meaning "feeling." In the Bible (I Chronicles 8:8), the wife of a member of the tribe of Benjamin. Hushim is a variant spelling. Used also as a masculine name.

Cicely A variant form of Cecilia. See Cecilia. Sisley is a variant spelling.

Cicily A variant form of Cecilia.

Cinderella From the French, meaning "ashes."

Cindy A pet form of Cynthia. See Cynthia. Sindy is a variant spelling.

Cipora A variant spelling of Tzipora. See Tzipora.

Ciporit A variant spelling of Tziporit. See Tziporit.

Cis, Ciss, Cissy Pet forms of Cecilia. See Cecilia.

Civia A variant spelling of Tzivya. See Tzivya.

Claire A French form of Clara. See Clara. Clare is a variant spelling. Clairene is a pet form. Le Clair and Le Claire are French forms.

Clairene A pet form of Claire. See Claire.

Clara From the Latin, meaning "clear, bright." Claire, Claretha, Clarette, Clarissa, Clarisse, and Clarita are variant forms.

Clarabella, Clarabelle Names compounded of the Latin *clarus*, meaning "bright," and *bella*, meaning "beautiful." Claribel is a variant spelling of Clarabelle.

Clare A variant spelling of Claire. See Claire. Used often as a masculine name.

Claretha A variant form of Clara. See Clara.

Clarette A variant form of Clara. See Clara. Also, from the Old French, meaning "clear (wine)," referring to a dry red wine.

Claribel A variant spelling of Clarabelle. See Clarabelle.

Clarice A variant spelling of Clarisse. See Clarisse.

Clarinda A pet form of Clara. See Clara. Clorinda is a variant form.

Clarine A pet form of Clara. See Clara.

Clarissa, Clarisse Italian forms of Clara. See Clara. Clarice is a variant spelling.

Clarita A Spanish form of Clara. See Clara.

Claudella A pet form of Claudia. See Claudia.

Claudette   A French pet form of Claudia. *See* Claudia.

Claudia   From the Latin, meaning "lame." Clodia is a variant form. Claudella, Claudette, and Claudine are pet forms.

Claudine   A French pet form of Claudia, popular in Switzerland. *See* Claudia.

Clea   A variant form of Chloe. *See* Chloe.

Cleantha   From the Greek, meaning "in praise of flowers."

Clematis   From the Greek, meaning "vine" or "twig."

Clementina   A variant form of Clementine. *See* Clementine.

Clementine   A French form of the Latin, meaning "merciful." The feminine form of Clement. Clementina is a variant form.

Cleo   A variant spelling of Clio. *See* Clio. Cleora is probably a variant form.

Cleona, Cleone   Feminine forms of Cleon. *See* Cleon (masculine section).

Cleora   Probably a variant form of Cleo. *See* Cleo.

Clio   From the Greek, meaning "to celebrate, glorify." In Greek mythology, the muse of history. Cleo is a variant spelling.

Clodia   A variant form of Claudia. *See* Claudia.

Cloe   A variant spelling of Chloe. *See* Chloe.

Clorinda   A variant form of Clarinda. *See* Clarinda.

Cloris   A variant spelling of Chloris. *See* Chloris.

Clotilda   From the Old German, meaning "famous in battle." Clotilde is a variant form.

Clotilde   A variant form of Clotilda. *See* Clotilda.

Cody   From the Latin, meaning "tail."

Colena   Probably a variant form of Colleen. *See* Colleen.

Colette   From the Latin, meaning "victorious." The French pet form of Nicole.

Colleen   From the Irish, meaning "girl." Colena and Collice are probably variant forms. Koleen is a variant spelling.

Collette   A variant spelling of Colette. *See* Colette.

Collice   Probably a variant form of Colleen. *See* Colleen.

Columbine   The name of any of a genus of plants in the buttercup family, so named because their flowers resemble a flock of doves.

Comfort   From the Middle English and Latin, meaning "to strengthen greatly."

Conetta   A pet form of Constance. *See* Constance.

Connie   A pet form of Constance. *See* Constance.

Constance   From the Latin, meaning "constant, firm, faithful." Conetta and Connie are pet forms.

Consuela, Consuelo   From the Latin, meaning "consolation."

Content   From the Latin, meaning "satisfied." A Puritan virtue name.

Cora   From the Greek, meaning "maiden." Also, a form of Corey. *See* Corey. Coretta and Corita are pet forms. Corinna and Corinne are variant forms.

Coral   From the Greek, meaning "small stone," usually red in color. Coralee and Coralie are variant forms.

Coralee   A variant form of Coral. *See* Coral. Also, a hybrid name of Cora and Lee. *See* Cora *and* Lee.

Coralie   A variant form of Coral. *See* Coral.

Cordelia   From the Celtic, meaning "daughter of the sea."

Cordelle   From the French, meaning "rope."

Coretta   A pet form of Cora. *See* Cora. Corette is a variant form.

Corette   A variant form of Coretta. *See* Coretta.

Corey   From the Gaelic, meaning "ravine, deep hollow." Cori, Corie, Correy, Corri, Corrie, Cory, and Corry are variant spellings. Cora is a variant form.

Cori, Corie   Variant spellings of Corey. *See* Corey.

Corinna, Corinne   From the Greek, meaning "hummingbird." Also, French forms of Cora. *See* Cora.

Corisande   From the Greek, meaning "one who sings in a chorus."

Corita   A pet form of Cora. *See* Cora.

Cornelia   From the Latin, meaning "cornell tree."

Correy   A variant spelling of Corey. *See* Corey.

Corri, Corrie   Variant spellings of Corey. *See* Corey.

Cory, Corry   Variant spellings of Corey. *See* Corey.

Cosima   From the Greek, meaning "universe, harmony."

Courtney   From the Old French, meaning "one who frequents the king's court."

Cozbi   A variant spelling of Kozvi. *See* Kozvi.

Crissie   A pet form of Christina. *See* Christina.

Crystal   From the Greek, meaning "clear, brilliant glass." Chrystal is a variant spelling.

Cybil, Cybill   From the Latin, meaning "soothsayer." Sibyl is a variant spelling.

Cyd   From the Old English, meaning "public hill."

Cyma   From the Greek and Latin, meaning "to sprout, grow, flourish." Sima and Syma are variant spellings.

Cymbalina   A variant form of Cymbaline. *See* Cymbaline.

Cymbaline Either from the Celtic, meaning "lord of the sun," or from the Greek, meaning "hollow vessel," from which the name of the musical instrument (cymbal) comes. Cymbalina is a variant form.

Cyndi A pet form of Cynthia. *See* Cynthia.

Cynthia From the Greek, meaning "from the cynthus." In Greek mythology, a mountain on which Artemis, goddess of the moon, was born. Hence, Cynthia came to mean "the moon personified." Cindy and Cyndi are pet forms.

Cyrilla From the Greek, meaning "lordly."

Daat (דַּעַת) From the Hebrew, meaning "knowledge, intelligence."

Dafna, Dafne (דַּפְנָה) Variant spellings of Daphne. *See* Daphne. Adopted as a Hebrew name.

Dafnit (דַּפְנִית) The Hebrew form of the Greek, Daphne. *See* Daphne. Daphnit is a variant spelling.

Dagania A variant spelling of Deganya. *See* Deganya.

Daganya A variant spelling of Deganya. *See* Deganya.

Dagmar From the Danish and German, meaning "bright day."

Dagmat (דַּגְמַת) From the Hebrew, meaning "model, image" or "exemplary, excellent."

Dahlia A variant spelling of Dalya. *See* Dalya. Also, a perennial plant with large flower heads, named for eighteenth-century Swedish botanist A. Dahl.

Daisy Usually taken as a nickname for Margaret. Derived from St. Margherita of Italy, who took the daisy (flower) as her symbol. Also, from the Anglo-Saxon, meaning "day's eye," symbolic of the dawn. Daysi is a variant spelling.

Dala, Dalah (דַּלָּה) From the Hebrew, meaning "hair" or "poor."

Dale From the Anglo-Saxon, meaning "dweller in a vale between hills." Commonly used as a masculine name.

Dalia A variant spelling of Dalya and Daliya. *See* Dalya *and* Daliya.

Dalit (דָּלִית) From the Hebrew, meaning "to draw water" or "bough, branch." Akin to Dalya.

Daliya (דַּלְיָה) A variant form of Dalya. *See* Dalya. Dalia is a variant spelling.

Dallas From the Old English, meaning "valley."

Dalores A variant spelling of Dolores. *See* Dolores.

Dalya (דַּלְיָה) From the Hebrew, meaning "branch, bough" or "to draw water." *See also* Dahlia. Dalia is a variant spelling. Daliya is a variant form. Akin to Dalit.

Dama From the Latin, meaning "lady." Damita is a diminutive form.

Dame From the Latin, meaning "lady."

Damita A Spanish form of Dama. *See* Dama.

Dana (דָּנָה) From the Latin, meaning "bright, pure as day." Also, from the Hebrew, meaning "to judge." Danette is a pet form.

Danette A pet form of Dana. *See* Dana.

Dania, Daniah Variant spellings of Danya. *See* Danya.

Daniela, Daniella (דָּנִיאֵלָה) Feminine forms of the masculine Daniel, meaning "God is my judge."

Daniele, Danielle Feminine spellings of the masculine Daniel, meaning "God is my judge."

Danit (דָּנִית) A feminine form of Daniel. *See* Daniel (masculine section).

Danita (דָּנִיתָה) A variant form of Daniel. *See* Daniel (masculine section).

Daniya (דָּנִיָה) A variant form of Danya. *See* Danya.

Dantel A feminine form of Dante. *See* Dante (masculine section).

Dantia A feminine form of Dante. *See* Dante (masculine section).

Danya (דָּנִיָה) A feminine form of Dan, meaning "judgment of the Lord." *See* Dan (masculine section). Dania, Daniah, and Donia are variant spellings. Daniya is a variant form.

Daphna A variant spelling of Daphne. *See* Daphne.

Daphne From the Greek, meaning "laurel or bay tree." In Greek mythology, Daphne is a nymph who escaped from Apollo by turning into a laurel tree. As a consequence, laurel leaves were worn by victors. Dafna, Dafne, and Daphna are variant spellings. Dafnit, Daphniela, Daphniella, and Dapna are variant forms.

Daphniela, Daphniella Variant forms of Daphne. *See* Daphne.

Daphnit A variant spelling of Dafnit. *See* Dafnit.

Dapna A variant form of Daphne. *See* Daphne.

Dara From the Middle English and the Old English, meaning "to dare," hence "a courageous person." Dare and Dareth are variant forms.

Darcie From the Celtic, meaning "dark." The masculine form is Darcy.

Darcy A variant spelling of Darcie. *See* Darcie.

Dare A variant form of Dara. *See* Dara.

Dareth A variant form of Dara. *See* Dara.

Daria The feminine form of the Persian Darius, meaning "wealth."

Darla From the Middle English, meaning "dear, loved one." Darleen, Darlene, and Darline are pet forms. Akin to Daryl.

Darleen, Darlene, Darline   Pet forms of Darla. *See* Darla. Akin to Daryl.

Darlyn   A variant form of Daryl. *See* Daryl.

Darona (דְּרוֹנָה)   A Hebrew form of the Greek, meaning "gift." Dorona is a variant spelling.

Daronit (דְּרוֹנִית)   A variant spelling of Doronit. *See* Doronit.

Daryl   From the Old English, meaning "dear, beloved." Akin to Darla and Darleen. Darlyn is a variant form.

Dasi (דָּסִי)   A pet form of Hadassah. *See* Hadassah. Dassi is a variant spelling.

Dasia   A variant pronunciation of Datya. *See* Datya.

Dassi   A variant spelling of Dasi. *See* Dasi.

Dati (דָּתִי)   From the Hebrew, meaning "religious, observant."

Datia, Datiah   Variant spellings of Datya. *See* Datya.

Datit (דָּתִית)   A variant form of Dati. *See* Dati.

Datiya (דָּתִיָּה)   A variant form of Datya. *See* Datya.

Datya (דָּתִיָה)   From the Hebrew, meaning "faith in God" or "law of the Lord." Akin to Dati. Datia and Datiah are variant spellings. Datiya is a variant form.

Davene   A feminine form of David, meaning "beloved, friend." *See* David (masculine section).

Davi   A feminine form of David. *See* David (masculine section).

Davida (דָּוִידָה)   A feminine form of David. *See* David (masculine section). Vida is a short form. Dovida is a variant spelling.

Davina   A Scottish form of David used in the seventeenth century. *See* David (masculine section).

Davir (דָּבִיר)   A variant form of Devir. *See* Devir.

Davita   A Spanish form of David. *See* David (masculine section).

Davrat (דָּבְרַת)   A variant form of Devora. *See* Devora. The name of a biblical city (Joshua 19:12).

Dawn   From the Old Norse and Old English, meaning "dawn."

Daya (דַּיָּה)   The Hebrew name of a bird, usually taken to mean "kite" or "bird of prey."

Daysi   A variant spelling of Daisy. *See* Daisy.

Dean, Deane   Feminine forms of Dean. *See* Dean (masculine section).

Deanna, Deanne   Variant forms of Diana or of Dinah. *See* Diana *and* Dinah. Deannie is a pet form.

Deannie   A pet form of Deanna. *See* Deanna.

Debbe, Debbi, Debby   Pet forms of Deborah. *See* Deborah.

Debera   A variant spelling of Debra, a form of Deborah. *See* Deborah.

Debi A pet form of Deborah. *See* Deborah.

Debora A variant spelling of Deborah. *See* Deborah.

Deborah A variant spelling of Devora. *See* Devora. Debora is a variant spelling. Debra and Dobra are variant forms. Debbe, Debbi, Debby, and Debi are pet forms.

Debra A variant form of Deborah. *See* Deborah. Debera is a variant spelling.

Decima From the Latin, meaning "tenth." Used for the name of the tenth child in a family.

Dee From the British, meaning "dark water." Also, a short form of Deena and Dinah, and a pet name for Dorothy and Doris.

Deena A variant spelling of Dinah. *See* Dinah. Also, from the Anglo-Saxon, meaning "from the valley." Dee is a short form.

Degana (דְּגָנָה) From the Hebrew, meaning "grain."

Degania, Deganiah Variant spellings of Deganya. *See* Deganya.

Deganit (דְּגָנִית) A variant form of Deganya. *See* Deganya.

Deganiya (דְּגָנִיָּה) A variant form of Deganya. *See* Deganya.

Deganya (דְּגָנְיָה) From the Hebrew, meaning "grain." Akin to Dagon, the chief god of the ancient Philistines, and later of the Phoenicians, represented as half man and half fish. Dagania, Daganya, Degania, and Deganiah are variant spellings. Deganit and Deganiya are variant forms.

Degula (דְּגוּלָה) From the Hebrew, meaning "honored" or "famous."

Dei'a (דֵּעָה) From the Hebrew, meaning "knowledge, understanding."

Deirdre From the Middle Irish, meaning "young girl." In Irish legend, a princess of Ulster who eloped to Scotland with her young lover. Diedra and Diedre are variant forms. Dierdre is a variant spelling.

Deka From the Greek, meaning "ten."

Delia From the Latin, referring to "an inhabitant of Delos (a small island in the Aegean, the legendary birthplace of Artemis and Apollo)."

Delila, Delilah (דְּלִילָה) From the Hebrew, meaning "poor" or "hair." In the Bible (Judges 16:4), a Philistine woman, the mistress of Samson. When Delila learned that the secret of Samson's strength was in his hair, she had his locks cut off and betrayed him to the Philistines.

Dell, Della, Delle Variant pet forms of Adela and Adeline. *See* Adela *and* Adeline.

Delores A Spanish spelling of Dolores. *See* Dolores.

Delpha From the Greek, meaning "dolphin." Akin to Delphinia.

Delta From the Greek *delta* and the Hebrew *dalet* (דָּלֶת), the fourth letter of both alphabets, meaning "door."

Demumit From the Hebrew, referring to a flower or plant called Adonis.

Dena   A variant spelling of Dinah. *See* Dinah.

Denice, Deniece, Deniese   Variant spellings of Denise. *See* Denise.

Denise   A feminine form of Denis, derived from Dionysius, the Greek god of wine and drama. *See* Denis (masculine section). Denice, Deniece, Deniese, and Denyse are variant spellings. Dennet is a variant form.

Denna   From the Anglo-Saxon, meaning "glen, valley." Also, a variant spelling of Dena. *See* Dena.

Dennet   A variant form of Denise. *See* Denise.

Denyse   A variant spelling of Denise. *See* Denise.

Deromit (דְּרוֹמִית)   From the Hebrew, meaning "south, southerly."

Deror (דְּרוֹר)   From the Hebrew, meaning "freedom." Dror is a variant spelling.

Derora, Derorah (דְּרוֹרָה)   From the Hebrew, meaning "flowing stream" or "bird (swallow)" or "freedom, liberty." Deroria and Derorit are variant forms.

Deroria (דְּרוֹרִיָה)   A variant form of Derora. *See* Derora.

Derorit (דְּרוֹרִית)   A variant form of Derora. *See* Derora.

Deva   Probably a variant form of Devora. *See* Devora.

Devash (דְּבַשׁ)   From the Hebrew, meaning "honey." Used also as a masculine name.

Devasha (דְּבָשָׁה)   From the Hebrew, meaning "honey." Akin to Duvsha.

Devera   A variant form of Devora. *See* Devora.

Devir (דְּבִיר)   From the Hebrew, meaning "sanctuary." Used also as a masculine name. Davir is a variant form.

Devira (דְּבִירָה)   A variant form of Devir. *See* Devir.

Devora, Devorah (דְּבוֹרָה)   From the Hebrew, meaning "swarm of bees" or "to speak kind words." Deborah and Dvora are variant spellings. *See* Deborah. In the Bible (Genesis 35:8, Judges 4:5), two charming characters were known by this name: 1) the nurse of Rebekah, and 2) the Prophetess-Judge, the wife of Lapidos, who lived about 1150 B.C.E. and led the revolt against the Canaanite king and his general, Sisera. Her victory song, "Song of Deborah," is one of the oldest poems preserved in Hebrew. Davrat, Deva, Devera, Devoranit, Devorit, Devra, and Dvera are variant forms. Dvoshke is a Yiddish form.

Devoranit (דְּבוֹרָנִית)   From the Hebrew, referring to a flower in the orchid family. Its center resembles a bee. Also, a variant form of Devora. *See* Devora.

Devorit (דְּבוֹרִית)   A variant form of Devora. *See* Devora. Dvorit is a variant spelling.

Devra   A variant form of Devora. *See* Devora.

Di   A pet form of Diana. *See* Diana.

Diahann A variant form of Diana. *See* Diana.

Diana From the Latin, meaning "divine" or "bright, pure as day." The moon goddess in Roman mythology. Deanna, Deanne, Diahann, Diane, Dianne, Diona, Dione, Dionne, and Dyan are variant forms. Di is a pet form. Dyana is a variant spelling.

Diandra From the Greek, meaning "flower with two stamens."

Diane, Dianne French forms of Diana. *See* Diana.

Diantha, Dianthe From the Greek and the Modern Latin, meaning "divine flower." In Greek mythology, the flower of Zeus.

Dicey A variant spelling of Dicie. *See* Dicie.

Dicia A variant form of Dicie. *See* Dicie.

Dicie From the British, meaning "risky, hazardous." Dicey is a variant spelling. Dicia is a variant form.

Dickla A variant spelling of Dikla. *See* Dikla.

Diedra, Diedre Variant forms of Deirdre. *See* Deirdre.

Dierdre A variant spelling of Deirdre. *See* Deirdre.

Dikla, Diklah (דִּקְלָה) The Aramaic form of the Hebrew, meaning "palm (date) tree." In the Bible (Genesis 10:27), a descendant of Noah. Dickla is a variant spelling. Diklit is a variant form.

Diklit (דִּקְלִית) A variant form of Dikla. *See* Dikla.

Dimona (דִּימוֹנָה) From the Hebrew, meaning "south." Akin to Divona.

Dina, Dinah (דִּינָה) From the Hebrew, meaning "judgment." In the Bible (Genesis 30:21), the daughter of Jacob and Leah. Dena and Deena are variant spellings. Dinah is not to be confused with Diana. Deanna and Deanne are variant forms. Dee is a short form.

Dinar (דִּינָר) From the Hebrew, meaning "coin."

Dinia A variant spelling of Dinya. *See* Dinya.

Dinya (דִּינְיָה) From the Hebrew, meaning "judgment of the Lord." Dinia is a variant spelling.

Diona, Dione, Dionne Greek forms of the Latin Diana. *See* Diana.

Dionetta, Dionette Pet forms of Diona. *See* Diona.

Dita (דִּיתָה) A pet form of Yehudit (Judith). *See* Yehudit.

Ditza, Ditzah (דִּיצָה) From the Hebrew, meaning "joy." Diza and Dizah are variant spellings.

Divla, Divlah (דִּבְלָה) From the Hebrew, meaning "a pressed fig cake." Divlata and Divlatah are variant forms.

Divlata, Divlatah (דִּבְלָתָה) Variant forms of Divla. *See* Divla.

Divona, Divonah (דִּיבוֹנָה) From the Hebrew, meaning "south." Akin to Dimona.

Dixie From the Old English, meaning "dike, wall." Also, a pet form of Benedicta. *See* Benedicta.

Diza, Dizah Variant spellings of Ditza. *See* Ditza.

Dobe A pet form of Devora. *See* Devora.

Dobra, Dobrah Variant forms of Deborah. *See* Deborah.

Doda, Dodah (דּוֹדָה) From the Hebrew, meaning "friend, beloved" or "aunt."

Dodi, Dodie (דּוֹדִי) From the Hebrew, meaning "my friend, my beloved." Also, a pet form of Dorothy.

Dodo A pet form of Dorothy. *See* Dorothy.

Dody A variant spelling of Dodi. *See* Dodi.

Dolley A variant spelling of Dolly. *See* Dolly.

Dollie A variant spelling of Dolly. *See* Dolly.

Dolly A variant form of Dorothy. *See* Dorothy. Also, an independent name from the Old English, meaning "doll." Dolley and Dollie are variant spellings.

Dolores A Christian name from the Latin, meaning "lady of sorrows." Dalores and Delores are variant spellings.

Domenica A variant spelling of Dominica. *See* Dominica.

Dominica The feminine form of Dominic, meaning "belonging to the Lord." Domenica is a variant spelling. Dominique is a variant form.

Dominique The French form of Dominica. *See* Dominica.

Donella A pet form of Donna. *See* Donna.

Donia A variant spelling of Danya. *See* Danya.

Donita A Spanish pet form of Donna. *See* Donna.

Donna From the Latin and Italian, meaning "lady of nobility." Donni and Donnis are variant forms. Donella and Donita are pet forms.

Donni, Donnis Variant forms of Donna. *See* Donna.

Dor (דּוֹר) From the Hebrew and Aramaic, meaning "generation" or "period of time."

Dora A diminutive form of Dorothy. *See* Dorothy. Doraleen and Doralene are pet forms.

Doraleen, Doralene Pet forms of Dora. *See* Dora.

Doran, Dorann Compounded of Dora and Ann. *See* Dora *and* Ann.

Dorcas, Dorcia From the Greek, meaning "gazelle."

Dore A German form of Dorothea. *See* Dorothea. Used also as a masculine name.

Dorea A variant form of Doris. *See* Doris.

Doreen, Dorene   Variant pet forms of Dorothy and its diminutive Dora. *See* Dorothy.

Doretta   A combination of Dora and Etta. *See* Dora *and* Etta.

Dorette   A French form of Dorothy. *See* Dorothy.

Doria, Dorie   Variant forms of Doris. *See* Doris.

Dorinda   An invented name styled after Belinda.

Doris   From the Greek, meaning "sacrificial knife." Also, a mythological character, the wife of Nereus, "mother of sea gods." Some authorities claim Doris means "bountiful," one who is blessed with many talents and good qualities. Dorris is a variant spelling. Dorea, Doria, and Dorie are variant forms. Dee is a pet form.

Dorit (דּוֹרִית)   From the Greek, meaning "to heap, pile" or "dwelling place." Also, from the Hebrew, meaning "generation." Dorith, Doritt, and Dorrit are variant spellings.

Dorita   A pet form of Dorothy. *See* Dorothy.

Dorith   A variant spelling of Dorit. *See* Dorit.

Doritt   A variant spelling of Dorit. *See* Dorit.

Doriya   A variant form of Dorya. *See* Dorya.

Dorma   From the Latin, meaning "to sleep."

Dorona (דּוֹרוֹנָה)   From the Greek, meaning "gift." Darona is a variant spelling. Doronit is a variant form.

Doronit (דּוֹרוֹנִית)   A variant form of Dorona. *See* Dorona. Daronit is a variant spelling.

Dorotea   The Spanish form of Dorothy. *See* Dorothy.

Dorothea   A variant form of Dorothy. *See* Dorothy.

Dorothee   A variant spelling of Dorothy. *See* Dorothy.

Dorothy   From the Greek, meaning "gift of God." The original form is Theodora. Dora, Dorothea, Dorotea, Dore, Doreen, Dorene, and Dorette are among the many variant forms. Dodo, Dodi, Dollie, Dolly, Dot, Dottie, Dorri, Dorrie, and Dorita are among the common pet forms. Dorothee is a variant spelling.

Dorri, Dorrie   Pet forms of Dorothy. *See* Dorothy.

Dorris   A variant spelling of Doris. *See* Doris.

Dorrit   A variant spelling of Dorit. *See* Dorit.

Dorya (דּוֹרְיָה)   From the Hebrew, meaning "generation of God." Doria is a variant spelling. Doriya is a variant form.

Dot, Dottie, Dotty   Pet forms of Dorothy. *See* Dorothy.

Dova (דּוֹבָה)   A variant form of Doveva. *See* Doveva.

Doveva (דּוֹבְבָה) From the Hebrew, meaning "graceful, to move gracefully like a bear *(dov)"* or "to speak." Dovevet is a variant form. Akin to Dovit.

Dovevet (דּוֹבֶבֶת) A variant form of Doveva. *See* Doveva.

Dovida A variant spelling of Davida. *See* Davida.

Dovit (דּוֹבִית) From the Hebrew, meaning "bear." Dov is the masculine form. Akin to Doveva.

Dreama From the Middle English and the Old English, meaning "joy, music."

Dror A variant spelling of Deror. *See* Deror.

Duba (דֻּבָּה) From the Hebrew, meaning "bear."

Dudait (דּוּדָאִית) From the Hebrew, meaning "mandrake."

Dulce A variant form of Dulcie. *See* Dulcie.

Dulcea A variant spelling of Dulcie. *See* Dulcie.

Dulcee A variant spelling of Dulcie. *See* Dulcie.

Dulcie From the Latin, meaning "charming, sweet." Dulcea, Dulcee, and Dulcy are variant spellings. Dulce is a variant form.

Dulcy A variant spelling of Dulcie. *See* Dulcie.

Dumia A variant spelling of Dumiya. *See* Dumiya.

Dumiya (דּוּמִיָּה) From the Hebrew, meaning "silent" or "to resemble." Dumia is a variant spelling.

Dumont From the French, meaning "from the mountain."

Durene From the Latin, meaning "enduring, lasting."

Dushe (דּוּשֶׁע) A Yiddish pet form of Devora. *See* Devora.

Duvsha (דּוּבְשָׁה) From the Aramaic, meaning "honey." Akin to Devasha.

Dvera A variant form of Devora. *See* Devora.

Dvora A variant spelling of Devora. *See* Devora.

Dvorit (דְּבוֹרִית) A variant spelling of Devorit. *See* Devorit.

Dvoshke (דְּוָואשְׁקֶע) A Yiddish form of Devora. *See* Devora.

Dyan A variant form of Diana. *See* Diana.

Dyana A variant spelling of Diana. *See* Diana.

Earla A feminine form of Earl. *See* Earl (masculine section).

Earlene A feminine form of Earl. *See* Earl (masculine section).

Eartha From the Old English, meaning "ground." Akin to Erda.

Ebony From the Greek, meaning "a hard, dark wood."

Edda From the Icelandic, meaning "poet" or "songwriter."

Ede A pet form of Edith. See Edith.

Edel (אײדל) From the Yiddish, meaning "gentle." Also spelled אײידעל.

Eder (עֵדֶר) From the Hebrew, meaning "flock, herd."

Edga The feminine form of Edgar. See Edgar (masculine section).

Edia, Ediah Variant spellings of Edya. See Edya.

Edie A popular Scottish pet form of Edith. See Edith.

Edina From the Anglo-Saxon, meaning "rich friend."

Edita A Spanish pet form of Edith. See Edith.

Edith From the Anglo-Saxon, meaning "rich, happy, prosperous" and "happy warrior." Edyth and Edythe are variant spellings. Editha is a variant form. Ede, Edie, and Edita are pet forms.

Editha A variant form of Edith. See Edith.

Edlyn From the Old English, meaning "happy (bubbling) brook."

Edna, Ednah (עֶדְנָה) From the Hebrew, meaning "delight, desired, adorned, voluptuous." Also, a contracted form of the Anglo-Saxon name Edwina, meaning "rich friend." Edna occurs first as a name in the Apocrypha, in the Book of Tobit (7:2).

Edva, Edvah Variant spellings of Adva. See Adva.

Edwarda A feminine form of Edward. See Edward (masculine section).

Edwina A feminine form of Edwin. See Edwin (masculine section).

Edya, Edyah (עֶדְיָה) From the Hebrew, meaning "adornment of the Lord." Edia and Ediah are variant spellings.

Edyth, Edythe Variant spellings of Edith. See Edith.

Eeva A Finnish spelling of Eva. See Eva.

Efa, Efah (עֵיפָה) From the Hebrew, meaning "darkness." In the Bible (I Chronicles 2:46), the concubine of Caleb. Used also as a masculine name. Eifa is a variant spelling.

Efie, Effie Pet forms of Euphemia. See Euphemia.

Efrat (אֶפְרָת) A variant form of Efrata. See Efrata.

Efrata (אֶפְרָתָה) From the Hebrew, meaning "honored, distinguished" or "fruitful." Also, from the Aramaic, meaning "mantle, turban." In the Bible (I Chronicles 2:19), the wife of Caleb ben Chetzron is called Efrat. Also, a site near Bethel (between Jerusalem and Bethlehem), where Rachel, the wife of Jacob, died and was buried. In Genesis 35:19, Efrata is used as a name for Bethlehem. David's father, Jesse, is called an Efrathite (I Samuel 17:12).

Efrona From the Hebrew, meaning "bird (of a species that sings well)." Ephrona is a variant spelling. Also, the feminine form of Efron. *See* Efron (masculine section).

Egla, Eglah (עֶגְלָה) From the Hebrew, meaning "heifer." In the Bible (II Samuel 3:5), the name of one of David's wives.

Egoza, Egozah (אֱגוֹזָה) From the Hebrew, meaning "nut, nut tree" or "palm tree."

Eidel (אֵיידֶעל) From the Yiddish, meaning "delicate, gentle."

Eifa A variant spelling of Efa. *See* Efa.

Eila, Eilah (אֵלָה) From the Hebrew, meaning "oak tree, terebinth tree." Ela, Elah, and Ayla are variant spellings.

Eilat (אֵילַת) From the Hebrew, meaning "gazelle" or "tree." A city in the eastern gulf of the Red Sea whose roots stretch back to Amatziah, king of Judah (II Kings 14:22). Elat is a variant spelling.

Eileen A popular Irish form of Helen. *See* Helen. Ilene is a variant form.

Eilona (אֵילוֹנָה) From the Hebrew, meaning "oak tree." Elona and Ilona are variant spellings.

Ela, Elah Variant spellings of Eila. *See* Eila.

Elain, Elaine French forms of Helen, meaning "light." *See* Helen. Also, from the Welsh, meaning "fawn, young hind." Elane and Elayne are variant spellings.

Elama (אֶלְעָמָה) From the Hebrew, meaning "God's people."

Elana A variant spelling of Ilana, meaning "tree."

Elane A variant spelling of Elaine. *See* Elaine.

Elat A variant spelling of Eilat. *See* Eilat.

Elayne A variant spelling of Elaine. *See* Elaine.

Elberta The feminine form of Elbert. *See* Elbert (masculine section).

Elda From the Middle English, meaning "old." Akin to Alda.

Eldora From the Spanish, meaning "gilded." A short form of Eldorado, an imaginary South American country fabled to be rich in gold.

Ele A pet form of Eleanor. *See* Eleanor.

Eleanor A variant Germanic form of Helen, from the Greek, meaning "light." Also from the Anglo-Saxon, meaning "fruitful." Akin to Lenore. Elenor, Elinor, and Elinore are variant spellings. Elenora, Ella, Elnora, Leonora, and Leonore are variant forms. Ele, Elie, Ellie, Lena, Lennie, Lenora, Lenore, Nell, Nella, Nellie, and Nelly are pet forms. Elen and Ellen are short forms.

Eleanora A variant form of Eleanor. *See* Eleanor.

Eleanore A variant spelling of Eleanor. *See* Eleanor.

Electra   From the Greek, meaning "shining one."

Elen   A variant spelling of Ellen. Also, a short form of Eleanor. *See* Eleanor.

Elena   From the Greek, meaning "light." The Italian form of Helen.

Elenor   A variant spelling of Eleanor. *See* Eleanor.

Elenora   A variant form of Eleanor. *See* Eleanor.

Eleora   A variant spelling of Eliora. *See* Eliora.

Elese   The Hawaiian form of Elsie. *See* Elsie.

Elfreda, Elfreida, Elfride   Variant spellings of Alfreda. *See* Alfreda.

Elia   A variant spelling of Elya. *See* Elya.

Eliana, Eliane, Elianna (אֱלִיעָנָה)   From the Hebrew, meaning "my God has answered."

Eliava, Eliavah (אֱלִיאָבָה)   From the Hebrew, meaning "my God is willing."

Elie   A pet form of Eleanor. *See* Eleanor.

Eliezra (אֱלִיעֶזְרָה)   From the Hebrew, meaning "my God is salvation."

Elik   A variant form of Elka. *See* Elka.

Elin   A variant spelling of Ellen. *See* Ellen.

Elinoa (אֱלִינוֹץ)   From the Hebrew, meaning "my God is omnipresent."

Elinoar (אֱלִינֹעַר)   From the Hebrew, meaning "my God is young" or "God of my youth."

Elinor   A variant spelling of Eleanor. *See* Eleanor.

Elinora   A variant spelling of Eleanora. *See* Eleanora.

Elinore   A variant spelling of Eleanor. *See* Eleanor.

Elinorr   A variant spelling of Elinor. *See* Elinor.

Eliora (אֱלִיאוֹרָה)   From the Hebrew, meaning "my God is light." Eleora is a variant spelling.

Eliraz (אֱלִירָז)   From the Hebrew, meaning "my God is my secret."

Elisa   A variant form of Elisabeth. *See* Elisabeth.

Elisabeta   The Hawaiian form of Elisabeth. *See* Elisabeth.

Elisabeth   A variant spelling of Elizabeth. *See* Elizabeth.

Elise   A pet form of Elisabeth. *See* Elisabeth.

Elisheva (אֱלִישֶׁבַע)   From the Hebrew, meaning "God is my oath." In the Bible (Exodus 6:23), the wife of Aarona and sister-in-law of Moses. Elizabeth is an Anglicized form. *See* Elizabeth.

Elissa   A pet form of Elisabeth. *See* Elisabeth.

Eliya (אֱלִיָה)   A feminine form of Eliyahu. *See* Eliyahu (masculine section).

Eliza   A short form of Elizabeth. *See* Elizabeth.

Elizabeth (אֱלִישֶׁבַע)   From the Hebrew, meaning "God's oath" or "God is an oath." The original Hebrew form is Elisheva, also spelled Elisheba. In the Bible (Exodus 6:23), the wife of Aaron, sister-in-law of Moses. The Greek translation of the Bible (Septuagint) renders Elisheva as Elisabeth, spelled with an *s*. However, the more common American spelling is Elizabeth. Few names have produced a greater variety of forms. These include: Babette, Bess, Bessie, Bessy, Bet, Beth, Betsey, Betsie, Betta, Bette, Bettina, Elisa, Eliza, Elsie, Elspeth, Ilsa, Isabel, Libby, Lilibet, Lilla, Lillah, Lisa, Lisbet, Lisbeth, Liz, Liza, Lizzie, Tetsy, and Tetty.

Elize   A short form of Elizabeth. *See* Elizabeth.

Elka, Elke   A pet form of Alice or Alexandra. *See* Alice *and* Alexandra. Elik, Elki, and Elkie are variant forms.

Elki, Elkie   Variant forms of Elka. *See* Elka.

Ella   From the Old German, meaning "all." Or, a variant form of Eleanor. *See* Eleanor. Ellette is a pet form.

Ellen   A short form of Eleanor. *See* Eleanor. Elin, Ellin, Ellyn, Ellynne, Elyn, and Elynn are variant spellings.

Ellette   A pet form of Ella. *See* Ella.

Ellie   A pet form of Eleanor. *See* Eleanor.

Ellin   A variant spelling of Ellen. *See* Ellen.

Ellyn, Ellynne   Variant spellings of Ellen. *See* Ellen.

Elma   From the Greek and Latin, meaning "pleasant, fair, kind." Alma is a variant spelling.

Elnora   A variant form of Eleanor. *See* Eleanor.

Eloise   A variant form of the French Heloise and Louise. *See* Louise.

Elona   A variant spelling of Eilona. *See* Eilona.

Elsa, Else   German pet forms of Elizabeth. *See* Elizabeth. Also, from the Anglo-Saxon, meaning "swan."

Elsie   A variant form of Elisabeth. *See* Elisabeth. Elese is the Hawaiian form.

Elspeth   A Scottish form of Elizabeth. *See* Elizabeth.

Elula (אֱלוּלָה)   A variant form of Elul. *See* Elul (masculine section).

Elva   From the Anglo-Saxon, meaning "elf."

Elverta   A variant form of Alberta. *See* Alberta.

Elvina   From the Anglo-Saxon, meaning "friend of elves."

Elvira   A Spanish form of the German, meaning "to close up completely."

Elya (אֶלְיָה)   From the Syriac and Hebrew, meaning "dirge, elegy." Ilya is a variant form. Elia is a variant form.

Elyca   A variant form of Elisabeth. *See* Elisabeth.

Elyce   A variant form of Elisabeth. *See* Elisabeth.

Elyn, Elynn   Variant spellings of Ellen. *See* Ellen. Also, short forms of Eleanor. *See* Ellen *and* Eleanor.

Elysa, Elyse   Variant forms of Elisabeth. *See* Elisabeth.

Elyssa, Elysse   Variant forms of Elisabeth. *See* Elisabeth.

Elza (עֶלְזָה)   From the Hebrew, meaning "joy."

Em   A pet form of Emma. *See* Emma.

Emaline   A variant form of Emily. *See* Emily.

Emanuela, Emanuella (עְמָנוּאֵלָה)   Feminine forms of Emanuel, meaning "God is with us." *See* Emanuel (masculine section). Imanuela, Imanuella, Immanuela, and Immanuella are variant spellings.

Eme   A variant form of Emma. *See* Emma.

Emele   The Hawaiian form of Emily. *See* Emily.

Emelin, Emelina, Emeline   Variant forms of Emily. *See* Emily.

Emerald, Emeralda, Emeraldine   From the Middle English and the Old French, meaning "a bright green precious stone."

Emet (אֶמֶת)   From the Hebrew, meaning "truth."

Emilia   A variant form of Emilie and Emily. *See* Emilie *and* Emily.

Emilie   From the Anglo-Saxon, meaning "flatterer." Or, a variant form of Emily. *See* Emily. Emilia is a pet form.

Emily   From the Latin, meaning "industrious" or "ambitious." Emele, Emelin, Emelina, Emeline, Emilia, Emilie, and Emmaline are variant forms. Emmie and Emmy are pet forms.

Emma   From the Anglo-Saxon, meaning "big one" or "grandmother." Ymma, Imma, and Eme are variant forms. Em, Emmie, and Emmy are popular pet forms.

Emmaline   A French form of Emily. *See* Emily.

Emmie, Emmy   Pet forms of Emily or Emma. *See* Emily *and* Emma.

Emuna, Emunah (אֱמוּנָה)   From the Hebrew, meaning "faith, faithful."

Ena   A variant spelling of Ina. Or, a pet form of Eugenia. *See* Ina *and* Eugenia.

Enid   From the Anglo-Saxon, meaning "fair," or from the Celtic, meaning "soul, life."

Ephrat, Ephrata   Variant spellings of Efrat and Efrata. *See* Efrat *and* Efrata.

Ephrona   A variant spelling of Efrona. *See* Efrona.

Erana (עֲרָנָה)   From the Hebrew, meaning "energetic, industrious, alert." Eranut is a variant form.

Eranut (עֲרָנוּת) A variant form of Erana. *See* Erana.

Erda From the German, meaning "earth." Akin to Eartha.

Erela (אֶרְאֵלָה) From the Hebrew, meaning "angel" or "messenger." Also, a variant form of Ariela, meaning "lion of God."

Eretz (אֶרֶץ) From the Hebrew, meaning "land, country, territory."

Erga (עֶרְגָּה) From the Hebrew, meaning "yearning, hope, longing."

Erica The feminine form of Eric, meaning "ever kingly, brave, powerful." *See* Eric (masculine section). Erika is a variant spelling.

Erika A variant spelling of Erica. *See* Erica.

Erin From the Irish, meaning "peace."

Erlinia A variant form of the masculine Earl. *See* Earl (masculine section).

Erma A variant spelling of Irma. *See* Irma.

Erna From the Anglo-Saxon, meaning "retiring, shy, reserved, peaceful." Or, a feminine form of Ernest. *See* Ernest (masculine section).

Ernesta, Ernestine Feminine forms of Ernest. *See* Ernest (masculine section).

Eshkola (אֶשְׁכּוֹלָה) From the Hebrew, meaning "cluster (of grapes)." Eshkol is the masculine form.

Eshkolit (אֶשְׁכּוֹלִית) From the Hebrew, meaning "grapefruit."

Esme From the Old French, meaning "esteemed."

Esranit (עֶשְׂרָנִית) A variant form of Esronit. *See* Esronit.

Esronit (עֶשְׂרוֹנִית) From the Hebrew, meaning "ten, tenth." Esranit is a variant form.

Essie A pet form of Esther. *See* Esther.

Esta, Estee Variant forms of Esther. *See* Esther.

Estella A Spanish form of Esther. *See* Esther.

Estelle A variant form of Esther. *See* Esther.

Ester, Esther (אֶסְתֵּר) From the Persian, meaning "star." In the Bible, Queen Esther is the central figure in the Book of Esther. She was the cousin and adopted daughter of Mordecai. Her Hebrew name, Haddasah, means "myrtle." Esta, Essie, Estella, Estelle, Etti, and Etty, are some of the variant forms. Ester is a modern spelling. Hester and its diminutive, Hetty, are Latinized forms of Esther. Astera is probably the original form. *See* Astera.

Estralita From the Spanish, meaning "little star."

Etana (אֵיתָנָה) From the Hebrew, meaning "strong." Etan is the masculine equivalent.

Ethel From the Anglo-Saxon, meaning "noble." The Old German word *adal*, and the modern German *edel*, are of the same origin. These gave rise to names such as Adele and Alice. The Yiddish name Edel is of the same origin.

Etka (עֶטְקָא) The Yiddish pet form of Ita and Yetta. *See* Ita *and* Yetta.

Etna (אָתְנָה)   From the Hebrew, meaning "hire, hired, for hire."

Etroga (אָתְרוֹגָה)   From the Hebrew, meaning "citron (etrog)."

Etta   A pet form of Harriet and Henrietta, meaning "mistress of the house, lord, ruler." See Harriet and Henrietta.

Etti, Etty   Pet forms of Esther. See Esther.

Etziona   A variant spelling of Etzyona. See Etzyona.

Etzyona (עֶצְיוֹנָה)   A feminine form of Etzyon. See Etzyon (masculine section). Etziona and Eziona are variant spellings.

Eudice   A variant spelling of Eudit. See Eudit. Also, a variant form of Yehudit. See Yehudit.

Eudit (יוּדִית)   A variant form of Yehudit (Judith). See Yehudit. Eudice is a variant spelling.

Eudora   From the Greek meaning "good gift."

Eugenia   From the Greek, meaning "well-born." Ina and Ena are pet forms. Eugenie is the French form.

Eugenie   The French form of Eugenia. See Eugenia.

Eulalia   From the Greek, meaning "sweet talk, good talk."

Eunice   From the Greek, meaning "happy victory."

Euphemia   From the Greek, meaning "good speech" or "well-spoken." Efie and Effie are pet forms.

Eva   A variant form of Eve. See Eve. Eeva and Iva are variant spellings.

Evadne   A variant form of Eve. See Eve.

Evalina, Evaline   Variant spellings of Evelina and Eveline. See Evelina and Eveline. Also pet forms of Eve.

Evangeline   From the Greek, meaning "bearer of glad tidings, messenger."

Eve (חַוָה)   The Latin and German form of Eve. Derived from the Hebrew meaning "life." In the Bible (Genesis 3:20), the wife of Adam, the first woman. Chava is the exact Hebrew equivalent. Eva and Evadne are variant forms. Evalina, Evaline, Evelina, Eveline, Evelyn, Evette, Evie, and Evita are pet forms.

Evelina, Eveline   Variant forms of the Old German Avelina. Also, pet forms of Eve. See Eve. Evalina and Evaline are variant spellings.

Evelyn   A pet form of Eve. See Eve.

Evette   A pet form of Eve. See Eve. Yvette is a variant spelling.

Evie   A pet form of Eve. See Eve. Evy is a variant spelling.

Evita   A Spanish pet form of Eve. See Eve.

Evona   A variant form of Yvonne. See Yvonne.

Evonne   A pet form of Eva and Evelyn. See Eva and Evelyn. Or, a variant form of Yvonne. See Yvonne.

Evrona (עֶבְרוֹנָה) From the Hebrew, meaning "overflowing" or "anger, fury." Evran is the masculine form. Avrona is a variant form.

Evy A variant spelling of Evie. *See* Evie.

Eyvonne A variant spelling of Yvonne. *See* Yvonne.

Eziona A variant spelling of Etzyona. *See* Etzyona.

Ezra (עֶזְרָא) Basically a masculine name. *See* Ezra (masculine section).

Ezraela, Ezraella (עֶזְרָאֵלָה) Feminine forms of the masculine Ezra, meaning "God is my help or support." *See* Ezra (masculine section).

Ezr'ela, Ezr'ella (עֶזְרָאֵלָה) Variant forms of Ezraela and Ezraella. *See* Ezraela.

Ezriela, Ezriella (עֶזְרִיאֵלָה) Variant forms of Ezraela and Ezraella. *See* Ezraela.

Fabia From the Greek, meaning "bean farmer." The feminine form of Fabian.

Fabrice From the French, meaning "a fabric product."

Faga A variant spelling of Feige. *See* Feige.

Faiga A variant spelling of Feige. *See* Feige. Also, from the Anglo-Saxon, meaning "the beautiful."

Faigel A variant spelling of Feigel. *See* Feigel.

Faith From the Anglo-Saxon, meaning "unswerving trust, hope." Faith, along with Hope and Charity, came to be used as a personal name after the Reformation. Fay and Faye are occasionally used as a short form.

Falice, Falicia Variant spellings of Felice, and Felicia. *See* Felice *and* Felicia.

Fania A pet form of Frances. *See* Frances.

Fanina From the Latin, meaning "flour, ground corn." Farista is a pet form.

Fannie, Fanny, Fannye Pet forms of Frances. *See* Frances.

Fanya A variant spelling of Fania. *See* Fania.

Farista A Spanish pet form of Farina. *See* Farina.

Farrah From the Arabic, meaning "wild ass."

Fawn From the Middle English, meaning "to be friendly," or from the Latin, meaning "young deer." Fawna, Fawne, and Fawnia are variant forms.

Fawna, Fawne Variant forms of Fawn. *See* Fawn.

Fawnia A French form of Fawn. *See* Fawn.

Fay, Faye From the Old French, meaning "fidelity." Also, from the Latin, meaning "fairy." Used occasionally as a short form of Faith. *See* Faith.

Fayette A pet form of Fay. *See* Fay.

Fayme From the Old English, meaning "fame."

Fedora From the Greek, meaning "divine gift."

Fee From the Middle English, meaning "fief, estate."

Feiga (פֵיגָא) A variant form of Feige. *See* Feige.

Feige (פֵייגֶע) From the Yiddish *fayg*, meaning "fig." Or, a variant form of Feigel, meaning "bird." Feiga is a variant form. Faga and Faiga are variant spellings.

Feigel (פֵייגְל) The Yiddish form of the German *Vogel*, meaning "bird." Faigel is a variant English spelling. Akin to Feige. Also spelled פֵייגֶל.

Felecia A variant spelling of Felicia. *See* Felicia.

Felice, Felicia From the Latin, meaning "happy, fortunate." Felicitas was the Roman goddess of good luck. Felicia was common in twelfth-century England as a feminine form of Felix. *See* Felix (masculine section). Falice and Felise are variant spellings. Falicia and Felecia are variant spellings of Felicia. Feliciana, Felicite, and Felicity are variant forms.

Feliciana A Spanish form of Felice. *See* Felice.

Felicite, Felicity French and Spanish forms of Felice. *See* Felice.

Feline From the Latin, meaning "cat."

Felise, Felisse Variant spellings of Felice. *See* Felice.

Felta From the Dutch, meaning "field, forest."

Fern, Ferne Feminine forms of Ferdinand. *See* Ferdinand (masculine section). Also, an Old English plant-name, and from the Anglo-Saxon, meaning "strong, brave."

Fernandina, Fernandine Feminine forms of Ferdinand. *See* Ferdinand (masculine section). *See also* Fern.

Fidelia From the Latin, meaning "faithful." Akin to Fidella.

Fidella From the Latin, meaning "faithful." Akin to Fidelia. Fidel is the masculine form.

Filomena From the Middle English, meaning "lover of songs."

Flavia From the Latin, meaning "yellow-haired, blond."

Fleur A French form of the Latin, meaning "flower." Flora is a variant form. *See* Flora. Fleurette is a pet form.

Fleurette A pet form of Fleur. *See* Fleur.

Flora From the Latin, meaning "flower." The Roman goddess of flowers and springtime. *See also* Florence *and* Fleur. Floria, Florida, and Floris are variant forms. Florrie, Floryn, and Flossie are pet forms.

Floreen A variant form of Florence. *See* Florence.

Florella A pet form of Florence. *See* Florence.

Floren A short form of Florence. *See* Florence.

Florence From the Latin, meaning "blooming, flowery, flourishing." Used also as a masculine name. Flo, Florella, Florrie, Floryn, and Flossie are pet forms. Floreen, Floren, Florenz, and Flower are variant forms.

Florenz A German form of Florence. *See* Florence.

Floria A variant form of Flora. *See* Flora.

Florida A Spanish form of Flora. *See* Flora.

Florinda A variant form of Flora. *See* Flora.

Floris A variant form of Flora. *See* Flora.

Florrie A pet form of Flora and Florence. *See* Flora *and* Florence.

Floryn A pet form of Flora and Florence. *See* Flora *and* Florence.

Flossie A pet form of Flora and Florence. *See* Flora *and* Florence.

Flower A rare form of Flora and Florence first used in the eighteenth century. Fleur is a popular French form. *See* Flora *and* Florence.

Fortuna In Roman mythology, the goddess of fortune. Akin to Fortunata.

Fortunata From the Latin, meaning "chance, good luck." *See also* Fortuna.

Fradel (פֿרײידל) A pet form of Frayda. *See* Frayda. Also spelled פֿרײידעל.

Fran A pet form of Frances. *See* Frances.

France A variant form of Frances. *See* Frances.

Frances From the Anglo-Saxon, meaning "free, liberal." The feminine form of the masculine Francis. Frances actually means "free-woman," while Francis means "free-man." The origin of these names dates back to the Franks, a confederacy of German tribes who for a long time battled with the Romans before settling permanently in Gaul, in the fifth century. France took its name from the Franks. France, Francesca, Francis, Francoise, and Frania are variant forms. Fania, Fannie, Fanny, Fannye, Fran, Francine, Frani, Frankie, and Ranny are pet forms.

Francesca An Italian form of Frances. *See* Frances.

Francine A pet form of Frances. *See* Frances.

Francis Used occasionally as a feminine name, but primarily a masculine form. *See* Frances.

Francoise A French form of Frances. *See* Frances.

Frani A pet form of Frances. *See* Frances.

Frania A variant form of Frances. *See* Frances. Fronia is a variant spelling.

Frankie A pet form of Frances. *See* Frances.

Frayda, Frayde From the Yiddish, meaning "joy." Fradel is a pet form. Freida and Freide are variant spellings.

Freda   A variant form of Frieda. *See* Frieda.

Fredda   A pet form of Frederica and Frieda. *See* Frederica *and* Frieda.

Freddie   A pet form of Frederica and Frieda. *See* Frederica *and* Frieda.

Freddye   A variant spelling of Freddie. *See* Freddie.

Frederica   The feminine form of Frederick, meaning "peaceful ruler." Fredda, Freddie, and Fritzi are pet forms.

Fredyne   A pet form of Frieda. *See* Frieda.

Freema   A variant form of Fruma. *See* Fruma.

Freida, Freide   Variant forms of Frieda. *See* Frieda. Also, variant spellings of Frayda. *See* Frayda.

Freya   In Norse mythology, the goddess of love and beauty.

Frida   A variant spelling of Frieda. *See* Frieda.

Frieda   From the Old High German, meaning "peace." Freda, Freida, Freide, and Friedia are variant forms. Fredda, Freddie, Fredyne, and Fritzi are pet forms.

Friedia   A variant form of Frieda. *See* Frieda.

Frimme (פְּרִימֶע)   A variant form of Fruma. *See* Fruma.

Fritzi   A pet form of Frieda and Frederica. *See* Frieda *and* Frederica.

Fronde   From the Latin, meaning "leafy branch."

Fronia   A variant spelling of Frania, a form of Frances. *See* Frances.

Fruma (פרוּמָא)   From the Yiddish, meaning "pious one." Freema and Frimme are variant forms.

Frume (פרוּמֶע)   A variant form of Fruma. *See* Fruma.

Gaalia   A variant spelling of Gaalya. *See* Gaalya.

Gaalya (גְּאַלְיָה)   From the Hebrew, meaning "God has redeemed." Gealya is a variant form.

Gabi (גַּבִּי)   A pet form of Gabriella. *See* Gabriella.

Gabriela, Gabriella   Anglicized feminine forms of Gavriela. *See* Gavriela.

Gabriele, Gabrielle   French forms of the Hebrew name Gavriela. *See* Gavriela.

Gachalilit (גַּחֲלִילִית)   From the Hebrew, meaning "glow worm." Gahalilit is a variant spelling.

Gada (גָּדָה)   The feminine form of Gad. *See* Gad (masculine section). Also, the name of a plant (coriander) that is grown in Israel. Gadit is a variant form.

Gadiel (גַּדִיאֵל) From the Hebrew, meaning "God is my fortune." A feminine variant form of Gad. *See* Gad (masculine section).

Gadiela, Gadiella (גַּדִיאֵלָה) Variant forms of Gadiel. *See* Gadiel.

Gadit (גַּדִית) A variant form of Gada. *See* Gada.

Gadya (גַּדְיָה) From the Hebrew, meaning "goat, kid."

Gae A variant spelling of Gay. *See* Gay.

Gafna (גַּפְנָה) The Aramaic form of Gefen. *See* Gefen. Gaphna is a variant spelling.

Gafnit (גַּפְנִית) A variant form of Gafna. *See* Gafna.

Gahalilit A variant spelling of Gachalilit. *See* Gachalilit.

Gail A short form of Abigail. *See* Abigail. Gale and Gayle are variant spellings.

Gailard From the Old French, meaning "strong, brave."

Gal (גַּל) From the Hebrew, meaning "mound, hill" or "wave" or "fountain, spring." *See also* Gail. Used also as a masculine name.

Gala (גַּלָה) A variant form of Gal. *See* Gal.

Gale A variant spelling of Gail. *See* Gail.

Gali (גַּלִי) A variant form of Gal. *See* Gal. Galit is a variant form.

Galia A variant spelling of Galya. *See* Galya.

Galila (גְּלִילָה) The feminine form of Galil. *See* Galil (masculine section). Also a variant form of Gelila. *See* Gelila.

Galina (גַּלִינָה) The Russian form of Helen. *See* Helen. Used in Israel as an Hebraic form.

Galit (גַּלִית) A variant form of Gali. *See* Gali.

Galiya (גַּלִיָה) A variant form of Galya. *See* Galya.

Galuta (גָּלוּתָה) From the Hebrew, meaning "exile."

Galya (גַּלְיָה) From the Hebrew, meaning "hill of God." Galia is a variant spelling. Galiya is a variant form.

Gamliela, Gamlielle (גַּמְלִיאֵלָה) Feminine forms of Gamliel. *See* Gamliel (masculine section). Gamlielit is a variant form.

Gamlielit (גַּמְלִיאֵלִית) A variant form of Gamliela. *See* Gamliela.

Gana (גַּנָּה) From the Hebrew, meaning "garden." Ganit is a variant form.

Gania A variant spelling of Ganya. *See* Ganya.

Ganit (גַּנִּית) From the Hebrew, meaning "defender." Also, a variant form of Gana. *See* Gana.

Ganya (גַּנְיָה) From the Hebrew, meaning "garden of the Lord." Gania is a variant spelling.

Gaphna A variant spelling of Gafna. *See* Gafna.

Garland From the Old French, meaning "wreath of flowers." Garldina is a pet form.

Garldina A pet form of Garland. *See* Garland.

Garna (גָּרְנָה) From the Hebrew, meaning "silo, granary." Akin to Garnit.

Garnet From the Middle English and the Latin, meaning "pomegranate."

Garniata From the French, meaning "to garnish, adorn."

Garnit (גָּרְנִית) From the Hebrew, meaning "granary." Akin to Garna.

Gat (גַּת) From the Hebrew, meaning "wine press." Gita is a variant form.

Gavi (גַּבִי) A pet form of Gavriela. *See* Gavriela.

Gavriela, Gavriella (גַּבְרִיאֵלָה) Feminine forms of Gabriel, meaning "God is my strength." There is a superstition that if parents who have lost several children give a new baby one of these names the baby will survive. *See also* Gabriel (masculine section). Gabriela, Gabriele, Gabriella, and Gabrielle are variant forms. Gavi is a pet form.

Gavrila, Gavrilla (גַּבְרִילָה) ' From the Hebrew, meaning "heroine, strong." *See also* Gavriela.

Gay From the Anglo-Saxon, meaning "gay, merry." Gae is a variant spelling.

Gayle A variant spelling of Gail. *See* Gail.

Gayora (גִּיאוֹרָה) From the Hebrew, meaning "valley of light."

Gazella From the Latin, meaning "gazelle, deer."

Gazit (גָּזִית) From the Hebrew, meaning "hewn stone."

Gealia A variant spelling of Gealya. *See* Gealya.

Gealya (גְּאַלְיָה) From the Hebrew, meaning "redeemed by God." Gealia is a variant spelling. Gaalya is a variant form.

Gedda From the Old English, meaning "javelin."

Gedera (גְּדֵרָה) From the Hebrew, meaning "wall" or "hedge."

Gedula, Gedulah (גְּדוּלָה) From the Hebrew, meaning "big, great, greatness."

Geela, Geelah Variant spellings of Gila. *See* Gila.

Geene A variant spelling of Jean. *See* Jean.

Gefen, Geffen (גֶּפֶן) From the Hebrew, meaning "vine." Used also as a masculine name. Gafna is an Aramaic form.

Gelalia A variant spelling of Gelalya. *See* Gelalya.

Gelalya (גְּלַלְיָה) A variant form of Gelila. *See* Gelila. Gelalia is a variant spelling.

Gelila, Gelilah (גְּלִילָה) From the Hebrew, meaning "boundary" or "rolled up," hence "rolling hills." Galila, Gelalya, and Geliliya are variant forms. *See also* Galil (masculine section).

Geliliya (גְּלִילְיָה) A variant form of Gelila. *See* Gelila.

Gemma From the Latin, meaning "swelling, bud" or "precious stone."

Gemula, Gemulah (גְּמוּלָה) From the Hebrew, meaning "repaid."

Gena A variant spelling of Gina. *See* Gina

Gendel (גֶּענְדְל) A Russian form of the Yiddish Hendel (from Hannah), used by Germans. Since Russia does not have an "h" sound, Hendel became Gendel. Also spelled גֶּענְדְעל.

Gene A pet form of Genevieve and Jean. *See* Genevieve *and* Jean.

Geneva, Genevia From the Old French and the Latin, meaning "juniper berry." Genna is a variant form.

Genevieve From the Celtic, meaning "white wave." Or, of French-German origin and equivalent to Winifred. Also, possibly compounded of two Old German words, *geno*, meaning "race," and *wefo*, meaning "woman." Gene and Genie are pet forms.

Genie A pet form of Genevieve. *See* Genevieve. Also a variant spelling of Jeanie. *See* Jeanie.

Genna A variant spelling of Jenna, a form of Jeanette. *See* Jeanette. Or, a variant form of Geneva. *See* Geneva.

Geona (גְּאוֹנָה) From the Hebrew, meaning "exaltation, pride, majesty" or "wisdom." Geonit is a variant form.

Geonit (גְּאוֹנִית) A variant form of Geona. *See* Geona.

Georgea A variant spelling of Georgia. *See* Georgia.

Georgeanne A hybrid of George and Anne. *See* George (masculine section) *and* Anne. Georgiana is a variant form.

Georgeene Variant pet forms of Georgia. *See* Georgia.

Georgess A variant form of Georgia. *See* Georgia.

Georgette A pet form of Georgia. *See* Georgia.

Georgia From the Greek, meaning "husbandman, farmer." The masculine George is the original form. *See* George (masculine section). Georgea and Georja are variant spellings. Georgess is a variant form. Georgea, Georgeena, Georgeene, Georgina, and Georgine are pet forms.

Georgiana A variant form of Georgeanne. *See* Georgeanne.

Georgina, Georgine Pet forms of Georgia. *See* Georgia.

Georja A variant spelling of Georgia. *See* Georgia.

Geraldene, Geraldine From the Old High German, meaning "spear-wielder, warrior." Geri, Gerrie, and Gerry are pet forms. The masculine Gerald is the original form of the name. Gerardene and Gerardine are variant forms.

Gerardene, Gerardine Variant forms of Geraldene. *See* Geraldene.

Geratzia (גְּרַצְיָה) From the Italian, meaning "gracious." Used in modern Israel.

Gerda From the Old High German, meaning "protected one."

Geremi A feminine form of Jeremy. *See* Jeremy (masculine section).

Geri A pet form of Geraldine and Gerardine. *See* Geraldine *and* Gerardine.

Germaine From the Middle English and the Latin, meaning "sprout, bud."

Gerrie, Gerry Pet forms of Geraldine and Gerardine. *See* Geraldine *and* Gerardine.

Gershona (גֵּרְשׁוֹנָה) The feminine form of Gershon. *See* Gershon (masculine section).

Gertrude From the Old High German, meaning "battlemaid" or "adored warrior." Truda, Trude, Trudi, and Trudy are pet forms.

Gerusha, Gerushah (גְּרוּשָׁה) From the Hebrew, meaning "exiled, expelled" or "stranger."

Geula, Geulah (גְּאוּלָה) From the Hebrew, meaning "redemption." Also spelled גְּאֻלָּה.

Gevat (גְּבָת) From the Hebrew, meaning "mound" or "height." Akin to Giva. *See* Giva.

Gevionit (גְּבִיעוֹנִית) A flower in the lilac family, found in Israel.

Gevira, Gevirah (גְּבִירָה) From the Hebrew, meaning "lady" or "queen."

Gevura, Gevurah (גְּבוּרָה) From the Hebrew, meaning "strength."

Ghila A variant spelling of Gila. *See* Gila.

Gia A short form of Regina. *See* Regina.

Gibora, Giborah (גִּבּוֹרָה) From the Hebrew, meaning "strong, heroine."

Gideona A variant form of Gidona. *See* Gidona.

Gidona (גִּדְעוֹנָה) The feminine form of Gidon. *See* Gidon (masculine section). Gideona is a variant form.

Gil (גִּיל) From the Hebrew, meaning "joy." Used also as a masculine name.

Gila, Gilah (גִּילָה) From the Hebrew, meaning "joy." Geela, Geelah, Ghila, and Gilla are variant spellings. Gili is a variant form.

Gilada, Giladah (גִּלְעָדָה) From the Hebrew, meaning "(the) hill is (my) witness" or "joy is forever." The masculine form is Gilad (Gilead).

Gilana, Gilanah (גִּילָנָה) From the Hebrew, meaning "joy" or "stage in life." Gilat and Gilit are variant forms.

Gilat (גִּילַת) A variant form of Gilana. *See* Gilana.

Gilberta The feminine form of Gilbert. *See* Gilbert (masculine section).

Gilda From the Celtic, meaning "servant of God," or from the Old English, meaning "gold, coated with gold." Akin to Golda.

Gili (גִּילִי) From the Hebrew, meaning "my joy." A variant form of Gila.

Gilia, Giliah Variant spellings of Giliya. *See* Giliya.

Gilit (גִּילִית) A variant form of Gilana. *See* Gilana.

Giliya, Giliyah (גִּילְיָה) From the Hebrew, meaning "my joy is in the Lord." Gilia and Giliah are variant spellings.

Gill From the Old English, meaning "girl." The original form is Gillian. Jill is a variant spelling. The name has become synonymous with "sweetheart," as in the expression, "Every Jack has his Jill (Gill)".

Gilla A variant spelling of Gila. *See* Gila.

Gimra, Gimrah (גִּמְרָה) From the Hebrew, meaning "to ripen, fulfill, complete."

Gina (גִּנָּה) From the Hebrew, meaning "garden." Also spelled גִינָה. Akin to Ginat. Also, a short form of Regina (but pronounced with a soft g). *See* Regina. Gena is a variant spelling.

Ginat (גִּינַת) From the Hebrew, meaning "garden." Akin to Gina.

Ginette A pet form of Virginia. *See* Virginia. Also, a variant form of Jeanette. *See* Jeanette.

Ginger A pet form of Virginia. *See* Virginia.

Ginnie, Ginny Pet forms of Virginia. *See* Virginia.

Giora (גִּיוֹרָה) From the Hebrew, meaning "stranger" or "convert."

Gioret (גִּיוֹרֶת) A variant form of Giora. *See* Giora.

Giovanna, Giovanina Italian forms of Johanna. *See* Johanna.

Gipsy A variant spelling of Gypsy. *See* Gypsy.

Gisa From the Anglo-Saxon, meaning "gift."

Gisela, Gisella From the Anglo-Saxon, meaning "the bright hope of the people" or "sword." Giselle is a variant form. Gizela is a variant spelling.

Giselle A variant form of Gisela. *See* Gisela.

Gita, Gitah (גִּתָּה) Variant forms of Gat. *See* Gat. Sometimes spelled גִּיתָּה. Also, a variant form of Gite. *See* Gite.

Gitat (גִּתַּת) From the Hebrew, meaning "one who plays the gitit (instrument)."

Gite (גִּיטֶע) From the Yiddish, meaning "good" or "good person."

Gitel, Gitele, Gittel (גִּיטל) From the Yiddish, meaning "good." Gitela is usually a pet form. *See* Gita. Also spelled גִּיטֶעל.

Gitit (גִּתִּית) From the Hebrew, meaning "cut off" or "wine presser." Also, a musical instrument mentioned in the Book of Psalms. *See* Gitat. Gita and Gitah are variant forms.

Giva, Givah (גִּבְעָה) From the Hebrew, meaning "hill, high place." Givona is a variant form.

Givola (גִּבְעוֹלָה)   From the Hebrew, meaning "bud."

Givona (גִּבְעוֹנָה)   A variant form of Giva. *See* Giva.

Giza (גִּזָּה)   From the Hebrew, meaning "cut stone" or "cut wool."

Gizela   A variant spelling of Gisela. *See* Gisela.

Gladys   A Welsh form of the Latin name Claudia, meaning "lame." Also, from the Celtic, meaning "brilliant, splendid."

Glenda   A feminine form of the Celtic Glen and Glenn, meaning "a narrow, secluded valley."

Glenna   The feminine form of Glenn. *See* Glenn (masculine section).

Glicke (גְּלִיקֶע)   From the Yiddish, meaning "luck." Akin to Glucke.

Glickel (גְּלִיקל)   A pet form of Glicke. *See* Glicke. Also spelled גְּלִיקֶעל.

Glora   From the Latin, meaning "glorious."

Gloria   From the Latin, meaning "glory." Gloriana and Glory are variant forms.

Gloriana   A variant form of Gloria. *See* Gloria.

Glory   A variant form of Gloria. *See* Gloria. Gloryette is a pet form.

Gloryette   A pet form of Glory. *See* Glory.

Glucke (גְּלוּקֶע)   From the Yiddish, meaning "luck." Akin to Glicke.

Gluckel (גְּלוּקל)   A pet form of Glucke. *See* Glucke. Also spelled גְּלוּקֶעל.

Glynda   A variant form of Glenda. *See* Glenda.

Glynis, Glynnis   From the British, meaning "glen, narrow valley."

Goelet (גּוֹאֶלֶת)   From the Hebrew, meaning "redeemer."

Gola (גּוֹלָה)   From the Hebrew, meaning "exile."

Golda (גּוֹלְדָה)   From the Old English and German, meaning "gold, golden." Akin to Gilda. Goldarina, Goldie, and Goldy are pet forms. Zlata is a Polish-Yiddish form.

Goldarina   A pet form of Golda. *See* Golda.

Goldie, Goldy   Pet forms of Golda. *See* Golda.

Gomer (גֹּמֶר)   From the Hebrew, meaning "to finish, complete." Used also as a masculine name. In the Bible, one Gomer was the son of Japhet and grandson of Noah (Genesis 10:2), and another was the wife of Hosea, the Prophet (Hosea 1:3).

Gozala (גּוֹזָלָה)   From the Hebrew, meaning "young bird."

Grace   From the Latin, meaning "grace." Gracie and Graciela are pet forms.

Gracie   A pet form of Grace. *See* Grace.

Graciela   A pet form of Grace. *See* Grace.

Grania   From the Latin, meaning "grain" or "granary."

Grazia   An Italian form of the Latin, meaning "grace." Grazina is a pet form.

Grazina   A pet form of Grazia. *See* Grazia.

Green, Greene   From the Old English, meaning "the color of growing grass." Used also as a masculine name.

Greer   From the Greek and Latin, meaning "guard, guardian."

Greta   A Swedish pet form of Margaret. *See* Margaret.

Gretchen   A German pet form of Margaret. *See* Margaret. Gretel is a variant form.

Gretel   A variant form of Gretchen. *See* Gretchen. Also, from the Old English, meaning "great."

Griselda   From the French, meaning "gray." Chriselda is a variant form.

Gula   A variant spelling of Geula. *See* Geula.

Gurit (גּוּרִית)   From the Hebrew, meaning "the young of an animal," and most often referring to the lion. Akin to the masculine Gur.

Gussie, Gussy   Popular pet forms of Augusta. *See* Augusta.

Guta (גּוּטָא)   A variant form of Gute. *See* Gute.

Gute (גּוּטֶע)   From the Yiddish, meaning "good" or "good person." Guta is a variant form. Gutel is a pet form.

Gutel (גּוּטֶל)   A pet form of Gute. *See* Gute. Also spelled גּוּטֶעל.

Gwen   From the Welsh, meaning "white, fair" or "beautiful and blessed." Gwyn, Gwynn, and Gwynne are variant forms. Gwen and Gwenne are variant spellings. Gwendaline, Gwendoline, Gwendowlyn, Wendy, and Wynne are pet forms.

Gwendaline, Gwendoline, Gwendolyn   Pet forms of Gwen. *See* Gwen.

Gwenn, Gwenne   Variant spellings of Gwen. *See* Gwen.

Gwyn, Gwynn, Gwynne   Variant forms of Gwen. *See* Gwen.

Gypsy   The name signifies a "bohemian" or "rover." One theory says Gypsies originally came from Egypt and Gypsy is a short form. Gipsy is a variant spelling.

Hada (הָדָה)   A pet form of Hadassa. *See* Hadassa.

Hadar (הָדָר)   From the Hebrew, meaning "ornamented, beautiful, honored." Primarily a masculine name. Hadara and Hadarit are variant forms. Also spelled הֲדַר.

Hadara (הֲדָרָה)   A variant form of Hadar. *See* Hadar. Hadura is a variant form.

Hadarit (הֲדָרִית)   A variant form of Hadar. *See* Hadar.

Hadas (הֲדַס)   A short form of Hadassa. *See* Hadassa.

Hadasha   A variant spelling of Chadasha. *See* Chadasha.

Hadassa, Hadassah (הֲדַסָּה)   From the Hebrew, meaning "myrtle tree," the symbol of victory. In the Bible (Esther 2:7), Hadassa is the Hebrew name of Esther, cousin of Mordecai. *See also* Esther. Hadas is a short form. Hada is a pet form. Hode, Hodeh, Hodel, and Hude are Yiddish forms.

Hadura (הַדּוּרָה)   From the Hebrew, meaning "ornamented" or "beautiful." Also, a variant form of Hadara. *See* Hadara.

Hadusha   A variant spelling of Chadusha. *See* Chadusha.

Hafshia   A variant spelling of Chafshiya. *See* Chafshiya.

Hafziba   A variant spelling of Hefziba. *See* Hefziba.

Hagar (הָגָר)   From the Hebrew, meaning "emigration, forsaken, stranger." In the Bible (Genesis 16:1), the concubine of Abraham and the mother of Ishmael.

Hagia, Haggiah   Variant spellings of Chagiya. *See* Chagiya.

Hagiga   A variant spelling of Chagiga. *See* Chagiga.

Hagit   A variant spelling of Chagit. *See* Chagit.

Hagiya   A variant spelling of Chagiya. *See* Chagiya.

Haifa   A variant spelling of Cheifa. *See* Cheifa.

Haile   A variant spelling of Haley. *See* Haley.

Haley   From the Norse, meaning "hero." Akin to Harold. Haile, Halie, Hallie, and Hally are variant spellings. Hollace is a variant form.

Haliaka   The Hawaiian form of Harriet. *See* Harriet.

Halie   A variant spelling of Haley. *See* Haley.

Halina   From the Hawaiian, meaning "resemblance." Also, a Polish form of Helen. *See* Helen.

Hallie, Hally   Variant spellings of Haley. *See* Haley.

Halutza   A variant spelling of Chalutza. *See* Chalutza.

Hamama   A variant spelling of Chamama. *See* Chamama.

Hamania   A variant spelling of Chamaniya. *See* Chamaniya.

Hamital   A variant spelling of Chamital. *See* Chamital.

Hamuda   A variant spelling of Chamuda. *See* Chamuda.

Hamutal   A variant spelling of Chamutal. *See* Chamutal.

Hana   A variant spelling of Chana. *See* Chana. Hanna and Hannah are variant spellings. Hanita is a pet form.

Hanatza (הַנָּצָה)   From the Hebrew, meaning "sprouting."

Hania   A variant spelling of Chaniya. *See* Chaniya. Haniya, Hannia, and Hanniah are variant spellings.

Hanina   A variant spelling of Chanina. *See* Chanina.

Hanit A variant spelling of Chanit. *See* Chanit.

Hanita A variant spelling of Chanita. *See* Chanita. Also, a pet form of Hana. *See* Hana.

Haniya A variant spelling of Chaniya. *See* Chaniya.

Hanna, Hannah Variant spellings of Hana. *See* Hana.

Hannia A variant spelling of Hania. *See* Hania.

Hanniah A variant spelling of Hania. *See* Hania.

Hanuka A variant spelling of Chanuka. *See* Chanuka.

Hanuna A variant spelling of Chanuna. *See* Chanuna.

Hanya A variant spelling of Chanya. *See* Chanya.

Hardie From the Middle English and Old French, meaning "bold, robust."

Harela (הַרְאֵלָה) The feminine form of Harel. *See* Harel (masculine section).

Haritza A variant spelling of Charitza. *See* Charitza.

Harmony From the Greek, meaning "blending into the whole."

Harri A pet form of Harriet. *See* Harriet.

Harriet, Harriette From the Old English, meaning "mistress of the house, ruler, lord." Harri, Hattie, Hatty, Hattye, Hetta, Hetty, and Etta are pet forms. Harry is the masculine form. Haliaka, Henrietta, and Henriette are variant forms.

Hartzit A variant spelling of Chartzit. *See* Chartzit.

Harutza A variant spelling of Charutza. *See* Charutza.

Harzit A variant spelling of Chartzit. *See* Chartzit.

Hashuva A variant spelling of Chashuva. *See* Chashuva.

Hasia A variant spelling of Chasya. *See* Chasya.

Hasida A variant spelling of Chasida. *See* Chasida.

Hasina A variant spelling of Chasina. *See* Chasina.

Hasna A variant spelling of Chasna. *See* Chasna.

Hasuda A variant spelling of Chasuda. *See* Chasuda.

Hasya A variant spelling of Chasya. *See* Chasya.

Hattie, Hatty, Hattye Pet forms of Harriet. *See* Harriet.

Hatzlacha (הַצְלָחָה) From the Hebrew, meaning "success."

Hava A variant spelling of Chava. *See* Chava.

Haviva A variant spelling of Chaviva. *See* Chaviva.

Havuka A variant spelling of Chavuka. *See* Chavuka.

Havuva A variant spelling of Chavuva. *See* Chavuva.

Haya   A variant spelling of Chaya. *See* Chaya.

Hayuta   A variant spelling of Chayuta. *See* Chayuta.

Hazel   From the Old English, meaning "hazel tree." Some scholars associate Hazel with Aveline, French for hazelnut. Among early peoples a wand made from a hazel tree was a symbol of authority. Hazelle is a pet form.

Hazelbelle   A combination of Hazel and Belle. *See* Hazel *and* Belle.

Hazelle   A pet form of Hazel. *See* Hazel.

Healani   From the Hawaiian, meaning "message from heaven."

Heather   From the Anglo-Saxon, meaning "heath, plant, shrub."

Hedda   From the German, meaning "strife, warfare." Hedy and Heddy are pet forms.

Hedia, Hediah   Variant spellings of Hedya. *See* Hedya.

Hedley   From the Old English, meaning "hiding place" or "meadowland."

Hedva   A variant spelling of Chedva. *See* Chedva.

Hedy, Heddy   Pet forms of Hedda, Hester, and Esther. *See* Hedda, Hester, *and* Esther.

Hedya (הֶדְיָה)   From the Hebrew, meaning "voice or echo of the Lord." Hedia and Hediah are variant spellings.

Hefziba, Hefzibah   Anglicized forms of Cheftzi-Ba. *See* Cheftzi-Ba. Hafziba, Hephziba, and Hephzibah are variant spellings. Hepziba and Hepzibah are variant forms.

Heidi   Probably a variant form of Hester, a derivative of Esther. *See* Esther. Heiki is the Hawaiian form.

Heifa   A variant spelling of Cheifa. *See* Cheifa.

Heiki   The Hawaiian form of Heidi. *See* Heidi.

Hela, Helah   Variant spellings of Chel'a. *See* Chel'a.

Helaine   A variant form of Helen. *See* Helen.

Helen   From the Greek, meaning "light." Eileen, Elaine, Eleanor, Ellen, Halina, Helaine, Helena, Helene, and Helina are among its many variant forms.

Helena   A variant form of Helen. *See* Helen.

Helene   The French form of Helen. *See* Helen.

Helenmae   A combination of Helen and Mae. *See* Helen *and* Mae.

Helga   From the Anglo-Saxon, meaning "holy."

Helina   The Hawaiian form of Helen. *See* Helen.

Hella   A variant form of Helen. *See* Helen.

Helly   A pet form of Helga. *See* Helga.

Helmit   A variant spelling of Chelmit. *See* Chelmit.

Helmonit   A variant spelling of Chelmonit. *See* Chelmonit.

Hemda   A variant spelling of Chemda. *See* Chemda.

Hemdia, Hemdiah   Variant spellings of Chemdiya. *See* Chemdiya.

Hen   A variant spelling of Chen. *See* Chen.

Hende (הֶעְנְדֶע)   A variant Yiddish form of Hene. *See* Hene.

Hendel   A variant Yiddish form of Hana (Chana). *See* Chana.

Hene, Heneh (הֶעְנֶע)   Yiddish forms of Chana (Hana). *See* Chana.

Henia   A variant spelling of Chenya. *See* Chenya.

Henna (הֶנָּא)   A Yiddish form of Hannah. *See* Hannah.

Henrietta, Henriette   Variant forms of Harriet. *See* Harriet. Etta is a pet form. Yenta is a Yiddish form.

Henya   A variant spelling of Chenya. *See* Chenya.

Hephziba, Hephzibah   Variant spellings of Hefziba. *See* Hefziba. Hepzi and Hepzia are pet forms.

Hepzi, Hepzia   Pet forms of Hephziba. *See* Hephziba.

Hepziba, Hepzibah   Variant forms of Hefziba. *See* Hefziba.

Herma   From the Latin, meaning "square stone pillar" or "milestone, signpost." Also, a feminine form of Herman. *See* Herman (masculine section).

Hermine   A variant form of Hermione. *See* Hermione.

Hermione   In Greek legend, the daughter of Menelaus and Helen of Troy. Akin to Hermes, who in Greek mythology was the messenger and servant of the other gods. Hermine is a variant form.

Hermona   A variant spelling of Chermona. *See* Chermona.

Herodias   The feminine form of Herod. *See* Herod (masculine section). The second wife of Herod Antipas and the mother of Salome.

Hertzela (הֶרְצְלָה)   The feminine form of Herzel, a popular masculine personal name which honors Theodor Herzl. *See* Herzl (masculine section). Hertzliya is a variant form.

Hertzliya (הֶרְצְלִיָה)   A variant form of Hertzela. *See* Hertzela. Herzlia and Herzliah are variant spellings. Hertzliya is a city in Israel.

Herut   A variant spelling of Cherut. *See* Cherut.

Heruta   A variant spelling of Cheruta. *See* Cheruta.

Herzlia, Herzliah   Variant spellings of Hertzliya. *See* Hertzliya.

Hester   The Latin form of Esther. *See* Esther.

Hesther   A variant form of Hester. *See* Hester.

Hestia   In Greek mythology, the goddess of the hearth. Akin to the Roman name Vesta.

Hetta A pet form of Harriet. *See* Harriet.

Hetty A pet form of Harriet. *See* Harriet. Also, a pet form of Hester. *See* Hester.

Hetzrona A variant spelling of Chetzrona. *See* Chetzrona.

Hiba A variant spelling of Chiba. *See* Chiba.

Hila (הִלָּה) From the Hebrew, meaning "praise." A feminine form of Hillel. Also, a variant spelling of Chila. *See* Chila. Hilla and Hillah are variant spellings.

Hilaire The French form of Hilary. *See* Hilary.

Hilana (הִלָנָה) A variant form of Hila. *See* Hila.

Hilary From the Greek and the Latin, meaning "cheerful." Also, from the Anglo-Saxon, meaning "protector." Hillary is a variant spelling. Hilaire is the French form.

Hilda, Hilde (הִילְדָה) From the German, meaning "battlemaid." Also, variant forms of Hildegard and Mathilda. *See* Hildegard *and* Mathilda. Hildy and Hili are pet forms. Used as a Hebrew name in Israel.

Hildegard, Hildegarde, Hildergarde From the German, meaning "warrior." Hilda, Hilde, and Hildy are variant forms.

Hildy A variant form of Hildegard. *See* Hildegard.

Hili (הִילִי) A pet form of Hilda and Hillela. *See* Hilda *and* Hillela.

Hilla, Hillah Variant spellings of Hila. *See* Hila.

Hillary A variant spelling of Hilary. *See* Hilary.

Hillela (הִלֵּלָה) The feminine form of Hillel. *See* Hillel (masculine section). Hili is a pet form.

Hilma Probably a variant form of Wilhelmina. *See* Wilhelmina.

Hina A variant spelling of China. *See* China.

Hinanit A variant spelling of Chinanit. *See* Chinanit.

Hinda From the German, meaning "hind, deer." A popular Yiddish name. Hindel and Hindelle are pet forms.

Hindel, Hindelle (הִינְדְל) Yiddish pet forms of Hinda. *See* Hinda. Also spelled הִינְדְעל.

Hinit A variant spelling of Chinit. *See* Chinit.

Hita A variant spelling of Chita. *See* Chita.

Hiyuta A variant spelling of Chiyuta. *See* Chiyuta.

Hode, Hodeh (הָאדֶע) Yiddish forms of Hadassah. *See* Hadassah.

Hodel (הָאדֶעל) A Yiddish pet form of Hadassah. *See* Hadassah.

Hodesh A variant spelling of Chodesh. *See* Chodesh.

Hodi (הֹודִי) A Yiddish form of Hadassah. *See* Hadassah.

Hodia, Hodiah   Variant spellings of Hodiya. *See* Hodiya.

Hodiya (הוֹדִיָה)   From the Hebrew, meaning "praise the Lord." Hodia and Hodiah are variant spellings. A masculine name in the Bible (I Chronicles 6:15).

Hogla, Hoglah   Variant spellings of Chogla. *See* Chogla.

Holiday   From the Anglo-Saxon, meaning "festive day, holiday."

Holis   A variant spelling of Hollace. *See* Hollace.

Hollace   A variant form of Haley. *See* Haley. Holis and Hollis are variant spellings.

Holli   A variant spelling of Holly. *See* Holly.

Hollis   A variant spelling of Hollace. *See* Hollace.

Holly, Hollye   From the Anglo-Saxon, meaning "holy." Also, the name of a plant with red berries that was hung on the door in ancient English homes, with the hope that it would bring luck. Holli is a variant spelling.

Honeah   A variant spelling of Honey. *See* Honey.

Honey   From the Anglo-Saxon, meaning "honey." Honeah is a variant spelling.

Honor   From the Latin, meaning "glory, respect." Honour is a variant spelling. Honora is a variant form. Honorine is a pet form.

Honora   A variant form of Honor. *See* Honor.

Honorine   A pet form of Honor. *See* Honor.

Honour   A variant spelling of Honor. *See* Honor.

Hope   From the Anglo-Saxon, meaning "trust, faith." First used as a Christian name by seventeenth-century Puritans, who delighted in adopting abstract virtues for names. Faith, Charity, Prudence, and Honour were some of the other names used.

Horia, Horiah (הוֹרִיָה)   From the Hebrew, meaning "teaching of the Lord."

Hortense   From the Latin, meaning "gardener."

Hosa   A variant spelling of Chosa. *See* Chosa.

Hude (הוּדֶע)   A Yiddish form of Hadassah. *See* Hadassah.

Hudel (הָאדל)   A pet form of Hude. *See* Hude. Also spelled הָאדְעל.

Huela   A feminine form of Hugh. *See* Hugh (masculine section).

Hula   A variant spelling of Chula. *See* Chula.

Hulda, Huldah   Variant spellings of Chulda. *See* Chulda.

Huma   A variant spelling of Chuma. *See* Chuma.

Humi   A variant spelling of Chumi. *See* Chumi.

Hushim   A variant spelling of Chushim. *See* Chushim.

Hyacinth   From the Greek, meaning "blue gem, sapphire."

Ianna The feminine form of Ian. *See* Ian (masculine section).

Ianthe From the Greek, possibly meaning "flower." In Greek mythology, a sea nymph, daughter of Oceanus and Tethys.

Ida From the Old English, meaning "fortunate warrior." Or, from the Old Norse, meaning "industrious." Also, from the Greek, meaning "happy." Idel, Idelle, and Idette are pet forms. Akin to Idonea.

Idalee A combination of Ida and Lee. *See* Ida *and* Lee.

Idel, Idelle Pet forms of Ida. *See* Ida.

Idena A hybrid name of Ida and Dena (Dinah). *See* Ida *and* Dena.

Idette A pet form of Ida. *See* Ida.

Idit (עִדִּית) A Yiddish form of the Hebrew name Yehudit (Judith). *See* Yehudit.

Idonea From the Old Norse, meaning "industrious." Akin to Ida.

Idra (אִדְרָא) From the Aramaic, meaning "flag" or "fig tree." The fig tree was symbolic of profound scholarship. Also, from the Hebrew and Aramaic, meaning "bone (skeleton) of a fish."

Idria A variant spelling of Idriya. *See* Idriya.

Idriya (אִדְרִיָה) From the Hebrew, meaning "duck." Idria is a variant spelling.

Ila A variant form of Ilit. *See* Ilit. Also, a pet form of Ilsa. *See* Ilsa.

Ilana (אִילָנָה) From the Hebrew, meaning "tree." Ilanit is a variant form.

Ilanit (אִילָנִית) A variant form of Ilana. *See* Ilana.

Ilene A variant form of Eileen. *See* Eileen.

Ilia A variant spelling of Ilya. *See* Ilya.

Ilisa, Ilise Variant forms of Elisabeth. *See* Elisabeth.

Ilit (עִלִּית) From the Aramaic, meaning "uppermost, superlative." Ila is a variant form.

Ilka A Scottish form of the Middle English, meaning "of the same class."

Ilona (אִילוֹנָה) From the Hebrew, meaning "oak tree." Eilona and Elona are variant spellings.

Ilsa, Ilse Variant forms of Elisabeth. *See* Elisabeth. Ila is a pet form.

Ilya (אִלְיָה) From the Syriac and Hebrew, meaning "dirge, elegy." Ilia is a variant spelling. Elya is a variant form.

Ilyse A variant form of Elisabeth. *See* Elisabeth.

Ima A variant spelling of Imma. *See* Imma. Yma is a variant spelling.

Imanuela, Imanuella Variant spellings of Emanuela. *See* Emanuela.

Imma (אִמָּא) From the Hebrew, meaning "mother." Also, a variant form of Emma, meaning "big one" or "grandmother." Ima is a variant spelling.

Imma Miriam (אִמָּא מִרְיָם) From the Hebrew, meaning "mother Miriam." In the Talmud, the mother of Abba Saul, a second-century scholar.

Immanuela, Immanuella Variant spellings of Emanuela. *See* Emanuela.

Imma Shalom (אִמָּא שָׁלוֹם) From the Hebrew, meaning "mother of peace." In the Talmud (Shabbat 116a), the wife of Rabbi Eliezer and the sister of Rabban Gamaliel.

Imogen, Imogene From the Latin, meaning "image, likeness."

Imuna, Imunah Variant spellings of Emuna. *See* Emuna.

Ina From the Latin, meaning "mother." A pet form of Eugenia. *See* Eugenia. Ena is a variant spelling.

Inbal (עִנְבָּל) From the Hebrew, meaning "clapper (of a bell)."

Inez From the Greek and Portuguese, meaning "pure." Also, a variant Portuguese form of Agnes. *See* Agnes.

Inga, Inge From the Old English, meaning "meadow" or "children, descendants." Inger is a variant form.

Inger A variant form of Inga. *See* Inga.

Ingrid Popular in Scandinavian countries. From the Old English, meaning "Ing's ride." In Norse mythology, Ing is the god of fertility and peace.

Iora From the Latin, meaning "gold." Also, possibly of Indian origin, meaning "sunshine."

Iphigene, Iphigenia In Greek mythology, a beautiful young girl snatched from the altar where she was to be sacrificed by Aretmis and carried to heaven.

Ipo From the Hawaiian, meaning "darling."

Irena A Polish form of Irene. *See* Irene. Irenka and Irina are variant forms.

Irene From the Greek, meaning "peace." Irena and Irenee are variant forms. *See* Irena. Rene is probably a variant form.

Irenee A variant form of Irene. *See* Irene.

Irenka A Slavic form of Irena. *See* Irena.

Irina A variant form of Irena. *See* Irena.

Iris (אִירִיס) In Greek mythology, the goddess of the rainbow. From the Latin, meaning "faith, hope." Also, the Hebrew name of a plant in the lily family.

Irit (עִירִית) From the Hebrew, meaning "animal fodder." Or, the name of a plant in the lily family.

Irma From the Anglo-Saxon, meaning "maid of high degree," connoting nobility. Erma is a variant spelling.

Isa A pet form of Isabel, used chiefly in Scotland. *See* Isabel.

Isaaca (יִצְחָקָה) The feminine form of Isaac, meaning "laughter." *See* Isaac (masculine section).

Isabeau   A French form of Isabel. *See* Isabel.

Isabel, Isabele, Isabella, Isabelle   Variant forms of Elisabeth, meaning "God's oath." *See* Elisabeth. Bella is a short form. Isobel is a variant spelling.

Isadora, Isidora   Feminine forms of the masculine Isadore, meaning "gift of Isis" in the Greek. Isis was the Egyptian moon goddess.

Isobel   A variant Scottish spelling of Isabel. *See* Isabel.

Isolda, Isolde   Probably from the Old High German, meaning "to rule." Also, possibly from the Celtic, meaning "fair one."

Israela   A variant spelling of Yisraela. *See* Yisraela.

Israelit   A variant spelling of Yisraelit. *See* Yisraelit.

Isr'ela   A variant spelling of Yisr'ela. *See* Yisr'ela.

Isr'elit   A variant spelling of Yisr'elit. *See* Yisr'elit.

Ita (אִיטָא)   From the Celtic, meaning "thirsty." Also, a corrupt Yiddish form of Yehudit (Judith). *See* Yehudit. Also, a Yiddish form of Yetta. *See* Yetta.

Itai (אִתַּי)   From the Aramaic, meaning "timely."

Iti (אִתִּי)   From the Hebrew, meaning "with me." Itti is a variant spelling.

Itia, Itiah   Variant spellings of Itiya. *See* Itiya.

Itiel (אִתִּיאֵל)   From the Hebrew, meaning "God is with me." Itil is a variant form.

Itil (אִיתִּיל)   An abbreviated form of Itiel. *See* Itiel.

Itiya (אִיתִּיָה)   From the Hebrew, meaning "God is with me." Itia and Itiah are variant spellings.

Itka (אִיטְקֶע)   A pet form of the Yiddish Ita. *See* Ita.

Itta   A variant spelling of Ita. *See* Ita.

Itti   A variant spelling of Iti. *See* Iti.

Iva   A variant spelling of Eva. *See* Eva.

Ivana, Ivanna   Feminine forms of Ivan, the Russian form of John. *See* John (masculine section).

Iverna   From the Old English, meaning "bank, shore."

Ivette   A variant spelling of Yvette. *See* Yvette.

Ivria, Ivriah   Variant spellings of Ivriya. *See* Ivriya.

Ivrit (עִבְרִית)   From the Hebrew, meaning "Hebrew (language)." Ivrita is a variant form.

Ivrita (עִבְרִיתָה)   A variant form of Ivrit. *See* Ivrit.

Ivriya (עִבְרִיָה)   The feminine form of Ivri, meaning "Hebrew," the original form by which Jews have been known dating back to Abraham. Literally, Ivri means "from the other side (of the river Euphrates)," from where Abraham came. Ivria and Ivriah are variant spellings.

Ivy   From the Middle English, meaning "vine (of the ginseng family)." Also, from the Greek, meaning "clinging."

Izetta   Probably a pet form of Isabel. *See* Isabel.

Izevel (אִיזֶבֶל)   The original Hebrew form of Jezebel. *See* Jezebel.

Jacinta   From the Middle English and the Greek, meaning "a (reddish-orange) precious stone." Jacinth and Jacinthe are variant forms.

Jacinth   An English form of Jacinta. *See* Jacinta.

Jacinthe   A French form of Jacinta. *See* Jacinta.

Jackie   A pet form of Jacoba and Jacqueline. *See* Jacoba *and* Jacqueline.

Jacklyn, Jaclyn   Variant forms of Jacqueline. *See* Jacqueline.

Jacky   A pet form of Jacqueline. *See* Jacqueline.

Jacoba (יַעֲקֹבָה)   The feminine form of Jacob, meaning "to supplant" or "to protect." *See* Jacob (masculine section). Jacqueline is a variant form. Jackie and Jacobina are pet forms.

Jacobina   A Scottish pet form of Jacoba. *See* Jacoba.

Jacqueline   A French form of Jacoba. *See* Jacoba. Jackie, Jacquetta, Jacqui, Jacquie, and Jaquetta are pet forms. Jacklyn, Jaclyn, and Jaqualina are variant forms. Jacquelyn, Jacquelynne, and Jaqualine are variant spellings.

Jacquelyn, Jacquelynne   Variant spellings of Jacqueline. *See* Jacqueline.

Jacquetta   A pet form of Jacqueline. *See* Jacqueline. Jaquetta is a variant spelling.

Jacqui, Jacquie   Pet forms of Jacqueline. *See* Jacqueline.

Jada   From the Middle English and the Old Norse, meaning "horse," especially an old, worn-out (jaded) one. Also, from the French and Spanish, meaning "a hard stone (generally green in color)."

Jaen   A variant spelling of Yaen. *See* Yaen.

Jaffa   A variant spelling of Yafa. *See* Yafa.

Jafit   A variant spelling of Yafit. *See* Yafit.

Jaime, Jaimee, Jaimie   Feminine forms of James, derived from Jacob, meaning "to supplant" or "to protect." *See* James *and* Jacob (masculine section). Jamie is a variant spelling.

Jamese   A French feminine form of James. *See* James (masculine section).

Jamesena, Jamesina   Feminine pet forms of James. *See* James (masculine section).

Jamie A variant spelling of Jaime. *See* Jaime.

Jan A pet form of Janice or Jeanette. *See* Janice *and* Jeanette.

Jane A variant English form of Johanna. *See* Johanna. Also, a feminine form of John. *See* John (masculine section). Until the sixteenth century Joan was the popular feminine form of John. Jane replaced it in popularity in the centuries that followed. Janice is a variant form. Janean, Janeane, Janee, Janel, Janell, Janella, Janerette, Janey, Jani, Janina, Janine, Janita, Jenerette, and Jenine are pet forms. *See also* Johanna.

Janean, Janeane Variant pet forms of Jane. *See* Jane.

Janee A pet form of Jane. *See* Jane.

Janel, Janell, Janella Pet forms of Jane. *See* Jane.

Janerette A pet form of Jane. *See* Jane.

Janet An English and Scottish form of Johanna. *See* Johanna.

Janetta An English form of Johanna. *See* Johanna. Akin to Janet.

Janette A variant spelling of Janet. *See* Janet.

Janey A pet form of Jane. *See* Jane.

Jani A pet form of Jane. *See* Jane.

Janice A variant form of Jane. *See* Jane. Jan is a pet form. Janiece and Janis are variant spellings. Jenise is a variant form.

Janie A pet form of Jane. *See* Jane.

Janiece A variant spelling of Janice. *See* Janice.

Janina, Janine Pet forms of Jane. *See* Jane.

Janis A variant spelling of Janice. *See* Janice.

Janita A Spanish pet form of Jane. *See* Jane.

Janna A pet form of Johanna. *See* Johanna.

Jantina A Dutch form of Johanna. *See* Johanna.

Jaonne A variant form of Joan. *See* Joan.

Jaqualina A variant form of Jacqueline. *See* Jacqueline.

Jaqualine A variant spelling of Jacqueline. *See* Jacqueline.

Jaquetta A variant spelling of Jacquetta. *See* Jacquetta.

Jara A Slavonic form of Gertrude. *See* Gertrude.

Jardena A variant spelling of Yardena. *See* Yardena.

Jardenia A variant spelling of Yardeniya. *See* Yardenia.

Jaredene The feminine form of Jared. *See* Jared (masculine section).

Jasmina, Jasmine A Persian flower-name, usually referring to a flower in the olive family. *See also* Yasmin.

Jean, Jeane Scottish forms of Johanna. *See* Johanna. Jeanice is a variant form. Jene is a variant spelling.

Jeanetta A variant form of Jeanette. *See* Jeanette.

Jeanette A French form of Johanna. *See* Johanna. Jeanetta and Jenat are variant forms. Jeannette is a variant spelling. Jeanie and Jeanine are pet forms.

Jeanice A variant form of Jean. *See* Jean.

Jeanie A pet form of Jean. *See* Jean.

Jeanine A pet form of Jean. *See* Jean. Jeannine is a variant spelling.

Jeanne A French form of Johanna. *See* Johanna.

Jeannette A variant spelling of Jeanette. *See* Jeanette.

Jeannine A variant spelling of Jeanine. *See* Jeanine.

Jedidia, Jedidiah Variant spellings of Yedidya. *See* Yedidya.

Jehane, Jehanne French forms of Johanna. *See* Johanna.

Jehosheba A variant spelling of Yehosheva. *See* Yehosheva.

Jemima A variant spelling of Yemima. *See* Yemima.

Jemina A variant spelling of Yemina. *See* Yemina.

Jen A short form of Jeannette. *See* Jeannette. Also, a pet form of Jennifer.

Jenat A variant form of Jeanette. *See* Jeanette.

Jene A variant spelling of Jean. *See* Jean.

Jenerette A pet form of Jane. *See* Jane.

Jenine A pet form of Jane. *See* Jane.

Jenise A variant form of Janice. *See* Janice.

Jenna A variant form of Jeanette. *See* Jeanette. Genna is a variant spelling.

Jennie A pet form of Jean, Jeanette, and Jennifer. Jinny is a variant form. Also, a variant spelling of Jenny.

Jennifer From the Welsh name Guinever, which later became Winifred. *See* Winifred. Jen, Jennie, and Jenny are pet forms.

Jennilee A name created by combining Jennifer and Lee. *See* Jennifer *and* Lee.

Jenny An English and Scottish form of Johanna. *See* Johanna. Also, a variant spelling of Jennie. *See* Jennie.

Jeri, Jerri Pet forms of Geraldene. *See* Geraldene.

Jerriann A name created by combining Jerri and Ann. *See* Jerry (masculine section) *and* Ann.

Jerrilyn A name created by combining Jerri and Lyn. *See* Jerry (masculine section) *and* Lyn.

Jerusalem (יְרוּשָׁלַיִם) The Anglicized form of Yerushalayim. *See* Yerushalayim.

Jerusha, Jerushah   Variant spellings of Yerusha. *See* Yerusha.

Jessica   A variant form of Jessie. *See* Jessie.

Jessie   A Scottish form of Johanna. *See* Johanna. Or, a feminine form of Jesse. *See* Jesse (masculine section).

Jethra (יִתְרָה)   A feminine form of Jethro, meaning "abundance, riches." *See* Jethro (masculine section). Akin to Yitra.

Jetta   From the Old French and the Latin, meaning "a hard variety of black coal which takes a high polish."

Jewel, Jewell   From the Old French, meaning "joy."

Jezebel (אִיזֶבֶל)   An Anglicized form of the Hebrew, meaning "unexalted" or "impure." In the Bible (I Kings 16:31), the wicked wife of Ahab, king of Israel. Izevel is the original Hebrew form.

Jill   A variant spelling of Gill. *See* Gill.

Jinny   A Scottish form of Jenny. *See* Jenny.

Jinx   An invented name. Jynx is a variant spelling.

Joan   A variant form of Johanna. *See* Johanna.

Joann, Jo Ann   Short forms of Joanna. *See* Joanna. Joanne is a variant spelling.

Joanna   A short form of Johanna. *See* Johanna. In the New Testament (Luke 3:27), the wife of Chuza, King Herod's steward.

Joanne   A variant spelling of Joann. *See* Joann.

Jo-Anne   A hybrid name compounded of Jo (Josephine) and Ann(e). *See* Josephine *and* Ann(e). Also, a variant spelling of Joann. *See* Joann.

Jobina, Jobyna   Feminine forms of Job. *See* Job (masculine section).

Jocelin, Joceline   German forms of the Hebrew Jacoba, the feminine form of Jacob, meaning "supplanted." Akin to Jacqueline. Also, from the Latin, meaning "just, honest." Akin to Justina. Jocelyn, Jocelyne, Joscelin, Josceline, Joscelyn, and Joslyn are variant spellings. Joscelind is a variant form.

Jocelyn, Jocelyne   Variant spellings of Jocelin. *See* Jocelin.

Jochebed, Jocheved   Variant spellings of Yocheved. *See* Yocheved.

Jodette   A French form of Jodi or Jocelin. *See* Jodi *and* Jocelin.

Jodi, Jodie, Jody   Pet forms of Judith. *See* Judith. Also, pet forms of Josephine. *See* Josephine.

Joela, Joella, Joelle (יוֹאֵלָה)   Feminine forms of Joel, meaning "God is willing." *See* Joel *and* Yoel (masculine section). *See also* Yoela.

Joellen   A variant form of Joelynn. *See* Joelynn.

Joelynn   A name created by combining Joseph and Ellen. *See* Joseph (masculine section) *and* Ellen. Joellen is a variant form.

Joette   A pet form from the masculine Joseph. *See* Joseph.

Johanina   A Portuguese form of Johanna. *See* Johanna.

Johanna (יוֹחָנָה)   A German and English form of the Hebrew masculine name Yochanan, meaning "God is gracious." Yochana is the Hebrew feminine form of Yochanan. Akin to Chana. Among its many variant forms are Jane, Janetta, Joan, Jone (English); Janet, Jenny (English, Scotch); Jean, Jeane, Jessie (Scotch); Joanna (English, Scotch, Polish); Jeanne, Jeanette (French); Juana, Juanita (Spanish); Jantina (Dutch); Johanina, Jovanna (Portuguese); Giovanna, Giovanina (Italian). The Yiddish name Yachna is a derivative form.

Johanne   A variant form of Johanna. *See* Johanna.

Johnna   A variant form of Johanna. *See* Johanna.

Johnnie   A pet form of Johanna. *See* Johanna.

Joia   An early form of Joyce (thirteenth century). *See* Joyce.

Joice   A variant spelling of Joyce. *See* Joyce.

Jolan   A short form of Jolande. *See* Jolande.

Jolande   A variant spelling of Yolande. *See* Yolande. Jolan is a short form.

Jolene   A pet form of Jolie. *See* Jolie.

Joletta   A pet form of Jolie. *See* Jolie.

Jolie   A French form of the Middle English, meaning "high spirits, good humor, pleasant." Jolene and Joletta are pet forms. Joliet is a variant form.

Joliet   A variant form of Juliet or Jolie. *See* Juliet *and* Jolie.

Jona, Jonah (יוֹנָה)   Feminine forms of Jonah. *See* Jonah (masculine section). Variant spellings of Yona. *See* Yona.

Jonat   A variant spelling of Yonat. *See* Yonat.

Jonata   A variant spelling of Yonata. *See* Yonata.

Jonati   A variant spelling of Yonati. *See* Yonati.

Jone   An Old English form of Johanna. *See* Johanna.

Jonina   A variant spelling of Yonina. *See* Yonina.

Jonit, Jonita   Variant spellings of Yonit and Yonita. *See* Yonit.

Jonnalee   A hybrid form combining Johanna and Lee. *See* Johanna *and* Lee.

Jonnie   A pet form of Johanna. *See* Johanna.

Jordana, Jordena (יַרְדְּנָה)   Feminine forms of Jordan. *See* Jordan (masculine section). Akin to Yardena. Jordi and Jordie are pet forms.

Jordi, Jordie   Pet forms of Jordana. *See* Jordana.

Joscelin   An Old French form of Jocelin. *See* Jocelin.

Joscelind   A variant form of Jocelin. *See* Jocelin.

Josceline   An Old French form of Jocelin. *See* Jocelin.

Joscelyn   A variant spelling of Joscelin. *See* Jocelin.

Josefa, Josepha   Variant spellings of Yosifa. *See* Yosifa.

Josephine   A feminine French form of Joseph. *See* Joseph (masculine section). Jo, Josette, Josie, and Pepita are pet forms.

Josette   A pet form of Josephine or Jocelyn. *See* Josephine *and* Joceline.

Josie   A pet form of Josephine or Joceline. *See* Josephine *and* Joceline.

Josifa, Josipha   Variant spellings of Yosifa. *See* Yosifa.

Joslyn   A variant spelling of Jocelin. *See* Jocelin.

Jovanna   A Portuguese form of Johanna. *See* Johanna.

Jovita   From the Latin, meaning "jovial."

Joy   A short form of Joyce. *See* Joyce.

Joya   A variant form of Joyce. *See* Joyce.

Joyce   From the Latin, meaning "merry." Joice is a variant spelling. Joya is a variant form. Joy is a short form.

Juana   A Spanish form of Johanna. *See* Johanna.

Juanita   A Spanish form of Johanna. *See* Johanna. Nita is a short form.

Judi, Judie (יוּדִי)   Pet forms of Judith. *See* Judith.

Judith (יְהוּדִית)   An Anglicized form of Yehudit. *See* Yehudit. Jodi, Jodie, Jody, Judi, Judie, and Judy are pet forms.

Judy   A pet form of Judith. *See* Judith.

Jule, Jules   Variant forms of Julia. *See* Julia.

Julia   From the Greek, meaning "soft-haired," symbolizing youth. The feminine form of Julian and Julius. *See* Julian *and* Julius (masculine section). Jule, Jules, Julian, Juliana, and Julienne are variant forms. Julie, Juliet, and Juliette are pet forms.

Julian, Juliana   Variant forms of Julia. *See* Julia. Also, may be derived from Gillian, meaning "girl." *See* Gill.

Julie   A pet form of Julia. *See* Julia.

Julienne   The French form of Julia. *See* Julia.

Juliet   A French pet form of Julia. *See* Julia. Joliet is a variant form.

Julieta   A variant form of Julia. *See* Julia.

Juliette   A pet form of Juliet. *See* Juliet.

June   From the Latin, meaning "ever youthful."

Junez   An invented name. A combination of June and Inez. *See* June *and* Inez.

Justina, Justine   Feminine forms of Justin, meaning "just, honest." *See* Justin (masculine section).

Kaaren   A variant spelling of Karen. *See* Karen.

Kadia, Kadiah, Kadya (כַּדְיָה)   From the Hebrew, meaning "pitcher."

Kaile, Kaille   Variant forms of Kelila. *See* Kelila. Kaylee and Kayley are variant spellings.

Kaimana   A Hawaiian name, meaning "diamond."

Kalanit (כַּלָנִית)   A cup-shaped plant with colorful flowers seen along the Israeli countryside.

Kaley   A variant form of Kelly. *See* Kelly.

Kalia   A variant form of Kelila. *See* Kelila.

Kama (קָמָה)   From the Hebrew, meaning "ripened, mature grain."

Kana (כַּנָּה)   From the Hebrew, meaning "plant."

Kanara (כַּנָּרָה)   From the Hebrew, meaning "harpist" or "canary." Akin to Kanarit.

Kanarit (כַּנָּרִית)   From the Hebrew, meaning "canary."

Kandi   A variant spelling of Candy. *See* Candy.

Kanit (קָנִית)   From the Hebrew, meaning "songbird." Akin to Kanara and Kanarit.

Kara   A pet form of Katherine. *See* Katherine.

Kareen   A variant spelling of Karen. *See* Karen.

Karen   A Danish form of Katherine. *See* Katherine. Caren, Carin, Kaaren, Kareen, Karin, Karon, and Karyn are variant spellings.

Kari   A variant spelling of Carrie. *See* Carrie.

Karin   A variant spelling of Karen. *See* Karen.

Karina   A variant spelling of Carina. *See* Carina.

Karita   A variant spelling of Carita. *See* Carita.

Karla   A feminine form of Karl. *See* Karl (masculine section). Also, a variant spelling of Carla. Karleen and Karlene are pet forms.

Karleen   A pet form of Karla. *See* Karla.

Karlene   A pet form of Karla. *See* Karla.

Karma   A variant spelling of Carma. *See* Carma. Akin to Kerem.

Karmel   A variant spelling of Carmel. *See* Carmel.

Karmela   A variant spelling of Carmela. *See* Carmela.

Karmeli   A variant spelling of Carmeli. *See* Carmeli.

Karmelit   A variant spelling of Carmelit. *See* Carmelit.

Karmia   A variant spelling of Karmiya. *See* Karmiya.

Karmil (כַּרְמִיל)   From the Hebrew, meaning "red, crimson."

Karmit   A variant spelling of Carmit. *See* Carmit.

Karmiya   A variant spelling of Carmia. *See* Carmia.

Karna   A variant spelling of Carna. *See* Carna.

Karnei-Yael (קַרְנֵי-יָעֵל)   From the Hebrew, meaning "antelope horns."

Karni   A variant spelling of Carni. *See* Carni.

Karnia   A variant spelling of Carnia. *See* Carnia.

Karniela, Karniella   Variant spellings of Carniela. *See* Carniela.

Karnit   A variant spelling of Carnit. *See* Carnit.

Karol, Karole   Variant spellings of Carol. *See* Carol, Karol, Karole.

Karolina   The Polish form of Karolyn. *See* Karolyn.

Karolyn   A variant spelling of Carolyn and Caroline. *See* Caroline. Karolina is a variant form.

Karon   A variant spelling of Karen. *See* Karen.

Karyl   A variant spelling of Carol. *See* Carol.

Karyn   A variant spelling of Karen. *See* Karen.

Kasia, Kassia   Variant Polish forms of Katherine. *See* Katherine.

Kasimira   From the Slavic, meaning "command for peace."

Kaspit (כַּסְפִּית)   From the Hebrew, meaning "silver."

Kasse   A variant form of Katherine. *See* Katherine.

Katania, Kataniya (קְטַנְיָה)   From the Hebrew, meaning "small." Katan is the masculine form.

Kate   A pet form of Katherine. *See* Katherine.

Kath   A pet form of Katherine. *See* Katherine.

Katha   A pet form of Katherine. *See* Katherine.

Katharina   A variant spelling of Katherine. *See* Katherine.

Katharine   A variant spelling of Katherine. *See* Katherine.

Kathe   A pet form of Katherine. *See* Katherine.

Katherine   From the Greek, meaning "pure, unsullied." Catherine is the more popular spelling. *See* Catherine. Also spelled Katharina, Katharine, Kathrene, and Kathryn. Karen, Karin, Kasia, Kasse, Kassia, Katrina, Katrine, Katrinka, Katrinke, and Kay are variant forms. Kara, Katania, Kate, Kath, Katha, Kathe, Kathie, Kathy, Kati, Katie, Katina, Ketina, Katy, Kelly, Kit, and Kitty are pet forms.

Kathie   A pet form of Katherine. *See* Katherine.

Kathleen   A variant spelling of Cathleen.

Kathrene   A variant spelling of Katherine.

Kathryn   A variant spelling of Katherine. *See* Katherine.

Kathy   A pet form of Katherine. *See* Katherine.

Kati, Katie   Pet forms of Katherine. *See* Katherine.

Katina   A Slavic pet form of Katherine. *See* Katherine.

Katrina, Katrine   Variant forms of Katherine. *See* Katherine.

Katrinka, Katrinke   Slavic forms of Katherine. *See* Katherine.

Katy   A pet form of Katherine. *See* Katherine.

Kay   From the Greek, meaning "rejoice," or a form of Katherine, meaning "purity." *See* Katherine.

Kayla, Kayle (קײלֶע)   Variant forms of Kelila. Or, a Yiddish form of Celia. *See* Kelila *and* Celia.

Kaylee, Kayley   Variant spellings of Kaile. *See* Kaile.

Kedma (קֶדְמָה)   From the Hebrew, meaning "east, eastward."

Keely   A variant form of Kelly. *See* Kelly.

Kefira (כְּפִירָה)   From the Hebrew, meaning "young lioness."

Kelda   From the Old Norse, meaning "fountain, spring."

Kelila (כְּלִילָה)   From the Hebrew, meaning "crown " or "laurel." Kalia, Kaile, Kaille, Kayla, Kayle, Kyla, and Kyle are variant forms used as Yiddish names.

Kelley, Kelli   Variant spellings of Kelly. *See* Kelly.

Kelly   A variant form of Kelt (also spelled Celt), the name of an ancient people in Central and Western Europe who were antecedents of the Gaelic families of Europe. Kelley and Kelli are variant spellings. Kaley and Keely are variant forms. *See also* Kelton. Also, a pet form of Katherine. *See* Katherine.

Kelton   From the Celtic, meaning "a town inhabited by Celts." Akin to Kelly. Also, from the Old English, meaning "keel town, a town where ships are built."

Kelula (כְּלוּלָה)   A variant form of Kelila. *See* Kelila.

Ken   A pet form of Kenna and the masculine Kenneth. *See* Kenna *and* Kenneth (masculine section).

Kendis   A variant form of Kenna. *See* Kenna.

Kendra   A variant form of Kenna. *See* Kenna.

Kendy   A feminine form of Kenneth. *See* Kenneth (masculine section).

Kenna   From the Old English, meaning "head" or "children." Also, from the Old Norse, meaning "to know, have knowledge." Kendis and Kendra are variant forms. Ken is a pet form.

Kerem (כֶּרֶם)   From the Hebrew, meaning "vineyard." Carma is an Aramaic form. *See* Carma. Akin to Carmel. *See* Carmel.

Keren (קֶרֶן) From the Hebrew, meaning "horn" (of an animal)." Keryn is a variant spelling.

Keren-Hapuch (קֶרֶן־הַפּוּךְ) From the Hebrew, meaning "horn of antimony (a black eye-paint used as a beautifier)." In the Bible (Job 42:14), one of Job's daughters. Translated as "Amalthea's horn" in the Greek translation of the Bible (Septuagint). In Greek mythology, Amiltai (also called Amalthea) is the goat whose horn overflowed with riches.

Keret (קֶרֶת) From the Hebrew, meaning "city" or "settlement."

Kerry A variant spelling of Carrie. See Carrie.

Keryn A variant spelling of Keren. See Keren.

Kesarit (קֵסָרִית) A Hebrew form of the feminine form of the Latin name Caesar, Caesar, meaning "to cut."

Keshet (קֶשֶׁת) From the Hebrew, meaning "bow, rainbow."

Keshisha (קְשִׁישָׁה) From the Hebrew, meaning "old, elder."

Keshuva (קְשׁוּבָה) From the Hebrew, meaning "hear, listen."

Kessem (קֶסֶם) From the Hebrew, meaning "magic."

Ketana (קְטַנָּה) From the Hebrew, meaning "small."

Ketifa (קְטִיפָה) From the Hebrew and Arabic, meaning "to pluck (usually ripened fruit)" and "velvet." Ketipha is a variant spelling.

Ketina (קְטִינָא) From the Aramaic, meaning "minor" or "small child." Also, a pet form of Katherine. See Katherine. Also spelled קְטִינָה.

Ketipha A variant spelling of Ketifa. See Ketifa.

Ketura, Keturah (קְטוּרָה) From the Hebrew, meaning "burned (usually incense)" or "perfumed." In the Bible (Genesis 25:1), Abraham's wife.

Ketzia, Ketziah (קְצִיעָה) From the Hebrew, meaning "cassia, powdered bark," with a cinnamon-like fragrance. Possibly, a variant form of Kida. See Kida. In the Bible (Job 42:14), the second daughter of Job. Kezi, Kezzi, Kezzie, and Kezzy are pet forms. Kezia, and Keziah are variant spellings.

Kevuda (כְּבוּדָה) From the Hebrew, meaning "precious" or "respected."

Kezi A pet form of Ketzia. See Ketzia.

Kezia, Keziah Variant spellings of Ketzia. See Ketzia.

Kezzi, Kezzie, Kezzy Pet forms of Ketzia. See Ketzia.

Kida (קִדָּה) A spice-producing plant, usually referred to as cassia. In the Bible (Exodus 30:24), it provided an ingredient in the production of sacred oil for use in the Tabernacle. See also Ketzia.

Kim A pet form of Kimberley. See Kimberley.

Kimberley, Kimberly A name adopted from kimberlite, a type of rock formation often containing diamonds. Kimberly is the diamond-mining center of

South Africa. Kim is a pet form.

Kin From the Old English and the Old Norse, meaning "to produce," hence "offspring, relatives."

Kinneret (כִּנֶּרֶת) The Hebrew name of the Sea of Galilee—a lake in northern Israel. Probably from the Hebrew, meaning "harp."

Kiria, Kiriah Variant spellings of Kirya. *See* Kirya.

Kirsten From the Old English, meaning "stone church." Kirsti, Kirstie, and Kirsty are pet forms.

Kirsti, Kirstie, Kirsty Norwegian pet forms of Kirsten. *See* Kirsten.

Kirya (קִרְיָה) From the Hebrew, meaning "town, village." Kiria and Kiriah are variant spellings.

Kismet From the Arabic, meaning "fate, destiny."

Kit A pet form of Katherine. *See* Katherine.

Kitra (כִּתְרָה) From the Aramaic, meaning "crown." Akin to Kitron.

Kitron (כִּתְרוֹן) A feminine form of the masculine Keter, meaning "crown." Akin to Kitra.

Kitty A pet form of Katherine. *See* Katherine.

Kochava (כּוֹכָבָה) From the Hebrew, meaning "star, pertaining to the stars." Kochavit and Kochevet are variant forms.

Kochavit (כּוֹכָבִית) A variant form of Kochava. *See* Kochava.

Kochevet (כּוֹכֶבֶת) A variant form of Kochava. *See* Kochava.

Koleen A variant spelling of Colleen. *See* Colleen.

Kolia A variant spelling of Kolya. *See* Kolya.

Kolya (קוֹלְיָה) From the Hebrew, meaning "God's voice." Kolia is a variant spelling.

Koranit (קוֹרָנִית) From the Hebrew, meaning "thistle."

Korenet (קוֹרֶנֶת) From the Hebrew, meaning "to shine, emit rays."

Kozbi A variant spelling of Kozvi. *See* Kozvi.

Kozvi (כָּזְבִּי) From the Hebrew, meaning "lie, falsehood." In the Bible (Numbers 25:15), a Midianite woman. Cozbi and Kozbi are variant spellings.

Kreindel (קְריינדל) A pet form of Kreine. *See* Kreine. Also spelled קריינדעל.

Kreine (קְריינֶע) A Yiddish form of the German *Krone*, meaning "crown." Kreindel is a pet form.

Kriss, Krissie Pet forms of Kristin and Kristine. *See* Kristin.

Krist, Krista Short forms of Kristian. *See* Kristian.

Kristian A variant form of Christina. *See* Christina. Krist and Krista are short forms.

Kristie   A pet form of Kristine. *See* Kristine.

Kristin, Kristine   Variant forms of Christine. *See* Christine. Kriss, Krissie, Kristie, and Kristy are pet forms.

Kristy   A pet form of Kristine. *See* Kristine.

Kyla, Kyle   Variant forms of Kelila. *See* Kelila. Also from the Greek, meaning "two-handled drinking cup." Kylia is a variant form. Kylene is a pet form.

Kylene   A pet form of Kyla. *See* Kyla.

Kylia   A variant form of Kyla. *See* Kyla.

Kyrene   From the Greek, meaning "Lord" or "God."

LaBelle   From the French, meaning "beautiful one."

LaDean   From the French, meaning "dean." *See* Dean.

Lady   From the Old English, meaning "lady, mistress."

Lahela   The Hawaiian form of Rachel. *See* Rachel.

Laila   A variant spelling of Leila. *See* Leila.

Laili, Lailie   Variant spellings of Leili and Leilie. *See* Leili.

Laliv (לָלִיב)   Possibly a variant form of Lulava. *See* Lulava.

Lamarr   From the Latin and French, meaning "of the sea."

Lamorna   From the Middle English, meaning "morning."

Lana   From the Latin, meaning "woolly." Also, a pet form of Alana. *See* Alana.

Lanai   From the Hawaiian, meaning "veranda, terrace."

Lancey, Lanci, Lancie   Feminine forms of Lance. *See* Lance (masculine section).

Lani   From the Hawaiian, meaning "sky."

La Nora   A variant form of Nora. *See* Nora.

Lara   A variant spelling of Laura. *See* Laura. In Roman mythology, a nymph punished by Jove because of her talkativeness.

Laraine   From the Latin, meaning "sea-bird."

Laris, Larisa, Larissa   From the Latin, meaning "cheerful."

Lark   From the Middle English, referring to "a bird of a family of songbirds," the most common being the meadowlark.

Lasca   From the Arabic, meaning "army" or "soldier."

Lassie   From the Middle English, meaning "young girl, maiden." Popular in Scotland.

Latifa (לְטִיפָה)   From the Hebrew, meaning "gentle slap" or "caress."

Laura   A variant form of Laurel. From the Latin, meaning "laurel (a symbol of victory)." Lara, Lora, and Loura are variant spellings. Lauraine, Laure, and Lauren are variant forms. Laurestine, Lauretta, Laurette, Lauri, Laurie, and Lolly are pet forms.

Lauraine   A variant form of Laura. *See* Laura.

Laure   A variant form of Laura. *See* Laura.

Laurel   From the Latin, meaning "laurel (a symbol of victory)." Laura and Laurice are variant forms. Loral and Lorrell are variant spellings.

Lauren   A variant form of Laura. *See* Laura.

Laurestine   A pet form of Laura. *See* Laura.

Lauretta, Laurette   Pet forms of Laura. *See* Laura.

Lauri, Laurie   Pet forms of Laura. *See* Laura. Loree is a variant spelling.

Laurice   A variant form of Laurel. *See* Laurel.

Lauve   From the Old English, meaning "lord." Also, from the Old French, meaning "to wash."

Laverne   From the Latin and French, meaning "spring, springlike" or "to be verdant."

Lavi (לָבִיא)   From the Hebrew, meaning "lion." Primarily a masculine name.

Lavinia   From the Latin, meaning "woman of Rome."

Lawrie   A feminine form of Lawrence. *See* Lawrence (masculine section). Akin to Laura. *See* Laura.

Layish (לַיִשׁ)   From the Hebrew, meaning "lion." In the Bible (I Samuel 25:44), the father of Michal's second husband. Primarily a masculine name.

Laylie   A variant spelling of Leili. *See* Leili.

Lea   A French form of Leah. *See* Leah. Also, from the Old English, meaning "meadow."

Leah (לֵאָה)   From the Hebrew, meaning "to be weary." Also, from the Assyrian, meaning "mistress, ruler." In the Bible (Genesis 29:17), the daughter of Laban and the first of Jacob's four wives. Lea is a variant spelling and also a French form. Leia is the Hebrew form. Lia is an Italian form. Lea and Lee are pet forms.

Leala   From the Middle English and the Latin, meaning "legal, loyal."

Leana   A variant form of Liana. *See* Liana.

Leanne   A name created by combining Leah and Anne. *See* Leah *and* Anne. Also, a variant form of Lianne.

Leanor, Leanore   Variant forms of Eleanor. *See* Eleanor.

Leather   From the Old English, meaning "oracle."

Leatrice   A name created by combining Leah and Beatrice. *See* Leah *and* Beatrice.

Le Clair, Le Claire   French forms of Claire. *See* Claire.

Leda   In Greek mythology, a Spartan queen, the mother of Helen of Troy. Lida is a variant spelling. Lidia is a variant form.

Lee   From the Anglo-Saxon, meaning "field, meadow." Also, a pet form of Leah. *See* Leah. Leigh is a variant spelling. Lea is the original form.

Leean   A hybrid form of Lee and Ann. *See* Lee *and* Ann.

Leeba   A variant spelling of Liba. *See* Liba.

Lei   A pet form of Leilani. *See* Leilani.

Leia (לֵאָה)   The Hebrew form of Leah. *See* Leah.

Leiana   A name created by combining Leah and Anna. *See* Leah *and* Anna.

Leigh   A variant spelling of Lee. *See* Lee.

Leila, Leilah (לַיְלָה)   From the Arabic and Hebrew, meaning "dark Oriental beauty" or "night." Among the Persians Leila was used as a name meaning "dark-haired." Laila and Leyla are variant spellings.

Leilani   From the Hawaiian, meaning "heavenly flower." Lelani is a variant spelling. Lei is a pet form.

Leili, Leilie (לֵילִי)   From the Hebrew, meaning "my night." Laili, Lailie, and Laylie are variant spellings. Akin to Leila.

Lela   From the Anglo-Saxon, meaning "loyal, faithful." Lelia is a variant form.

Leland   From the Old English, meaning "meadowland." Akin to Lea.

Lelani   A variant spelling of Leilani. *See* Leilani.

Lelia   A variant form of Lela. *See* Lela.

LeMyra   A variant form of Myra. *See* Myra.

Lena   A pet form of Eleanor, Helen, and Magdalene. *See* Eleanor, Helen, *and* Magdalene. Also, from the Hebrew, meaning "to sleep, dwell," and from the Old English, meaning "farm."

Lenis   From the Latin, meaning "gentle, mild."

Lennie   A pet form of Eleanor. *See* Eleanor.

Lenora, Lenore   Pet forms of Eleanor. *See* Eleanor.

Leola   From the Anglo-Saxon, meaning "deer," connoting swiftness.

Leoma   A variant form of Leona. *See* Leona.

Leona   From the Greek, meaning "lion-like." Akin to the masculine Leo. *See* Leo (masculine section). Leonia and Leota are variant forms. Leonie is a pet form. Akin to Leontine.

Leonarda   A feminine form of Leonard. *See* Leonard (masculine section).

Leonia A variant form of Leona. *See* Leona.

Leonie A pet form of Leona. *See* Leona.

Leonora, Leonore Variant forms of Eleanor. *See* Eleanor.

Leontine, Leontyne From the Latin, meaning "lion-like." Akin to Leona.

Leora A variant spelling of Liora. *See* Liora.

Leorit A variant spelling of Liorit. *See* Liorit.

Leota A variant form of Leona. *See* Leona.

Lera Possibly derived from the French *le roi,* meaning "the king."

Leron A variant spelling of Liron. *See* Liron. Lerone is a variant spelling.

Lerone A variant spelling of Leron. *See* Leron.

Lesley, Leslie From the Anglo-Saxon, meaning "meadowland."

Lesta A feminine form of Lester. *See* Lester (masculine section).

Leta Probably a form of Elizabeth. *See* Elizabeth.

Letha A pet form of Elizabeth. *See* Elizabeth.

Letifa (לְטִיפָה) A variant form of Latifa. *See* Latifa.

Letitia From the Latin, meaning "joy." Lettie, Letty, Tisha, and Titia are pet forms.

Lettie, Letty Pet forms of Elizabeth. *See* Elizabeth. Also, pet forms of Letitia. *See* Letitia.

Leuma (לְאוּמָה) From the Hebrew, meaning "nation."

Leumi (לְאוּמִי) From the Hebrew, meaning "national" or "my nationality."

Levana (לְבָנָה) From the Hebrew, meaning "white" or "moon." Used also as a masculine name in the Bible. Livana is a variant spelling. Akin to Livna.

Levani From the Fijian, meaning "anointed with oil."

Levia, Leviah (לְבִיאָה) From the Hebrew, meaning "lioness of the Lord." In the Bible (Ezra 19:2), used as a figure of speech for Mother Israel. Also, a feminine form of Levi and spelled לְוָה. *See* Levi (masculine section).

Levina From the Middle English, meaning "to shine."

Leviva (לְבִיבָה) From the Hebrew, meaning "pancake."

Levona (לְבוֹנָה) From the Hebrew, meaning "frankincense," a white spice used in the sacrificial system. Levonat is a variant spelling.

Levonat (לְבוֹנַת) A variant form of Levona. *See* Levona.

Lexi A pet form of Alexandra. *See* Alexandra.

Leyla A variant spelling of Leila. *See* Leila.

Li (לִי) From the Hebrew, meaning "to me." Also, a variant spelling of Lee. *See* Lee.

Lia   The Italian form of Leah. *See* Leah.

Liana   From the French, meaning "to bind, wrap around." Akin to the Latin form, meaning "a tree with creeping vines." Lianne is a variant form.

Lianne   A variant form of Liana. *See* Liana.

Liat (לִיאַת)   From the Hebrew, meaning "you are mine."

Liba (לִיבָּא)   A variant form of Libe. *See* Libe.

Libbie, Libby   Diminutive forms of Elizabeth. *See* Elizabeth.

Libe (לִיבֶּע)   A Yiddish form of the German *Liebe*, meaning "love." Also, from the Hebrew *lev*, meaning "heart." Leeba is a variant spelling. Libi, Libke, Libkeh, and Luba are variant forms.

Liberty   From the Latin, meaning "free."

Libi (לִיבִּי)   A variant form of Liba. *See* Liba.

Libke, Libkeh (לִיבְּקֶע)   Yiddish pet forms of Liba. *See* Liba. Lipke is a variant spelling.

Licia   A pet form of Alicia (Alice). *See* Alice.

Lida   A variant spelling of Leda. *See* Leda.

Lidia   A variant form of Leda. *See* Leda.

Lidon (לִידוֹן)   From the Hebrew, meaning "judgment is mine."

Li-Dror (לִי־דְּרוֹר)   From the Hebrew, meaning "freedom is mine."

Lieba (לִיבָּא)   A variant form of Liebe. *See* Liebe.

Liebe (לִיבֶּע)   From the Yiddish, meaning "loved one." Used also as a masculine name. Akin to Libe.

Li-Hi (לִי־הִיא)   From the Hebrew, meaning "she is mine."

Lila (לִילָה)   A flower-name of Persian origin, relating to the lilac flower. Lilah is a variant spelling. Also, from the Hebrew, meaning "she is mine." Also, a variant form of Lilian.

Lilac   From the Arabic and the Persian, meaning "bluish," with special reference to the hardy shrubs or trees of the olive family with their bluish and lavender flowers. *See also* Lilach.

Lilach (לִילָךְ)   From the Hebrew, meaning "you are mine." Also, the Hebrew word for Lilac. *See* Lilac.

Lilah   A variant spelling of Lila. *See* Lila.

Lili, Lilia   Variant forms of Lilian. *See* Lilian.

Lilian   From the Greek and Latin, meaning "lily" or a variant form of Lilibet. (Queen Elizabeth was nicknamed Lilibet.) Lila, Lili, Liliana, Liliane, Lilias, Lilita, Lilli, and Lilly are variants. Lillian and Lilyan are variant spellings.

Liliana   The Hawaiian form of Lilian. *See* Lilian.

Liliane   A variant form of Lilian. *See* Lilian.

Lilias A variant form of Lilian. *See* Lilian.

Lilibet A pet form of Elizabeth. *See* Elizabeth.

Lilis A variant form of Lilith. *See* Lilith.

Lilit (לִילִית) The Hebrew form of Lilith. *See* Lilith. Lillit is a variant spelling.

Lilita A pet form of Lilian. *See* Lilian.

Lilith From the Assyrian and Babylonian, meaning "of the night." In ancient Semitic folklore, a female demon, the first wife of Adam before the creation of Eve. Lilit is the Hebrew form. Lillith is a variant spelling. Lillus is a variant form.

Lilli A pet form of Lillian. *See* Lillian.

Lillian A variant spelling of Lilian. *See* Lilian.

Lillit A variant spelling of Lilit. *See* Lilit.

Lillith A variant spelling of Lilith. *See* Lilith.

Lillus A variant form of Lillith. *See* Lillith.

Lilly A pet form of Lillian. *See* Lillian.

Lilo From the Hawaiian, meaning "to be generous."

Lily A pet form of Lilian. *See* Lilian.

Lilyan A variant spelling of Lilian. *See* Lilian.

Lilybeth A hybrid name of Lily (Lilian) and Beth (Elizabeth). *See* Lilian *and* Elizabeth.

Limor (לִימוֹר) From the Hebrew, meaning "to exchange."

Limur (לִימוּר) A variant form of Limor. *See* Limor.

Lin A variant spelling of Linn. *See* Linn.

Lina A pet form of Carolina and Adelina. *See* Caroline *and* Adeline. Also, a variant form of Linit. *See* Linit.

Linda From the Latin and Spanish, meaning "handsome, pretty." Or, from the Anglo-Saxon, meaning "lovely or gentle maid." Some authorities maintain that Linda is derived from the Old German, meaning "serpent." Also, a pet form of Belinda. *See* Belinda. Linde, Lynda, and Lynde are variant spellings.

Linde A variant spelling of Linda. *See* Linda.

Linden From the Old English and the German, meaning "linden tree."

Lindsay, Lindsey From the Old English, meaning "camp near the stream."

Linit (לִינִית) From the Hebrew, meaning "rest, sleep." Lina is a variant form.

Linita A Spanish pet form of Belinda. *See* Belinda.

Linn, Linne From the Welsh, meaning "waterfall, lake." Lin, Lyn, and Lynne are variant spellings. Linnet and Linnette are pet forms.

Linnet, Linnette From the Latin and Old French, meaning "flax or flaxen-haired." Also, pet forms of the Welsh name Linn.

Linur (לִינוּר) From the Hebrew, meaning "I have light."

Lior (לִיאוֹר) From the Hebrew, meaning "my light" or "I have light."

Liora (לִיאוֹרָה) From the Hebrew, meaning "light, light is mine." Leora is a variant spelling.

Liorit (לִיאוֹרִית) A variant form of Liora. See Liora. Leorit is a variant spelling.

Lipke, Lipkeh (לִיפְּקֶע) Variant spellings of the Yiddish Libke. See Libke.

Liran (לִירָן) A variant form of Liron. See Liron.

Liraz (לִירָז) From the Hebrew, meaning "I have a secret."

Lirit (לִירִית) A Hebrew form of the Greek, meaning "lyrical, musical, poetic."

Liron (לִירוֹן) From the Hebrew, meaning "song is mine." Used also as a masculine name. Leron, Lerone, and Lirone are variant spellings.

Lirona (לִירוֹנָה) A variant form of Liron. See Liron.

Lirone A variant spelling of Liron. See Liron.

Lisa A pet form of Elizabeth. See Elizabeth.

Lisann A name created by combining Lisa and Ann. See Lisa and Ann.

Lise A pet form of Elizabeth. See Elizabeth.

Lisette A pet form of Elizabeth. See Elizabeth. Also, a variant form of Louise. See Louise.

Lisl A variant form of Elizabeth. See Elizabeth.

Lissa A pet form of Elizabeth and Melissa. See Elizabeth and Melissa.

Lisse A variant spelling of Lissa. See Lissa.

Lita A short form of Lolita. See Lolita.

Lital (לִיטַל) From the Hebrew, meaning "dew (rain) is mine."

Livana A variant spelling of Levana. See Levana.

Livia A short form of Olivia. See Olivia.

Liviya A variant form of Levia. See Levia.

Livna (לִבְנָה) From the Hebrew, meaning "white." In the Bible (Joshua 10:29), the name of a city captured by Joshua. Akin to Levana. Livnat and Livona are variant forms.

Livnat (לִבְנַת) A variant form of Livna. See Livna.

Livona (לִבוֹנָה) A variant form of Livna. See Livna. Also, a variant spelling of Levona. See Levona.

Livya (לִוְיָה) From the Hebrew, meaning "crown."

Liza A pet form of Elizabeth. See Elizabeth.

Lizbeth A pet form of Elizabeth. See Elizabeth.

Lize   A variant spelling of Liza. *See* Liza.

Lizette   A pet form of Elizabeth. *See* Elizabeth.

Lizzie, Lizzy   Pet forms of Elizabeth. *See* Elizabeth.

Lodema   A variant form of Lodemia. *See* Lodemia.

Lodemia   From the Old English, meaning "canal, stream." Lodema is a variant form.

Lodia   A feminine form of Lod. *See* Lod (masculine section).

Loia   A variant spelling of Loya. *See* Loya.

Lois   From the Greek, meaning "good, desirable."

Lola   A pet form of the Italian Carlotta. *See* Carlotta. Loleta and Lolita are pet forms.

Loleta   A pet form of Lola. *See* Lola.

Lolita   A pet form of Lola. *See* Lola. Lita is a short form.

Lolly   A pet form of Laura. *See* Laura.

Lona   From the Middle English, meaning "alone."

Lora   From the Latin, meaning "she who weeps, sorrowful." Or, from the Old High German, meaning "famous warrior." Also, a variant spelling of Laura. *See* Laura. Loraine, Lorinda, Lorrin, and Loryn are variant forms. Lorene, Lori, and Lorine are pet forms.

Loraine   A variant form of Lora. *See* Lora. Lorraine is a variant spelling.

Loral   A variant spelling of Laurel. *See* Laurel.

Loran, Lorann   A hybrid of Laura and Ann. *See* Laura *and* Ann.

Loree   A variant spelling of Laurie. *See* Laurie.

Lorelei   From the German, meaning "melody, song." Lorelie is a variant spelling.

Lorelie   A variant spelling of Lorelei. *See* Lorelei.

Loren   From the Latin, meaning "crowned with laurel (the symbol of victory)."

Lorene   A pet form of Lora. *See* Lora.

Loretta, Lorette   From the Anglo-Saxon, meaning "ignorant." Also, variant spellings of Lauretta and Laurette.

Lori   A pet form of Lora. *See* Lora.

Lorice   From the Latin, meaning "thong." In ancient Rome, a leather corselet worn by Roman soldiers. Also, a short form of Chloris. *See* Chloris.

Lorinda   A variant form of Lora. *See* Lora.

Lorine   A pet form of Lora. *See* Lora.

Lorna   From the Anglo-Saxon, meaning "lost, forlorn, forsaken."

Lorraine   A variant spelling of Loraine. *See* Loraine.

Lorrell   A variant spelling of Laurel. *See* Laurel.

Lorrin   A variant form of Lora. *See* Lora.

Lo Ruchama, (לֹא רֻחָמָה)   From the Hebrew, meaning "compassionless." The symbolic name of the Prophet Hosea's daughter (Hosea 1:6).

Loryn   A variant form of Lora. *See* Lora.

Lotta, Lotte   Pet forms of Charlotte. *See* Charlotte.

Lottie   A pet form of Charlotte. *See* Charlotte.

Louisa   From the Anglo-Saxon, meaning "hero" or "refuge of the people, warrior, prince." Louise is a popular French form. Louis is the masculine equivalent. Luisa and Luise are other variant forms. Lula and Lulu are pet forms.

Louise   A French form of Louisa. *See* Louisa.

Loura   A variant spelling of Laura. *See* Laura.

Lourana   A hybrid name combining Loura (Laura) and Anna. *See* Laura *and* Anna.

Loya (לוֹיָה)   From the Hebrew, meaning "ornamented, ornamental." Loia is a variant spelling.

Luana   From the Hawaiian, meaning "to be at leisure."

Luann   A hybrid name combining Louise and Ann. *See* Louise *and* Ann.

Luba (לוּבָּא)   A variant Yiddish form of Liba. *See* Liba.

Lucania   From the Latin, meaning "fish."

Lucette   A pet form of Lucile. *See* Lucile.

Luci   A pet form of Lucile. *See* Lucile.

Lucia   From the Latin, meaning "to shine." A feminine form of Lucian. Akin to Lucile. Luciana, Lucinda, and Lucy are variant forms. Lucina and Lucine are pet forms.

Luciana   A variant form of Lucia. *See* Lucia.

Lucie   A pet form of Lucile. *See* Lucile.

Lucile, Lucille   From the Latin, meaning "light, light-bringing, daybreak." Lucette, Luci, Lucie, Lucine, and Lucy are pet forms. Akin to Lucia.

Lucina   A pet form of Lucia. *See* Lucia.

Lucinda   An English form of Lucia. *See* Lucia.

Lucine   A pet form of Lucia and Lucile. *See* Lucia *and* Lucile.

Lucy   An English form of Lucia. *See* Lucia. Also, a pet form of Lucile.

Luella   A hybrid of Louise and Ella. *See* Louise *and* Ella.

Luisa An Italian and Spanish form of Louise. *See* Louise.

Luise A variant French form of Louise. *See* Louise.

Lula A pet form of Louise. *See* Louise.

Lulava (לוּלָבָה) From the Hebrew, meaning "palm branch." Adapted from the word *lulav*.

Lulie From the Anglo-Saxon, meaning "soothing, comforting."

Lulu A pet form of Louise. *See* Louise.

Luna From the Latin, meaning "moon" or "shining one." Lunetta and Lunette are pet forms.

Lunetta, Lunette Pet forms of Luna. *See* Luna.

Lupe From the Latin, meaning "wolf." Lupita is a pet form.

Lupita A pet form of Lupe. *See* Lupe.

Lurleen From the Old Norse, meaning "war horn." Lurline is a variant spelling.

Lurline A variant spelling of Lurleen. *See* Lurleen.

Luza (לוּזָה) From the Hebrew, meaning "bush" or "almond tree."

Lycoris From the Greek, meaning "lamp, light."

Lyda A Greek place-name, meaning "maiden from Lydia." Lydda is a variant spelling. Lydia is a variant form.

Lydda A variant spelling of Lyda. *See* Lyda.

Lydia A variant form of Lyda. *See* Lyda.

Lyn A variant spelling of Linn. *See* Linn. Lynell and Lynette are pet forms.

Lynda A variant spelling of Linda. *See* Linda.

Lynde A variant spelling of Linda. *See* Linda.

Lyndell A pet form of Lyn. *See* Lyn.

Lynell A pet form of Lyn. *See* Lyn.

Lynette A pet form of Lyn. *See* Lyn.

Lynn, Lynne Variant spellings of Linn. *See* Linn.

Lynwood From the Old English, meaning "lake in the woods."

Lynx From the Old English and the German, meaning "to shine." An animal with shining eyes.

Lyris From the Greek, meaning "lyre, harp."

Lys A pet form of Elisabeth. *See* Elisabeth.

Lysandra From the Greek, meaning "to free, liberate."

Lytle From the Greek, meaning "to loosen, free."

Maacha (מַעֲכָה) From the Hebrew, meaning "to press, squeeze, rub." In the Bible (II Samuel 3:3), one of King David's wives. Used also as a masculine name.

Maanit (מַעֲנִית) From the Hebrew, meaning "marker" or "frame."

Maayan (מַעְיָן) From the Hebrew, meaning "fountain, spring." Mayana is a variant form.

Mabel From the Latin, meaning "my beautiful one," or from the Old Irish, meaning "merry." Mable is a variant spelling. Mabella and Mabelle are variant forms.

Mabella, Mabelle Variant forms of Mabel. *See* Mabel.

Mable A variant spelling of Mabel. *See* Mabel.

Machalat (מָחֲלַת) From the Hebrew, meaning "weak" or "sick." In the Bible (Genesis 28:9), one of Esau's wives, and a daughter of Ishmael. Also, the wife of Rehoboam, king of Judah (I Chronicles 11:18).

Machla (מַחְלָה) From the Hebrew, meaning "fat." In the Bible (Numbers 36:11), a daughter of Zelophechad. Mahla is a variant spelling.

Madalynne A variant form of Magdalene. *See* Magdalene.

Madeena A variant form of Magdalene. *See* Magdalene. Also, from the Arabic, meaning "city."

Madelaine A variant form of Magdalene. *See* Magdalene.

Madeleine, Madeline French forms of Magdalene. *See* Magdalene.

Madelon A variant form of Magdalene. *See* Magdalene.

Madelyn A variant form of Magdalene. *See* Magdalene.

Madge A pet form of Margaret. *See* Margaret. Mady is a pet form. Midge is a variant form.

Madra From the Latin, meaning "mother." Madrona is a variant form.

Madrona A variant form of Madra. *See* Madra.

Mady A pet form of Madge or Magdalene. *See* Madge *and* Magdalene.

Mae A variant form of Mary and a variant spelling of May. *See* Mary *and* May.

Maeve An Irish form of Mavis. *See* Mavis.

Mag A pet form of Margaret or Magdalene. *See* Margaret *and* Magdalene.

Magda A pet form of Magdalene. *See* Magdalene. Also, a pet form of the Hebrew Migdala. *See* Migdala.

Magdalen A variant spelling of Magdalene. *See* Magdalene.

Magdalena A variant form of Magdalene. *See* Magdalene.

Magdalene From the Greek, meaning "of Magdala." In biblical times, Magdala was a town on the Sea of Galilee. Akin to Migdal. *See* Migdal. In the New

Testament, Mary Magdalene is mentioned in the Book of Luke (8:2). Magdalen and Magdaline are variant spellings. Madalynne, Madeena, Madelaine, Madeleine, Madeline, Madelon, Madelyn, and Magdalena are variant forms. Lena, Mady, Mag, Madge, and Magda are pet forms.

Magdaline   A variant spelling of Magdalene. *See* Magdalene.

Magena (מָגֵנָּה)   From the Hebrew, meaning "covering" or "protector." Akin to Megina. Magina is a variant form.

Maggie   A pet form of Margaret. *See* Margaret.

Magina (מָגִנָּה)   A variant form of Magena. *See* Magena.

Magna   From the Latin, meaning "great."

Magnolia   Referring to trees and shrubs of the magnolia family, named for French botanist Pierre Magnol (1638-1705). Also, from the Latin, meaning "big laurel tree."

Mago   A pet form of Margo. *See* Margo.

Mahalia   From the Aramaic and Arabic, meaning "fat (fatlings)" or "marrow, brain." Mehalia is a variant spelling.

Mahina   From the Hawaiian, meaning "moon."

Mahira (מְהִירָה)   From the Hebrew, meaning "swift, energetic."

Mahla   A variant spelling of Machla. *See* Machla.

Mahola   A variant spelling of Mechola. *See* Mechola.

Mai   A Slavonic form of Maria. *See* Maria.

Maia (מָאיָה, מָיָה)   In Roman mythology, goddess of the earth and growth. Romans offered sacrifices on the first day of May. *See also* May. Maya is a variant spelling. Used as a modern Hebrew name.

Maida, Maide   From the Anglo-Saxon, meaning "maiden." Maidie is a variant form.

Maidie   A variant form of Maida. *See* Maida.

Maire   An Irish form of Mary. *See* Mary. Moira and Moirae are variant forms.

Mairead   An Irish form of the Old French, meaning "magistrate."

Mairin   An Irish form of Mary. *See* Mary.

Maisie   From the British, meaning "field." Also, a Scottish pet form of Margaret. *See* Margaret. Mysie is a variant form.

Majesta   From the Latin, meaning "majesty, sovereign power."

Makabit (מַכַּבִּית)   The feminine form of Maccabee. From the Hebrew, meaning "hammer." Also spelled מְקַבִּית.

Makala   From the Hawaiian, meaning "myrtle."

Makeda (מָקֵדָה)   From the Hebrew, meaning "cup" or "bowl." In the Bible (Joshua 15:41), a place-name in the territory of Judah, near Beth Horon.

Maksima (מַקְסִימָה) From the Hebrew, meaning "enchanting" or "diviner, performer of miracles." Maxima is a variant spelling.

Mala From the Norman-French, meaning "bad." Also, from the Old English, meaning "meeting place."

Malach (מַלְאָךְ) From the Hebrew, meaning "angel" or "messenger." Used also as a masculine name.

Malbina (מַלְבִּינָה) From the Hebrew, meaning "to whiten," or "embarrass."

Malia The Hawaiian form of Mary. *See* Mary.

Malinda A variant spelling of Melinda. *See* Melinda. Also, a short form of Marcelinda. *See* Marcelinda.

Malka, Malkah (מַלְכָּה) From the Hebrew, meaning "queen."

Malkia, Malkiah Variant spellings of Malkiya. *See* Malkiya.

Malkit (מַלְכִּית) From the Hebrew, meaning "queen, queenly."

Malkiya (מַלְכִּיָּה) From the Hebrew, meaning "queen of God." Malkia and Malkiah are variant spellings.

Malkosha (מַלְקוֹשָׁה) From the Hebrew, meaning "last rain."

Malvina A feminine form of Melvin, meaning "servant" or "chief." Also, from the Anglo-Saxon, meaning "friendly toiler" or "famous friend."

Malvinda A variant feminine form of Melvin. *See* Melvin (masculine section).

Mamie A pet form of Mary. *See* Mary.

Mana (מָנָה) From the Hebrew, meaning "part, portion." Mania and Menat are variant forms.

Manachat (מָנַחַת) From the Hebrew, meaning "peace, rest."

Mancheima, Manchema Variant forms of Menachema. *See* Menachema.

Manda A pet form of Amanda. *See* Amanda.

Mandy A pet form of Amanda. *See* Amanda.

Manette A pet form of Marion. *See* Marion.

Mangena (מַנְגְּנָה) From the Hebrew, meaning "song, melody."

Mangina (מַנְגִּנָה) From the Hebrew, meaning "song, melody."

Mania A variant form of Mana. *See* Mana.

Manuela A Spanish feminine form of Manuel. *See* Manuel (masculine section).

Mara, Marah (מָרָה) From the Hebrew, meaning "bitter, bitterness." In the Bible (Ruth 1:20), Naomi says, "Do not call me Naomi [meaning 'pleasure'], call me Mara [meaning 'bitterness'], for the Lord has sent me a bitter lot."

Maralyn A variant spelling of Marilyn. *See* Marilyn.

Marata (מָרָתָה) From the Aramaic, meaning "bitter." Akin to Mara.

Marcelinda A variant form of Marcella. *See* Marcella. Malinda is a short form.

Marcella From the Latin, meaning "brave, martial" or "hammer." The feminine counterpart of Mark. Marcelinda, Marcelyn, Marcia, Marcilen, and Marisela are variant forms.

Marcelyn A variant form of Marcella. *See* Marcella.

Marcha A variant form of Marcia. *See* Marcia.

Marcia A variant form of Marcella. *See* Marcella. Marcha, Marcie, and Marcy are variant forms. Marsha and Marshe are variant spellings.

Marcie A variant form of Marcia. *See* Marcia.

Marcilen A variant form of Marcella. *See* Marcella.

Marcy A variant form of Marcia. *See* Marcia.

Mardell From the Old English, meaning "meadow near the sea (or lake)." Maridel and Meridel are variant forms.

Mardeth A variant form of Martha. *See* Martha.

Mardi A pet form of Martha. *See* Martha.

Mardut (מַרְדּוּת) From the Hebrew, meaning "rebellion."

Mare From the Latin, meaning "sea."

Maree A variant spelling of Marie. *See* Marie.

Mareea A variant spelling of Maria. *See* Maria.

Maren, Marena From the Latin, meaning "sea." Akin to Marina.

Marenda A variant form of Miranda. *See* Miranda.

Margalit (מַרְגָּלִית) A Hebrew form of the Greek Margarit, meaning "pearl." Akin to Margaret. Margolis is a variant pronunciation.

Margalita (מַרְגָּלִיתָה) A variant form of Margalit. *See* Margalit.

Margalith A variant spelling of Margalit. *See* Margalit.

Marganit (מַרְגָּנִית) A plant with blue, gold, and red flowers that is common in Israel. Marganita is a variant form.

Marganita (מַרְגָּנִיתָה) A variant form of Marganit. *See* Marganit.

Margaret From the Greek, meaning "pearl" or "child of light." Marjorie is a Scottish version, and Margery is an English form. Additional variations include Greta, Gretchen, Madge, Mae, Maggie, Maisie, May, Margareta, Margaretta, Margo, Marguerita, Marguerite, Meg, Peg, and Peggy.

Margarete A German form of Margaret. *See* Margaret.

Margaretta A Spanish pet form of Margaret. *See* Margaret.

Margarita   A Spanish form of Margaret. *See* Margaret.

Marge   A pet form of Margaret. *See* Margaret.

Margea (מָרְגְּעָה)   From the Hebrew, meaning "peace."

Margene   A variant form of Margaret. *See* Margaret.

Margerie   A variant spelling of Margery. *See* Margery.

Margery   A variant form of Margaret. *See* Margaret. Margerie, Marjary, Marjorie, and Marjory are variant spellings.

Marget   A pet form of Margaret. *See* Margaret.

Margherita   An Italian form of Margaret. *See* Margaret.

Margiad   A Welsh form of Margaret. *See* Margaret.

Margie   A pet form of Margaret. *See* Margaret.

Margita   A short form of Margarita. *See* Margarita.

Margo   A variant form of Margaret. *See* Margaret. Mago is a pet form.

Margolis   A variant pronunciation of Margalit. *See* Margalit.

Marguerita   A Spanish form of Margaret. *See* Margaret.

Marguerite   A French form of Margaret. *See* Margaret.

Margy   A pet form of Margaret. *See* Margaret.

Mari   A variant spelling of Mary. *See* Mary.

Maria   A variant form of Mary. *See* Mary. Mareea and Mariah are variant spellings. Mai is a Slavonic form.

Mariah   A variant spelling of Maria. *See* Maria. Or, a variant spelling of Moriah. *See* Moriah.

Mariamne   An early form of Mary. First used by Flavius Josephus, a first-century Jewish historian.

Marian, Mariane, Marianne   Variant hybrid forms of Mary and Ann. *See* Mary *and* Ann.

Maribel   A variant form of Mary, meaning "beautiful Mary."

Maribeth   A hybrid name of Mary and Beth. *See* Mary *and* Beth.

Maridel   A variant form of Mardell. *See* Mardell.

Marie   The French and Old German form of Mary. *See* Mary. Maree is a variant spelling. Mariesa, Mariessa, and Marion are pet forms.

Mariel   A Dutch form of Mary. *See* Mary.

Mariele   A variant form of Mary. *See* Mary.

Mariene   A variant form of Marion. *See* Marion.

Mariesa, Mariessa Pet forms of Marie. *See* Marie.

Marietta An Italian pet form of Mary. *See* Mary.

Mariette A French pet form of Mary. *See* Mary.

Marigold From the Middle English, compounded of Marie and "gold," hence "Marie's (Mary's) gold flower." A variety of annual plant with yellow, red, and orange flowers. Marygold is a variant spelling.

Marika A Slavonic pet form of Mary. *See* Mary.

Marilu A hybrid of Mary and Louise. *See* Mary *and* Louise.

Marilyn, Marilynn Variant forms of Mary, meaning "Mary's line" or "descendants of Mary." *See* Mary. Maralyn, Marylin, and Maryline are variant spellings. Marlyn is a contracted form.

Marina, Marinna From the Latin, meaning "sea." Rina is a pet form. Akin to Maren. Marna and Marne are variant forms. Marni is a pet form.

Marion A pet form of the French name Marie. Also, a variant form of Mary. *See* Mary. Often used as a nickname for Molly. Manette and Mariene are variant forms.

Mariquita A variant form of Mary. *See* Mary.

Maris, Marisa, Marise From the Latin, meaning "sea." Meris is a variant spelling of Maris. Marissa is a variant spelling of Marisa. Marisela is a variant form.

Marisela A Spanish form of Maris and Marcella. *See* Maris *and* Marcella.

Marissa A variant spelling of Marisa. *See* Marisa.

Marita A pet form of Martha. *See* Martha.

Marjarie, Marjary Variant spellings of Marjorie. *See* Marjorie.

Marjorie, Marjory Variant spellings of Margery, popular in Scotland. *See* Margery.

Marla A variant form of Marleen. *See* Marleen.

Marleen A Slavic form of Magdalene. *See* Magdalene. Marlene is a variant spelling. Marla, Marlena, Marlo, Marlowe, and Marlys are variant forms. Marlie is a pet form.

Marlena A variant form of Marleen. *See* Marleen.

Marlene A variant spelling of Marleen. *See* Marleen.

Marlie A pet form of Marleen. *See* Marleen.

Marlo A variant form of Marleen. *See* Marleen.

Marlowe A variant form of Marleen. *See* Marleen.

Marlyn A contracted form of Marilyn. *See* Marilyn.

Marlys A variant form of Marleen. *See* Marleen.

Marna, Marne A variant form of Marina. *See* Marina.

Marni A pet form of Marina. *See* Marina.

Marnina (מַרְנִינָה)   From the Hebrew, meaning "rejoice."

Marona   From the Hebrew, meaning "flock of sheep." Maron is the masculine form.

Marquita, Marquite   From the French, meaning "awning, canopy."

Marsha, Marshe   Variant spellings of Marcia. *See* Marcia.

Marta   A variant form of Martha. *See* Martha.

Martelle   A French feminine form of Martin. *See* Martin (masculine section).

Martha (מָרְתָּה)   From the Aramaic, meaning "sorrowful" or "mistress." Mardeth, Marta, Marthe, and Merta are variant forms. Mardi and Marita are pet forms.

Marthe   A French form of Martha. *See* Martha.

Martina, Martine   Feminine forms of Martin. *See* Martin (masculine section).

Marva (מַרְוָה)   From the Hebrew, referring to a plant of the mint family.

Marvel, Marvella   From the Middle English and the Latin, meaning "to wonder, admire."

Mary   The Greek form of Miryam (Miriam), from the Hebrew, meaning "sea of bitterness or sorrow." Also, from the Chaldaic, meaning "mistress of the sea." Among the most common foreign forms are Marie, Marion, and Manette in the French and Scotch; Maria, Mariquita, and Marita in the Spanish; Mair in the Welsh; Maire, Maura, Maureen, Moira, Moya, and Muire in the Irish; Marya in the Polish. Minnie is a Scottish form that was in widespread use in England in Victorian times. Molly and Polly are pet forms currently used in England and America, as are Minnie, May, Moll, Molly, and Min. Mari is a variant spelling.

Marya   A Russian and Polish form of Mary. *See* Mary.

Maryanne   A hybrid of Mary and Anne. *See* Mary *and* Anne.

Maryashe (מַרְיַאשֶׁע)   A Yiddish form of Miriam. *See* Miriam.

Marybeth   A hybrid of Mary and Beth. *See* Mary *and* Beth.

Marygold   A variant spelling of Marigold. *See* Marigold.

Maryland   One of the original thirteen American states, named for Queen Henrietta Maria, wife of Charles I, and meaning "land of Mary."

Marylin, Maryline   Variant spellings of Marilyn. *See* Marilyn.

Maryrose   A hybrid of Mary and Rose. *See* Mary *and* Rose.

Masada (מָסָדָה)   From the Hebrew, meaning "foundation" or "support." Metzada and Metzadah are the original Hebrew forms.

Maseit, Maset (מַשְׂאֵת)   From the Hebrew, meaning "gift."

Mashena (מַשְׁעֵנָה)   From the Hebrew, meaning "resting place" or "support."

Maskia   A variant spelling of Maskiya. *See* Maskiya.

Maskit (מַשְׂכִּית)   From the Hebrew, meaning "portrait" or "engraving." Maskia is a variant form.

Maskiya (מַשְׂכִּיָה) A variant form of Maskit. *See* Maskit.

Masua (מַשׂוּאָה) From the Hebrew, meaning "signal, torch."

Matama (מַטְעַמָה) From the Hebrew, meaning "tasty food, delicacy."

Matana (מַתָּנָה) From the Hebrew, meaning "gift."

Matat (מַתָּת) From the Hebrew, meaning "gift."

Mathilda, Mathilde From the Old High German, meaning "powerful in battle," or from the Anglo-Saxon, meaning "battlemaid." Matilda is a variant spelling. Matti, Mattie, Matty, Mattye, Matya, Maud, and Maude are pet forms. Hilda and Hilde are variant forms.

Matilda A variant spelling of Mathilda. *See* Mathilda.

Matkonet (מַתְכֹּנֶת) From the Hebrew, meaning "number" or "measure" or "format."

Matmona (מַטְמוֹנָה) From the Hebrew, meaning "treasure."

Matnat (מַתְנַת) From the Hebrew, meaning "gift."

Matred (מַטְרֵד) From the Hebrew, meaning "to pursue" or "to continue without interruption." In the Bible (Genesis 36:39), the mother-in-law of Hadar, king of Edom.

Matrona (מַטְרוֹנָה) From the Latin, meaning "matron" or "noble woman."

Matti, Mattie Pet forms of Mathilda. *See* Mathilda.

Matty, Mattye Pet forms of Mathilda. *See* Mathilda.

Matya A pet form of Mathilda. *See* Mathilda.

Matzhelet (מַצְהֶלֶת) From the Hebrew, meaning "shout of joy."

Matzila (מַצִּילָה) From the Hebrew, meaning "savior."

Matzlicha (מַצְלִיחָה) From the Hebrew, meaning "successful."

Maud, Maude French pet forms of Mathilda. *See* Mathilda. Maudene is a pet form.

Maudene A pet form of Maude. *See* Maude.

Maura A form of Mary commonly used in Ireland. Also, from the Celtic, meaning "dark." Maureen, Maurine, Maurella, and Morina are variant forms.

Maureen, Maurine Variant forms of Maura. *See* Maura. Morine is a variant spelling. Mo is a pet form.

Maurella A variant form of Maura. *See* Maura.

Mauve The French form of the Latin name for a plant of the mallow family.

Mavis A bird-name that evolved in France from an Old English word meaning "song-thrush." Maeve is an Irish form.

Maxa A feminine form of Max. *See* Max.

Maxene A variant spelling of Maxine. *See* Maxine.

Maxima   A variant spelling of Maksima. *See* Maksima.

Maxime   A feminine form of Maximilian. *See* Maximilian (masculine section). Maxine is a variant form.

Maxine   A variant form of Maxime. *See* Maxime.

May   A pet form of Mary and Margaret. *See* Mary *and* Margaret. Also, from the Old English, meaning "flower (daisy)." Mae is a variant spelling. Mei is the Hawaiian form.

Maya   A variant spelling of Maia. *See* Maia.

Mayana (מַעְיָנָה)   A variant form of Maayan. *See* Maayan.

Mazal (מַזָּל)   From the Hebrew, meaning "star," connoting "good luck." Mazala and Mazalit are variant forms.

Mazala (מַזָּלָה)   A variant form of Mazal. *See* Mazal.

Mazalit (מַזָּלִית)   A variant form of Mazal. *See* Mazal.

Mazhira (מַזְהִירָה)   From the Hebrew, meaning "to shine, shining."

Mea (מֵאָה)   A variant spelling of Mia. *See* Mia. Also, from the Hebrew, meaning "one hundred" or "century."

Mechola (מְחוֹלָה)   From the Hebrew, meaning "dance." Mahola is a variant spelling.

Mechubada (מְכֻבָּדָה)   From the Hebrew, meaning "honored, respected."

Medina (מְדִינָה)   From the Hebrew, meaning "country" or "province."

Meg   A pet form of Margaret. *See* Margaret.

Megan   A Welsh form of Margaret. *See* Margaret.

Megina (מְגִינָה)   From the Hebrew, meaning "covering" or "protector." Akin to Magena.

Mehalia   A variant spelling of Mahalia. *See* Mahalia.

Mehira (מְהִירָה)   From the Hebrew, meaning "swift" or "energetic."

Mei   The Hawaiian form of May. *See* May.

Meifaat (מֵפַעַת)   A variant form of Mofaat. *See* Mofaat.

Meira (מְאִירָה)   From the Hebrew, meaning "light." A feminine form of Meir. *See* Meir (masculine section). Meiri and Meirit are variant forms.

Meirav   A variant spelling of Merav. *See* Merav.

Meiri (מְאִירִי)   A variant form of Meira. *See* Meira. Meirit is a variant form.

Meirit (מְאִירִית)   A variant form of Meiri. *See* Meiri.

Meirona (מֵרוֹנָה)   From the Aramaic, meaning "sheep," or from the Hebrew, meaning "troops, soldiers." Merona is a variant spelling.

Meital (מֵיטַל)   From the Hebrew, meaning "dew drops."

Melabevet (מְלַבֶּבֶת) From the Hebrew, meaning "enticing, endearing."

Melanie From the Greek, meaning "black, dark in appearance." Melantha and Melloney are variant forms.

Melantha A variant form of Melanie. *See* Melanie.

Melba A variant feminine form of Melvin. *See* Melvin (masculine section). A variant form of Melva.

Mele The Hawaiian form of Mary. *See* Mary.

Melesina A pet form of Millicent. *See* Millicent.

Melevine A feminine form of Melvin. *See* Melvin (masculine section).

Melicent A variant form of Millicent. *See* Millicent.

Melina From the Greek, meaning "song."

Melinda From the Greek and Old English, meaning "gentle." Malinda is a variant spelling. Linda and Mindy are pet forms.

Melissa, Melisse From the Greek, meaning "bee, honey." Also, pet forms of Millicent. *See* Millicent. Lissa, Lisse, and Melita are pet forms. Melleta is a variant form.

Melita An Italian pet form of Melissa. *See* Melissa.

Melleta A variant form of Melissa. *See* Melissa.

Melloney A variant form of Melanie. *See* Melanie.

Melody, Melodye From the Greek, meaning "melody, song."

Melora From the Greek, meaning "golden apple," which in some cultures is the orange.

Melosa From the Greek, meaning "melody."

Melva A feminine form of Melvin. *See* Melvin (masculine section). Melba is a variant form.

Melveen, Melvene Feminine forms of Melvin. *See* Melvin (masculine section).

Melvina A feminine form of Melvin. *See* Melvin (masculine section) *and* Malvina.

Menachema (מְנַחֶמָה) From the Hebrew, meaning "comfort, comforter." A feminine form of the masculine Menachem.

Menachemya (מְנַחֶמְיָה) From the Hebrew, meaning "comfort of the Lord." Menahemia and Menahemiah are variant spellings.

Menahemia, Menahemiah Variant spellings of Menachemya. *See* Menachemya.

Menat (מְנָת) A variant form of Mana. *See* Mana.

Menora, Menorah (מְנוֹרָה) From the Hebrew, meaning "candelabrum."

Menucha (מְנוּחָה) From the Hebrew, meaning "peace, rest." Menuha is a variant spelling.

Menuha A variant spelling of Menucha. See Menucha.

Meona, Meonah (מְעוֹנָה) From the Hebrew, meaning "dwelling place," with special reference to the Temple.

Meora, Meorah (מְאוֹרָה) From the Hebrew, meaning "light."

Merav (מֵרַב) From the Hebrew, meaning "contender, warrior" or "to increase, multiply." In the Bible (I Samuel 14:49), the eldest daughter of King Saul and his wife Achinoam, and the sister of Michal. Meirav is a variant spelling.

Mercedes From the Latin, meaning "mercy, pity." Used also as a masculine name.

Merchava (מֶרְחָבָה) From the Hebrew, meaning "expanse."

Merchavia, Merchaviah Variant spellings of Merchavya. See Merchavya.

Merchavya (מֶרְחַבְיָה) From the Hebrew, meaning "space of the Lord" or "expanse." Merchavia and Merchaviah are variant spellings.

Mercia A variant form of Mercy. See Mercy.

Mercille A French form of Mercy. See Mercy.

Mercy From the Latin, meaning "reward, payment," and from the Late Latin, meaning "pity, favor." Mercia and Mercille are variant forms.

Meredith From the Celtic, meaning "protector of the sea." Used also as a masculine name.

Meri (מְרִי) From the Hebrew, meaning "rebellious" and "bitterness." Akin to Miryam. Merrie is a variant spelling.

Meridel A variant form of Mardell. See Mardell.

Merie A variant spelling of Meri. See Meri.

Merima (מְרִימָה) From the Hebrew, meaning "uplifted, raised up."

Meris A variant spelling of Maris. See Maris.

Merit, Merritt From the Latin, meaning "to deserve" or "to have value."

Merla A variant form of Merle. See Merle.

Merle From the Latin and the French, meaning "bird (blackbird)." Merla and Merril are variant forms. Murle is a variant spelling.

Merlin From the Old High German, meaning "falcon."

Meroma (מְרוֹמָה) From the Hebrew, meaning "elevated, high" or "noble."

Merona A variant spelling of Meirona. See Meirona.

Merrie From the Anglo-Saxon, meaning "joyous, pleasant." Merry is a variant spelling. Also, a variant spelling of Meri. See Meri. Merrielle and Merris are variant forms. Merrita is a pet form.

Merrielle A variant form of Merrie. See Merrie.

Merril, Merrill Variant forms of Muriel and Merle. *See* Muriel *and* Merle. Merryl, Meryl, and Meryle are variant spellings. Also used as masculine names.

Merris A variant form of Merrie. *See* Merrie.

Merrita A pet form of Merrie. *See* Merrie.

Merry A variant spelling of Merrie. *See* Merrie.

Merryl A variant spelling of Meryl. *See* Meryl.

Merta A variant form of Marta (Martha). *See* Martha.

Meryl, Meryle Variant spellings of Merril. *See* Merril.

Meshulemet (מְשֻׁלֶּמֶת) From the Hebrew, meaning "peaceful" or "complete." In the Bible (II Kings 21:19), the wife of King Manasseh of Israel.

Metuka (מְתוּקָה) From the Hebrew, meaning "sweet."

Metzada, Metzadah (מְצָדָה) The original Hebrew forms of Masada. *See* Masada.

Meusheret (מְאֻשֶּׁרֶת) From the Hebrew, meaning "fortunate" or "blessed."

Meuza (מְעֻזָּה) From the Hebrew, meaning "strength."

Mevorechet (מְבוֹרֶכֶת) From the Hebrew, meaning "blessed."

Mia A short form of Michaela. *See* Michaela. Mea is a variant spelling.

Mica A short form of Michal. *See* Michal.

Michael (מִיכָאֵל) Used occasionally as a feminine name. *See* Michael (masculine section).

Michaela (מִיכָאֵלָה) The feminine form of Michael. *See* Michael (masculine section). Mia is a short form.

Michaelann A hybrid of Michael and Ann. *See* Michael *and* Ann.

Michaele The feminine form of Michael. *See* Michael (masculine section).

Michal (מִיכַל) A contracted form of Michael, meaning "Who is like God?" In the Bible (II Samuel 6:23), the daughter of King Saul, and wife of David. Mica is a short form. Michalla, Michayahu, Michel, Michele, and Michelle are variant forms. Mickey and Micki are pet forms.

Michala, Michalla (מִיכָלָה) Variant forms of Michal. *See* Michal.

Michayahu (מִיכָיָהוּ) A variant form of Michal. *See* Michal. In the Bible (II Chronicles 13:2), the wife of Rehoboam, king of Judah.

Michel, Michele, Michelle Variant French forms of Michal. *See* Michal.

Mickey, Micki Pet forms of Michal. *See* Michal.

Midge A variant form of Madge. *See* Madge.

Miette From the French, meaning "small sweet things."

Mifracha (מִפְרָחָה) From the Hebrew, meaning "to fly, flight." Mifrachat and Mufrachat are variant forms.

Mifrachat (מְפָרַחַת) A variant form of Mifracha. *See* Mifracha.

Migda (מִגְדָּה) From the Hebrew, meaning "choice thing, gift" or "excellent." Akin to Migdana.

Migdala (מִגְדָּלָה) From the Hebrew, meaning "fortress, tower." Magda is a pet form. Akin to Magdalene.

Migdana (מִגְדָּנָה) From the Hebrew, meaning "gift." Akin to Migda.

Mignon From the French, meaning "delicate, graceful, petite."

Milca, Milcah A variant spelling of Milka. *See* Milka.

Milda From the Middle English, meaning "mild." Akin to Milena.

Mildred From the Anglo-Saxon, meaning "gentle of speech" or "gentle counselor." Mili, Millie, Milly, and Mindy are pet forms.

Mildrid A variant spelling of Mildred. *See* Mildred.

Milena From the Old High German, meaning "mild, peaceful." Akin to Milda.

Milet (מְלֵאת) From the Hebrew, meaning "fullness, abundance" or "border, rim." Based on a word in Song of Songs 5:12.

Mili (מִילִי) A modern Israeli name compounded of *mi* and *li*, meaning "Who is for me?" Also, a variant spelling of Millie, a pet form of Millicent and Mildred. *See* Millicent *and* Mildred.

Miliama The Hawaiian form of Miryam. *See* Miryam.

Milka (מִלְכָּה) From the Hebrew, meaning "divine" or "queen." Akin to Malka. In the Bible (Genesis 11:29), the wife of Nachor, brother of Abraham. Milca and Milcah are variant spellings.

Millet A variant spelling of Milet. *See* Milet.

Millicent From the Old French and the Old High German, meaning "work" or "strong." Also, from the Latin, meaning "sweet singer." Melicent is a variant form. Melesina, Melissa, Mili, Millie, Milly, Mollie, Molly, and Mollye are pet forms.

Millie, Milly Pet forms of Millicent and Mildred. *See* Millicent *and* Mildred.

Mim (מִים) A pet form of Miryam. *See* Miryam. Also, from the Anglo-Saxon, meaning "martial." Mimi is a variant pet form.

Mimi (מִימִי) A variant pet form of Mim. *See* Mim.

Mina A variant spelling of Minna. *See* Minna.

Mincha (מִנְחָה) From the Hebrew, meaning "gift." Minha is a variant spelling.

Mindel (מִינְדִל) A Yiddish pet form of Wilhelmina. *See* Wilhelmina. Also spelled מִינְדְּעל.

Mindy A pet form of Melinda and Mildred. *See* Melinda *and* Mildred.

Minerva The Roman goddess of wisdom. Akin to Athena in Greek mythology.

Minette   A French pet form of Mary. *See* Mary.

Minha   A variant spelling of Mincha. *See* Mincha.

Minke   A pet form or Minna. *See* Minna.

Minna   A pet form of Wilhelmina. *See* Wilhelmina. Mina is a variant spelling. Minke and Minnie are pet forms.

Minnie, Minny   Pet forms of Minna, Miriam, and Wilhelmina. *See* Minna, Miriam, *and* Wilhelmina. Also, from the Scotch, meaning "mother."

Minta   From the Greek, meaning "mint (an aromatic leaf)."

Mira (מִירָה)   A pet form of Miryam. *See* Miryam. Mirra is a variant spelling. Mirit is a variant form.

Mirabel, Mirabell, Mirabelle   From the Latin, meaning "of great beauty" or "wonderful, glorious." Mirabella is a variant form. Mirella is a short form.

Mirabella   A variant form of Mirabel. *See* Mirabel.

Miranda   From the Latin, meaning "wonderful," or "adored one." Marenda is a variant form.

Mirel, Mirele (מִירל)   Yiddish pet forms of Miryam. *See* Miryam. Also spelled מִירעל.

Miri (מִירִי)   A short form of Miryam and Mirit. *See* Miryam *and* Mirit.

Miriam   The Anglicized spelling of Miryam. *See* Miryam. Minnie is a pet form. Mishke is a Yiddish form.

Miril (מִירִיל)   A Yiddish pet form of Miryam. *See* Miryam.

Mirit (מִירִית)   From the Hebrew, meaning "sweet wine." Also, a variant form of Mira. *See* Mira.

Mirra   A variant spelling of Mira. *See* Mira.

Mirtza (מִרְצָה)   From the Hebrew, meaning "energetic" or "satisfied."

Miryam (מִרְיָם)   From the Hebrew, meaning "sea of bitterness, sorrow." Or, from the Chaldaic, meaning "mistress of the sea." In the Bible (Exodus 15:20), the sister of Moses and Aaron. Mary is an English form. Miriam is an Anglicized spelling. Mary is a New Testament spelling. In the Bible, Miryam is also used as a masculine name. Akin to Meri and and Meria. Maryasha and Mishke are Yiddish forms. Mim, Mimi, Mira, Mirel, Mirele, Mirit, Mollie, Molly, and Mollye are pet forms.

Mishbacha (מִשְׁבָּחָה)   From the Hebrew, meaning "choice" or "excellent." Mishbachat is a variant form.

Mishbachat (מִשְׁבַּחַת)   A variant form of Mishbacha. *See* Mishbacha.

Mishke (מִישְׁקֶע)   A Yiddish form of Miriam. *See* Miryam.

Mishmeret (מִשְׁמֶרֶת)   From the Hebrew, meaning "guard-house" or "observation tower."

Missie   A modern American name, meaning "young girl."

Misty   From the Old English, meaning "obscure, covered with mist."

Mitala (מִתְעָלָה)   From the Hebrew, meaning "channel" or "stream."

Mittie   A pet form of Margaret. *See* Margaret.

Mitzhala (מִצְהָלָה)   From the Hebrew, meaning "shouts of joy" or "bray (of horses)."

Mitzi   A pet form of Mary. *See* Mary.

Mitzpa, Mitzpah (מִצְפָּה)   From the Hebrew, meaning "tower" or "observation post." Mizpa and Mizpah are variant spellings.

Mivtechet (מִבְטַחַת)   From the Hebrew, meaning "assured" or "secure."

Mizpa, Mizpah   Variant spellings of Mitzpa. *See* Mitzpa.

Mo   A pet form of Maureen. *See* Maureen.

Moana   From the Hawaiian, meaning "ocean, open sea."

Modesta, Modeste   From the Latin, meaning "shy, modest." Modestine is a pet form.

Modestine   A pet form of Modesta. *See* Modesta.

Mofaat (מוֹפַעַת)   From the Hebrew, meaning "appearance." Meifaat is a variant form.

Mog   A pet form of Margaret. *See* Margaret.

Moina   From the Celtic, meaning "gentle, soft." Moyna is a variant spelling.

Moira, Moirae   In Greek mythology, the goddess of destiny and fate. Also, variant forms of Maire, the Irish form of Mary. *See* Mary. Moyra is a variant spelling. Myra is a variant form.

Molada (מוֹלָדָה)   From the Hebrew, meaning "homeland, birthplace." Used also as a masculine name. Akin to Moledet.

Molechet (מוֹלֶכֶת)   From the Hebrew, meaning "ruler" or "queen." In the Bible (I Chronicles 7:18), a descendant of Manasseh.

Moledet (מוֹלֶדֶת)   From the Hebrew, meaning "homeland, birthplace." Akin to Molada.

Mollie, Molly, Mollye   Pet forms of Mary, Millicent, and Miriam. *See* Mary, Millicent *and* Miriam.

Momi   From the Hawaiian, meaning "pearl."

Mona   From the Irish, meaning "noble." Also, from the Greek, meaning "alone," and from the Latin, meaning "advisor." Monna is a variant spelling. Monica and Monique are variant forms.

Monday   From the Old English, meaning "moon's day." Used in the Middle Ages for children born on a Monday. Monete and Monette are pet forms.

Monete, Monette   French pet forms of Monday. *See* Monday.

Monica   A variant form of Mona. *See* Mona.

Monique A French form of Mona. *See* Mona.

Monna A variant spelling of Mona. *See* Mona.

Montina From the Latin, meaning "of the mountain."

Mor (מוֹר) From the Hebrew, meaning "myrrh."

Morag (מוֹרַג) From the Hebrew, meaning "threshing board." Used also as a masculine name.

Moran (מוֹרָן) From the Hebrew, meaning "teacher" or "spear." Akin to Moranit.

Moranit (מוֹרָנִית) From the Hebrew, meaning "spear." Akin to Moran.

Morasha (מוֹרָשָׁה) From the Hebrew, meaning "legacy."

Morena A variant form of Maura. *See* Maura.

Morgan From the Welsh, meaning "sea dweller." Used most often as a masculine name.

Moria, Moriah Variant spellings of Moriya. *See* Moriya. Mariah is a variant form.

Moriel (מוֹרִיאֵל) From the Hebrew, meaning "God is my teacher."

Morine A variant form of Maureen. *See* Maureen.

Morit (מוֹרִית) From the Hebrew, meaning "teacher."

Moriya (מוֹרִיָּה) From the Hebrew, meaning "teacher." In the Bible (Genesis 22:2), the name of the mountain where Abraham prepared to sacrifice his son Isaac. Moria and Moriah are variant spellings.

Morna From the Middle English and the German, meaning "morning." Akin to Morrow. Also, from the Celtic and the Gaelic, meaning "gentle, beloved." Myra and Myrna are variant forms.

Morrisa The feminine form of Morris. *See* Morris (masculine section).

Morrow From the Old English and the German, meaning "morning." Akin to Morna.

Moryat (מָרְיַת) From the Hebrew, meaning "bitter."

Moshaa (מוֹשָׁעָה) From the Hebrew, meaning "salvation."

Moshit (מוֹשִׁית) The feminine form of Moshe. *See* Moshe (masculine section).

Moyna A variant spelling of Moina. *See* Moina.

Moyra A variant spelling of Moira. *See* Moira.

Mufrachat (מֻפְרַחַת) A variant form of Mifracha. *See* Mifracha.

Murial A variant spelling of Muriel. *See* Muriel.

Muriel From the Irish, meaning "bright sea," or from the Middle English, meaning "merry." Also, a Greek form of Myron. *See* Myron (masculine section). Murial is a variant spelling. Merril and Merrill are variant forms.

Murle   A variant spelling of Merle. *See* Merle.

Musette   From the Old French, meaning "to play music."

Mushit (מוּשִׁית)   From the Hebrew, meaning "to feel."

Myra   From the Greek and Arabic, meaning "myrrh." Also, a variant form of Moira. *See* Moira.

Myrna   From the Greek and Arabic, meaning "myrrh." Also, a variant form of Morna. *See* Morna. Akin to Myra.

Myrtilla   From the Middle Latin, meaning "myrtle." *See* Myrtle.

Myrtle   From the Persian, meaning "myrtle tree," a symbol of victory.

Mysie   A variant form of Maisie. *See* Maisie.

Na'a, Na'ah (נָאָה)   From the Hebrew, meaning "beautiful, pleasant."

Naama, Naamah (נַעֲמָה)   From the Hebrew, meaning "pleasant, beautiful." In the Bible (I Kings 14:21), the mother of King Rehoboam.

Naamana (נַעֲמָנָה)   From the Hebrew, meaning "pleasant."

Naami (נָעֳמִי)   A variant form of Naama. *See* Naama. In the Bible (Ruth 1:2), the mother-in-law of Ruth. Naomi is the Anglicized form.

Naamia, Naamiah   Variant spellings of Naamiya. *See* Naamiya.

Naamit (נַעֲמִית)   From the Hebrew, meaning "an ostrich-like bird." Also, a variant form of Naama. *See* Naama.

Naamiya (נַעֲמִיָה)   From the Hebrew, meaning "pleasant, sweet." Naamia and Naamiah are variant spellings.

Naara, Naarah (נַעֲרָה)   From the Hebrew, meaning "girl, maiden." In the Bible (I Chronicles 4:5), the wife of a member of the tribe of Judah.

Nacha (נֶחָה)   From the Hebrew, meaning "rest." Akin to Nachat.

Nachala (נַחֲלָה)   From the Hebrew, meaning "territory" or "inheritance." Nachalat is a variant form.

Nachalat (נַחֲלַת)   A variant form of Nachala. *See* Nachala.

Nachat (נַחַת)   From the Hebrew, meaning "rest." Akin to Nacha.

Nachmania, Nachmaniah   Variant spellings of Nachmaniya. *See* Nachmaniya.

Nachmanit (נַחְמָנִית) A variant form of Nachmaniya. *See* Nachmaniya.

Nachmaniya (נַחְמָנִיָּה) From the Hebrew, meaning "comfort." The feminine form of Nachmani. Nachmanit is a variant form. Nachmania and Nachmaniah are variant spellings.

Nachmi (נַחְמִי) A pet form of Nechama. *See* Nechama.

Nada From the Slavic, meaning "hope." Nadia, Nadie, Nadine, and Nadya are variant forms.

Nadan (נָדָן) From the Hebrew, meaning "dowry" or "that which is due by law." Nadin is a variant form.

Nadia A variant form of Nada. *See* Nada.

Nadian A variant spelling of Nadyan. *See* Nadyan.

Nadie A variant form of Nada. *See* Nada.

Nadin A variant form of Nadan. *See* Nadan.

Nadine A French form of Nada. *See* Nada.

Nado A variant form of Nada. *See* Nada.

Nadya (נַדְיָה) A Hebrew form of Nada, used in Israel. *See* Nada.

Nadyan (נַדְיָן) From the Hebrew, meaning "pond" or "brook (in which clothes are washed)." Nadian is a variant spelling.

Nafshiya (נַפְשִׁיָה) From the Hebrew, meaning "soul" or "friendship."

Naftala (נַפְתָּלָה) From the Hebrew, meaning "to wrestle." A feminine form of Naftali.

Naftalya (נַפְתַּלְיָה) A variant form of Naftala. *See* Naftala.

Nagida (נְגִידָה) From the Hebrew, meaning "noble one" or "prosperous one." Negida is a variant form.

Nahara (נְהָרָה) From the Hebrew and Aramaic, meaning "light." Nehara and Nehora are variant forms.

Naia From the Greek, meaning "to flow." Naiad is a variant form.

Naiad A variant form of Naia. *See* Naia.

Naida The Russian form of the Greek Naiad. *See* Naiad.

Nan, Nana Pet forms of Nancy. *See* Nancy.

Nancy A pet form of Hannah. *See* Hannah. Nan and Nana are variant forms.

Nanella A name created by combining Nancy and Ella. *See* Nancy *and* Ella.

Nanette A pet form of Anna and Hannah. *See* Anna *and* Hannah. Nanine is a variant pet form. Ninette is a variant form.

Nani From the Hawaiian, meaning "glory, splendor."

Nanine A variant pet form of Nanette. *See* Nanette.

Nanna A pet form of Hannah. *See* Hannah.

Naoma A variant form of Naomi. *See* Naomi.

Naomi (נָעֳמִי) The Anglicized form of Naami, meaning "beautiful, pleasant, delightful." In the Bible (Ruth 1:2), the mother-in-law of Ruth, a Moabitess who converted to Judaism. Naoma is a variant form.

Nara From the Celtic, meaning "happy." Also, from the Old English, meaning "north."

Narcissa From the Greek, meaning "self-love." In Greek mythology, a beautiful youth who falls in love with his own reflection in a spring and then changes into a narcissus plant. Narcisse is a variant spelling. Narcisus is a variant form. Narkis and Narkisa are Hebrew forms.

Narcisse A variant spelling of Narcissa. *See* Narcissa.

Narcisus A variant form of Narcissa. *See* Narcissa.

Narda From the Greek, meaning "spikenard," an Asiatic plant that yields an ointment. Nirda is a variant form.

Nardinon A variant form of Narda. *See* Narda.

Nardit A variant form of Narda. *See* Narda.

Narkis (נַרְקִיס) A Hebrew form of Narcissa. *See* Narcissa.

Narkisa (נַרְקִיסָה) A variant form of Narcissa. *See* Narcissa.

Nasia A variant spelling of Nasya. *See* Nasya.

Nastasya A Russian form of Anastasia. *See* Anastasia.

Nasya (נַסְיָה) A variant form of Nesya. From the Hebrew, meaning "miracle of the Lord." Nasia is a variant spelling.

Nata From the Latin, meaning "to swim." Also, from the Sanskrit, meaning "dancer."

Natala, Natalia Variant Russian forms of Natalie. *See* Natalie. Natasha is a pet form.

Natalie A French and German form of the Latin, meaning "to be born." A name often given to children born on Christmas Day. Natala, Natalia, Natalya, and Nathalie are variant forms.

Natalya A variant form of Natalie. *See* Natalie.

Natania, Nataniah Variant spellings of Natanya. *See* Natanya

Nataniela, Nataniella, Natanielle (נְתַנְיְאֵלָה) Variant feminine forms of Nataniel (Nathaniel). *See* Nataniel (masculine section).

Natanya (נְתַנְיָה) The feminine form of Natan (Nathan). *See* Natan (masculine section). Natania, Nataniah, and Nathania are variant spellings.

Natasha A Russian pet form of Natalia. *See* Natalia.

Natel A variant form of Natalie. *See* Natalie.

Nathalia   A variant form of Natalie. *See* Natalie.

Nathalie   A variant form of Natalie. *See* Natalie.

Nathania   A variant spelling of Natanya. *See* Natanya.

Nathaniella, Nathanielle   Variant spellings of Nataniela. *See* Nataniela.

Nava (נָאוָה)   From the Hebrew, meaning "beautiful, pleasant." Navit is a variant form. Akin to Naveh.

Naveh (נָאוֶה)   From the Hebrew, meaning "beautiful." Akin to Nava.

Navit (נָאוִית)   A variant form of Nava. *See* Nava.

Nayer   From the Persian, meaning "sunshine." Also, from the Old English, meaning "one who works on water" or "sailor."

Neala   An Irish feminine form of Neal. *See* Neal (masculine section).

Nebula   From the Latin, meaning "vapor, cloud, mist."

Necha (נֶחָה)   A Yiddish pet form of Nechama. *See* Nechama. Also, from the Hebrew, meaning "rest." Akin to Nacha.

Nechama (נֶחָמָה)   From the Hebrew, meaning "comfort." Nehama is a variant spelling. Nahum is the masculine equivalent. Nachmi, Necha, and Neche are pet forms.

Neche (נֶעְחֶע)   A Yiddish pet form of Nechama. *See* Nechama.

Nechocha (נְכוֹחָה)   From the Hebrew, meaning "straightforward, honest."

Nechona (נְכוֹנָה)   From the Hebrew, meaning "right, proper."

Nechushta (נְחֻשְׁתָּא)   From the Aramaic, meaning "copper, bronze." In the Bible (II Kings 24:8), the mother of Jehoiakim, king of Judah. Nehushta is a variant spelling.

Neda   From the British, meaning "sanctuary, retreat." Nedda is a variant spelling.

Nedavia, Nedaviah   Variant spellings of Nedavya. *See* Nedavya.

Nedavya (נְדַבְיָה)   From the Hebrew, meaning "generosity of the Lord." Nedavia and Nedaviah are variant spellings.

Nedda   A variant spelling of Neda. *See* Neda.

Nedira (נְדִירָה)   From the Arabic, meaning "rare."

Nediva (נְדִיבָה)   From the Hebrew, meaning "noble, generous."

Nedra   From the Old English, meaning "lower, below the surface of the earth."

Needara, Ne'edara (נֶאֱדָרָה)   From the Hebrew, meaning "noble" or "glorified." Neederet is a variant form.

Neederet, Ne'ederet (נֶאֱדֶרֶת)   A variant form of Needara. *See* Needara.

Neemana, Ne'emana (נֶאֱמָנָה)   From the Hebrew, meaning "truthful, faithful." Neemenet is a variant form.

Neemenet, Ne'emenet (נֶאֱמֶנֶת) A variant form of Neemana. *See* Neemana.

Neena A variant spelling of Nina. *See* Nina.

Neetzala (נֶאֱצָלָה) From the Hebrew, meaning "perfect, perfected." Neetzelet is a variant form.

Neetzelet (נֶאֱצָלֶת) A variant form of Neetzala. *See* Neetzala.

Negba (נֶגְבָּה) From the Hebrew, meaning "south."

Negida (נְגִידָה) A variant spelling of Nagida. *See* Nagida.

Negiha (נְגִיהָה) From the Hebrew, meaning "fluorescent."

Negida (נְגִידָה) A variant form of Nagida. *See* Nagida.

Nehama A variant spelling of Nechama. *See* Nechama.

Nehara (נְהָרָה) A variant form of Nehora. *See* Nehora.

Nehedara (נֶהְדָּרָה) From the Hebrew, meaning "beautiful." Nehederet is a variant form.

Nehederet (נֶהְדֶּרֶת) A variant form of Nehedara. *See* Nehedara.

Nehira (נְהִירָה) A variant form of Nehora. *See* Nehora.

Nehora (נְהוֹרָה) From the Aramaic, meaning "light." Nehara, Nehira, and Nehura are variant forms.

Nehura (נְהוּרָה) A variant form of Nehora. *See* Nehora.

Nehushta A variant spelling of Nechushta. *See* Nechushta.

Neila, Neilah, Neilla (נְעִילָה) From the Hebrew, meaning "closing, sealing up." The name of the final service on the Day of Atonement.

Neima (נְעִימָה) From the Hebrew, meaning "melody."

Neira (נְאִירָה) From the Aramaic, meaning "light."

Nelda An invented name, meaning unknown.

Nelia A feminine form of Neil. *See* Neil (masculine section). Or, a variant form of Nell. *See* Nell.

Nell, Nella Pet forms of Eleanor and Helen. *See* Eleanor *and* Helen. Nelia and Nellene are variant forms.

Nellene A variant form of Nell. *See* Nell.

Nellie A pet form of Eleanor. *See* Eleanor.

Nellwyn From the Old English, meaning "friend of Nell." *See* Nell.

Nelly A pet form of Eleanor. *See* Eleanor.

Nema A variant spelling of Nima. *See* Nima.

Nemera (נְמֵרָה) From the Hebrew, meaning "leopard."

Nena A variant spelling of Nina. *See* Nina.

Neola   From the Greek, meaning "new."

Neoma   Possibly from the Greek, meaning "pasture in the woods."

Neora (נְאוֹרָה)   From the Aramaic and Hebrew, meaning "light" or "shine." Nehora is a variant form.

Nera (גֵרָה)   From the Hebrew, meaning "light" or "candle."

Nerdi (גֵרְדִּי)   From the Hebrew, meaning "my spice."

Neria, Neriah   Variant spellings of Neriya. See Neriya.

Nerisa, Nerissa   Variant spellings of Nerita. See Nerita.

Nerita   From the Greek, meaning "sea snail." Nerisa and Nerissa are variant forms.

Neriya (גֵרְיָה)   From the Hebrew, meaning "light of the Lord." Neria and Neriah are variant spellings.

Ner-li (גֵר־לִי)   From the Hebrew, meaning "I have light" or "the light is mine."

Nesha   A variant form of Nessa. See Nessa.

Neshama (נְשָׁמָה)   From the Hebrew, meaning "soul." Nishmia is a variant form.

Nesia   A variant spelling of Nesya. See Nesya.

Nesicha (נְסִיכָה)   From the Hebrew, meaning "royalty" or "princess."

Nessa   From the Old Norse, meaning "promontory, headland." Nesha is a variant form.

Nessia, Nessiah   Variant spellings of Nesya. See Nesya.

Nessie   A Welsh pet form of Agnes. See Agnes.

Nest, Nesta   Welsh pet forms of Agnes. See Agnes.

Nesya (נֵסְיָה)   From the Hebrew, meaning "miracle of God." Nesia, Nesiah, Nessia, and Nessiah are variant spellings. Nasya and Nisya are variant forms.

Neta (נֶטַע)   From the Hebrew, meaning "plant, shrub." Used also as a masculine name. Netia is a variant form. Netta is a variant spelling.

Netana (נְתָנָה)   From the Hebrew, meaning "gift."

Netanela (נְתַנְאֵלָה)   From the Hebrew, meaning "gift of God."

Netania, Netaniah   Variant spellings of Netanya. See Netanya.

Netaniela, Netaniella (נְתַנִיאֵלָה)   From the Hebrew, meaning "the gift of God."

Netanya (נְתַנְיָה)   From the Hebrew, meaning "gift of God." Netania, Netaniah, Nethania, and Nethaniah are variant spellings.

Nethania, Nethaniah   Variant spellings of Netanya. See Netanya.

Neti (נְטָעִי)   From the Hebrew, meaning "plant." Netti is a variant spelling.

Netia (נְטִיעָה)   A variant form of Neta. *See* Neta.

Netina (נְתִינָה)   From the Hebrew, meaning "gift."

Netiva (נְתִיבָה)   From the Hebrew, meaning "path, road."

Netta   A variant spelling of Neta. *See* Neta.

Netti   A variant spelling of Neti. *See* Neti.

Nettie, Netty   Pet forms of Antoinette and Annette. *See* Antoinette *and* Annette.

Neva   From the Spanish, meaning "snow." Or, from the Old English, meaning "new." Also, a variant spelling of Niva. *See* Niva.

Nevet (נֶבֶט)   From the Hebrew, meaning "sprout."

Nevia, Neviah (נְבִיאָה)   From the Hebrew, meaning "seer, Prophet."

Nevona, Nevonah (נְבוֹנָה)   From the Hebrew, meaning "wise" or "intelligent."

Nezira, Nezirah (נְזִירָה)   From the Hebrew, meaning "Nazirite."

Neziriya (נְזִירִיָה)   A variant form of Nezira. *See* Nezira.

Nicci   An Italian form of the Latin, meaning "victory." Akin to the masculine Nicholas. Nichelle is a variant form.

Nichbada (נִכְבָּדָה)   From the Hebrew, meaning "honored, respected."

Nichelle   A variant form of Nicci. *See* Nicci.

Nicola, Nicole   Italian and French feminine forms of Nicholas. *See* Nicholas (masculine section). Nicolette is a pet form. Nicolle is a variant spelling of Nicole. Colette is a pet form.

Nicolette   A pet form of Nicola. *See* Nicola.

Nicolle   A variant spelling of Nicole. *See* Nicole.

Niga (נִיגָה)   A variant form of Noga. *See* Noga.

Nika   A Russian feminine form of Nicholas. *See* Nicholas (masculine section).

Nilbava (נִלְבָּבָה)   From the Hebrew, meaning "kind, good-natured." Nilbevet is a variant form.

Nilbevet (נִלְבֶּבֶת)   A variant form of Nilbava. *See* Nilbava.

Nili (נִילִי)   From the Hebrew, meaning "a plant in the pea family that yields indigo." *See* Nili (masculine section). Nilit is a variant form.

Nilit (נִילִית)   A variant form of Nili. *See* Nili.

Nima (נִימָה)   From the Hebrew, meaning "thread, hair." Nema is a variant spelling. Also spelled נִימָא.

Nina (נִינָה)   A French and Russian pet form of Anne (from Nanine). *See* Anne. Also, from the Spanish meaning "young girl," from the Babylonian meaning "goddess of the deep water," and from the Hebrew meaning "granddaughter" or "great-granddaughter." Neena is a variant spelling.

Ninette   A variant form of Nanette. *See* Nanette.

Ninon   A French form of Anne. *See* Anne.

Nira (נִירָה)   From the Hebrew, meaning "uncultivated field."

Nirda (נִרְדָה)   A variant form of Narda. *See* Narda.

Nirdi (נִרְדִי)   A variant form of Narda. *See* Narda.

Nirdit (נִרְדִית)   From the Hebrew, meaning "spice, perfume."

Nirel (נִירְאֵל)   From the Hebrew, meaning "uncultivated field" or "light of God." Used also as a masculine name.

Nirit (נִירִית)   An annual plant with yellow flowers, found in Israel.

Nirtza (נִרְצָה)   From the Hebrew, meaning "desirable." Nirza is a variant spelling.

Nirza   A variant spelling of Nirtza. *See* Nirtza.

Nisa, Nissa (נִסָה)   From the Hebrew, meaning "to test."

Nishmia   A variant spelling of Nishmiya. *See* Nishmiya.

Nishmiya (נִשְׁמִיָה)   A variant form of Neshama. *See* Neshama.

Nisia, Nisiah   Variant spellings of Nisya. *See* Nisya.

Nisya (נִסְיָה)   A variant form of Nesya. *See* Nesya. Nisia and Nisiah are variant spellings.

Nita (נִיטַע)   From the Hebrew, meaning "to plant." Also, a short form of Juanita and Anita. *See* Juanita *and* Anita.

Nitza, Nitzah (נִצָה)   From the Hebrew, meaning the "bud of a flower." Niza and Nizah are variant English spellings. Also spelled נִיצָה. Nitzana, Nitzania, and Nitzanit are variant forms.

Nitzana (נִצָּנָה)   A variant form of Nitza. *See* Nitza. Nizana is a variant English spelling. Also spelled נִיצָנָה.

Nitzanit (נִצָּנִית)   A variant form of Nitza. *See* Nitza. Also spelled נִיצָנִית.

Nitzaniya (נִצָּנִיָה)   A variant form of Nitza. *See* Nitza.

Nitzcha (נִצְחָה)   From the Hebrew, meaning "victory" or "eternity." Nitzchit, Nitzchiya, and Nitzchona are variant forms.

Nitzchit (נִצְחִית)   A variant form of Nitzcha. *See* Nitzcha.

Nitzchiya (נִצְחִיָה)   A variant form of Nitzcha. *See* Nitzcha. Nitzhia is a variant spelling.

Nitzchona (נִצְחוֹנָה)   A variant form of Nitzcha. *See* Nitzcha.

Nitzhia   A variant spelling of Nitzchiya. *See* Nitzchiya.

Nitzra (נִצְרָה)   From the Hebrew, meaning "guard." Nizra is a variant spelling.

Niva (נִיבָה)   From the Hebrew, meaning "speech." Neva is a variant spelling.

Nivchara (נִבְחָרָה) From the Hebrew, meaning "choice, chosen." Nivcheret is a variant form.

Nivcheret (נִבְחֶרֶת) A variant form of Nivchara. *See* Nivchara.

Nixie From the German, meaning "water sprite." In mythology a Nixie was half-girl and half-fish. Used also as a pet form of Berenice. *See* Berenice.

Niza, Nizah A variant spelling of Nitza. *See* Nitza.

Nizana A variant spelling of Nitzana. *See* Nitzana.

Nizra A variant spelling of Nitzra. *See* Nitzra.

Nizria, Nizriah Variant spellings of Nizriya. *See* Nizriya.

Nizriya (נְזְרִיָה) From the Hebrew, meaning "Nazirite of the Lord." Nizria and Nizriah are variant spellings.

Noa (נוֹעָה) From the Hebrew, meaning "tremble, shake." In the Bible (Numbers 26:33), a daughter of Zelophehad. Also spelled נוֹעַ.

Noada (נוֹעָדָה) From the Hebrew, meaning "appointed" or "prepared."

Noadia, Noadiah Variant spellings of Noadya. *See* Noadya.

Noadya (נוֹעַדְיָה) From the Hebrew, meaning "appointed by God." In the Bible (Nehemiah 6:14), a Prophetess. Noadia and Noadiah are variant spellings.

Noam (נֹעַם) From the Hebrew, meaning "sweet, pleasant." Used primarily as a masculine name.

Noaza (נוֹעֲזָה) From the Hebrew, meaning "courageous" or "audacious."

Nodeleya (נוֹדְלְיָה) From the Hebrew, meaning "let us praise God."

Noel From the French, meaning "Christmas." Used also as a masculine name.

Noelene, Noelle Pet forms of Noel. *See* Noel.

Nofiya (נוֹפִיָה) From the Hebrew, meaning "beautiful panorama" or "God's beautiful landscape." Nophia is a variant spelling.

Noga (נֹגַה) From the Hebrew, meaning "morning light, dazzle, brightness." Niga and Nogahat are variant forms.

Nogahat (נוֹגַהַת) A variant form of Noga. *See* Noga.

Noia A variant spelling of Noya. *See* Noya.

Noit, No'it (נוֹאִית) From the Hebrew, meaning "plant."

Nokomis An American Indian name, meaning "moon daughter."

Nola From the Celtic, meaning "famous." Nolan and Noland are masculine forms.

Nolina The Hawaiian form of Noreen. *See* Noreen.

Noma The Hawaiian form of Norma. *See* Norma.

Nona From the Latin, meaning "ninth." Noni and Nonie are variant forms.

Noni, Nonie   Variant forms of Nona. *See* Nona.

Nophia   A vairant spelling of Nofia. *See* Nofia.

Nora, Norah   From the Latin, meaning "honor, respect." The original form, Honoria, was widely used in England in the Middle Ages. La Nora is a variant form. Noreen is a popular form. *See* Noreen.

Norberta   The feminine form of Norbert. *See* Norbert (masculine section).

Noreen   A variant Irish form of Nora. *See* Nora. Nolina, Noreen, and Norina are variant forms. Norene and Norine are variant spellings.

Norella   A hybrid of Nora and Ella. *See* Nora *and* Ella.

Norene   A variant spelling of Noreen. *See* Noreen.

Norie   A pet form of Nora. *See* Nora.

Norina, Norine   Variant forms of Noreen. *See* Noreen.

Norma   From the Latin, meaning "exact to the pattern, normal, peaceful."

Notera (נוֹטְרָה)   From the Hebrew, meaning "guard, protector." Noteret is a variant form.

Noteret (נוֹטֶרֶת)   A variant form of Notera. *See* Notera.

Notzeret (נוֹצֶרֶת)   From the Hebrew, meaning "guard."

Nova   From the Latin, meaning "new." A type of star that increases and decreases in brightness from time to time. Novia is a variant form.

Novia   A variant form of Nova. *See* Nova.

Noya (נוֹיָה)   From the Hebrew, meaning "beautiful, ornamented." Noia is a variant spelling.

Nufar (נוּפָר)   From the Hebrew, meaning "a plant (that grows in water)." Nuphar is a variant spelling.

Nuphar   A variant spelling of Nufar. *See* Nufar.

Nura (נוּרָא)   From the Aramaic, meaning "light."

Nureen (נוּרִין)   Possibly from the Hebrew, meaning "light." Also, a variant form of Noreen. *See* Noreen.

Nurit (נוּרִית)   A plant with red and yellow flowers common in Israel. Nurita is a variant form.

Nurita (נוּרִיתָה)   A variant form of Nurit. *See* Nurit.

Nurya (נוּרְיָא)   From the Aramaic, meaning "light of the Lord." Also spelled נוּרְיָה.

Nydia   From the Latin, meaning "haven of refuge."

Nysa, Nyssa   From the Greek, meaning "goal."

Octavia From the Latin, meaning "eighth." The eighth girl in a Roman family was often named Octavia. Octavius is the masculine form. Tavi and Tavia are pet forms.

Oda, Odah (אוֹדָה) From the Greek and Hebrew, meaning "song."

Odeda (עוֹדְדָה) From the Hebrew, meaning "strong, courageous." The feminine form of Oded.

Odedia A variant form of Odeda. See Odeda.

Odele From the Greek, meaning "ode, melody." Also, from the Danish, meaning "otter." Odelet and Odeleya are variant forms. Odell is a variant spelling. Odetta is a pet form.

Odelet A variant form of Odele. See Odele.

Odeleya (אוֹדְלְיָה) From the Hebrew, meaning "I will prase God." Also, a variant form of Odele. See Odele. Odelia is a variant spelling.

Odelia A variant spelling of Odeleya. See Odeleya.

Odell A variant spelling of Odele. See Odele.

Odera (עוֹדְרָה) From the Hebrew, meaning "plough."

Odetta A pet form of Odele. See Odele.

Odette A variant form of Odetta. See Odetta.

Odiya (אוֹדִיָה) From the Hebrew, meaning "song of God." Akin to Oda.

Ofera (עוֹפָרָה) From the Hebrew, meaning "lead, (the metal)."

Oferet (עוֹפֶרֶת) A variant form of Ofera. See Ofera.

Ofira (אוֹפִירָה) From the Hebrew, meaning "gold," derived from Ofir, a place-name in the Bible (I Kings 10:11). Ophira is a variant spelling.

Ofna (אָפְנָה) From the Aramaic, meaning "appearance" or "style." Aphna is a variant spelling.

Ofnat (אָפְנַת) From the Hebrew, meaning "wheel." Ophnat is a variant spelling.

Ofra (עָפְרָה) From the Hebrew, meaning "young mountain goat" or "young deer." Afra, Aphra, and Ophra are variant spellings. Used also as a masculine name (I Chronicles 4:14).

Ofrat (עָפְרַת) A variant form of Ofra. See Ofra. Afrat, Aphrat, and Ophrat are variant spellings.

Ofrit (עָפְרִית) A variant form of Ofra. See Ofra. Also, a Hebrew plant-name. Afrit, Aphrit, and Ophrit are variant English spellings. Also spelled עוֹפְרִית.

Oganya (עוֹגַנְיָה) A variant form of Ogenya. See Ogenya.

Ogenya (עוֹגֶנְיָה) From the Aramaic and Greek, meaning "anchor" or "to tie." Oganya is a variant form. Ogen is the masculine form.

Ohad (אֹהַד)   From the Hebrew, meaning "love." In the Bible (Genesis 46:10), a masculine name. *See* Chad (masculine section).

Ohela (אוֹהֱלָה)   From the Hebrew, meaning "tent." The feminine form of Ohel. *See* Ohel (masculine section).

Oholiav (אָהֳלִיאָב)   From the Hebrew, meaning "father (God) is my tent (protector)" or "father's tent." In the Bible (Exodus 36:2), an associate of Betzalel.

Oholiva (אָהֳלִיבָה)   A variant form of Oholiav. *See* Oholiav.

Oholivama (אָהֳלִיבָמָה)   From the Hebrew, meaning "tent of the high place." In the Bible (Genesis 36:2), a wife of Esau.

Oholo (אָהֳלָה)   From the Hebrew, meaning "her tent."

Ola, Olah (עוֹלָה)   From the Hebrew, meaning "immigrant," or from the Old Norse, meaning "ancestor."

Olga   From the Russian and Old Norse, meaning "holy" or "peace." Some authorities relate Olga to Oliver, meaning "olive," the symbol of peace.

Olinda   Possibly a variant form of Yolanda. *See* Yolanda.

Olive   From the Latin, meaning "olive," the symbol of peace. Livia, Livya, Nola, and Olivia are variant forms.

Olivia   A variant form of Olive. *See* Olive.

Oliye   A pet form of Olive. *See* Olive.

Omega   From the Greek, meaning "great."

Omer (עֹמֶר)   From the Hebrew, meaning "bundle of cut wheat." Omri is a variant form. Primarily a masculine name.

Omri (עָמְרִי)   A variant form of Omer. *See* Omer.

Omrit (עָמְרִית)   A variant form of Omer. *See* Omer.

Ona   Probably from the British *oni*, meaning "from the river." Or, a variant form of Oona. *See* Oona.

Oneida   From the Iroquois tribal language, meaning "standing rock." Onetha is a variant form.

Onetha   A variant form of Oneida. *See* Oneida.

Oona   An Old Irish variant form of the Latin Una, meaning "the one." Ona, Onnie, and Unity are variant forms.

Opal   From the Sanskrit, meaning "jewel."

Ophelia   From the Greek, meaning "to help" and "serpent."

Ophira   A variant spelling of Ofira. *See* Ofira.

Ophnat   A variant spelling of Ofnat. *See* Ofnat.

Ophra   A variant spelling of Ofra. *See* Ofra.

Ophrat   A variant spelling of Ofrat. *See* Ofrat.

Ophri   A variant spelling of Ofri. *See* Ofri.

Ophrit   A variant spelling of Ofrit. *See* Ofrit.

Or (אוֹר)   From the Hebrew, meaning "light." Used also as a masculine name.

Ora, Orah (אוֹרָה)   From the Hebrew, meaning "light." Also, from the Latin, meaning "gold." Orit is a variant form.

Oralee (אוֹרָה־לִי)   From the Hebrew, meaning "my light" or "I have light." Orali is a variant spelling. Orlee and Or-lee are variant forms.

Orali (אוֹרְלִי)   A variant spelling of Oralee. *See* Oralee.

Oralia   From the Latin, meaning "margin, border."

Oretha   A variant spelling of Aretha. *See* Aretha.

Oria   From the Latin, meaning "Orient, the East."

Oriana   From the Celtic, meaning "golden girl."

Oriel   From the Old French and the Latin, meaning "gold." Oriole is a variant form.

Oriente   From the Latin, meaning "direction of the sunrise."

Oriole   A variant form of Oriel. *See* Oriel. A species of American bird with bright plumage.

Orit (אוֹרִית)   A variant form of Ora. *See* Ora.

Orlean, Orleans   French forms of the Latin, meaning "gold."

Orleana   A variant form of Orlean. *See* Orlean.

Or-Lee, Orlee (אוֹר־לִי)   From the Hebrew, meaning "light is mine." Also spelled Orli.

Orlene   A variant spelling of Orlean. *See* Orlean.

Orli (אוֹרְלִי)   A variant spelling of Or-lee. *See* Or-lee.

Orlit (אוֹרְלִית)   A variant form of Or-lee. *See* Or-lee.

Orly   A variant spelling of Orli. *See* Orli.

Orma   A pet form of Ormanda. *See* Ormanda.

Ormanda   A variant feminine form of Armand. *See* Armand (masculine section).

Orna (אָרְנָה)   From the Hebrew, meaning either "let there be light" or "pine tree." Arna is a variant spelling. Also spelled אוֹרְנָה.

Ornat (אָרְנַת)   A variant form of Orna. *See* Orna.

Ornette   A pet form of Orna. *See* Orna.

Orni (אָרְנִי)   From the Hebrew, meaning "pine tree." Ornina, Orninit, and Ornit are variant forms.

Ornina (אָרְנִינָה)   A variant form of Orni. *See* Orni.

Orninit (אָרְנִינִית)   A variant form of Orni. *See* Orni.

Ornit (אָרְנִית)   A variant form of Orni. *See* Orni. Also spelled אוֹרְנִית.

Orpa, Orpah (עָרְפָּה)   From the Hebrew, meaning "to flee, to turn one's back." In the Bible (Ruth 1:4), a Moabite woman, the wife of Kilyon, son of Elimelech and Naomi. Also spelled עָרְפָּה.

Oryn   A feminine form of Orin. *See* Orin (masculine section).

Oshrat (אָשְׁרַת)   From the Hebrew, meaning "fortunate."

Osma   From the Old English, meaning "hero" and "protection." A variant form of the masculine Osmund.

Osnat   A variant spelling of Asnat. *See* Asnat.

Ottalie, Ottilie   Variant Swedish forms of the masculine Otto. *See* Otto (masculine section).

Ottilia   A variant form of Ottalie. *See* Ottalie.

Otzara (אוֹצָרָה)   From the Hebrew, meaning "treasure, wealth." Ozara is a variant spelling.

Ova   From the Latin, meaning "egg."

Oz (עֹז)   From the Hebrew, meaning "strength." Also, the name of a bird mentioned in the Talmud.

Ozara   A variant spelling of Otzara. *See* Otzara.

Ozera (עוֹזֶרָה)   From the Hebrew, meaning "help, helper."

Page, Paige   From the Italian, meaning "boy attendant, servant." Used also as a masculine name.

Palma   From the Latin, meaning "palm tree," so named because its leaves resemble the palm of the hand. Palmeda, Palmer, and Palmira are variant forms.

Palmeda   A variant form of Palma. *See* Palma.

Palmer   An occupational name derived from Palma. *See* Palma.

Palmira, Palmyra   Variant forms of Palmer. *See* Palmer *and* Palma.

Paloma   A Spanish name from the Latin, meaning "dove." Akin to Columba.

Pam   A diminutive form of Pamela. *See* Pamela.

Pamela   From the Greek and the Anglo-Saxon, meaning "loved one" or "all sweetness." Coined by Sir Philip Sidney for a character in his *Arcadi* (1590). Pam is a popular diminutive. Pamelia is a variant form.

Pamelia   A variant form of Pamela. *See* Pamela.

Pamelyn   A hybrid of Pamela and Lyn. *See* Pamela *and* Lyn.

Pandora   From the Greek, meaning "very gifted." In Greek mythology, the first woman who, out of curiosity, opened a sealed box and permitted human ills to escape into the world.

Panfila, Panphila   From the Greek, meaning "loved by all."

Pansy   An English flower-name derived from the French and meaning "to think." Shakespeare used the phrase, "Pansies for thought."

Paola   A Spanish form of Paula. *See* Paula.

Pascha, Pasha   From the Greek, derived from the Hebrew *pesach*, meaning "paschal lamb" and "to pass over." Pashell is probably a variant form.

Pashell   Probably a variant form of Pascha. *See* Pascha.

Pat   A pet form of Patricia. *See* Patricia.

Patia   A variant form of Patricia. *See* Patricia.

Patience   From the Latin, meaning "to suffer."

Patrice   A variant form of Patricia. *See* Patricia.

Patricia   The feminine form of Patrick. *See* Patrick (masculine section). Patia and Patrice are variant forms. Pat, Patsy, Patti, Pattie, and Patty are pet forms.

Patsy   A pet form of Patricia. *See* Patricia.

Patti, Pattie, Patty   Pet forms of Patricia. *See* Patricia.

Paula   The feminine form of Paul. *See* Paul (masculine section). Paola and Pavla are variant forms. Paulette, Paulina, and Pauline are pet forms.

Paulette   A French pet form of Paula. *See* Paula.

Paulina, Pauline   Paulina is the Spanish form of the French Pauline. Both are pet forms of Paula, the feminine form of Paul. *See* Paul (masculine section).

Pavla   A Russian form of Paula. *See* Paula.

Paz (פָּז)   From the Hebrew, meaning "gold." Paza and Pazit are variant forms.

Paza (פָּזָה)   A variant form of Paz. *See* Paz.

Pazia, Paziah   Variant spellings of Pazya. *See* Pazya.

Pazit (פָּזִית)   A variant form of Paz. *See* Paz.

Paziya (פָּזִיָה)   A variant form of Pazya. *See* Pazya.

Pazya (פַּזְיָה)   From the Hebrew, meaning "God's gold." Pazia and Paziah are variant spellings. Paziya is a variant form.

Peale   From the Latin, meaning "peace."

Pearl   From the Latin and Middle English, meaning "pearl." Akin to Margaret. *See* Margaret. Perle is a variant spelling. Perla is a variant form. Pearlie, Peg, Peggie, and Peggy are pet forms.

Pearlie A pet form of Pearl. *See* Pearl.

Pearliemae A hybrid of Pearlie and Mae. *See* Pearlie *and* Mae.

Pearline A pet form of Pearl. *See* Pearl.

Peduia A variant spelling of Peduya. *See* Peduya.

Pedut (פְּדוּת) From the Hebrew, meaning "redemption." Akin to Peduya.

Peduya (פְּדוּיָה) From the Hebrew, meaning "redeemed." Peduia is a variant spelling. Akin to Pedut.

Pe'era (פְּאֵרָה) From the Hebrew, meaning "adornment" or "praise."

Peer-Li, Pe'er-Li (פְּאֵר־לִי) From the Hebrew, meaning "I am adorned."

Peg, Peggie, Peggy Pet forms of Margaret and Pearl. *See* Margaret *and* Pearl. Peig and Pegeen are Irish forms. Pegi is a variant spelling of Peggy.

Pegeen An Irish form of Peggy. *See* Peggy.

Pegi A variant spelling of Peggy. *See* Peggy.

Peig An Irish form of Peg. *See* Peg.

Pelagia From the Greek, meaning "sea."

Pelia, Peliah (פְּלִיאָה) From the Hebrew, meaning "wonder, miracle."

Penelope From the Greek, meaning "worker in cloth" or "silent worker." Penney, Pennie, and Penny are pet forms.

Peni, Penie Pet forms of Penina. *See* Penina.

Penina, Peninah (פְּנִנָּה) From the Hebrew, meaning "coral" or "pearl." In the Bible (I Samuel 1:2), the wife of Elkanah. Penini is a variant form. Akin to Peninit. Also spelled פְּנִינָה. Peni and Penie are pet forms.

Penini (פְּנִינִי) A variant form of Penina. *See* Penina.

Peninia A variant spelling of Peniniya. *See* Peniniya.

Peninit (פְּנִינִית) From the Hebrew, meaning "pearly, pearliness." Peniniyut is a variant form.

Peniniut A variant spelling of Peniniyut. *See* Peniniyut.

Peniniya (פְּנִנִיָּה) From the Hebrew, meaning "hen." Peninia is a variant spelling.

Peniniyut (פְּנִינִיּוּת) A variant form of Peninit. *See* Peninit.

Penney, Pennie, Penny Pet forms of Penelope. *See* Penelope.

Penthea From the Greek, meaning "fifth." Often given to the fifth child in a family.

Penuya (פְּנוּיָה) From the Hebrew, meaning "single, unmarried."

Peony From the Greek, Paion, an epithet for Apollo, physician of the gods. A flower of the buttercup family with medicinal properties.

Pepita A Spanish pet form of Josephine. *See* Josephine. Peppy is a pet form.

Pepper From the Latin, describing "a condiment derived from a plant." Used also as a masculine name.

Peppy A variant form of Pepita. *See* Pepita.

Perach (פֶּרַח) From the Hebrew, meaning "blossom" or "flower." Perah is a variant spelling. Akin to Pericha and Pircha.

Perah A variant spelling of Perach. *See* Perach.

Perfecta A Spanish form of the Latin, meaning "perfect."

Peri (פְּרִי) From the Hebrew, meaning "fruit." Also, a variant spelling of Perri. *See* Perri.

Pericha (פְּרִיחָה) From the Hebrew, meaning "blossom, growth, flower." Akin to Perach and Pircha.

Perla A variant form of Pearl. *See* Pearl.

Perle A variant spelling of Pearl. *See* Pearl.

Perpetua From the Latin, meaning "constant, everlasting."

Perri A pet form of Perrin. *See* Perrin. Peri is a variant spelling.

Perrin, Perrine Variant forms of Peter. *See* Peter (masculine section). Perri is a pet form.

Peshe (פֶּעשֶׁע) A Yiddish form of Bashe. *See* Bashe.

Pessel (פֶּעסֶעל) A Yiddish form of Bashe. *See* Bashe.

Peta A pet form of Petra. *See* Petra.

Petie A feminine form of Peter. *See* Peter (masculine section). Petty is a variant spelling.

Petite From the French, meaning "small." Petit is the masculine form.

Petra A feminine form of Peter. *See* Peter (masculine section). Peta is a pet form. Petrina is a Russian form.

Petrina A Russian form of the Greek Petra. *See* Petra.

Petty A variant spelling of Petie. *See* Petie.

Petula From the Latin, meaning "impatient."

Petunia From the French *petun*, referring to plants of the nightshade variety.

Peuta (פְּעוּטָה) From the Hebrew, meaning "small."

Phebe A variant spelling of Phoebe. *See* Phoebe.

Phila From the Greek, meaning "love."

Philana From the Greek, meaning "lover of mankind."

Philantha From the Greek, meaning "lover of flowers."

Philena, Philina From the Greek, meaning "lover of mankind." Phillina is a variant spelling.

Philippa From the Greek, meaning "lover of horses." Philip is the masculine form. Pippa is an Italian pet form. Phillippa is a variant spelling.

Phillina A variant spelling of Philina. *See* Philina.

Phillippa A variant spelling of Philippa. *See* Philippa.

Philyra From the Greek, meaning "to love the lyre," hence "to be musical."

Phoebe From the Greek, meaning "bright, shining one." In Greek mythology, the moon goddess. Akin to Diana in Roman mythology. Phebe is a variant spelling. Phoebus is the masculine counterpart.

Phyl A pet form of Phyllis. *See* Phyllis.

Phylis, Phyliss Variant spellings of Phyllis. *See* Phyllis.

Phyllie A pet form of Phyllis. *See* Phyllis.

Phyllis From the Greek, meaning "little leaf, green bough." Phylis and Phyliss are variant spellings. Phyl and Phyllie are pet forms.

Pia From the Latin, meaning "pious."

Pier A feminine form of Pierre, the French form of Peter. *See* Peter (masculine section).

Pili (פְּלָאִי) From the Hebrew, meaning "miraculous."

Pippa An Italian pet form of Philippa. *See* Philippa.

Pircha (פִּרְחָה) From the Hebrew, meaning "blossom" or "flower." Pirha is a variant spelling. Akin to Perach, Pericha, and Pirchiya. Pirchit is a variant form.

Pirchia A variant spelling of Pirchiya. *See* Pirchiya.

Pirchit (פִּרְחִית) A variant form of Pircha. *See* Pircha.

Pirchiya (פִּרְחִיָּה) From the Hebrew, meaning "blossom" or "flower." Pirchia is a variant spelling. Akin to Pircha.

Pirha A variant spelling of Pircha. *See* Pircha.

Pita (פִּיתָה) From the Hebrew and Arabic, meaning "bread." Also spelled פִּתָּה.

Piuta A variant spelling of Piyuta. *See* Piyuta."

Piyuta (פִּיּוּטָה) A Hebrew form of the Greek, meaning "poet, poetry."

Placida, Placidia From the Latin, meaning "to please, to placate."

Pleasance, Pleasant From the Middle French, meaning "agreeable, delightful."

Plennie From the Latin, meaning "full, complete."

Poda, Podah (פּוֹדָה) From the Hebrew, meaning "redeem, redeemer."

Polly A variant form of Molly, which was at one time a popular form of Mary. Mary is the Greek form of Miryam. *See* Miryam.

Ponchita, Ponchitta   From the Spanish, meaning "cloak, cape."

Pomona   From the Latin, meaning "apple, fruit." In Roman mythology, the goddess of fruit trees and their products.

Poppy   From the Latin, referring to "a plant that yields juice from which opium is made."

Pora (פּוֹרָה)   From the Hebrew, meaning "fruitful." Porat, Poriel, and Poriya are variant forms.

Porachat (פּוֹרַחַת)   From the Hebrew, meaning "to blossom." Akin to Pora.

Porat (פּוֹרָת)   A variant form of Pora. See Pora.

Poria, Poriah   Variant spellings of Poriya. See Poriya.

Poriel (פּוֹרִיאֵל)   A variant form of Pora, meaning "fruit of God."

Poriya (פּוֹרִיָה)   A variant form of Pora. See Pora. Poria and Poriah are variant spellings.

Portia   From the Latin, meaning "hog."

Pow   From the Thai, meaning "fish."

Prima   From the Latin, meaning "first choice, premium."

Primrose   From the French and Latin, meaning "first rose." Used mostly in Scotland.

Priscilla   From the Latin, meaning "ancient, old."

Prudence   From the Latin, meaning "prudent, cautious." Prue is a pet form.

Prue   A pet form of Prudence. See Prudence.

Pua, Puah (פּוּעָה)   From the Hebrew, meaning "to groan, cry out." In the Bible (Exodus 1:15), a Hebrew midwife. Also from the Hawaiian, meaning "flower, blossom."

Quanda   From the Old English, meaning "companion" or "queen."

Queena   A variant form of Queenie. See Queenie.

Queenie   A nickname for Regina, from the Latin meaning "queen." Queena is a variant form.

Quella   From the Old English, meaning "kill."

Quenby   From the Old English, meaning "queen's castle."

Quilla   From the Middle English, meaning "quill."

Quinn   From the Old English, meaning "queen."

Quinta   From the Latin, meaning "fifth." A name usually given to the fifth child in a family, if a girl, or to the fifth girl in a family.

Raanana (רַעֲנָנָה)   From the Hebrew, meaning "fresh, luscious" or "beautiful." Ranana is a variant spelling.

Rachaela (רָחֵלָה)   A variant form of Rachel. *See* Rachel.

Rachaele   A variant spelling of Rachel. *See* Rachel.

Rachav (רָחָב)   From the Hebrew, meaning "large, extended, spacious." In the Bible (Joshua 2:1), a harlot in Jericho who aided the spies sent in by Joshua. Rahab is an Anglicized spelling.

Rachel (רָחֵל)   From the Hebrew, meaning "ewe," a symbol of purity and gentility. In the Bible (Genesis 29:16), the wife of Jacob and sister of Leah. Rahel and Rachelle are variant spellings. Rachaela, Rachaele, Rachela, Racheli, Rahil, Raquel, Rechel, and Recheli are variant forms. Rae, Ray, and Raye are pet forms.

Rachela (רָחֵלָה)   A variant form of Rachel. *See* Rachel.

Racheli (רָחֵלִי)   A variant form of Rachel. *See* Rachel.

Rachelle   A variant spelling of Rachel. *See* Rachel.

Rachmona (רַחְמוֹנָה)   A variant form of Ruchama. *See* Ruchama.

Radella   A French form of the German, meaning "counsel." Radinka is a Russian form.

Radinka   A Russian form of Radella. *See* Radella.

Rae   A pet form of Rachel. *See* Rachel.

Rafaela, Rafaele   Variant spellings of Refaela. *See* Refaela.

Rafia   A variant spelling of Rafya. *See* Rafya.

Rafya (רָפְיָה)   From the Hebrew, meaning "the healing of the Lord." Rafia and Raphia are variant spellings.

Rahab   A variant spelling of Rachav. *See* Rachav.

Rahel   A variant spelling of Rachel. *See* Rachel.

Rahil   A variant form of Rachel. *See* Rachel.

Raina (רֵיינָא)   From the Latin, meaning "to rule." Akin to Regina. Also, a variant spelling of the Yiddish Rayna. *See* Rayna. Raine and Rana are variant forms. Rane is a variant spelling.

Raine (רֵיינֶע)   A variant form of Raina. *See* Raina.

Raisa (רײַזָא) From the Yiddish, meaning "rose." Raissa and Raisse are variant spellings. Akin to Raisel.

Raise (רײַזֶע) A variant form of Raisa. See Raisa.

Raisel A pet form of Raise. See Raise.

Raissa, Raisse Variant spellings of Raisa. See Raisa.

Raize A variant spelling of Raise. See Raise.

Raizel (רײַזֶעל) A variant spelling of Raisel. See Raisel. Also spelled רײזל.

Raizi (רײַזִי) A pet form of Raizel. See Raizel.

Rakefet (רָקֶפֶת) A plant that flourishes in rocky places. Probably of Syriac origin.

Ralna A feminine form of Roland. See Roland (masculine section).

Rama (רָמָה) From the Hebrew, meaning "lofty, exalted." Also, the name of a precious ruby-colored stone. Also, a place-name mentioned in the Bible (Nehemiah 11:33). Rami, Ramit, and Ramot are variant forms.

Rami (רָמִי) A variant form of Rama. See Rama.

Ramit (רָמִית) A variant form of Rama. See Rama.

Ramona A short form of the Anglo-Saxon Raymonda, meaning "peace" or "protection." See Raymonda.

Ramot (רָמוֹת) A variant form of Rama. See Rama.

Ramzia A variant spelling of Ramziya. See Ramziya.

Ramziya (רָמְזִיָה) From the Hebrew, meaning "to signal." Ramzia is a variant spelling. Rimzia is a variant form.

Rana A variant form of Raina. See Raina.

Ranana A variant spelling of Raanana. See Raanana.

Randa A feminine form of Randall. See Randall (masculine section). Randy is a pet form.

Randall Used primarily as a masculine name. See Randall (masculine section).

Randee, Randi Variant spellings of Randy. See Randy.

Randy A feminine pet form of Randolph. See Randolph (masculine section). Also, a pet form of Randa. See Randa. Randee and Randi are variant spellings.

Rane A variant spelling of Raina. See Raina.

Rani (רָנִי) From the Hebrew, meaning "my song."

Ranit (רָנִית) From the Hebrew, meaning "joy" or "song." Ranita is a variant form.

Ranita (רָנִיתָה) A variant form of Ranit. See Ranit.

Ranny A pet form of Frances. See Frances.

Ranya (רַנְיָה) From the Hebrew, meaning "song of the Lord." Rania is a variant spelling.

Raomi (רָאוֹמִי) A variant form of Reuma. *See* Reuma.

Raoul A variant form of Randolph and Ralph. *See* Randolph *and* Ralph (masculine section).

Rapa From the Hawaiian, meaning "moonbeam."

Raphaela A variant spelling of Refaela. *See* Refaela.

Raphia A variant spelling of Rafya. *See* Rafya.

Raquel A variant Spanish form of Rachel. *See* Rachel.

Raske (רַאסְקֶע) A Yiddish form of Rachel. *See* Rachel.

Ravina (רְבִינָה) A feminine usage of the masculine Ravina. *See* Ravina (masculine section).

Ravit (רָבִית) A variant form of Ravital. *See* Ravital.

Ravital (רְבִיטָל) From the Hebrew, meaning "my master (God) is my dew (provider)." Ravit is a variant form.

Raviva (רְבִיבָה) From the Hebrew, meaning "rain, raindrops."

Ray, Raye Pet forms of Rachel. *See* Rachel. Also, from the Celtic, meaning "grace, gracious."

Raya (רֵעָ) From the Hebrew, meaning "friend."

Raymonda The feminine form of Raymond. *See* Raymond (masculine section). Ramona is a short form.

Rayna (רֵיינָא) A Yiddish form of Catherine and Catherina, meaning "pure, clean." Raina, Rayne, Reina, Reine, and Reyna are variant spellings.

Rayne (רֵיינָע) A variant form of Rayna. *See* Rayna.

Rayzel A variant spelling of Raisel. *See* Raisel.

Raz (רָז) From the Aramaic, meaning "secret." Used also as a masculine name.

Razi (רָזִי) From the Hebrew, meaning "my secret." Used also as a masculine name.

Razia, Raziah Variant spellings of Raziya. *See* Raziya.

Raziela (רָזִאֵלָה) From the Hebrew, meaning "God is my secret" or "secret of God." Akin to Raziya.

Razil A variant spelling of Raisel. *See* Raisel.

Razilee A variant spelling of Razili. *See* Razili.

Razili (רָזִילִי) From the Aramaic and Hebrew, meaning "my secret." Razilee is a variant spelling.

Razina (רָזִינָה) An Hebraicized form of Rosina. *See* Rosina.

Raziya (רָזִיָה) From the Hebrew, meaning "secret of the Lord." Akin to

Raziela. Razia and Raziah are variant spellings.

Reade   From the Old English, meaning "to counsel, advise."

Reatha   A variant form of Marguerita. *See* Marguerita. Akin to Retha and Rita. Reitha is a variant spelling.

Reba   A pet form of Rebecca. *See* Rebecca. Also, a variant spelling of Reva. *See* Reva.

Rebecca (רִבְקָה)   From the Hebrew, meaning "to tie, bind." Fattened animals were tied and prepared for slaughtering. Rivka is the original Hebrew form. *See* Rivka. In the Bible (Genesis 24:15), the wife of Isaac and the mother of Jacob and Esau. Reba is a pet form, as are Riki, Rivai, Rivvy, Beckie, and Becky. In some versions of the Bible Rebecca is called Rebekah.

Rechana   A variant form of Reichana. *See* Reichana.

Rechela (רְחֵלָה)   A variant form of Rachel. *See* Rachel.

Recheli (רְחֵלִי)   A variant form of Rachel. *See* Rachel.

Reda   A variant form of Rita. *See* Rita.

Re'ema (רְאֵמָה)   From the Hebrew, meaning "reindeer."

Reena   A variant spelling of Rina. *See* Rina.

Reeta   A variant spelling of Rita. *See* Rita.

Refaela (רְפָאֵלָה)   From the Hebrew, meaning "God has healed." The feminine form of Refael. Rafaele, Raphaela, and Raphaele are variant spellings.

Refua (רְפוּאָה)   From the Hebrew, meaning "healing" or "succor." Rofi is a variant form. Rephua is a variant spelling.

Regan   A variant form of Regina. *See* Regina.

Regina   From the Latin, meaning "to rule," hence "queen." Also, from the Anglo-Saxon, meaning "pure." Regan is a variant form. Rena is a short form.

Rehana   A variant spelling of Reichana. *See* Reichana.

Reia Rei'a (רֵעַ)   From the Hebrew, meaning "friend." Primarily a masculine name.

Reichana (רֵיחָנָה)   From the Hebrew, meaning "sweet-smelling." Also, the name of a plant with a spicy odor. Rechana is a variant form. Rehana is a variant spelling.

Reida   A variant form of Rita. *See* Rita.

Reina, Reine   Variant spellings of Rayna. *See* Rayna.

Reisel   A variant spelling of Raisel. *See* Raisel.

Reita   A variant spelling of Rita. *See* Rita.

Reitha   A variant spelling of Reatha. *See* Reatha.

Reizel   A variant spelling of Raisel. *See* Raisel.

Remazia, Remaziah   Variant spellings of Remazya. *See* Remazya.

Remazya (רְמַזְיָה) From the Hebrew, meaning "sign from the Lord." Remazia and Remaziah are variant spellings. Ramziya and Rimzia are variant forms.

Rena A short form of Regina or Serena. *See* Regina *and* Serena. Also, a variant spelling of Rina. *See* Rina.

Renana (רְנָנָה) From the Hebrew, meaning "joy" or "song." Renanit and Renina are variant forms.

Renanit (רְנָנִית) A variant form of Renana. *See* Renana.

Renata From the Latin, meaning "to be born again."

Renatia A variant spelling of Rinatya. *See* Rinatya.

Renatya A variant spelling of Rinatya. *See* Rinatya.

Rene, Renee French forms of Renata. *See* Renata. May also be a variant form of Irene. *See* Irene. Renette and Renita are pet forms.

Renette A French pet form of Rene. *See* Rene.

Renina (רְנִינָה) A variant form of Renana. *See* Renana.

Renita A Spanish pet form of Rene. *See* Rene.

Rephaela A variant spelling of Refaela. *See* Refaela.

Rephua A variant spelling of Refua. *See* Refua.

Retem (רֶתֶם) A variant form of Rotem. *See* Rotem.

Retha A short form of Marguerita. *See* Marguerita. Akin to Rita.

Reubena A variant spelling of Reuvena. *See* Reuvena.

Reuel (רְאוּאֵל) From the Hebrew, meaning "Behold, God!" Used primarily as a masculine name.

Reuma (רְאוּמָה) From the Aramaic, meaning "antelope." A feminine form of R'em, meaning "wild ox." In the Bible (Genesis 22:24), the concubine of Nachor, Abraham's brother. Raomi is a variant form.

Reuvena (רְאוּבֵנָה) From the Hebrew, meaning "Behold, a son!" The feminine form of Reuven. Reubena is a variant spelling.

Reva (רְבַע) From the Hebrew, meaning "rain" or "one-quarter, a fourth." Used also as a diminutive form of Rebecca. Reba is a variant spelling.

Revaia A variant spelling of Revaya. *See* Revaya.

Revaya (רְוָיָה) From the Hebrew, meaning "satisfied, sated." Revaia is a variant spelling.

Revital (רְוִיטַל) From the Hebrew, meaning "saturated with dew."

Reviva (רְבִיבָה) From the Hebrew, meaning "dew" or "rain."

Rexana The feminine form of Rex, meaning "king." *See* Rex (masculine section).

Rexella A feminine pet form of Rex. *See* Rex (masculine section).

Reyna A variant spelling of Rayna. *See* Rayna.

Reysel A variant spelling of Raisel. *See* Raisel.

Rhea From the Greek, meaning "protector of cities," or "a poppy (flower)."

Rheta A variant spelling of Rita. *See* Rita. Also, from the Greek, meaning "one who speaks well."

Rhina A Spanish pet form of Katrina. *See* Katrina.

Rhoda From the Greek, meaning "rose." Akin to Rose. *See* Rose. Rhode and Rhodeia are variant forms.

Rhode A variant form of Rhoda. *See* Rhoda.

Rhodeia A variant form of Rhoda. *See* Rhoda.

Rhona A hybrid of Rose and Anna. *See* Rose *and* Anna. Also, a variant spelling of Rona.

Rhonda From the Celtic, meaning "powerful river." Rhonnie is a pet form.

Rhonnie A pet form of Rhonda. *See* Rhonda.

Ria From the Spanish, meaning "small river."

Rica A pet form of Ricarda. *See* Ricarda. Also, a pet form of Patricia and Roberta. *See* Patricia *and* Roberta.

Ricarda A feminine Italian form of Ricardo (Richard). *See* Richard (masculine section).

Richarda A feminine form of Richard. *See* Richard (masculine section). Richela is a pet form.

Richela A pet form of Richarda. *See* Richarda.

Richenda A feminine form of Richard. *See* Richard (masculine section).

Richia A feminine form of Richard. *See* Richard (masculine section).

Ricka, Ricki, Ricky Pet forms of Patricia, Rebecca, Ricarda, and Roberta. *See* Patricia, Rebecca, Ricarda, *and* Roberta.

Riesa A pet form of Theresa. *See* Theresa.

Rifka (רִיפְקָא) A Yiddish form of Rivka. *See* Rivka.

Rifke (רִיפְקֶע) A Yiddish form of Rivka. *See* Rivka.

Riki (רְקִי) A variant spelling of Ricki. *See* Ricki. Also, a pet form of Rebecca. *See* Rebecca.

Rikma (רִקְמָה) From the Hebrew, meaning "woven."

Rikuda (רִקּוּדָה) From the Hebrew, meaning "to prance" or "to dance."

Rilla From the Dutch and Low German, meaning "little stream."

Rimon (רִימוֹן) From the Hebrew, meaning "pomegranate." Used also as a masculine name. Also spelled רִמוֹן.

Rimona (רִמוֹנָה) The feminine form of Rimon. *See* Rimon.

Rimzia (רִמְזִיָה) A variant form of Ramziya. *See* Ramziya.

Rina (רִנָּה) From the Hebrew, meaning "joy." Rinat is a variant form. Rena, Renna, and Rinna are variant spellings. Also, a pet form of Marina.

Rinat (רִינַת) A variant form of Rina. *See* Rina.

Rinatia A variant spelling of Rinatya. *See* Rinatya.

Rinatya (רִנַּתְיָה) From the Hebrew, meaning "song of the Lord." Renatia, Renatya, and Rinatia are variant spellings.

Rinda A pet form of Dorinda. *See* Dorinda.

Rinna A variant spelling of Rina. *See* Rina.

Risa A pet form of Theresa. *See* Theresa.

Rishona (רִאשׁוֹנָה) From the Hebrew, meaning "first."

Rishpa (רִשְׁפָּה) From the Hebrew, meaning "burning coal" or "spark." Rishpona is a variant form.

Rishpona (רִשְׁפּוֹנָה) A variant form of Rishpa. *See* Rishpa.

Rita From the Sanskrit, meaning "brave" or "honest." Also, a short form of Marguerita. *See* Marguerita. Akin to Retha. Reda and Reida are variant forms. Reeta and Rheta are variant spellings.

Ritma (רִתְמָה) A variant form of Rotem. *See* Rotem.

Ritzpa, Ritzpah (רִצְפָּה) From the Hebrew, meaning "floor, pavement." In the Bible (II Samuel 3:7), the daughter of Aya, one of King Saul's concubines.

Riva (רִיבָה) From the Old French, meaning "bank, coast, shore." Also, a pet form of Rivka. *See* Rivka.

Rivana A variant form of River. *See* River.

Rivca A variant spelling of Rivka. *See* Rivka.

Rivcka A variant spelling of Rivka. *See* Rivka.

Rivi (רִיבִי) A variant form of Reva. Also, a pet form of Rivka. *See* Rivka.

Rivka, Rivke (רִבְקָה) From the Hebrew, meaning "to bind." The original form of Rebecca. *See* Rebecca. Rifka, Rifke, Rivca, and Rivcka are variant spellings. Riva is a pet form.

Rivvy (רִיבִי) A pet form of Rivka. *See* Rivka.

Ro'a (רֹאה) From the Hebrew, meaning "to see" or "seer."

Roanna, Roanne A hybrid of Rose and Ann. *See* Rose *and* Ann.

Robbi, Robbie Pet forms of Roberta. *See* Roberta.

Roberta The feminine form of Robert. *See* Robert (masculine section). Bobbe, Rica, Ricky, Robbi, Robbie, Robin, and Robyn are pet forms. Bunny is a nickname.

Robin, Robyn Pet forms of Roberta. *See* Roberta.

Rochel (רָאחל) A Yiddish form of Rachel. *See* Rachel. Also, a variant spelling of Rochelle. *See* Rochelle.

Rochella A variant form of Rochelle. *See* Rochelle.

Rochelle From the Old French, meaning "small rock." Rochel is a variant spelling. Rochella is a variant form. Rochette is a pet form.

Rochette A French pet form of Rochelle. *See* Rochelle.

Roderica A feminine form of Roderick. *See* Roderick (masculine section).

Rofi (רֹפִי) A variant form of Refua. *See* Refua.

Rolanda A feminine form of Roland. *See* Roland (masculine section).

Rolene, Rollene Feminine forms of Roland. *See* Roland (masculine section).

Roma (רוּמָה) From the Hebrew, meaning "heights, lofty, exalted." Also, the city of Rome, named for Romulus. In Roman mythology, Romulus was one of the sons of Mars. *See* Romulus (masculine section). Romaine, Romana, Romit, and Romy are variant forms. *See* also Romema.

Romaine A variant form of Roma. *See* Roma. Romayne is a variant spelling.

Romana A variant form of Roma. *See* Roma.

Romayne A variant spelling of Romaine. *See* Romaine.

Romelda From the German, meaning "Roman warrior." Romilda is a variant form.

Romema (רוּמֶמָה) From the Hebrew, meaning "heights, lofty, exalted." Romemit, Romemiya, Romit, and Romiya are variant forms. Akin to Roma.

Romemit (רוּמֶמִית) A variant form of Romema. *See* Romema.

Romemiya (רוּמֶמְיָה) A variant form of Romema. *See* Romema.

Romia A variant spelling of Romiya. *See* Romiya.

Romilda A variant form of Romelda. *See* Romelda.

Romit (רוּמִית) A variant form of Roma. *See* Roma.

Romiya (רוּמְיָה) A variant form of Romema. *See* Romema. Romia is a variant spelling.

Romola The Italian feminine form of Romulus. *See* Romulus (masculine section).

Romy A variant form of Roma. *See* Roma.

Ron (רוֹן) From the Hebrew, meaning "song" or "joy." Ronit is a variant form. Rona, Ronela, Ronella, Ronena, Roni, Ronit, Roniya, and Ronli are variant forms.

Rona (רֹנָה) From the Gaelic, meaning "seal," or from the Hebrew, meaning "joy." Also, a feminine form of Ronald. *See* Ronald (masculine section). Rhona is a variant spelling. Also spelled רוֹנָּה.

Ronalda A feminine form of Ronald. *See* Ronald (masculine section).

Ronee   A feminine pet form of the masculine Ronald. *See* Ronald (masculine section).

Ronela, Ronella (רוֹנְאֵלָה)   Variant forms of Ron. *See* Ron. From the Hebrew, meaning "joy of the Lord" or "song of the Lord." Akin to Roniya.

Ronena (רוֹנְנָה)   From the Hebrew, meaning "song" or "joy."

Roni (רוֹנִי)   A variant form of Ron. *See* Ron. From the Hebrew, meaning "my song" or "my joy." Used also as a masculine name.

Ronia   A variant spelling of Roniya. *See* Roniya.

Ronit (רוֹנִית)   A variant form of Ron. *See* Ron. Ronnit is a variant spelling.

Roniya (רוֹנִיָה)   A variant form of Ron. *See* Ron. From the Hebrew, meaning "joy of the Lord" or "song of the Lord." Akin to Ronela. Ronia is a variant spelling.

Ronli (רוֹנְלִי)   A variant form of Ron. *See* Ron. From the Hebrew, meaning "joy is mine."

Ronne, Ronni, Ronnie   Feminine pet forms of Ronald. *See* Ronald (masculine section). Ronny is a variant spelling.

Ronnit   A variant spelling of Ronit. *See* Ronit.

Ronny   A variant spelling of Ronnie. *See* Ronnie.

Rori, Rory   Irish feminine forms of Roderick and Robert. *See* Roderick *and* Robert (masculine section). Often used as masculine names.

Rosa   A popular Italian form of Rose. *See* Rose.

Rosabel   From the Latin and French, meaning "beautiful rose." *See* Rose.

Rosaleen   A variant form of Rosalind. *See* Rosalind.

Rosalie   A variant French pet form of Rose. *See* Rose.

Rosalind   A pet form of Rose. *See* Rose. From the Latin, meaning "beautiful rose." Rosaleen, Rosalinda, Rosaline, Rosalyn, Roselee, and Roselyn are variant forms.

Rosalinda   A Spanish form of Rosalind. *See* Rosalind.

Rosaline   A variant form of Rosalind. *See* Rosalind.

Rosalyn   A variant form of Rosalind. *See* Rosalind. Roslyn is a variant spelling. Roz is a pet form.

Rosamond, Rosamund, Rosamunde   From the Latin, meaning "rose of the world." Also, from the Old High German, meaning "protector of the horse."

Rosanne   A hybrid of Rose and Anne. *See* Rose *and* Anne.

Rose   The English form of the Latin Rosa, meaning "rose." Among the many variant forms of this name are Rosa, Rosaleen, Rosalie, Rosalind, Rosalinde, Rosaline, Rosalyn, Rosamond, Rosebud, and Rosel. Among its many pet forms are Rosetta, Rosette, Rosi, Rosina, and Rosita.

Roseanna   A hybrid of Rose and Anna. *See* Rose *and* Anna.

Roseanne A hybrid of Rose and Anne. *See* Rose *and* Anne. Rozanne is a variant spelling.

Rosebud A variant form of Rose, meaning "bud of a rose."

Rosedale From the Old English, meaning "valley of roses."

Rosel, Roselle Pet forms of Rose. *See* Rose.

Roseleen A variant form of Rosalind. *See* Rosalind.

Rosellen A hybrid of Rose and Ellen. *See* Rose *and* Ellen.

Roselotta A variant form of Roselotte. *See* Roselotte.

Roselotte A hybrid of Rose and Lotte. *See* Rose *and* Lotte. Roselotta is a variant form.

Roselyn A variant form of Rosalind. *See* Rosalind.

Rosemary A hybrid of Rose and Mary. Used as a plant-name. In Shakespeare's time, the medicine made from the plant was believed to refresh the memory. Ophelia, in *Hamlet*, says: "There's Rosemary, that's for remembrance; pray, love, remember." *See* Rose *and* Mary.

Rosetta An Italian pet form of Rose. *See* Rose.

Rosette A French pet form of Rose. *See* Rose.

Rosi, Rosie Pet forms of Rose. *See* Rose.

Rosina, Rosine Pet forms of Rose. *See* Rose. Razina is an Hebraicized form. Rozina is a variant spelling.

Rosita A pet form of Rose. *See* Rose.

Roslyn A variant spelling of Rosalyn. *See* Rosalyn.

Rotam (רוֹתָם) A variant form of Rotem. *See* Rotem.

Rotem (רוֹתֶם) From the Hebrew. In the Bible (I Kings 19:5), a plant common to the southern (desert) parts of Israel. Also, from the Hebrew, meaning "to bind." Retem, Ritma, and Rotam are variant forms.

Rowan From the Old English, meaning "rugged land." Rowena is a variant form.

Rowena A variant form of Rowan. *See* Rowan. Also, from the Celtic, meaning "flowering white hair."

Roxane, Roxanna, Roxanne From the Persian, meaning "dawn" or "brilliant light." Roxine is a variant form. Roxy is a popular diminutive form.

Roxie A variant spelling of Roxy. *See* Roxy.

Roxine A variant form of Roxanne. *See* Roxanne.

Roxy A pet form of Roxanne. *See* Roxanne. Roxie is a variant spelling.

Royal, Royale From the Middle English and the Latin, meaning "king, royal."

Roz A pet form of Rosalyn. *See* Rosalyn.

Rozanne   A variant spelling of Roseanne. *See* Roseanne.

Rozina   A variant spelling of Rosina. *See* Rosina.

Rubetta, Rubette   Pet forms of Ruby. *See* Ruby.

Ruby   From the Latin and French, meaning "red, reddish," usually referring to a deep-red precious stone. Rubetta and Rubette are pet forms.

Ruchama (רוּחָמָה)   From the Hebrew, meaning "comfort" or "compassion." Rachmona is a variant form. Ruhama is a variant spelling. In the Bible (Hosea 1:6), Lo-Ruchama is a symbolic name. Also spelled רֻחָמָה.

Rudelle   From the Old High German, meaning "famous one." Akin to Rue.

Rue   From the Old High German, meaning "fame." Akin to Rudelle. Ruey is a variant form.

Ruey   A variant form of Rue. *See* Rue. Or, a pet form of Reuel. *See* Reuel.

Ruhama   A variant spelling of Ruchama. *See* Ruchama.

Rula   From the Middle English and the Latin, meaning "ruler."

Ruma (רוּמָה)   From the Hebrew, meaning "heights."

Rumya (רוּמְיָה)   From the Hebrew, meaning "heights of the Lord." Popular among Yemenites.

Runa   From the Old Norse, meaning "to flow, cause to run."

Ruperta   The feminine form of Rupert. *See* Rupert (masculine section).

Rut (רוּת)   The Hebraicized form of Ruth. *See* Ruth. Ruti is a pet form.

Ruth   From the Syriac and Hebrew, meaning "friendship." Rut is the exact Hebrew form. In the Bible (Book of Ruth), Ruth is a Moabitess who marries Naomi's son. She is renowned for her loyalty to Judaism even after the death of her husband.

Ruthanna   A hybrid of Ruth and Anna. *See* Ruth *and* Anna.

Ruti (רוּתִי)   A pet form of Rut. *See* Rut.

Saada (סַעֲדָה)   From the Hebrew, meaning "support, help." Popular in Oriental communities. Akin to the masculine Saadya.

Saba (סָבָּא)   From the Hebrew and Aramaic, meaning "old, aged." Sava is a variant form. Used also as a masculine name.

Sabaria   A variant form of Tzabaria. *See* Tzabaria.

Sabina, Sabine   Feminine forms of the Latin Sabin, meaning "of the Sabines." The Sabines were an ancient Italian people who conquered the Romans in 290 B.C.E. Savina is a variant form.

Sabra (סַבְרָה)   The Hebrew name for a native-born Israeli. From the Arabic, meaning "thorny cactus." Used primarily as a feminine name, but occasionally as a masculine name. Also spelled צַבְּרָה.

Sabrina   A pet form of Sabra. *See* Sabra. Savrina is a variant spelling. Zabrina is a variant form.

Sacha   A pet form of Alexandra, popular in Russia. *See* Alexandra. Used also as a masculine name.

Sada   A variant form of Sadie. *See* Sadie. Also, from the Old English, meaning "seed."

Sadella, Sadelle   Pet forms of Sadie. *See* Sadie.

Sadi   A modern spelling of Sadie.

Sadie   A pet form of Sarah. *See* Sarah. Once popular among Roman Catholics as a pet form of Mercedes, meaning "Mary of the Mercies." Sadi, Sady, and Sadye are variant spellings. Sada is a variant form.

Sadira (סָדִירָה)   From the Arabic and Hebrew, meaning "organized, regulated." Also, the Arabic name of a constellation. Sedira is a variant form.

Sady, Sadye   Variant spellings of Sadie. *See* Sadie.

Saffron   From the Arabic, meaning "crocus," a plant with purple flowers. The dried, aromatic stigmas of this plant are used in coloring and flavoring foods.

Sahara (סַהֲרָא)   From the Arabic and Aramaic, meaning "moon."

Salcha (סַלְחָה)   From the Hebrew, meaning "forgiving" or "gracious." Popular in Oriental communities.

Salchan (סַלְחָן)   From the Hebrew, meaning "one who forgives."

Salena, Salina   From the Latin, meaning "salt."

Salida   From the Old German, meaning "happiness, joy." Selda, Selde, and Zelda are variant Yiddish forms.

Salit (סַלְעִית)   From the Hebrew, meaning "rock, rocky." The name of a desert bird indigenous to the southern part of Israel, where it inhabits the craggy hills. Silit is a variant form.

Sallie, Sally   Variant forms of Sarah. *See* Sarah.

Salma (שַׁלְמָה)   From the Hebrew, meaning "garment."

Salome   From the Hebrew, meaning "peaceful." In history, Salome Alexandra was the ruler of Judea from 76 to 67 B.C.E. She was succeeded by her husband, Alexander Yannai (Jannai). A sister of King Herod was also named Salome. Shelomit and Shulamit are Hebrew equivalents. The exact Hebrew name is שְׁלוֹמְצִיּוֹן.

Samantha Possibly a feminine form of Samuel. *See* Samuel (masculine section).

Samara From the Latin, meaning "seed of the elm."

Sami, Samie Feminine forms of Samuel. *See* Samuel (masculine section). Also a pet form of Samantha. *See* Samantha.

Samira From the Arabic, meaning "entertainer." Samir is a masculine form.

Samuela The feminine form of Samuel. *See* Samuel (masculine section). Shmuela is the equivalent Hebrew form.

Samye A variant spelling of Sami. *See* Sami.

Sande A pet form of Sandra. *See* Sandra.

Sanderalee A hybrid name of Sander and Lee. *See* Sander (masculine section) *and* Lee.

Sandi A pet form of Sandra. *See* Sandra.

Sandra A pet form of Alexandra. *See* Alexandra. Saundra is a variant spelling. Sande, Sandi, and Sandy are pet forms. Zandra is a variant form.

Sandy A pet form of Sandra. *See* Sandra.

Sansana (סַנְסָנָה) From the Hebrew, meaning "veins (skeleton) of the palm leaf."

Santina From the Latin, meaning "little saint."

Sapa (סָפָּה) A pet form of Yosefa (Josepha). *See* Yosefa. Also, from the Hebrew, meaning "couch."

Saphira (סַפִּירָה) From the Hebrew, meaning "sapphire." Akin to Sapir and Sapira.

Sapir (סַפִּיר) From the Hebrew, meaning "sapphire" or "precious stone." Used also as a masculine name. Sapira and Sapirit are variant forms. Akin to Saphira.

Sapira (סַפִּירָה) A variant form of Sapir. *See* Sapir.

Sapirit (סַפִּירִית) A variant form of Sapir. *See* Sapir.

Sara, Sarah (שָׂרָה) From the Hebrew, meaning "noble" or "princess." In the Bible (Genesis 17:15), the first of the matriarchs, Abraham's wife, whose original name was Sarai. Abraham and Sara were the parents of Isaac and Esau. Among Jews the name Sara was always popular, but among Christians it was rarely used before the Reformation (sixteenth century). Sareli, Sarina, Sarit, Sera, and Zara are variant forms. Sadie, Sadye, Sally, Saretta, and Sarette are pet forms. Sirel, Sorale, Sorali, Sorke, Sura, Surah, Tzirel, and Zirel are Yiddish forms.

Sarai (שָׂרַי) The original biblical form of Sara (Genesis 11:29). *See* Sara. Sari is a variant spelling.

Saran, Sarann, Saranne Hybrid forms of Sarah and Ann. *See* Sarah *and* Ann.

Sareli (שָׂרְאֵלִי) A variant form of Sara. *See* Sara. Also, a variant form of Yisrael (Israel). *See* Yisrael (masculine section).

Sarene A variant form of Sara. *See* Sara.

Saretta, Sarette Pet forms of Sara. *See* Sara.

Sari From the Hindi and Sanskrit, referring to an "outergarment" worn by Hindu women. Also, a variant spelling of Sarai. *See* Sarai.

Sarid (שָׂרִיד) From the Hebrew, meaning "escaped" or "saved."

Sarina, Sarine Variant forms of Sara. *See* Sara.

Sarit, Sarita (שָׂרִית) Variant forms of Sara. *See* Sara.

Sasgona (סַסְגּוֹנָא) From the Aramaic, meaning "colored, multicolored." The name of an animal whose skin was used for covering the Tabernacle.

Sasgoni (סַסְגּוֹנִי) From the Aramaic and Hebrew, meaning "multicolored."

Sasgonit (סַסְגּוֹנִית) A variant form of Sasgoni. *See* Sasgoni.

Sasha A variant spelling of Sacha. *See* Sacha.

Sasona (שָׂשׂוֹנָה) From the Hebrew, meaning "joy."

Saundra A variant spelling of Sandra. *See* Sandra.

Sava (סָבָא) A variant form of Saba. *See* Saba. Also spelled סָבָה.

Savannah From the Spanish, meaning "treeless plain."

Savina A variant form of Sabina. *See* Sabina.

Savion A variant spelling of Savyon. *See* Savyon.

Savlanut (סַבְלָנוּת) From the Hebrew, meaning "patience."

Savrina A variant form of Sabra. *See* Sabra.

Savta (סָבְתָּא) From the Aramaic, meaning "old" or "grandmother." Also spelled סבתה.

Savyon (סַבְיוֹן) A plant of the senecio genus. Savion is a variant spelling. Savyona is a variant form.

Savyona (סַבְיוֹנָה) A variant form of Savyon. *See* Savyon.

Saxon A Germanic name, from the Latin, meaning "sword, knife, stone."

Scarlet, Scarlett From the Middle English, meaning "red, ruby-colored."

Schifra A variant spelling of Shifra. *See* Shifra.

Scotia A feminine form of Scott. *See* Scott (masculine section).

Scotti A feminine form of Scott. *See* Scott (masculine section).

Season From the Latin, meaning "sowing, planting."

Sedera (סְדֵרָה) From the Hebrew, meaning "a row, a series of pillars."

Sedira (סְדִירָה) A variant form of Sadira. *See* Sadira.

Seema   From the Greek, meaning "sprout." Akin to Cyma. Sema is a variant spelling.

Sefach (סְפַח)   From the Hebrew, meaning "aftergrowth."

Segula (סְגֻלָּה)   From the Hebrew, meaning "treasure" or "precious." Also spelled סְגוּלָה.

Segura (סְגוּרָה)   From the Hebrew, meaning "locked, closed."

Sela (סֶלַע)   From the Greek and Hebrew, meaning "rock." Used also as a masculine name. Also, from the Hebrew, meaning "musical note" and spelled סֶלָה.

Selda, Selde   From the Anglo-Saxon, meaning "precious, rare," and from the Middle English, meaning "booth, hut." Also, a variant form of Salida. Zelda is a variant spelling.

Selena, Selene   From the Greek, meaning "moon." In Greek mythology, the goddess of the moon. Akin to Diana in Roman mythology. Selina is a variant spelling.

Selila (סְלִילָה)   From the Hebrew, meaning "path, road."

Selima, Selimah   Arabic feminine forms of Solomon, meaning "peace." *See* Solomon (masculine section).

Selina   A variant spelling of Selena. *See* Selena.

Selma   From the Celtic, meaning "fair."

Sema   A variant spelling of Seema. *See* Seema.

Semadar (סְמָדַר)   From the Hebrew, meaning "bud" or "blossom." Smadar is a variant form.

Semecha   A variant spelling of Semeicha. *See* Semeicha.

Semeicha (שְׂמֵחָה)   From the Hebrew, meaning "happy."

Semele   From the French, meaning "to sow." In Greek mythology, the mother of Dionysius.

Semira (סְמִירָה)   From the Hebrew, meaning "bristles."

Senait (סְנָאִית)   From the Hebrew, meaning "squirrel."

Senalda   From the Spanish, meaning "sign, symbol."

Senunit (סְנוּנִית)   From the Hebrew, describing a species of bird known for its sweet singing and swift flying.

Sera   A variant form of Sara. *See* Sara.

Serach (שֶׂרַח)   From the Hebrew, meaning "to be unrestrained, to be free" or "excess." In the Bible (Genesis 46:17), a daughter of Asher reputed (according to the Midrash) to be the person who showed Moses where Joseph's bones were hidden (in a coffin) in the Nile. Serah is a variant spelling.

Serafina   A variant spelling of Seraphina. *See* Seraphina.

Serah   A variant spelling of Serach. *See* Serach.

Seraphina, Seraphine (שְׂרָפִינָה)   From the Hebrew, meaning "to burn." Akin to the Serafim of the Bible, which are heavenly, winged creatures (angels) that surround the throne of God. Serafina is a variant spelling.

Serel (שֶׁעְרְעל)   A Yiddish form of Sara. *See* Sara.

Serena   From the Latin, meaning "peaceful" or "cheerful." Sirena is a variant spelling. Serepta is an Old English form. Rena is a short form.

Serepta   An Old English form of Serena. *See* Serena.

Seril (שֶׁעְרִיל)   A Yiddish form of Sara. *See* Sara.

Serita   A variant spelling of Sarita. *See* Sarita.

Setav (סְתָו)   From the Hebrew, meaning "autumn." Used also as a masculine name.

Setavanit (סְתָוָנִית)   The Hebrew name of a lily-like flower (colchicum).

Setavi (סְתָוִי)   From the Hebrew, meaning "autumnal."

Setavit (סְתָוִית)   From the Aramaic, meaning "autumnal."

Setura (סְתוּרָה)   From the Hebrew, meaning "sheltered, protected."

Sevilla   A variant form of Sibyl. *See* Sibyl.

Sevira (סְבִירָה)   From the Hebrew, meaning "reasonable."

Seya (שֶׂיָה)   From the Hebrew, meaning "lamb."

Shaanana (שַׁאֲנַנָּה)   From the Hebrew, meaning "tranquil, peaceful."

Shaaron   A variant spelling of Sharon. *See* Sharon.

Shachar (שַׁחַר)   From the Hebrew, meaning "dawn, morning." Shacharit, Shacharita, Shachariya, Shaharit, and Shaharita are variant forms. Shahar is a variant spelling. Used also as a masculine name.

Shacharia   A variant spelling of Shachariya. *See* Shachariya.

Shacharit (שַׁחֲרִית)   A variant form of Shachar. *See* Shachar.

Shacharita (שַׁחֲרִיתָה)   A variant form of Shachar. *See* Shachar.

Shachariya (שַׁחֲרִיָה)   A variant form of Shachar. *See* Shachar. Shacharia is a variant spelling.

Shachat (שַׁחַת)   From the Hebrew, meaning "corn grass."

Shadmit (שַׁדְמִית)   A variant form of Shedema. *See* Shedema.

Shafrira   From the Hebrew, meaning "tent, canopy" or "dwelling."

Shahar   A variant spelling of Shachar. *See* Shachar.

Shaharit   A variant spelling of Shacharit. *See* Shacharit.

Shaharita   A variant spelling of Shacharita. *See* Shacharita.

Shaina   A variant spelling of Sheina. *See* Sheina.

Shaindel   A variant spelling of Sheindel. *See* Sheindel.

Shaine   A variant spelling of Sheina. *See* Sheina.

Shalechet (שַׁלֶּכֶת)   From the Hebrew, meaning "Indian summer" or "fallen leaves."

Shalgia   A variant spelling of Shalgiya. *See* Shalgiya.

Shalgit (שַׁלְגִּית)   From the Hebrew, meaning "snow."

Shalgiya (שַׁלְגִּיָּה)   From the Hebrew, meaning "snow, snow-white." In Israel, a plant with white flowers. *See also* Shilga. Shalgia is a variant spelling.

Shalhevet (שַׁלְהֶבֶת)   From the Hebrew, meaning "flame."

Shalva, Shalvah (שַׁלְוָה)   From the Hebrew, meaning "peace, tranquility." Shalviya is a variant form.

Shalviya (שַׁלְוִיָּה)   A variant form of Shalva. *See* Shalva.

Shamira (שָׁמִירָה)   From the Hebrew, meaning "guard, protector."

Shana   A variant spelling of Shaina. *See* Shaina.

Shane   A variant spelling of Shaine. *See* Shaine.

Shanie   A pet form of Shaine. *See* Shaine.

Shannon   A feminine form of Sean. *See* Sean (masculine section).

Shapira (שַׁפִּירָא)   From the Aramaic, meaning "good." Used also as a masculine name.

Shareen   A variant form of Sharon. *See* Sharon.

Sharelle   A variant form of Sharon. *See* Sharon.

Shari   A pet form of Sharon. *See* Sharon.

Sharine   A pet form of Sharon. *See* Sharon.

Sharleen   A variant spelling of Charlene. *See* Charlene.

Sharlene   A variant spelling of Charlene. *See* Charlene.

Sharman   From the Middle English, meaning "plowshare" or "farmer."

Sharol   A variant form of Cheryl. *See* Cheryl.

Sharon (שָׁרוֹן)   From the Hebrew, meaning "plain, flat area." In the Bible, an area of ancient Palestine extending from Mount Carmel south to Jaffa where roses grew in abundance. The fertile soil was covered with oak trees. *Saronis* is the Greek word for oak, from which the name Sharon probably evolved. Occasionally used as a masculine name. Shareen, Sharelle, Sharona, Sharoni, Sharonit, and Sherran are variant forms. Shaaron, and Sharyn are variant spellings.

Sharona (שָׁרוֹנָה)   A variant form of Sharon. *See* Sharon.

Sharoni (שָׁרוֹנִי)   A variant form of Sharon. *See* Sharon.

Sharonit (שָׁרוֹנִית)   A variant form of Sharon. *See* Sharon.

Sharyn   A variant spelling of Sharon. *See* Sharon.

Shaula (שָׁאוּלָה)   A feminine form of Shaul (Saul). *See* Shaul (masculine section). Shaulit is a variant form.

Shaulit (שָׁאוּלִית)   A variant form of Shaula. *See* Shaula.

Shavcha (שָׁבְחָה)   From the Hebrew, meaning "praise."

Shayna   A variant spelling of Sheina. *See* Sheina.

Shayndel   A variant spelling of Sheindel. *See* Sheindel.

Shayne   A variant spelling of Sheina. *See* Sheina.

She'aga (שְׁאָגָה)   From the Hebrew, meaning "roar (of a lion)" or "cry."

Sheba   The Anglicized form of Sheva. *See* Sheva.

Shechina (שְׁכִינָה)   From the Hebrew, meaning "the Holy Spirit, God."

Shechora (שְׁחוֹרָה)   From the Hebrew, meaning "black." Shehora is a variant spelling.

Shedema (שְׂדְמָה)   From the Hebrew, meaning "farm." Shadmit is a variant form.

Sheena   A Gaelic form of Jane. *See* Jane.

She'era, She'erah (שְׁאָרָה)   From the Hebrew, meaning "remnant" or "survivor." In the Bible (I Chronicles 7:24), a daughter of Ephraim, son of Jacob.

Shehora   A variant spelling of Shechora. *See* Shechora.

She'ifa (שְׁאִיפָה)   From the Hebrew, meaning "breathing" or "lofty aspiration, yearning."

Sheila, Sheilah   Variant forms of Cecelia and Celia, introduced into Ireland by early Englishmen. *See* Cecelia. Shelagh is a variant form. Shiela and Shielah are variant spellings.

Sheina (שֵׁיינָא)   From the Yiddish, meaning "beautiful." Shaina, Shaine, Shane, and Shayna are variant spellings. Sheindel is a popular pet form. Shona, Shoni, and Shonie are variant forms.

Sheindel (שֵׁיינְדֵל)   A pet form of Sheina. *See* Sheina. Also spelled Shaindel and Shayndel, in English and שֵׁיינְדֵעל in Yiddish.

Shekeda (שְׁקֵדָה)   From the Hebrew, meaning "almond tree." Shekedia is a variant form.

Shekedia   A variant spelling of Shekediya. *See* Shekediya.

Shekediya (שְׁקֵדְיָה)   From the Hebrew, meaning "almond tree."

Shekufa (שְׁקוּפָה)   From the Hebrew, meaning "frame, framework," or from the Aramaic, meaning "threshold" or "window."

Shelagh   An Irish form of Sheilah. *See* Sheilah.

Shelavia   A variant spelling of Shelavya. *See* Shelavya.

Shelavya (שְׁלַבְיָה) From the Hebrew, meaning "to be bound" or "joined." Shelavia is a variant spelling.

Shelby Used primarily as a masculine name. *See* Shelby (masculine section).

Sheli (שֶׁלִי) From the Hebrew, meaning "mine, belonging to me." Shelli is a variant spelling.

Shelia A variant spelling of Sheliya. *See* Sheliya.

Sheliya (שֶׁלְיָה) From the Hebrew, meaning "God is mine." Shelia is a variant spelling.

Shelley, Shelly Irish pet forms of Cecelia. *See* Cecelia. Shelli is a variant spelling. Used also as a masculine name.

Shelli A variant spelling of Shelley and Sheli. *See* Shelley *and* Sheli.

Shelomit A variant spelling of Shlomit. *See* Shlomit.

Shelom-Tzion, Shelom-Zion Variant spellings of Shlom-Tziyon. *See* Shlom-Tziyon.

Shemamit (שְׁמָמִית) From the Hebrew, meaning "lizard" or "spider."

Shemuela A variant spelling of Shmuela. *See* Shmuela.

Shemura (שְׁמוּרָה) From the Hebrew, meaning "hidden" or "protected."

Shena A Gaelic form of Jane. *See* Jane.

Sher A variant spelling of Cher. *See* Cher.

Sheral A variant form of Cheryl. *See* Cheryl.

Shere A pet form of Cheryl and Charlotte. *See* Cheryl *and* Charlotte.

Sheree A variant form of Cheryl. *See* Cheryl.

Sherelle, Sherrelle A variant spelling of Cheryl. *See* Cheryl.

Sheri A variant spelling of Cheri. *See* Cheri.

Sherran A variant form of Sharon. *See* Sharon.

Sherrie, Sherry, Sherrye Variant forms of Caesrina, the feminine form of the Latin Caesar, meaning "king"; hence, Sherry means "queen." Sheryl, Sheryle, and Cheryl are variant forms.

Sheryl, Sheryle Variant forms of Sherry. Also spelled Cheryl. *See* Cheryl.

Shetila (שְׁתִילָה) From the Hebrew, meaning "plant" or "nursling." Shotela, Shetula, and Shotelet are variant forms.

Shetula (שְׁתוּלָה) A variant form of Shetila. *See* Shetila.

Sheva (שֶׁבַע) From the Hebrew, meaning "oath." Used in the Bible as a masculine name only. Also, a pet form of Batsheva. *See* Batsheva. Sheba is the Anglicized form.

Shevivia A variant spelling of Shevivya. *See* Shevivya.

Sheviviya (שְׁבִיבְיָה) A variant form of Shevivya. *See* Shevivya.

Shevivya (שְׁבִיבְיָה) From the Hebrew, meaning "spark of God." Shevivia is a variant spelling. Sheviviya is a variant form.

Shibolet (שִׁבּוֹלֶת) From the Hebrew, meaning "grain stalk." Shiboleth is a variant spelling.

Shiboleth A variant spelling of Shibolet. *See* Shibolet.

Shidra (שִׁדְרָה) From the Hebrew, meaning "spine, backbone."

Shiela, Shielah Variant spellings of Sheila. *See* Sheila.

Shifa (שִׁפְעָה) From the Hebrew, meaning "abundance."

Shiffie, Shiffy Pet forms of Shifra. *See* Shifra.

Shifra, Shifrah (שִׁפְרָה) From the Hebrew, meaning "good, handsome, beautiful," or from the Aramaic, meaning "trumpet." In the Bible (Exodus 1:15), a Hebrew midwife. Schifra is a variant spelling.

Shikma (שִׁקְמָה) From the Hebrew, meaning "sycamore tree." Shikmona is a variant form.

Shikmona (שִׁקְמוֹנָה) A variant form of Shikma. *See* Shikma.

Shilga (שִׁלְגָה) From the Hebrew, meaning "snow." Talga and Shilgit are variant forms. *See also* Shalgiya.

Shilgit (שִׁלְגִית) A variant form of Shilga. *See* Shilga.

Shilo (שִׁילֹה) Primarily a masculine name. *See* Shilo (masculine section).

Shimat (שִׁמְעָת) From the Hebrew, meaning "hearing" or "report." In the Bible (II Kings 12:22), the mother of the murderer of King Joash.

Shimona (שִׁמְעוֹנָה) The feminine form of Shimon. *See* Shimon (masculine section). Simeona and Simona are variant forms.

Shimra (שִׁמְרָה) From the Hebrew, meaning "guarded, protected." Shimrat is a variant form.

Shimrat (שִׁמְרָת) From the Aramaic, meaning "protected, guarded." A variant form of Shimra.

Shimria, Shimriah Variant spellings of Shimriya. *See* Shimriya.

Shimrit (שִׁמְרִית) From the Hebrew, meaning "guarded, protected." In the Bible (II Chronicles 24:26), a Moabite, the mother of one of Joash's murderers.

Shimriya (שִׁמְרְיָה) From the Hebrew, meaning "God is my protector."

Shimshona (שִׁמְשׁוֹנָה) The feminine form of Shimshon (Samson). *See* Samson (masculine section).

Shiphra A variant spelling of Shifra. *See* Shifra.

Shir (שִׁיר) From the Hebrew, meaning "song." Used also as a masculine name.

Shira, Shirah (שִׁירָה) From the Hebrew, meaning "song."

Shirel (שִׁירְאֵל) From the Hebrew, meaning "God's song."

Shirl   A pet form of Shirley. *See* Shirley.

Shir-Lee (שִׁיר-לִי)   From the Hebrew, meaning "song is mine." Shirlee is a variant spelling.

Shirlee   A variant spelling of Shirley. *See* Shirley. Also, a variant spelling of Shir-lee. *See* Shir-lee.

Shirley   From the Old English, meaning "from the white meadow."

Shirli (שִׁירְלִי)   From the Hebrew, meaning "song is mine." Shirlee is a variant spelling.

Shita (שִׁטָּה)   From the Hebrew, and Arabic, meaning "acacia tree" or "pea-thorn."

Shlomit (שְׁלוֹמִית)   From the Hebrew, meaning "peaceful." In the Bible (Leviticus 4:24), the daughter of Divri of the tribe of Dan. Shelomit is a variant spelling. Salome is the Anglicized form. Akin to Shulamit. *See* Salome. Used also as a masculine name.

Shlom-Tziyon (שְׁלוֹם-צִיּוֹן)   From the Hebrew, meaning "peace of Zion." Another name for Salome, wife of King Alexander Yannai (Jannai), who reigned after his death. Shelom-Tzion and Shelom-Zion are variant spellings.

Shmuela (שְׁמוּאֵלָה)   The feminine form of Shmuel (Samuel). *See* Shmuel (masculine section). Samuela is the Anglicized form. Shemuela is a variant spelling.

Shomera (שׁוֹמֵרָה)   From the Hebrew, meaning "guard." Shomrona, Shomrit, and Shomriya are variant forms.

Shomria, Shomriah   Variant spellings of Shomriya. *See* Shomriya.

Shomrit (שׁוֹמְרִית)   A variant form of Shomera. *See* Shomera.

Shomriya (שׁוֹמְרִיָה)   A variant form of Shomera. *See* Shomera.

Shomrona (שׁוֹמְרוֹנָה)   A variant form of Shomron, the capital of the kingdom of Israel in the eighth and ninth centuries B.C.E.

Shona, Shoni, Shonie   Variant forms of Sheina. *See* Sheina.

Shoshan (שׁוֹשָׁן)   From the Hebrew, meaning "lily," or from the Egyptian and Coptic, meaning "lotus." Shoshana and Shoshanah are variant forms. *See also* Shoshan (masculine section).

Shoshana, Shoshanah (שׁוֹשַׁנָּה)   Variant forms of Shoshan. *See* Shoshan. Used also as a synonym for "rose." In the Midrash (Leviticus Raba 22), a generic name for "flower." *See also* Chavatzelet. Susanna (Latin), Susanne (French), and Susan (English) are variant forms.

Shoshe (שָׁאשֶׁע)   From the Yiddish, meaning "sweet." Akin to Zisse.

Shotela (שׁוֹתֵלָה)   A variant form of Shetila. *See* Shetila.

Shotelet (שׁוֹתֶלֶת)   A variant form of Shetila. *See* Shetila.

Shprintza (שְׁפְּרִינְצָא)   A Yiddish form of Esperanza. From the Esperanto, meaning "hope." Shprinza and Shprinze are variant spellings. Shprintzel is a pet form.

Shprintze (שְׁפְּרִינְצֶע)   A variant form of Shprintza. See Shprintza.

Shprintzel (שְׁפְּרִינְצֶל)   A pet form of Shprintza or Shprintze. See Shprintza. Also spelled שְׁפְּרִינצֶעל.

Shprinza, Shprinze   Variant spellings of Shprintza and Shprintze. See Shprintza and Shprintze.

Shua (שׁוּעָא)   From the Aramaic, meaning "salvation" or possibly "opulence." In the Bible (I Chronicles 7:32), a member of the tribe of Asher.

Shuala (שׁוּעָלָה)   From the Hebrew, meaning "fox."

Shula (שׁוּלָה)   A pet form of Shulamit. See Shulamit.

Shulamit (שׁוּלַמִּית)   From the Hebrew, meaning "peace, peaceful." Akin to Shlomit. Salome is a variant form. Shulamith is a variant spelling. Shula and Shuly are pet forms. In the Bible (Song of Songs 7:1), a name used as an allusion to Avishag Hashunamit, reputed to be the most beautiful girl in Israel. She served King David in his old age (I Kings 1:3).

Shulamith   A variant spelling of Shulamit. See Shulamit.

Shuly (שׁוּלִי)   A pet form of Shulamit. See Shulamit.

Shunamit (שׁוּנַמִּית)   From Shunam, the name of a city in the territory of Issachar (II Kings 4:8). The home of Avishag Hashunamit. See also Shulamit.

Shuni (שׁוּנִי)   From the Hebrew and Aramaic, meaning "rock, boulder (on the seacoast)." Used as a masculine name in the Bible (Genesis 46:16). Shunit is a variant form.

Shunit (שׁוּנִית)   A variant form of Shuni. See Shuni.

Shura (שׁוּרָה)   From the Hebrew, meaning "row, line."

Sibil   A variant spelling of Sibyl. See Sibyl.

Sibilla   A variant form of Sibil. See Sibil.

Sibley   From the Old English, meaning "having one parent in common."

Sibyl   From the Greek, meaning "counsel of God." Also, from the Old Italian, meaning "wise old woman." Sibil, Sybil, Sybille, Sybyl, and Sybyle are variant spellings. Sevilla, Sibilia, and Sybella are variant forms.

Sicel   A variant spelling of Sisel. See Sisel.

Sid   A pet form of Sydney. See Sydney.

Sidi   Probably a pet form of Sydel. See Sydel.

Sidne   A variant spelling of Sydney. See Sydney.

Sidney   A variant spelling of Sydney. See Sydney.

Sidona (סִידוֹנָה)   From the Hebrew, meaning "calcium."

Sidonya (סִידוֹנְיָה)   From the Hebrew, meaning "to ensnare, entice."

Sidra (סִדְרָה)   From the Latin, meaning "starlike." Also, from the Hebrew, meaning "order, sequence" or "weekly portion."

Sigal (סִיגָל)   From the Hebrew, meaning "treasure." Akin to Segula.

Sigalit (סִגָלִית)   A variant form of Sigal. See Sigal.

Sigaliya (סִגָלִיָה)   A variant form of Sigal. See Sigal.

Sigla (סִגְלָה)   A variant form of Sigal. See Sigal.

Siglia, Sigliah   Variant spellings of Sigliya. See Sigliya.

Siglit (סִגְלִית)   A variant form of Sigal. See Sigal.

Sigliya (סִגְלִיָה)   A variant form of Sigal. See Sigal. Siglia and Sigliah are variant spellings.

Signa   From the Latin, meaning "signal, sign." Syna is a variant form.

Sigrid   A feminine form of Siegfried. See Siegfried (masculine section).

Silit (סְלְעִית)   A variant form of Salit. See Salit.

Silona (סִילוֹנָה)   From the Greek and Hebrew, meaning "conduit (carrying water)" or "stream." Silon is a masculine form. Silonit is a variant form.

Silonit (סִילוֹנִית)   A variant form of Silona. See Silona.

Silva   A variant form of Sylvia. See Sylvia.

Silvania, Silvanna   Variant forms of Sylvia. See Sylvia.

Silvano   A feminine form of Silvanus. See Silvanus (masculine section).

Silvia   A variant spelling of Sylvia. See Sylvia.

Sima (סִימָה)   From the Aramaic, meaning "treasure." Simona is a variant form.

Simajean   A hybrid of Sima and Jean. See Sima and Jean.

Simcha (שִׂמְחָה)   From the Hebrew, meaning "joy." Used also as a masculine name. Simha is a variant spelling. Simchona, Simhona, Simchit, and Simhit are variant forms.

Simchit (שִׂמְחִית)   A variant form of Simcha. See Simcha. Simhit is a variant spelling.

Simchona (שִׂמְחוֹנָה)   A variant form of Simcha. See Simcha. Simhona is a variant spelling.

Simeona   A variant form of Shimona. See Shimona.

Simha   A variant spelling of Simcha. See Simcha.

Simhit   A variant spelling of Simchit. See Simchit.

Simhona   A variant spelling of Simchona. See Simchona.

Simona   A feminine form of Simon. See Simon (masculine section). Also, a variant form of Sima. See Sima.

Simone A French form of Simon. *See* Simon (masculine section) *and* Shimona.

Sindy A fanciful spelling of Cindy. *See* Cindy.

Siona (שִׁיאוֹנָה) From the Hebrew, meaning "peak, height." Also, a variant spelling of Tziona (Ziona), meaning "excellent," and spelled צִיּוֹנָה.

Sirel (שִׁירְל) A Yiddish form of Sara. *See* Sara. A variant English spelling of Tzirel and Zirel. Also spelled שִׁירְעל.

Sirena A variant spelling of Serena. *See* Serena. Or, from the Greek, meaning "rope," hence "one who ensnares."

Sirke (שִׁירְקֶע) A Yiddish pet form of Sara. *See* Sara.

Sirkel (שִׁירְקל) A Yiddish pet form of Sara. *See* Sara. Also spelled שִׁירְקעל.

Sisel (סִיסל) From the Yiddish, meaning "sweet." Zisel and Sicel are variant English spellings. Also spelled סִיסעל.

Sisi (שִׁישִׁי) A pet form of Cecilia. *See* Cecilia. Also, from the Hebrew, meaning "my joy." Sissie and Sissy are variant spellings.

Sisley A variant spelling of Cicely. *See* Cicely.

Siss (שִׁיש) From the Hebrew, meaning "joy." Also, a pet form of Cecilia. *See* Cecilia.

Sissela A pet form of Cecelia. *See* Cecelia.

Sissie, Sissy Variant spellings of Sisi. *See* Sisi.

Sitria A variant spelling of Sitriya. *See* Sitriya.

Sitriya (סִתְרִיָה) From the Hebrew, meaning "protected by the Lord." Sitria is a variant spelling.

Sivan (סִיוָן) The ninth month after the Jewish New Year, corresponding to May-June. In the Zodiac, its sign is Gemini ("twins"). Used also as a masculine name. Sivana is a variant form.

Sivana (סִיוָנָה) A variant form of Sivan. *See* Sivan.

Sivia A variant form of Tzivya. *See* Tzivya.

Sloan, Sloane From the Celtic, meaning "warrior."

Smadar (סְמָדַר) A variant form of Semadar. *See* Semadar.

Snira (שְׁנִירָה) From the Hebrew, meaning "snowcap (of a mountain)."

Sofia An Italian form of Sophia. *See* Sophia.

Solace From the Latin, meaning "to comfort."

Soma From the Greek, meaning "body." Also, the name of an intoxicating plant.

Sona From the Latin, meaning "to sound."

Sondra A variant spelling of Sandra. *See* Sandra.

Sonia   A variant form of Sophia. *See* Sophia. Zonya is a variant form.

Sonja, Sonya   Slavic forms of Sonia. *See* Sonia.

Soozie   A variant spelling of Suzy. *See* Suzy.

Sophia   From the Greek, meaning "wisdom, wise one." Sonia, Sonja, Sonya, Soph, Sophie, Sophy, and Zophia are variant forms.

Sophie   A French form of Sophia. *See* Sophia.

Sophy   An English form of Sophie. *See* Sophie.

Sorale (שְׂרָאלֶע)   A Yiddish pet form of Sarah. *See* Sarah. Also spelled שְׂרָלֶע.

Sorali, Soralie, Soroli (שְׂרָאלִי)   Yiddish pet forms of Sarah. *See* Sarah. Also spelled שְׂרָלִי.

Soreka (שׂוֹרֵקָה)   From the Hebrew, meaning "vine," mentioned in the Bible (Isaiah 5:2).

Sorke (שְׂרְקֶע)   A Yiddish pet form of Sara. *See* Sara.

Spring   From the German, meaning "to leap."

Stacey, Stacy   Irish forms of the Greek name Anastasia, meaning "resurrection, revival." *See* Anastasia. Used also as a masculine name.

Stacia, Stacie   Variant pet forms of Anastasia. *See* Anastasia.

Star   From the Old English, meaning "star."

Staria   A variant form of Star. *See* Star.

Starletta   A pet form of Star. *See* Star.

Starr   A variant spelling of Star. *See* Star.

Stefana, Stefania   Feminine forms of Stephen. *See* Stephen (masculine section).

Stefanie, Stefenie   Feminine forms of Stephen. *See* Stephen (masculine section).

Stella   From the Latin, meaning "star." Esther is the Persian form of Stella.

Stephane   A variant spelling of Stephanie. *See* Stephanie.

Stephania, Stephanie, Stephenie   Feminine forms of Stephen. *See* Stephen (masculine section).

Stevana, Stevena   Feminine forms of Steven. *See* Steven (masculine section).

Storm   From the Anglo-Saxon, meaning "tempest." Stormie and Stormy are pet forms.

Stormie, Stormy   Pet forms of Storm. *See* Storm.

Su   A pet form of Susan. *See* Susan.

Sudy   From the Old English, meaning "south, from the south."

Sue   A pet form of Susan. *See* Susan.

Suella A hybrid of Sue (Susan) and Ella. *See* Susan *and* Ella.

Suellen A hybrid of Sue (Susan) and Ellen. *See* Susan *and* Ellen.

Sugar From the Sanskrit, meaning "pebble, sweet crystal."

Sukey A pet form for Susan popular in the mid-nineteenth century. *See* Susan.

Sura, Surah (שׂוּרָא) Yiddish forms of Sarah. *See* Sarah.

Susan (שׁוֹשַׁנָה) From the Hebrew, meaning "lily." *See also* Shoshan. Su, Sue, Sukey, Susette, Susi, Susie, Susy, Suzette, and Suzy are pet forms. Susanna, Susannah, Susanne, Suzanne, and Suzette are variant forms.

Susanna, Susannah Variant forms of Susan. *See* Susan.

Susanne A variant form of Susan. *See* Susan.

Susette A pet form of Susan. *See* Susan.

Susi, Susie, Susy Pet forms of Susan. *See* Susan.

Suzanne A variant form of Susan. *See* Susan.

Suzette A French form of Susan. *See* Susan.

Suzy A pet form of Susan. *See* Susan. Soozie, Susi, Susie, and Susy are variant spellings.

Swana From the German, meaning "swan."

Sybella A variant form of Sibyl. *See* Sibyl.

Sybil, Sybille Variant spellings of Sibyl. *See* Sibyl.

Sybyl, Sybyle Variant spellings of Sibyl. *See* Sibyl. Sybylla is a variant form.

Sybylla A variant form of Sybyl. *See* Sybyl.

Syd, Sydel, Sydelle Variant pet forms of Sydney. *See* Sydney.

Sydney A feminine form of the masculine Sidney. *See* Sidney (masculine section). Sidney is a variant feminine spelling. Syd, Sydel, and Sydelle are variant pet forms. Sidney is a variant spelling.

Sylva, Sylvana From the Latin, meaning "forest." Akin to Sylvia. *See* Sylvia.

Sylvi A Norwegian form of Sylvia. *See* Sylvia.

Sylvia From the Latin, meaning "forest" or "one who dwells in the woods." Akin to Sylva and Sylvana. Sylvan is the original masculine form. Silvia is a variant spelling. Silva, Silvania, Silvanna, Sylvi, and Sylvie are variant forms.

Sylvie A Norwegian form of Sylvia. *See* Sylvia.

Syma A variant spelling of Cyma, Seema, and Sima. *See* Cyma, Seema, *and* Sima.

Syna A variant form of Signa. *See* Signa.

Syril A variant spelling of Cyril. *See* Cyril (masculine section). *See also* Cyrilla.

Taafe   A variant spelling of Taffy. *See* Taffy.

Tabitha   From the Greek and Aramaic, meaning "gazelle."

Tabora   A variant spelling of Tavora. *See* Tavora.

Tace   A variant form of Tacita. *See* Tacita.

Tachan (תַּחַן)   From the Hebrew, meaning "prayer, petition."

Tacita   From the Latin, meaning "to be silent." Tace is a variant form.

Tafat (טָפַת)   From the Hebrew, meaning "to drip, trickle." In the Bible (I Kings 4:11), a daughter of King Solomon. Taphat is a variant spelling.

Taffy   The Welsh form of Vida, a variant form of David. *See* David (masculine section). Taafe is a variant spelling.

Taga (תַּגָּה)   From the Aramaic and Arabic, meaning "crown."

Tal (טַל)   From the Hebrew, meaning "dew."

Tala (טָלָה)   From the Aramaic and Hebrew, meaning "patched" or "spotted."

Talal (טְלַל)   From the Hebrew, meaning "covering of dew." Talila is a variant form.

Talga (טַלְגָה)   From the Aramaic, meaning "snow." Shilga is a variant form.

Tali (טַלִי)   From the Hebrew, meaning "my dew."

Talia   A variant spelling of Talya. *See* Talya.

Talila (טְלִילָה)   A variant form of Talal. *See* Talal.

Tal-Li (טַל-לִי)   From the Hebrew, meaning "dew is mine."

Tallula, Tallulah   An American Indian name generally taken to mean "running water."

Talma (תַּלְמָה)   From the Hebrew, meaning "mound, hill."

Talmit (תַּלְמִית)   A variant form of Talma. *See* Talma.

Talmona (טַלְמוֹנָה)   From the Ethiopic and Aramaic, meaning "to oppress" or "injure." Talmonit is a variant form.

Talmonit (טַלְמוֹנִית)   A variant form of Talmona. *See* Talmona.

Talmor (תַּלְמוֹר)   From the Hebrew, meaning "heap of myrrh (spice)."

Tal-Or, Talor (טַל-אוֹר)   From the Hebrew, meaning "morning dew." Tal-Ora is a variant form.

Tal-Ora, Talora (טַל-אוֹרָה)   A variant form of Tal-Or. *See* Tal-Or. Also spelled טַלְאוֹרָה.

Talya (טַלְיָה)   From the Hebrew, meaning "dew." Akin to Tal. Also, from the Aramaic, meaning "lamb" and spelled טַלְיָא. Talia is a variant spelling.

Tama, Tamah (תַּמָּה)   From the Hebrew, meaning "wonder, surprise" or "whole, complete."

Tamar (תָּמָר) From the Hebrew, meaning "palm tree" or "upright, righteous, graceful." In the Bible (Genesis 38:6), the granddaughter of Judah and his Canaanite wife, Shua, the daughter of Er. Tamara, Tamarah, and Temara are variant forms. Used also as a masculine name.

Tamara, Tamarah From the East Indian, meaning "spice." Also, a variant form of Tamar. *See* Tamar.

Tami, Tammy Feminine forms of Thomas. *See* Thomas (masculine section).

Tana A variant form of Dana. *See* Dana.

Tangye From the Old Norse, meaning "dagger."

Tania A variant spelling of Tanya. *See* Tanya.

Tanith From the Old Irish, meaning "estate."

Tanka Probably from the Portuguese, meaning "tank" or "pond."

Tansy A pet form of Anastasia. *See* Anastasia.

Tanya From the Russian, meaning "fairy queen." Tania is a variant spelling.

Taphat A variant spelling of Tafat. *See* Tafat.

Tapuach (תַּפּוּחַ) From the Hebrew, meaning "apple." Tapuha is a variant spelling. Tapucha is a variant form.

Tapucha (תַּפּוּחָה) A variant form of Tapuach. *See* Tapuach.

Tapuha A variant spelling of Tapucha. *See* Tapucha.

Tara From the French and Aramaic, referring to a unit of measurement. Also, from the Aramaic, meaning "throw" or "carry."

Tari (טָרִי) From the Hebrew, meaning "fresh, ripe, new." Akin to Teriya.

Tarshisha (תַּרְשִׁישָׁה) From the Greek, meaning "from the sea." Refers to a precious pearl that comes from the sea. *See also* Tarshish (masculine section).

Tasha A short form of Natasha. *See* Natasha. Also, from the Arabic, meaning "cup."

Tate From the Anglo-Saxon, meaning "to be cheerful." Used also as a masculine name.

Tatum A variant form of Tate. *See* Tate.

Tauba, Taube (טוֹיבֶּע) Yiddish forms of the German, meaning "dove." Toby and Toibe are variant forms.

Tavi A variant form of the masculine form David. *See* David (masculine section). Also, a pet form of Octavia. *See* Octavia.

Tavita A pet form of Tavi. *See* Tavi. Akin to Tevita. Also, a pet form of Octavia.

Tavora (תָּבוֹרָה) A variant form of Tavor (Tabor). In the Bible (Judges 4:6), a mountain southwest of the Sea of Galilee. Tabora is a variant spelling.

Taylor An Anglo-Saxon occupational name, meaning "tailor." Used also as a masculine name.

Tebita   A variant spelling of Tevita. *See* Tevita.

Techia   A variant spelling of Techiya. *See* Techiya.

Techiya (תְּחִיָּה)   From the Hebrew, meaning "rebirth, resurrection." Techia and Tehia are variant spellings.

Techiya-Yehudit (תְּחִיָּה־יְהוּדִית)   From the Hebrew, meaning "rebirth of the Jewish people."

Techula, Techulah (תְּכוּלָה)   From the Hebrew, meaning "blue" or "purple."

Techuna, Techunah (תְּכוּנָה)   From the Hebrew, meaning "prepared, preparation" or "trait, characteristic." Tehuna and Tehunah are variant spellings.

Teena, Te'ena (תְּאֵנָה)   From the Hebrew, meaning "fig."

Tegan   From the Celtic, meaning "doe."

Tehia   A variant spelling of Techiya. *See* Techiya.

Tehila, Tehilla (תְּהִלָּה)   From the Hebrew, meaning "praise, song of praise" or "prayer."

Tehora (טְהוֹרָה)   From the Hebrew, meaning "pure, clean."

Tehuna, Tehunah   Variant spellings of Techuna. *See* Techuna.

Teima, Te'ima (טְעִימָה)   From the Hebrew, meaning "tasty."

Tekuma, Tekumah (תְּקוּמָה)   From the Hebrew, meaning "rebirth, revival."

Telat (תְּלַת)   From the Aramaic and Arabic, meaning "three."

Telalit (טְלָלִית)   From the Hebrew, meaning "covering."

Teli (טְלִי)   From the Aramaic and Hebrew, meaning "my lamb."

Tellus   From the Latin, meaning "earth." In Roman mythology, the goddess of the earth.

Tema (טֶעמְא)   A Yiddish form of Tamar. *See* Tamar.

Temana (תֵּימָנָה)   From the Hebrew, meaning "the left side," hence "the south, southward." Temania is a variant spelling.

Temania   A variant spelling of Temana. *See* Temana. Also, from the Aramaic, meaning "eight."

Temara (תְּמָרָה)   A variant form of Tamar. *See* Tamar.

Temima (תְּמִימָה)   From the Hebrew, meaning "whole, honest."

Temira (תְּמִירָה)   From the Hebrew, meaning "tall." Also, from a second Hebrew root, meaning "hidden, secret," and spelled סְמִירָה.

Templa   From the Latin, meaning "temple, sanctuary."

Temura, Temurah (תְּמוּרָה)   From the Hebrew, meaning "substitute."

Tenuva, Tenuvah (תְּנוּבָה)   From the Hebrew, meaning "fruit" or "produce."

Teresa   The Spanish and Italian form of Theresa. *See* Theresa.

Teresina, Teresita   Pet forms of Theresa. *See* Theresa.

Teri   A pet form of Theresa. *See* Theresa.

Teria, Teriah   Variant spellings of Teriya. *See* Teriya.

Terita   From the Latin, meaning "third."

Teriya (טְרִיָה)   From the Hebrew, meaning "fresh, ripe, new." Akin to Tari. Teria and Teriah are variant spellings.

Terranda   From the Latin, meaning "man's earth."

Terri, Terrie   Pet forms of Theresa. *See* Theresa.

Terrill   A variant form of Terry. *See* Terry.

Terry   A pet form of Theresa. *See* Theresa.

Teruda (טְרוּדָה)   From the Hebrew, meaning "burdened."

Terufa, Terufah (תְּרוּפָה)   From the Hebrew, meaning "healing." Terupha is a variant spelling.

Teruma, Terumah (תְּרוּמָה)   From the Hebrew, meaning "offering, gift."

Terupha   A variant spelling of Terufa. *See* Terufa.

Teshua, Teshuah (תְּשׁוּעָה)   From the Hebrew, meaning "salvation."

Teshura, Teshurah (תְּשׁוּרָה)   From the Hebrew, meaning "gift."

Tess, Tessie   Pet forms of Theresa. *See* Theresa.

Tetsy   A variant form of Elizabeth. *See* Elizabeth.

Tetty   A pet form of Elizabeth. *See* Elizabeth.

Teura (תְּאוּרָה)   From the Hebrew, meaning "display of lights."

Tevita (טְבִיתָא)   A Fijian form of Davida. *See* Davida. Also, the Aramaic form of Tzevi (צְבִי). Tebita is a variant spelling.

Tevuna, Tevunah (תְּבוּנָה)   From the Hebrew, meaning "understanding."

Thaddea   A feminine form of Thaddeus. *See* Thaddeus (masculine section).

Thadine   A variant form of Thaddea. *See* Thaddea.

Thalassa   From the Greek, meaning "sea."

Thalia   From the Greek, meaning "luxurious, flourishing."

Thana   From the Greek, meaning "death." In Greek mythology, Thanatos is death personified.

Thea   A short form of Althea. *See* Althea.

Theadora   A variant spelling of Theodora. *See* Theodora.

Theda   A variant form of Theodora. *See* Theodora.

Thelma   From the Greek, meaning "nursling, infant."

Theoda   A pet form of Theodora. *See* Theodora.

Theodora   The feminine form of Theodore. *See* Theodore.

Theola From the Greek, meaning "divine."

Theophila From the Greek, meaning "beloved of God."

Thera A variant form of Theresa. *See* Theresa.

Theresa, Therese From the Greek, meaning "harvester, farmer." Teresa is a variant spelling used in Italy and Spain. Tracey and Tracy are variant English forms. Zita is a pet form.

Thomasa The feminine form of Thomas. *See* Thomas (masculine section).

Thomasina, Thomasine, Thomassine Feminine forms of Thomas. *See* Thomas (masculine section).

Thora From the Norse, meaning "thunderer," a feminine form of Thor, the god of war in Norse mythology.

Tifara (תִּפְאָרָה) From the Hebrew, meaning "beautiful" or "glory." Tiphara is a variant spelling. Tiferet is a variant form.

Tiferet (תִּפְאֶרֶת) A variant form of Tifara. *See* Tifara.

Tiffany From the Latin, meaning "three, the trinity." Also, from the Greek, meaning "manifestation of God."

Tifracha (תִּפְרָחָה) From the Hebrew, meaning "bunch of flowers." Tifrachat is a variant form.

Tifrachat (תִּפְרַחַת) A variant form of Tifracha. *See* Tifracha.

Tigra (תִּגְרָה) From the Hebrew, meaning "strife, contention, war."

Tikva (תִּקְוָה) From the Hebrew, meaning "hope." In the Bible (II Kings 22:14), used only as a masculine name. *See* Tikva (masculine section).

Tilda A pet form of Mathilda. *See* Mathilda.

Tilla A variant form of Tillie. *See* Tillie.

Tillamae A hybrid of Tilla and Mae. *See* Tilla *and* Mae.

Tillie, Tilly Pet forms of Mathilda. Also, from the Latin, meaning "graceful linden tree."

Timi A pet form of Timora. *See* Timora.

Timna (תִּמְנָה) From the Hebrew, meaning "to count," and from a second Hebrew root, meaning "to deny, prevent."

Timora (תִּמּוֹרָה) From the Hebrew, meaning "tall" (like the palm tree). Timura is a variant form.

Timothea From the Greek, meaning "honoring God." Timothy is the masculine form.

Timura A variant form of Timora. *See* Timora.

Tina A pet form of names such as Christina *and* Bettina.

Tiphara A variant spelling of Tifara. *See* Tifara.

Tira (טִירָה) From the Syriac, meaning "sheepfold," or from the Hebrew, meaning "enclosure" or "encampment."

Tiri (טִירִי) A variant form of Tira. *See* Tira.

Tirtza (תִּרְצָה) From the Hebrew, meaning "willing, pleasing." Tirza is a variant spelling. In the Bible (Numbers 26:33), one of the five daughters of Zelophehad.

Tirza, Tirzah (תִּרְזָה) From the Hebrew, meaning either "cypress tree" or "willing, desirable." In the Bible, the capital of Samaria. Also, a variant spelling of Tirtza. *See* Tirtza.

Tisha A pet form of Patricia. *See* Patricia.

Tishbacha (תִּשְׁבָּחָה) From the Hebrew, meaning "praise, praised."

Tita A variant form of Titania. *See* Titania.

Titania From the Greek, meaning "great one."

Tiva (טִיבָה) From the Hebrew, meaning "good."

Tivona (טִבְעוֹנָה) From the Hebrew, meaning "lover of nature."

Tivoni (טִבְעוֹנִי) A variant form of Tivona. *See* Tivona.

Toba A variant spelling of Tova. *See* Tova. Akin to the masculine Tobias.

Tobelle A pet form of Toba. *See* Toba.

Tobey A variant form of Toba. *See* Toba.

Tobi A variant spelling of Toby. *See* Toby.

Tobit A variant spelling of Tovit. *See* Tovit.

Toby A pet form of Toba. *See* Toba.

Tochelet (תּוֹחֶלֶת) From the Hebrew, meaning "hope." Tohelet is a variant spelling.

Tohelet A variant spelling of Tochelet. *See* Tochelet.

Toibe, Toibeh (טוֹיבֶּע) From the Yiddish, meaning "dove." Akin to Toba.

Toinette A short form of Antoinette. *See* Antoinette.

Tomasa The Spanish feminine form of Thomas. *See* Thomas (masculine section).

Tomer A variant form of Tamar. *See* Tamar.

Tommi A feminine pet form of Thomas. *See* Thomas (masculine section).

Toni A pet form of Antoinette. *See* Antoinette.

Tonia A variant form of Toni. *See* Toni.

Tony A variant spelling of Toni. *See* Toni.

Topaza From the Greek, referring to "a yellow variety of sapphire."

Tora, Torah (תּוֹרָה) From the Hebrew, meaning "Holy Scripture, Bible."

Tori (תּוֹרִי)   From the Hebrew, meaning "my turtledove."

Totie   A variant form of Dottie, a pet form of Dorothy. *See* Dorothy.

Tottie   A pet form of Charlotte. *See* Charlotte. Also, a pet form of Dorothy. *See* Dorothy.

Tousha   A pet form of Natasha. *See* Natasha.

Tova, Tovah (טוֹבָה)   From the Hebrew, meaning "good." Toba, Tovat, Tovit, and Tuvit are variant forms.

Tovat (טוֹבַת)   A variant form of Tova. *See* Tova.

Tovit (טוֹבִית)   From the Hebrew, meaning "good." In the Apocrypha, the heroine of the Book of Tobit. Tobit is a variant spelling. Used also as a masculine name.

Toyah   From the Scottish, meaning "a woman's headdress with flaps that hang over the shoulder."

Tracee   A variant spelling of Tracy. *See* Tracy.

Tracey   A variant spelling of Tracy. *See* Tracy.

Tracy   From the Anglo-Saxon, meaning "brave." Tracy may also be a pet form. Used also as a masculine name.

Trella   A short form of Estrella, the Spanish form of Esther. *See* Esther.

Tressa   A German form of Theresa. *See* Theresa.

Trestel (טרעסטל)   A Yiddish form of the German *troest*, meaning "consolation." Also spelled טרעסטעל.

Tricia   A pet form of Patricia. *See* Patricia.

Trina   A short form of Katrina. *See* Katrina.

Trish, Trisha   Pet forms of Patricia. *See* Patricia. Tricia is a variant spelling.

Trix, Trixie, Trixy   Pet forms of Beatrice and Beatrix. *See* Beatrice *and* Beatrix.

Truda, Trude   Pet forms of Gertrude. *See* Gertrude.

Trudel   A Dutch contraction of Gertrude. *See* Gertrude.

Trudi, Trudy   Pet forms of Gertrude. *See* Gertrude.

Trula   Probably a variant form of Gertrude. *See* Gertrude.

Tumi (תֻּמִי)   From the Hebrew, meaning "whole, complete."

Tushia   A variant spelling of Tushiya. *See* Tushiya.

Tushiya (תּוּשִׁיָּה)   From the Hebrew, meaning "wisdom of God" or "good counsel." Tushia is a variant spelling. Also, a variant pet form of Natasha. *See* Natasha.

Tuvit (טוּבִית)   A variant form of Tova. *See* Tova.

Tybal, Tyballa   From the Old English, meaning "holy place (where sacrifices are brought)."

Tyna, Tyne   From the British, meaning "river."

Tzabara (צְבָּרָה)   From the Arabic, meaning "cactus." Tzabar (Sabra) is the masculine form. Tzabariya is a variant form.

Tzabaria   A variant spelling of Tzabariya. See Tzabariya.

Tzabariya (צְבָּרִיָה)   A variant form of Tzabara. See Tzabara.

Tzadika (צְדִיקָה)   From the Hebrew, meaning "pious" or "righteous." Zadika is a variant spelling.

Tzafnat (צְפְנָת)   From the Hebrew, meaning "hidden treasure." Zafnat is a variant spelling.

Tzafona (צְפוֹנָה)   From the Hebrew, meaning "north," or "hidden." Zafona is a variant spelling.

Tzafra (צָפְרָה)   From the Aramaic, meaning "morning." Zafra is a variant English spelling. Also spelled צַפְרָא.

Tzafrira (צָפְרִירָה)   From the Aramaic, meaning "morning breeze" or "demons of the morning." Zafrira is a variant spelling. Tzafririt and Zafririt are variant forms.

Tzafririt (צָפְרִירִית)   A variant form of Tzafrira. See Tzafrira. Zafririt is a variant spelling.

Tzahala (צָהֲלָה)   From the Hebrew, meaning "joy, rejoicing." Zahala is a variant spelling.

Tzalcha (צְלְחָה)   From the Hebrew, meaning "successful."

Tzameret (צְמֶרֶת)   From the Hebrew, meaning "head, leader," referring particularly to the top branch of a tree. Zameret is a variant spelling.

Tzara (צָרָה)   From the Hebrew, meaning "trouble, anguish."

Tzechira (צְחִירָה)   A variant form of Tzechora. See Tzechora.

Tzechora (צְחוֹרָה)   From the Hebrew, meaning "white."

Tzechorit (צְחוֹרִית)   A variant form of Tzechora. See Tzechora.

Tzedaka (צְדָקָה)   From the Hebrew, meaning "charity" or "righteousness."

Tze'elit (צָאֱלִית)   The Hebrew word for "jujube."

Tzefira (צְפִירָה)   From the Hebrew, meaning "morning" or "crown." Zefira is a variant spelling.

Tzehuva (צְהוּבָה)   From the Hebrew, meaning "golden."

Tzeira (צְעִירָה)   From the Hebrew, meaning "young."

Tzeitel (צײטעל)   A variant form of Tzeitl. See Tzeitl.

Tzeitl (צײטל)   A Yiddish form of Sara and Tzipora. See Sara and Tzipora. Zeitl and Zeitel are variant spellings. Tzeitel is a variant form.

Tzelil (צְלִיל) From the Hebrew, meaning "tone, sound,"and also "cake, round loaf."

Tzelila (צְלִילָה) From the Hebrew, meaning "descent" or "bright, clear." Zelila is a variant spelling. Tzelili and Zelili are variant forms.

Tzelili (צְלִילִי) A variant form of Tzelila. See Tzelila.

Tzemecha (צְמֶחָה) A variant form of Tzemicha. See Tzemicha.

Tzemicha (צְמִיחָה) From the Hebrew, meaning "flowering" or "growth." Zemicha is a variant spelling.

Tzertel (צֶערְטֶעל) A variant Yiddish form of Sara and Tzipora. See Sara and Tzipora. Zertel and Zertl are variant spellings. Tzertl is a variant form.

Tzertl (צֶערְטל) A variant spelling of Tzertel. See Tzertel.

Tzerua (צְרוּעָה) From the Hebrew, meaning "sick" or "wounded." In the Bible (I Kings 11:26), the mother of King Jeroboam. Zerua is a variant spelling.

Tzeruya (צְרוּיָה) From the Hebrew, meaning "pointed with *tzere*" [vowel]. Zeruya is a variant spelling.

Tzevia A variant spelling of Tzeviya. See Tzeviya.

Tzeviya (צְבִיָה) From the Hebrew, meaning "gazelle."

Tzifriya (צִפְרִיָה) From the Hebrew, meaning "ornithologist."

Tzifrona (צִפְרוֹנָה) A variant form of Tzifriya. See Tzifriya. Zifrona and Ziphrona are variant spellings.

Tzila (צִילָה) From the Hebrew, meaning "shade" or "shadow." Zila is a variant spelling.

Tzili (צִילִי) From the Hebrew, meaning "my shadow." Zili is a variant spelling.

Tzimchona (צִמְחוֹנָה) From the Hebrew, meaning "vegetarian." Zimchona is a variant spelling.

Tzina (צִינָה) From the Hebrew, meaning "covering" or "protection." Zina is a variant spelling.

Tziona A variant spelling of Tziyona. See Tziyona.

Tzionit (צִיוֹנִית) A variant form of Tziona. See Tziona. Zionit is a variant spelling.

Tziparta (צִפָּרְתָּא) From the Aramaic, meaning "hummingbird."

Tzipeh (צִיפֶּע) A Yiddish form of Tziporah, meaning "bird." Zipeh, Zippe, and Tzippe are variant spellings.

Tzipia A variant spelling of Tzipiya. See Tzipiya.

Tzipiya (צִפִּיָה) From the Hebrew, meaning "hope." Zipia is a variant spelling.

Tzipora, Tziporah (צִפּוֹרָה) From the Hebrew, meaning "bird."In the Bible (Exodus 2:21), the wife of Moses. Cipora, Zipora, Ziporah, Zippora, and

Zipporah are variant spellings. Tzipori is a variant form.

Tziporen (צִפּוֹרֶן)   From the Hebrew, meaning "clove, spice" or "carnation."

Tziporet (צִפֹּרֶת)   A variant form of Tzipora. A term of endearment for a woman.

Tzipori (צִפּוֹרִי)   From the Hebrew, meaning "my bird." Zipori is a variant spelling.

Tziporit (צִפּוֹרִית)   A variant form of Tzipora. See Tzipora.

Tzippe   A variant spelling of Tzipeh. See Tzipeh.

Tzirel (צִירֶעל)   A Yiddish form of Sara. See Sara. Also, from the German, meaning "jewelry, ornament." Zirel is a variant spelling.

Tziril (צִירִיל)   A variant form of Tzirel. See Tzirel.

Tzivia   A variant spelling of Tzivya. See Tzivya.

Tzivya (צִבְיָה)   From the Hebrew, meaning "deer, gazelle." In the Bible (II Kings 12:2), the mother of King Yehoash. Tzivia and Civia are variant spellings.

Tziyona (צִיּוֹנָה)   From the Hebrew, meaning "excellent." The feminine form of Zion. In the Bible (II Samuel 5:7), a place-name, the residence of King David. Zeona and Ziona are variant spellings.

Tzofi (צוֹפִי)   From the Hebrew, meaning "scout" or "guard." Zofi is a variant spelling. Tzofit, Tzofiya, Zofia, and Zofit are variant forms.

Tzofia   A variant spelling of Tzofiya. See Tzofiya.

Tzofit (צוֹפִית)   From the Hebrew, meaning "scout" or "guard." Also, the name of a small bird. Zofit is a variant spelling.

Tzofiya (צוֹפִיָּה)   A variant form of Tzofi. See Tzofi. Tzofia and Zofia are variant spellings.

Tzur-El (צוּר-אֵל)   From the Hebrew, meaning "God is a rock, God is strength." Zur-El is a variant spelling.

Tzuria   A variant spelling of Tzuriya. See Tzuriya.

Tzurit (צוּרִית)   From the Hebrew, meaning "rock." Zurit is a variant spelling.

Tzuriya (צוּרִיָה)   From the Hebrew, meaning "God is a rock, God is strength." Tzuria and Zuria are variant spellings.

Uda   A variant form of Uta. See Uta.

Udia   A variant spelling of Udiya. See Udiya.

Udiya (אוּדִיָה)   From the Hebrew, meaning "ember (fire) of God." Udia is a variant spelling.

Ufara (עוּפָרָה)   From the Hebrew, meaning "to lead, leader." Uphara is a variant spelling.

Ula   A pet form of Ulrica. *See* Ulrica.

Ulani   From the Hawaiian, meaning "gay."

Ulema   From the Arabic, meaning "to know, to be learned."

Ulla (עוּלָא)   From the Middle English, meaning "to fill (a cask to the brim)." Also, from the Aramaic, meaning "superior." In the Talmud (Berachot 62a), a fourth-century Palestinian scholar.

Ulrica   From the German, meaning "ruler over all." Ulric is the masculine form. Ula is a pet form.

Uma (אָמָה)   From the Hebrew, meaning "nation."

Umarit (אוּמָרִית)   From the Hebrew, meaning "sheaf."

Una   From the Latin, meaning "the one." Oona is a popular Irish variant form. Ona and Unity are variant forms.

Undina, Undine   From the Latin, meaning "wave."

Unity   From the Latin Una, meaning "the one."

Uphara   A variant spelling of Ufara. *See* Ufara.

Urania   From the Greek, meaning "heaven."

Uranit (אוּרָנִית)   From the Hebrew, meaning "light."

Urbana, Urbanna   From the Latin, meaning "city." Urban is the masculine form.

Uriela, Uriella (אוּרִיאָלָה)   From the Hebrew, meaning "light of the Lord" or "flame (fire) of God."

Urilla   Probably a French form of the masculine Uriah, meaning "God's light." *See* Uriah (masculine section).

Urit (אוּרִית)   From the Hebrew, meaning "light" or "fire." Urith is a variant spelling.

Urith   A variant spelling of Urit. *See* Urit.

Uriti   A variant form of Urit. *See* Urit.

Ursa   A short form of Ursala. *See* Ursala.

Ursala   From the Latin, meaning "she-bear." Ursel, Ursina, and Ursine are variant forms. Ursula and Ursule are variant spellings. Ursa is a short form.

Ursel   A variant form of Ursala. *See* Ursala.

Ursina, Ursine   Variant forms of Ursula. *See* Ursula.

Ursula, Ursule   Variant spellings of Ursala. *See* Ursala.

Urte   From the Latin, meaning "stinging or spiny plant."

Ushara (אוּשָׁרָה)   From the Hebrew, meaning "fortunate." Usheret and Ushriya are variant forms.

Usheret (אוּשָׁרָת)   A variant form of Ushara. *See* Ushara.

Ushria   A variant spelling of Ushriya. *See* Ushriya.

Ushriya (אוּשְׁרִיָּה)   From the Hebrew, meaning "fortunate of God" or "blessed of the Lord." *See* Ushara. Ushria is a variant spelling.

Uta   Probably from the Spanish tribal name Yutta, meaning "mountain dweller." Uda is a variant form.

Uza, Uzza (עֻזָּה)   From the Hebrew, meaning "strength."

Uziela, Uziella (עֻזִיאֵלָה)   From the Hebrew, meaning "my strength is the Lord."

Uzit (עֻזִּית)   From the Hebrew, meaning "strength."

Val   A pet form of Valerie. *See* Valerie. Also, a pet form of Valda. *See* Valda.

Valari   A variant form of Valerie. *See* Valerie.

Valda   From the German, meaning "battle heroine." Val is a pet form.

Valencia   A Spanish form of Valeria. *See* Valeria. Valentia is a variant spelling. Also, a Spanish place-name.

Valentia   A variant spelling of Valencia. *See* Valencia.

Valentine   From the Latin, meaning "healthy, strong." Used originally as a masculine form.

Valeria   From the Latin, meaning "to be strong." Valerie is a variant French form. *See* Valerie.

Valerie   A French form of the Latin name Valeria, meaning "to be strong." Valari is a variant form. Val is a pet form. Valery and Valri are variant spellings.

Valery   A variant spelling of Valerie. *See* Valerie.

Valeska   From the Slavic, meaning "glory."

Valora   A variant form of Valeria. *See* Valeria.

Valri   A variant spelling of Valerie. *See* Valerie.

Vana   From the British, meaning "high."

Vanessa   From the Greek, meaning "butterfly."

Vania   A feminine form of Ivan. *See* Ivan (masculine section).

Vanora   From the Celtic, meaning "white wave."

Varda (וַרְדָּה)   From the Hebrew, meaning "rose." Vardina, Vardit, Vardiya, and Vered are variant forms.

Vardia   A variant spelling of Vardiya. *See* Vardiya.

Vardina (וַרְדִינָה) A variant form of Varda. *See* Varda.

Vardit (וַרְדִּית) A variant form of Varda. *See* Varda.

Vardiya (וַרְדִּיָה) A variant form of Varda. *See* Varda. Vardia is a variant spelling.

Vashti (וַשְׁתִּי) From the Persian, meaning "beautiful." In the Bible (Esther 1:9), the wife of King Ahasuerus of Persia.

Veda From the Sanskrit, meaning "sacred understanding." The Veda are the sacred books of the Hindus.

Vedis From the Singhalese, meaning "hunter."

Vega From the Arabic, meaning "the falling," referring to a very bright star in the constellation Lyra.

Vela From the Latin, meaning "to wish, desire." Also, a constellation in the Southern Milky Way. Vella is a variant spelling.

Velda, Veleda From the Middle Dutch, meaning "field."

Velika From the Slavic, meaning "great."

Velinda A variant form of Belinda. *See* Belinda.

Vella A variant spelling of Vela. *See* Vela.

Velma A pet form of Wilhelmina. *See* Wilhelmina. Vilma is a variant form.

Velva A name derived from "velvet." *See* Velvet.

Velvela (וֶלְוֶולֹא) A feminine form of the Yiddish Velvl, meaning "wolf." *See* Velvel in masculine section.

Velvet From the Latin, meaning "shaggy hair, wool."

Vena From the Latin, meaning "vein."

Venda From the Latin, meaning "to love."

Veneta A variant form of Venetia. *See* Venetia.

Venetia From the Latin, meaning "a woman of Venice." Veneta and Venita are variant forms.

Venita A variant form of Venetia. *See* Venetia. Vinita is a variant spelling.

Ventura From the Spanish, meaning "good fortune."

Venus From the Latin, meaning "to love." In Greek mythology, the goddess of love and beauty.

Vera From the Latin, meaning "truth." Also, from the Russian, meaning "faith." Vira is a variant spelling.

Verda A variant form of Verdi. *See* Verdi.

Verdi From the Old French, meaning "green, springlike." Verda is a variant form.

Vered (וֶרֶד)   From the Hebrew, meaning "rose." Used also as masculine name. *See* Varda.

Verena, Verina   From the Latin, meaning "one who venerates God" or "sacred wisdom." Verna is a variant form.

Verita   From the Latin, meaning "truth." Akin to Verity.

Verity   From the Latin, meaning "truth." Akin to Verita.

Verna   A variant form of Verena. *See* Verena. Also, a variant form of Verne. *See* Verne. Virna is a variant spelling.

Verne   From the Latin, meaning "spring-like." Literally, "to grow green." Verna and Verona are variant forms. Vernee, Vernie, and Vernita are pet forms.

Vernee, Vernie, Vernita   Pet forms of Verne. *See* Verne.

Verona   A variant form of Verne. *See* Verne.

Veronica   A variant form of Berenice, meaning "bringer of victory." Also, from the Latin, meaning "truthful, faithful." Nicky is a pet form.

Vesma   From the Latin, meaning "vessel, vase." Vesna is a variant form.

Vesna   A variant form of Vesma. *See* Vesma.

Vespera   An Old French form of Esther, meaning "star."

Vesta   In Roman mythology, the goddess of fire.

Vevila   From the Celtic, meaning "harmonious."

Vi   A pet form of Violet and Victoria. *See* Violet *and* Victoria.

Vici, Vicki, Vicky   Variant pet forms of Victoria. *See* Victoria. Viqui is a variant spelling.

Victoria   From the Latin, meaning "victorious." Victor is the masculine form. Vi, Vici, Vicki, Vicky, Victorina, Victorine, Vikki, Vikkie, and Vikky are pet forms.

Victorina, Victorine   Pet forms of Victoria. *See* Victoria.

Vida   A pet form of Davida. *See* Davida. Also, a variant form of Vita. *See* Vita.

Vidonia   From the Latin, meaning "vine."

Viena, Vienna   From the Middle English and the Old French, meaning "to invite, vie with (in competitive games)."

Vikki, Vikkie, Vikky   Pet forms of Victoria. *See* Victoria.

Vila   An Italian form of the Latin, meaning "country estate, farm."

Vilma   A variant form of Velma. *See* Velma.

Vilna   A pet form of Wilhelmina. *See* Wilhelmina.

Vincentia   From the Latin, meaning "to conquer." Vinnette is a pet form.

Vinita   A variant spelling of Venita. *See* Venita.

Vinnette A French pet form of Winifred. *See* Winifred. Also, a pet form of Vincentia. *See* Vincentia.

Viola From the Middle English and Latin, meaning "violet," a genus of plant with white, blue, purple, or yellow flowers. Violet is a variant form.

Violet A variant form of Viola. *See* Viola. Violeta, Violetta, and Violette are pet forms.

Violeta, Violetta, Violette Pet forms of Violet. *See* Violet.

Viqui A variant spelling of Vicki. *See* Vicki.

Vira A variant spelling of Vera. *See* Vera.

Virgie A pet form of Virginia. *See* Virginia.

Virgilia The feminine form of Virgil. *See* Virgil (masculine section).

Virginia From the Latin, meaning "virgin, pure" or "maiden." The feminine form of Virgil. *See* Virgil (masculine section). Virginie is a French form. Virgie is a pet form.

Virginie A French form of Virginia. *See* Virginia.

Viridis From the Latin, meaning "green, youthful, blooming."

Virna A variant spelling of Verna. *See* Verna.

Vita From the Latin, meaning "life, animated." Vida, Vivian, Vivien, and Vyvyan are variant forms.

Viveca From the Middle Latin, meaning "with living voice, by word of mouth." Also, from the Latin, meaning "lively."

Vivi From the Latin, meaning "alive."

Vivian, Viviana, Vivianna From the Latin, meaning "alive." Akin to Vita. *See* Vita. Vivien and Vivienne are French forms. Vyvyan is a variant spelling.

Vivien, Vivienne French forms of Vivian. *See* Vivian.

Volante An Italian form of the Latin, meaning "to fly."

Vyvyan A variant spelling of Vivian. *See* Vivian.

Walda From the Old High German, meaning "to rule." The feminine form of Waldo.

Wallis From the British, meaning "fortification."

Wanda From the Old Norse, meaning "young tree," or from the Anglo-Saxon, meaning "wanderer." Wandis is a variant form.

Wandis   A variant form of Wanda. *See* Wanda.

Wanette, Wannetta   From the Old English, meaning "young pale one." Also, an adaptation of Juanita. *See* Juanita.

Wanika   The Hawaiian form of Juanita. *See* Juanita.

Warrene   The feminine form of Warren. *See* Warren (masculine section).

Wasida   From the Old English, meaning "water."

Wenda   From the British, meaning "fair." Wendelin and Wendaline are pet forms.

Wendelin, Wendaline   Pet forms of Wenda *and* Gwendaline. *See* Wenda *and* Gwendaline.

Wendey, Wendi, Wendy   Pet forms of Genevieve and Gwendaline. *See* Genevieve *and* Gwendaline.

Wenona   From the Old English, meaning "joy, bliss." Also, an American Indian name, meaning "firstborn daughter."

Whaley   From the Old English, meaning "wall." Also, from the Middle English, meaning "large fish."

Wilda   From the Old English, meaning "willow."

Wilfreda   The feminine form of Wilfred. *See* Wilfred (masculine section).

Wilhelmina   The English and Dutch form of the masculine Wilhelm (the German form of William), meaning "warrior" or "ruler." *See* William (masculine section). Willa, Willene, Willi, Wilma, Wilmena, Wilmet, and Wilmette are pet forms. Mindel is a Yiddish form.

Willa   A pet form of Wilhelmina. *See* Wilhelmina.

Willene   A pet form of Wilhelmina. *See* Wilhelmina.

Willeta, Willetta, Willette   Feminine forms of William.   *See* William (masculine section).

Willi, Willie   Pet forms of Wilhelmina. *See* Wilhelmina.

Wilma   A pet form of Wilhelmina. *See* Wilhelmina.

Wilmena   A pet form of Wilhelmina. *See* Wilhelmina.

Wilmet, Wilmette   Pet forms of Wilhelmina. *See* Wilhelmina.

Win   A pet form of Winifred. *See* Winifred.

Winifred   From the Anglo-Saxon, meaning "friend of peace." Win, Winnie, Wyn, Wynna, and Wynne are pet forms.

Winnie   A pet form of Winifred. *See* Winifred.

Woodren   A feminine form of Woodrow. *See* Woodrow (masculine section).

Wyetta   A feminine form of Wyatt. *See* Wyatt (masculine section).

Wyn   A pet form of Gwendaline and Winifred. *See* Gwendaline *and* Winifred.

Wynna, Wynne   Pet forms of Gwendaline. *See* Gwendaline. Also, pet forms of Winifred. *See* Winifred. Wynelle and Wynette are variant forms.

Wynelle   A variant form of Wynna. *See* Wynna.

Wynette   A variant form of Wynna. *See* Wynna.

Xanthe   From the Greek, meaning "yellow."

Xena   From the Greek, meaning "great" or "stranger." Also, a variant form of Zena.

Xenia   From the Greek, meaning "hospitality" and "guest, stranger (to whom hospitality was extended)." Ximena is a variant form.

Ximena   A variant form of Xenia. *See* Xenia.

Xylia   A variant form of Sylvia. *See* Sylvia. Xylina is a variant form.

Xylina   A variant form of Xylia. *See* Xylia.

Yaa, Ya'a (יָאָה)   From the Hebrew, meaning "beautiful."

Yaakova (יַעֲקֹבָה)   The feminine form of Yaakov (Jacob), meaning "to supplant" or "to protect." *See* Yaakov *and* Jacob (masculine section). In the Bible (I Chronicles 4:36), Yaakova is a masculine name, a member of the tribe of Simeon. Presently, it is used exclusively as a feminine form.

Yaala (יַעֲלָה)   A variant form of Yael. *See* Yael.

Yaalat (יַעֲלַת)   A variant form of Yael. *See* Yael.

Yaalat-Chen (יַעֲלַת־חֵן)   From the Hebrew, meaning "graceful woman." *See* also Yael.

Yaalit (יַעֲלִית)   A variant form of Yael. *See* Yael.

Yaanit (יַעֲנִית)   A variant for of Yaen. *See* Yaen.

Yaara (יַעֲרָה)   From the Hebrew, meaning "honeycomb." Yaari and Yaarit are variant forms. Yara is a variant spelling.

Yaari (יַעֲרִי)   From the Hebrew, meaning "pertaining to the forest."

Yaarit (יַעֲרִית)   A variant form of Yaara. *See* Yaara.

Yachna (יַחְנָא)   A variant spelling of Yachne. *See* Yachne.

Yachne (יַחְנֶע)   A Yiddish form of Johanna. *See* Johanna.

Yael (יָעֵל)   From the Hebrew, meaning "to ascend" or "mountain goat." In the Bible (Judges 4:17), a Kenite woman in the time of Deborah who slew Sisera with a tent-pin. Jael is a variant spelling. Yaala, Yaalat, Yaalit, Yaela, Yaella, Ye'ela, and Ye'elit are variant forms.

Yaen (יָעֵן)   From the Hebrew, meaning "ostrich." Jaen is a variant spelling.

Yaela, Yaella   Variant forms of Yael. *See* Yael.

Yafa, Yaffa (יָפָה)   From the Assyrian and the Hebrew, meaning "beautiful." Yafit is a variant form

Yafo (יָפוֹ)   A seaport town in Israel (near Tel Aviv) once referred to as Joppa, and mentioned in the Bible (Joshua 19:46). Jaffa, Japha, Yaffa, and Yapha are variant spellings.

Yafit (יָפִית)   A variant form of Yafa. *See* Yafa. Jafit is a variant spelling.

Yahala (יָהֲלָה)   A variant form of Yahel. *See* Yahel.

Yahalai (יָהֲלַי)   A variant form of Yahel. *See* Yahel.

Yahali (יָהֲלִי)   A variant form of Yahel. *See* Yahel.

Yahaloma (יָהֲלוֹמָה)   A variant form of Yahel. *See* Yahel. Also, from the Hebrew, meaning "precious stone, diamond," and mentioned in the Bible (Exodus 28:18). Yahalomit is a variant form.

Yahalomit (יָהֲלוֹמִית)   A variant form of Yahaloma. *See* Yahaloma.

Yahava (יָהֲבָה)   A variant form of Yehava. *See* Yehava.

Yahel (יָהֵל)   From the Hebrew, meaning "to shine." Yahala, Yahalai, Yahali, and Yahaloma are variant forms.

Yaira (יָאִירָה)   From the Hebrew, meaning "to enlighten." The feminine counterpart of Yair. *See* Yair (masculine section).

Yakinton (יַקִנְתוֹן)   The Hebrew name for "hyacinth (plant)."

Yakira (יַקִירָה)   From the Hebrew, meaning "valuable, precious." Yekara and Yikrat are variant forms.

Yalta (יַלְתָּא)   The Aramaic form of Ayala. *See* Ayala. In the Talmud (Gitin 67a), the wife of Rabbi Nachman.

Yama (יָמָה)   From the Hebrew, meaning "toward the sea" or "westward." Refers to the Mediterranean Sea, which is to the west of Israel.

Yamit (יַמִית)   From the Hebrew, meaning "pertaining to the sea."

Yanocha (יָנוֹחָה)   From the Hebrew, meaning "to rest."

Yapha   A variant spelling of Yafa. *See* Yafa.

Yara   A variant spelling of Yaara. *See* Yaara.

Yarden (יַרְדֵּן)   From the Hebrew, meaning "Jordan." Used also as a masculine name.

Yardena (יַרְדֵּנָה)   The feminine form of Yarden (Jordan). *See* Yarden (masculine section). Jardena is a variant spelling.

Yardenia   A variant spelling of Yardeniya. *See* Yardeniya.

Yardeniya (יַרְדְּנִיָה)   From the Hebrew, meaning "garden of the Lord." Jardenia and Yardenia are variant spellings.

Yarkona (יַרְקוֹנָה)   The feminine form of Yarkon, meaning "green." *See* Yarkon (masculine section). The Yarkona, a bird with golden-green feathers, is found in southern Israel.

Yarona (יָרוֹנָה)   From the Hebrew, meaning "to sing."

Yasmeen   A variant spelling of Yasmin. *See* Yasmin.

Yasmin, Yasmine (יַסְמִין)   From the Persian, meaning "a plant in the olive family." *See also* Jasmine. Yasmeen is a variant spelling. Yasmina is a variant form.

Yasmina (יַסְמִינָה)   A variant form of Yasmin. *See* Yasmin.

Yatva (יָטְבָה)   From the Hebrew, meaning "good." In the Bible (II Kings 21:19), a place-name. Yatvat and Yatvata are variant forms.

Yatvat (יָטְבַת)   A variant form of Yatva. *See* Yatva.

Yatvata (יָטְבָתָה)   A variant form of Yatva. *See* Yatva.

Yavn'ela (יַבְנְאֵלָה)   From the Hebrew, meaning "God builds." The feminine counterpart of Yavne'el. *See* Yavne'el (masculine section).

Yechezkela (יְחֶזְקֵאלָה)   The feminine form of Yechezkel (Ezekiel). *See* Yechezkel (masculine section).

Yechiela, Yechiella (יְחִיאֵלָה)   From the Hebrew, meaning "may God live." Feminine forms of Yechiel. *See* Yechiel (masculine section).

Yedida, Yedidah (יְדִידָה)   From the Hebrew, meaning "friend" or "beloved." In the Bible (II Kings 22:1), the mother of Josiah, king of Judah. Yedidya is a variant form.

Yedidia, Yedidiah   Variant spellings of Yedidya. *See* Yedidya.

Yedidya (יְדִידְיָה)   From the Hebrew, meaning "friend of God" or "beloved of God." In the Bible (II Kings 22:1), the mother of King Josiah. Jedidia, Jedidiah, Yedidia, and Yedidiah are variant spellings.

Ye'ela (יְעֵלָה)   A variant form of Yael. *See* Yael.

Ye'elit (יְעֵלִית)   A variant form of Yael. *See* Yael.

Yefefia   A variant spelling of Yefeifiya. *See* Yefeifiya.

Yefeifiya (יְפֵהפִיָה)   From the Hebrew, meaning "beautiful." Yefefia is a variant spelling.

Yegaala (יְגָאֵלָה)   A variant form of Yigaela. *See* Yigaela.

Yehava (יְהָבָה)   From the Hebrew, meaning "gift."

Yehezkela   A variant spelling of Yechezkela. *See* Yechezkela.

Yehoadan (יְהוֹעַדָן)   From the Hebrew, meaning "God has adorned." In the Bible (II Kings 14:2), the wife of Yoash, king of Judah, and the mother of Amatziah.

Yehoshavat (יְהוֹשַׁבְעַת) A variant form of Yehosheva, mentioned in II Chronicles 22:11. *See* Yehosheva.

Yehosheva (יְהוֹשֶׁבַע) From the Hebrew, meaning "God has sworn; God's oath." In the Bible (II Kings 11:2), a daughter of Yoram, king of Judah. Yehoshavat is a variant form, referring to the same person. Jehosheba is a variant spelling.

Yehudit (יְהוּדִית) From the Hebrew, meaning "praise." In the Bible (Genesis 26:31), the wife of Esau. Eudice, Idit, Yudit, and Yuta are variant forms. Judith is the Anglicized form. *See* Judith. Dita and Yudi are pet forms.

Yeira, Yeirah (יְאִירָה) From the Hebrew, meaning "light."

Yekara, Yekarah (יְקָרָה) Variant forms of Yakira. *See* Yakira.

Yemima (יְמִימָה) Possibly related to the Arabic, meaning "dove." In the Bible (Job 42:14), a daughter of Job. Jemima is a variant spelling.

Yemina (יְמִינָה) From the Hebrew, meaning "right hand," signifying strength. Jemina is a variant spelling.

Yenika (יְנִיקָה) From the Hebrew, meaning "sapling" and "nursling."

Yenta (יֶענְטָא) A Yiddish form of Henrietta. *See* Henrietta. Or, from the French Gentille and Yiddishized as Yentille. May also be a Yiddish form of the Spanish Juanita. Yente is a variant form.

Yente (יֶענְטֶע) A variant form of Yenta. *See* Yenta.

Yentel (יֶענְטל) A pet form of Yente. *See* Yente. Also spelled יֶענְטעל.

Yentele (יֶענְטֶעל) A pet form of Yente. *See* Yente.

Yentil (יֶענְטִיל) A pet form of Yente. *See* Yente.

Yeora (יְאוֹרָה) From the Hebrew, meaning "light."

Yeriot (יְרִיעוֹת) From the Hebrew, meaning "draperies." In the Bible (I Chronicles 2:18), the daughter of Caleb ben Chetzron.

Yeruchama (יְרוּחָמָה) From the Hebrew, meaning "compassion." Yerucham is the masculine form.

Yerusha (יְרוּשָׁה) From the Hebrew, meaning "inheritance." In the Bible (II Chronicles 17:1), the wife of King Uziah of Judah, and the mother of King Jotham. Jerusha is a variant spelling. In II Kings 15:33, the Hebrew name is spelled יְרוּשָׁא.

Yerushalayim (יְרוּשָׁלַיִם) A biblical place-name. Early on, the capital of all Israel; later, the capital of the Southern Kingdom. Probably from the Assyrian, meaning "city of peace" or "foundation of peace." Jerusalem is an Anglicized form.

Yerushel (יְרוּשֶׁעל) A Yiddish form of Yerusha. *See* Yerusha.

Yeshana (יְשָׁנָה) From the Hebrew, meaning "old, ancient."

Yeshara (יְשָׁרָה) From the Hebrew, meaning "straight" or "honest."

Yeshisha (יְשִׁישָׁה)   From the Hebrew, meaning "old."

Yeshiva (יְשִׁיבָה)   From the Hebrew, meaning "resting place" or "school."

Yeshua (יְשׁוּעָה)   From the Hebrew, meaning "salvation."

Yetta   A pet form of Henrietta. *See* Henrietta. Yitta is a variant form.

Yifa, Yif'a (יִפְעָה)   From the Hebrew, meaning "beauty" or "splendor." Yif'at is a variant form.

Yifat, Yif'at (יִפְעַת)   A variant form of Yif'a. *See* Yif'a.

Yigaala (יִגְאָלָה)   From the Hebrew, meaning "to redeem."

Yigaela (יִגְאֵלָה)   From the Hebrew, meaning "redemption." Yigael is the masculine form.

Yigala (יִגְאָלָה)   From the Hebrew, meaning "to redeem." Yigaala is a variant form.

Yikrat (יִקְרַת)   A variant form of Yakira. *See* Yakira.

Yimna (יִמְנָה)   Possibly related to the Arabic, meaning "good fortune" or "right side." In the Bible (Genesis 46:17), used as a masculine name.

Yisha (יִשְׁעָה)   From the Hebrew, meaning "salvation."

Yishva (יִשְׁוָה)   From the Hebrew, meaning "ballast" or "stabilizer."

Yiska (יִסְכָּה)   From the Hebrew, meaning "anointed." In the Bible (Genesis 11:29), the wife of Chever the Kenite.

Yisra   A variant spelling of Yitra. *See* Yitra.

Yisraela (יִשְׂרָאֵלָה)   A variant form of Yisr'ela. *See* Yisr'ela.

Yisraelit (יִשְׂרָאֵלִית)   A variant form of Yisraela. *See* Yisraela.

Yisr'ela (יִשְׂרְאֵלָה)   From the Hebrew, meaning "Israeli" or "Jew." The feminine form of Yisrael. Yisraela and Yisr'elit are variant forms.

Yisr'elit (יִשְׂרְאֵלִית)   A variant form of Yisr'ela. *See* Yisr'ela.

Yitra (יִתְרָה)   From the Hebrew, meaning "wealth, riches." Yitro is the masculine form. *See* Yitro (masculine section). Yisra is a variant spelling. Akin to Jethra.

Yitta (יִטָא)   A variant Yiddish form of Yetta. *See* Yetta.

Yitte (יִטֶע)   A variant Yiddish form of Yetta. *See* Yetta.

Yizr'ela (יִזְרְאֶאלָה)   From the Hebrew, meaning "God will plant."

Yma   A variant spelling of Ima. *See* Ima.

Yochana (יוֹחָנָה)   From the Hebrew, meaning "God is gracious." A feminine form of Yochanan.

Yochani (יוֹחָנִי)   From the Hebrew, meaning "gracious one." In the Talmud (Sota 22b), the daughter of a widow.

Yochebed   A variant spelling of Yocheved. *See* Yocheved.

Yocheved (יוֹכֶבֶד)   From the Hebrew, meaning "God's glory." In the Bible

(Exodus 6:20), the wife of Amram and the mother of Moses, Aaron, and Miriam. Jochebed, Jocheved, and Yochebed are variant spellings.

Yoela (יוֹאֵלָה) From the Hebrew, meaning "God is willing." The feminine form of Yoel. *See* Yoel. Yoelit is a variant form. Used also as a masculine name. Joela is a variant spelling.

Yoelit (יוֹאֵלִית) A variant form of Yoela. *See* Yoela.

Yolanda, Yolande Possibly, a form of the Old French name Violante, a derivative of Viola. *See* Viola. Or, from the Latin, meaning "modest, shy." Also, a variant form of the Greek Eolande, meaning "dawn." Jolande is a variant spelling.

Ymma A variant form of Emma. *See* Emma.

Yona, Yonah (יוֹנָה) From the Hebrew, meaning "dove." Primarily a masculine name. *See* Yona (masculine section). Jona is a variant spelling. Yonat, Yonata, Yonati, Yonina, Yonit, and Yonita are variant forms.

Yonat (יוֹנַת) A variant form of Yona. *See* Yona. Jonat is a variant spelling.

Yonata (יוֹנָתָה) A variant form of Yona. *See* Yona. Jonata is a variant spelling.

Yonati (יוֹנָתִי) From the Hebrew, meaning "my dove." Jonati is a variant spelling. Also, a variant form of Yona. *See* Yona.

Yonina (יוֹנִינָה) A variant form of Yona. *See* Yona. Jonina is a variant spelling.

Yonit (יוֹנִית) A variant form of Yona. *See* Yona. Jonit is a variant spelling.

Yonita (יוֹנִיתָה) A variant form of Yona. *See* Yona. Jonita is a variant spelling.

Yosefa A variant spelling of Yosifa. *See* Yosifa.

Yoseifa (יוֹסֵפָה) A variant form of Yosifa. *See* Yosifa.

Yosepha A variant spelling of Yosifa. *See* Yosifa.

Yosifa (יוֹסִיפָה) A feminine form of Yosef (Joseph). *See* Yosef *and* Joseph (masculine section). Josefa, Josepha, Josifa, Josipha, Yosefa, Yosepha, and Yosipha are variant spellings.

Yosipha A variant spelling of Yosifa. *See* Yosifa.

Yovela (יוֹבְלָה) From the Hebrew, meaning "jubilee" or "rejoicing." The feminine form of Yovel. *See* Yovel (masculine section).

Yudi A pet form of Yehudit. *See* Yehudit.

Yudit (יוּדִית) A short form of Yehudit. *See* Yehudit.

Yuta (יוּטָא) A Yiddish form of Yehudit (Judith). *See* Yehudit.

Yute (יוּטֶע) A variant form of Yuta. *See* Yuta.

Yutke (יוּטְקֶע) A Yiddish form of Yehudit (Judith). *See* Yehudit.

Yve A feminine form of Yves. *See* Yves (masculine section).

Yvette A feminine form of Yves. *See* Yves (masculine section). Also, a Welsh form of Evan. *See* Evan (masculine section). Ivette is a variant spelling.

Yvonne A French form of Yves. *See* Yves (masculine section).

Zabrina A variant form of Sabrina. *See* Sabrina.

Zadika A variant spelling of Tzadika. *See* Tzadika.

Zafnat A variant spelling of Tzafnat. *See* Tzafnat.

Zafona A variant spelling of Tzafona. *See* Tzafona.

Zafra A variant spelling of Tzafra. *See* Tzafra.

Zafrira A variant spelling of Tzafrira. *See* Tzafrira.

Zafririt A variant spelling of Tzafririt. *See* Tzafririt.

Zahala A variant spelling of Tzahala. *See* Tzahala.

Zahara (זֶהֱרָה) From the Hebrew, meaning "to shine." Zahari, Zaharira, Zaharit, and Zoheret are variant forms.

Zahari (זֶהֲרִי) A variant form of Zahara. *See* Zahara.

Zaharira (זֶהֲרִירָה) A variant form of Zahara. *See* Zahara.

Zaharit (זֶהֲרִית) A variant form of Zahara. *See* Zahara.

Zahava A variant spelling of Zehava. *See* Zehava.

Zahavi A variant spelling of Zehavi. *See* Zehavi.

Zaka, Zakah (זַכָּה) From the Hebrew, meaning "bright, pure, clear." Zakit is a variant form. Akin to Zakiya.

Zakia, Zakiah Variant spellings of Zakiya. *See* Zakiya.

Zakit (זַכִּית) A variant form of Zaka. *See* Zaka.

Zakiya (זַכִּיָּה) From the Hebrew, meaning "pure, clean." Akin to Zaka. Zakia and Zakiah are variant spellings.

Zameret A variant spelling of Tzameret. *See* Tzameret.

Zandra A variant form of Sandra. *See* Sandra.

Zaneta, Zanetta Russian forms of Johanna. *See* Johanna.

Zara, Zarah (זָרָה) Variant forms of Sarah. *See* Sarah. Also, from the Arabic, meaning "dawn," and from the Hebrew, meaning "stranger." Zora is a variant spelling. *See* Zora.

Zariza (זְרִיזָה) A variant form of Zeriza. *See* Zeriza.

Zayat (זַיָּת) From the Hebrew, meaning "one who raises olives."

Zayit (זַיִת) From the Hebrew, meaning "olive." Used also as a masculine name. Zeita and Zeta are variant forms.

Zaza (זָזָה) From the Hebrew, meaning "movement." Zazu is a variant form.

Zazu A variant form of Zaza. *See* Zaza.

Zeena A variant spelling of Zina. *See* Zina.

Zeeva A variant spelling of Ziva. *See* Ziva.

Ze'eva, Zeeva (זְאֵבָה) From the Hebrew, meaning "wolf." Zeva is a variant spelling. Zev and Ze'ev are masculine forms.

Zefira A variant spelling of Tzefira. *See* Tzefira.

Zehara (זְהָרָה) From the Hebrew, meaning "light, brightness." Zehorit is a variant form.

Zehari (זְהָרִי) A variant form of Zohar. *See* Zohar.

Zehava (זְהָבָה) From the Hebrew, meaning "gold, golden." Zahava is a variant spelling. Zehovit, Zehuva, and Zehuvit are variant forms.

Zehavi (זְהָבִי) A variant form of Zehava. *See* Zehava.

Zehavit (זְהָבִית) A variant form of Zehava. *See* Zehava.

Zehira (זְהִירָה) From the Hebrew, meaning "guarded, careful, cautious."

Zehorit (זְהוֹרִית) A variant form of Zehara. *See* Zehara. Also, from the Hebrew, meaning "red-colored thread or fabric."

Zehovit (זְהוֹבִית) A variant form of Zehava. *See* Zehava.

Zehuva (זְהוּבָה) From the Hebrew, meaning "gilded." Akin to Zehava.

Zehuvit (זְהוּבִית) A variant form of Zehava. *See* Zehava.

Zeira (זְעִירָא) From the Aramaic, meaning "small."

Zeita (זֵיתָה) An Aramaic variant form of Zayit. *See* Zayit.

Zeitana (זֵיתָנָה) A variant form of Zeita. *See* Zeita. Zetana is a variant spelling.

Zeitel A variant spelling of Tzeitl. *See* Tzeitl.

Zeitl A variant spelling of Tzeitl. *See* Tzeitl.

Zekena (זְקֵנָה) From the Hebrew, meaning "old, ancient."

Zekifa (זְקִיפָה) A variant form of Zekufa. *See* Zekufa.

Zekufa (זְקוּפָה) From the Hebrew, meaning "upright." Zekifa is a variant form.

Zelda (זֶעלְדֶע) A variant spelling of Selda. *See* Selda. Also, a Yiddish form of the Old German Salida. *See* Salida.

Zelia From the Latin, meaning "zealous." Zella is a variant form.

Zelila A variant spelling of Tzelila. *See* Tzelila.

Zelili A variant form of Tzelila. *See* Tzelila.

Zella A variant form of Zelia. *See* Zelia.

Zemicha A variant spelling of Tzemicha. *See* Tzemicha.

Zemira (זְמִירָה) From the Hebrew, meaning "song, melody."

Zemora, Zemorah (זְמוֹרָה) From the Hebrew, meaning "branch, twig."

Zena A short form of Zenana. *See* Zenana. Zenia and Xena are variant forms.

Zenana   From the Persian, meaning "woman." Zena is a short form.

Zenda   From the Persian, meaning "sacred."

Zenia   A variant form of Zena. See Zena.

Zenobia   From the Greek, meaning "sign, symbol."

Zeona   A variant spelling of Ziona. See Ziona.

Zephira   A variant spelling of Tzefira. See Tzefira.

Zephyr   From the Greek, meaning "the west wind."

Zeriza (זְרִיזָה)   From the Hebrew, meaning "energetic, industrious." Zariza is a variant form.

Zertel   A variant spelling of Tzertel. See Tzertel.

Zerua (זְרוּעָה)   From the Hebrew, meaning "planted, seeded."

Zeruia   A variant spelling of Tzeruya. See Tzeruya.

Zeta   A variant spelling of Zeita. See Zeita.

Zetana   A variant spelling of Zeitana. See Zeitana.

Zetta   A variant spelling of Zeta. See Zeta.

Zeva   A variant spelling of Ze'eva. See Ze'eva.

Zevida (זְבִידָה)   From the Hebrew, meaning "gift."

Zevuda (זְבוּדָה)   A variant form of Zevida. See Zevida. In the Bible (II Kings 23:36), the mother of Jehoiakim, king of Judah.

Zevula (זְבוּלָה)   From the Hebrew, meaning "dwelling place" or "palace."

Zia (זִיע)   From the Hebrew, meaning "to tremble." Primarily a masculine name.

Zichria, Zichriah   Variant spellings of Zichriya. See Zichriya.

Zichrini (זִכְרִינִי)   A variant form of Zichriya. See Zichriya. Primarily a masculine name. Zichroni is a variant form.

Zichriya (זִכְרִיָה)   From the Hebrew, meaning "remembrance." A plant of the Myosotis genus that bears blue flowers (probably the forget-me-not). Zichrini is a variant form. Zichria and Zichriah are variant spellings.

Zichrona (זִכְרוֹנָה)   From the Hebrew, meaning "remembrance."

Zichroni (זִכְרוֹנִי)   A variant form of Zichrini. See Zichrini.

Zifria   A variant spelling of Tzifriya. See Tzifriya.

Zifrona   A variant spelling of Tzifrona. See Tzifrona.

Zila, Zilla, Zillah   Variant spellings of Tzila. See Tzila.

Zili, Zilli   Variant spellings of Tzili. See Tzili.

Zilpa, Zilpah (זִלְפָּה)   From the Hebrew, meaning "to drop, trickle" or "youthful." In the Bible (Genesis 29:24), one of Jacob's wives and the handmaid of Leah. Zylpha is a variant form. Zulpha is probably a variant form.

Zimchona   A variant spelling of Tzimchona. *See* Tzimchona.

Zimra (זִמְרָה)   From the Hebrew, meaning "choice fruit" or "song of praise." Zemora and Zimrat are variant forms.

Zimrat (זִמְרַת)   A variant form of Zimra. *See* Zimra.

Zimria, Zimriah   Variant spellings of Zimriya. *See* Zimriya.

Zimriya (זִמְרִיָה)   From the Hebrew, meaning "songfest."

Zina   A variant form of Zinnia. *See* Zinnia. Zeena is a variant spelling.

Zinnia   A variety of plant with colorful flowers, named for German botanist J.G. Zinn (died 1759). Zina is a variant form.

Ziona   A variant spelling of Tziona. *See* Tziona. Zeona is a variant spelling.

Zionit   A variant spelling of Tzionit. *See* Tzionit.

Zipeh   A variant spelling of Tzipeh. *See* Tzipeh.

Ziphrona   A variant spelling of Tzifrona. *See* Tzifrona.

Zipia   A variant spelling of Tzipya. *See* Tzipya.

Zipora, Zippora   Variant spellings of Tzipora. *See* Tzipora.

Zipori   A variant spelling of Tzipori. *See* Tzipori.

Zippe   A variant spelling of Tzipeh. *See* Tzipeh.

Zippora   Variant spellings of Tzipora. *See* Tzipora.

Zira, Zirah (זִירָה)   From the Hebrew, meaning "arena."

Zirel   A variant spelling of Tzirel. *See* Tzirel.

Zisse (זִיסֶע)   From the Yiddish, meaning "sweet." Used also as a masculine name. Soshe is a variant form.

Zissele (זִיסֶעלֶע)   A pet form of Zisse. *See* Zisse.

Zita   A pet form of Theresa. *See* Theresa.

Ziva (זִיוָה)   From the Hebrew, meaning "brightness, brilliance, splendor." Zivi and Zivit are variant forms. Zeeva is a variant spelling.

Zivanit (זִיוָנִית)   From the Hebrew. A plant-name in the lily family.

Zivi (זִיוִי)   A variant form of Ziva. *See* Ziva.

Zivit (זִיוִית)   A variant form of Ziva. *See* Ziva.

Zlata (זְלאַטאַ)   A Polish-Yiddish form of Golda. *See* Golda.

Zlate (זְלאַטֶע)   A variant form of Zlata. *See* Zlata.

Zoe   From the Greek, meaning "life." In a third-century Greek translation of the Bible by Alexandrian Jews, Eve (Chava), meaning "life," is translated as Zoe.

Zofi   A variant spelling of Tzofi. *See* Tzofi.

Zofia   A variant spelling of Tzofiya. *See* Tzofiya.

Zofit   A variant spelling of Tzofit. *See* Tzofit.

Zohar (זֹהַר)   From the Hebrew, meaning "light, brilliance." Also spelled זֹהַר. Used also as a masculine name. Zehari is a variant form.

Zoheret (זוֹהֶרֶת)   A variant form of Zahara. From the Hebrew, meaning ''she shines.'' *See* Zahara.

Zona (זוֹנָה)   From the Hebrew, meaning "prostitute."

Zonya   A variant form of Sonia. *See* Sonia.

Zophia   A variant form of Sophia. *See* Sophia.

Zora   A variant spelling of Zara. *See* Zara. Zorana, Zoreen, Zoreene, and Zorene are pet forms. Zorna is a variant form. Also a variant form of Aurora. *See* Aurora.

Zorachat (זוֹרַחַת)   From the Hebrew, meaning "she shines, she is bright."

Zorana   A pet form of Zora. *See* Zora.

Zoreen, Zoreene, Zorene   Pet forms of Zara. *See* Zara.

Zorna   A variant form of Zora. *See* Zora.

Zuelia   A variant form of Zulema. *See* Zulema.

Zuleika   A variant form of Zulema. *See* Zulema.

Zulema   From the Arabic name Suleima, meaning "peace." Akin to Shalom. Zuelia and Zuleika are variant forms.

Zulpha   Probably a variant form of Zilpah. *See* Zilpah.

Zur-El   A variant spelling of Tzur-El. *See* Tzur-El.

Zuria   A variant spelling of Tzuriya. *See* Tzuriya.

Zurit   A variant spelling of Tzurit. *See* Tzurit.

Zylpha   A variant form of Zilpah. *See* Zilpah.

HEBREW NAME VOCABULARY

HEBREW NAME VOCABULARY
(Yiddish names are in italics)

Detailed information about most of these names will be found in the body of this work.

Abandoned
FEMININE: Azuva
Able
MASCULINE: Yuchal
Abode See also Dwelling
MASCULINE: Shechanya
Abundance, Abundant See also Rich, Riches
MASCULINE: Hotir, Petuel, Shefa, Shifi, Yefet, Yeter, Yitra, Yitran, Yitro
FEMININE: Milet, Shifa, Yitra
Acacia
FEMININE: Shita
Academy
FEMININE: Yeshiva
Account (to account for)
MASCULINE: Chashavya, Chashuv
Achievement
MASCULINE: Gemarya, Gemaryahu
Acquire
MASCULINE: Cain, Kenan, Konen, Zevina
Act, Actions See also Deed, Deeds
MASCULINE: *Basha,* Gemarya, Gemaryahu
FEMININE: Asya
Add See also Increase
MASCULINE: Yosef, Yosefus, Yosi, Yosiel, Yosifel, Yosifus, Yosifya, Yossi
FEMININE: Yosifa
Admiration
FEMININE: Ahada
Adorn, Adorned, Adornment See also Beautiful, Majestic
MASCULINE: Adaya, Adi, Adiel, Adin, Adna, Hadar, Hadur, Heder, Meudan, Meutar, Remalyahu
FEMININE: Ada, Adaya, Adena, Adi, Adie, Adiella, Adin, Atura, Edia, Ed-

na, Edya, Hadar, Hadara, Hadarit, Pe'era, Pe'er-Li, Yehoadan
Advise, Advisor
MASCULINE: Melitz, Ye'utz, Yoetz
Aftergrowth
MASCULINE: Lakish, Sefach
Agitate, Agitation See also Industrious
MASCULINE: Yaziz, Ziruz, Ziza
Agree, Agreeable
MASCULINE: Yishva, Yishvi
FEMININE: Ava
Air
MASCULINE: Avira
FEMININE: Avirit
Alabaster
MASCULINE: Bahat, Shisha, Sisa
FEMININE: Bahat
Alert
MASCULINE: Martizin, Meretz
FEMININE: Erana, Eranut
Alike See Comparable
Almond
MASCULINE: Etz-Shaked, Luz, Shaked
FEMININE: Luza, Shekeda, Shekediya
Alone
MASCULINE: Yachid
Alter See Change
Amaryllis
MASCULINE: Narkis
Ambassador
MASCULINE: Chashmon, Chashmonai
Anchor
MASCULINE: Agnon, Ogen
FEMININE: Aguna, Oganya, Ogenya
Ancient See also Old
MASCULINE: Alter, Kadmiel, Kedem, Kedma, Yeshisha
Angel
MASCULINE: Malach

FEMININE: Arela, Arella, Erela, Malach, Seraphina

Anger, Angry
MASCULINE: Achimaatz, Avimaatz, Evron, Hamam, Maatz, Otzem, Tzahuv
FEMININE: Evrona

Anklet
FEMININE: Achsa

Anointed
MASCULINE: Mashiach
FEMININE: Yiska

Another
MASCULINE: Acher

Answer
FEMININE: Eliana

Ant
MASCULINE: Nemalya, Nemuel, Nimli

Antelope
MASCULINE: Raam, Re'em
FEMININE: Karnei-Yael, Reuma

Anxious
MASCULINE: Doeg

Apostate
MASCULINE: Meshovav, Shovav

Appearance
FEMININE: Afna, Mofaat, Ofna

Apple
MASCULINE: Bivai
FEMININE: Tapuach, Tapucha

Appointed See also Chosen
FEMININE: Noada, Noadya

Appropriate
MASCULINE: Yeshavya, Yoshavya

Arena
FEMININE: Zira

Arise See also Establish, Resurrect
MASCULINE: Kemuel, Kimum, Yakim, Yekamam, Yekamya

Armor
MASCULINE: Shiryon, Siriya, Siriyon

Army See also Troops, Warriors
MASCULINE: Meron
FEMININE: Chila

Artisan See also Craftsman
MASCULINE: Oholiav

Ascend See also Increase
MASCULINE: Eli, Yaal, Yala
FEMININE: Alita, Aliya

Ask, Asked See Borrow

Aspiration See also Hope
FEMININE: She'ifa

Ass See Donkey

Assemble, Assembly
MASCULINE: Amiasaf, Kehat, Kohelet, Moadya, Noad, Noadya

Assessment, Assessor
MASCULINE: Shuma

Assistance
MASCULINE: Gamliel

Association See also Circle
MASCULINE: Chever, Chevron, Chug, Chugi

Atmosphere
MASCULINE: Aviva

Attractive See also Beautiful
MASCULINE: Maksim

Atonement
MASCULINE: Kapara

Author See also Scribe
MASCULINE: Safra, Sofer

Autumn
MASCULINE: Setav
FEMININE: Setav

Awake
MASCULINE: Eran, Er, Shaked, Tirya
FEMININE: Tiri

Awe See also Fear
FEMININE: Yirat

Badger (Animal)
MASCULINE: Shafan, Tachash, Yishpan

Bald
MASCULINE: Karcha, Kareach, Korach

Ball
MASCULINE: Kadur, Kaduri

Balm, Balsam
MASCULINE: Tzeri
FEMININE: Tzeruya

Banner
MASCULINE: Dagul, Degel, Diglai

Barren
MASCULINE: Eker, Ekron, Shefi, Shefo, Yishpa

Basket
MASCULINE: Keluv, Keluvai, Salai, Sali, Salu, Teneh

Beach
FEMININE: Shunit

Beam
MASCULINE: Ov

Bear
MASCULINE: Ber, Beryl, Dov, Dubi
FEMININE: Dova, Doveva, Dovit, Duba, Duvit

Beautiful, Beauty See also Delightful
MASCULINE: Adin, Hadar, Kalil, Melabev, Naeh, Naom, Naveh, Nechmad, Ne'edar, Noi, Pe'er, Per, Raanan, Shafer, Shapir, Shapira, Shefer, Shifron, Yafe, Yafim, Yefet
FEMININE: Baile, Bayle, Bela, Hadura, Na'a, Naama, Naamana, Naami, Naamiya, Nava, Nehedara, Nehederet, Nofiya, Noya, Ranana, Shayna,

Shayndel, Vashti, Ya'a, Yafa, Yafit, Yefeifiya

Bee
FEMININE: Davrat, Devora, Devoranit, Devorit, Dushe, Dvoshke

Behold See also Look
MASCULINE: Navot, Nevat, Nevayot
FEMININE: Reuel, Reuvena

Belief, Believe See also Faithful
MASCULINE: Yaamin
FEMININE: Emuna

Beloved See also Love, Friend
MASCULINE: Ahuv, Ahuvam, Ahuvya, Bildad, Chaviv, Chavivam, Chavivel, Chavivi, Chavivya, Chovav, Chuba, David, Dekel, Didi, Dodi, Dodo, Eldad, Nilbav, Ohad, Ohed, Yadid, Yakar, Yakir, Yedid, Yedidya, Yido
FEMININE: Ahava, Ahuda, Ahuva, Ahuvya, Amita, Chaviva, Chavuka, Davida, Doda, Dod, Lieba, Yedida

Beseech
MASCULINE: Pelalya

Bestow
MASCULINE: Yehozavad, Zevadya, Zevadyahu

Betroth, Betrothal
FEMININE: Arusa

Bible
FEMININE: Tora

Big See also Great
MASCULINE: Gadol, Gedalya, Gidel

Bind See Tie
MASCULINE: Asir, Ater, Isur, Rotam
FEMININE: Retem, Rifka, Rifke, Ritma, Rivka, Rotem, Shelavya

Bird, Birdlike
MASCULINE: Aya, Deror, Derori, Dror, Efron, Gozal, Paruach, Shachaf, Tavas, Tzipor, Yarkon, Zamir
FEMININE: Aya, Chagla, Daya, Efrona, Faiga, Feigel, Gozala, Kanarit, Salit, Senunit, Silit, Tzifriya, Tzipeh, Tzipora, Tzipori, Tziporit, Tzofit

Birthplace See Homeland

Bitter
MASCULINE: Merari, Meraya
FEMININE: Mara, Marata, Marati, Meri, Mira, Miri, Miril, Mirit, Miryam, Moryat

Black
MASCULINE: Achumai, Ashchur, Cham, Chumi, Guni, Kush, Pinchas, Shachor, Tziltai
FEMININE: Shechora

Blemish
MASCULINE: Dofi

Blessed, Blessing See also Chosen, Fortune
MASCULINE: Anshel, Anshil, Asher, Barachel, Baruch, Bechiel, Ben-Baruch, Bendit, Benesh, Beracha, Berachya, Berechya, Berechyahu, Beruchiel, Bruchel, Mevorach, Selig, Yeverechya, Yeverechyahu, Yevorach, Zelig
FEMININE: Ashera, Asherit, Ashra, Ashrat, Ashria, Beracha, Berucha, Beruchiya, Beruchya, Mevorechet

Blonde See also Yellow, Gold
MASCULINE: Zahavi, Zahuv
FEMININE: Zehuva

Blossom See also Bud, Flower, Fruitful
MASCULINE: Pekach, Peachya, Tzemach
FEMININE: Perach, Pericha, Pircha, Pirchit, Pirchiya, Porachat

Blue
FEMININE: Techula

Boat
MASCULINE: Sira
FEMININE: Aniya

Bold See also Courageous, Strong
MASCULINE: Noaz
FEMININE: Noaza

Bone See also Skeleton
FEMININE: Idra

Border See Boundry

Born
MASCULINE: Achilud

Borrow, Borrowed See also Asked
MASCULINE: Metushael, Mishael, Shaul, Shealtiel
FEMININE: Shaula, Shaulit

Bottle
MASCULINE: Bakbuk, Bakbukiya, Bakbukya, Buki

Bound See also Tied
MASCULINE: Anuv, Asir

Boundary
MASCULINE: Efes, Galil, Galili
FEMININE: Galila, Gelila, Gelilya, Milet

Bow
MASCULINE: Kashti, Kish, Kishoni
FEMININE: Keshet

Boy See also Youth, Lad
MASCULINE: Bachur, Naarai, Naari, Naarya

Branch
MASCULINE: Choter, Netzer, Sarig, Tzemach
FEMININE: Anefa, Anufa, Zemora

Brave
MASCULINE: Kalev

Breach
MASCULINE: Shever
Bread See also Food
MASCULINE: Lachma, Lachmi, Lechem, Zemel
FEMININE: Bet-Lechem
Break See also Breach
MASCULINE: Peresh, Peretz
Breath, Breathing
MASCULINE: Hevel, Nafish
FEMININE: She'ifa
Bribe
MASCULINE: Shalmai, Shalmon
Bridge
MASCULINE: Geshur
Bright, Brightness See also Brilliance, Shine
MASCULINE: Avner, Bahir, Barak, Bazak, Bezek, Feibush, Feivel, Meir, Meiri, Noga, Zahir, Zahur, Zerach, Zerachya, Ziv, Zivan, Zivi
FEMININE: Behira, Dana, Meira, Noga, Ora, Tzelila, Tzelili, Zaka, Zakit, Zakiya, Ziva, Zivanit, Zivi, Zivit
Brilliance See also Bright, Shine, Shining
MASCULINE: Ziv, Zivi, Zohar
FEMININE: Ziva, Zivi, Zivit, Zohar, Zohara, Zoheret
Bristles
MASCULINE: Zifa
FEMININE: Semira
Bronze
MASCULINE: Ard, Ardi, Arod, Arodi
FEMININE: Arda, Ardona, Aruda, Nechushta
Brook See also Stream
MASCULINE: Arnon
FEMININE: Arnona, Nadyan
Broom
MASCULINE: Rotem
Brother, Brotherhood
MASCULINE: Ach, Acha, Achai, Achav, Achban, Achi, Achiam, Achiasaf, Achiav, Achida, Achidan, Achidod, Achiem, Achiezer, Achiezev, Achihud, Achikar, Achilud, Achiman, Achimoto, Achina, Achinadav, Achiner, Achinoam, Achipelet, Achira, Achivam, Achisamach, Achisar, Achishachar, Achishai, Achishalom, Achisar, Achishur, Achitov, Achituv, Achiya, Achiyahu, Achli, Achva, Achyan, Achyo, Echud, Eichi, Yechiach, Yoach
Brown
FEMININE: Breindel, Breine, Brina, Brine, Brune

Bud See also Blossom, Flower, Plant
MASCULINE: Givol, Nitzan, Peka
FEMININE: Givola, Nitza, Nitzana, Nitzanit, Nitzaniya, Semadar
Build, Builder
MASCULINE: Bani, Benaya, Benayahu, Buni, Yavnel, Yavniel, Yivneya
FEMININE: Bona, Yavn'ela
Bundle See Sheaf
Burden, Burdened
MASCULINE: Amali, Amasya, Amel, Amos, Masa, Ula
FEMININE: Teruda
Burn, Burned
MASCULINE: Gacham
FEMININE: Baara, Ketura
Burst See also Breach, Break
MASCULINE: Peretz
Bush
MASCULINE: Eshchad, Sneh
FEMININE: Luza
Buttercup
FEMININE: Nurit
Butterfly
MASCULINE: Parpar
Buy
MASCULINE: Elkan, Elkana, Elki

Cactus
MASCULINE: Sabra, Tsabar, Tzabar
FEMININE: Sabariya, Sabra, Savrina, Tzabara, Tzabariya, Tzabrina
Cage See Basket
Call
MASCULINE: Korei
Calcium
FEMININE: Sidona
Calloused
MASCULINE: Geshan
Calm See Peace, Rest
Camel
MASCULINE: Becher, Gamal, Gamla
Canal
MASCULINE: Peleg
Canary
FEMININE: Kanara, Kanarit
Candelabrum See also Light
FEMININE: Menora
Canopy
MASCULINE: Chupa, Shafrir
FEMININE: Shafrira
Cape See also Garment
FEMININE: Aderet
Capital
FEMININE: Bira, Biranit, Biriya
Captivity
MASCULINE: Shevaya

Caress
MASCULINE: Latif
FEMININE: Letifa

Carnation
FEMININE: Tziporen

Cassia
FEMININE: Ketzia, Kida

Castle See also Palace
MASCULINE: Armon, Armoni, Devir
FEMININE: Armona, Armonit

Casualty
MASCULINE: Nefeg

Catch
MASCULINE: Chatifa

Cautious
MASCULINE: Zahir
FEMININE: Zehira

Cease
MASCULINE: Chadlai

Cedar
MASCULINE: Arza, Arzi, Beros, Erez, Erez-Yisrael, Oren
FEMININE: Ariza, Arna, Arza, Arzit, Berosa, Orna, Ornat, Orni, Orninit, Ornit

Celebration See Rejoice

Chance See also Lot
MASCULINE: Goral

Change
MASCULINE: Chalafta, Chalfan, Chalfon, Chalifa, Shoni, Tachkemoni, Tachlifa, Yamir

Chant See Sing

Characteristic
FEMININE: Techuna

Charity
MASCULINE: Getz, Getzel, Tzidkiya
FEMININE: Tzedaka

Chest
MASCULINE: Aran, Aron

Chief See also Leader
MASCULINE: Katzin

Child See also Boy and Girl
MASCULINE: Chur, Churai, Churi

Choice, Chosen See also Excellent, Select
MASCULINE: Adif, Bechiel, Bocher, Mivchar, Nivchar, Yivchar
FEMININE: Bara, Bechira, Bechura, Migda, Migdana, Mishbacha, Mishbachat, Nivchara, Nivcheret, Yivchar, Zimra, Zimrat, Zimriya

Chrysanthemum
FEMININE: Chartzit

Circle
MASCULINE: Chug, Chugi, Dur, Gozan, Zeira, Zera

Circumcision
MASCULINE: Nemalya, Nemuel, Nimli

Citizen
MASCULINE: Ezrach, Ezrachi

Citron
FEMININE: Etroga

City
MASCULINE: Ir

Clapper (of a bell)
FEMININE: Inbal

Clean, Cleanse See also Pure
MASCULINE: Misham, Zakai
FEMININE: Berura, Beruriya, *Raina, Rayna, Reine, Reyna*

Clear See also Clean, Pure
MASCULINE: Barur, Mevorar, Tzalil, Tzalul
FEMININE: Berura, Berurit, Beruriya, Berurya, Tzelila

Clever See also Crafty
MASCULINE: Cheilev, Chelbo, Chelev

Clod (of earth)
MASCULINE: Regev

Close
MASCULINE: Ater
FEMININE: Neila, Segura

Cloud See Vapor

Cluster (of grapes)
MASCULINE: Eshkol
FEMININE: Eshkola

Coal
FEMININE: Rishpa, Rishpona, Ritzpa

Coast
MASCULINE: Chupam
FEMININE: Riva

Coat See also Covering, Garment
FEMININE: Adra

Coin
MASCULINE: Zara
FEMININE: Dinar

Cold
MASCULINE: Bered

Collector (of proverbs)
MASCULINE: Kehat, Kohelet

Collector (of taxes)
MASCULINE: Gabai

Color, Colorful
MASCULINE: Guni
FEMININE: Sasgona, Sasgonit

Combat See also War, Warrior
MASCULINE: Gera

Comet
MASCULINE: Shavit

Comfort, Comforter See also Consolation
MASCULINE: Latif, *Manin, Mann, Mannes,* Menachem, Menachem-Tziyon,

Menachem-Mendel, Nachman, Nachmani, Nachmiel, Nachum, Nechemya, Nechum, Nechunya, Nocham, Nocheim, Nochem, Tanchum, Tanchuma, Yerucham

FEMININE: Nachmanit, Nachmaniya, Menachema, Menachemya, *Necha,* Nechama, *Neche,* Ruchama

Command, Commandments
MASCULINE: Elitzav

Commit, Committed
MASCULINE: Aduk
FEMININE: Aduka

Companion See also Friend
MASCULINE: Iti, Itai, Itiel

Comparable, Compare
MASCULINE: Micha, Michael
FEMININE: Michal

Compassion, Compassionate See also Comfort, Consolation, Grace, Mercy
MASCULINE: Chanan, Chanani, Chananya, Chanaton, Chaniel, Chanin, Chanina, Chaninon, Chanita, Chanun, Racham, Rachaman, Rachamim, Rachim, Rachmiel, Rachum, Rechum, Rechumei, Rechumi, Yachon, Yerucham
FEMININE: Rachmona, Ruchama, Yeruchama

Complain
MASCULINE: Yalon, Yalun

Complet, Completion See also Peace
MASCULINE: Gomer, Meshulam, Shalman, Shalum, Tam
FEMININE: Gimra, Gomer, Meshulemet

Conceal, Concealed
MASCULINE: Alemet

Conduit
MASCULINE: Silon
FEMININE: Silona, Silonit

Confidence
FEMININE: Bitcha

Congeal
MASCULINE: Gamad, Gamada, Gamda

Consecrated See also Dedicated, Sacred
MASCULINE: Charim, Chermon, Chermoni

Consolation See also Comfort
MASCULINE: Nacham, Nechemya, Nocham, Tanchum
FEMININE: Nachmaniya, Nachmant, Nachmi, Nechami, Nehama, *Trestel*

Constellation, Heavenly
MASCULINE: Ashvat

Contempt
MASCULINE: Buz, Buzi

Contention See also Strife, War
MASCULINE: Medan, Midian, Rivai, Yehoyariv, Yeravam
FEMININE: Tigra

Cony (animal)
MASCULINE: Shafan

Coral
MASCULINE: Almog
FEMININE: Almoga

Corn See also Grain
FEMININE: Shachat

Correspondence
MASCULINE: Agron

Couch
FEMININE: Sapa

Counsel, Counselor
MASCULINE: Pele-Yoetz, Tachkemoni, Ye'utz, Yoetz
FEMININE: Tushiya

Count See also Reckon, Time
MASCULINE: Idan, Iddo, Ido

Country See also Land
MASCULINE: Artzi
FEMININE: Artzit, Eretz, Medina

Courage, Courageous See also Strong
MASCULINE: Abiri, Chutzpit, Noaz
FEMININE: Noaza, Odeda

Courteous See also Polite
MASCULINE: Adiv

Covenant
MASCULINE: Brit, Brit-El

Cover, Covering See also Canopy
FEMININE: Talal, Talila, Tal-Li, Telalit, Tzina

Craftsman
MASCULINE: Oholiav

Crafty See also Clever, Cunning
MASCULINE: Chelbo, Naftali

Create, Creation, Creative See also Establish, Fashion
MASCULINE: Asael, Asaya, Assi, Asiel, Elasa, Maaseiya, Maaseiyahu, Yaasai, Yaasiel

Creep
FEMININE: Chulda

Crimson
MASCULINE: Shani
FEMININE: Karmil

Crippled See Lame

Crocus
MASCULINE: Chavatzinya

Crown, Crowned See also Decorated, Royalty, Wreath
MASCULINE: Atir, Atur, Eter, Kalil, Kasriel, Katriel, Keter, Kitron, Meutar, Taga, Tzeri, Zeira, Zer
FEMININE: Atara, Ateret, Atura, Kelila,

Kelula, Kitra, Kitron, *Kreindel, Krei-
ne*, Livya, Taga, Tzefira
Cruel
MASCULINE: Tarfon
Cry, Cry Out *See also* Lament
MASCULINE: Yovav, Tzahal
FEMININE: Pua, Puah, She'aga
Culture, Cultured *See also* Educated,
Enlightened
MASCULINE: Meir, Naor, Neorai
Cup
FEMININE: Makeda
Cure
FEMININE: Segula, Sigalit, Sigla, Sigliya
Curse
MASCULINE: Kalai
Cut, Cut Off
MASCULINE: Bavai, Gidon, Gidoni
FEMININE: Gitit, Giza, Kesarit
Cute *See* Precious
Cylinder *See* Circle
MASCULINE: Galil, Galili
FEMININE: Galila
Cypress *See also* Tree
MASCULINE: Bros
FEMININE: Tirza

Daffodil
FEMININE: Irit
Dainty *See* Delicate
Dance
FEMININE: Mechola, Rikuda
Daring *See* Bold
Dark, Darkened, Darkness
MASCULINE: Adar, Ard, Chachaliah,
Chachalya, Chachila, Chumi, Efa,
Efah, Eifa, Eifai, Kedar, Kush, Pin-
chas, Pinhas, Tzalmon
FEMININE: Adara, Chachila, Efa, Ha-
chila, Laila, Leili
Date, Date Tree
MASCULINE: Dekel
FEMININE: Dikla
Daughter
MASCULINE: Betuel
FEMININE: *Bashe,* Basya, Bat, Bat-Ami,
Bat-Chen, Bat-El, Batela, Bat-Eli,
Bat-Galim, Bat-Shachar, Bat-Shem,
Bat-Sheva, Bat-Shir, Bat-Shua, Bat-
Tziyon, Batya, Bat-Yam, Bet, Betuel,
Betuiel, Biya, Reuvat
Dawn *See also* Morning
MASCULINE: Achishachar, Avishachar,
Ben-Shachar, Shachar, Shecharya,
Shacharayim
FEMININE: Shachar, Shacharit, Shacha-
rita, Shachariya

Day
MASCULINE: Yemuel
Dear (beloved)
MASCULINE: Chaviv, Yakar, Yakir
FEMININE: Chaviva, Tziporet
Death
MASCULINE: Achimot
Deceit
MASCULINE: Mirma
Decorated
MASCULINE: Me'udan, Me'utar
Dedicate, Dedicated, Dedication
MASCULINE: Chanoch, Chanuka
FEMININE: Chanuka
Deed, Deeds *See also* Act, Actions
MASCULINE: Amasa, Maaseiya
Deep
MASCULINE: Amok
Deer *See also* Gazelle, Hart
MASCULINE: Ayal, Ayalon, Ben-Tzvi,
Efer, Efron, *Hersh, Hershel,* Hertzl,
Herz, Hirsh, Hirshel, Ofar, Ofer,
Ofra, Ofri, Ophri, Tzevi, Tzeviel
FEMININE: Afra, Aphra, Ayala, Ayelet,
Hertzela, Hertzliya, *Hinda, Hinde,
Hindel,* Ofra, Re'ema, Tzivya
Defend, Defender *See also* Protection,
Protector
MASCULINE: Gonen
Delicacy, Delicate
MASCULINE: Mishmana
FEMININE: Adina, Anuga, Eidel, Matama
Delight, Delightful *See also* Beautiful,
Desire, Joy, Pleasure
MASCULINE: Aden, Adna, Adni, Avi-
noam, Cheiletz, Cheletz, Eden, Ei-
den, Maadai, Maadiya, Naeh, Noam
FEMININE: Adina, Naa, Naama
Deliverance *See also* Salvation
MASCULINE: Achipelet, Elifelet
Den
FEMININE: Chamital, Chamutal
Depart
MASCULINE: Uzal
Dependable *See also* Honest, Upright
MASCULINE: Avishur
Depraved *See* Foolish
Depth
MASCULINE: Shucha
Descend, Descendant
MASCULINE: Nachat, Yarden, Yarden-
Li, Yared, Yered
FEMININE: Tzelila, Tzelilit, Yardena,
Yardeniya
Desire, Desirable *See also* Beautiful,
Precious, Will
MASCULINE: Chamadel, Chamadya,

Chamdiel, Chamud, Chefetz, Chei-
fetz, Chemdad, Chemdan, Chemdi-
ya, Chemed, Evi, Nechman, Ratzon,
Yetzer, Yitzri
FEMININE: Ava, Chamuda, Cheftzi,
Cheftzi-Ba, Cheftziya, Chemda, Nir-
tza
Despise
MASCULINE: Bavi
Destroy, Destroyer
MASCULINE: Amishoa, Balak, Yishma
Destruction
MASCULINE: Avdima, Avdimei, Avdimi
Destructive
MASCULINE: Ido
Dew See also Rain, Sustenance
MASCULINE: Avital, Avtalyon, Lital, Or-
tal, Or-Tal, Raviv, Tal, Tali, Tal-Or,
Talor, Tal-Shachar
FEMININE: Avital, Avtalya, Chamital,
Chamutal, Meital, Ravital, Revital,
Reviva, Tal, Tali, Talal, Talila, Tal-
Or, Tal-Ora, Talya
Diamond
MASCULINE: Yahalom
FEMININE: Yahaloma, Yahalamit
Dig
MASCULINE: Chefer, Cheifer, Koresh
FEMININE: Chulda
Diligent See also Industrious
MASCULINE: Charutz
Dirge
FEMININE: Alya, Elya, Ilya
Disappear
MASCULINE: Chalfon
Disaster
MASCULINE: Achitofel
Diseased
MASCULINE: Achlai
Display See Exhibit
FEMININE: Te'ura
Disrepute
MASCULINE: Ikavod
Distinguished See also Illustrious
MASCULINE: Chasuv
FEMININE: Chashiva, Chashuva
Distorted
MASCULINE: Akashya
Distress
MASCULINE: Baana
Disturb, Disturbed
MASCULINE: Achran
FEMININE: Tzara
Divide
MASCULINE: Perida, Peruda
Divine See also God, Godly
FEMININE: Milka

Diviner
MASCULINE: Nachshon
Doctor
MASCULINE: Ashi, Ashyan, Assi
Doe See also Deer
FEMININE: Ayala, Ayelet, *Hinda, Hindel,
Hindl*
Dog
MASCULINE: Kalev
Doll
FEMININE: Buba, Bubati
Donkey
MASCULINE: Chamor, Ira, Irad, Irai,
Iram, Iran, Iri, Iru
Dove See also Turtledove
MASCULINE: Tor, Yona
FEMININE: Avi-Yona, *Taube, Teibel, Tei-
vel, Toba, Toibe*, Yemima, Yona,
Yonat, Yonata, Yonati, Yonina, Yo-
nit, Yonita
Dowry See also Gift
MASCULINE: Mohar, Zavad, Zavdi, Zav-
diel, Zavud
FEMININE: Nadan
Draperies
FEMININE: Yeriot
Draw
MASCULINE: Meshech, Moshe
FEMININE: Dalit, Dalya
Dried Up, Dry
MASCULINE: Yavesh
Drip, Drop
FEMININE: Tafat, Zilpa
Driver
MASCULINE: Movil
Duck
MASCULINE: Barvaz
FEMININE: Idriya
Dwarf
MASCULINE: Gamad, Gamada
Dwell, Dwelling See also Abode
MASCULINE: Avgar, Dor, Dori, Dur,
Duriel, Gur, Maon, Yeshevav, Zevul,
Zevulun
FEMININE: Meona, Shafrira, Zevula

Ear See also Hearing
MASCULINE: Ozni
Earth See also Soil
MASCULINE: Adam, Admata, Artza, Re-
gev
FEMININE: Adama
East, Eastward
MASCULINE: Kadmiel, Kedem, Kedma
FEMININE: Kedma
Echo
MASCULINE: Hed, Hedi

FEMININE: Hedya

Educate, Educated, Educator See also Trained
MASCULINE: Chanoch, Chanuka, Maskil
FEMININE: Chanuka

Eight
FEMININE: Temanya

Elder, Eldest See also Old
MASCULINE: Bachir, Becher, Bechor, Bechorat, Bichri, Shneur
FEMININE: Bakura, Bechira, Bechora, Bikura, Keshisha

Elegy See also Dirge
FEMININE: Alya, Elya, Ilya

Embarrass See also White, Whiten
MASCULINE: Malbin

Ember See also Flame
FEMININE: Udya

Emblem See also Signs
MASCULINE: Degel, Nisan, Nisim

Embrace
MASCULINE: Chavakuk

Embroider, Embroidery See Weave, Weaving

Emerald
MASCULINE: Bareket
FEMININE: Bareket

Encampment See also Enclosure
FEMININE: Chaniya, Tira, Tiri

Enchant, Enchanter, Enchanting
MASCULINE: Maksim
FEMININE: Maksima

Enclosure See also Envelop, Fortress, Protection
MASCULINE: Betzer, Bitzaron, Chetzrai, Chetzron, Chupa, Chupam, Gedor, Gidron, Lotan
FEMININE: Afeka, Efrat, Gana, Ganit, Ganya

Endearing
MASCULINE: Melabev

Enemy
MASCULINE: Iyov

Energetic See also Industrious
MASCULINE: Martzin, Meretz
FEMININE: Erana, Eranut, Mirtza, Zariza, Zeriza

Engrave, Engraving
FEMININE: Churshit, Maskit, Maskiya

Enlighten, Enlightened See also Culture, Educated
MASCULINE: Maskil, Naor, Neora, Neorai

Envelop See also Enclosure
MASCULINE: Lotan

Equal
MASCULINE: Yoshavya

Era See also Time
MASCULINE: Idan

Erect See also Upright
MASCULINE: Dekel, Itamar, Zakuf

Escape See also Save, Saved
MASCULINE: Palti, Paltiel, Pelatya, Pelet, Piltai, Yaflel
FEMININE: Sarid

Establish, Established See also Create, Firm, Support
MASCULINE: Achikam, Adabel, Azrikam, Elayakim, Elyakum, Elika, Kananyahu, Kaneyu, Kayam, Kemuel, Kimum, Komem, Konanya, Yachin, Yakim, Yechanya, Yechanyahu, Yehoyachin, Yehoyakim, Yekamya, Yeriel, Yeriya, Yoyachin

Esteem, Esteemed See also Exalted
MASCULINE: Ne'edar

Eternal, Eternity
MASCULINE: Amiad, Avi-Ad, Aviad, Ben-Ad, Benad, Cheiled, Cheldai, Cheled, Elad, Elada, Eliad, Elam, Liad, Netziach, Nitzchi, Nitzchan
FEMININE: Nitzcha, Nitzchiya, Nitzchona

Evil
MASCULINE: Achira, Beria

Ewe
FEMININE: Rachel

Exalt, Exalted See also Lofty
MASCULINE: Achiram, Adar, Adonikam, Adoniram, Amiram, Atalya, Atlai, Chiram, Chirom, Gaon, Ila, Ne'edar, Ram, Rama, Rami, Ramya, Rom, Romem, Romi, Segev, Seguv, Yehoram, Yidgal, Yigdalyahu, Yirmeyahu, Yoram, Zevulun
FEMININE: Geona, Geonit, Ram, Rama, Rami, Ramit, Ramot, Roma, Romema, Romemit, Romemiya, Romit, Romiya

Excel, Excellence, Excellent
MASCULINE: Ben-Tziyon, Ilai, Magdiel, Meged, Mehader, Mehudar, Meshubach, Mishbach, Tziyon, Yitran, Yitro
FEMININE: Adifa, Degula, Idit, Ila, Ilit, Yehudit

Exchange
FEMININE: Limor, Limur

Exhibit See Display

Exile, Exiled
MASCULINE: Golyat, Yagli, Zerubavel
FEMININE: Galuta, Gerusha, Gola

Exist See also Live
MASCULINE: Yehu

Expanse
MASCULINE: Rechavam, Rechavia, She-
tach
FEMININE: Merchava, Merchavya
Explore
MASCULINE: Bidkar
Eyes
MASCULINE: Einan, Eini, Einon, Eli-Ei-
nai, Enon

Face
MASCULINE: Peniel, Penuel, Yefuneh
Faith, Faithful
MASCULINE: Amitai, Amitan, Amnon,
Heiman, Heman, Neeman, Omen
FEMININE: Amana, Amania, Emuna, Er-
ga, Imuna, Iris, Neemana, Neemenet
False, Falsehood
FEMININE: Kazbi
Fame, Famous See also Reputation
MASCULINE: Noda, Shevach
FEMININE: Degula
Farm, Farmer See also Field, Land
MASCULINE: Bustanai, Chaklai, Cho-
reish, Choresh, Shadmon, Yagev,
Yogev, Zoreia
FEMININE: Shadmit, Shedema
Fast See Quick
Fat
MASCULINE: Achlav, Cheilev, Chelbo,
Eval, Machlon
FEMININE: Machla
Father
MASCULINE: Aba, Abahu, Abaye, Ab-
ba-Yadan, *Aberlin,* Av, Avdan, Av-
gar, Avi, Aviad, Aviam, Aviasat, Avi-
az, Avichai, Avichen, Avida, Avidror,
Aviel, Avifelet, Avigal, Avigdor, Avi-
hu, Avihud, Avikam, Avikar, Avi-
maatz, Avimael, Avimelech, Avimi,
Avin, Avina, Avinadav, Avinaim, Avi-
natan, Aviner, Avinoam, Avior, Avi-
tal, Avituv, Avitzedek, Aviur, Aviya,
Aviyam, Avizemer, Avner, Avraham,
Avram, Avrom, *Avrum, Avrumel,
Avrumke,* Avtalyon, Avuha, Avuya,
Bremil, Eliav, *Fromel,* Liav, Papa,
Papai, Papos, Yechiav, Yeshevav,
Yoav
FEMININE: Avi, Avia, Avichayil, Avichen,
Aviel, Aviela, Avigayil, Aviem, Avi-
gal, Avigdora, Avirama, Avishag, Avi-
tal, Aviya, Avrahamit, Avramit, Avu-
ya
Fault See Blemish
Favor, Favored
MASCULINE: Meyuchas

Fear, Fearful
MASCULINE: Chatat, Sered
Feel, Feelings
MASCULINE: Chusha, Chushai, Chu-
sham, Chushiam, Chushiel, Chu-
shim, Mushi
FEMININE: Chushim, Mushit
Festival, Festive
MASCULINE: Chagai, Chagi, Chagiga
FEMININE: Chagiga, Chagit, Chagiya
Field See Plough
Fig
MASCULINE: Divlayim
FEMININE: Divla, Divlata, *Feige,* Idra,
Te'ena
Fight See also Contend
MASCULINE: Yisrael
Fin
MASCULINE: Snapir
Fire See also Flame
MASCULINE: Ashbel, Aviur, Esh, *Feivel,*
Lahav, Nur, Nuri, Nuriya, Nuriel,
Shraga, Ud, Udi, Udiel, Yoshiya,
Yoshiyahu
FEMININE: Uriela, Urit
Firm
MASCULINE: Sharar
First, First-born
MASCULINE: Becher, Bechor, Rishon,
Yiftach
FEMININE: Rishona
Fish See also Fruitful
MASCULINE: Dag, *Fishel, Fishke, Fish-
kin, Fishlin*
Fit See also Proper, Suited
MASCULINE: Naot
Flame See also Fire, Light, Torch
MASCULINE: Gacham, Lahav, Lapid,
Lapidos, Reshef, Shedeur, Ur, Uri,
Uriel, Uriya, Uriyahu
FEMININE: Avuka, Shalhevet, Uriela,
Urit
Flee
MASCULINE: Bariach
FEMININE: Orpa
Flight, Fly, Fly Away
MASCULINE: Paruach
FEMININE: Afa, Aya, Mifracha, Mifra-
chat, Mufrachat
Flint
MASCULINE: Shamir
Flock
MASCULINE: Eder, Edri, Maron
FEMININE: Eder
Floor
FEMININE: Ritzpa

Flour
MASCULINE: Kimchi
Flow, Flowing
MASCULINE: Deror, Derori, Dror, Drori, Tzif, Tzuf
Flower See also Blossom, Bud, Plant
MASCULINE: Admon, Mifrach, Nitzan, Parchi, Perach, Perachya, Pirchai, Savyon, Segel, Shoshan, Shushan, Yasmin
FEMININE: *Bluma, Blume,* Chamaniya, Chavatzelet, Chelmit, Chelmonit, Demumit, Devoranit, Gevionit, Kalanit, Nirit, Nurit, Nurita, Odem, Ofrit, Perach, Pericha, Pircha, Pirchit, Pirchiya, Setavanit, Setavit, Shoshana, Tifracha, Tifrachat, Tzemecha, Tzemicha, Tziporen, *Yachne,* Yasmin, Yasmina
Flourescent
FEMININE: Negiha
Flute
MASCULINE: Chalil
Foam
FEMININE: Aphrodit
Fodder
MASCULINE: Irit
Folly
MASCULINE: Achitofel
Food See also Bread, Grain
MASCULINE: Shever
FEMININE: Bet-Lechem, Matama
Foolish
MASCULINE: Naval
FEMININE: Chel'a
Forest
MASCULINE: Yaar, Yaari, Yara
FEMININE: Yaara, Yaarit
Forever See also Eternal
Forget, Forgetful
MASCULINE: Menashe, Menashi, Menashya
Forgive, Forgiving
FEMININE: Salcha, Salchan
Format
FEMININE: Matkonet
Forsaken
MASCULINE: Almon, Menashe
FEMININE: Almana, Azuva, Hagar, Yisma
Fortress See also Enclosure
MASCULINE: Bira, Biranit, Biriyah, Chamat, Cheilon, Maon
Fortunate, Fortune See also Happy, Luck
MASCULINE: Adna, *Anshel, Anshil,* Asher, Ashri, Gad, Gadi, Gadiel,

Maimon, Mashel, Mazal-Tov, Meushar, Osher, Oshri, Yimna
FEMININE: Ashera, Asherit, Ashrat, Ashriya, Gadiel, Gadiela, Gadit, Meusheret, Oshrat, Ushara, Usheret, Ushriya
Foundation
MASCULINE: Eshed, Sheresh
FEMININE: Masada, Metzada
Fountain See Spring, Water
Four, Fourth
MASCULINE: Arba, Raviya, Reva
Fox
MASCULINE: Shual
FEMININE: Shuala
Fragrance, Fragrant See also Incense
MASCULINE: Bosem
FEMININE: Ketziya
Frame
FEMININE: Maanit, Shekufa
Fraternal, Fraternity See also Brotherhood
MASCULINE: Achyan
Free, Freedom
MASCULINE: Admata, Amidror, Avidror, Cherut, Chofesh, Dror, Drori, Dror-Li, Lidror, Magen Deror, Mesha, Ramya, Rechavam, Rechavya
FEMININE: Chafshiya, Cherut, Cheruta, Chufshit, Derora, Deroria, Derorit, Dror, Li-Dror, Sera, Serach
Fresh
MASCULINE: Raanan
FEMININE: Raanana, Teriya
Friend, Friendly, Friendship See also Beloved, Companion
MASCULINE: Aluf, Alvan, Amit, Amitai, Amitan, Amiti, Chovav, Chovev, David, Dodi, Edad, Elidad, Itai, Iti, Itie'i, Latif, Medad, Raya, Regem, Rei'a, Rei'i, Reuel, Yadid, Yedid, Yedidya
FEMININE: Achava, Amit, Amita, Rut
Fruit, Fruitful
MASCULINE: Bar-Ilan, Efraim, *Fishel, Fishke, Fishkin, Fishlin, Fravim, Froikin, Froyim,* Periel, Porat, Poriel, Periel, Pura
FEMININE: Peri, Pora, Porachat, Porat, Poriel, Poriya, Tenuva
Fugitive
MASCULINE: Achipelet
Full, Fullness See Abundance
Furrow See also Plough, Plow
MASCULINE: Bartholomew, Nir, Nirel, Niriel, Niriya, Talmai, Talmi, Telem
FEMININE: Nira, Nirel, Talma
Fury See Anger

Future, Future Time
MASCULINE: Ataya, Atid
FEMININE: Atida

Galley
MASCULINE: Eshban
Garden, Gardener See also Farm, Farmer
MASCULINE: Bustan, Bustanai, Gan, Gani, Gina, Ginat, Gintoi, Ginton
FEMININE: Gana, Ganit, Ganya, Gina, Ginat, Yardeniya
Garment See also Weave, Weaver
MASCULINE: Ben-Chur, Salma, Salmai, Salmon, Samla, Samlai, Shet, Simla
FEMININE: Salma
Gate
MASCULINE: Baba, Bava, Shaarya, Shearya
FEMININE: Bava
Gather See also Ingathering
MASCULINE: Amiasaf, Asaf, Aviasaf, Evyasaf
Gazelle See also Deer
MASCULINE: Eilat, Elat
FEMININE: Eilat
Generation
MASCULINE: Amidor, Avidor, Dor, Dori
FEMININE: Dor, Dorit, Dorya
Generous
MASCULINE: Nadav, Nadiv, Nedavya
FEMININE: Nedavya, Nediva
Gentle See also Gracious, Kind
MASCULINE: Adin, Adiv
FEMININE: Adina, Adiva, *Eidel*
Gift, Giving
MASCULINE: Achiman, Achishai, Amishai, Amizavad, Avinatan, Avisha, Avishai, Doran, Doron, Doroni, Dosetai, Elinatan, Elnatan, Elzavad, Imishai, Matan, Matanya, Mati, Matityah, Matityahu, Matnai, Natan, Nataniel, Netana, Netanel, Netanela, Netaniel, Netaniela, Netanya, Netina, Shai, Teruma, Tesher, Tshura, Yatniel, Yehonatan, Yahav, Yatniel, Yishai, Yonaton, Zavda, Zavdi, Zavdiel, Zavud, Zevid, Zevida
FEMININE: Darona, Daronit, Dorona, Doronit, Matana, Matat, Matnat, Migda, Migdana, Mincha, Natanya, Netana, Netanela, Netaniela, Netanya, Netina, Teruma, Teshura, Yehava, Zevida, Zevuda
Girl See also Maiden
FEMININE: Alma, Aluma, Bethula, Betula, Naara, Riva, Rivi, Tzeira

Gleaners, Gleaning
MASCULINE: Nemesh, Nimshi
Gloomy
MASCULINE: Chachalya
Glorified, Glorious, Glory See also Esteemed, Exalted, Honor
MASCULINE: Amihod, Amihud, Hadar, Hod, Hodiya, Ish-Hod, Nedar, Ne'edar, Nehedar, Pe'er, Per, Segev, Yafia, Zeviel, Zevieli
FEMININE: Adra, Tifara, Tiferet, Yocheved
Glow Worm
FEMININE: Gachalilit
Goat
MASCULINE: Afanya, Afra, Afri, Efer, Efron, Gad, Gadi, Gadiel, Ofer, Ofra, Ofri, Seya, Terach, Tzofar, Yaala, Yala, Zimri
FEMININE: Gadya, Yaala, Yaalat, Yaalat-Chen, Yaalit, Yael, Yaela, Ye'ela, Ye'elit
God, Godlike
MASCULINE: Achazya, Achazyahu, Achihud, Achiya, Adabel, Adael, Adayan, Adiel, Adlai, Adon, Adonikam, Adoniram, Adoniya, Adoram, Adriel, Ahuvya, Amarya, Amaryah, Amasya, Amatzya, Amdiel, Amishadai, Arel, Areli, Ariel, Arik, Asael, Asarel, Asaya, Atalya, Avdel, Avdiel, Aviel, Aviezer, Avishai, Aviya, Avriel, Avuya, Asanya, Azarya, Azazyahu, Aziel, Azriel, Bechiel, Berachya, Berechya, Betuel, Elad, Elada, Elasa, Eldad, Eliata, Eliel, Eliya, Eliyahu, Elihu, Elishua, Elpaal, Erel, Etel, Gamliel, Imanuel, Itai, Itiel, Lael, Lemuel, Micha, Michael, Seriel, Yechiel, Yoel
FEMININE: Bat El, Betuel, Eliya, Gamliela, Gamlielit, Imanuela, Michaela, Michal, Shechina, Yoela
Gold, Golden
MASCULINE: Elifaz, Mei-Zahav, Nemesh, Nimshi, Ofar, Ofir, Paz, Pazi, Upaz, Zahav, Zahavi, Zehavi
FEMININE: *Golda*, Ofira, Paz, Paza, Pazit, Paziya, Pazya, Tzehuva, Zehava, Zehavit, Zehuva, Zehuvit, *Zlate*
Good, Goodness See also Blessed, Righteous
MASCULINE: Achitov, Achituv, Amituv, Avituv, Bechiel, Benesh, Ben-Tov, Ben-Tovim, *Bonesh, Bunim*, Elituv, Evyatar, *Gutkind, Gutman*, Ish-Tov, Litov, Magdiel, Meged, Metav, Metiv, Tabai, Tavi, Tiv, Tivon, Tov, Tovat,

Tovi, Toviel, Tovim, Toviya, Tovishi-lem, Tov-Shilem, Tuvi, Tuviya, Tuvi-yahu, Yatva
FEMININE: *Gita, Gite, Gitel, Gitil, Guta, Gute, Gutel,* Shapira, Tiva, *Toibe,* Tova, Tovat, Tovit, Tuvit, Yatva, Yatvat, Yatvata

Good-natured
MASCULINE: Nilbav

Good Tidings
MASCULINE: Mevaser

Goose, Gosling
MASCULINE: Gozal

Grace, Graceful, Gracious See also Compassionate
MASCULINE: Adiv, Amichen, Avichen, Ben-Chanan, Ben-Chen, Chanamel, Chana, Chanan, Chananel, Chanani, Chaniel, Chanina, Chanun, Chanan-ya, Chasdiel, Chen, Chen-Melech, Chinan, Chisda, Chonen, Choni, Chonyo, Elchanan, Elnadav, Yeho-chanan, Yehonadav, Yochanan, Yo-nadav
FEMININE: Adiva, Chana, Chanina, Cha-nita, Chanuna, Chanya, Chen, Chen-ya, China, Doveva, Dovevet, *Gera-tzia, Hene,* Salchan, Yochana

Grain See also Food, Wheat
MASCULINE: Dagan, Kelaya, Shevar
FEMININE: Chita, Degana, Deganit, De-ganya, Kama, Shibolet

Granery
FEMININE: Garna, Garnit

Grandfather
MASCULINE: Aviav, Avimi, Saba, Zeide

Grandmother
FEMININE: Aviem, *Bobbe, Bubbe,* Savta

Grandson
MASCULINE: Nin

Grape, Grape Presser See also Vine, Wine
MASCULINE: Anav, Anavi, Eshkol, Gitai, Giti
FEMININE: Anava, Eshkola

Grapefruit
FEMININE: Eshkolit

Grass
MASCULINE: Dashe, Rotem

Great, Greatness
MASCULINE: Atalya, Evyatar, Gadol, Gedalya, Gedalyahu, Gedil, Gedula, Gidel, Michael
FEMININE: Gedula, Rachav

Green See also Luxuriant
MASCULINE: Yarkon
FEMININE: Yarkona

Greetings See also Tidings
FEMININE: Besora, Besura

Groundkeeper
FEMININE: Chetzrona

Grove
MASCULINE: Eshel, Pardes

Grow, Growth See also Sprout
MASCULINE: Atlai, Miklot, Rotem, Tze-mach, Yanuv, Yifrach, Yifracham, Yigdal, Yitzmach
FEMININE: Atalya, Atlit, Tzemicha

Guard, Guardian See also Protector
MASCULINE: Eri, Mishmar, Natron, Nat-ronai, Nitron, Noter, Notzar, No-tzer, Shemaram, Shemarya, Shemer, Shimrai, Shimrat, Shimri, Shimron, Shitrai, Shmaram, Shmarya, Shomer, Shoter, Tzefi, Tzefo
FEMININE: Mishmeret, Nitzra, Notera, Noteret, Notzeret, Samara, Sham-ira, Shimra, Shimrat, Shimrit, Shim-riya, Shomera, Shomrit, Shomriya, Shomrona, Tzofi, Tzofit, Tzofiya

Gully
MASCULINE: Eshban

Habitation
MASCULINE: Eldar

Hail
MASCULINE: Bered

Hair
MASCULINE: Esav
FEMININE: Dala, Delila, Nima

Halo
FEMININE: Childa

Hammer
MASCULINE: Helem, Makabi, Patish
FEMININE: Makabit

Handful, Hands
MASCULINE: Chofni, Yedaya

Happiness, Happy See also Joy, Plea-sure
MASCULINE: *Anshel, Anshil,* Asher, Big-vai, Gad, Gadi, Osher
FEMININE: Semeicha, *Zelde*

Harbor See also Port
MASCULINE: Nemali Nemalya, Nemuel, Nimli, Shuni
FEMININE: Chaifa, Cheifa

Harness
MASCULINE: Rotam

Harp
FEMININE: Kanara, Kinneret

Hart See also Deer
MASCULINE: *Hersh, Hershel, Hertz, Hirsh, Hirshel,* Tzvi
FEMININE: Tzivya

Harvest
MASCULINE: Asif, Katzir
Haste See also Fast, Speed
MASCULINE: Maharai
Hate, Hated
MASCULINE: Bavai, Iyov
Head
MASCULINE: Koppel, Rosh
Heal, Healer, Healing See also Medicine, Physician
MASCULINE: Asa, Assi, Marpei, Rafa, Rafael, Rafi, Rafu, Rafael, Refaya, Refi, Yaakov
FEMININE: Rafaela, Rafela, Rafya, Refaela, Refua, Rofi, Terufa, Yaakova
Heap
MASCULINE: Dur, Gal, Galal
Hear, Hearing
MASCULINE: Avishama, Azanya, Azanyahu, Elishama, Hoshama, Ishmael, Mishma, Oz, Ozni, Shama, Shamua, Shima, Shimi, Shimon (and variations Shimke, Shimel, Shimme, Shimi) Shema, Shemaya, Shemuel, (and variations Shmelke, Shmul, Shmulke, Shmulik, Sanvil, Zanvil, Zavel, Zavil), Shimi, Shimon, Yaazanya, Yishmael, Yishmaya
FEMININE: Keshuva, Shimat, Shimona, Shmuela
Heart
MASCULINE: Kalev, Leib, Lev
FEMININE: Libi
Heaven See Heights
Hebrew
MASCULINE: Ivri
FEMININE: Ivrit, Ivriya
Hedge
FEMININE: Gedera
Heel
MASCULINE: Akiva, Akuv
Heifer
FEMININE: Egla
Height, Heights See also Mountain
MASCULINE: Aharon, Alyan, Aram, Marom, Merom, Ram, Rami, Ramya, Rom, Romen
FEMININE: Gevat, Giva, Rama, Ramit, Roma, Romema, Romemit, Romemiya, Romit, Romiya, Ruma, Rumya, Siona
Help See also Salvation, Support
MASCULINE: Achiezer, Amiezer, Aviezer, Aviezri, Avishua, Azarel, Azarya, Azaryahu, Azriel, Azrikam, Elazar, Elezri, Eliezer, Ezer, Ezra, Ezri, Hadarezer, Hoshaya, Iezer, Imanuel,

Lesser, Lezer, Oshaya, Ozer, Saadya, Utai, Yoezer
FEMININE: Eliezra, Ezraela, Ez'rela, Ezriela, Ozera, Saada
Herd See Flock
Hero See also Protector
MASCULINE: Abir, Abiri, Aviram, Gavrel, Gavri, Gavriel, Gevaram, Gever, Gibar, Gibor
Hide, Hidden, Hiding
MASCULINE: Alemet, Amon, Chavaya, Cheifa, Kamus, Lot, Lotan, Nachbi, Tamir, Tzefanya
FEMININE: Shemura, Tzafnat, Tzafona
High See also Height
MASCULINE: Aram
FEMININE: Meroma
Hill See also Mound, Mountain
MASCULINE: Aharon, Chaga, Chagai, Chagiya, Gal, Gali, Galil, Galya, Geva, Gilad, Giva, Givon, Givton, Harel, Maresha, Talmi, Talmai, Tel, Tilom
FEMININE: Gal, Gali, Galit, Galya, Gilada, Giva, Givona, Talma, Talmi
Hold
MASCULINE: Akiva, Akuv, Yehoachaz
Hole
MASCULINE: Chori
Holy, Holy Day (Holiday)
MASCULINE: Chaga, Devir, Dvir, Kadish, Kadosh, Pesach, Shabtai, Tamir, Yom-Tov, Zak
FEMININE: Devira, Chagit, Chagiya
Homeland See also Birthplace
FEMININE: Molada, Moledet
Honest See also Honor, Right, Upright
MASCULINE: Avishur, Kenanya, Kenanyahu, Konanya, Konen, Nachon, Ne'eman, Sharar, Tam, Yashar
FEMININE: Nechona, Yeshara
Honey See also Bee
MASCULINE: Devash, Yidbash
FEMININE: Devash, Devasha, Devora, Duvsha
Honor, Honorable, Honored See also Adore, Respect, Upright
MASCULINE: Atzil, Efrat, Kavud, Mechubad, Meishar, Meshar, Meushar, Mokir, Nichbad, Zeviel, Zevieli, Zevul, Zevulun, Zivion
FEMININE: Atzila, Efrat, Efrata, Mechubada, Nichbada
Hope, Hopeful See also Wait
MASCULINE: Tikva
FEMININE: Erga, Shprintze, Shprintzel, Tikva, Tochelet, Tzipiya

Horizon
FEMININE: Afeka
Horn
MASCULINE: Shofar, Yuval
FEMININE: Karin, Karna, Karniel, Karnei-Yael, Karni, Karniel, Karniela, Karnit, Karniya, Keren
Horse, Horseman, Horsemanship
MASCULINE: Chayil, Ish-Chayil, Peresh, Rechev, Reichav, Sisera, Susi
Hostile See Angry
House See also Palace
MASCULINE: Avgar, Betuel, Bitan
Hot
MASCULINE: Cham, Chama, Chami, Chamuel
FEMININE: Chamama, Chuma, Chumi
Hot Spring
MASCULINE: Chamat
Humble
MASCULINE: Anuv
FEMININE: Anava
Husband
MASCULINE: Baal
Hyacinth
FEMININE: Yakinton
Hymn See also Song
MASCULINE: Hamnuna

Illustrious
MASCULINE: Adir, Adiv, Avihud
FEMININE: Adira, Adiva
Image
MASCULINE: Betzalel, Michael
FEMININE: Dagmar, Maskit, Maskiya, Michaela
Immigrant
FEMININE: Olah
Important
MASCULINE: Chashuv
FEMININE: Chashuva
Imprison, Imprisoned
MASCULINE: Agnon, Asir, Ogen
FEMININE: Aguna
Impure
FEMININE: Izevel
Incarcerate, Incarcerated See also Bind
MASCULINE: Asir, Isur
Incense See also Perfume, Spice
MASCULINE: Machat
FEMININE: Levona, Livnat, Livneh
Increase See also Add
MASCULINE: Efrayim, Eliasaf, Elyasaf, Ephraim, Fish, Fishel, Fishlin, Gamliel, Gedalya, Gedil, Yeravam, Yosef, Yosifel, Yosifya, Yossel, Yossi
FEMININE: Merav, Yoseifa, Yosifa

Industrious Industry See also Create, Creative, Energetic
MASCULINE: Asael, Asiel, Eiran, Eran, Mahir, Ziruz, Ziza
FEMININE: Amalia, Amela, Charutza, Erana, Eranut
Ingathering See also Gather
MASCULINE: Elyasaf, Evyasaf
Inheritance
MASCULINE: Morash
FEMININE: Morasha, Nachala, Nachalat, Yerusha, Yerushel
Iniquity See also Sin
MASCULINE: Onan
Innocent See also Pure
MASCULINE: Amizakai, Zakai
Insult
MASCULINE: Alvan
Intellectual, Intelligence, Intelligent
MASCULINE: Bina, Ish-Sechel, Maskil
Interpret, Interpreter See also Advice, Advisor
MASCULINE: Melitz
Investigation
FEMININE: Bakara
Iron See also Strength
MASCULINE: Barzilai, Peled, Pildash
Israel
MASCULINE: Iser, Iserl, Sriel, Srol, Srul, Srully, Yesarel, Yisrael
FEMININE: Yisraela, Yisraelit
Ivory
MASCULINE: Bahat, Shashai, Sheishai, Sheishan, Sheshai, Sheshan
FEMININE: Bahat

Jasmin
MASCULINE: Yasmin
FEMININE: Yasmin, Yasmina
Jealous
MASCULINE: Elkana
Jew
MASCULINE: Yehuda, Yudel
FEMININE: Dita, Yehudit
Jewelry See also Ornaments
MASCULINE: Ravid
Join, Joined
MASCULINE: Levi
FEMININE: Leviya, Shelavya
Jordan
MASCULINE: Yarden
FEMININE: Yarden, Yardena
Joy See also Happiness
MASCULINE: Alitz, Aliz, Avigal, Bilga, Bilgai, Chedvi, Ditz, Eletz, Elez, Eliran, Gil, Gila, Gildad, Gil-Ad, Gilam, Gili, Gil-Li, Gilon, Marnin, Masos,

Mitzhal, Ranen, Rani, Ranon, Rina, Ron, Ronel, Roni, Ronli, Sason, Semach, Simcha, Simchon, Simchoni, Sisa, Sisi, Tzahal, Tzahalon, Yachdiel, Yagil, Yitzchak, Yitzhal
FEMININE: Alisa, Aliza, Avigal, Avigayil, Chedva, Ditza, Elza, Gil, Gila, Gilana, Gilat' Gili, Gilit, Giliya, *Frayda, Freida*, Matzhelet, Mitzhala, Noam, Ranit, Ranita, Ranya, Renana, Renanit, Renina, Rina, Ron, Rona, Ronela, Ronena, Roni, Ronit, Roniya, Ronli, Sasona, Semecha, Simcha, Simchit, Simchona, Tzahala

Jubilee
MASCULINE: Yovel, Yuval
FEMININE: Yovela

Judge, Judgment See also Justice, Law
MASCULINE: Avidan, Dan, Dana, Dani, Dani-Am, Daniel, Danin, Dayan, Dinai, Dotan, Eflal, Elial, Elishafat, Elishama, Shafat, Shefatya, Shiftan, Shofet, Yadin, Yadon, Yadun, Yehoshafat, Yoshafat, Yudan, Zavdi, Zavdiel
FEMININE: Daniela, Danit, Danita, Danya, Dena, Dina, Dinya, Donya, Lidon

Juice, Juicy
MASCULINE: Asis
FEMININE: Asisa, Asisya

Jujube
MASCULINE: Tze'el
FEMININE: Tze'elit

Just, Justice See also Judge, Judgment
MASCULINE: Achidan, Achitzedek, Adlai, Amidan, Elitzedek, Palal, Pelalya, Tzadok, Tzidkiya, Yosher

Keepsake
MASCULINE: Natron, Natronai, Nitron
Kid See Goat
Kind, Kindness See also Compassion, Gracious
MASCULINE: Chasadel, Chasadya, Chasdiel, Chasid, Chesed, Chisda, Chisdai
FEMININE: Nilbava, Nilbevet

King See also Majesty, Royal, Royalty
MASCULINE: Achimelech, Avimelech, Daryavesh, Elimelech, Malkam, Malki, Malkiel, Malkiram, Malkishua, Malki-Tzedek, Malkiya, Maluch, Melech

Know, Knowledge See also Intelligence, Understanding, Wisdom
MASCULINE: Agur, Avida, Bina, Bun, Buna, Dael, Datan, Datiel, Deuel,

Egron, Eldaa, Eli-Yada, Elyada, Yada, Yadua, Yavin, Yedaya, Yediael, Yediel, Yehoyada, Yoyada
FEMININE: Daat, Dei'a

Lad See Boy
Lady
FEMININE: Gevira
Lamb
MASCULINE: Lemel, Talya
FEMININE: Avtalya, Seya, Talya, Teli
Lame See also Crippled
MASCULINE: Ater, Paseach, Pesach, Pesachya
Lament See also Cry
MASCULINE: Yovav
Lamp
MASCULINE: Aviner
Land See also Country
MASCULINE: Artzi
FEMININE: Artzit, Eretz
Landscape
FEMININE: Nofiya
Large See Great
Last, Latest
MASCULINE: Acharon, Beteira
Laughter
MASCULINE: Tzachi, Yitzchak (and variations *Eisik, Eizik, Itzig, Itzik, Itzl, Sekel, Sikel, Zekl*)
FEMININE: Yitzchaka
Laurel
FEMININE: Dafna, Dafnit, Dafniela
Law See also Judge
MASCULINE: Datan, Datiel, Dayan, Dinai, Dotan
FEMININE: Nadan, Nadin, Tora, Tori
Lay Aside
MASCULINE: Atzalya, Atzalyahu, Atzel
Lead, Leaden
FEMININE: Ofera, Oferet, Ufara
Lead, Leader See also Head
MASCULINE: Alef, Ovil, Raba, Rav, Rava, Shashai, Solel
FEMININE: Alufa, Mindel, *Minne*, Tzameret
Leaf
MASCULINE: Alei
FEMININE: Shalechet
Leap See also Jump
MASCULINE: Tzofar
Left-hand, Left-handed
MASCULINE: Binyamin, Samla
FEMININE: Binyamina
Legacy See Inheritance
Lemon
MASCULINE: Limon

Leopard
MASCULINE: Namer, Namir
FEMININE: Nemera
Lexicon See also Knowledge
MASCULINE: Egron
Life, Live, Living
MASCULINE: Amichai, Amidar, Amram, Avichai, Bachya, Bar-Yocha'i, Ben-Chai, Chai, Chaim, Chayim, Chiel, Chiva, Elchai, Elichai, Elkayam, Feitel, Omri, Yechiel, Yehu, Yichye, Yochai, Yocha'i
FEMININE: Achiya, Chava, Chaya, Chayei-Sara, Chayuta, Chiyuta, Techiya, Yechiela
Light, Lightning See also Bright, Brilliance, Radiant
MASCULINE: Achiner, Amior, Aviner, Avior, Aviur, Avner, Barak, Bareket, Barkai, Bazak, Bezek, Elior, Feibush, Feivel, Iyar, Leor, Lior, Maor, Meir, Meiri, Mendel, Nakdimon, Nahir, Nahor, Nahur, Naor, Nehor, Nehorai, Ner, Neri, Neriya, Neriyahu, Ner-li, Nerva, Noga, Or, Oran, Or-Chayim, Ori, Orli, Or-Li, Oron, Or-Tal, Or-Tziyon, Oryan, Or-Yesh, Shachar, Shacharya, Sheragai, Shneur, Shraga, Shragai, Ur, Uri, Uriah, Uriel, Uriya, Uriyahu, Ur-Malki, Uryon, Yair, Zeharya, Zerachya, Ziv, Zivi, Zohar
FEMININE: Am-Or, Behira, Eliora, Gayora Leora, Leorit, Lior, Liora, Liorit, Linur, Meira, Meirat, Meiri, Meirit, Meora, Negia, Nehara, Nehira, Nehura, Neira, Neora, Nera, Neria, Ner-Li, Nirel, Noga, Nura, Nurya, Or, Ora, Orali, Orli, Orlit, Ornat, Orit, Orlit, Orna, Ornina, Orninit, Ornit, Uranit, Uriela, Urit, Yeira, Yeora, Zohar
Like See Comparable, Resemble
Lilac
FEMININE: Avivit, Gevionit, Lilach
Lily
MASCULINE: Shoshan, Shushan
FEMININE: Chavatzelet, Chavatzelet-Hasharon, Shoshan, Shoshana
Linguist
MASCULINE: Bilshan
Lion
MASCULINE: Arel, Areli, Ari, Ariav, Ariel, Arik, Arye, Aryeh, Ben-Gurion, Gur, Gur-Ari, Gur-Aryeh, Guri, Guria, Guriel, Guryon, Kefir, Label, Lavi, Layb, Layish, Leib, Leibel, Lei-

bush, Lev, Levia, Loib
FEMININE: Ariel, Ariela, Kefira, Levia
Listen See Hear
Live See also Life
MASCULINE: Avichai, Elchai, Elichai, Elkayam, Yechi, Yechiach, Yechi-Ach, Yechiam, Yechi-Am, Yechiav, Yechiel, Yechieli, Yechishalom, Yechi-Shalom, Yechya, Yichye, Yehu
FEMININE: Chaya, Chayei-Sara, Chayuta, Yechiela
Lizzard
FEMININE: Shemamit
Loathe
MASCULINE: Gaal
Locust
MASCULINE: Chagav, Gazam
Lodge
MASCULINE: Malon
Lofty See also Honorable, Noble
MASCULINE: Achiram, Marom, Zevul, Zevulun
FEMININE: Romema, Romemya
Loins
MASCULINE: Chaltzon, Cheletz
Long
MASCULINE: Aricha, Aryoch, Erech
Look See also See
MASCULINE: Nevat
Loosen
MASCULINE: Yirmiya, Yirmiyahu
Lord See also Noble, Nobility
MASCULINE: Adir, Adon, Adoniya, Azarel, Chirom, Yisrael
Loss
MASCULINE: Avdima, Avdimei, Avdimi
Lotus
MASCULINE: Arnan, Chagav
FEMININE: Shoshan
Love
MASCULINE: Ahava, Ahud, Ahuv, Bildad, Dodai, Ehud, Gottlieb, Liber, Narkis, Ohad, Ohev, Yedidia, Yedidya
FEMININE: Ahada, Ahava, Ahavat, Ahuva, Aphrodit, Chiba, Chibat-Tziyon, Liba, Libe, Lipkeh
Loyal See Faithful, Honest
Lucid See also Clear
MASCULINE: Tzalil, Tzalul
Luck See also Fortune
MASCULINE: Gad, Maimon, Mazal, Mazal-Tov, Siman-Tov, Yimna
FEMININE: Glicke, Glickel, Glucke, Gluckel, Mazal, Mazala, Mazalit
Luckless See also Misfortune
MASCULINE: Asna

FEMININE: Asnat

Luxuriant, Luxuriate, Luxurious
MASCULINE: Aden, Adni, Eden, Eiden, Raanan

Lyrical, Lyrics *See also* Song
MASCULINE: Liron, Li-Ron

Magic
MASCULINE: Cheresh
FEMININE: Kessim

Maiden
FEMININE: Alma, Aluma, Alumit, Betula, Reva

Maimed
MASCULINE: Gidi, Gidon
FEMININE: Gidona

Majestic, Majesty *See also* Noble, Nobility, Royalty
MASCULINE: Achihud, Achimelech, Adir, Adriel, Avihud, Elihud, Gaon, Geuel, Ish-Hod
FEMININE: Adira, Geona, Geonit

Make *See* Create
MASCULINE: Elpaal

Male *See* Man
MASCULINE: Zakur

Man, Mankind
MASCULINE: Adam, Ben-Azai, Ben-Gever, Enosh, Gavriel, Gavirol, Gever

Mandrake
MASCULINE: Dodai, Dudai
FEMININE: Dudait

Mane
MASCULINE: Rama

Mantle
FEMININE: Efrat

Master
MASCULINE: Adon, Adonikam, Adoram, Aluf, Baal, Mar

Mature *See also* Old, Oldest, Ripe
FEMININE: Bakura, Bikura, Kama

Me, Mine
MASCULINE: Li
FEMININE: Iti, Itiel, Itiya, Li, Liad, Liam, Liav, Li-Hi, Linur, Liron, Lital, Litov, Sheli, Sheliya

Meadow
MASCULINE: Hevel

Measurement
MASCULINE: Aryoch

Medicine *See also* Heal, Healing
MASCULINE: Marpei

Melody *See also* Song
MASCULINE: Zamir, Zemarya, Zemer, Zemira, Zimran, Zimri, Zimroni
FEMININE: Ariana, Negina, Neima, Zemira, Zimra, Zimrat, Zimriya

Memory *See also* Remembrance
MASCULINE: Zachur, Zecharya, Zecharyahu, Zecher, Zichri

Merchandise
MASCULINE: Machir, Michri, Sechora

Merchant
MASCULINE: Avitagar

Mercy *See also* Kindness
MASCULINE: Ben-Chesed, Elchanan, Yerachmiel

Messiah
MASCULINE: Mashiach, Moshia
FEMININE: Shilo

Messenger *See also* Servant
MASCULINE: Aharon, Aharoni, Aron, Malach, Malachi, Maluch, Metushelach, Mevaser, Mevaser-Tov
FEMININE: Malach

Meteor
MASCULINE: Elgavish

Might, Mighty *See also* Strength
MASCULINE: Achiram, Adoram, Adonikam, Amiaz, Amir, Amiram, Amotz, Amram, Avram, Ben-Guryon, El-Gibbor, Eliram, Oz-Tziyon
FEMININE: Amtza, Ariel

Milk
MASCULINE: Achlav

Miracle, Miracle Worker, Miraculous
MASCULINE: Nes, Nisan, Nisi, Nisim, Palu, Pelaya, Pele
FEMININE: Maksima, Nasya, Nesya, Nisya, Peliya, Pili

Misfortune
MASCULINE: Asna, Tavor

Mistress
FEMININE: Marta

Modest *See* Humble

Month, Monthly
MASCULINE: Yarchinai, Sivan
FEMININE: Chodesh, Elula, Maya, Sivana

Moon
MASCULINE: Levanon, Yarchi, Yaroach, Yerach
FEMININE: Levana, Sahara

Morning *See also* Dawn, Light
MASCULINE: Achishachar, Avishechar, Ben-Shachar, Tzafrir, Tzafriri, Tzafrit
FEMININE: Tzafra, Tzafrira, Tzafirit, Tzefira

Mother
FEMININE: Imma

Mother of Pearl *See also* Pearl
MASCULINE: Tzedef

Mound *See also* Heap, Hill, Mountain
MASCULINE: Gal, Galal, Gali, Gilad

Giladi, Talmai, Talmi, Tel, Tel-Chai, Telem, Tilon
FEMININE: Gevat, Giva
Mountain See also Hill
MASCULINE: Aharon, Gal, Gali, Haran, Harel, Sinai
FEMININE: Chermona, Harela, Horiya
Mourner, Mourning
MASCULINE: Onan
Mouse
MASCULINE: Achbor
Mouth
MASCULINE: Pinchas, *Pinkus, Pinya,* Pua
Movement
MASCULINE: Zaza
Multitude
MASCULINE: Aviasaf, Avraham, Avram, *Avrom, Avrum, Avrumel, Avrumke,* Shefa, Shifi
Music, Musical See also Melody, Song
MASCULINE: Tzelil, Yedutun
FEMININE: Lirit, Liron, Lirona, Mangena, Negina
Myrrh See Spice
FEMININE: Mor, Talmor
Myrtle
MASCULINE: Hadas
FEMININE: Hadas, Hadassa, *Hodel*
Mystery
FEMININE: Eliraz

Name See also Reputation
MASCULINE: Ben-Shem, Kalman, Shamai, Shem, Shemaya, Shemi, Shem-Tov
FEMININE: Bat-Shem
Narcissus
FEMININE: Chelmit, Chelmonit, Narkis, Narkisa
Nation See also People
MASCULINE: *Aberlin,* Ahuvam, Amiad, Amiaz, Amichai, Amichen, Amida, Amidar, Amidror, Amiezer, Amihud, Amikam, Amikar, Aminadav, Amior, Amiram, Amiran, Amiron, Amishadai, Amishalom, Amishar, Amishav, Amishoa, Amituv, Amitzedek, Amitzur, Aniam, Aviam, Avichal, Avishalon, Avishamar, Avishar, Avishua, Avishur, Avitagar, Avraham, Avram, *Avrom, Avrum, Avrumel, Avrumke,* Baram, Barami, Dani-Am, Leumi, Yechiam, Yekamam, Yifracham
FEMININE: Leuma, Leumi, Uma
Natural, Nature
MASCULINE: Tivo

FEMININE: Tivona, Tivoni
Navy
MASCULINE: Tzi
Nazirite
FEMININE: Nezira, Nizriya
Near
MASCULINE: Kariv
Neck
FEMININE: Arpa
Negligent
MASCULINE: Chadlai
Negro See Dark
Neighbor, Neighborhood
MASCULINE: Shachna, Shechanya
Nephew
MASCULINE: Achyan
New
FEMININE: Chadasha, Chadusha
Night
FEMININE: Laila, Lilit
Noble, Nobility
MASCULINE: Achinadav, Achiram, Adar, Adir, Adon, Aminadav, Ard, Chirom, Ish-Hod, Nadiv, Ne'etzal, Yehonadav, Yisrael, Yonadav
FEMININE: Adena, Adina, Adira, Adoniya, Atzila, *Edel, Eidel,* Matrona, Nagida, Nediva, Needara, Neederet, Sara, Yisraela
Noise
MASCULINE: Kish, Kishoni
North, Northward
MASCULINE: Tzefanya
FEMININE: Tzafona
Nostril
MASCULINE: Nachor
Nothingness
MASCULINE: Efes
Nourish
MASCULINE: Yekutiel, Zan
Number
MASCULINE: Mispar, Muna
Number One
MASCULINE: Alef
Nursling See Plant
Nut
FEMININE: Egoza

Oak
MASCULINE: Alon, Armon, Eila, Ela, Elon
FEMININE: Alona, Eila, Eilona, Ela, Elona
Oath
MASCULINE: Ashbei, Nadir, Nidri, Sheva
FEMININE: *Basha, Bashe,* Batsheva, Bat-Sheva, *Bayle,* Bela, Elisheva, Sheva, Yehoshavat, Yehosheva

Observant *See also* Religious
MASCULINE: Aduk
FEMININE: Aduka

Observation Tower
MASCULINE: Bachan

Offer, Offering *See also* Gift, Sacrifice
MASCULINE: Eli
FEMININE: Teruma

Offspring
MASCULINE: Nun

Oil
MASCULINE: Yitzhar

Ointment
MASCULINE: Rekach

Old *See also* Ancient, Elder, Eldest
MASCULINE: *Alter*, Kadamiel, Kedem, Kedma, Saba, Yashish, Yeshishai, Sava, Zaken, Zeira
FEMININE: *Alte, Baile*, Bilha, Keshisha, Yeshana, Yeshisha, Zekena

Olive
MASCULINE: Zayit, Zeitam, Zeitan, Zetam, Zetan
FEMININE: Zayit, Zeita, Zeitana

Omnipresent
FEMININE: Elinoa

Onion
MASCULINE: Batzlit, Batzlut

Onyx
MASCULINE: Shoham

Open
MASCULINE: Petachya, Yiach, Yiftach-El

Oppress, Oppression
MASCULINE: Anat, Eshek, Iyov, Talmon
FEMININE: Talmona, Talmonit

Opulent, Opulence
FEMININE: Bathshua, Bat-Shua, Shua

Oracle
MASCULINE: Devir, Divri

Orator
MASCULINE: Divri

Orchard
MASCULINE: Bustan, Ginat

Orchid
FEMININE: Devoranit

Order
MASCULINE: Sadir, Sidra
FEMININE: Sidra

Organize
FEMININE: Sedira

Ornament *See* Treasure

Orphan
MASCULINE: Yitma, Yotam

Ornament, Ornamented *See also* Decorated, Jewelry
MASCULINE: Adaya, Adi, Adiel, Adin, Atir, Atur, Eter, Ravid

FEMININE: Adi, Adiella, Hadar, Hadara, Hadarit, Hadura, Loya

Orthodox *See also* Observant

Ostrich
MASCULINE: Yaen
FEMININE: Naamit, Yaanit, Yaen

Over, Overflowing
MASCULINE: Ever, Evron, Tzif, Tzuf
FEMININE: Evrona

Overreach
MASCULINE: Akuv

Owner
MASCULINE: Achuzam, Baal

Ox, wild
MASCULINE: Arad, Ard, Ardi

Page
MASCULINE: Dapi

Pain
MASCULINE: Onan, Yabetz
FEMININE: Chila

Palace *See also* Castle
MASCULINE: Armon, Armoni, Bitan, Seraya, Serayahu
FEMININE: Chavila

Palm, Palm tree
MASCULINE: Dekel, Dikla, Itamar, Miklot, Tamar
FEMININE: Dikla, Diklit, Egoza, Lulava, Sansana, Tamar, Tamara, Timora, Timura, Tomer

Pancake
FEMININE: Leviva

Parable
MASCULINE: Achichud

Park *See also* Garden
MASCULINE: Ben-Karmi, Kerem
FEMININE: Carma, Carmelit

Partridge
FEMININE: Chogla

Pass Away
MASCULINE: Chalfon, Shovek

Pass Over
MASCULINE: Ever, Paseach, Pesach, Pesachya

Patch
FEMININE: Tala

Path
MASCULINE: Nativ, Shoval, Solel
FEMININE: Netiva, Selila

Patience
FEMININE: Savlanut

Pavillion
FEMININE: Bitaniya

Peace, Peaceful
MASCULINE: Achishalom, Amishalom, Avishalom, Avshalom, Getzel, Ish-Shalom, Margia, Margoa, Menucha,

Meshulam, *Salaman, Salman, Salmen,* Sar-Shalom, Shalem, Shalev, Shalmai, Shalmiya, Shalom, Shanan, Shela, Shelemya, Shelumiel, Shilem, Shilo, Shlomo, Sholom, Shlomi, Tov-Shilem, Yechi-Shalom, *Zalke, Zalkin, Zalkind, Zalman*
FEMININE: Achishalom, Margea, Menucha, Meshulemet, Shaanana, Shalva, Shalviya, Shelomit, Shlomit, Shlom-Tzion, Shula, Shulamit, Shuly

Peacock
MASCULINE: Tavas

Pearl
MASCULINE: Dar, Darda, Penini, Tzedef
FEMININE: Margalit, Margalita, Penina, Penini, Peninit, *Perl*

Pedigree *See* Favor, Favored

People *See also* Nation
MASCULINE: Ami, Amiasaf, Amiaz, Amichai, Amichen, Amidan, Amidar, Amidor, Amidror, Amiel, Amihud, Amikam, Amikar, Aminadav, Amior, Amiram, Amiran, Amishadai, Amishar, Amishav, Amishoa, Amiram, Amram, Aniam, Ben-Ami, Ben-Tziyon, El-Ami, Lo-Ami
FEMININE: Amiela, Amya, Bat-Ami, Bat-Tziyon, Elana, Eliam

Perfect, Perfected, Perfection
MASCULINE: Kalul, Meshelemya, Meshulam, Michael, Yotam
FEMININE: Neetzala, Neetzelet, Nitzala, Nitzelet

Perfume, Perfumed *See also* Incense, Spice
MASCULINE: Bosem, Mivsam, Yivsam
FEMININE: Basma, Basmat, Bosma, Bosmat, Bosemet, Ketura, Livnat, Livneh, Tzeruya

Pierce
MASCULINE: Deker

Pine
MASCULINE: Oran
FEMININE: Orna, Ornat, Orni

Pioneer
MASCULINE: Chalutz, Chalutzel
FEMININE: Chaluz

Pious *See also* Holy
MASCULINE: Chasdiel, Chasid, Chesdai, *Frommel,* Yekutiel
FEMININE: Chasuda, *Frume,* Tzadika

Pitcher
MASCULINE: Kadi
FEMININE: Kadya

Pity *See also* Compassion
MASCULINE: Yerachm'el, Yerachmiel, Yerocham

Plain (open field)
MASCULINE: Sharon
FEMININE: Sharon, Sharona, Sharoni, Sharonit

Plant *See also* Flower
MASCULINE: Admon, Avgar, Chavakuk, Ezrach, Ezrachi, Iris, Narkis, Neta, Netiya, Nitai, Notea, Nufar, Shalmon, Shalmon, Shatil, Shatul, Shetel, Tzemach, Yahali, Yahel, Yizr'el, Zichrini, Zoreia
FEMININE: Afrit, Atzmoni, Avi-Yona, Chelmit, Chelmonit, Dalia, Gada, Gadit, Iris, Kalanit, Kana, Kida, Marganit, Marganita, Marva, Narkis, Neta, Netia, Nili, Nilit, Nita, Noit, Nufar, Nurit, Nurita, Rakefet, Rechana, Retem, Ritma, Rotem, Savyon, Savyona, Shetila, Shetula, Shotela, Shotelet, Yasmin, Yasmina, Yenika, Yizr'ela, Zerua, Zichriya, Zivanit

Plateau
MASCULINE: Tavla, Tavlai

Play (an instrument)
FEMININE: Chula, Gitat

Pleasant *See also* Beautiful, Good, Sweet
MASCULINE: Achinoam, Adin, Adiv, Avi-Naim, Elnaam, Mehader, Mehudar, Naam, Naaman, Naim, Noam, Shefer, Shifron
FEMININE: Achinoam, Adiva, Naamiya, Ne'ima

Plough, Ploughed
MASCULINE: Nir, Niram, Nirel, Niriel, Niriya, Nirya, Padon, Yanir
FEMININE: Churshit, Nira, Nirit, Odera

Pluck
MASCULINE: Ara
FEMININE: Ketifa

Plunder
MASCULINE: Shelef

Poet, Poetry
FEMININE: Piuta

Pomegranate
MASCULINE: Rimon
FEMININE: Rimon, Rimona

Ponder
MASCULINE: Chashavya, Chashuv

Poor
MASCULINE: Anav
FEMININE: Anava, Dala, Delila

Poplar
FEMININE: Livnat, Livneh

Port *See also* Harbor
MASCULINE: Chaifa, Cheifa

Portion
MASCULINE: Chelek, Chelkai, Chilkiya
FEMININE: Chelkat, Mana, Menat

Possession
MASCULINE: Achuzat, Kayin, Kenan, Nachliel
FEMININE: Achuza, Beula

Pot
MASCULINE: Tamach, Temach

Praise
MASCULINE: Hila, Hilai, Hilan, Hili, Hillel, Mahalalel, Mehulal, Noda, Omar, Seled, Shevach, Yahud, Yehalelel, Yehuda, Yehudi, *Yidel*, Yishbach, *Yudel, Yudke*
FEMININE: Hila, Hilana, Hillela, Hodiya, Nodeleya, Odeleya, Shavcha, Tehila, Tishbacha, Yehudit, Yudit

Pray, Prayer See also Praise
MASCULINE: Atar, Eflal, Elipal, Pagiel, Palal, Tachan, Techina
FEMININE: Ateret, Atira, Tachan, Tehila

Preacher
MASCULINE: Kehat, Kohelet

Precious See also Desirable
MASCULINE: Amikar, Avikar, Chamadel, Chamdiel, Chamud, Chemdad, Chemdan, Chemed, Leshem, Nofech, Penini, Safir, Sapir, Shoham, Shovai, Tarshish, Yahalom
FEMININE: Bareket, Chamuda, Chemda, Kevuda, Sapir, Sapira, Sapirit, Yahaloma, Yahalomit, Yakira, Yekara, Yikrat

Prepare, Prepared, Preparation
MASCULINE: Arach, Ataya, Atid
FEMININE: Noada, Techuna

Preservation, Preserve
MASCULINE: Yekutiel

Press
MASCULINE: Maacha
FEMININE: Maacha

Prestige, Prestigious See also Noble
MASCULINE: Sagiv

Price
MASCULINE: Mechir

Pride
MASCULINE: Gaon
FEMININE: Geona, Geonit

Priest
MASCULINE: Kahana, Kohen

Prince, Princely See also Ruler
MASCULINE: Achiram, Achisar, Aluf, Asarel, Asarela, Asriel, Avinadav, Avisar, *Isril, Isser, Isserl*, Nadav, Nadivi, Nagid, Nasi, Nedavya, Rosen, Sar, Sar-Shalom, Seriel, *Srol, Srul, Srule, Srulik*, Yisrael
FEMININE: Nagida, Yisr'ela

Princess See also Noble, Ruler

FEMININE: Alufa, Chashmona, Chashmonit, Sara, Sarai,Sareli, Sarit, *Sirel, Sirkel, Sorale, Soralie, Tzirel*, Yisraela

Prison, Prisoner See also Imprisoned
MASCULINE: Asir, Mishmar

Problem
MASCULINE: Abaye

Produce
FEMININE: Tenuva

Progenitor
MASCULINE: Molid

Prolific See Fruitful

Proper See also Fit, Suited
MASCULINE: Naot

Property
MASCULINE: Mikneiyahu

Prophet See also Seer
MASCULINE: Chozai
FEMININE: Chazona, Neviya

Propagate See also Increase
MASCULINE: Nun

Proselyte
MASCULINE: Ger, Ger-Tzedek

Prosperous See Successful

Prostitute
FEMININE: Zona

Protect, Protection, Protector See also Provider, Support
MASCULINE: Akiva, Alexander, Alexandri, Avifelet, Avigdor, Betzalel, Bitzaron, Chasun, Elitzafan, Eltzafan, Gonen, Lot, Lotan, Machaseh, Machseiya, Magen, Meigein, Mishan, Shemer, Shimrai, Shimrat, Shimri, Shimron, Shmaram, Shmarya, Shomer, Sistri, Tzelafchad, Tzilai, Tzipiyon, Yaakov, Yachmai, Yahali, Yahel, *Yankel*
FEMININE: Avigdora, Chasya, Chosa, Magena, Megina, Setura, Shamira, Shemura, Shimra, Shimrat, Shimriya, Sitriya, Tzina, Yaakova, Zehira

Provider See also Support
MASCULINE: Aviman, Avisamach

Prune
MASCULINE: Zomeir

Pure See also Clean, Clear
MASCULINE: Amizakai, Barur, Tzach, Zach, Zachi, Zakai
FEMININE: Berura, Beruriya, Berurya, *Rayna, Reina*, Tehora, Zaka, Zait, Zakiya

Purple
MASCULINE: Argaman
FEMININE: Techula

Pursue, Pursuit
MASCULINE: Redifa
FEMININE: Matred
Python
MASCULINE: Piton

Quarrel
MASCULINE: Yariv, Yerivai
Queen, Queenly
FEMININE: Malka, Malkiela, Malkit, Malkiya, Milka, Molechet
Question
MASCULINE: Abaye
Quick
MASCULINE: Chatil, Maher, Mahir
Quiet See also Peace, Rest
MASCULINE: Manoach
FEMININE: Shalva, Shalviya

Radiant See also Light, Shine
MASCULINE: Zohar
FEMININE: Ziva
Rain See also Dew
MASCULINE: Dalfon, Geshem, Malkosh, Matri, Raviv, Yorai
FEMININE: Malkosha, Lital, Ravital, Reviva
Rainbow
MASCULINE: Kashti
FEMININE: Keshet
Raise See also Exalt
MASCULINE: Gidalti, Gidel, Yarom, Yarum, Yirmeya, Yirmeyahu
FEMININE: Merima, Meroma
Ram
MASCULINE: Ayal
Ransom See Redeem
Rare
FEMININE: Nedira
Raven
MASCULINE: Orev
Ready
MASCULINE: Atai, Ataya, Atid
Reasonable
FEMININE: Sevira
Rebel, Rebellion, Rebellious
MASCULINE: Mardut, Mered, Nimrod
FEMININE: Mardut, Meri
Rebirth See also Resurrection, Revival
FEMININE: Techiya, Techiya-Yehudit, Tekuma
Recalcitrant
MASCULINE: Shovav
Reckon
MASCULINE: Edan, Idan, Ido
Recompense
FEMININE: Gemula

Red, Reddish
MASCULINE: Admon, Almog, Chachalia, Chamran, Chemdan, Edom, Tzachar, Tzochar
Redeem, Redeemer, Redemption See also Ransom
MASCULINE: Egal, Elgaal, Gaalya, Gaalyahu, Gealva, Goel, Hagoel, Pedael, Pedat, Pedatzur, Pedaya, Pedayahu, Yagael, Yagel, Yagli, Yifdeya, Yigael, Yigal
FEMININE: Gealya, Geula, Goelet, Pedut, Peduya, Poda, Yegaala, Yifdeya, Yigaela, Yigala
Reed See also Stalk
MASCULINE: Agmon, Kaniel, Kenaz, Kini
Refresh
MASCULINE: Nafish
Refuge See also Protection
MASCULINE: Adalya, Adlai, Chasiel, Chosa, Luz
Refugee
MASCULINE: Sarid
Reindeer
MASCULINE: Re'em
FEMININE: Re'ema
Rejoice, Rejoicing See also Joy
MASCULINE: Agel, Agil, Amishar, Seled, Simchon, Simchoni, Yagel, Yagil, Yaron, Yasis, Yismach
FEMININE: Marnina, Tzahala
Relative
MASCULINE: Kariv
Release
MASCULINE: Yishbak
Religious
MASCULINE: Aduk
FEMININE: Aduka, Datit, Datiya, Datya
Remain, Remainder
MASCULINE: Sarid
Remembering, Remembrance See also Memory
MASCULINE: Zecharya, Zecharyahu, Zichroni
FEMININE: Zichrini, Zichriya, Zichrona, Zichroni
Repair
MASCULINE: Bidkar, *Mendel*
Repatriate See also Return
MASCULINE: Shear-Yashuv, Yashiv, Yeshavam, Yoshivya, Yov
Reputation See also Name
MASCULINE: Ben-Shem, Noda, Shama, Shema, Shem-Tov, Shima, Shimi, Shimon, Shmaya
FEMININE: Bat-Shem

Resemble
MASCULINE: Dama, Michael
FEMININE: Dumiya, Michaela, Michal

Reserve
MASCULINE: Atalya, Atalyahu, Atzel

Reside
MASCULINE: Amidar

Respect, Respected See also Honor, Honored
MASCULINE: Ben-Shem, Mokir
FEMININE: Kevuda

Respectable
MASCULINE: Adalya

Respond
MASCULINE: Elyashiv

Rest See also Peace, Quiet
MASCULINE: Manoach, Menucha, Noach, Nocha, Shabat, Shabtai, Teradyon, Yalon, Yalun, Yanoach, Yashen
FEMININE: Chania, Chaniya, Linit, Manachot, Mashena, Menucha, Nacha, Nachat, Yanocha

Resting Place
MASCULINE: Malon, Manoach, Shevna, Shevanya
FEMININE: Yeshiva

Restore, Restorer
MASCULINE: Amikam, Oded

Restrain, Restraint
MASCULINE: Achaz, Achazai, Achazya, Achazyan, Achzai, Akavya, Akiva, Yaakov

Resurrection See also Rebirth, Revival
MASCULINE: Achikam, Amikam, Avikam, Elyashiv, Elyashuv
FEMININE: Techiya

Retreat
MASCULINE: Gachar

Return, Returnee See also Repatriate, Restore, Resurrect, Revive
MASCULINE: Amishav, Elyashuv, Shear-Yashuv, Shevi, Shevna, Shevuel, Shovi, Shuvael, Yashuv, Yeshuvam, Yoshivya, Yov

Reveal See also Uncover
MASCULINE: Yagel, Yair

Revenge
MASCULINE: Elnakam

Revere, Reverend
MASCULINE: Omar

Revival See also Rebirth, Resurrection
MASCULINE: Achikam, Amikam, Amishav
FEMININE: Techiya, Tekuma

Reward See also Gift
MASCULINE: Atanya, Etnan, Etni, Gamliel, Gamul, Gemala, Gemali, Gema-

liel, Sachar, Shalem, Shalman, Shelumiel, Shilem, Yimla, Yisachar
FEMININE: Gemliela, Gamlielit, Gemula

Rich See also Valuable, Wealthy
MASCULINE: Achikar, Ashir
FEMININE: Ashira, Bat-Shua, Batshua

Riddle See Parable

Right, Righteous, Righteousness See also Justice, Upright
MASCULINE: Amidan, Amitzedek, Chasid, Elitzedek, Eltzedk, Meshar, Nachon, Tzadik, Tzadkiel, Tzadok, Tzedekya, Tzidkiya, Tzidkiyahu, Yehotzadak, Yotzadak
FEMININE: Chasida, Tamar

Right hand, Right-handed See also Strength, Support
MASCULINE: Binyamin, Teman, Temani, Yamin, Yemin, Yimna
FEMININE: Binyamina, Yemina, Yimna

Ring
MASCULINE: Tabaot
FEMININE: Tabaat

Ripe, Ripen
FEMININE: Bakura, Bikura, Gimra, Kama

Rise, Rise Up See also Ascend
MASCULINE: Idi, Ido, Yaziz

River
MASCULINE: Yeor, Yeori

Road
MASCULINE: Rechov
FEMININE: Selila

Rock See also Protector, Strength
MASCULINE: Achitzur, Amitzur, Avitzedek, Avitzur, Avniel, Chalamish, Elitzur, Even, Sela, Shamir, Tzeror, Tzur, Tzuri, Tzuriel, Tzurishadai, Tzuriya
FEMININE: Avna, Salit, Shuni, Shunit, Silit, Tzur-El, Tzurit, Tzuriya

Rod See also Staff
MASCULINE: Miklot

Roll, Rolled up, Rolling
MASCULINE: Galil, Galili, Gilalai
FEMININE: Galila, Gelia

Root
MASCULINE: Sheresh

Rose
MASCULINE: Etzbonit, Vardi, Vardimon, Vardinon, Vered
FEMININE: Raise, Raisel, Raizel, Rayzel, Reisel, Varda, Vardina, Vardit, Vardiya, Vered

Row
MASCULINE: Yetur
FEMININE: Sedera, Shura

Royalty *See* King, Prince, Princess, Queen, Ruler

Rule, Ruler *See also* King, Prince
MASCULINE: Aluf, Baal, Elrad, Melech, Moshel, Nagid, Rozen, Sar, Yamlech, Yisrael
FEMININE: Alufa, *Raine*, Sara, Sarit

Run
MASCULINE: Ratz

Sabbath *See* Rest

Sacred *See also* Consecrated, Dedicated
MASCULINE: Chermon, Chermoni, Tamir
FEMININE: Chermona

Sacrifice
MASCULINE: Zevach, Zevachya

Saffron *See also* Plant
MASCULINE: Karkom

Salvation *See also* Help
MASCULINE: Achipelet, Aviezer, Avishua, Ben-Ezra, Eliasaf, Elisha, Elishua, Elyasaf, Hosheia, Isa, Mosha, Mosha, Moshe, Oshiya, Pelatya, Pelatyahu, Piltai, Shua, Yehoshua, Yesha, Yeshaya, Yeshayahu, Yeshua, Yoezer
FEMININE: Moshaa, Shua, Teshua, Yisha

Sanctification, Sanctify *See also* Sanctuary, Holy
MASCULINE: Devir, Kadish, Zak

Sanctuary *See also* Holy
MASCULINE: Devir
FEMININE: Davir, Devir, Devira

Sapling *See* Plant

Sapphire
MASCULINE: Sapir
FEMININE: Sapir, Sapira, Sapirit

Sarcophagus
MASCULINE: Aran

Satisfied, Satisfy
FEMININE: Revaya

Save, Savior *See also* Protector, Redeemer
MASCULINE: Ashi, Atzalya, Avifelet, Chamuel, Chamul, Elishua, Hitzilyahu, Hoshaya, Melatya, Moshe, Palti, Paltiel, Paltoi, Pelatya, Pelet, Yaflet, Yishi, Yisho, Yoshiya, Yoshiyahu
FEMININE: Matzila

Saw
MASCULINE: Shur

Scab
MASCULINE: Garev

Scar
MASCULINE: Tzelek

Scarlet
MASCULINE: Shani, Tola

Scatter
MASCULINE: Yazer

Scholar
MASCULINE: Aluf, Arza, Arzi, Erez

School
MASCULINE: Sidra

Scout *See also* Guard
MASCULINE: Chazo, Roeh, Ro'i
FEMININE: Tzofai, Tzofi, Tzofit, Tzofiya

Scribe
MASCULINE: Sofer

Sea *See also* Water
MASCULINE: Avigal, Aviyam, Livyatan
FEMININE: Bat-Galim, Bat-Yam, Yama, Yamit

Seagul
MASCULINE: Shachaf, Shachafit

Seal
MASCULINE: Chotam

Seashore
MASCULINE: Chaifa, Cheifa, Shuni

Secret *See also* Hidden
MASCULINE: Raz, Razi, Raziel, Sitri, Sodi, Tamir
FEMININE: Eliraz, Liraz, Raz, Razi, Raziela, Raziya

Secure, Security *See also* Protection
MASCULINE: Betach, Mivtach, Mivtachyahu, Mivtzar, Shalev, Shela, Shilo
FEMININE: Mivtechet

See, Seer *See also* Prophet
MASCULINE: Chason, Chazael, Chazaya, Chaziel, Chazon, Chozai, Elra'i, Elroi'i, Navot, Nevat, Re'aya, Roeh, Ro'i, Yachaziel, Yachazya, Yiriya
FEMININE: Nevia, Roa

Seed
MASCULINE: Zera

Seedling *See* Plant

Select, Selected *See also* Chosen
MASCULINE: Nivchar

Senior
MASCULINE: *Shneur*

Senseless *See* Foolish

Sensuality
MASCULINE: Chushai, Chushiam, Chushiel

Serpent
MASCULINE: Nachash, Nachshon, Saraf

Servant, Server *See also* Messenger
MASCULINE: Avda, Avdel, Avdi, Avdel, Avdon, Eved, Malach, Malachi, Maluch, Ovad, Ovadya, Ovadyahu, Oved, Potifar, Potifera, Put, Putiel, Shamash, Shimshai, Shimshon

FEMININE: Amaa, Shimshona
Settlement
MASCULINE: Chetzrai, Chetzron
FEMININE: Keret
Shade, Shaded, Shadow *See also* Protected
MASCULINE: Betzalel, Tziltai
FEMININE: Tzila, Tzili
Shame
MASCULINE: Ish-Boshet
Sharp
MASCULINE: Chadad, Charif
Sheaf
MASCULINE: Amir, Omer, Omri
FEMININE: Omrit, Umarit
Shear
MASCULINE: Gazaz, Gazez, Giza
Sheep, Shepherd
MASCULINE: Ro'i, Shepsel, Talya, Zimri
FEMININE: Merona
Shine, Shining *See also* Bright, Glorified, Radiant
MASCULINE: Aharon, Aron, Hillel, Meir, Yafiya, Yarach, Yitzhar, Yizhar, Yizrach, Yizrachya, Zharai, Zahir, Zahur, Zarchi, Zerach, Zerachya, Ziv, Zivan, Zivi, Zohar, Zoreiach
FEMININE: Korenet, Mazhira, Noga, Yahala, Yahaloma, Yaholomit, Yanel, Zahara, Zahari, Zaharira, Zaharit, Zehara, Zehari, Zehorit, Zohar, Zohara, Zorachat, Zoheret, Zorachat
Ship
FEMININE: Ania, Aniya
Shoot *See* Branch
Short
MASCULINE: Nanas, Nanos
Shoulder
MASCULINE: Shechem
Shout *See also* Cry Out
MASCULINE: Tzahal, Tzahalon
Shut
MASCULINE: Ater
Sick
FEMININE: Achlai, Machalat, Tzerua
Sieve
MASCULINE: Arbel
Sight
MASCULINE: Peniel, Reuven
Sign *See also* Emblem, Signal, Symbol
MASCULINE: Nisan, Nisi, Nissim, Remez, Rimzi, Samal, Siman-Tov
FEMININE: Remazya, Simona
Signal *See also* Sign
FEMININE: Masua, Ramziya, Rimziya
Silence
MASCULINE: Duma

FEMININE: Dumiya
Silk
MASCULINE: Meshi
Silo *See* Granary
Silver
MASCULINE: Kaspi, Kesef
FEMININE: Kaspit
Sin, Sinner *See also* Iniquity
MASCULINE: Alva, Onan
FEMININE: Alva, Avishag
Sing, Singing, Song *See also* Melody
MASCULINE: Achishar, Aharon, Aharoni, Amiran, Amiron, Amishar, Ana, Anaya, Aron, Avishar, Avizemer, Avron, Eliran, Liron, Lirona, Ranen, Ranon, Ron, Ronel, Ronen, Roni, Ronli, Ronon, Shir, Shiron, Uni, Yaron, Yashir, Yoran, Zamir, Zemarya, Zemer, Zemira, Zimra, Zimran, Zimri, Zimroni
FEMININE: Anat, Arni, Arnina, Arninit, Arnit, Liron, Lirona, Mangena, Mangina, Oda, Odiya, Rani, Ranit, Ranita, Raniya, Ranya, Renana, Ron, Ronela, Roni, Ronit, Roniya, Ronli, Shir, Shira, Shirel, Shiri, Shir-Lee, Shirli, Yarona
Six
MASCULINE: Sheshet
Skeleton
MASCULINE: Shaldon
Slaughter
MASCULINE: Tevach
Sleep *See* Rest
Small
MASCULINE: Katan, Tzuar, Yaktan, Yoktan, Z'eira, Zera, Zuta, Zutai, Zutei, Zutra
FEMININE: Katania, Ketana, Ketina, Peuta, Zeira
Smooth
MASCULINE: Zishva, Yishvi
Snake
MASCULINE: Achan, Shefifon
Snatch
MASCULINE: Yachat
Snow
FEMININE: Shalgit, Shalgiya, Shilga, Shilgit, Shilgiya, Snira, Talga
Soldier *See also* Troops
MASCULINE: Chayil, Gad, Gadi
Son
MASCULINE: Bani, Baram, Barami, Ben, Ben-Ami, Ben-Asor, Ben-Baruch, Ben-Carmi, Ben-Chai, Ben-Chanan, Ben-Gever, Ben-Guryon, Ben-Karmi, Ben-Oni, Ben-Tzvi, Ben-Tziyon,

Ben-Yishai, Beni, Beno, Ben-Nun, Bni, Bno, Buni, Bunni, Hevel, Nun, Reuven, *Zindel, Zundel*
Song *See* Melody, Sing
Songbird *See also* Canary
FEMININE: Bat-Shir, Kanit
Soothsayer, Soothsaying
MASCULINE: Anan, Anani, Ananya
Sorrow
MASCULINE: Ben-Oni
Soul
FEMININE: Nafshiya, Neshama, Nishmiya
South
MASCULINE: Darom, Nagiv, Negev, Teman, Temani
FEMININE: Deromit, Dimona, Divona, Negba
Spark
MASCULINE: Zik
FEMININE: Rishpa, Rishpona, Shevivya, Temana
Speak, Speech
MASCULINE: Amarya, Amaryahu, Dovev, Imri, Maloti, Milalai, Niv, Omer, Siach, Suach, Yaniv, Nanuv
FEMININE: Amira, Doveva, Dovevet, Neva, Na
Spear *See also* Armor
MASCULINE: Sirya, Siryon
FEMININE: Chanit, Chanita, Chinanit, Chinit, Moran, Moranit
Speed *See also* Swift
MASCULINE: Maharai, Mahari
Spice, Spicy *See also* Incense, Perfume
MASCULINE: Mivsam, Mor, Nardimon, Nerd, Rechan, Tzeri
FEMININE: Bosemet, Bosma, Bosmat, Ketziya, Kida, Levona, Mor, Nardimon, Nerdi, Nirdi, Nirdit, Rechana, Tamara, Tziporen
Spider
FEMININE: Shemamit
Spine
FEMININE: Shira
Spirit
MASCULINE: Aviri
Splendor, Splendid *See also* Adornment, Majestic
MASCULINE: Hadar, Hadaram, Hadarezer, Hadriel, Heder, Hod, Hodiya, Naim, Nehedar
FEMININE: Yifa, Yifat, Ziva, Zivi, Zivit
Spread
MASCULINE: Radai, Yazer, Yeziel
Spring, Springtime *See also* Water
MASCULINE: Aviv, Avivi, Silon, Tamuz

FEMININE: Aviva, Avivi, Avivit, Maayan, Mayana, Silona, Silonit
Sprinkle
MASCULINE: Yeziya, Zerika
Sprout, *See also* Grow, Growth
MASCULINE: Miklot, Nun, Shatil, Shelach, Shetil, Shilchi
FEMININE: Hanatza, Nevet
Squirrel
MASCULINE: S'nai
FEMININE: Senait
Staff *See also* Rod
MASCULINE: Miklot
Stag *See also* Deer
MASCULINE: Ayal, Ayalon
Stalk *See also* Reed
FEMININE: Shibolet
Star
MASCULINE: Bar-Kochva, Kochav, Kochavi, Kochva, Mazal, Mazal-Tov, Siman-Tov, Yaish
FEMININE: Ayelet-Hashachar, Barkait, Barkat, Ester, Kochava, Kochavit, Kochevet, Mazal, Mazala, Mazalit
Stately *See also* Tall, Upright
MASCULINE: Tamir, Timur, Tomer
Steadfast
FEMININE: Tzuriya
Stone
MASCULINE: Even, Even-Ezer, Regem, Sapir
FEMININE: Gazit
Stork
FEMININE: Chasida
Storm *See also* Wind
MASCULINE: Saar
Stout *See* Fat
Straight
FEMININE: Yeshara
Strange, Stranger
MASCULINE: Geri, Gershom, Gershon, Giora, Golyat
FEMININE: Gershona, Gerusha, Giora, Gioret, Hagar, Zara
Stream *See also* Brook Water
MASCULINE: Arnan, Arnon, Mitala, Yaval, Yoval, Yuval, Zerem
FEMININE: Afeka, Arnona, Arnonit
Strength, Strong *See also* Iron, Might, Mighty
MASCULINE: Abir, Abiri, Achitzur, Adir, Amatzya, Amiram, Amitz, Amitza, Amotz, Amtzi, Ariav, Atzmon, Aviaz, Avichayil, Aviram, Avitzedek, Avitzur, Avniel, Az, Azai, Azan, Azaz, Azi, Azazyahu, Aziel, Aziz, Aziza, Azriel, Ben-Azzai, Ben-Chayil, Ben-

Gever, Ben-Gurion, Binyamin, Boaz, *Chaikel, Chatzkel,* Chaltzon, Chasin, Chason, Chayil, Cheifa, Cheilem, Cheili, Cheletz, *Chezkel,* Chizki, Chizkiya, Chizkiyahu, Chosen, Eitan, Eliaz, Eliram, Elitzur, Eluzai, Eluzi, Etan, Gabi, Gavital, *Gavrel,* Gavri, Gavriel, Gavriol, Gevaram, Gevarya, Gever, Gibar, Gibor, Gil-On, Gover, Gur, Guri, Guriel, Guron, *Haskel,* Ido, Ish-Chayil, Izuz, *Keskel,* Layish, Lion, Maazya, Makabi, Maoz, Maoziya, Ometz, On, Otni, Otniel, Otzem, Oz, Oz-Tzion, Ozer, Sagi, Sagiv, Shamir, Sharir, Sherira, Uz, Uza, Uzi, Uziel, Uziya, Yaoz, Yaaziel, Yaaziyahu, Yechezkel, Yechizkiya, Yoash, Yoaz
FEMININE: Abira, Abiri, Adira, Alma, Amitza, Amitzya, Amtza, Atzma, Atzmona, Avichayil, Avirama, Aza, Aziaz, Aziza, Azriela, Chasina, Chasna, Eitana, Etana, Gavriela, Gavrila, Gevura, Gibora, Meuza, Nili, Odeda, Odedya, Uza, Uziela, Uzit, Yechezkela

Strife *See also* War, Warrior
MASCULINE: Madai, Medan, Midyan

Strip Off
MASCULINE: Batzlut

Stubborn
MASCULINE: Akashya, Ikesh

Stupid
MASCULINE: Kislon

Style
FEMININE: Ofna

Substitute
MASCULINE: Tachat
FEMININE: Temura

Succeed, Success, Successful *See also* Victory
MASCULINE: Matzliach, Yatzliach, Yitzlach
FEMININE: Hatzlacha, Matzlicha, Tzalcha

Suck, Suckle
MASCULINE: Machi, Miza, Yanik

Suited *See also* Fit, Proper
MASCULINE: Naot

Summit *See also* Height
MASCULINE: Amir

Sun *See also* Shine
MASCULINE: Charsom, Koresh, Shamash, Shimshon, *Zundel*
FEMININE: Chamaniya, Simshona

Superb, Superlative
MASCULINE: Adif

FEMININE: Ilit

Superior *See also* Excellent
FEMININE: Adifa, Ulla

Supplant
MASCULINE: Akavel, Akavya, Akiva, Yaakov
FEMININE: Yaakova

Support *See also* Help, Protect, Provider, Save, Sustain
MASCULINE: Achisamach, Amdiel, Amiezer, Amitzur, Aviezer, Avierzi, Avisamach, Avitzur, Eliakum, Elyakim, Elyakum, *Getzel, Goetz,* Mashen, Parnas, Saad, Saadya, Semachyahu, Soed, Somech, Yehoachaz, Yehoyachin, Yehoyakim, Yismachya, Yismachyahu, Yoshiya, Yoshiyahu, Yoyachin
FEMININE: Mashena, Saada

Survivor
FEMININE: She'era

Swarthy
MASCULINE: Cham, Chama

Swear
MASCULINE: Ashbei

Sweet, Sweetness *See also* Beautiful, Delightful, Goodness, Pleasant
MASCULINE: Avinoam, Elnaam, Magdiel, Matok, Meged, Naam, Naaman, Naim, Noam, Reichana, *Syshe,* Tabbai, Yivsam, *Zisel, Zishe, Ziskind, Zusa, Zus, Zushe, Zusman*
FEMININE: Metuka, Mirit, *Sisel, Zisele, Zisse, Zusa*

Swift
MASCULINE: Boaz
FEMININE: Mahira

Sycamore
MASCULINE: Shakmon, Shikmon
FEMININE: Shikma, Shikmona

Symbol *See also* Sign
MASCULINE: Samal

Sympathetic
MASCULINE: Ahud

Tail
FEMININE: Alya

Talent
MASCULINE: Mechonan, Mechonen

Tall *See also* Stately
MASCULINE: Amir, Chatil, Sagiv, Tamir, Tamur, Timur, Tomer
FEMININE: Tamar, Tamira, Temira, Timora, Timura

Tamarish *See also* Tree
MASCULINE: Eshel

Tan
MASCULINE: Tzochar
Tasty
FEMININE: Te'ima
Teach, Teacher, Teaching
MASCULINE: Aharon, Alef, Likchi, Moran, Morenu, Mori, Moriel, Rabban, Rabi, Rav, Ravi, Yeriel, Yeriya, Yora, Yorai, Yore
FEMININE: Horiya, Mora, Moran, Moriel, Morit, Moriya
Tear
MASCULINE: Pashchur
Tempest See also Storm, Wind
MASCULINE: Saar
Ten, Tenth
MASCULINE: Ben-Asor
FEMININE: Esranit, Esronit
Tent
MASCULINE: Ohel, Oholi, Oholiav, Yahali, Yahel
FEMININE: Ohela, Oholiav, Oholiva, Oholivama, Shafrira
Terebinth See also Oak
FEMININE: Ayla, Eila
Territory
MASCULINE: Chilkiya, Chilkiyahu, Galil, Galili
FEMININE: Galilya, Nachala, Nachalat
Thankfulness
MASCULINE: Toda
Think
MASCULINE: Chashavya, Chashuv, Seviram
Third See also Three
MASCULINE: Shelesh
Thistle
FEMININE: Koranit
Thorn
MASCULINE: Kotz
FEMININE: Chochit
Thornbush
FEMININE: Asnat
Three See also Third
MASCULINE: Shelosha, Shilsha, Shlosha
FEMININE: Telat
Thresh, Threshing
MASCULINE: Dishon, Garon, Morag
FEMININE: Morag
Threshold
MASCULINE: Saf
Throat
MASCULINE: Garon
Thunder
MASCULINE: Raam, Raamya
Tie See also Bind
MASCULINE: Anuv, Isur

FEMININE: Rivka
Time, Timely
MASCULINE: Atai, Ataya, Atid, Edan, Idan, Ido, Itai, Tor
FEMININE: Itai, Itiel, Itiya
Tiny See also Small
FEMININE: Ketana, Minkche
Tomb
MASCULINE: Gadish
Tora
FEMININE: Tora
Torch See also Flame
MASCULINE: Lapid, Ud, Udi, Udiel
FEMININE: Avuka, Masua
Torn
MASCULINE: Tarfon
Touch, Touching
MASCULINE: Mushi
Tower
MASCULINE: Migdal
FEMININE: Magda, Migdala, Mitzpa
Trained See Educated
Tranquil, Tranqility See Peace
Traveller
MASCULINE: Orach
Treasure
MASCULINE: Atir, Matmon, Michman, Otzar, Segel, Sima, Simai, Tzefanya
FEMININE: Adiya, Matmona, Otzara, Segula, Sigal, Sigalit, Sigla, Sigliya, Sima
Tree
MASCULINE: Almog, Alon, Amir, Arza, Arzi, Bar-Ilan, Bros, Eila, Eilon, Ela, Elon, Erez, Eshel, Etzion, Etzioni, Ilan, Ilan-Chai, Ilan-Tov, Luz, Oren, Shaked, Tidhar, Tzameret
FEMININE: Almuga, Alona, Ariza, Arna, Arza, Arzit, Ayla, Egoza, Eila, Ela, Etzyona, Ilana, Ilanit, Ilona, Livnat, Livneh, Shikma, Shikmona
Tremble
MASCULINE: Zia
FEMININE: Noa, Zia
Troops See also Army, Soldiers, Warriors
MASCULINE: Gad, Gadi, Meron
FEMININE: Merona
Trouble, Troubled See Disturbed
Trumpet
MASCULINE: Bazuka
FEMININE: Shifra
Trustworthy
MASCULINE: Amin
FEMININE: Amina
Truth See also Honest
MASCULINE: Amit, Amitai, Amitan, Emet, Sharar

FEMININE: Amita, Emet

Turban
FEMININE: Efrat

Turtledove
FEMININE: Tori

Twig
MASCULINE: Serug

Twin, Twins
MASCULINE: Sivan, Tom, Tomi
FEMININE: Sivan, Sivana

Uncle
MASCULINE: Achav, Achiam, Achiem, Achuav, Dodi, Dodo

Uncover
FEMININE: Eira, Era

Under
MASCULINE: Tachat

Understanding See also Know, Knowledge, Wisdom
MASCULINE: Bina, Bun, Buna, Ish-Sechel, Navon, Yavin, Yediel
FEMININE: Bina, Buna, Tevuma

Unfathomable
MASCULINE: Amok

Unfortunate See Misfortune

Unite, Unity
MASCULINE: Chever, Chevron, Echud, Yachad

Uplift
MASCULINE: Yirmiya,Yirmiyahu

Upright See also Honest, Stately
MASCULINE: Achishur, Avishur, Dekel, Itamar, Konanya, Konen, Tamir, Timur, Tomer, Yashar, Yesher, Yeshurun, Zakif, Zakuf
FEMININE: Amida, Tamar, Zekifa, Zekufa

Useless
MASCULINE: Taval

Valley
MASCULINE: Emek, Gai, Gayora, Geichazi

Valuable See also Precious, Wealthy
MASCULINE: Achikar, Yakar, Yakir
FEMININE: Yakira, Yekara

Vanity
MASCULINE: Hevel

Vanish
MASCULINE: Chalfan, Chalfon

Vapor
MASCULINE: Adda, Anan, Anani, Ananya, Hevel

Vegetarian
FEMININE: Tzimchona

Vegetation See also Growth, Sprout, Garden
MASCULINE: Lotam, Lotem, Shalmon

Veil
MASCULINE: Re'elya

Vest
MASCULINE: Efod

Victor, Victorious, Victory See also Eternal, Warrior
MASCULINE: Gevarya, Gevaryahu, Gover, Netzach, Netziach, Nitzchan, Nitzchi, Shua
FEMININE: Nitzcha, Nitzchiya, Nitzchona

Vigorous See also Strength
MASCULINE: Ira, Irad, Iram, Iran, Iri, Iro, On, Onam, Onan

Village
FEMININE: Kirya

Vine, Vineyard See also Wine
MASCULINE: Ben-Karmi, Carmel, Carmeli, Carmi, Dalit, Gafni, Gefanya, Gefen, Karmel, Karmeli, Karmi, Karmiel, Karmeli, Kerem, Pardes
FEMININE: Gafna, Gafnit, Gefen, Karma, Karmel, Karmela, Karmelit, Karmiel, Karmiela, Karmit, Karmiya, Kerem, Soreka

Violet
FEMININE: Sigliya

Vision See also See, Seer
MASCULINE: Chezyon, Geichazi

Visit, Visitation
FEMININE: Bakara

Vocabulary
MASCULINE: Agron

Voice See also Speech
MASCULINE: Kolya
FEMININE: Kolya

Voluptuous See also Fat
FEMININE: Adina

Vulture
MASCULINE: Aya

Wagon
MASCULINE: Eglon, Tzoveva
FEMININE: Agala

Wait See also Hope
MASCULINE: Yachel, Yachil, Yachl'el, Yachl'eli

Wall
MASCULINE: Achishur, Avishur, Dafna, Gada, Shur
FEMININE: Gedera

Walk
MASCULINE: Darkon, Divon, Shuach

Wander, Wanderer *See also* Stranger
MASCULINE: Aminad
War, Warrior *See also* Contention, Strength, Strife, Victor
MASCULINE: Gad, Gadi, Gadiel, Gavriel, Gevarya, Gevaryahu, Gibor, Gidon, Gidoni, Ish-Chayil, Madai, Medan, Meron, Mindel, Mordechai, Nimrod
FEMININE: *Breindel, Brineh, Brune,* Gidona, Merav, Tigra
Warm, Warmth *See* Hot
Watch *See* Guard, Protect
Water *See also* Sea, Spring, Stream
MASCULINE: Aviyam, Beri, Chamat, Dalfon, Delaya
FEMININE: Afeka, Bat-Yam, Yaval
Water Drawer, Water Drawing
MASCULINE: Delaya, Silon
FEMININE: Silona, Silonit
Waterfall
MASCULINE: Eshed
FEMININE: Ashdoda
Wave *See also* Sea
MASCULINE: Avigal, Gal, Galal, Gali, Yanai
FEMININE: Adva, Bat-Galim, Gal, Gala, Gali, Galit, Galva
Way
MASCULINE: Shoval
Weak
MASCULINE: Bilhan, Kehat, Kilayon
FEMININE: Amuma, *Baila*, Bilha, Leah, Leia
Wealth, Wealthy
MASCULINE: Ashir, Daryavesh, Etzer, Hotir, Huna, Matmon, On, Osher, Oshri, Yishai, Yitro
FEMININE: Ashira, Yitra
Weapon
MASCULINE: Shelach, Shelachel, Shilchi
Weary
FEMININE: Leah, Leia
Weasel
FEMININE: Chulda
Weave, Weaver, Weaving
MASCULINE: Arig, Ben-Chur, Gardi, Oreg, Rekem
FEMININE: Rikma
Weep
MASCULINE: Iyov
Well *See also* Water
MASCULINE: B'era, B'eri, Maayan
FEMININE: B'era, B'erit
West, Western
MASCULINE: Maarav
FEMININE: Yama

Wheat
FEMININE: Chita
Wheel
MASCULINE: Ofnat
Whisper
MASCULINE: Dovev, Lochesh
White, Whiten *See also* Fair
MASCULINE: Alvan, Chari, Laban, Lavan, Levanon, Livna, Livneh, Livni, Malbin, Tzachar, Tzecharya
FEMININE: Livnat, Livona, Malbina, Tzechira, Tzechora, Tzechorit
Whole *See also* Peace, Perfect
MASCULINE: Kalil, Kalu, Meshulam, Mishlam, Shalem
FEMININE: Temima, Tumi
Widower
MASCULINE: Almon
Will, Willing *See also* Agreeable, Desire
MASCULINE: Yitzri, Yoav, Yoel, Yoela
FEMININE: Ava, Eliava, Tirtza, Yoela
Wind *See also* Storm, Tempest
MASCULINE: Saar
Wine, Winery *See also* Vine, Vineyard
MASCULINE: Gefanya, Giti, Gitai, Sava, Seva
FEMININE: Gat, Gita, Gitit
Winter
MASCULINE: Eli-Choref
FEMININE: Setavit
Wisdom *See also* Knowledge, Understanding
MASCULINE: Avida, Bina, Buna, Chatzkel, Ish-Sechel, Navon, Utz, Zavin, Yosha
FEMININE: Chochma, Geona, Geonit, Tushiya
Wise *See also* Wisdom
MASCULINE: Chacham, Chachmon, Chachmoni, Haskel, Navon
FEMININE: Nevona
Withdraw
MASCULINE: Atzalya, Atzalyahu, Atzel, Bariach, Chaltzon, Cheletz, Nachbi
Withhold
MASCULINE: Atzalya, Atzalyahu, Atzel, Timma, Yimna
Witness
MASCULINE: Adael, Adaya, Adi, Adlai, Aviad, Eidi, Elad, Eliad, Elied, Lada, Ladan, Udi, Yoad, Yoed
Wolf
MASCULINE: *Lopez, Lupo, Seff, Velvel, Volf, Walk, Wilk, Wolpe, Wulf, Zavel,* Ze'ev, Ze'evi, *Zev, Ziff*
FEMININE: Zeeva

Wonder
MASCULINE: Tema
FEMININE: Pelia, Tama
Wonder See Beautiful, Miraculous
Wool, Woolly
MASCULINE: Tzameret, Tzemari
Word
MASCULINE: Amarya, Amaryahu, Imra, Imri, Omer
Work, Worker
MASCULINE: Amal, Amali, Amasa, Amel, Mahir
FEMININE: Amal, Amalya, Amela
World
MASCULINE: Cheiled, Cheldai, Cheled
Worm
MASCULINE: Tola
Worrisome, Worry
MASCULINE: Doeg
Worshipper
MASCULINE: Avda, Avdon
Worthy
MASCULINE: Ya'e
Wreath See also Crown
MASCULINE: Ativ, Zeira, Zer, Zera, Zeri
Wrestle, Wrestler
MASCULINE: Chavakuk, Naftali

FEMININE: Naftala, Naftalya
Wrought See also Create, Creation
MASCULINE: Elasa, Elpaal

Yearn, Yearning
MASCULINE: Yachel, Yachil
FEMININE: Erga
Yoke See Burden
Young See Youth
Youth, Youthful
MASCULINE: Aviv, Avrech, Bachur, Becher, Bichri, Elinoar, Ira, Irad, Iram, Iran, Iri, Iro, Ofer, Yafet, Yefet, Zuta, Zutai, Zutra
FEMININE: Elinoar, Gurit, Tzeira

Zealous
MASCULINE: Elkana
Zinc
MASCULINE: Ivtzan
Zion
MASCULINE: Ben-Tziyon, Oz-Tziyon, Tziyon
FEMININE: Bat-Tziyon, Tziona, Tzionit
Zoo
MASCULINE: Beivar, Bevar

Bibliography

Ames, Winthrop *What Shall We Name the Baby?* New York; Simon & Shuster, 1935.

Bardsley, Charles *English Surnames*. London: Chatto & Windus, 1884.

— — —*Curiosities of Puritan Nomenclature*. London: 1897.

— — —*The Romance of the London Directory*. London: 1879.

Baring, Gould S. *Family Names and Their Story*. London: 1932.

Barr, George. *Who's Who in the Bible*. New York: Jonathan David Publishers, 1975.

Blackie, C. *Dictionary of Place Names*. London: John Murray, 1887.

Bowman, William D. *The Story of Surnames*. London: 1932.

Burnham, S.M. *Our Names*. Boston: A. I. Bradley Co., 1900.

Burton, Dorothy. *A New Treasury of Names for the Baby*. New York: Prentice Hall, 1961.

Brown, Driver & Briggs. *Hebrew and English Lexicon of the Old Testament*. New York: Houghton Mifflin Co., 1907.

Edmunds, F. *Traces of History in the Names of Places*. London: Longmans, Green and Co., 1872.

Fisher, Henry W. *Girls' Names*. New York: Fisher's Foreign Letters, Publishers, 1910.

Grussi, A.M. *Chats on Christian Names*. Boston: The Stratford Co. 1925.

Kolatch, Alfred J. *These Are the Names*. New York: Jonathan David, 1948.

— — —*The Name Dictionary*. New York: Jonathan David, 1967.

— — —*Names for Boys and Girls*. New York: Jonathan David, 1968.

— — —*Names for Pets*. New York: Jonathan David, 1971.

— — —*Who's Who in the Talmud*. New York: Jonathan David, 1964.

Lambert, E. and Pei, M. *Our Names*. New York: Lothrop, 1962.

Latham, Edward *Dictionary of Names, Nicknames, and Surnames*. London: 1904.

Loughead, F. *Dictionary of Given Names*. Glendale, California: Arthur Clark, 1966.

Moody, Sophy *What Is Your Name?* London: Richard Bentley, 1863.

Mordacque, L.H. *History of the Names of Men, Nations and Places*. Vol. I (1862), and Vol. II (1964). London: John Russel Smith, Publisher.

Palmer G., and Lloyd, N., *Exploring Names*. London: Oldham Books, 1964.

Sleigh, L. and Johnson, C. *The Book of Boys*. New York: Thomas Y. Crowell, 1962.

——— *The Book of Girls*. New York: Thomas Y. Crowell, 1962.

Smith, Elsdon *American Surnames*. New York: Chilton, 1970.

——— *Naming Your Baby*. New York: Chilton, 1970.

Stewart, George R. *American Place-Names*. New York: Oxford, 1970.

Swan, H. *Girls' Christian Names*. London.

Taggart, Jean *Pet Names*. New York: Scarecrow Press, 1962.

Wagner, Leopold *Names and Their Meaning*. London: T. Fisher Unwin, 1893.

——— *More About Names*. London: T. Fisher Unwin, 1893.

Weekley, Ernest *Surnames*. London: John Murray, Second Edition, 1927.

Wells, Evelyn *What to Name the Baby*. New York: Doubleday, 1946.

——— *A Treasury of Names*. New York: Duell, Sloan & Pearce, 1946.

Withycombe, E.G. *The Oxford Dictionary of English Christian Names*. New York: Oxford University Press, 1945.

Yonge, Charlotte M. *History of Christian Names*. London: MacMillan (1884).